European Politics

This book arises out of a specially commissioned issue of *West European Politics* marking the journal's 30th anniversary. It examines the profound changes in the European political landscape over the last three decades, including the fall of Communism; progressive European integration; territorial restructuring; public sector reforms at European, national, regional and local levels; changes in democratic participation, protest, elections, political communication, political parties and party competition; and challenges to the welfare state. This book also discusses how political science has responded to these changes in terms of its substantive focus, concepts, methods and theories. Many of the 17 contributions included identify important challenges for the future, including those stemming from EU integration, the reduced electoral accountability of politicians, the problematic legitimation of party government and the sharpening of the edges of the state. Contributors include K. M. Anderson, F. G. Castles, C. Crouch, M. Egeberg, M. Ferrera, K. H. Goetz, L. Hooghe, E. M. Immergut, R. F. Inglehart, M. Keating, H.-D. Klingemann, H. Kriesi, M. Lodge, J. Lovenduski, P. Mair, G. Marks, Y. Mény, L. Morlino, H. Obinger, V. A. Schmidt, P. C. Schmitter, and G. Smith.

This book was published as a special issue of *West European Politics*.

Klaus H. Goetz is Professor of German and European Politics and Government at the University of Potsdam and a Visiting Fellow at the European Institute, LSE.

Peter Mair is Professor of Comparative Politics, European University Institute.

Gordon Smith is Professor Emeritus of Government at the LSE.

European Politics

Pasts, presents, futures

Edited by Klaus H. Goetz, Peter Mair and
Gordon Smith

Routledge
Taylor & Francis Group
LONDON AND NEW YORK

First published 2009 by Routledge
2 Park Square, Milton Park, Abingdon, Oxon, OX14 4RN

Simultaneously published in the USA and Canada
by Routledge
270 Madison Avenue, New York, NY 10016

Routledge is an imprint of the Taylor & Francis Group, an informa business

Transferred to Digital Printing 2010

© 2009 Edited by Klaus H. Goetz, Peter Mair and Gordon Smith

Typeset in Times by Value Chain, India

British Library Cataloguing in Publication Data
A catalogue record for this book is available from the British Library

ISBN10: 0-415-48455-3 (hbk)
ISBN10: 0-415-60213-0 (pbk)

ISBN13: 978-0-415-48455-8 (hbk)
ISBN13: 978-0-415-60213-6 (pbk)

Contents

Acknowledgements

This special issue of *West European Politics* has been compiled to mark the 30th anniversary of its publication. First drafts of nearly all of the papers included were presented at a three-day workshop held at the European University Institute in Florence in January 2007. We wish to thank the President of the EUI, Professor Yves Mény, for agreeing to host this event and for the generous financial support he arranged. We would also like to thank our Publishers – Routledge – and the University of Potsdam for additional funding. Laszlo Bruszt (EUI), Jack Hayward (University of Hull) and Mark Thatcher (LSE) acted as discussants at the workshop, and we are grateful for the many helpful suggestions they made. Liz Webb at the EUI coped splendidly with the complex arrangements that such an event entails. We were especially pleased to welcome Stephanie Wright in Florence. She has, for many years, carried most of the administrative burden that comes with editing the journal; her contribution has been invaluable.

In celebrating 30 years of *West European Politics*, we wish to remember two fine gentlemen and their very close association with the journal: Vincent Wright, the co-founding editor, who sadly passed away in 1999; and Frank Cass (1930–2007), our long-time Publisher, who unstintingly supported the journal for nearly three decades.

KHG
PM
GS

Foreword

YVES MÉNY

Both *West European Politics* and the European University Institute in Florence are celebrating (or have just done so) their 30th anniversaries. The two events are apparently disconnected, even if the characteristics in common are many. It is perhaps a sign of the times that the need for more interaction, more exchange between scholars, and more 'European' training was felt at that time, in the 1970s. Another major initiative, the creation of ECPR in 1970, is another testimony to the underground transformation that we are better able to understand and interpret today.

With the benefit of 30 years' hindsight, I am struck by the magnitude of the changes that have occurred both in our privileged domain of observation, research and analysis, i.e., in European politics itself, and in our profession, political science.

All of the contributions in this special issue focus on the many and sometimes dramatic changes that have affected the continent as a whole and within each unit of comparison. Many of these changes are endogenous, but I believe that in most instances Europe has been more reactive than proactive. The European integration process, for example, might appear as a genuine impulse from within to avoid further 'fratricidal' wars, but the American drive, as well as the fear of Russia, were probably just as powerful as the visionary concepts offered by Schuman, Monnet and others. The same could be said about the fall of the Berlin Wall and the successive integration of the former Soviet-dominated countries. Western Europe did little to contribute to this revolution and had willy-nilly to adjust.

Today we could say that globalisation, probably the most radical challenge that Europe has to face, again puts Europe on the defensive. For the first time in history, Europe is not the engine and the main actor of a worldwide enterprise in economic and cultural terms. Not only is Europe not the driving force, but the very phenomenon with which we are confronted is challenging the foundations – traditional and more recent – of European politics, including the centrality of the nation state, the supremacy of state over market, the welfare consensus and the separation of state and religion.

At this point, we could deliberate if it still makes sense to continue to name a journal *West European Politics* given that the Europe of today is the fusion/reunification of the two parts of a once-divided continent. Should we not draw conclusions from the 30 years of change analysed in this volume? On reflection, I believe it is correct to stick to the flag that was hung up so successfully 30 years ago, and not only for commercial or sentimental reasons.

In many ways, and in spite of differences and peculiarities, everything and everybody is now 'western': politically and economically Eastern and Central Europe have chosen to adhere to the basic rules, values, conventions and practices of both the market and democracy. The notion of 'Western' today has lost its remaining geographical connotation and keeps mainly its political meaning. So long life to *West European Politics*!

The transformation which affects the profession is no less impressive even if its pace is slower – as often happens in academic life. More and more, teaching, curricula, scientific references and professional careers are becoming Europeanised. We are still far from the dreams of a European academic space that is equivalent to the American model, but we are on the way. In its limited capacity, the EUI tries to contribute to and push for such an evolution. The ECPR has worked for more than 30 years in the same direction, and *WEP* has done the same. Indeed, *WEP* has always played a major role in introducing emerging scholars to the study of comparative European politics, and has often offered these younger generations one of their first and most successful international publishing outlets. When looking at the relationship between these three initiatives from the 1970s, I am fascinated by the growing interplay between people, in particular in the young generation, who are, by now, European players and not only British, French, Italian or German. The present volume is a vivid testimony to this trend, and most of the contributors in one way or another have crossed the roads of ECPR or the EUI at some point of their academic life. *Splendide isolement* is not only a luxury that nobody can afford, but is an ever-poorer excuse for not addressing the challenges ahead of us. Europe, in particular on the academic front, cannot satisfy itself with being a laggard or a follower.

Yves Mény is President of the European University Institute and a former Chairman of ECPR. He has served on the editorial board of WEP since 1986.

Notes on Contributors

Karen M. Anderson is Associate Professor of Political Science at Radboud University Nijmegen. She has written widely on the politics of welfare state change, the relationship between welfare states and labour markets, and trade unions as political actors. Her most recent book is *The Handbook of Western European Pension Politics* (co-editor, 2006).

Francis G. Castles is Professor of Social and Public Policy at the University of Edinburgh, and Adjunct Professor of Political Science at the Research School of Social Sciences, Australian National University. His recent books include *Australia Reshaped* (co-editor, 2002), *The Future of the Welfare State* (2004), *Federalism and the Welfare State* (co-editor, 2005) and *The Disappearing State?* (editor, 2007).

Colin Crouch is Professor of Government and Public Management at Warwick Business School and a Fellow of the British Academy. He previously taught at Oxford, LSE and the EUI. His recent books include *Changing Governance of Local Economies* (co-author, 2004), *Capitalist Diversity and Change* (2005) and *Diversity of Democracy* (co-editor, 2006).

Morten Egeberg is Director of ARENA-Centre for European Studies and Professor of Political Science, University of Oslo. He is a Member of the Norwegian Academy of Science and Letters. Recent publications include *Multilevel Union Administration* (editor, 2006) and *Towards a New Executive Order in Europe* (co-editor, special issue of *West European Politics*, 2008).

Maurizio Ferrera is Professor of the Theory and Politics of the Welfare State at the State University of Milan. He also directs the Research Unit on European Governance (URGE) in Turin and is deputy-director of the POLEIS Centre for Comparative Political Studies at Bocconi University. His recent publications include *The Future of European Welfare States* (co-author, 2004), *The Boundaries of Welfare* (2005) and *Le Politiche Sociali* (co-author, 2006).

Klaus H. Goetz holds the Chair in German and European Politics and Government at the University of Potsdam. He has been a Visiting Professor at Humboldt University Berlin, the Institute of Advanced Studies, Vienna, and the Institute of Social Sciences, University of Tokyo. His most recent books include *Germany, Europe and the Politics of Constraint* (co-editor, 2003) and *Governing after Communism: Institutions and Policies* (co-author, 2006).

Liesbet Hooghe is Zachary Taylor Smith Professor in Political Science at the University of North Carolina in Chapel Hill, and Chair in Multilevel Governance at the Free University Amsterdam. She is Chair of the European Union Studies Association for 2007–9. She recently edited and co-edited special issues of *European Union Politics* and *Acta Politica* on Euroscepticism. Amongst other books, she has published *The European Commission and the Integration of Europe* (2002).

Ellen M. Immergut is Professor of Comparative Politics at Humboldt University, Berlin. She has published widely on institutional theory and comparative public policy. Her most recent publications include *The Handbook of Western European Pension Politics* (co-editor, 2006) and a special issue of *Governance* on institutional change in Japan and Europe (co-editor, 2006).

Ronald F. Inglehart is Research Professor at the Center of Political Studies, University of Michigan, and is Chairman of the Executive Committee of the World Values Survey. His recent books include *Modernization and Post-Modernization* (1997), *Sacred and Secular* (co-author, 2004) and *Modernization, Cultural Change and Democracy* (co-author, 2005).

Michael Keating is Professor of Political and Social Sciences at the European University Institute and is a Fellow of the Royal Society of Edinburgh. His recent books include *The Regional Challenge in Central and Eastern Europe* (co-editor, 2003), *The Government of Scotland* (2005), *European Integration and the Nationalities Question* (co-editor, 2006) and *Devolution and Public Policy* (co-editor, 2006).

Hans-Dieter Klingemann is Professor Emeritus of Political Science at the Free University Berlin and was for many years director of research at the Social Science Research Centre Berlin. His recent books include *A New Handbook of Political Science* (co-editor, 1998), *Democracy and Political Culture in Eastern Europe* (co-editor, 2006), *Mapping Policy Preferences II* (co-author, 2006) and *The State of Political Science in Western Europe* (editor, 2007).

Hanspeter Kriesi is Professor of Comparative Politics at the Department of Political Science, University of Zurich. He is director of the Swiss national research programme on the 'Challenges to Democracy in the 21st Century'. His recent books include *Social Movements in a Globalizing World* (co-editor, 1999), *The Blackwell Companion to Social Movements* (co-editor, 2005), and *Direct Democratic Choice* (2005).

Martin Lodge is Reader in Political Science and Public Policy at the London School of Economics and Political Science. He is Reviews Editor of *West*

European Politics. His recent books include *On Different Tracks* (2002), *Regulatory Innovation* (co-editor, 2005) and *The Politics of Public Service Bargains* (co-author, 2006).

Joni Lovenduski is Anniversary Professor of Politics at Birkbeck College, University of London. She is Convenor of the European section of the Research Network on Gender, Politics and the State (RNGS), a cross-national collaborative project that investigates the impact of women's movements on public policy. Her recent books include *Women in Parliament* (co-author, 2005), *Feminizing Politics* (2005) and *State Feminism and the Political Representation of Women* (2005).

Peter Mair is Professor of Comparative Politics at the European University Institute, Florence, and at Leiden University, Netherlands. His most recent books include *Representative Government in Modern Europe* (co-author, 4th ed., 2005) and *Political Parties and Electoral Change* (co-editor, 2004). His earlier book with Stefano Bartolini *Identity, Competition and Electoral Availability* has recently been reissued in the ECPR Classics Series.

Gary Marks is Burton Craige Distinguished Professor of Political Science at the University of North Carolina in Chapel Hill, and Chair in Multilevel Governance at the Free University Amsterdam. His many publications include recently edited and co-edited special issues of *Electoral Studies* and *Acta Politica*, and *European Integration and Political Conflict* (co-editor, 2004).

Leonardo Morlino is Professor of Political Science at the Istituto Italiano di Scienze Umane (SUM, Florence, Italy), Director of the Research Centre on Southern Europe in Florence and Director of the doctoral programme in Political Science at SUM. His most recent books include *Assessing the Quality of Democracy* (2005), *Partiti e caso italiano* (2005), *Europeizzazione e rappresentanza territoriale. Il caso italiano* (2006), and *Party Change in Southern Europe* (co-editor, 2007).

Herbert Obinger is Professor of Public and Social Policy at the University of Bremen, where he works on the transformation of the welfare state. His recent books include *Politik und Wirtschaftswachstum* (2004), *Federalism and the Welfare State* (co-editor, 2005), and *Sozialstaat Österreich zwischen Kontinuität und Umbau* (co-author, 2006).

Vivien A. Schmidt is Jean Monnet Professor of European Integration and Associate Chair in the Department of International Relations at Boston University. Her recent books include *Welfare and Work in the Open Economy* (2 volumes, co-editor, 2000), *The Futures of European Capitalism*

(2002), *Policy Change and Discourse in Europe* (co-editor, 2005), and *Democracy in Europe: The EU and National Polities* (2006).

Philippe C. Schmitter is Professorial Fellow at the European University Institute, Florence, and Visiting Professor at the Central European University, Budapest. He is currently working on the emerging Euro-polity, the consolidation of democracy in Southern and Eastern Europe, and post-liberal democracy. His most recent publications include *How to Democratize the European Union* (2000) and *The Future of Democracy in Europe* (co-author, 2004).

Gordon Smith is Professor Emeritus of Government at the London School of Economics and Political Science. He is the founding editor of *West European Politics* and also co-founded the journal *German Politics*. His books include *Politics in Western Europe* (5th ed., 1989) and *Democracy in Western Germany* (3rd ed., 1986).

Trajectories of European Politics:
An Introduction

KLAUS H. GOETZ, PETER MAIR and GORDON SMITH

The first issue of *West European Politics* (*WEP*) was published in February 1978 under the joint editorship of Gordon Smith and Vincent Wright. The journal had been initially conceived when both editors were lecturing at the London School of Economics, where they were jointly responsible for a new MSc degree in West European politics. At that time, the range of journals dealing with comparative European politics was considerably more limited than is now the case. The standard national political science journals, including *American Political Science Review* and *Political Studies*, were well established, but usually included only a small number of comparative European papers. The same was true even for the more explicitly comparative journals, including the US-based *Comparative Politics* and *Comparative Political Studies*, both founded in 1968, and *World Politics*. Moreover, almost none of these journals paid much attention to the politics of the smaller European democracies, which was to become a particular concern of *WEP*. The smaller democracies also tended to be sidelined by the two leading journals in European politics at the time. The *Journal of*

Common Market Studies, founded in 1963, was devoted almost exclusively to the study of European integration, while the *European Journal of Political Research*, launched in 1973 as the official journal of the newly-established European Consortium for Political Research, tended primarily towards quantitative and cross-national studies. For *WEP*, what mattered was a more conventional, case-oriented comparative politics that would cover the small as well as the large democracies – ranging across the whole of what was then Western Europe.

The range of papers included in the very first issue of the new journal reflected this basic approach. In addition to two reflective essays by Ralf Dahrendorf and Altiero Spinelli marking the launch of the journal – both were members of the first editorial advisory board – there were separate papers on politics in West Germany, Spain and France, a fourth paper on Britain's relations with the European Community and a fifth on Scandinavian social democracy. There was also a short report on a recent election in Norway, as well as a series of book reviews covering publications in comparative politics, national politics, and European integration, including two books concerned with current politics in West Germany, and a third dealing with East Germany.

From one perspective that first issue might not seem very remote. Indeed, among the eight original contributors were scholars who continue to contribute to the journal today. John Madeley, the author of the Norwegian election report, recently co-edited a special issue of *WEP* dealing with 'Church and State in Contemporary Europe' (Madeley and Enyedi 2003), while Francis G. Castles, who contributed the paper on Scandinavian social democracy, is also contributing to this 30th anniversary issue. From another perspective, however, and particularly from the perspective of any young graduate students coming to comparative European politics for the first time, this was another Europe – a now foreign continent where things were done very differently. Take the recent special issue on church and state, for example. This was the second special issue on the theme of religion to be carried by *WEP*, the first being on 'Religion in West European Politics', edited by Suzanne Berger (1982). Berger's issue included three papers on religion and politics in France, her own particular interest, and one each on Italy, Spain, England and the Netherlands. John Madeley – again – contributed a paper on Protestant Europe, and a paper by Brian Smith dealt with the lessons that Western Europe might draw from experiences in Allende's Chile. This was, by any standard, a narrowly circumscribed world. By 2003, in contrast, the special issue on church and state included not only a number of chapters on the familiar West European cases, now expanded to include Ireland and Greece, but also chapters dealing with Poland, Hungary and the Czech Republic. France, which had received the lion's share of attention in 1982, was now handled in the context of a single comparative contribution that also included Britain and Germany. By 2003, in other words, *WEP*, despite its name, was dealing with a new Europe.

To appreciate the extent to which the European political landscape has been recast during the past 30 years, it is worth recalling briefly how the main contours looked just three decades ago. Europe was divided sharply between the Western liberal democracies and the Communist bloc. Germany, Europe's largest nation, was also divided by the Cold War. In the West, Greece, Portugal and Spain were still very much in the process of post-authoritarian transition and consolidation. The EU had nine members, with the Southern enlargements of the 1980s still some years off, and with direct elections to the European Parliament due to begin in 1979. As regards the largest Western European states, the UK was yet to experience Thatcherism and France was yet to undergo the Socialist experiment of the first Mitterrand presidency and its subsequent policy reversals. In Germany, it would be a further four years before the beginning of the Kohl chancellorship, which was to last 16 years and witness German unification. In Italy, the Christian Democratic Party controlled the political system as it had done throughout the post-war period, but was now also having to deal with a powerful Communist party, and with the demands of the so-called historic compromise. This was the heyday of Eurocommunism, with the US State Department expressing particular concerns about possible Communist party involvement in the governments of NATO allies.

Thirty years later, this picture has been profoundly altered. The demise of Soviet Communism rendered obsolete the old West–East divide – hitherto a fundamental structuring principle of European politics; it also led directly to the emergence of a host of new or reborn European states, including, inter alia, the Baltic states of Estonia, Latvia and Lithuania; the Czech and Slovak Republics; and the states that emerged from the break-up of Yugoslavia. In the study of democratic transition and consolidation, the focus shifted, accordingly, from Southern Europe to Central and Eastern Europe. The European Union has grown from 9 to 27 members (as of 1 January 2007); it has experienced a massive extension of the *acquis communautaire*; and its membership has become immensely more diverse (see Mair and Zielonka 2002). Amongst the largest European states, the political system of the UK has been profoundly affected by Thatcherism and, since 1997, the New Labour government. France underwent 14 years of Socialist rule under President Mitterrand, massive nationalisations followed by privatisation, repeated attempts at overcoming its centralist state tradition, and saw the rise of a populist extreme right, culminating, in 2002, in a presidential election that saw the incumbent Jacques Chirac competing in a second-round run-of against the leader of the *Front National*. Germany was reunited during the Kohl chancellorship, and, in 1998, for the first time in the Federal Republic's history, a government of the left was formed that did not include one of the bourgeois parties. In Italy, both the right and the left were comprehensively transformed, prompting many commentators to speak of the birth of a second Italian republic, and leading to a process of alternation in government that was completely without precedent in Italian democratic history (Bull and Rhodes 2007). In all of these countries, as in the smaller European democracies, we have also seen the emergence of a new inter-communal tension between native and immigrant groups, as well as an increasingly conflictual divide between Christian and Muslim communities in particular.

These changes in both the political landscape and social structure of Europe continue to provide extremely rich material for scholars of European politics, as do the changes that have been wrought in some of the key dimensions of domestic political systems. Most of these changes have been charted and analysed in various ways and to varying extents in the pages of *WEP*. Among the topics which have been extensively covered during the past three decades have been the transformation of the European state through progressive European integration; the redrawing of the boundaries between public and private (nationalisation and, later, privatisation), as well as the readjustment of territorial boundaries through decentralisation, regionalisation and federalisation; changes in patterns of democratic participation, protest, elections and political communication; the changing character of political parties and changing patterns of party competition; the new challenges faced by European welfare states; and changes in the organisation and style of executive government.

At the same time as the building blocks of the traditional political systems have changed, new modes of enquiry have been initiated at the scholarly level, new overarching themes have emerged, and traditional concerns have waned or have sometimes been reinvigorated. One of the most important of the new themes is the study of Europeanisation, for which a special issue was organised (Goetz and Hix 2000), whilst interest in the more traditionally-focused study of territory, state and nation-building in Europe has been reawakened in the aftermath of the break-up of the Communist bloc. New perspectives have been opened up both in respect of comparison across space (e.g. comparative studies of democratisation in Southern and Central and Eastern Europe) and across time. This has also stimulated the search for broader comparative patterns ('worlds', 'families', 'clusters'). Within the much expanded field of comparative policy analysis, new topics of inquiry have emerged and have attracted much attention in the pages of *WEP* in recent years, including, for example, new modes of regulation, and new approaches have been developed to look at more familiar questions, including discourse analysis.

Next to political events as key forces of change in what we study, disciplinary developments have affected how we study European politics. As expected, there has, of course, been innovation in concepts; in methods (notably through advances in quantitative and statistical techniques and novel combinations of quantitative and qualitative methods); and in terms of theoretical approaches – as Immergut and Anderson (2008) argue in this volume, the impact of the new institutionalism on the study of European politics deserves special attention. Improved access to quantitative data, drastically reduced costs of data analysis and, owing to the passage of time, the availability of longer time series have all helped to bolster the empirical bases of research. In this respect, comparative European politics has mirrored developments in contemporary empirical political science more generally. At least one further development specific to Europe-focused research should be mentioned, that is, the growing fusion between comparative politics approaches and international relations initially in the study of European integration and, increasingly, in analyses of the impact of integration on the member states.

How we study the politics of Europe has also been decisively influenced by changes in the organisational capacities of European political science. As Klingemann (2008) shows in his evaluation of developments in the discipline, the political science communities in Europe are now much more closely integrated and internationalised than three decades ago, as witnessed, for example, by the ever-expanding scope of the European Consortium of Political Research; the systematic promotion of Europe-wide networking notably through the EU Framework programmes; the proliferation of new Europe-focused political science journals; the growing geographical mobility of European scholars; the standardisation of training and curricula, now reaching down to the undergraduate level through the Bologna process; and, finally, by the growing acceptability of English as the principal language of scholarly communication. Equally, links between European and North American scholars have gained in intensity, not least in the context of professional associations such as the European Community Studies Association (now European Union Studies Association), founded in the US in 1988. There has also been a rapid process of 'professionalisation' associated with an ever-growing number of PhD and post-doctoral programmes, on the one hand, most of which are international in character, and an increased level of specialisation, on the other hand, facilitated by the growing number of scholars in the field and by the rise of specialised journals.

It is not difficult to detect the trajectories of change in the study of European politics; but it is a more demanding undertaking to identify their precise effects on the intellectual pursuit of political analysis. It is this question that lies at the heart of this anniversary issue of *WEP*. Indeed, with this special anniversary collection we intend to address the developments which emerge from the intersection of two distinct processes: the new comparative politics of the new Europe, on the one hand, the main contours of which have been already sketched above, and the new ways of studying this new comparative European politics, on the other. As Martin Shapiro (1995: 3) has suggested in an assessment of American political science, 'there is often some confusion between changes in the real world and changes in the political science learning about it'. In other words, and as Michael Keating (2008) emphasises in his evaluation of territorial politics, we need to know how much of what we see as new developments in the real world is genuinely new, and how much is new because we have learned to ask new questions, or because we have applied new skills.

The first answer we get is clearly unequivocal in this regard, in that Colin Crouch (2008) charts the marked shift that has been experienced in the past 30 years in terms of social trends in Europe, with a clear and quite pervasive decline in traditional industrial and agricultural employment, and with the emergence of a new post-industrial occupational structure. For Crouch, the weight of the traditional nineteenth- and twentieth-century social order has become substantially diminished, with the office replacing the factory as the new paradigmatic organizational form, extending across different sectors and across the public/private divide, producing a hierarchy of managers and professionals and a large junior administrative and clerical workforce. These multiple gradations have not yet produced cleavages resembling those between manual workers and managers that helped frame twentieth-century politics, except, as he notes, for the tendency 'for lower levels of office hierarchies to be heavily female, upper levels male, producing a gender rather than a class division. It is therefore relevant that gender has become more important than class in many political debates in recent times'.

A second key change that has taken place both in Europe and further afield is the victory of democracy. Just a few years prior to the launch of *WEP*, as Leonardo Morlino (2008) recalls in his contribution, the third wave of democracy began in Portugal, and by now it has embraced most of the European continent. This shift in real world politics has also had major implications for the empirical theory of democracy, as Morlino argues, both in terms of the efforts to understand the so-called 'hybrid regimes', or the 'electoral' or 'illiberal' democracies, and in terms of our understanding of the democratisation process itself. The global shift towards democracy has also placed the issue of the quality of democracy on the research agenda, and the question of how quality might be measured with quantifiable and finite indicators.

For Michael Keating (2008), the issue of territory in European politics is less a newly discovered theme and more a revival of earlier concerns. During the 1960s and early 1970s, as he notes in his essay, territorial politics tended to be neglected by comparative political science scholarship on the grounds that it was giving way to function as a principle of social and political organization. Since the mid-1970s, by contrast, territorial political movements have been making a substantial impact in European politics, and this has led to renewed attention within the discipline. The incorporation of East-Central Europe into the democratic world has also encouraged the revival of scholarly attention to territorial politics, and with this has come the realisation that it is differences in the manner in which states have evolved that provides the key to understanding the new spatial tensions.

For Maurizio Ferrera (2008), the last 30 years have witnessed a turbulent transition in welfare states from a 'golden age' of expansion to a more sober 'silver age' of permanent austerity, a shift that has resulted from external pressures and from the internal transformations of domestic economies and social structures. In common with a number of the essays in this volume, Ferrera contrasts the contemporary situation with the very distinctive situation that prevailed during the so-called *trente glorieuses*, a period which ran from the late 1940s to the late 1970s, and that was brought to a more or less abrupt end by the second oil shock and the ending of the Bretton Woods agreement. In retrospect, whether seen from the perspective of welfare states, as in the case of Ferrera's essay, or in terms of party government and the politics of organized interests, as in Mair's (2008) and Schmitter's (2008) essays, it is this moment which appears decisive, since it is from this point on that the partisan political management of more or less protected economies begins to fray. With the end of embedded liberalism, in short, there came a transformation in the trajectories of European politics. This conjuncture may also have served as one of the key stimuli in encouraging a robust scholarship in the field of welfare states in Europe. Indeed, Ferrera concludes his essay by arguing that comparative welfare state research has proved to be one of the liveliest fields of political economy – a field marked by important analytical and theoretical advances as well as by the accumulation of systematic empirical knowledge concerning some of the key institutions of the European political landscape.

Scholarship on the European Union was often less lively than this, particularly in the late 1970s and early 1980s. As Liesbet Hooghe and Gary Marks (2008) point out, *WEP* was launched at a moment in which the EU itself, as well as its scholarship, was in the doldrums, and both the institutions and the study were only to come to life again in the late 1980s. Indeed, by the end of the 1980s the field of EU research was attracting some of the very best scholarship in international relations and comparative politics. Hooghe and Marks offer a substantial and comprehensive analysis of how political science has treated the Union over the years, and chart the development of the institutions and their implication for politics, both domestic and transnational. Writing in the immediate wake of a period of 'sustained politicization, of public debates, mobilization of populist parties, and referendums on Europe', they emphasise how self-reflexive the process of European integration actually is, being one that is subject to various attempts at purposeful manipulation. They point out that political leaders who have suffered from referendums may well want to change the process, although it is also the case, as both the French and the Dutch experiences tells us, that these leaders might simply want to change the process of ratification. Let us keep integration, one can imagine them arguing, but let us change how it looks. This is perhaps one route to keeping their citizens on side.

Ronald Inglehart has been the dominant figure in the fields of political culture and value change for as long as *WEP* has existed. His early research was already well-known and cited widely in the early 1970s, and his path-breaking volume *The Silent Revolution* was published in 1977, the year prior to *WEP*'s launch. In his contribution to this anniversary issue (2008) he revisits the hypotheses that he originally advanced in the early 1970s regarding intergenerational value change and looks at a variety of European and global data to see the extent to which these hypotheses have been borne out. His conclusion is confirmatory and convincing. Using cohort analysis, the comparison of value preferences in rich and poor countries, and the trends that can be derived from surveys conducted over the past 35 years, he emphasises how major cultural changes are occurring, and how they reflect a process of intergenerational change and increasing levels of existential security. Nor, as he concludes, is this a uniquely West European phenomenon, although it is particularly pronounced in this region. Rather, this process of culture change occurs whenever and wherever the formative experience of the younger generations are substantially different from those that shaped the older generations.

This is also a lesson that might be drawn from studying the changing patterns of political participation over the past decades, although Hanspeter Kriesi's analysis (2008) of these patterns uses quite different terms to those of Inglehart. Kriesi here emphasises the role of collective actors and political elites in determining patterns of individual political participation. His framework of analysis also underlines the changes in the political context which have taken place over the past 30 years and which have modified the conditions for both conventional and unconventional political participation. These include the increasing role of the media in politics and the decline of party command over voters. Other institutional changes reduce electoral accountability, with some far-reaching, if sometimes ambiguous, conse-quences. Here too, as with Ferrera and other contributors, there is the sense of a crucial watershed being passed some time after the end of the *trente glorieuses*, a shift which has consequences not only for the policy-making process, the concern of Ferrera (2008) and Lodge (2008) among others, but also, as is emphasised by Kriesi, for the way in which citizens can connect to the political system.

One of the ways in which these connections have changed is that they have become more feminised, that is, they have changed in gender terms, an argument which lies at the core of the contribution by Joni Lovenduski (2008), and that also figures in the analyses by Crouch, Kriesi and others. Lovenduski looks at two related elements in this process. In the first place, she highlights the relative neglect and marginalisation of gender issues in the comparative European politics of the late 1970s and 1980s. But although, as she argues, the study of gender and politics has now become established in West European universities and although it is a thriving and varied subfield, it continues to be ignored by mainstream European political science. Even now, she concludes, 'most European political scientists tolerate but do not engage the theories, concepts and research generated by feminist scholars'. In the second part of her paper she reports on a tight empirical analysis of the impact of the women's policy agencies on the policy process. Drawing on unique cross-national European data, she shows how these agencies have helped to make Western European democracies more democratic by fostering the participation of women's movement advocates in decision-making processes and by helping meet women's movement demands.

The connections between citizens and the state have also changed in many other ways, of course, and in a broad-ranging and speculative contribution, Philippe Schmitter (2008) offers an inventory of the full variety of ways in which these changes might have affected the organisation and mobilisation of interests. Distinguishing between political parties, associations and movements, he traces the potential challenges to each category of interest organisation as well as the potential explanations for these challenges. Echoing the points raised by Kriesi, he underlines the importance of individuation, on the one hand, and the loss of traditional party control, on the other. This is not to suggest that parties will necessarily fade away, however, or that they will be replaced by associations or movements. In the past, these three forms of representation have grown together and supported each other and hence nothing suggests that they cannot also decline together in the present. That said, there clearly has been a widespread loosening of the links between interests and organizations in contemporary Europe.

Peter Mair (2008) is also pessimistic about the position and role of parties. Tracing a shift in the status and capacities of party government since the end of the *trente glorieuses*, he reviews evidence of the changing pattern of party competition, the decline of partisanship in policy-making, and the convergence of parties in the various European polities into a mainstream consensus. He also reviews the evidence for declining partisanship within the electorate. The final section of his article looks at the way the literature has specified the conditions for party government, and argues that these have been undermined in such a way that it is now almost impossible to imagine party government in contemporary Europe either functioning effectively or sustaining complete legitimacy.

One of the symptoms of party government weakness can be seen, of course, in the 'agencification' and fragmentation of national governments, which is one of the key topics addressed by Morten Egeberg (2008) in his essay. Echoing Hooghe and Marks, Egeberg also shows how the development of the EU, due to its peculiar institutional architecture, takes quite another direction than traditional intergovernmental cooperation, and thus also comes to challenge governments in an unprecedented way. This also impacts on national agencies and governments, which become part of two administrations – the national as well as the Union administration. Egeberg concludes that the centrifugal forces present at the very heart of national governments in Europe are at least partly the result of the 'emancipation' of the European Commission as a new executive centre. The Commission itself has become more similar to national governments in terms of structure and functions and has at the same time become more independent of national governments. In this sense, he concludes, we might even speak of a kind of 'pre-parliamentary system' at the EU level.

Change of a different, and perhaps also more muted, order is discussed by Klaus Goetz (2008) in his contribution on governance and governability. During the 1970s, when *WEP* was being launched, analyses of state and government in Western Europe were preoccupied with crises of govern-ability and legitimacy. By the end of the 1980s, and after the Mitterrand and Thatcher experiences, the notion of 'governance' came to be regarded as the dominant institutional response to problems of governability. This shift from government to governance may well have been overstated, however, and Goetz argues more sceptically that governance is actually less widespread and consequential in Europe than its proponents suggest. Viewed historically, governance does not indicate a shift from government but towards government, as the core institutions of the state build up capacity to deal authoritatively and hierarchically with new governing challenges.

One such capacity is regulatory capacity, the issue that Martin Lodge (2008) addresses in his contribution, reviewing a literature that usually takes its lead from a seminal article by Majone (1994), published in this journal. As Lodge suggests, Majone's argument was based on a diagnosis of two key trends, one being an overall shift towards the use of legal authority or regulation over the other tools of stabilisation and redistribution, and the other being the European Commission's expansionist role through the use of influence over policy content. Indeed, here too, as with Egeberg's analysis, we see a major, albeit sometimes indirect, effect of the European Commission on forms and styles of government at the national level. Since the mid-1990s, as Lodge goes on to argue, it has become commonplace to say we live in the age of the regulatory state, an age characterised by privatisation of public services, the establishment of quangos, and the formalisation of relationships within policy domains. Governance may not have replaced government, as Goetz insists, but an understanding of the new regulatory state is central to our broader understanding of how the state itself had changed, particularly in its relationship to business and its citizens, and in its distribution of coercive authority.

This is also the essence of the argument advanced by Vivien A. Schmidt (2008), who finds that there is much that has changed in European political economy over the past 30 years, both in terms of the political economic realities and the scholarly explanations of those realities. She argues that national economic policies and the policy-making process have undergone major transformations, largely in response to the twin pressures of globalization and Europeanization – two of the factors also emphasised by Schmitter. For Schmidt, these pressures have led to significant alterations in the role of the state, the importance of business, and the power of labour. Political economists, in their turn, have also changed their focus over time, first taking labour out of the equation, and then bringing the state back in, while later devaluing the state in the light of globalisation and Europeanisation and putting the firm to the centre. Only recently has attention come back to the state and to labour.

The substantive contributions to this anniversary issue of *WEP* are concluded by a reassessment by Francis G. Castles and Herbert Obinger (2008) of the continued validity of the notion of 'worlds' or 'clusters' of nations. When *WEP* was first launched, public policy analysts as well as students of political organisations and political behaviour frequently worked with the idea of families of polities – the Anglo-American democracies, the Low countries, the Nordic area, southern Europe, and so on. Indeed, many of the earlier contributions to the journal worked explicitly with such regional frames. Thirty years on, in an era of policy convergence and globalization, Castles and Obinger ask whether distinct worlds still persist, whether policy antecedents cluster in the same ways as policy outcomes, and whether the enlargement of the EU has led to an increase in the number of worlds constituting the wider European polity. Their conclusions are against expectations, in that they find that country clustering is now probably more pronounced than in the past, that it is, in large part, structurally determined, and that a quite distinct post-Communist family of nations has now joined the other, more traditional worlds.

One of the purposes of stock-taking exercise such as this is not only to look at changes in the real world, but also at changes in how scholars have approached that reality in their analyses. In other words, are newly discovered phenomena genuinely new, or only newly discovered? And what is the added value of the new modes of inquiry that have been applied in comparative European politics over the past three decades? Has there been an opening up and a greater pluralisation of approaches, or has there been a narrowing of theoretical perspectives in the study of European politics? In addressing these questions, this anniversary issue is rounded off with two pieces oriented more explicitly towards the patterns and capacities of scholarship in the field. Ellen M. Immergut and Karen M. Anderson (2008) emphasise the affinities between the traditional approaches to the study of West European politics, on the one hand, and the newly emergent, or newly branded, school of historical institutionalism, on the other. They suggest that there are four phases of scholarship that can be identified: the foundational ideas of the late 1970s and early 1980s; the evolution of these ideas from structuralism to institutionalism in the late 1980s and early 1990s; the more radical revision under the turbulent 1990s and early 2000s; and the emerging future patterns that can be seen at the end of the first decade of the 2000s.

In the final essay, Hans-Dieter Klingemann (2008) looks at the changing capacities of the discipline over this same period, beginning with the legacy of the political and social context in which European political science developed after World War II, and then going on to look at the degree of institutionalisation of political science as an academic discipline in Europe.

He then offers an assessment of the professional organisation and communication structures of the discipline, before concluding with an evaluation of the capacity to represent the discipline's education and research interests in the wider European area.

Of course, no single publication, even one as voluminous as the present and written by such a distinguished set of authors, can possibly claim to chart the diverse pasts and contested presents of European politics comprehensively and in detail. But it can provide a map to help students of European politics – both novices and 'old hands' – to understand 'how we got here' and to appreciate not just the immense breadth and depth of contemporary scholarship on European politics, but also to discern common trends and undercurrents, which can easily be masked by ever-increasing specialisation in the themes, methods and theoretical approaches of scholarly enquiry. Yet, for all the emphasis on path-dependencies in the evolution of European political systems, pasts and presents are likely to be unreliable guides to the futures of European politics, as sharp reversals in developmental trajectories over the past three decades have underlined. Many contributions to this volume contain troubling messages about the future, whether it concerns the EU integration project (Hooghe and Marks), the reduced electoral accountability of political decision-makers (Kriesi), the challenged legitimation of party government (Mair) or the sharpening of the edges of the state (Goetz). As yet, these developments do not appear sufficiently portentous to signal a 'systemic crisis' equivalent to the one which so preoccupied analysts some 30 years ago. But there is no reason to assume that changes in the politics of Europe over the coming the coming years should be any less profound, unexpected and, at times, traumatic, than they have been during the past three decades.

References

Berger, S., ed. (1982). *Religion in West European Politics*, special issue of *West European Politics*, 5:2.

Bull, M., and M. Rhodes, eds. (2007). *Italy: A Contested Polity*, special issue of *West European Politics*, 30:4.

Castles, F.G., and H. Obinger (2008). 'Worlds, Families, Regimes: Country Clusters in European and OECD Area Public Policy', *West European Politics*, 31:1–2, 321–44.

Crouch, C. (2008). 'Change in European Societies since the 1970s', *West European Politics*, 31:1–2, 14–39.

Egeberg, M. (2008). 'European Government(s): Executive Politics in Transition?', *West European Politics*, 31:1–2, 235–57.

Ferrera, M. (2008). 'The European Welfare State: Golden Achievements, Silver Prospects', *West European Politics*, 31:1–2, 82–107.

Goetz, K.H. (2008). 'Governance as a Path to Government', *West European Politics*, 31:1–2, 258–79.

Goetz, K.H., and S. Hix, eds. (2000). *Europeanised Politics? European Integration and National Political Systems*, special issue of *West European Politics*, 23:4.

Hooghe, L., and G. Marks (2008). 'European Union?', *West European Politics*, 31:1–2, 108–29.

Immergut, E.M., and K.M. Anderson (2008). 'Historical Institutionalism and West European Politics', *West European Politics*, 31:1–2, 345–69.

Inglehart, R.F. (2008). 'Changing Values among Western Publics from 1970 to 2006', *West European Politics*, 31:1–2, 130–46.

Keating, M. (2008). 'Thirty Years of Territorial Politics', *West European Politics*, 31:1–2, 60–81.

Klingemann, H.-D. (2008). 'Capacities: Political Science in Europe', *West European Politics*, 31:1–2, 370–96.

Kriesi, H. (2008). 'Political Mobilisation, Political Participation and the Power of the Vote', *West European Politics*, 31:1–2, 147–68.

Lodge, M. (2008). 'Regulation, The Regulatory State and European Politics', *West European Politics*, 31:1–2, 280–301.

Lovenduski, J. (2008). 'State Feminism and Women's Movements', *West European Politics*, 31:1–2, 169–94.

Madeley, J.T.S., and Z. Enyedi, eds. (2003). *Church and State in Contemporary Europe: The Chimera of Neutrality*, special issue of *West European Politics*, 26:1.

Mair, P. (2008). 'The Challenge to Party Government', *West European Politics*, 31:1–2, 211–34.

Mair, P., and J. Zielonka, eds. (2002). *The Enlarged European Union: Diversity and Adaptation*, special issue of *West European Politics*, 25:2.

Majone, G. (1994). 'The Rise of the Regulatory State in Europe', *West European Politics*, 14:3, 77–101.

Morlino, L. (2008). 'Democracy and Changes: How Research Tails Reality', *West European Politics*, 31:1–2, 40–59.

Schmidt, V.A. (2008). 'European Political Economy: Labour Out, State Back In, Firm to the Fore', *West European Politics*, 31:1–2, 302–20.

Schmitter, P.C. (2008). 'The Changing Politics of Organized Interests', *West European Politics*, 31:1–2, 195–210.

Shapiro, M. (1995). 'Of Interests and Values: The New Politics and the New Political Science', in Marc K. Landy and Martin A. Levin (eds.), *The New Politics of Public Policy*. Baltimore: Johns Hopkins University Press.

Change in European Societies since the 1970s

COLIN CROUCH

Sociology lags considerably behind political science in its comparative research on European societies. The reason lies partly in the dependence of modern social science on quantitative data bases. These tend to be collected nationally, by national agencies, and the informal phenomena studied by much sociology are highly vulnerable to different national definitions. Some of the same problems beset political science, but there are more formal institutions that, even when they differ across countries, can at least be understood in relation to each other. The situation has begun to improve in recent years, as more data are collected by the European Commission, and as a number of large, multinational research projects have been launched. There is now a European Sociological Association, and two major general journals (*European Sociological Review* and *European Societies*) that carry the continent's name in their titles, in addition to some specialised ones in related fields (like urban studies).

Enough material exists to enable us to talk broadly about the major changes that have taken place during these decades across western Europe, but also to some extent central and eastern Europe too. Attention will here be concentrated on those social trends that seem particularly salient for the study of politics. My starting point will be occupational structure. Although this dominant theme of classical sociology has tended to be neglected by much recent research in favour of such areas as deviance, gender and the formation of identities, working life remains fundamental to social organisation and in particular to politics. In fact, the theme of gender is easily accessed through consideration of changes in occupations, and considerable attention will be devoted to it here. This leads in turn to consideration of the family, then on to other aspects of demography including immigration and cultural diversity. This relates clearly to the final theme that will be discussed: the state of religion in Europe. In the conclusions some of the political implications of these, discussed through the article, will be brought together.

Occupational Change

Although the gradual decline of industrial employment in favour of various kinds of services had been predicted since the mid-twentieth century, and 'post-industrial society' had been proclaimed since the early 1970s (Bell 1973), European politics around the time of the founding of *West European Politics* was still firmly rooted in industrialism. This was especially the case in the southern parts of western Europe and in France, where the move from rural agricultural employment to urban and industrial was still taking place while the shift into services was also beginning. But the generalisation holds true in the north, and even in the oldest industrial nation, the United Kingdom, for the making of a population engaged in industrial work had been part of the same process that had produced the forms of the modern polity and its characteristic institutions of mass parties, rational bureaucratic public administration and, less generally, democracy. So powerful were the forces engaged in forging these historically unique forms of both working life and politics that subsequent changes leave us with the implications of 'post-industrialism' rather with a social form definable in its own terms. Alongside this, contemporary political organisation reflects the decline of the politics of industrial society rather than the rise of anything new.

The story in the eastern half of the continent is clearly different, but less so than for politics as such. Here too a central issue of previous decades had been the shaping of an industrial population, even more emphatically so than in the west, as the initial state of rural 'backwardness' was more intense, and the political determination to industrialise more all-embracing. The same drive also produced a deliberate avoidance of post-industrial tendencies, as a result of which the former state-socialist countries 'rejoined'

Europe as thoroughgoing examples of industrialising societies while their western neighbours had already departed considerably from that social form.

Table 1 presents data for all countries that had produced broadly comparable statistics around the time in the mid-1970s when *West European Politics* was launched. Although it was then still common to consider 'services' as a single 'tertiary' sector, it is possible to examine data for three of what have become known as the four services sectors, distinguished more or less by their distance from manufacturing (Crouch 1999: ch. 4). The table therefore shows, separately for men and women, employment in five of the six sectors:

I.   *Agriculture and mining*;
II.   *Manufacturing, public utilities and construction*;
III. *Distribution*; the movement of the products of industry and therefore still close to manufacturing activities: transport and all sales activities (including shops); postal services and telecommunications. Unfortunately, until recent years it has been common to include within these activities many of those that we now identify as sector VI (below);
IV.   *Business services*: activities that are not themselves part of the manufacturing process, but which are important to it: banks, insurance, and other financial activities; legal services; various design and consultancy activities; cleaning, security and maintenance. (The growth of this sector includes some quite illusory shifts from manufacturing to services, as manufacturing firms concentrating on their core business have sub-contracted, rather than employed directly, ancillary services.)
V.   *Social and community services*, that is services considered to contribute to some general good going beyond the individuals who receive them (like education or health). In some cases it is not easy to identify an individual user (maintenance of the environment; police services). Because of their communal character, many of these services have historically been provided by public authorities.
VI.   *Personal services*, considered to benefit solely the individuals who consume them: cultural and sporting entertainment, domestic cleaning, repair of domestic goods, etc. It is not possible to distinguish this sector in aggregated statistics until the late 1990s, parts of it being included in sector III.

Outside southern and eastern Europe, only Ireland had a primary (largely agricultural) sector employing more than 20 per cent of the workforce at that time, though it was still above 10 per cent in Austria, Finland, France and Norway. Manufacturing, construction, etc was the largest sector in all countries except Greece. It employed more than 40 per cent in Austria and West Germany, as well as three eastern European countries (Bulgaria,

TABLE 1
EUROPEAN OCCUPATIONAL STRUCTURES, c. 1975 (%)

	I	II	III (VI)	IV	V	Total
Austria						
M	7.3	30.0	13.0	2.4	8.9	61.6
F	6.0	10.4	10.0	2.3	9.6	38.3
Total	**13.3**	**40.4**	**23.0**	**4.7**	**18.5**	**99.9**
Belgium						
M	3.9	30.0	14.6	3.5	14.3	66.3
F	0.9	8.0	8.5	2.0	14.0	33.4
Total	**4.8**	**38.0**	**23.1**	**5.5**	**28.3**	**99.7**
Bulgaria						
M	12.6	24.1	8.0	0.2	8.2	53.1
F	12.9	16.8	6.7	0.5	10.0	46.9
Total	**25.5**	**40.9**	**14.7**	**0.7**	**18.2**	**100.0**
Czechoslovakia 1980						
M	7.8	30.4	7.2	0.5	7.5	53.4
F	5.5	18.9	9.1	0.7	12.5	46.7
Total	**13.3**	**49.3**	**16.3**	**1.2**	**20.0**	**100.1**
Denmark						
M	6.9	24.9	12.9	3.3	10.9	58.9
F	2.6	7.5	8.4	2.9	19.7	41.1
Total	**9.5**	**32.4**	**21.3**	**6.2**	**30.6**	**100.0**
Finland						
M	8.2	25.6	11.2	1.7	6.5	53.2
F	6.7	10.5	11.7	3.2	14.7	46.8
Total	**14.9**	**36.1**	**22.9**	**4.9**	**21.2**	**100.0**
France						
M	7.8	28.5	13.1	3.4	10.6	63.4
F	3.1	9.3	8.1	2.8	13.4	36.7
Total	**10.9**	**37.8**	**21.2**	**6.2**	**24.0**	**100.1**
Germany (East) 1981						
M	2.5	28.2	11.1	4.3	12.6	58.7
F	1.5	9.8	10.7	4.1	15.0	41.1
Total	**4.0**	**38.0**	**21.8**	**8.4**	**27.6**	**99.8**
Germany (West)						
M	4.4	32.8	11.0	2.7	11.9	62.8
F	3.6	11.5	9.2	2.4	10.5	37.2
Total	**8.0**	**44.3**	**20.2**	**5.1**	**22.4**	**100.0**
Greece 1977						
M	19.3	23.1	17.1	2.0	8.3	69.8
F	14.5	5.5	3.9	1.0	5.3	30.2
Total	**33.8**	**28.6**	**21.0**	**3.0**	**13.6**	**100.0**
Hungary						
M	13.8	26.5	9.1	0.0	6.6	56.0
F	8.9	17.4	7.6	0.0	10.1	44.0
Total	**22.7**	**43.9**	**16.7**	**0.0**	**16.7**	**100.0**
Ireland						
M	21.1	24.2	15.1	1.4	10.3	72.1
F	2.1	6.7	6.2	1.4	11.8	28.2
Total	**23.2**	**30.9**	**21.3**	**2.8**	**22.1**	**100.3**
Netherlands 1977						
M	5.1	30.8	15.6	4.8	16.3	72.6

(continued)

TABLE 1
(Continued)

	I	II	III (VI)	IV	V	Total
F	1.0	3.9	6.9	2.4	13.4	27.6
Total	**6.1**	**34.7**	**22.5**	**7.2**	**29.7**	**100.2**
Norway						
M	7.4	28.2	14.5	2.4	10.1	62.6
F	2.8	6.1	10.2	2.0	16.4	37.5
Total	**10.2**	**34.3**	**24.7**	**4.4**	**26.5**	**100.1**
Portugal						
1978						
M	15.8	25.2	10.8	1.3	7.6	60.7
F	14.5	10.1	5.4	0.6	8.6	39.2
Total	**30.3**	**35.3**	**16.2**	**1.9**	**16.2**	**99.9**
Spain						
1977						
M	16.1	30.2	14.4	2.6	8.4	71.7
F	5.8	6.8	7.4	0.6	7.7	28.3
Total	**21.9**	**37.0**	**21.8**	**3.2**	**16.1**	**100.0**
Sweden						
M	5.2	28.0	11.9	2.8	9.8	57.7
F	1.7	8.0	9.2	2.5	21.0	42.4
Total	**6.9**	**36.0**	**21.1**	**5.3**	**30.8**	**100.1**
UK						
M	3.5	29.0	13.1	2.9	12.5	61.0
F	0.6	9.6	10.1	2.9	15.8	39.0
Total	**4.1**	**38.6**	**23.2**	**5.8**	**28.3**	**100.0**

Czechoslovakia and Hungary), though not East Germany. Everywhere else, except Greece, it employed between 30 and 40 per cent. Its position within the world of male employment was even more significant. Only in some central European countries did female employment exceed a third of the total for the sector.

Distributive services and communications accounted for 20–25 per cent of the workforce throughout almost all western Europe, but less in central Europe and Portugal. It employed relatively high proportions of women except in Greece, Ireland, the Netherlands and Portugal, while women formed a majority in Czechoslovakia and Finland. Business services were a very small sector almost everywhere. Emerging as the clear second in size to manufacturing was employment in the largely public social and community services sector. In two Scandinavian countries (Denmark and Sweden) this was already employing more than 30 per cent of the workforce. Unlike the other sectors, this one was dominated by female employment: only in Belgium, West Germany, Greece, the Netherlands and Spain were women in a minority, and in Finland and Sweden they clearly dominated the sector. The relative size of this sector, combined with the higher levels of female employment in sector II in parts of central Europe, largely determines the gender structure of the workforce at this period. In only three countries – Bulgaria, Czechoslovakia and Finland – did women constitute more than 45 per cent of employment. In Ireland, the Netherlands, Spain they accounted for less than 30 per cent, with Greece barely above that level.

In general the mid-1970s constitute the peak of male industrial employment and the mid-twentieth century forms of politics associated with it. Challenging the industrial sector, as it were, is sector V: where the former is primarily male, concerned with the politics of production, and (in the west) largely privately owned, the latter is mainly female, mainly in public ownership and generating a politics of service provision.

The equivalent situation around 1990 is shown in Table 2. This year is both halfway through the intervening period and immediately following the collapse of the Soviet bloc. The classification base for reporting occupational structure is the same as in 1975, but data are available for more countries.

Agriculture and mining remain important in most central and southern European countries as well as Ireland, but are generally declining. Sector II is also declining, but remains the biggest single one in all but the Scandinavian and some north-western European countries (as well as the isolated case of Lithuania), where sector V is now the biggest. (In two south-eastern countries, Croatia and Greece, the distributive sector is larger than both these.) The countries with the most dominant industrial sectors are all in central Europe, with only Austria and West (but not East) Germany joining them at over 35 per cent of all employment. Only Norway has gone below having 25 per cent of employment in sector II. The distributive sector remains at between 20 and 29 per cent for all western European countries, rather less for most central ones – particularly Lithuania and Romania. Business services remains a small sector, but exceeds 10 per cent in the three commercially oriented economies of the Netherlands, Switzerland and the UK. Sector V accounts for more than 20 per cent except for Croatia, Greece, Romania and Slovakia. The Nordic countries, France, Belgium and the Netherlands have reached 35 per cent working in this sector, as has East but not West Germany. Only in Greece and Italy does this sector not have a female majority. In the economy overall women have achieved a 45 per cent presence in two kinds of country: all the Nordics (and, almost, the UK) and the majority of central Europeans. There is a sharp difference in the profile of these two groups: in the first female employment is concentrated in a large sector V with a low presence in sector II; in the latter many women also work in manufacturing.

By the end of the period, 2005, it begins to be possible to examine sector VI in its own right. Table 3 therefore finally gives data for all six sectors. With the collapse of industrial employment in parts of central Europe, there has been some rise in the role of agriculture there; in Bulgaria and Romania this sector has again become the largest one. With the exception of Italy and Portugal, only central European countries still have more than 30 per cent of their workforce in the industrial sector. Germany, for so long the epitome of an industrial economy, has finally become dominated by services sectors

TABLE 2
EUROPEAN OCCUPATIONAL STRUCTURES, c. 1990 (%)

	I	II	III (VI)	IV	V	Total
Austria						
M	4.7	28.5	12.8	3.2	9.9	59.1
F	4.3	8.1	12.2	3.2	13.2	41.0
Total	9.0	36.6	25.0	6.4	23.1	100.1
Belgium						
M	2.2	22.4	14.2	5.1	16.4	60.3
F	0.7	5.4	9.5	3.6	20.5	39.7
Total	2.9	27.8	23.7	8.7	36.9	100.0
Bulgaria						
1992						
M	10.0	20.7	11.0	0.3	10.0	52.0
F	6.8	16.5	8.8	0.9	15.1	48.1
Total	16.8	37.2	19.8	1.2	25.1	100.1
Croatia						
1991						
M	9.3	27.2	11.7	1.5	7.3	57.0
F	6.2	15.1	9.1	2.0	10.7	43.1
Total	15.5	42.3	20.8	3.5	18.0	100.1
Czech Republic						
M	7.4	28.5	7.5	0.6	8.3	52.3
F	4.5	17.8	9.9	1.0	14.5	47.7
Total	11.9	46.3	17.4	1.6	22.8	100.0
Denmark						
M	4.2	20.4	12.6	4.8	12.0	54.0
F	1.3	7.6	9.3	4.2	23.6	46.0
Total	5.5	28.0	21.9	9.0	35.6	100.0
Finland						
M	5.5	22.5	12.0	3.6	9.3	52.9
F	2.9	8.3	10.9	4.5	20.6	47.2
Total	8.4	30.8	22.9	8.1	29.9	100.1
France						
M	4.0	22.3	13.6	5.0	12.7	57.6
F	2.0	7.4	9.4	4.6	19.1	42.5
Total	6.0	29.7	23.0	9.6	31.8	100.1
Germany (East)						
1991						
M	5.3	23.5	8.1	1.7	13.6	52.2
F	2.8	11.3	9.6	2.2	22.0	47.9
Total	8.1	34.8	17.7	3.9	35.6	100.1
Germany (West)						
1991						
M	2.5	28.2	11.6	4.3	12.6	59.2
F	1.5	9.8	10.7	4.1	15.0	41.1
Total	4.0	38.0	22.3	8.4	27.6	100.3
Greece						
1977						
M	13.6	21.1	16.9	2.9	10.0	64.5
F	10.5	6.4	7.6	2.0	9.0	35.5
Total	24.1	27.5	24.5	4.9	19.0	100.0
Hungary						
1991						
M	11.1	23.4	10.4	0.0	9.6	54.5
F	6.5	13.4	10.5	0.0	15.2	45.6
Total	17.6	36.8	20.9	0.0	24.8	100.1

(continued)

TABLE 2
(*Continued*)

	I	II	III (VI)	IV	V	Total
Ireland						
M	14.4	21.6	15.1	4.4	11.6	67.1
F	1.3	6.2	8.3	3.7	13.7	33.2
Total	**15.7**	**27.8**	**23.4**	**8.1**	**25.3**	**100.3**
Italy						
M	6.7	23.3	18.0	2.5	15.0	65.5
F	3.3	7.8	8.7	1.7	13.0	34.5
Total	**10.0**	**31.1**	**26.7**	**4.2**	**28.0**	**100.0**
Lithuania 1989						
M	12.0	24.2	6.7	2.5	6.3	51.7
F	6.4	16.2	8.2	2.1	15.4	48.3
Total	**18.4**	**40.4**	**14.9**	**4.6**	**21.7**	**100.0**
Netherlands						
M	3.5	21.7	14.6	6.2	16.3	62.3
F	1.3	4.3	9.1	4.0	19.2	37.9
Total	**4.8**	**26.0**	**23.7**	**10.2**	**35.5**	**100.2**
Norway						
M	5.4	18.9	13.9	4.0	13.0	55.2
F	2.0	4.9	11.9	3.4	22.8	45.0
Total	**7.4**	**23.8**	**25.8**	**7.4**	**35.8**	**100.2**
Poland 1992						
M	13.7	22.5	8.3	0.3	10.1	54.9
F	11.2	9.4	8.0	1.1	15.6	45.3
Total	**24.9**	**31.9**	**16.3**	**1.4**	**25.7**	**100.2**
Portugal						
M	9.7	22.8	12.2	2.9	10.2	57.8
F	9.0	10.9	7.8	1.6	13.1	42.4
Total	**18.7**	**33.7**	**20.0**	**4.5**	**23.3**	**100.2**
Romania						
M	15.5	24.5	8.2	0.1	5.5	53.8
F	16.7	16.7	5.4	0.3	7.2	46.3
Total	**32.2**	**41.2**	**13.6**	**0.4**	**12.7**	**100.1**
Slovakia						
M	9.3	27.9	7.5	3.1	5.0	52.8
F	5.0	17.3	9.5	3.0	12.6	47.4
Total	**14.3**	**45.2**	**17.0**	**6.1**	**17.6**	**100.2**
Slovenia 1991						
M	8.2	25.1	9.0	2.6	7.9	52.8
F	6.8	16.9	8.9	2.5	12.3	47.4
Total	**15.0**	**42.0**	**17.9**	**5.1**	**20.2**	**100.2**
Spain						
M	9.3	27.3	16.3	3.5	10.8	67.2
F	3.5	5.9	9.6	1.7	12.3	33.0
Total	**12.8**	**33.2**	**25.9**	**5.2**	**23.1**	**100.2**
Sweden						
M	2.7	22.3	12.0	4.7	10.4	52.1
F	0.9	6.7	9.4	3.9	27.1	48.0
Total	**3.6**	**29.0**	**21.4**	**8.6**	**37.5**	**100.1**
Switzerland						
M	3.1	23.8	15.2	7.8	11.0	60.9
F	1.2	6.7	12.2	5.1	14.0	39.2
Total	**4.3**	**30.5**	**27.4**	**12.9**	**25.0**	**100.1**

(*continued*)

TABLE 2
(Continued)

	I	II	III (VI)	IV	V	Total
UK						
1993						
M	2.1	22.0	14.3	6.7	9.9	55.0
F	0.6	7.1	12.2	6.1	18.9	44.9
Total	**2.7**	**29.1**	**26.5**	**12.8**	**28.8**	**99.9**

(Mayer and Hillmert 2003). Italy and Portugal, along with Ireland and Spain, are also the only western economies where this sector still employs more than sector V, while Latvia is the only central European case of sector V being larger than sector II. In the Netherlands, Norway and the UK sector III is now larger than sector II. In western Europe the transition to post-industrial society may be said to be complete. The business services sector, while still small, has grown rapidly, being more than 15 per cent of employment in Ireland, Netherlands, Sweden, Switzerland and the UK. This sector has now begun to grow in central Europe, remaining very small only in Greece and Portugal. Sector V now accounts for more than 35 per cent of employment in Scandinavia and Belgium. It remains much lower in both central and southern Europe, giving a very clear geo-political character to this sector's position. We can for the first time inspect employment in personal services. In a mixed group of countries – south-west Europe together with Austria, Croatia, France and Ireland – it accounts for more than 5 per cent. Like many other services sectors, it is dominated by female employment, the sole exception being Ireland.

Overall, female employment has only exceeded 50 per cent in one small country – Estonia – but it is more than 45 per cent in all but nine countries, and is over 40 per cent in all except Greece and Italy. In general the process of change in eastern and central Europe since the collapse of state socialism can be seen as moving towards the social structures of western countries. However, the state socialist economies had higher proportions of women in work than did most western European ones; in this respect they resembled the Nordic countries, the UK and USA more closely than they did the countries that make up the bulk of the pre-enlargement EU. In the majority of central European cases, 'Westernisation' has involved a reduction or stagnation in women's labour force participation, despite the gradual shift towards more services employment that might imply feminisation. This is mainly because cuts in public spending have hit services that care for young children and the elderly, tasks which then tend to fall on women. At the same time female labour-force participation has been rising in the west, suggesting a true two-sided convergence between the different parts of Europe on this issue, rather than just a movement towards western patterns in CEE.

TABLE 3
EUROPEAN OCCUPATIONAL STRUCTURES, c. 2005 (%)

	I	II	III	IV	V	VI	Total
Austria							
M	3.1	21.7	11.8	6.3	9.5	2.4	54.8
F	2.5	5.9	10.3	6.3	15.9	4.4	45.3
Total	**5.6**	**27.6**	**22.1**	**12.6**	**25.4**	**6.8**	**100.1**
Belgium 2003							
M	1.4	19.8	13.4	7.6	13.1	1.7	57.0
F	0.5	5.0	8.1	5.7	22.0	1.8	43.1
Total	**1.9**	**24.8**	**21.5**	**13.3**	**35.1**	**3.5**	**100.1**
Bulgaria 2002							
M	16.1	15.1	10.2	2.0	7.1	1.6	52.1
F	13.3	11.0	7.7	1.9	11.7	2.4	48.0
Total	**29.4**	**26.1**	**17.9**	**3.9**	**18.8**	**4.0**	**100.1**
Croatia							
M	8.9	20.2	12.3	3.2	8.0	2.6	55.2
F	7.9	8.9	8.9	3.1	12.4	3.6	44.8
Total	**16.8**	**29.1**	**21.2**	**6.3**	**20.4**	**6.2**	**100.0**
Czech Republic							
M	3.8	26.8	11.2	4.1	8.5	1.8	56.2
F	1.4	11.8	9.4	3.9	15.2	2.3	44.0
Total	**5.2**	**38.6**	**20.6**	**8.0**	**23.7**	**4.1**	**100.2**
Denmark 2002							
M	2.5	18.2	13.1	7.1	11.2	1.1	53.2
F	0.8	6.2	8.2	5.4	24.6	1.6	46.8
Total	**3.3**	**24.4**	**21.3**	**12.5**	**35.8**	**2.7**	**100.0**
Estonia							
M	4.7	21.0	11.8	4.6	6.9	0.8	49.8
F	1.9	12.4	10.5	4.0	18.5	3.0	50.3
Total	**6.6**	**33.4**	**22.3**	**8.6**	**25.4**	**3.8**	**100.1**
Finland							
M	3.5	19.6	11.5	6.9	9.7	1.1	52.3
F	1.4	5.9	7.9	6.4	23.7	2.5	47.8
Total	**4.9**	**25.5**	**19.4**	**13.3**	**33.4**	**3.6**	**100.1**
France							
M	2.9	18.7	11.6	7.1	11.8	2.2	54.3
F	1.1	5.6	8.3	6.1	21.1	3.7	45.9
Total	**4.0**	**24.3**	**19.9**	**13.2**	**32.9**	**5.9**	**100.2**
Germany (All)							
M	1.9	22.2	10.8	6.9	11.7	1.6	55.1
F	0.8	7.2	9.0	6.3	19.2	2.5	45.0
Total	**2.7**	**29.4**	**19.8**	**13.2**	**30.9**	**4.1**	**100.1**
Greece							
M	7.2	18.1	15.4	4.7	11.4	4.0	60.8
F	5.1	4.2	8.7	4.5	11.9	4.9	39.3
Total	**12.3**	**22.3**	**24.1**	**9.2**	**23.3**	**8.9**	**100.1**
Hungary							
M	4.0	22.5	12.1	4.5	9.1	1.8	54.0
F	1.3	10.0	10.1	4.5	17.6	2.3	45.8
Total	**5.3**	**32.5**	**22.2**	**9.0**	**26.7**	**4.1**	**99.8**
Ireland							
M	11.0	20.7	4.6	7.9	6.2	5.1	55.5
F	4.7	8.3	6.3	7.1	16.6	1.5	44.5
Total	**15.7**	**29.0**	**10.9**	**15.0**	**22.8**	**6.6**	**100.0**

(*continued*)

TABLE 3
(*Continued*)

	I	II	III	IV	V	VI	Total
Italy							
M	3.1	23.8	13.2	7.3	10.6	2.7	60.7
F	1.4	6.9	7.3	5.9	14.1	3.8	39.4
Total	**4.5**	**30.7**	**20.5**	**13.2**	**24.7**	**6.5**	**100.1**
Latvia							
M	7.7	18.2	12.4	3.1	9.3	0.8	51.5
F	3.9	8.5	12.4	3.5	18.1	2.0	48.4
Total	**11.6**	**26.7**	**24.8**	**6.6**	**27.4**	**2.8**	**99.9**
Lithuania							
M	8.5	19.1	12.2	2.5	8.0	0.8	51.1
F	5.5	10.3	10.3	2.7	17.8	2.3	48.9
Total	**14.0**	**29.4**	**22.5**	**5.2**	**25.8**	**3.1**	**100.0**
Netherlands							
M	2.4	16.8	12.6	9.3	11.9	2.0	55.0
F	1.0	3.9	9.0	6.5	22.4	2.2	45.0
Total	**3.4**	**20.7**	**21.6**	**15.8**	**34.3**	**4.2**	**100.0**
Norway 2000							
M	4.2	16.1	13.5	6.7	11.7	1.2	53.4
F	1.3	4.1	9.2	4.6	25.2	2.3	46.7
Total	**5.5**	**20.2**	**22.7**	**11.3**	**36.9**	**3.5**	**100.1**
Poland							
M	10.5	21.4	11.5	4.0	7.4	0.7	55.5
F	6.9	8.1	9.5	3.8	14.8	1.4	44.5
Total	**17.4**	**29.5**	**21.0**	**7.8**	**22.2**	**2.1**	**100.0**
Portugal							
M	5.9	22.0	11.6	4.0	7.9	2.2	53.6
F	5.7	9.2	7.9	3.5	13.9	6.3	46.5
Total	**11.6**	**31.2**	**19.5**	**7.5**	**21.8**	**8.5**	**100.1**
Romania							
M	18.0	18.6	8.7	1.9	7.3	0.6	55.1
F	14.7	11.3	7.0	1.6	9.3	1.1	45.0
Total	**32.7**	**29.9**	**15.7**	**3.5**	**16.6**	**1.7**	**100.1**
Slovakia							
M	4.4	26.8	10.2	4.0	8.7	1.5	55.6
F	1.5	11.7	8.6	3.5	15.9	3.2	44.4
Total	**5.9**	**38.5**	**18.8**	**7.5**	**24.6**	**4.7**	**100.0**
Slovenia							
M	5.2	25.2	9.7	4.6	7.7	1.7	54.1
F	4.1	11.7	7.8	4.5	15.3	2.7	46.1
Total	**9.3**	**36.9**	**17.5**	**9.1**	**23.0**	**4.4**	**100.2**
Spain							
M	4.2	24.4	12.4	5.7	9.3	3.6	59.6
F	1.6	5.0	8.7	5.5	12.6	7.1	40.5
Total	**5.8**	**29.4**	**21.1**	**11.2**	**21.9**	**10.7**	**100.1**
Sweden							
M	1.7	17.5	11.9	9.2	10.7	1.3	52.3
F	0.5	4.4	7.0	6.4	28.0	1.5	47.8
Total	**2.2**	**21.9**	**18.9**	**15.6**	**38.7**	**2.8**	**100.1**
Switzerland							
M	2.6	17.6	10.7	10.4	11.5	1.6	54.4
F	1.3	5.2	9.4	6.6	20.8	2.3	45.6
Total	**3.9**	**22.8**	**20.1**	**17.0**	**32.3**	**3.9**	**100.0**

(*continued*)

TABLE 3
(*Continued*)

	I	II	III	IV	V	VI	Total
UK							
M	1.3	17.4	12.9	8.7	11.2	2.1	53.6
F	0.4	4.4	9.3	7.0	22.8	2.7	46.6
Total	**1.7**	**21.8**	**22.2**	**15.7**	**34.0**	**4.8**	**100.2**

Political Implications of Occupational Change

Political sociology has long recognised the implications for political cleavages, voting patterns and party organisation of the decline of manual and rise of non-manual work. But this change is easily confused with some of the implications of sectoral change. The class structure of industrialising society, on which the political cleavages surrounding democratisation were based in virtually all Europe, was itself an extension of the social order of the factory: a small owning and managing group, assisted by a junior administrative and clerical team, both separated by working environment from a manual workforce, which was itself divided by one or two broad skill demarcations. Although only a minority of the adult population anywhere ever worked in factories of this kind (an even smaller minority if account is taken of both genders), it provided the language and perceptual apparatus through which the whole population was structured, particularly for political purposes. This factory-based social structure emerged from the private practices of employers, but became embedded in government practice as much twentieth century social policy (e.g. pensions, social insurance and industrial relations institutions, qualification systems for vocational education) took on its assumptions about how industrial populations were to be classified. This further ramified their use in political organisation and the structuring of cleavages.

Post-industrial occupational structure challenges this situation in two ways. The more obvious is the fact that the nineteenth and twentieth century social order of the factory now accounts for an even smaller part of the workforce than it did when it was dominant. Less obviously, but perhaps more important, is the fact that there is no single equivalent paradigm sector in the new economy. To a considerable extent the office has replaced the factory as the paradigm organisational form, extending across several sectors and across the public/private divide. This produces a hierarchy of managers and professionals (the relative size of these groups varying considerably), and a large junior administrative and clerical workforce that may be larger or smaller than the professional one. The multiple gradations of this structure have so far not produced cleavages resembling those between manual workers and administrative staff that generated the politics of the twentieth century, except that there is a strong tendency for lower levels of office hierarchies to be heavily female, upper levels male, producing a gender rather than a class division. It is therefore relevant that gender has become more important than class in many political debates in recent times (Lovenduski this volume).

The role of the office varies in the different sectors from being the central location of organisations' activities (the business services sector, public administration) to being, as it is in the factory, ancillary (much of distribution, education, health, personal services). Also, the various services sectors have rather different internal structures. In two of them (business services and social and community services) the 'mass' workforce primarily comprises professionally qualified workers. In the distributive and private services sectors there is considerable heterogeneity, but there is often a less skilled workforce more like the factory model, though it is ambiguously definable as manual. The only one of these sectors large enough to be a potential paradigm is social and community services, but throughout Europe (and elsewhere in the advanced world) the majority provision of these services is funded by the state rather than through market forces. (This remains largely true even if service delivery is privatised.) It is difficult for a non- or only partially market sector to stand as the paradigm form of work organisation in societies where work is primarily rooted in markets.

A further form of division within contemporary workforces concerns different contract statuses, with some persons enjoying salaried positions and some security of employment, while others are in a number of precarious positions: temporary contracts, highly insecure tenure, certain kinds of self-employment (including 'false' self-employment), and indeed illegal employment, which plays a larger role in many economies than is usually acknowledged (Schneider 1997, 2002). These divisions between the relatively secure and the insecure often correspond to demographic divisions. The young and the old are both likely to concentrate in precarious jobs, an extreme case being the concentration of the young in temporary contracts in Spain. Ethnic minorities and recently arrived immigrants are likely to be heavily concentrated in insecure locations, including the black economy. In central and southern Europe women are also often in insecure jobs; in northern Europe they are more likely to be in fairly secure but part-time posts.

This emerging pattern of occupational divisions has a number of implications for politics in European countries. Should we see post-industrial society as one without major cleavages, as some have argued? Or, do cleavages exist, but are not achieving direct political expression because they are not acquiring explicit form in ways that are amenable to political mobilisation? If that is the case, are they acquiring implicit expression; that is, are political issues around work being politically presented in non-occupational forms? Alternatively again, do cleavages in post-industrial societies exist, but in fields unrelated to work? These questions go well beyond the scope of the present discussion, but the issues raised here provide essential background for addressing issues of political cleavage and organisation. Coverage of political sociology questions in the first 30 years of *West European Politics* usually drew on a Rokkanian framework of the sociology of twentieth century cleavages, but often to record their political decline (Crewe 1983; Wolinetz 1979). However, only one article, and an early one (Ersson and Lane 1981), actually discussed the decline of industrial and the rise of services employment. And there has been little that analyses the potential implications of the new structures being erected as opposed to those of the decline of the old. Some authors insisted that social structure has become less important than movements based on value orientations (Flanagan and Dalton 1984), but others provided evidence to contest this (Reiter 1993). If anything, the strongest arguments have come from those showing that, though the old cleavages might be declining, in the absence of anything clearly replacing them they retain considerable importance (Mair 1984).

These discussions have of course concentrated on west European politics. In those countries that experienced a state socialist period there was, at the level of official ideology and social policy organisation, an 'inverted' class structure, whereby manual workers were represented as the key group to be served by public policy, though the structures created to give expression to this special status did not have an autonomous capacity to express the group's self-defined interests (Kivinen 2006). The collapse of that system has therefore produced considerable confusion in the articulation of occupational interests, which feeds through into the rather unstable character of post-socialist party structures. This is not simply a result of the suppression of autonomous political organisation during dictatorships *per se*: following the collapse of reactionary dictatorships in Greece, Portugal and Spain, democratic party politics rapidly acquired a familiar western European, occupation-based form (Montero 1998). It was the particular distinctiveness of state socialist class structure that makes it difficult to establish relationships between occupational structure and political cleavage in CEE countries today, even though that structure remains less subject to post-industrial fragmentation than those of western European countries.

Changes in Gender Roles

As already indicated, one of the candidates for consideration as a new source of cleavage in post-industrial societies is gender, partly as an occupationally related category, partly *sui generis*. Overall, incomes are higher in business services and social and community services than in other sectors, probably because of the different educational levels of most workers in these sectors (Crouch 1999: chs. 5, 6). However, even though more women work in these higher-paying sectors than men, their incomes are on average lower than men's. Clearly, women are found predominantly in the lower-grade positions. Among older generations this may partly reflect the fact that male educational achievements used to be superior to female. However, virtually everywhere this has been subject to major change, and among younger generations the genders' educational performances have been reversed (Shavit and Blossfeld 1993). Another, and continuing, reason for women occupying the lower rungs in hierarchies is of course that their working careers are interrupted by child-bearing and, in several countries, associated periods of either part-time work or temporary exit from the labour force. This is changing as several factors increase the opportunities for women to enter the paid workforce, these factors operating very diversely in different European countries.

First, the automation of the kitchen that took place in the west with the growth of electrical domestic appliances during the post-war decades of growing prosperity raised the productivity of domestic labour just as factory automation did to industrial labour.

Second, families throughout Europe today have fewer children, reducing the quantity of childcare needed (Blossfeld 1995).

Third, particularly in eastern Europe where there was far less kitchen automation, women acquired the 'double burden' of doing their housework when they finished their paid jobs for the day; sometimes their husbands may have shared these tasks, but not often (Pollert 1999). Indeed, there is also research evidence in western Europe that men have been slow to accept that their wives' engagement in paid work implies many additional domestic duties for themselves. In some countries (particularly the Netherlands and the UK) women tend to work part-time in paid employment and part-time at housework and childcare.

Fourth, other family members might help as a family obligation, for example grandmothers helping mothers with childcare. Finally, other people (nearly always other women) might carry out the employed woman's domestic tasks by themselves being paid to do the work. It is this last that leads to the employment-creating spiral of women's employment (Esping-Andersen 1999). The jobs that are created by this last process are in childcare and in other care services for the sick and the elderly that have traditionally been performed as unpaid domestic tasks by women. These services can be organized in very different ways, with major implications for how the work is reported in official statistics. These are often jobs in the community and social services sector, or in personal services, including food preparation, replacing domestic labour. But some of these activities are traded informally among women (Mingione 1991). For example, cleaners and child-minders are usually paid informally by the women who employ them; they have no contract of employment, do not appear in any lists of persons employed, and are not registered as taxpayers. The size of this kind of female employment is therefore under-estimated in official statistics.

As Tables 1–3 have shown, there remains considerable diversity among countries in their patterns of female employment. Most can be explained in the following ways. Some countries, particularly the Nordic ones but to some extent also the UK, developed extensive direct services within the welfare state. These countries have evinced particularly strong growth of women's employment in the social and community sector (Esping-Andersen 1999), with secondary effects as the women recruited by this expansion created further demand for female labour services as carers, etc. Rather similarly, during the state socialist period in central and eastern Europe places of employment provided childcare facilities for working mothers, the carers being other employed women. Elsewhere in Europe, the welfare state placed a stronger emphasis on transfer payments (pensions, disability and sickness allowances, etc) than on direct service provision (for example, Germany, Italy) (Daly 2000; von Wahl 2006). This restricted primary job growth among women, and therefore the multiplier process was also weaker. In these countries, primarily those in which the Roman Catholic Church had a strong influence on social policy, acceptance of inter-generational family obligations remains strong, and women are likely to carry out as unpaid domestic work the activities that enable their daughters, nieces, or sisters to enter the labour force. The work is being carried out just as much as if it was being rewarded, but as with the informal economy it does not register in the job statistics.

As the tables also show, these divergences among countries are relatively recent. In the 1970s there was less variation in women's employment between the various parts of western Europe, except for the south (Crouch 1999: ch. 2; Naumann 2006). High levels of female paid work were found only in central Europe. It was from the late 1960s onwards that nearly every democratic country in western Europe started to see a major growth in welfare state expenditure. Countries differed in the size and speed of that growth, but more importantly they differed (as has been noted) in the form of the expenditure, with major implications for whether it created primarily female employment in social and community services. These differences are beginning to decline now, as female participation in formal employment in these services is growing virtually everywhere, and in western Europe very few if any political forces pursue policies that would deliberately inhibit women's employment. But past legacies remain prominent.

As already noted, the trajectory in CEE has been different. Particularly in Poland, Catholic social policy has been able to exert political influence only since the collapse of state socialism. This has resulted in a number of policies that discourage female employment, bringing female participation down from its formerly high levels (Pollert 1999).

Returning to the west, the turn of the decade of the 1960s and 1970s also saw, in almost all these countries, a major development in women's consciousness, with a significant and enduring feminist movement that was to have, and continues to have, extensive implications for politics and policy. The relationship between the two factors – the growth in social services employment and feminism – is complex. Neither can be said to have 'caused' the other, but they have combined with major consequences.

Although there are many examples of gender-based social movements and pressure groups, there are very few gender-based political parties. Given that political allegiances tend to be rooted in various forms of social segregation, it is difficult in societies where men and women live together for gender to articulate its conflicts in party form.

There have however long been gender differences in political loyalties. For most of the twentieth century, where democracy existed women tended more than men did to ally themselves to right-of-centre parties, especially those with links to Christian churches (Mayer and Smith 1985). There are two good sociological reasons for this. First, left-of-centre parties usually defined themselves in relation to the concerns of manual workers in manufacturing industry, who were predominantly male. Second, in the twentieth century division of labour between the genders, women's lives were mainly centred on family, home and local community, the values of which were strongly upheld by churches. These differences were only of emphasis: some women were in paid employment, or even if they were not, they shared the life perspectives of their husbands. Also, in Catholic countries specifically Christian labour movements struggled against secular ones for the allegiance of males too. But an overall difference between men and women did exist.

These patterns have changed considerably in the past two decades. In most European polities gender difference in voting patterns and political allegiances have either disappeared or even been reversed (Northcutt and Flaity 1985). The rise in female labour-force participation, and (in western Europe) the decline in both religious observation and in churches' insistence on women having primarily domestic roles, have undermined the former basis of segregation. Meanwhile, as noted, women dominate employment in social and community services, and left-of-centre parties are particularly associated with supporting public funding of these services: these factors taken together lead women to vote increasingly for these parties.

Demographic Trends and Family Changes

Alterations in women's position have been among a number of major changes in the structure and behaviour of families. These need to be set in the context of wider changes in population patterns. As Table 4 shows, western Europeans are living longer than they did a few decades ago. The trend is not so strong, particularly among men, in central and eastern European countries. In some of these, and in Russia, the economic dislocation of the early 1990s led male life expectancy to go down.

As death rates decline, so do birth rates (see Table 5, which shows total fertility for women of child-bearing age in a number of European countries). This generalisation holds across the whole continent, and the current pattern of low birth rates distinguishes Europeans from most other world regions: only Japan shows similar patterns.

TABLE 4
LIFE EXPECTANCY AT BIRTH, CENTRAL AND WESTERN EUROPEAN
COUNTRIES, 1960–2002

	Males		Females	
	1960	**2005**	**1960**	**2005**
Austria	66.2	75.8	72.7	81.7
Belgium	67.7	75.1	73.5	81.1
Bulgaria	67.8	68.9	71.4	75.6
Croatia	64.3	70.5*	69	77.8*
Czech R.	67.9	72.1	73.4	78.7
Denmark	70.4	74.8	74.4	79.5
Estonia	64.3	65.3	71.6	77.1
Finland	65.5	74.9	72.5	81.5
France	66.9	75.6	73.6	82.9
Germany	**	75.6*	**	81.3*
Greece	67.3	75.4	72.4	80.7
Hungary	65.9	68.4	70.1	76.7
Ireland	68.1	75.2	71.9	80.3
Italy	67.2	76.8	72.3	82.9
Latvia	65.2	64.8	72.4	76
Lithuania	64.9	66.3	71.4	77.5
Netherlands	71.5	76	75.3	80.7
Norway	71.6	76.4	76	81.5
Poland	64.9	70.4	70.6	78.3*
Portugal	61.2	73.8	66.8	80.5
Romania	64.2	67.5	67.7	74.8
Slovakia	68.4	69.9	72.7	77.8
Slovenia	66.1	72.7	72	80.5
Spain	67.4	75.7	72.2	83.1
Sweden	71.2	77.7	74.9	82.1
Switzerland	68.7	77.8	74.5	83
UK	67.9	75.7*	73.7	80.4*

Source: Eurostat, Population Statistics 2004.
*Croatia 2000; Germany, Poland (female) and UK 2001.
**No comparable figures available for the two Germanies of that period.

The geography of European demography contains some paradoxes. Until the decades here under review, birth rates in southern Europe were considerably higher than in northern. This was easily explicable: industrialisation and growing prosperity started first in north-west Europe; and across the world and over time a strong association between modernisation and declining fertility is one of the safest generalisations in the social sciences. Also, much of southern Europe is Roman Catholic, and that church had maintained an opposition to artificial contraception long after Protestant churches had abandoned it. Birth rates were also low in central and eastern Europe, which were less industrialised than much of the west, but these countries were engaged in a rapid industrialisation process.

The following twin processes then seem to have reversed some of these generalisations (Crouch 1999: ch 7). First, the welfare state developments described above in relation to the Nordic countries and, to a lesser extent, France and the UK, began to make it easier for women to combine work

TABLE 5

TOTAL FERTLITY RATES, CENTRAL AND WESTERN EUROPEAN COUNTRIES,
1960–2002

	1960	2002
Austria	2.69	1.4
Belgium	2.56	1.62
Bulgaria	2.31	1.21
Croatia	2.21	1.23
Czech R.	2.11	1.17
Denmark	2.57	1.72
Estonia	2.16*	1.37
Finland	2.72	1.72
France	2.73	1.89
Germany	2.37	1.31
Greece	2.28	1.25
Hungary	2.02	1.3
Ireland	3.76	1.97
Italy	2.41	1.26
Latvia	1.74*	1.24
Lithuania	2.6	1.24
Netherlands	3.12	1.73
Norway	2.91	1.75
Poland	2.98	1.24
Portugal	3.1	1.47
Romania	2.33	1.26
Slovakia	3.07	1.19
Slovenia	2.18	1.21
Spain	2.86	1.25
Sweden	2.2	1.65
Switzerland	2.44	1.4
UK	2.72	1.64

Source: Eurostat, Population Statistics 2004.
*Estonia 1970; Latvia 1965.

with motherhood. Birth rates began to rise. Second, couples in southern Europe, Germany and other countries that were not pursuing employment-friendly social care policies, who were just as keen to exercise freedom in their lifestyles as their northern counterparts, did so by reducing the number of children for whom they would have to be responsible. By the 1990s the highest birth rates in western Europe were in Scandinavia, the lowest in Italy and Spain – a complete historical reversal.

Meanwhile, the upheavals in CEE countries have simply accentuated past trends to low birth rates. If these had previously been a result of the female 'double burden', since the change of regime they have resulted also from the high level of economic uncertainty. Birth rates in this part of Europe are lower even than in the south.

Smaller Households

In nearly all European countries, young people are forming couples later and having fewer children. This trend then joins with others to produce another change: households are becoming smaller. The other causes include a growing tendency for young adults and elderly people to live by themselves rather than in the same accommodation as other members of their families. This is the result of increased general prosperity, improving house-purchase loan systems, and (important for elderly people) both improved health in old age and improving care facilities. There is, however, diversity within this common trend. For example, in southern and eastern Europe birth rates are lower than in the north-west; but young adults are more likely to live with their parents. Causes of these developments are clearly complex.

Decreased household size also results from a common tendency towards a decline in the number of married people. This has several causes: the rise in the age of marriage discussed above; an increase in the number of couples who do not have a formal marriage; and a rise in divorce. These phenomena can be seen in all European countries, and in the rest of the industrialised world. There is again considerable diversity, however. Divorce rates in particular are far higher in northern and eastern Europe than in the south. On the other hand, growing longevity in most parts of Europe means that couples who stay together can expect to have more years together before widowhood.

The Ageing of the Population

Greater longevity combined with low birth rates produce what is often called the ageing of the population, as the average age rises. Western Europe and Japan are experiencing this in a way unparalleled elsewhere in the world or in human history (for an exploration of its implications applied to one country, Germany, see Mayer and Hillmert, 2003). This theme primarily enters political debate in the form of a so-called pensions crisis: if the proportion of the population in work falls in relation to the proportion living on retirement pensions, there are problems for the funding of pension schemes that rely on the earnings of today's workers to fund the incomes of today's pensioners (Ferrera and Rhodes 2000). However, it is less often noticed that low birth rates also mean reduced numbers of the dependent young, and therefore reduced pressure on childcare and education budgets. A major demographic crisis of public spending occurs only if *both* elderly and child populations are high, with an earlier dip in birth rates having produced a small working and tax-paying population. This is not the case in contemporary Europe.

Also less noticed is the contribution that a large generation of relatively wealthy retired people make to sustaining their adult, working children at a time of increased economic insecurity. The prolonged period of post-war full employment, accompanied by major improvements in state retirement pension provision immediately after World War II and then again after the 1970s have meant that, for the generations that entered the workforce during that era, old age has not been a time of poverty. This has been a remarkable change from previous generations. In most western European countries this was also a period of growth in home ownership. The majority of today's elderly among ordinary working people have considerably more financial resources than their predecessors. The role of this stabilising force in a contemporary economy and labour market characterised by uncertainty is a subject that would repay research.

This factor is likely to prevent the emergence of a generational cleavage (Goerres 2007). Such a cleavage is sometimes predicted because of the ostensible conflict between those enjoying good pensions and those who come after them, funding those pensions from their taxes while probably not being able to look forward to having such pensions themselves. In addition, younger people are aware that if their parents do not have sound pensions, the burden of their care will probably fall on them. They are therefore more likely to respond by insisting on the maintenance of generous pensions and their continuation until their own generation, rather than welcome tax cuts that could follow a reduction in pension cover. This logic probably explains why campaigns against cuts in pensions for public employees in France have attracted sympathy from parts of the public who do not themselves benefit from them (Bonoli 1997).

Immigration and Cultural Pluralism

Extensive immigration into western Europe from less prosperous parts of the world has been a long-standing phenomenon. In recent years this has extended to the Nordic countries, Italy and Spain. The latter, for so long countries of emigration, have found themselves attractive to people in northern Africa, which is geographically close. Following the collapse of the Soviet bloc, there are now major movements of people from eastern and central Europe towards the west, and from eastern towards central Europe.

Unlike the migrations of the 1960s, which took place when there were labour shortages in western Europe, these new movements are taking place at a time when there is high unemployment in much of the latter region. Meanwhile, half a century of immigration into some parts of western Europe has produced second and third generations of people descended from immigrants, but born and brought up in Europe, sometimes intermarrying and forming new families with people from the host society. Although such cultural mixing has always been a characteristic of many European countries, this longer European history has also been marked by major episodes of intolerance and bloodshed. Elements of this continue to dog the creation of multicultural societies today, as dominant majorities and immigrant or post-immigrant minorities try to come to terms with each other. These difficulties sometimes create major political issues, and anti-immigrant parties, or factions within existing parties, have become among the major innovations on the party-political scene (Messina 1990; *West European Politics* 1994, 2006; Joppke 2007).

In some cases these new cultural issues affect societies where tension still exists from older patterns of difficult relations between majorities and older settled minorities. Difficulties in relations between Catholics and Protestants in Northern Ireland and between Basques and Spaniards in northern Spain have been among the most persistent in western Europe. It is however in eastern and central Europe that this kind of tension remains strongest. During the 1990s the former state of Yugoslavia collapsed under the weight of extreme violence bordering on attempted genocide among its diverse cultural and religious (Catholic, Orthodox, and Muslim) populations. Elsewhere such issues as the place of Hungarians in Romania, of Turks in Bulgaria, of Russians in the Baltic states, of Gypsies in many countries, continue to produce means of political mobilisation, sources of discrimination and occasional outbursts of violence.

The Decline of European Religion

While there is debate about what indicators should be used, there is little doubt that religion is an institution in major decline throughout Europe – except among some of the immigrant communities mentioned above. This trend became manifest first in a decline in attendance at religious services by people who continued to regard themselves as believers. More recently, though, there has also been a decline even in affirmations of a belief in God (Halman *et al.* 2005; *West European Politics* 2003). Further, the European situation contrasts very considerably with that in the USA, where religious belief, church attendance, and the political power of religious organisations have been growing very strongly indeed. Europe, along with Japan, stands out as a world region of religious decline at a time when the institution is rising in prominence in the USA, the Islamic world, and some other areas.

There are however important differences in the patterns. In the UK, and more recently the Netherlands, religious observance of all kinds has sunk to very low levels. In the Nordic countries, while regular church attendance is the lowest in the world, large majorities of the population are confirmed into the church and opt to pay a voluntary religious tax to fund their churches. In some other countries, including Italy, Ireland, and Poland, church attendance remained high until the past decade or so (Halman *et al.* 2005).

The decline in Poland is particularly striking, as the Catholic Church had been a major source of Polish national identity during the years of Soviet domination, and had played a major part in undermining the state socialist regime (Anderson 2003). It had been widely expected that there would be a major Christian renaissance, not only in Poland, but throughout central and eastern Europe, where churches (variously Orthodox, Catholic, and Lutheran) had remained a stable symbol of popular identity during years of disorientation. At the level of political influence this has often been the case, religious leaders acquiring a dominant role in social policy in particular. However, this trend has contradicted that in popular behaviour.

In fact, in Poland and elsewhere the Christian churches have declined rapidly in central and eastern Europe following the fall of communism, as those countries have joined a general European trend.

In general the history of religion in modern Europe has followed a clear pattern (Martin 2005). Where the dominant church made strong demands on the loyalty of populations and exercised a major political influence, people became divided between supporters of that church role and outright opponents of it. This was largely the case with the Catholic Church, and also of Calvinist Protestant churches, which tend to flourish in embattled situations where Protestants face strong Catholic and/or secular or other opposition (the Netherlands, Scotland, Northern Ireland, to some extent Switzerland; and outside Europe in South Africa). National churches that became content to express the common life of a nation state without making political claims other than securing their own quiet position in that life tended to attract neither the support nor the hostility to which the Catholic Church was liable. Declining numbers took an interest in their activities, but few bothered to challenge their claim to a quiet place in national life. This has been the fate of the Church of England in England and the Lutheran churches in the Nordic countries. In a somewhat different way, it has also been the pattern in eastern Europe, where the Orthodox Church takes the form of a number of national churches.

Where religions of various kinds express the identity of people against, or at least separately from, an alien political power, that religion can attract powerful loyalties as in the dominant Catholic case (Anderson 2003). Here however this is without the antagonism attracted by a church's exercise of power over people, as it is experienced as an alternative to a more remote political authority. What such religions have to fear is the passing into insignificance of the identity that they express. There are many, varied examples of this phenomenon. The Catholic Church has been in this position where a Catholic population has been dominated by non-Catholics – as in Ireland (long dominated by the British) and Poland (dominated, among others, by the Russians). Those countries did not experience strong secularist movements. Long after Greek independence from Turkey, the Greek Orthodox Church still plays a similar role for Greeks.

Religions today often play this powerful cultural identity role for ethnic minorities, and an earlier expression of internal local cultural diversity is replacing that of regionalism in many European societies today. Jews have long been an example of this. Following the more recent waves of immigration, Islam, Hinduism, Buddhism, the distinctive forms of Christianity found in Africa and the Caribbean, and some others, have provided valuable identities among immigrant groups and their descendants, becoming important constituents of the cultural pluralism mentioned above. Typically, therefore, ethnic minorities have far higher patterns of religious observance than native populations.

Conclusion

The societies of central and eastern Europe have joined the general history of capitalist economic development when it is at a moment of considerable change. The late nineteenth and twentieth century economy built around male workers in manufacturing industry is giving way to one based on various services. This is a particularly strong challenge for the former state socialist countries, as services played a small role in their economies. Meanwhile, both parts of Europe have left behind them the forms of economic organisation that provided basic security to their working populations in the decades after World War II: Keynesian demand management in the west, a centrally planned economy in the east. Both now face the more turbulent global market economy. The struggle among populations for security in this context partly takes the form of the protective role of the welfare state, stronger in northern Europe than anywhere else, and partly that of different levels of security provided by different forms of work contract and associated labour rights. To some extent these areas become fields of distributional and therefore political conflict, as different demographic and occupational categories achieve different levels of social rights.

For most of the nineteenth and twentieth centuries the politics of most European countries was shaped by two major conflictual forces. The first was struggle between religions, or between religion and secularism. The second was class struggle. The party systems of Europe still bear the imprint of these struggles more than of any other. But they all refer to events of the past. This is not because there are no struggles over religion and class in twenty-first century society, but they concern different issues. First, relations between ethnic and religious minorities and their host societies take the form of potential clashes between cultures rather than religious conflict in the strict sense. Second, the class conflicts around which party politics is organised still concern the role of the industrial working class.

The political agenda has responded to change. Issues of globalisation and the transition of employment forms from those designed for large-scale manufacturing to those designed around the new services sector are important everywhere, from the prosperous economies of western Europe to those in the centre and the east entering the scene of these new issues while they are still embroiled in the transition from state socialist to capitalist economies. Changes in the role of women, and challenges for the welfare state created by both those changes and the wider shifts in employment patterns are similarly important. Immigration is also a political issue. In this last case both racist or populist parties or fractions of parties representing ethnic minorities have certainly entered the political stage. But otherwise party structures and rhetoric have remained largely static. The new issues of the transition to the services economy, and the new social groups forged by them, have so far found little autonomous expression. In the west this may be reflected in growing popular apathy towards politics and an apparent growing gulf between political classes and the mass of the population. In central and eastern Europe we see a difficulty in establishing stable party structures that might express people's conflicts and aspirations, and instead a rapidly changing series of personal cliques formed around individual political leaders.

References

Anderson, J. (2003). 'Catholicism and Democratic Consolidation in Spain and Poland', *West European Politics*, 26:1, 137–56.

Bell, D. (1973). *The Coming of Post-Industrial Society*. New York: Basic Books.

Blossfeld, H.-P., ed. (1995). *The New Role of Women. Family Formation in Modern Societies*. Boulder, CO: Westview.

Bonoli, G. (1997). 'Pension Politics in France: Patterns of Co-operation and Conflict in Two Recent Reforms', *West European Politics*, 20:4, 111–24.

Crewe, I. (1983). 'The Electorate: Partisan Dealignment Ten Years On', *West European Politics*, 6:4, 183–215.

Crouch, C. (1999). *Social Change in Western Europe*. Oxford: Oxford University Press.

Daly, M. (2000). 'A Fine Balance. Women's Labour Market Participation in International Comparison', in F.W. Scharpf and V.A. Schmidt (eds.), *Welfare and Work in the Open Economy. Vol. II: Diverse Responses to Common Challenges*. Oxford: Oxford University Press, 467–510.

Ersson, S., and J.-E. Lane (1981). 'The Socio-Economic Structures of European Democracies', *West European Politics*, 4:1, 120–33.

Esping-Andersen, G. (1999). *Social Foundations of Postindustrial Economies*. Oxford: Oxford University Press.

Ferrera, M., and M. Rhodes (2000). 'Recasting European Welfare States: Introduction', *West European Politics*, 23:2, 1–10.

Flanagan, S.C., and R.J. Dalton (1984). 'Parties under Stress: Realignment and Dealignment in Advanced Industrial Societies', *West European Politics*, 7:1, 7–23.

Goerres, A. (2007). Can We Reform the Welfare State in Times of 'Grey' Majorities? The Myth of an Electoral Opposition between Younger and Older Voters in Germany, MPIfG Working Paper 07/5. Cologne: MPIfG.

Halman, L., R. Luijkx and van M. Zundert (2005). *Atlas of European Values*. Leiden: Tilburg University.

Joppke, C. (2007). 'Beyond National Models: Civic Integration Policies for Immigrants in Western Europe', *West European Politics*, 30:1, 1–22.

Kivinen, M. (2006). 'Classes in the Making? The Russian Social Structure in Transition', in G. Therborn (ed.), *Inequalities of the World*. London: Verso, 247–94.

Mair, P. (1984). 'Party Politics in Contemporary Europe: A Challenge to Party?', *West European Politics*, 7:4, 170–84.

Martin, D. (2005). *On Secularisation: Towards a Revised General Theory*. Aldershot: Ashgate.

Mayer, K.-U., and S. Hillmert (2003). 'New Ways of Life and Old Rigidities? Changes in Social Structures and Life Courses and Their Political Implications', *West European Politics*, 26:4, 79–100.

Mayer, L., and R.E. Smith (1985). 'Feminism and Realignment: Female Electoral Behaviour in Western Europe', *West European Politics*, 8:4, 38–49.

Messina, A.M. (1990). 'Political Impediments to the Resumption of Labour Migration in Western Europe', *West European Politics*, 13:1, 31–46.

Mingione, E. (1991). *Fragmented Societies*. Oxford: Blackwell.

Montero, J.R. (1998). 'Stabilizing the Democratic Order: Electoral Behaviour in Europe', *West European Politics*, 21:4, 53–79.

Naumann, I. (2006). 'Childcare Politics in the West German and Swedish Welfare States from the 1950s to the 1970s', unpublished PhD thesis, European University Institute, Florence.

Northcutt, W., and J. Flaity (1985). 'Women, Politics and the French Socialist Government', *West European Politics*, 8:4, 50–70.

Pollert, A. (1999). *Transformation at Work in the New Market Economies of Central and Eastern Europe*. London: Sage.

Reiter, H.L. (1993). 'The Rise of the "New Agenda" and the Decline of Partisanship', *West European Politics*, 16:2, 89–104.

Schneider, F. (1997). 'The Shadow Economies of Western European Europe', *Journal of the Institute of Economic Affairs*, 17, 42–8.

Schneider, F. (2002). *The Size and Development of the Shadow Economy of 22 Transition and 21 OECD Countries*. Linz: Forschungsinstitute für Zukunft der Arbeit.

Shavit, Y., and H.-P. Blossfeld, eds. (1993). *Persistent Inequality. Changing Educational Attainment in Thirteen Countries*. Boulder, CO: Westview.

Von Wahl, A. (2006). 'Gender Equality in Germany: Comparing Policy Change across Domains', *West European Politics*, 29:3, 461–88.

West European Politics (1994). *Special Issue on the Politics of Immigration*, 17:2.

West European Politics (2003). *Special Issue on Religion and Politics*, 26:1.

West European Politics (2006). *Special Issue on Immigration Control*, 29:2.

Wolinetz, S.B. (1979). 'The Transformation of Western European Party Systems Revisited', *West European Politics*, 2:1, 4–28.

Democracy and Changes: How Research Tails Reality

LEONARDO MORLINO

As in other fields of research the burden of research tradition has been influential in empirical democratic theory. Consequently, there have always been new studies that continue building on previous published work. As a result, there has been no significant gap between reality and research, particularly when we consider the years when papers and manuscripts began to circulate and to be read, rather than the years of publication of related articles and books.[1] Thus, in the case of European and non-European democracies at the end of the 1960s and early 1970s we should take into account popular mobilisation, demand for participation and civil rights, activism of workers' movements, dissatisfaction and protest, instability and military coups d'état as the key phenomena of those years and we can immediately trace the related analyses of democratic crises and stability, participation and so on to work by Huntington (1968), Crozier *et al.* (1975), Barnes and Kaase (1976), Linz and Stepan (1978), and many others.[2] When we pay attention to the diffusion of democracy from Southern Europe, where the process began in the second half of the 1970s, to Latin America in the 1980s and Eastern Europe as well Asia and parts of Africa in the 1990s and later, we find related research on democratisation, consolidation and the analyses of more ambiguous cases of pseudo, façade or minimal democracy.

One consequence of such consistency between reality and empirical research is that if we compare the empirical theory of democracy as it was 30 or so years ago and as it is today, we see enormous differences that result from research on new phenomena, especially democratisation. Given that it is impossible to do full justice to this theme within the limited scope of this present paper, I will present instead some of the key themes that have changed the contemporary empirical theory of democracy by 'tailing' reality. Thus, first, I will pick up the old, recurrent question of the definition of democracy, which has been reshaped by the tripling of the number of democracies during the last 30 years (see Puddington 2007). Second, the phenomenon of the hybrid regime will be addressed with all its problems of empirical uncertainty, instability and intractability. These two issues can be summarised in two questions: after these decades has a theory, a quasi theory or at least a good theoretical framework for democratisation processes emerged? and in the light of the diffusion of democracy and the impossibility of openly challenging this kind of regime, are we able to assess the quality of democracy empirically?

Definitional Conundrums

We know that definitions are necessary compasses for empirical research. We are also aware that terms such as democracy have an empirical reference and, at the same time, a normative, ideal connotation. Consequently, for decades 'democracy' has been an essentially contested concept. But when the regimes that we label as democratic neared 100 (90 in 2006) and an additional 58 transitional cases of partially free regimes can be taken into consideration (Puddington 2007), then the definitional conundrums are modified accordingly. Collier and Adcock (1999: 562) remind us that 'concepts, definitions, and operationalisation may evolve with changes in the goals and context of research' and, as noted above, the goals and context of research changed because of key events and processes taking place in the real world.[3] Thus, first, we need a minimal definition that suggests when, in a transitional process, we can consider a regime to be democratic or not. Second, in trying to capture the complexities of a transitional period the possibility of measuring or grading the various steps can also be useful; that is, a regime can become democratic in some respects and remain authoritarian in others, although in the long run the various dimensions tend to converge in one direction or another. Third, if democracy is left as 'the only game in town' and consequently is no longer challenged as such, then the procedural definitions that prove so important in a different period as an empirically solid reference point within the liberal tradition are no longer very useful, and hence an analysis of the 'content' of democracy may appear more interesting for empirical research. Fourth, if we have so many democracies, the empirical analysis of the actual implementation of the main democratic values or tenets, or, better, an analysis of the *quality* of democracy, seems an obvious goal. This, however, implies some standard or a sort of 'maximal' definition of democracy as a frame of reference in the development of quality.

The problem of the minimal definition of democracy was already analysed by democratic theory (see e.g. Dahl 1971). Consequently, we are on safe ground when proposing that a regime has to be considered a minimal democracy if it has at least universal adult suffrage; recurring, free, competitive and fair elections; more than one political party; and more than one source of information. An important addition was made to this definition by Schmitter and Karl (1993: 45–6), who stress that democratic institutions, existing rights and also the decision-making process should *not* be constrained by non-elected elites and external powers. When considered jointly, all six characteristics are clearly demanding, and especially the four adjectives attached to elections are weighty. To what extent, for example, is the phenomenon of 'recurring, free, competitive and fair' elections undermined by allegations of corruption even in those democracies that have been consolidated for decades? As Diamond (2002: 28) recalls,

> often particularly difficult are judgments about whether elections have been free and fair, both in the ability of opposition parties and candidates to campaign and in the casting and counting of the votes. In other cases, the element of 'more than one source of information' is difficult to meet if we only make reference to TV broadcasts. Or in yet other countries a decision-making process not constrained by an army, which ironically can be formed by democratic officers – see the Turkish case – is difficult to achieve.

This same discussion shows how important it is to take account of the problem addressed by Collier and Adcock (1999) on the two possible paths when dealing with research on democracy: dichotomy and gradation. Although they emphasise (1999: 561–2) that 'research that focuses on democratization as a well-bounded event and on classical subtypes of democracy favors dichotomies', actual research in the field suggested how a graded approach can be more appropriate in the empirical analysis of transitions to democracy. The key point seems to be that with this kind of research, measurement is not always possible and analysis has necessarily to be qualitative. Consequently, falling back upon classifications and typologies – not dichotomous ones – as substitutes for quantitative measures is the only feasible path.

A graded approach to democracy is also useful in at least two additional domains of research. The first has again been pointed out by Collier in a piece written with Levitsky (1997), where they show that adjectives may serve to cancel part of the meaning of democracy. Therefore, we have 'diminished subtypes': 'The subtype thus expresses the idea of a gradation away from democracy. The use of diminished subtypes presents an interesting alternative to employing an ordinal scale' (Collier and Adcock 1999: 560). A second important domain of research concerns the analysis of the quality/qualities of democracy (see below). In this, whenever possible, the use of gradation is essential to understand the extent to which the quality under scrutiny is present in a democracy. Here again the key problem is the actual possibility of adopting measurement or, if this not possible, classifications, i.e. 'nominal scales'.

As mentioned above, a third conundrum refers to another long and heated debate in the past on democracy as 'form' and as 'substance'. The prevailing conclusion of that debate in empirical theory considered the definition of democracy as form or, better, as procedure to be preferable to democracy as substance (see e.g. Schumpeter 1954, Dahl 1971, Kelsen 1981, Bobbio 1984). Such a conclusion was complemented by the so-called 'not reversible' relationships between freedom, as civil and political rights, and equality, where following the experiences of Northern Europe vis-à-vis Eastern Europe the key point was that no kind of equality can be achieved if there is no actual guarantee of civil and political rights as a pre-requisite (see Sartori 1987). The consequence of this has been not only a growing attention to substantive aspects in the research that in our fields has been mirrored by the enormous developments in policy studies, welfare rights included, but also to political equality as suggested by the most recent book by Dahl (2006) and to the ways of complementing equality and freedom by giving to democracy a substantive important content, as in Ringen (2007).

Finally, the last salient debate and related conundrum we would like to point out here concern the possibility of proposing a 'maximal' definition of democracy that would complement the minimal one and facilitate the analysis of democratic quality (see below). Rather than summarising and discussing an extended debate involving scholars from political philosophy, political science, political sociology, political economy, and political theory as the bridging field among those disciplines, we will single out the most salient aspects for empirical research. To begin with, a maximal, ideal definition of democracy is at least inappropriate and unnecessary: ideals and normative tenets are at a high level of abstraction. They are by themselves unattainable and above all in continuous change and adaptation. In addition, the ideal definition we need has to have the requisite of being empirically 'related' or detectable, that is, we need a notion that sets up a standard, a benchmark and consequently the relative gap with reality can be empirically assessed. In this perspective two well-known examples of normative definitions, that of May (1978: 1) on the necessary consistency between governmental decisions and the preferences of people affected by them, and that of Dahl (1971: 1) on the continuous responsiveness of government to the preferences of its citizens, considered politically as equals, are particularly relevant as they do not indicate a 'maximal definition' by pointing to substantive and procedural aspects. However, they cannot be accepted because of the insurmountable difficulties in the actual empirical analysis in detecting the 'preferences' of citizens on the more and more complex issues of a modern democracy.

A different path is that of recalling the main values that a contemporary democracy is supposed to implement with its policies. For most authors these are freedom and equality/solidarity. The attainment of those values helps to establish the autonomy of an individual, which, according to other authors (see e.g. Held 1989, esp. ch. 9), is a key element in an ideal democracy. This can lead to a definition of a 'good' democracy as 'the set of institutions that create the best opportunities to carry out freedom and equality' or in a more developed way 'a stable institutional structure that realises the liberty and equality of citizens through the legitimate and correct functioning of its institutions and mechanisms'. Thus, a good democracy is a broadly legitimated regime that completely satisfies its citizens. When institutions have the full backing of civil society, they can pursue democratic values. If, in contrast, the institutions must postpone their objectives and expend energy and resources on consolidating and maintaining their legitimacy, crossing even the minimum threshold for democracy becomes a remarkable feat. Second, in a good democracy the citizens themselves have the power to check and evaluate whether the government pursues the objectives of liberty and equality according to the rule of law. They can monitor the efficiency of the application of the laws in force, the efficacy of the decisions made by government, and the political responsibility and accountability of elected officials in relation to the demands expressed by civil society. All this implies that the different levels of government, such as the local, regional, national and supranational (especially for European countries), cannot be overlooked (see also Morlino 2004).

The Salience of Ambiguity: Hybrid Regimes

S.E. Finer (1970: 441–531) was one of the first scholars to specify the existence of *façade democracies* or *semi-democracies* – indicating regimes that are no longer authoritarian, but not yet minimally democratic, and that have institutions that are recurrent in a democracy, such as a constitutional charter and elections, but where the former is not actually implemented and the latter are largely constrained. Later scholars such as Rouquié (1975) and O'Donnell and Schmitter (1986), who had a Spanish background or were working on Latin American countries, labelled these ambiguous cases *dictablandas* and *democraduras*. In this sense, the notion of *hybrid regimes* has been present in the classic political science literature for some years, and the most important change in recent years in this regard is to do with the sheer size and variety of the phenomenon. To recall again the Freedom House data (Puddington 2007), in 2006 the number of regimes defined as partly free was 58, i.e. some 30 per cent of all independent polities in the world today.

For Croissant and Merkel (2004: 1), 'diminished sub-types of democracy (illiberal democracies, defective democracies and so on) have begun to become the new predominant trend in democracy theory and democratization studies'. In a similar vein, Epstein *et al.* (2006: 556 and 564–5) assert that '[Partial democracies] account for an increasing portion of current regimes and the lion's share of regime transitions' while adding that 'we have little information as to the factors that would lead partial democracies to either slide down to autocracy or move up to full democracy...the determinants of the behavior of the partial democracies elude our understanding...the factors affecting transitions out of partial democracy remain poorly understood'. It is also clear that there are almost as many labels for this phenomenon as there are studies: from the semi-consolidated democracies mentioned by *Freedom House* to partial democracy (Epstein *et al.* 2006), electoral democracy (Diamond 1999), illiberal democracy (Zakaria 1997), defective democracies (Merkel 2004), competitive authoritarianism (Levitsky and Way 2002), electoral authoritarianism (Schedler 2006), semi-authoritarianism (Ottaway 2003) and so on.

Merkel and Croissant (2000) also take a step towards a classification of those regimes. Thus, under the category of *defective democracies* they include: 'exclusive' democracies, which offer only limited guaranties for political rights; 'dominated' democracies, in which powerful groups use their influence to condition and limit the autonomy of elected leaders; and 'illiberal' democracies, which offer only partial guarantees on civil rights. Diamond (2002) goes in the same direction when breaking down hybrid regimes into four categories on the basis of the degree of competitiveness: hegemonic electoral authoritarian, competitive authoritarian, electoral democracy and a residual category of 'ambiguous regimes'. The failure to ensure a minimum level of civil rights in three categories keeps them below the minimum threshold requirement for classification as minimally democratic. Electoral democracies also fail to overcome the threshold of a minimal democracy if the definition suggested above is applied with reference to non-constrained decisions by non-elected elites and external powers (see above).

Looking at the most recurrent empirical cases Morlino (2003: ch. 1) contends that the two most recurrent hybrid regimes are *protected democracy* and *limited democracy*. In the first model the limits to the effective expression of civil and political rights come from the political role of the army or police in the country or from an external power. This is the 'dominated' democracy of Croissant and Merkel, with specific characteristics due to the fact that the 'powerful groups' are clearly identified. *Limited democracy* is a case where universal adult suffrage and competitive elections – multiparty elections with incumbent leaders chosen as a result of those elections – are undermined by the lack of effective guarantee of civil and political rights for most or many people with monopolised, not independent information, and with in some cases a lack of actual political opposition. In such a regime competition is limited and some parties, be they extremist religious or of the extreme radical left, are not allowed to participate in electoral competition.

Hybrid regimes can also be seen from a different perspective. In fact, their main characteristic is that they do not have – any more – some of the key aspects of authoritarianism, such as limited pluralism, low participation and mobilisation from above, the presence of traditional ambiguous mentalities, some extent of institutional structuration (see Linz 1975; Morlino 2003), while at the same time have not yet acquired all the aspects of a minimal democracy. They are diminished models of both regimes because a process of change is under way. Therefore, they can be labelled *transitional regimes*, although the direction of transition is not necessarily linear toward democracy. On the contrary, reversals of direction as well as long stalemates are recurrent. From this perspective, however, the classification of a changing, highly unstable political arrangement is not so relevant. More interesting is an analysis that pays attention to the process. Thus, we may have at the beginning *liberalisation*, that is, 'the partial opening of an authoritarian system short of choosing governmental leaders through freely competitive elections' (Huntington 1991: 9). During liberalisation at least the two key aspects of authoritarianism, limitation of pluralism and participation managed from above, are changed in an empirically detectable way, with the toleration of new political actors who are opposed to the existing regime or with manifestations of uncontrolled participation. Oppositions, of course, are basically accepted, but they are excluded from any involvement in government. A hegemonic party may still control the political arena and is able to win elections with or without manipulation. The electoral law is manipulative in favour of the authoritarian leaders or a clientelistic party. The justification of a regime on the ground of traditional mentalities often disappears. Police suppression may gradually fade away. Existing authoritarian institutions may become hollowed out and remain only on paper, without any actual activity (see also Morlino 1998). Then, if there is no deadlock or reversal but again change, there is a proper *transition*, which refers to a fluid and uncertain period when new democratic structures are about to emerge, while some of the structures of the old regime still exist. Above all, it is not yet clear what regime is going to be installed – a democratic one, or even another form of authoritarianism, perhaps a less repressive one. Tilly (1978) might call it a situation of *dual sovereignty*, meaning that there is still ongoing competition or conflict for supremacy in the coercive-political arena between two different actors or coalitions of actors. During the transition, aspects of minimal democracy begin to appear, such as opposition, a number of parties and competitive or semi-competitive elections. Again, if there is no deadlock or reversal, *installation* of democracy is inaugurated to meet the main requisites for a minimal democracy. Attention to these three processes might make more meaningful the analysis of hybrid regimes and replace a possibly unhelpful classification in a situation of high instability where a regime can switch from one cell to another in a week or a month.

Does a Theory of Regime Change Exist? Can it Exist?

The question of whether a theory of regime change exists has been present for years in the classic literature in political science, but has been recast more recently in the new context of democratisation. To my knowledge the most appropriate reply is still the one suggested by O'Donnell and Schmitter (1986: 3): 'We did not have at the beginning, nor do we have at the end of this lengthy collective endeavor, a "theory" to test or to apply to the case studies'. Some years ago, in a still relevant review of the democratisation literature Valerie Bunce (2000) made a significant advance by distinguishing between theoretical propositions at a high level of generalisation and regional propositions. Bunce concludes that five large generalisations have been proposed. The first regards a high level of economic development as a guarantee of democratic continuity; the second concerns the centrality of political leaders in the founding and designing of democracy; the third stresses the benefits of parliamentary systems rather than presidential ones for 'the continuation of the democratic governance'; the fourth considers the salience of the settlements of 'national and state questions' for 'the quality and survival of democracy'; and the fifth concerns the key importance of rule of law for a fully fledged democracy. In addition, regional generalisations relate to the salience of 'pacting', that is, of reaching agreements and accommodation in the democratic transitions of Southern Europe and Latin America; the advantages of breaking with the past in Eastern Europe; the high correlation between democratisation and economic reform in a capitalist direction in Eastern Europe; and the threat to democracy in Latin America and post-socialist Europe because of the weakness of the rule of the law. We can easily agree that these propositions cannot form any theory of democratic transition, whether general or regional.

Some further progress had been made in this direction and has to be acknowledged. First of all, much earlier than the review by Bunce, Krassner (1984) with his reference to *punctuated equilibria* – and later Berins Collier and Collier (1991) with their reference to *critical junctures* and Pierson (2000) with his emphasis on *path dependence* – constituted some of the most important attempts to develop a theory of political change, albeit at a high level of abstraction. Pierson, for example, using terms borrowed from economics and with reference to the other two studies, attempts to sketch out a general theory based on a few key propositions: 'specific patterns of timing and sequence matter'; 'a wide range of social outcome are often possible'; 'large consequences may result from relatively small and contingent events'; 'particular courses of action, one introduced, are often virtually difficult or impossible to reverse even if their consequences prove to be disastrous'; 'political development is punctuated by critical moments and junctures which shape the basic contours of social life'; and, finally, in the political realm the high density of institutions, the central role of collective action, the complexity and opacity of politics, compounded by the short time horizon of politicians and the 'stickiness' of politics, make path dependence a relevant and important theory in this regard. Following Pierson, Mahoney (2001) made an attempt to apply such a theory to some cases of democratisation in Central America. Despite its salience, however, it is very difficult to consider the attempts by Krasser, Berins Collier and Collier, and Pierson as constituting a good or even adequate theory of democratisation or of democratic transition.

Within the perspective of analysing and explaining change at a high level of abstraction Goodin (1996: 24–5) more usefully refers to the three basic ways in which institutions can change: accident, evolution, and conscious intervention. Accordingly, one could say that the first transitions to democracy came by accident; transitions with strong characteristics of continuity like the Mexican, the Brazilian and the Chilean show an evolutionary path; and the discontinuous transitions brought about by different and identifiable actors in other cases can be seen as the result of conscious intervention. Thelen and Steinmo (1992: 16–18) have also pointed to the four 'sources of institutional dynamism': first, broad changes in socio-economic or political context that make previously latent institutions more salient; second, changes in socio-economic context or political balance that 'produce a situation in which old institutions are put in service of different ends, as new actors come into play who pursue their (new) goal through existing institutions'; third, exogenous changes that 'produce a shift in the goal or strategies being pursued within existing institutions'; and fourth, 'political actors adjust their strategies to accommodate changes in the institutions themselves' through a dramatic change or 'piecemeal change'. Thanks to these theoretical proposals an initial modelling of institutional change is achieved. But we are still some way from a theory of any kind.

The fact is that when someone tries to give substance to theoretical ambitions in this field, the research almost inevitably advances by breaking down the analysis into a few key but different questions. The main ones include: how to explain the crisis and fall of the previous non-democratic regime; whether there are recurrent modes of transition; why some institutions are created rather than others, e.g. why a presidential regime rather than a parliamentarian regime; and what is the best institutional design to implement during the transition as a means of achieving a stable democracy. There can be no general theory to reply to these questions.

Linz and Stepan (1996) and O'Donnell et al. (1986) seem to have been aware of this since the beginning. Here we can add that their analyses, as well as those of other scholars working on multiple cases in Southern Europe and Latin America, focus in particular on the main characteristics of the previous regime, the important role performed by 'pacts' or elite agreements on the institutions that need to be built, recalled by Bunce as a key regional generalisation, the 'resurrection' of civil society, the limited role of political parties, the salience of contingent consensus on institutions, the great uncertainties of the entire process of transition, and the importance of first, founding elections. That is, what all these authors actually propose is a theoretical framework that points to key aspects that are considered recurrent in the cases being analysed and consequently useful for understanding those variegated countries. In such a framework actors, institutions, timing and the very notion of process play the central role in analysing the countries in two geo-political areas, Southern Europe and Latin America.

Huntington (1991: 30) appears to follow a different path by setting a temporally and spatially defined explanatory goal ('to explain why, how and with what consequences a group of roughly contemporaneous transitions to democracy occurred in the 1970s and the 1980s'). He then goes on to mention explicitly five changes which he sees as the main explanatory factors of transitions in about 30 countries in those decades: the legitimacy problems of previous authoritarian regimes, especially in connection with poor domestic performance, the global economic growth during the 1960s, the basic changes in the doctrine and activity of the Catholic Church, the new policies of external actors (the EU, the USA, and the breakdown of the USSR), and 'snowballing' or demonstration effects (Huntington 1991: 45–6). That is, within a multi-causal explanation a small number of cultural, economic and international aspects are considered key.

When a systematic explanation of Southern European and Latin American cases is attempted (see Morlino 2003) the political traditions of the country stand out as a key factor. More precisely, the key variables are the organisation and control of civil society by a hegemonic party and the consequent manipulated participation through which the regime was able to destroy the social structure and the previous political and social identifications, the consequent socialisation and re-socialisation carried out by party organisations and other ancillary organisations to create new loyalties and identifications, and the suppression of the opposition. These variables were relevant as during the transition they heavily conditioned the subsequent activation of a democratic civil society with its social and political structures. That is, an authoritarian regime that has been able to carry out effective policies of socialisation and suppression may leave a passive, weak, fragmented, poorly organised civil society during the subsequent transition.

The change of polity boundaries and consequently of territory and population took place in several Eastern European cases, but not in the Southern European and Latin American transitions. Moreover, the analyses of the Southern European and Latin American cases totally ignored economic factors. These are, on the other hand, very relevant in Eastern Europe. Southern Europe had no equivalent problem of changing the economic system from a collectivist one to a capitalist one with market and private property (Pridham 1984). But again the considerable attention devoted to the relationships between economic and political aspects in Eastern Europe leads us to reconsider similar relationships in Southern Europe. It is an obvious mistake to think that there are no differences between an economy coexisting with an authoritarian regime and an economy coexisting with a democracy. With some exceptions (see especially Ethier 1990), most analyses of Southern European transitions simply overlooked those important aspects, and for example – to mention just one feature – they largely glossed over the reshaping of the relationships between more or less organised interests and parties and between those interests and the bureaucracy with or without a large public sector.

International factors are at the core of other analyses of transitions, for example in the research by Whitehead (1996), who points to three mechanisms of 'contagion', 'control' and 'consent'. Linz and Stepan (1996: 72–81) also discuss the salience of the foreign policies of other countries – the USA for one – together with 'Zeitgeist' and 'diffusion'. However, in general, attention to the role of external actors in the transitions and consolidation of democracy is a more recent development, particularly when the Eastern European cases and above all the enlargement of the European Union have been studied (see Pridham *et al.* 1994; but also Mair and Zielonka 2002; Pevehouse 2002; Schimmelfennig and Sedelmeier 2005; and many others).

A rational choice approach has also been applied, although in a limited way (see e.g. Przeworski 1986; Colomer 1995), to the transition process, with again close attention paid to elites and their choice and strategies. The building of democratic institutions is basically the product of those strategies and choices. The analysis by Colomer should be emphasised, not only for the theoretical approach he applies but also because it is an analysis of a case, Spain, to which some theoretical mechanisms are applied with useful improvement in understanding as a result. More generally, Spain is the case that has attracted most attention from a number of scholars who have developed some kind of theoretical proposals working just on that case. Fishman (1990), Share (1987) and Gunther (see especially Gunther *et al.* 2004) are only some of the authors who have been working especially on Spain. Moreover, some of the theoretical frameworks or propositions formulated for Spain have also influenced the analysis of Latin American and even Eastern European cases investigated by other authors. The recurring reference to pacts, the moderation of elites, the resurrection of civil society, the salience of memory of the past and even some of the regional propositions mentioned by Bunce emerge from this close attention paid to Spain.

In addition to the theoretical framework or to the emphasis on specific mechanisms that characterise some transitions, there have been a few attempts to develop models or patterns of transition. Stepan (1986), Karl and Schmitter (1991), Munck and Skalnik Leff (1997) and Berins Collier

(1999) are some of the main authors who have proposed those models. Some of the differences among them are simply explained by the different cases considered. For example, Stepan (1986) and Berins Collier (1999) also include the classic Western European cases of the past in addition to Southern and Eastern European ones; Karl and Schmitter (1991) and also Munck and Skalnik Leff (1997) encompass the Latin American transitions as well as the Eastern European ones of the early 1990s. The similarities of those attempts lie in the fact that all the authors quoted above mainly focus their analysis on two macro-variables: the actors of transition, be they the authoritarian incumbent elites or those of the opposition, and the strategies pursued by them, be they accommodating or conflictual ones. For example, according to Munck and Skalnik Leff, the resulting models are four: the 'revolution from above', if the actors of transition are the authoritarian elites who pursued a conflictual strategy of confrontation; the 'conservative reform', if those elites chose agreements and compromises; the 'social revolution', if counter-elites were at the core of transition and pursued a conflictual strategy; and the 'reform from below', if counter-elites at the core of transition adopted an accommodating strategy. The advantages and limits of such models are fairly evident and connected. One of the main points is that the most immediate understanding of a country is counter-balanced by a strong simplification of a great number of relevant aspects. In addition, the adoption of mixed models is very common. Consequently, there is a strong simplification complemented by a loss of theoretical efficacy that would have been to some extent rescued with the 'pure' models. On the whole, despite a few attempts, the 'impossibility' of a general or regional theory to deal with the transition to democracy or to some other regime is confirmed.

To conclude by coming back to the question addressed in the title of this section, a general theory of regime change or democratisation, even temporally bound, cannot exist if we really want to understand the cases we research, if for no other reason than the complexities and the large differences that exist among the various cases. But there is an additional important reason for this, which is nicely captured by March and Olsen (1989: 65–6) when they write: 'institutional change rarely satisfies the prior intentions of those who initiate it...Change cannot be controlled precisely...there are frequently multiple, not necessarily consistent, intentions,...intentions are often ambiguous...initial intent can be lost'. These words are particularly telling when the 'carnation revolution' triggered by the *golpe* of Portuguese captains and a number of other examples are considered.

A Controversial Frontier: The Quality of Democracy

After all the years spent within social sciences aimed at developing and professing good methodological standards in empirical research, it may seem disturbing to suggest that a normative topic can be investigated empirically. But this is possible because of full-grown social science: once the empirical methodology, be it quantitative or qualitative, is established on more solid ground, working on a normative topic can be even more enjoyable and certainly more relevant. The 'how' is the key challenge here, but looking into democracies to assess their quality is clearly becoming more and more the object of empirical research.

In fact, a number of authors have crossed this frontier. A first group led by David Beetham (1994) carefully developed the notion of 'auditing' for political analysis. As Weir and Beetham (1999: 4) put it: 'audit is a systematic assessment of institutional performance against agreed criteria and standards, so as to provide a reasonable authoritative judgment as how satisfactory the procedures and arrangements of the given institutions are'. The auditing procedure should follow four steps: to identify appropriate criteria for assessment; to determine standards of good or best practice which provide a benchmark for the assessment; to assemble the relevant evidence from both formal rules and informal practices; to review the evidence in the light of the audit criteria and defined standards to reach a systematic assessment. A number of authors followed Beetham in developing the experience of auditing in other countries (see e.g. Beetham *et al.* 2002a, 2002b; Sawer 2001, 2007; see also Klug *et al.* 1996; Landman 2006). There are still two key open questions in this approach: is there a shorter and more effective path to analyse democratic quality, since the one suggested by auditing is empirically very cumbersome and complex? Are there better 'agreed criteria and standards' than those set up by Beetham (popular control and political equality of citizens as basic tenets, and free and fair elections, accountable government, civil and political liberties and democratic society as key more specific aspects)?

The most interesting replies to the first question come from the work of Altman and Perez-Linan (2002) and Lijphart (1999). Both develop a quantitative comparative strategy. Some differences also emerge vis-à-vis the definition of good democracy proposed in the first section and consequently in the dimensions of variation and related indicators. Altman and Perez-Linan refer to three aspects that draw on Dahl's concept of polyarchy (civil rights, participation, and competition). Consistent with his notion of consensus democracy, Lijphart includes indicators such as female representation, electoral participation, satisfaction with democracy, and corruption. Once applied, these indicators show how a consensus democracy can have a higher quality.

A reply to the second question is suggested by Morlino (2004) and Diamond and Morlino (2005). In addition to the definition of 'good' democracy suggested in the first section, a more developed notion of *quality* is considered necessary. A survey of the use of the term in the industrial and marketing sectors suggests three different meanings: (a) quality is defined by the established procedural aspects associated with each product: a 'quality' product is the result of an exact, controlled process carried out according to precise, recurring methods and timing; here the emphasis is on the *procedure*; (b) quality consists in the structural characteristics of a product, be it the design, materials, or functioning of the good, or other details that it features; here, the emphasis is on the *content*; (c) the quality of a product or service is indirectly derived from the satisfaction expressed by the customer, by their requesting the same product or service again, regardless of either how it is produced or what the actual contents are, or how the consumer goes about acquiring the product or service; according to this meaning the quality is based on *result*. Thus, the three different notions of quality are grounded in procedures, contents or results. Each has different implications for empirical research.

Starting from these premises, we have to assess the main dimensions of variation. There are at least six possible dimensions on which good democracies might vary and which should be at the core of empirical analysis. The first three are procedural dimensions. First, there is the *rule of law*. As O'Donnell (2005: 4–5) recalls, under a rule of law all citizens are equal before the law, which is fairly and consistently applied to all by an independent judiciary, and the laws themselves are clear, publicly known, universal, stable, and non-retroactive. These characteristics are fundamental for any civil order and a basic requirement for democratic consolidation, along with other such cognate features of a constitutional order as civilian control over the military and the intelligence services and an elaborated network of other agencies of horizontal accountability that complement the judiciary.

The second and third procedural dimensions concern the two main forms of accountability. In general, accountability corresponds to the obligation of elected political leaders to answer for their political decisions when asked by citizen-electors or other constitutional bodies. Schedler (1999: 17) suggests that accountability has three main features: information, justification, and punishment/compensation. The first element, information on a political act or series of acts by a politician or political body (the government, parliament, and so on), is indispensable for attributing responsibility. The second – justification – refers to the reasons furnished by the governing leaders for their actions and decisions. The third, punishment/compensation, is the consequence drawn by the elector or whatever other person or body following an evaluation of the information, justifications, and other aspects and interests behind the political act. All three of these elements require the existence of a public dimension characterised by pluralism and independence and the real participation of a range of individual and collective actors. The two kinds of accountability are electoral and inter-institutional. Vertical or electoral accountability refers to electors being able to make their elected officials responsible for their actions. This first type has a periodic nature, and is dependent on the various national, local and, if they exist, supra-national election dates. The voter decides and either awards the incumbent candidate or slate of candidates with a vote in their favour, or else punishes them by voting for another candidate, abstaining from the vote, or by nullifying the ballot. The actors involved in vertical accountability are the governor and the governed, and are thus politically unequal. Horizontal or inter-institutional accountability is when governors are responsible to other institutions or collective actors that have the expertise and power to control the behaviour of the governors. In contrast to vertical accountability, the actors are for the most part political equals. Inter-institutional accountability is relatively continuous, being formally or substantially formalised by law. In practice, it is usually manifest in the monitoring exercised by the governmental opposition in parliament, by the various assessments and rulings emitted by the court system, if activated, and by constitutional courts, agencies of auditing, central banks, and other bodies of a similar purpose that exist in democracies. Political parties outside of parliament also exercise this kind of control, as do the media and other intermediary associations, such as unions and employers' associations (see Morlino 2004).

The fourth dimension of variation concerns the responsiveness or correspondence of the political decisions to the desires of the citizens and civil society in general, that is the capacity to satisfy the governed by executing the policies that correspond to their demands. This dimension is analytically related to accountability. Indeed, judgements on responsibility imply that there is some awareness of the actual demands, and that the evaluation of the government's response is related to how its actions either conform to or diverge from the interests of its electors. Perhaps the most effective method for measuring responsiveness is to examine the legitimacy of government – i.e. the citizens' *perception* of responsiveness, rather than the reality – and consequently to use survey analysis for doing that.

The final two dimensions of variation are substantive in nature. The first is the full respect for rights expanded through the achievement of a range of freedoms. The second is the progressive implementation of greater political, social, and economic equality. Freedom and equality, however they are understood, are necessarily linked to accountability and responsiveness. Indeed, a higher implementation of freedom and equality for citizens and civil society lies in the sphere of those representative mechanisms. In addition, effective rule of law is also indispensable for a good democracy. The rule of law is intertwined with freedom in the respect for all of those laws that directly or indirectly sanction those rights and their concrete realisation.

Two more dimensions can be considered: participation and competition (see Diamond and Morlino 2005). No regime can be a democracy unless it grants all adult citizens formal rights of political participation, including the franchise. But a good democracy must ensure that all citizens are in fact able to make use of these formal rights to influence the decision-making process: to vote, to organise, to assemble, to protest, and to lobby for their interests. With regard to participation, democratic quality is high when we in fact observe extensive citizen participation not only through voting but in the life of political parties and civil society organisations, in the discussion of public policy issues, in communicating with and demanding accountability from elected representatives, in monitoring the conduct of public office-holders, and in direct engagement with public issues at the local community level. As for competition, democracies vary in their degree of competitiveness – in the openness of access to the electoral arena by new political forces, in the ease with which incumbents can be defeated, and in the equality of access to the mass media and campaign funding on the part of competing political parties. Depending on the type of electoral system, democracies may allow for more or less decisive electoral alternation as well (see Diamond and Morlino 2005). These two dimensions deserve a special theoretical status. In fact one of the main conclusions we reached in our research (see again Diamond and Morlino 2005) is that 'competition and participation are engines of democratic quality', that is, they are the conditions that best explain the development of other dimensions once some degree of rule of law exists.

The main subjects of such a 'good' democracy are the citizen-individuals, the territorial communities, and the various forms of associations with common values, traditions, or aims. In this sense, the possibility for good democracy exists not only in the case of a defined territory with a specific population controlled by state institutions under a democratic government, but also for wider-ranging entities such as the European Union. The main point is that the above-named subjects are at the heart of a democracy in which the most important processes are those that work from the bottom up, and not vice versa. In this way, the transfer of the analytical dimensions from the national level to the supra-national level – though not uncomplicated and without difficulty – is possible. The key is to hold constant the same elements characteristic of each dimension.

Finally, such a multidimensional analysis is also justified by the possibility of accepting in this way a pluralist notion of quality. That is, the content, the procedure and the result correspond to three different conceptions of quality and each conception has its own ground in terms of values and ideals. In other words, if the notion of democratic quality has to become a legitimate topic of empirical research then the multidimensionality is essential to capture it empirically and to acknowledge at the same time that there are different equally possible, normative notions of quality.

'Men – and Women – at Work'

Although partial, the picture delineated in these pages seems adequate to support the first main assertion of this article: that the wave of democratisation, which began more than 30 years ago in Southern Europe, emerging later in Latin America, Eastern Europe and in some areas of Asia and Africa and still going on, with ups and downs, has been fundamentally changing the main themes of empirical democratic theory. If we had the space to deal with another theme such as typology of democracies, we would have shown how an analytical operation like this one is largely changed if there are 90 units to classify, as there are at the beginning of this century, rather than 20 or 30, as was the case only a decade or so ago. Moreover, meaningfully classifying the much higher number of units that have been changing and becoming more complex over the years is virtually impossible if we do not want to accept a quantitative approach. In such a situation a different strategy may seem more fruitful, that is, the multiple, specific configurations where every case is seen by itself, but along a few recurring dimensions that are the same for all cases (see also Mair 2008). The second point to stress is: new phenomena emphasise the salience of some definitions rather than others and, on the whole, stress the necessity of adapting definitions to different research goals. Here we need to pay attention to the difficulties of analysing ambiguous realities such as hybrid regimes that are becoming more and more salient; the constitutive impossibility of achieving a theory of democratic change; and, in the end, the promise of intellectual rewards in a new growing subfield, such as the analysis of democratic quality. There are no proper conclusions to draw here as we are only 'men and women at work', operating in a continuously changing social and political environment that we try to understand with the same obstinate continuity.

Notes

1. Note that some of the best known books of these years, for example, those by Linz and Stepan (1978), O'Donnell *et al.* (1986), and Gunther, Diamandouros and Puhle (1995), were known since 1975, 1981, and 1991 respectively in the form of conference papers.
2. Here a recurring and interesting aspect can be stressed: the crisis of democracies of the 1970s gives the opportunity to reassess the crises of democracies of the 1920s and 1930s in Europe.
3. On the several definitions of democracy related to different research goals, see also Morlino (2003: ch. 1).

References

Altman, D.A., and A. Perez-Linan (2002). 'Assessing the Quality of Democracy: Freedom, Competitiveness, and Participation in 18 Latin American Countries', *Democratization*, 9:2, 85–100.
Barnes, S., and M. Kaase, eds. (1976). *Political Action*. London: Sage Publications.
Beetham, D., ed. (1994). *Defining and Measuring Democracy*. London: Sage Publications.
Beetham, D., S. Bracking, I. Kearton and S. Weir (2002). *The IDEA Handbook on Democracy Assessment*. The Hague: IDEA/Kluwer Law International.
Beetham, D., Iain Byrne, Pauline Ngan and S. Weir (2002). *Democracy Under Blair*. London: Politico's.

Berins Collier, R. (1999). *Pathways toward Democracy: The Working Class and Elites in Western Europe and Latin America*. New York: Cambridge University Press.

Bobbio, N. (1984). *Il futuro della democrazia*. Torino: Einaudi.

Bunce, V. (2000). 'Comparative Democratization: Big and Bounded Generalizations', *Comparative Political Studies*, 33:6–7, 703–34.

Collier Berins, R., and D. Collier (1991). *Shaping the Political Arena: Critical Junctures, the Labor Movement, and Regime Dynamics in Latin America*. Princeton, NJ: Princeton University Press.

Collier, D., and R. Adcock (1999). 'Democracy and Dichotomies: A Pragmatic Approach to Choices About Concepts', *Annual Review of Political Science*, 2, 537–65.

Collier, D., and S. Levitsky (1997). 'Democracy with Adjectives: Conceptual Innovation in Comparative Research', *World Politics*, 49:3, 430–51.

Colomer, J.M. (1995). *Game Theory and Transition to Democracy. The Spanish Model*. Aldershot: Edward Elgar.

Croissant, A., and W. Merkel (2004). 'Introduction: Democratization in the Early Twenty-First Century', special issue on 'Consolidated or Defective Democracy? Problems of Regime Change', *Democratization*, 11:5, 1–9.

Crozier, M., S.P. Huntington and J. Watanuki (1975). *The Crisis of Democracy*. New York: New York University Press.

Dahl, R.A. (1971). *Poliarchy. Participation and Opposition*. New Haven, CT: Yale University Press.

Dahl, R.A. (2006). *Political Equality*. New Haven, CT: Yale University Press.

Diamond, L. (1999). *Developing Democracy: Toward Consolidation*. Baltimore, MD: Johns Hopkins University Press.

Diamond, L. (2002). 'Elections Without Democracy: Thinking About Hybrid Regimes', *Journal of Democracy*, 13:2, 25–31.

Diamond, L., and L. Morlino, eds. (2005). *Assessing the Quality of Democracy*. Baltimore, MD: Johns Hopkins University Press.

Epstein, D.L., Robert Bates, Jack Goldstone, Ida Kristensen and Sharyn O'Halloran (2006). 'Democratic Transitions', *American Journal of Political Science*, 50:3, 551–69.

Ethier, D., ed. (1990). *Democratic Transition and Consolidation in Southern Europe, Latin America and Southeast Asia*. Basingstoke: Macmillan.

Finer, S. (1970). *Comparative Government*. Harmondsworth: Penguin Books.

Fishman, R. (1990). *Working Class Organization and the Return to Democracy in Spain*. Ithaca, NY and London: Cornell University Press.

Goodin, R.E. (1996). 'Institutions and Their Design', in R.E. Goodin (ed.), *The Theory of Institutional Design*. Cambridge: Cambridge University Press, 1–53.

Gunther, R., N. Diamandouros and H.J. Puhle, eds. (1995). *The Politics of Democratic Consolidation: Southern Europe in Comparative Perspective*. Baltimore, MD: The Johns Hopkins University Press.

Gunther, R., J.R. Montero and J. Botella (2004). *Democracy in Modern Spain*. New Haven, CT: Yale University Press.

Held, D. (1989). *Political Theory and the Modern State: Essays State, Power and Democracy*. Cambridge: Polity Press.

Huntington, S.P. (1968). *Political Order in Changing Societies*. New Haven, CT: Yale University Press.

Huntington, S.P. (1991). *The Third Wave. Democratization in the Late Twentieth Century*. Norman, OK and London: University of Oklahoma Press.

Karl, T., and P.C. Schmitter (1991). 'Modes of Transition in Latin America, Southern Europe and Eastern', *International Social Science Journal*, 128:May, 269–84.

Kelsen, H. (1981). *La democrazia*. Bologna: Il Mulino.

Klug, F., K. Starmer and S. Weir (1996). *The Three Pillars of Liberty: Political Rights and Freedoms in the UK*. London: Routledge.

Krassner, S. (1984). 'Approaches to the State: Alternative Conceptions and Hystorical Dynamics', *Comparative Politics*, 16:1, 223–46.

Landman, T. (2006). *Studying Human Rights*. London: Routledge.

Levitsky, S., and L.A. Way (2002). 'Elections Without Democracy: The Rise of Competitive Authoritarianism', *Journal of Democracy*, 13:2, 51–65.

Lijphart, A. (1999). *Patterns of Democracy. Government Forms and Performance in Thirty-Six Countries*. New Haven, CT: Yale University Press.

Linz, J.J. (1975). 'Authoritarian and Totalitarian Regimes', in F.I. Greenstein and N.W. Polsby (eds.), *Handbook of Political Science, vol. III: Macropolitical Theory*. Reading, MA: Addison Wesley.

Linz, J.J., and A. Stepan, eds. (1978). *The Breakdown of democratic regimes*. Baltimore: Johns Hopkins University Press.

Linz, J.J., and A. Stepan (1996). *Problems of Democratic Transition and Consolidation. Southern Europe, South America and Post-communist Europe*. Baltimore, MD: Johns Hopkins University Press.

Mahoney, J. (2001). *The Legacies of Liberalism: Path Dependence and Political Regimes in Central America*. Baltimore: John Hopkins University Press.

Mair, P. (2008). 'Democracies', in Daniele Caramani (ed.), *Comparative Politics*. Oxford: Oxford University Press.

Mair, P., and J. Zielonka, eds. (2002). *The Enlarged European Union*, special issue of *West European Politics*, 25:2.

March, J.G., and J.P. Olsen (1989). *Rediscovering Institutions. The Organizational Basis of Politics*. New York and London: The Free Press and Collier Macmillan.

May, J.D. (1978). 'Defining Democracy: A Bid for Coherence and Consensus', *Political Studies*, 26.

Merkel, W. (2004). 'Embedded and Defective Democracies', special issue on 'Consolidated or Defective Democracy? Problems of Regime Change', *Democratization*, 11:5, 33–58.

Merkel, W., and A. Croissant (2000). 'Formal Institutions and Informal Rules of Defective Democracies', *Central European Political Science Review*, 1:2, 31–47.

Morlino, L. (1998). *Democracy between Consolidation and Crisis. Parties, Groups and Citizens in Southern Europe*. Oxford: Oxford University Press.

Morlino, L. (2003). *Democrazie e Democratizzazioni*. Bologna: Il Mulino.

Morlino, L. (2004). 'Good' and 'Bad' Democracies: How to Conduct Research into the Quality of Democracy', *Journal of Communist Studies and Transition Politics*, 20:1, 5–27.

Munck, G., and C. Skalnik Leff (1997). 'Modes of Transition and Democratization: South America and Eastern Europe in Comparative Perspective', *Comparative Politics*, 29:3, 343–62.

O'Donnell, G. (2005). 'Why the Rule-of-Law Matters, in L. Diamond and L. Morlino (eds.), *Assessing the Quality of Democracy*. (2005). Baltimore, MD: Johns Hopkins University Press.

O'Donnell, G., and P.C. Schmitter (1986). 'Transitions from Authoritarian Rule. Tentative Conclusions about Uncertain Democracies', in G. O'Donnell, P.C. Schmitter and L. Whitehead (eds.), *Transition from Authoritarian Rule*. Baltimore, MD: The Johns Hopkins University Press.

O'Donnell, G., P.C. Schmitter and L. Whitehead, eds. (1986). *Transition from Authoritarian Rule: Southern Europe*. Baltimore, MD: The Johns Hopkins University Press.

Ottaway, M. (2003). *Democracy Challenged: The Rise of Semi-Authoritarianism*. Washington, DC: Carnegie Endowment for International Peace.

Pevehouse, J.C. (2002). 'Democracy from Outside-in? International Organizations and Democratization', *International Organization*, 56:3, 515–49.

Pierson, P. (2000). 'Increasing Return, Path Dependence and the Study of Politics', *American Political Science Review*, 94:2, 251–67.

Pridham, G. (2000). *The Dynamics of Democratization: A Comparative Approach*. London: Continuum.

Pridham, G., ed. (1984). *The New Mediterranean Democracies: Regime Transition in Spain, Greece and Portugal*, special issue of *West European Politics*, 7:2.

Pridham, G., E. Herring and G. Sanford, eds. (1994). *Building Democracy? The International Dimension of Democratisation in Eastern Europe*. Leicester and London: Leicester University Press.

Przeworski, A. (1986). 'Some Problems in the Study of the Transition to Democracy', in G. O'Donnell, P.C. Schmitter and L. Whitehead (eds.), *Transitions from Authoritarian Rule*. Baltimore, MD: The Johns Hopkins University Press.

Puddington, A. (2007). 'The 2006 Freedom House Survey', *Journal of Democracy*, 18:2, 125–37.

Ringen, S. (2007). *What is Democracy for: On Freedom and Moral Government*. Princeton, NJ: Princeton University Press.

Rouquié, A. (1975). 'L'Hipothèse "Bonapartiste" et l'Emergence des Sistèmes Politiques Semicompetitifs', *Revue Française de Science Politique*, 25:6, 1077–111.

Sartori, G. (1987). *Theory of Democracy Revisited*. New York: Chatham House Publishers.

Sawer, M., ed. (2001). *Elections: Full, Free and Fair*. Leichhardt: Federation Press.

Sawer, M. (2007). 'Democratic Values: Political Equality?', Democratic Audit of Australia, Australian National University Discussion Paper 9/07, http://democratic.audit.anu.edu.au

Schedler, A. (1999). 'Conceptualizing Accountability', in A. Schedler, L. Diamond and M. Plattner (eds.), *The Self-Restraining State: Power and Accountability in New Democracies*. Boulder, CO: Lynne Rienner.

Schedler, A., ed. (2006). *Electoral Authoritarianism: The Dynamics of Unfree Competition*. Boulder, CO: Lynne Rienner.

Schimmelfennig, F., and U. Sedelmeier, eds. (2005). *The Europeanization of Central and Eastern Europe*. Ithaca, NY and London: Cornell University Press.

Schmitter, P.C., and T. Karl (1993). 'What Democracy is . . . and is Not', in L. Diamond and M. Plattner (eds.), *The Global Resurgence of Democracy*. Baltimore, MD: Johns Hopkins University Press.

Schumpeter, J. (1954). *Capitalism, Socialism and Democracy*. London: Allen & Unwin.

Share, D. (1987). 'Transitions to Democracy and Transitions through Transaction', *Comparative Political Studies*, 19:4, 525–48.

Stepan, A. (1986). 'Paths toward Redemocratization: Theoretical and Comparative Considerations', in G. O'Donnell, P.C. Schmitter and L. Whitehead (eds.), *Transitions from Authoritarian Rule. Comparative Perspective*. Baltimore, MD: The Johns Hopkins University Press.

Thelen, K., and S. Steinmo (1992). 'Historical Institutionalism in Comparative Politics', in S. Steinmo, K. Thelen and F. Longstreth (eds.), *Structuring Politics. Historical Institutionalism in Comparative Analysis*. Cambridge: Cambridge University Press.

Tilly, C. (1978). *From Mobilization to Revolution*. Reading, MA: Addison Wesley.

Weir, S., and D. Beetham (1999). *Political Power and Democratic Control in Britain*. London: Routledge.

Whitehead, L. (1996). 'Three International Dimensions of Democratization', in L. Whitehead (ed.), *The International Dimensions of Democratization. Europe and the Americas*. Oxford: Oxford University Press, 3–25.

Zakaria, F. (1997). 'The Rise of Illiberal Democracy', *Foreign Affairs*, November/December, 76:6, 22–43.

Thirty Years of Territorial Politics

MICHAEL KEATING

In 1974, when *West European Politics* was perhaps a glimmer in the eye of its founding editors, there appeared the paperback edition of Samuel Finer's *Comparative Government* in which the author asserted that 'Britain too has had its "nationalities" problem, its "language" problem, its "religious" problem, not to speak of its "constitutional" problem. These are problems no more' (Finer 1974: 137).[1] In retrospect, we can see this work, and similar ones from other parts of Europe, as the culmination of a literature on national integration that had been developing since the nineteenth century and which, as so often happens, reached its peak just as the conditions were changing. Our understanding of territorial politics has indeed been radically transformed in the 30 years of *WEP*'s existence.

For much of the twentieth century, the dominant paradigm for the understanding of territory and politics was provided by theories of national integration and assimilation, closely associated with a particular view of modernity. This was seen as replacing old social roles, norms and forms of community with a new division of labour so that territorial divisions would give way to functional ones. As Emil Durkheim (1964: 187) asserted 'we can almost say that a people is as much advanced as territorial divisions are superficial'. After the Second World War, national integration linked with diffusionist theories, notably in the work of Karl Deutsch, who saw national states as being formed around centres, which gradually extended their reach into peripheries, absorbing them economically, culturally and politically. Centres, being 'modern', have history on their side and the result is 'sovereign governments which have no critical regional or community cleavages' (Deutsch 1966: 80). The mechanisms, for Deutsch, are social rather than political so that 'it is communities which make governments' rather than the other way around. The process is limited at the point at which state-building projects meet each other, or where there are deep-rooted cleavages, in which case there will be secession and the creation of an independent state, so leaving the principle of the homogeneous state intact. It is striking, in retrospect, how much this has in common with neo-functionalist theories of European integration, which also emphasised the role of economic and social exchange and diffusion, with political structures following.

The neglect of territory, especially in the English-language literature, was exacerbated by the behaviourist revolution from the 1950s and the attempt to establish a universal science of politics and arrive at explanations while, in the famous formulation of Przeworski and Teune (1970), eliminating proper names. The reaction to the political culture studies of the 1960s with their ethnocentric biases reinforced this tendency, as did the rise of rational choice with its resolutely individualistic ontology. From this perspective, any territorial variation in political behaviour could be reduced to universal variables which just happened to have an uneven incidence across territories and could have nothing to do with territory itself. At best, territories could be included in analyses as dummy variables, pending their resolution into proper variables.

Historians were equally tied to a vision of national integration and an often teleological view of the formation of the national state. In the nineteenth century they were often nationalistic, emphasising 'natural' boundaries, and celebrating the unity of the people against internal and external foes, but even the more scientific historians would write of the 'unification' of Germany or Italy as though these were a mere fulfilment of national destiny. The nineteenth century saw the making of the Westphalian myth, the idea that the treaties of Münster and Osnabruck in 1648 had established independent, sovereign states (Osiander 1994, 2001). It is hard to know which has caused more confusion, the idea of the Westphalian state during the first three-quarters of the twentieth century, or the large literature on its supposed replacement since then.

Social scientists are often victims of their data as well as their theoretical frameworks and most social and political data have appeared in national sets. Thus the nation-state has become the default unit of analysis of social and political change, of the advance of liberalism and democracy and of modernity itself. Yet this is not all. A strong normative element permeated many of these interpretations and this has by no means disappeared. The creation of the unified national state was identified with 'modernity' in a very broad sense and resistance to it thus logically qualified as anti-modern. Seymour Martin Lipset (1985) included peripheral nationalisms among his 'revolts against modernity', while in France a long tradition associated regionalism with anti-revolutionary reaction and clericalism. An underlying theme of much work in the field has been that territorial resistance to the state is a problem and that sustaining national unity is self-evidently a good thing. J.S. Mill in the nineteenth century, insisting on the superiority of large, consolidated states, has his counterpart in the late twentieth century in Ralph Dahrendorf (1995, 2000) extolling the virtues of large nations while dismissing small nations aspiring to statehood (or even measures falling short of this) as backward. Taking these various disciplinary contributions together, it is hard to resist the conclusion that social scientists have been the organic intellectuals of the consolidated nation-state as much as they have been impartial analysts of it.

Perhaps the most revealing example of the implicit priority given to the nation-state is the lack of serious analysis of the term itself. In some European cultures the identification of the two is so strong that the compound term is not necessary. In French, for example, *Etat* and *nation* are two expressions of the same community, one institutional and the other more social and political.[2] In English, the linking of the two may refer to cases where the state and the nation are indeed co-terminous, as opposed to the multinational state, in which they are not. In fact, however, it usually refers to states that are sovereign, which is a different matter altogether. Yet this does not stop political scientists using the term as though it were unproblematic.

Bringing Territory Back In

Finer wrote just as a new wave of territorial politics was about to hit the United Kingdom. In the elections of 1974, a clutch of nationalist (and unionist) MPs was elected from the peripheral nations of the United Kingdom. The regional–national question became a major preoccupation for Spain's post-Francoist democracy. Revived movements in Brittany, Corsica and Languedoc put the myth of the indivisible French Republic in question, while Belgium moved towards a complex system of community and regional politics. For a while, such movements could be dismissed yet again as evidence of retarded modernity or, in the case of Scotland, evidence of opportunism and greed (North Sea oil was just beginning to flow). As the phenomenon persisted and spread, however, this standard response was increasingly inadequate and a search began for new ways of understanding.

When social scientists start to talk of a phenomenon in a new way, it is often difficult to know whether the phenomenon has changed, whether they have just noticed something, or whether they have merely found new analytical tools and a new vocabulary. In recent years political science has been gripped by a tendency to insist both that the world has changed radically and that we need new concepts to understand it. This is often accompanied by a rather simplified and stylised view of the world as it was before, in order to emphasise the contrast. Territorial politics has not been immune to this, with an outburst of writing about multilevel governance, spatial rescaling, post-Westphalian orders, post-nationalism, the end of territory and the borderless world. This is contrasted with the old world, as though the myths of the unitary and integrated nation-state represented a concrete reality. These new concepts do not always travel well across space; they travel hardly at all across time. It thus becomes very difficult indeed to tell what has actually changed and what has not. A good understanding of territorial politics in the last 30 years demands that we have concepts that do travel and a sound grasp of the history of the territorial state and the different ways of telling that history.

Among the earliest efforts to readdress the territorial state and confront the simply assimilationist theories was the work of Stein Rokkan in the 1960s and 1970s (Flora *et al.* 1999). Among Rokkan's contributions two stand out: he problematised the question of state formation and integration and showed that it was often partial; and he addressed the problem on a European scale, refusing to be trapped in pre-given national categories. Lipset and Rokkan (1967) started off in a rather traditional modernist mode, but noted that the integration process was often incomplete, leaving territorial cleavages, which however are a subordinate element in politics. In his later writings Rokkan more fully incorporated the territorial dimension. Rokkan and Urwin (1983) note that the processes of military–adminis-trative, of economic and of cultural system-building in the state may not coincide, creating complex patterns of territorial politics. So one region may be politically subordinate but economically powerful and culturally strong (as for example Catalonia in Spain). Peripheral territories were not necessarily assimilated but could survive within the national state, either at the edge of the state system or at the interface between state-building projects.

Charles Tilly's (1990, 1994) work also problematises the formation of the national state and discards the teleological bias of earlier accounts. He sees state formation based on two principles, coercion and capital. Large states emerged where rulers could coerce populations; where they encountered economically strong cities they had to bargain with them, allowing territorial autonomy. Spruyt (1994) argues that the emergence of the consolidated nation-state was not historically inevitable and that city-states and urban leagues might have won out. These works are valuable not only for their reinterpretation of history but in drawing attention to the way in which the diverse elements of the territorial polity might be separated. The nineteenth century, with its emphasis on security, did see the triumph of the nation-state but in changed circumstances we can imagine a re-separation of the various elements of territorial politics and their reconfiguration in new forms.

From the 1970s there was some work on regional political economy (Tarrow *et al.* 1978) which was to blossom in the 1990s (see below). The main contribution of this was to show that territorial distinctiveness was not merely the legacy of a pre-modern or pre-industrial past but was reproduced in industrial societies. A stream of Italian literature on the *questione meridionale* (southern question) sought to show how the conditions of Italian unification had systematically disadvantaged the south and sustained a territorial cleavage within the unified state (Salvadori 1976; Galasso 1978; Lo Curto 1978; Mori 1981). What was not anticipated at this time was that the next challenge to Italian unity would come from the developed north but from the 1990s a literature did develop to account for this revolt of the wealthy (Mannheimer 1991; Diamanti 1993; Biorcio 1997; Cento Bull and Gilbert 2001).

Another challenge to the modernist story of national integration and progress came in the 1970s from the left. Many of the territorial movements of that time were radical in their politics, protesting against exploitation by big states and big capital. Since the left in the mid-twentieth century had been rather centralist, an ideological rationalisation was required and this was provided in the form of uneven development theory. Capitalism, in this view, does not destroy territorial differences but rather reinforces them, favouring some territories over others. With anti-colonial struggles having rehabilitated nationalism on the left in the 1960s, it was incorporated in the form of 'internal colonialism', a process by which the state in collusion with big capital exploited workers in the peripheral parts of the state, reducing them to a position of dependence. The idea had its origins in the work of Gramsci (1978a, b) and his analysis of Italian unification but was reintroduced in France by Occitan activist Robert Lafont (1967) in the aftermath of the Algerian independence war. It was also reintroduced, via Latin America and *dependencia* theory this time, by Michael Hechter (1975), in a thoroughly confused account of the making of the United Kingdom. Scottish Marxist Tom Nairn (1977, 1997) also drew heavily on theories of under- and over-development to explain the rise of nationalism in the European periphery. Internal colonialism did not survive as a theory. It relied on an unconvincing analogy between European state formation and colonialism in Africa and Asia, and was a product of its times, the aftermath of de-colonisation. Uneven development, however, remained as a central element in the understanding of territorial politics, its persistence and change, to be strengthened by new theories of economic development from the 1990s.

Territorial Management

The approaches discussed above still tended in some cases to view territory as the legacy of the past, evidence of failed or incomplete integration, with the underlying assumption that the integrated national state is the normal state of affairs and that it is the deviation from this that needs to be explained. Others suffered from a certain determinism in which deep social and economic structures dictated integration or disintegration of the political superstructure. The next phase of the study of territorial politics gave a more central place to politics itself and to the strategic actions of state elites and territorial actors.

The French school of sociology of organisations produced a series of studies in the 1960s and 1970s on local systems and central–local dynamics in the supposedly monolithic Napoleonic state. The main insight is that centralisation, far from destroying territorial politics, merely recreates it in new forms. The key figures are the *notable*, a politician with local roots operating in national politics, and the territorial administrators of the central state, particularly the prefects. These serve as territorial inter-mediaries, conveying local demands to the centre and bending central decrees in their local application. This is not merely a legacy of the past but reproduces and modernises itself over successive regimes. So the old notables of nineteenth century France, rooted in traditional society, gave way to a new class of notables under the Third Republic from 1870, with a different class basis and drawing their power precisely from their relation-ship with the central state. The Fifth Republic after 1958 gradually pushed aside many of the notables of the Fourth Republic as the Gaullists established local roots; but these in turn developed similar practices of mediation in new conditions. Successive efforts by the French state to decentralise are, from this perspective, evidence not of a will to give power to the localities but of the desire of the centre to emancipate itself from local influence and regain its own autonomy. The most elaborate account of the French system from this perspective is Pierre Grémion's (1976) *Le pouvoir périphérique*. By the mid-1980s some members of this school had taken the analysis so far as almost to destroy the idea of the central state altogether, presenting a highly pluralistic world of local adaptation and discretion (for example Dupuy and Thoenig 1985). Tarrow (1977) compared the role of politicians as territorial intermediaries in France and Italy.

Jim Bulpitt's (1983) account of the United Kingdom also addresses the issue of central autonomy, with his concept of the 'dual polity', in which the centre would look after high politics, while leaving the management of local affairs to trusted collaborators, the condition being that the 'right chaps' were in charge. This strategy of 'territorial management' ensured the integrity of the state while avoiding entanglement in local politics. Rokkan and Urwin (1983) pursued the theme of territorial accommodation in a comparative context, showing how states responded to territorial pressures with party political responses, economic policy responses, and institutional concessions. They also produced a typology of territorial state forms to replace the conventional unitary–federal dichotomy. These were the unitary state; the union state, formed from an amalgam of territories some of which keep their distinctive features; mechanical federalism, with similar decentralised structures across the state and a strong centre; and organic federalism, built from below with limited central power. Although this typology has been cited repeatedly since, and the union state has become a standard term in the British debate, nobody has ever really elaborated on it or developed it theoretically and operationally.

State and Regional Nationalism (Keating 1988) placed territorial management at the centre of an analysis of the United Kingdom, France, Italy and Spain. The central questions were how states come together *and* how they stay together. Socio-economic disparities among territories are not enough to explain territorial politics, since at that time Italy had no significant regionalist movements; rather politics must be central to the explanation. States pursue territorial management strategies through party-political incorporation; centre–periphery intermediation through political and bureaucratic channels including clientelistic networks; policy concessions, notably but not exclusively in economic policy; and institutional decentralisation. Peripheral actors do not always favour regional autonomy, since this may prejudice their privileged access to the centre. Changing internal and external conditions alter the strategic interests and calculations of centres and peripheries. For example the creation and closing of national markets in the late nineteenth century made centres into peripheries and vice versa, as did the opening of European and global markets 100 years later. Tariff policy was thus a key issue in territorial politics in the first era of globalisation, creating new constellations of territorial and sectoral interests. Territorial distinctiveness is thus not something overcome once and for all, but creates and recreates itself in each generation. Penetration of the state into territories as it extends its reach threatens the old system of intermediation, creating a crisis of territorial representation, a challenge to the state and a reconfiguration of territorial politics. Such crises occurred in the late nineteenth century, a time of great territorial mobilisation and again in the late 1960s and early 1970s. In the latter case, one cause was the new phase of territorial management represented by modernising regional policies, intended to integrate declining and under-developed territories into national economies within the overall Keynesian strategy of macroeconomic management. These were presented as essentially technical, and of benefit to all by maximising national output. Yet, delivered by the central state, they disrupted existing patterns of territorial intermediation. Indeed, governments explicitly sought new territorial interlocutors among the dynamic and modernising elements, what the French called the *forces vives*. This produced reactions within the regions and a new wave of territorial mobilisation, itself taking various forms, from a defence of old modes of production to alternative policies for development. Work with Barry Jones and others (Keating and Jones 1985; Jones and Keating 1995) showed how European integration was similarly destabilising existing modes of territorial management, depriving states of key instruments of accommodation and creating new alliances of winners and losers.

The 1980s also saw a re-reading of some of the old evidence for territorial integration. For example, the nationalisation of politics in the form of the spread of party systems through national territories might be evidence for social and political homogenisation and thus for homogenisation of electoral preferences. Alternatively, it might be evidence that parties were able to adapt to different territorial contexts, absorbing local interests. The Italian Communists were able to penetrate the south after abandoning their old prejudices and adopting land reform (Tarrow 1977), while the Christian Democrats assumed different images from one part of the country to another. French notables working within national parties could bend policy to local interests, while in the United Kingdom a state-wide party system did not suppress territorial politics, merely channelled it in particular ways (Keating 1975; Miller 1983). In Germany, the Social Democrats were never able to penetrate Bavaria, but from 1966 built up a formidable presence in North Rhine-Westphalia, an area previously hostile to them despite the presence of a large Protestant working class (Rohe 1990b). The Christian Democrats were built from the bottom as a coalition of local forces, adapted to their local environments (Rohe 1990a). Scottish Conservatism, previously weak, flourished in the mid-twentieth century, a fact that was at one time taken as evidence of territorial homogenisation; but then it collapsed. These trends, it must be emphasised, cannot be explained merely by the uneven distribution of socio-economic groups across state territories. There is a territorial factor at work. It is striking that electoral studies in English have tended since their inception to concentrate on socio-economic status together with religion and ethnicity, leaving territorial effects as a residual to explain any remaining anomalies, so filtering territory out of the analysis. In France, on the other hand, accounts of election results tend to start with territorial differentiation, reflecting the strong tradition of political geography and the later development of survey research. Only recently have political scientists begun to put the two types of approach together.

Historians also escaped from their national frameworks during the 1980s and 1990s, with a revival of regional history and questioning of the statist teleologies (Applegate 1999). This coincides with a strengthening of comparative history and of the history of Europe. Norman Davies' (1997) *Europe* consciously breaks with the national categories as well as the western European focus of previous accounts of state-building, while his later *The Isles* (1999) is one of a number of books tackling the English and state-centric teleological bias of earlier accounts of the United Kingdom. Fernand Braudel's (1986) last book is an iconoclastic analysis of the myths of the natural emergence of the French nation-state.

Braudel and others of the *Annales* school, who started with territorial communities and studied the emergence and working of local societies in their entirety, rather than extrapolating downwards from the nation-state, have had some influence beyond history and beyond France. Marc Abélès (1989) *Jours tranquilles en '89* is an ethnographic account of the building of power on a local basis in a French region, from someone who deliberately avoided informing himself about the formal structures of government in advance. These ethnographic approaches have gradually made an impact in political science, modifying its universalist assumptions and efforts to eliminate territory.

The Regional and the Local

'Territorial politics' in Europe has come to refer to the territorial construction of the state, national integration and disintegration and the 'regional' level. Yet a separate tradition exists, of local government and urban studies, also focused on territory but using different theoretical and methodological tools. Only recently have the two begun to come together.

Local government studies, in contrast to the study of territorial politics, have tended to be national. There are very few comparative accounts, as opposed to edited collections of country studies and there is a continued insistence on national exceptionalism. It has been linked to public administration, with a certain tendency to depoliticisation and the search for efficiency. During the 1960s and 1970s there was something of an obsession with structures, reflecting the frenzied reform activity of that era as governments sought to modernise administration. From the 1970s questions of power came back, often framed by organisation theory. This reflected the evolution of public administration as well as the influence of the French school, brought into the United Kingdom notably in the work of Rod Rhodes (1999). Some works have spanned the regional and the local using the general frame of intergovernmental relations (an idea originating in US federalism). Indeed the special issue of *West European Politics* in 1987 devoted to territorial politics is largely about this (Rhodes and Wright 1987); Cole and John (1995) adopt a similar perspective for comparing France and Britain. From the 1980s, public choice approaches from the United States came in, posing a series of critical questions about the assumptions of the structural reformers of the 1960s. While the latter had largely favoured big structures and consolidation of municipalities in the interests of planning and efficiency, public choice emphasised the benefits of fragmentation and competition, inspired by the earlier work of Tiebout (1956). Meanwhile, urban sociology was alive and well but made surprisingly little impact on political science until later (with exceptions such as Saunders 1980).

The 1990s saw the import of urban political economy approaches from the United States. The central insight of this school is that local governments are dependent on private business for investment and that this constrains their ability to make autonomous policy decisions. Paul Peterson's *City Limits* (1981) is the classic statement of the structural necessity to defer to investors at the cost of restraining social expenditures.

Logan and Molotch (1987) are less deterministic and coined the phrase 'growth coalition' to refer to the constellation of interests within cities who promote the idea that the city has a unified interest in growth and property development. Clarence Stone's (1989) concept of urban regime is a more subtle way of grasping the balance of public authority and business power that governs American cities. Paul Kantor (1988) identified the central dilemma of American local government, which is pressured by the need to attract and retain investment on the one hand, implying pro-business policies, low taxes and low social expenditure; and the existence of pluralistic social movements on the other, demanding spending and redistribution. These structural theories of power replaced the earlier 'community power studies' pitching pluralists against elitists. The community power debate collapsed amid methodological arguments and had made rather little impact in Europe. Urban political economy was to be a more influential export.

There was some reluctance among Europeans to accepting the importance of private power in urban politics, given the concern of political scientists with the state and local government, and of sociologists with urban social movements. Yet the private sector has indeed been important, in the form of the development industry and in arrangements like the French *sociétés d'économie mixte*. Many European countries have compulsory membership of Chambers of Commerce, which in turn have important responsibilities in planning and infrastructure provision. There are, of course, significant differences from the United States, notably the role of the central state, which not only regulates and constrains local governments, but also protects them from market pressures. The application of the American model of the urban regime to Europe is discussed in Keating (1991), Harding (1999) and Stoker and Mossberger (1994) and US–Europe comparisons in urban political economy are presented in Savitch and Kantor (2002). Perhaps the most important effect of this import, however, was to bring together urban political analysis and regional studies, which had also been moving in the same direction.

The New Regionalism

The 1990s saw a strong revival of regional studies across a range of disciplines and talk of a 'new regionalism' (for overviews see Balme 1996; Keating 1998; Caciagli 2003). This was a response both to the events and trends of the times and to new intellectual approaches. The broad context is the transformation of the state and government, the loss of some capacities and the search for others, and the demystification of the state with the end of the Cold War and a more sophisticated understanding of its historical contingency. One result has been a literature on the end of territory (Badie 1995), the borderless world and the network society (Castells 1997). Indeed it would appear that trends in economic development (globalisation),

technology (instant communication) and society (individualism) are breaking the territorial frame for both society and politics. Yet another literature
stresses both de-territorialisation and re-territorialisation, at new spatial
scales, below, above and across the state.

One explanation is functional. The classic modernist notion that function
and territory are alternative principles of social organisation and behaviour,
with the former destined to triumph, was already questioned by the work of
the 1970s and 1980s showing the persistence and reinvention of territorial
frames alongside functional differentiation. Politics is always both
functional and territorial, although the dominant (and therefore unpro-
blematised) territorial frame of the nation state sometimes caused us to
forget it. By the 1990s observers were noting a spatial rescaling (Brenner
2004; Brenner et al. 2003) in which functions were changing their territorial
scale (Balme 1995). One perhaps surprising example concerns culture and
language. It might appear that modern communications technology, by
facilitating contact across space, would sunder the link between territory
and language, allowing minority cultures to survive in the virtual world. Yet
we see that minority languages are increasingly territorialised, strengthening
in their core areas and retreating elsewhere. The reason is that living culture
requires face-to-face casual contact, and needs institutions such as schools,
social services and administration, which are themselves territorial.

By far the best-documented example, however, concerns economic
development. A large literature has developed on the increased importance
of space for economic development and change. Previously, space was
usually conceptualised as distance – from raw materials and markets – and a
matter of cost, which could be compensated by subsidies for producers in
disadvantaged areas. There was, it is true, an older tradition of industrial
districts, in which the proximity of suppliers and producers gave a mutual
advantage and Alfred Marshall had even suggested that there may be some
cultural factor at work or, as he put it, 'something in the air'. The new
approaches build on this, stressing the social construction of territories and
productive systems. They draw on economic sociology and the new
literature on varieties of capitalism to show how local societies provide
the conditions for successful development (Bagnasco and Trigilia 1993;
Amin and Thrift 1994; Storper 1997; Cooke and Morgan 1998; Scott 1998;
Crouch et al. 2001). Key concepts are social capital, trust and networks.
Most of this literature comes from sociology and geography and the
political angle is not always well addressed. It has had a substantial influence
on governments and the European Commission. The old top-down regional
policies, based on direction of industry, subsidies, tax incentives and
infrastructure, has given way to a decentralised model in which the emphasis
is on what regions can do for themselves. This is combined with an emphasis
on inter-regional competition so that instead of occupying complementary
roles in a national division of labour, regions compete (for investment,
technology and markets) in a national, European and global frame.

This has obvious affinities with the literature on urban political economy and should lend itself to a political analysis of who runs these new regional spaces, what policies are pursued and who wins and loses. There are some occasional analyses on these lines (Keating *et al.* 2003) but by and large the field is left to sociologists, whose main interest is co-operation, rather than to political scientists, who specialise in conflict and distribution. There is also a tendency in some of the new regionalist literature to concentrate on success stories, themselves often idealised and, indeed to wishful thinking about the possibility, given the right spatial scale, to achieve the perfect balance between economic competitiveness and social integration. A severe criticism is given by Lovering (1999).

There is a longstanding literature on stateless nations and national minorities in Europe, including many case studies and some comparative work. For a long time this stood apart from the literature on regionalism, based rather in the general literature on nationalism, emphasising cultural issues and occasionally betraying rather primordialist assumptions (Connor 1994). There are now points of contact between these literatures, encouraged by the interlinking of the movements themselves and stateless nations and national minorities have used new regionalist themes to stake out a claim for functional autonomy without necessarily demanding independence (Keating 2004).

Comparative work on regionalism and political parties did not really start until the late 1990s, but there is now a growing literature (De Winter and Tursan 1998; Hough and Jeffery 2006). This emphasises both the role of the party competition in articulating territorial interests and forcing governments to respond, and the effects of institutional decentralisation on party alignments.

Globalisation and European Integration

An important part of the new regionalism concerns the external context, of globalisation and European integration. This underpins the paradigm of the competitive region, an idea that has much analytical value but which risks reifying the territory unless we engage in a systematic analysis of its social and political composition. As in other fields, there is an argument over whether European integration represents an accentuation of globalisation; whether it serves to modify its impact; or indeed whether it is a bit of both. There has been a huge literature on territorial politics and European integration, most of it concerning regions since the 1980s (Keating and Jones 1985; Petschen 1993; Bullman 1994; Jones and Keating 1995; Krämer 1998).

One unfortunate but persistent tendency has been to concentrate on the EU's own regional policy through the Structural Funds and to assume that the Commission is engaged in a strategy to by-pass the nation-state and refashion the political geography of Europe. The temptation is obvious.

Structural Funds have 'regional' written all over them, and they appear to be a discreet policy instrument amenable to analysis; this makes them particularly inviting as a PhD topic. It is true that the Structural Funds have been the subject of contestation among regions, member states and the Commission since the 1980s (Hooghe and Keating 1994) but the polity-building aspects of the policy should not be exaggerated. The funds flow largely through national governments, the policy is managed between them and the Commission, and they operate at a variety of scales involving a multiplicity of actors. They are symbolically used by regional entrepreneurs to claim success in attracting resources, but their substantive impact is impossible to disentangle from other funding flows. Experience among member states has varied (Hooghe 1996). Where states already have strong regional policy instruments, the Structural Funds have been incorporated into them. States with weak regional policy instruments have often used the Structural Fund programmes as the basis for their own programmes, as in Spain or Italy (Fargion *et al*. 2006) but this is a matter of state discretion, not European imposition. As for the Commission, no evidence has ever been produced of a plan to by-pass nation-states and create a Europe of the Regions. More important has been their role in diffusing the new ideas of regional development, emphasising local initiative, networks and 'soft' factors such as research and development rather than the 'hard' infrastructure that characterised regional policy in the Keynesian era.

Another area that has attracted great interest is cross-border co-operation, again, perhaps, because there is an EU programme. It is true that European integration has transformed borders but the assumption that the removal of the economic and even the physical border will lead to political restructuring and the emergence of cross-border spaces is misleading. Indeed it is curious that, after neo-functionalism has been largely rejected as a way of understanding European integration in general, it has come back into work on the regions. Work in this field also suffers from a lack of comparative analysis and a theoretical basis, tending to descriptive case studies and to taking the promoters' intentions as evidence of what has actually happened. There is now a second generation of studies, at a more sophisticated level, showing how border and boundaries are constantly renegotiated in daily life (Scott 1999; Bray 2004). National borders are still in place and indeed the European project guarantees that they will not be moved as happened so often in the past. Yet they do not enclose the totality of social, economic and political systems as (at least in theory) they once did. This links with new conceptions of space in social geography in which territories are not seen as bounded and fixed but as open-ended and often indeterminate (Paasi 2002). Territory does matter, but it is not to be reified.

In a broader perspective, the conjuncture of state transformation from above through European integration and from below through the new regionalism has created a stimulating research agenda. It has reminded scholars of the historical contingency of the nation-state form and stimulated the search for precedents. It has raised a series of important normative questions about sovereignty and legitimacy once the nation-state ceases to be their unique source. Parties representing stateless nations and national minorities have taken advantage of the reshaping of political space by the European project, often abandoning traditional notions of sovereignty and adapting to the new dispensation (Lynch 1996; De Winter and Gomez-Reino 2002; Keating 2004). Sometimes this involves nothing more than the aspiration to become another member state of the EU but more often it has implied a rethinking of the whole concept of independence and a move to a post-sovereign stance (MacCormick 1999; Keating 2001). There is a literature, notably in Spain, exploring the new meanings for self-determination and multinational accommodation in the emerging complex order (Jáuregui 1997; Requejo 1998).

Bartolini (2004), from a Rokkanian perspective, has shown how the partial unpacking of territory under the impact of Europe has separated systems previously bounded by the nation-state, allowing partial exit from national politics for selected groups. There is a literature on the complex patterns of intergovernmental relations where three levels are involved (Bullman 1994; Hooghe 1995) and studies of policy making in sectoral fields (Borzel 2002). Since the Europe of the Regions movement (both politically and in academic discussion) peaked in the mid-1990s, there has been a more realistic approach to all of this, accepting that European integration has affected territorial politics but that the state is still very much there. Scholarship has also de-emphasised the radically new element in all of this, seeing the conjunction of Europe and the regions as the latest phase in a story of territorial politics that has run throughout the history of the nation-state, rather than contrasting it with an idealised unitary polity that never really existed.

The impact of globalisation and European integration is reflected also in urban studies, notably in the concept of the global city (Sassen 2000; Scott 2001). This shows how cities are integrated into global networks, reducing their dependence on national support systems and sustaining a division of labour which is itself global in scope. Trade flows, technology and migration link these cities to the global order, but impose new patterns of social segregation and inequality. Critics have complained that this is a general-isation from a very few cities, and Le Galès (2002) has argued that the European city has its own characteristics, notably the domination of small and medium-sized urban settlements, often with deep historical roots, in contrast to the continuous rise and fall of American cities.

Regional Government

In the last 30 years, all the large European states and some of the smaller ones have put in place systems of regional or 'meso' government (Mény 1982; Sharpe 1993); the exception being Germany which already had it. This responds to the functional restructuring discussed above and the needs of the state for new instruments for territorial management. In the 1970s the emphasis was on planning, co-ordination and public investment. Since the 1990s it is more on competitive regionalism and self-help. Regional government has also become the preferred response to the demands of cultural and nationality movements. The new century has also seen a revival of the idea of metropolitan government for city-regions.

Regional government is such a heterogeneous phenomenon that some have doubted the utility of the general term (Le Galès and Lesquene 1997). Yet it provides an obvious object for study. There are numerous accounts of its origins and development, but many fewer on its actual workings. Studies have also tended to be bounded by national traditions. In Italy there is still a domination by constitutional lawyers (for example the annual reports of the Istituto di Studi sui Sistemi Regionali Federali e sulle Autonomie "Massimo Severo Giannini" (ISSiFRA)) while Spanish scholars have broken free of this (Moreno 1997; Aja 2003). French scholars continue in the organisational analysis tradition. Germans use theories of co-operative federalism. There is a lack of comparative work, with a few exceptions (Négrier and Jouve 1998; Thorlakson 2003). There is also a lack of research on the impact of regional government on public policy. Where policy is considered, the focus is usually on intergovernmental relations, an important part of the federal tradition, but not the whole story. This may be a legacy of the old state-bound framework of political science, in which regional government is assessed as a contribution to the working of the state rather than a system in its own right and of the regional planning origins of regional studies. There is some work on devolution in the United Kingdom (Adams 2001; Adams and Schmueker 2005; Keating 2005), a growing literature on Spain (Subirats and Gallego 2002), very little on Italy and almost nothing on Belgium (but see de Rynck 2002). There is a literature on regional economic development but so far little on the impact of regionalism on the welfare state (but see Ferrera 2005; McEwen and Moreno 2005; Keating and McEwen 2006). Nor is there much work on regional interest articulation or on how changing spatial scales shifts the power balance among groups and sectors.

The Other Europe

The study of territorial politics and the evolution of the state has been dominated by the example of western Europe. There is a general acceptance that the history of the state in eastern and central Europe is different, states there being formed from the break-up of empire rather than the consolidation of territory. Yet this distinction is not perfect, since there are secession states in western Europe, while Poland was formed as a large consolidated state at a rather early stage of history, before being partitioned and reappearing in the twentieth century. There are few over-arching accounts of state development and territory in central-eastern Europe, although Caramani (2003) has produced a Rokkanian historical analysis. Since the fall of Communism, regionalism in the other Europe has attracted a certain amount of attention and the following general findings. State history since the Second World War has differed from that in western Europe, so that we do not see the emergence of territories and territorial management through regional policy and gradual institutionalisation of regions. Nationality politics tends to take the form of national minorities, that is groups who have an external homeland somewhere else (such as Hungarians in Slovakia) rather than of minority nations seeking self-government within the state (as in Scotland or Catalonia). There has not therefore been a convergence of new regionalism and nationality politics. In the early period of accession negotiations, the European Commission appeared to suggest that the candidate countries should have regional structures in place in order to meet membership requirements and to manage Structural Funds. This was taken up by interests within the candidate countries pushing for regionalisation, although it was never clear whether the Commission was pressing for regional government or just regional administration. In 2000 there was a sharp change in policy and the Commission told candidate countries that the Structural Funds would have to be managed centrally (Keating 2003; Hughes *et al.* 2004; Agh 2005). Europe has thus become a force for centralisation. Regional government was nonetheless established in Poland and the Czech Republic while in Hungary non-elected regional machinery was put in place with a promise eventually to move to elected government. Yet national governments are jealous of their recently recovered sovereignty and power and talk of federalism or radical decentralisation is taboo. It is likely, therefore, that the new member states will remain distinct in their territorial structures and that it is not valid to extrapolate experience of the old member states to them.

Where Are We Now?

The study of territorial politics has come a long way in the last 30 years. Territory has been reintegrated into political analysis rather than systematically reduced to the residual. There has been learning and cross-fertilisation across social science disciplines and the literatures on the different spatial scales and different facets of the phenomenon are talking to each other. Over-determinate theories, whether of national integration, disintegration or Europe of the Regions, have been moderated. Yet have we arrived at a new shared understanding, a paradigm or set of common analytical tools? This is much less certain.

The term multilevel governance has been much in vogue as a way of capturing the new dynamic (Hooghe and Marks 2001; Bache and Flinders 2004). I have never been happy with this term and the more debate continues the less enlightening it becomes. 'Governance' itself has multiple meanings and is notoriously difficult to operationalise. For some it is a broad term for social regulation and collective action, including 'government' as one of its forms. For others it is narrower than government, referring to a specific mode of policy making through negotiation rather than hierarchy; it is thus one form that government might take. For others again, it is an alternative to government; indeed some people insist that we are moving away from government towards governance. Obviously, it is impossible for us to get to grips with multilevel governance (MLG) unless we first specify in which sense we are using governance itself (see Goetz this volume). The sense in which the term is used by the MLG theorists seems to be the third, that is a move away from government to governance. This raises the old problem of how to use a new concept to analyse a new phenomenon and compare it to what went before. If there is no conceptual continuity between past and present, how can we compare them? Governance analysts customarily resolve this problem by devising a fictional world before governance in which there was a unitary, centralised state autonomous of social interests, and comparing it with a world of governance in which policy is negotiated and bargained. Yet this is nothing new, since we have had decades of debate about the role of interests, about corporatism and the interlinking of public and private interests. There may indeed have been changes in the power and role of the state and organised interests over time, but this would require us to retain common concepts and variables so as to study these changes.

Much the same can be said about multilevel governance. It is almost invariably defined as a new state of affairs by reference to a stylised account of the centralised and unitary nation state. Yet everything in this paper so far suggests that territorial politics has always been present. It has changed its form over time, but tracking these changes requires common concepts, not a conceptual break from one era to another. If the concept of governance in MLG is unclear, that of levels is even more so. They seem variously to be spatial, organisational or even individual so that any complex organisation can be described as an example of MLG. Our concern in this paper has not been about organisational complexity but about the role of territory in political analysis and the way in which it shapes politics, institutions and policy. Political science, sociology and geography have gradually been developing concepts that travel across time and space that enable us to grasp the elusive factor of territory and its changing manifestations. We have made a lot of progress but we are not there yet.

Notes

1. This not only contradicted my upbringing from childhood, it also provided a foil for a doctoral thesis that I was then completing on politics in Scotland demonstrating the continued resilience of territorial politics within the unitary state.
2. Some ten years ago I published a book called *Nations against the State*. It translated well into Spanish but for the French translation the title had to be changed, since *Nations contre l'Etat* was considered an oxymoron.

References

Abélès, Marc (1989). *Jours Tranquilles en '89: ethnologie politique d'un département français.* Paris: Odile Jacob.

Adams, John, and Peter Robinson, eds. (2002). *Devolution in Practice. Public Policy Differences within the UK.* London: Institute for Public Policy Research.

Adams, John, and Katie Schmueker, eds. (2005). *Devolution in Practice 2006.* London: Institute for Public Policy Research.

Ágh, Attila (2005). *Institutional Design and Regional Capacity-Building in the Post-Accession Period.* Budapest: Hungarian Centre for Democracy Studies.

Aja, Eliseo (2003). *El estado autonómico. Federalismo y hechos diferenciales.* Madrid: Alianza.

Amin, A., and N. Thrift, eds. (1994). *Globalization, Institutions, and Regional Development in Europe.* Oxford: Oxford University Press.

Applegate, Celia (1999). 'A Europe of Regions: Reflections on the Historiography of Sub-National Places in Modern Times', *American Historical Review*, 104:4, 1157–82.

Bache, Ian, and Matthew Flinders, eds. (2004). *Multi-level Governance.* Oxford: Oxford University Press.

Badie, Bertrand (1995). *La fin des territoires. Essai sur le désordre international et sur l'utilité sociale du respect.* Paris: Fayard.

Bagnasco, Arnaldo, and Carlo Trigilia (1993). *La construction sociale du marché. Le défi de la troisième Italie.* Cachan: Editions de l'Ecole Normale Supérieur de Cachan.

Balme, Richard (1996). 'Pourquoi le gouvernement change-t-il d'échelle', in Richard Balme (ed.), *Les politiques du néo-régionalisme.* Paris: Economica, 11–40.

Bartolini, Stefano (2004). 'Old and New Peripheries in the Process of European Territorial Integration', in Christopher K. Ansell and Giuseppe di Palma (eds.), *Restructuring Territoriality. Europe and the United States Compared.* Cambridge: Cambridge University Press, 19–44.

Biorcio, Roberto (1997). *La Padania promessa.* Milan: Il Saggiatore.

Börzel, Tanja (2002). *States and Regions in the European Union: Institutional Adaptation in Germany and Spain.* Cambridge: Cambridge University Press.

Braudel, Fernand (1986). *L'identité de la France. Espace et Histoire.* Paris: Arthaud-Flammarion.

Bray, Zoe (2004). *Living Boundaries. Frontiers and Identities in the Basque Country.* Brussels: PIE-Peter Lang.

Brenner, Neil (2004). *New State Spaces. Urban Governance and the Rescaling of Statehood.* Oxford: Oxford University Press.

Brenner, Neil, Bob Jessop, Martin Jones and Gordon McLeod (2003). 'Introduction: State Space in Question', in Neil Brenner, Bob Jessop, Martin Jones and Gordon McLeod (eds.), *State/Space. A Reader.* Oxford: Blackwell, 1–26.

Bullman, Udo, ed. (1994). *Die Politik der dritten Ebene. Regionen im Europa der Union.* Baden-Baden: Nomos.

Bulpitt, James (1983). *Territory and Power in the United Kingdom. An Interpretation.* Manchester: Manchester University Press.

Caciagli, Mario (2003). *Regioni d'Europa. Devoluzioni, regionalismi, integrazione europea.* Bologna: Il Mulino.

Caramani, Daniele (2003). 'State Administration and Regional Construction in Central Europe: A Comparative-Historical Perspective', in Michael Keating and James Hughes (eds.), *The Regional Challenge in Central and Eastern Europe. Territorial Restructuring and European Integration.* Brussels: Presses interuniversitaires européenes/Peter Lang, 21–50.

Castells, Manuel (1989). *The Network Society.* Oxford: Blackwell.

Castells, Manuel (1997). *The Power of Identity.* Oxford: Blackwell.

Cento Bull, Anna, and Mark Gilbert (2001). *The Lega Nord and the Northern Question in Italian Politics.* London: Palgrave.

Cole, Alastair, and Peter John (1995). 'Local Policy Networks in France and Britain: Policy Co-ordination in Fragmented Political Systems', *West European Politics*, 18:4, 89–109.

Connor, Walker (1994). *Ethnonationalism: The Quest for Understanding*. Princeton, NJ: Princeton University Press.

Cooke, Philip, and Kevin Morgan (1998). *The Associational Economy. Firms, Regions, and Innovation*. Oxford: Oxford University Press.

Crouch, Colin, Patrick le Galès, Carlo Trigilia and Helmut Voelzkow (2001). *Local Production Systems in Europe. Rise or Demise?*. Oxford: Oxford University Press.

Dahrendorf, Ralph (1995). 'Preserving Prosperity', *New Statesman and Society*, 13/29 December, pp.36–40.

Dahrendorf, Ralph (2000). 'La sconfitta della vecchia democrazia', *La Repubblica*, 12 January.

Davies, Norman (1997). *Europe. A History*. London: Pimlico.

Davies, Norman (1999). *The Isles. A History*. London: Macmillan.

De Rynck, Stafaan (2002). *Changing Public Policy: The Role of the Regions*. Brussels: PIE/Peter Lang.

De Winter, Lieven, and Margarita Gomez-Reino Cachafeiro (2002). 'European Integration and Ethnoregionalist Parties', *Party Politics*, 8:4, 483–503.

De Winter, Lieven, and Huri Türsan, eds. (1998). *Regionalist Parties in Western Europe*. London: Routledge.

Deutsch, K.W. (1972). *Nationalism and Social Communication: An Inquiry into the Foundations of Nationality*. Cambridge, MA: MIT Press.

Diamanti, Ilvo (1993). *La lega : geografia, storia e sociologia di un nuovo soggetto politico*. Roma: Donzelli.

Dupuy, François, and Jean-Claude Thoenig (1985). *L'administration en miettes*. Paris: Fayard.

Durkheim, Emil (1964). *The Division of Labour in Society*. New York: Free Press.

Fargion, Valeria, Leonardo Morline, and Stefania Profeti, eds. (2006). *Europeizzazione e rappresentanza territoriale*. Bologna: Il Mulino.

Ferrera, Maurizio (2005). *The Boundaries of Welfare. European Integration and the New Spatial Politics of Social Protection*. Oxford: Oxford University Press.

Finer, S.E. (1974). *Comparative Government*. Harmondsworth: Penguin.

Flora, Peter, Stein Kuhnle, and Derek Urwin, eds. (1999). *State Formation Nation-Building and Mass Politics in Europe: The Theory of Stein Rokkan*. Oxford: Oxford University Press.

Galasso, G. (1978). *Passato e presente del meridionalismo*. Naples: Guida.

Gramsci, Antonio (1978a). 'Some aspects of the southern question', in Quentin Hoare (ed.), *Antonio Gramsci: Selections from Political Writings (1921–26)*. London: Lawrence and Wishart, 441–62.

Gramsci, Antonio (1978b). 'Operai e contadini', from L'Ordine Nuovo, 3 January 1920, in V. Lo Curto (ed.), *La questione meridionale*, 2nd edition. Florence: D'Anna.

Grémion, Pierre (1976). *Le pouvoir périphérique. Bureaucrates et notables dans le système politique français*. Paris: Seuil.

Harding, Alan (1999). 'Review Article: North American Urban Political Economy, Urban Theory and British Research', *British Journal of Political Science*, 29, 673–98.

Hechter, Michael (1975). *Internal Colonialism. The Celtic Fringe in British National Development, 1536–1966*. London: Routledge and Kegan Paul.

Hooghe, Liesbet (1995). 'Subnational Mobilisation in the European Union', *West European Politics*, 18.3, 175–98.

Hooghe, Liesbet, ed. (1996). *Cohesion Policy and European Integration. Building Multi-Level Governance*. Oxford: Clarendon.

Hooghe, Liesbet, and Gary Marks (2001). *Multi-Level Governance and European Integration*. Lanham, MD: Rowman and Littlefield.

Hooghe, Liesbet, and Michael Keating (1994). 'The Politics of EU Regional Policy', *Journal of European Public Policy*, 1:3, 368–93.

Hough, Dan, and Charlie Jeffery, eds. (2006). *Devolution and Electoral Politics*. Manchester: Manchester University Press.

Hughes, James, Gwendolyn Sasse and Claire Gordon (2004). *Europeanization and Regionalization in the EU's Enlargement to Central and Eastern Europe.* London: Palgrave.

ISSiFRA, Instituto di studi sui sistemi regionali, federale e sulle autonomie 'Massimo Severo Giannini', *Rapporto annuale sullo stato del regionalismo in Italia,* yearly from 2002. Rome: ISSiFRA.

Jáuregui, Gurutz (1997). *Los nacionalismos minoritarios en la Unión Europea.* Barcelona: Ariel.

Jones, Barry, and Michael Keating, eds. (1995). *The European Union and the Regions.* Oxford: Clarendon.

Kantor, Paul, with S. David (1988). *The Dependent City. The Changing Political Economy of Urban America.* Glenview, IL: Scott Foresman.

Keating, Michael (1975). 'The Role of the Scottish MP', PhD thesis, Glasgow College of Technology and CNAA.

Keating, Michael (1988). *State and Regional Nationalism. Territorial Politics and the European State.* London: Harvester-Wheatsheaf.

Keating, Michael (1991). *Comparative Urban Politics.* Aldershot: Edward Elgar.

Keating, Michael (1993). *Comparative Urban Politics. Power and the City in the United States, Canada, Britain and France.* Aldershot: Edward Elgar.

Keating, Michael (1996). *Nations against the State: The New Politics of Nationalism on Quebec, Catalonia and Scotland.* Basingstoke: MacMillan.

Keating, M. (1998). *The New Regionalism in Western Europe. Territorial Restructuring and Political Change.* Cheltenham: Edward Elgar.

Keating, Michael (2001). *Plurinational Democracy. Stateless Nations in a Post-Sovereignty Era.* Oxford: Oxford University Press.

Keating, Michael (2003). 'Regionalization in Central and Eastern Europe: The Diffusion of a Western Model?', in Michael Keating and James Hughes (eds.), *The Regional Challenge in Central and Eastern Europe. Territorial Restructuring and European Integration.* Brussels: Presses interuniversitaires européenes/Peter Lang, 51–68.

Keating, Michael (2004). 'European Integration and the Nationalities Question', *Politics and Society,* 3:1, 367–88.

Keating, Michael (2005). *The Government of Scotland. Public Policy Making after Devolution.* Edinburgh: Edinburgh University Press.

Keating, Michael, and Barry Jones, eds. (1985). *Regions in the European Community.* Oxford: Oxford University Press.

Keating, Michael, and Nicola McEwen, eds. (2006). *Devolution and Public Policy. A Comparative Perspective.* London: Taylor and Francis.

Keating, Michael, John Loughlin and Kris Deschouwer (2003). *Culture, Institutions and Economic Development. A Study of Eight European Regions.* Aldershot: Edward Elgar.

Krämer, Raimund, ed. (1998). *Regionen in der EuropäischenUnion.* Berlin: Berliner Debatte.

Lafont, Robert (1967). *La révolution régionaliste.* Paris: Gallimard.

Le Galès, Patrick (2002). *European Cities. Social Conflicts and Governance.* Oxford: Oxford University Press.

Le Galès, Patrick, and Christian Lesquesne, eds. (1997). *Les paradoxes des régions en Europe.* Paris: La Découverte.

Lipset, Seymour Martin (1985). 'The Revolt against Modernity', in *Consensus and Conflict. Essays in Political Sociology.* New Brunswick, NJ: Transaction, 253–94.

Lipset, Seymour Martin, and Stein Rokkan (1967). 'Cleavage Structures, Party Systems and Voter Alignments', in Seymour Martin Lipset and Stein Rokkan (eds.), *Party Systems and Voter Alignments.* New York: Free Press, 1–64.

Lo Curto, V., ed. (1978). *La questione meridionale.* Florence: D'Anna.

Logan, John, and Harvey Molotch (1987). *Urban Fortunes: The Political Economy of Place.* Berkeley: University of California Press.

Lovering, John (1999). 'Theory Led by Policy: The Inadequacies of the "New Regionalism"', *International Journal of Urban and Regional Research,* 23:2, 379–90.

Lynch, Peter (1996). *Minority Nationalism and European Integration*. Cardiff: University of Wales Press.

MacCormick, Neil (1999). *Questioning Sovereignty. Law, State and Nation in the European Commonwealth*. Oxford: Oxford University Press.

Mannheimer, Renato, ed. (1991). *La Lega Lombarda*. Milan: Feltrinelli.

McEwen, Nicola, and Luis Moreno, eds. (2005). *The Territorial Politics of Welfare*. London: Routledge.

Mény, Yves, ed. (1982). *Dix ans de régionalisme en Europe. Bilan et perspectivas*. Paris: Cujas.

Miller, William (1981). *The End of British Politics?* Oxford: Oxford University Press.

Moreno, Luís (1997). *La federalización de España. Poder político y territorio*. Madrid: Siglo Veintuno.

Mori, G., ed. (1981). *Autonomismo meridionale*. Bologna: Il Mulino.

Nairn, Tom (1977). *The Break-up of Britain. Crisis and Neo-Nationalism*. London: New Left Books.

Nairn, Tom (1997). *Faces of Nationalism. Janus Revisited*. London: Verso.

Négrier, Emmanuel, and B. Jouve, eds. (1998). *Que gouvernent les régions d'Europe? Échanges politiques et mobilisations*. Paris: L'Harmattan.

Osiander, A. (1994). *The States System of Europe, 1640–1990. Peacemaking and the Conditions of International Stability*. Oxford: Clarendon.

Osiander, Andreas (2001). 'Sovereignty, International Relations, and the Westphalian Myth', *International Organization*, 55:2, 251–287.

Paasi, Anssi (2002). 'Place and Region: Regional Worlds and Words', *Progress in Human Geography*, 26:6, 802–11.

Pasquier, Romain (2004). *La capacité politique des regions. Une comparaison France/Espagne*. Rennes: Presses Universitaires de Rennes.

Peterson, Paul (1981). *City Limits*. Chicago: University of Chicago Press.

Petschen, Santiago (1993). *La Europa de las regiones*. Barcelona: Generalitat de Catalunya.

Przeworski, Adam, and Henry Teune (1970). *The Logic of Comparative Social Inquiry*. New York: Wiley.

Putnam, Robert (1993). *Making Democracy Work. Civic Traditions in Modern Italy*. Princeton: Princeton University Press.

Requejo, Ferran (1998). *Reconeixement nacional, democràcia i federalisme. Alguns límits del model constitucional espanyol*. Barcelona: Fundació Ramon Trias Fargas.

Rhodes, R.A.W. (1999). *Control and Power in Central–Local Government Relations*. Aldershot: Ashgate.

Rhodes, R.A.W., and Vincent Wright (1987). 'Introduction', *West European Politics*, 10:4, special issue on *Tensions in Territorial Politics in Western Europe*, 1–20.

Rohe, Karl (1990a). 'German Elections and Party Systems in Historical Perspective: An Introduction', in Karl Rohe (ed.), *Elections, Parties and Political Traditions. Foundations of German Parties and Party Systems, 1867–1987*. New York: Berg, 1–26.

Rohe, Karl (1990b). 'Political Alignments and Realignments in the Ruhr, 1867–1987: Continuity and Change of Political Traditions in an Industrial Region', in Karl Rohe (ed.), *Elections, Parties and Political Traditions. Foundations of German Parties and Party Systems, 1867–1987*. New York: Berg, 107–44.

Rokkan, S. (1980). 'Territories, Centres, and Peripheries: Toward a Geoethnic–Geoeconomic–Geopolitical Model of Differentiation within Western Europe', in J. Gottmann (ed.), *Centre and Periphery. Spatial Variations in Politics*. Beverly Hills, CA: Sage, 163–204.

Rokkan, S., and D. Urwin (1982). 'Introduction: Centres and Peripheries in Western Europe', in S. Rokkan and D. Urwin (eds.), *The Politics of Territorial Identity. Studies in European Regionalism*. London: Sage, 1–18.

Rokkan, Stein, and Derek Urwin (1983). *Economy, Territory, Identity. Politics of West European Peripheries*. London: Sage.

Salvadori, M. (1976). *La questione meridionale*. Turin: Loescher.

Sassen, Saskia (2000). *The Global City: New York, London.* Tokyo and Princeton, NJ: Princeton University Press.

Sassen, Saskia (2001). 'Global Cities and Global City-Regions: A Comparison', in Allen J. Scott (ed.), *Global City-Regions. Trends, Theory, Policy.* Oxford: Oxford University Press, 78–95.

Saunders, Peter (1980). *Urban Politics. A Sociological Interpretation.* Harmondsworth: Penguin.

Savitch, H.V., and Paul Kantor (2002). *Cities in the International Marketplace.* Princeton, NJ: Princeton University Press.

Scott, Allen (1998). *Regions and the World Economy. The Coming Shape of Global Production, Competition, and Political Order.* Oxford: Oxford University Press.

Scott, Allen J., ed. (2001). *Global City-Regions. Trends, Theory, Policy.* Oxford: Oxford University Press.

Scott, James Wesley (1999). 'European and North American Contexts for Cross-border Regionalism', *Regional Studies*, 33:7, 605–17.

Sharpe, L.J., ed. (1993). *The Rise of Meso Government in Europe.* London: Sage.

Spruyt, H. (1994). *The Sovereign State and Its Competitors.* Princeton, NJ: Princeton University Press.

Stoker, Gerry, and Karen Mossberger (1994). 'Urban Regimes in Comparative Perspective', *Government and Policy*, 12:2, 195–212.

Stone, Clarence (1989). *Regime Politics. Governing Atlanta, 1946–1986.* Lawrence: University of Kansas Press.

Storper, Michael (1997). *The Regional World. Territorial Development in a Global Economy.* New York and London: Guildford.

Subirats, Joan, and Raquel Gallego, eds. (2002). *Veinte años de autonomías en España. Leyes, políticas públicas, instituciones y opinión pública.* Madrid: Centro de Investigaciones sociológicas.

Tarrow, Sydney (1977). *Between Center and Periphery. Grassroots Politicians in Italy and France.* New Haven, CT: Yale University Press.

Tarrow, Sydney, Peter Katzenstein, and Luigi Graziano, eds. (1978). *Territorial Politics in Industrial Nations.* New York: Praeger,.

Thorlakson, Lori (2003). 'Comparing Federal Institutions: Power and Representation in Six Federations', *West European Politics*, 26:2, 1–22.

Tiebout, Charles (1956). 'A Pure Theory of Local Expenditures', *Journal of Political Economy*, 64, 416–24.

Tilly, Charles (1990). *Coercion, Capital and European States, AD 990–1990.* Oxford: Blackwell.

Tilly, Charles (1994). 'Entanglements of European Cities and States', in C. Tilly and W.P. Blockmans (eds.), *Cities and the Rise of States in Europe, AD 1000 to 1800.* Boulder, CO: Westview.

The European Welfare State: Golden Achievements, Silver Prospects

The year 2008 marks the 30th anniversary of the second oil shock. In December 1978 the OPEC countries announced a new substantial price increase for crude oil, to be effective from 1979. This decision put a seal on the new terms of trade within the global economy and altered in irreversible ways the external economic foundations on which the so-called *Trente Glorieuses* had rested. A new phase was starting for the European economies and for the generous welfare states that had been laboriously built since World War II.

This historical watershed had implications not only for real-world social policy but also for its academic study. During the first half of the 1970s an articulated debate on the 'expansion' had gained momentum: why the *Trente Glorieuses*? In the wake of the two oil shocks a second and new debate took off: what is the nature of the 'crisis'? In the last 30 years these two debates have occupied a prominent position within the wider field of political economy. The 1980s and the first half of the 1990s were the heyday of comparative analyses of welfare state origins and expansion, while also witnessing the elaboration and refinement of 'crisis' arguments and diagnoses. Unsurprisingly, the latter have gained the centre stage during the last decade. In this latter period, however, both the expansion and the crisis discussions have tended to merge into a new grand debate on welfare state modernisation: what reforms are possible and effective? The metaphor of a 'silver age of permanent austerity', coined by Pierson (1998, 2001a) and Taylor-Gooby (2002), takes it for granted that a new historical phase has begun, in which social policy is systematically confronted with a novel set of constraints and problems and must find new ways for achieving its objectives.

Both the welfare state and the way of studying it have changed during the last 30 years: this article will try to give an idea of both dimensions of change. Since it is impossible to provide either a systematic analysis of factual developments or a comprehensive review of a huge literature, we will follow a middle course, moving back and forth between the two dimensions. In substantive terms, we will focus on three main topics:

- challenges: what have been the main pressures and dynamics that have led from the golden age of expansion to the silver age of permanent austerity?
- responses: what have been the main lines of institutional re-adaptation within European welfare states?[1]
- political correlations/implications of change: what has been the role of political dynamics in shaping welfare state developments? Has there been a shift in this role with the transition from the *Trente Glorieuses* to permanent austerity?

Before addressing these topics, a brief *tour d'horizon* is in order, i.e. a survey of the state of the art at the point of departure, the 1970s.

The Way We Were

The term *Trente Glorieuses* was coined by Jean Fourastié in 1979 in order to celebrate the rapid economic growth which quadrupled France's GDP between 1945 and 1975 (Fourastié 1979).[2] This expression was soon adopted by the international debate and in particular by scholars of the welfare state. There had been prolonged periods of economic boom earlier in history. But the true novelty of the *Trente Glorieuses* was indeed the spectacular expansion of this new institution.

At the beginning of the 1950s social security expenditure was still below 10 per cent of GDP in most European countries. By the early 1970s many countries (such as Belgium, Denmark, France, Germany, Italy, the Netherlands, and Sweden) had come to pass the 20 per cent mark and most of the remaining ones had already surpassed 15 per cent (Flora *et al.* 1983–87). The vast majority, if not the totality, of the population had come to be included in social protection schemes for all the 'standard risks': old age, disability, and bereavement; sickness, maternity, and work injuries; unemployment and family dependants. At least in terms of eligibility, European welfare states had 'grown to limits' (Flora 1986–87): they had reached or were about to reach their widest possible domestic boundaries, coinciding with the whole citizenry. During the 'golden age' (another well-known metaphor to denote the 1945–75 period) the more localised systems of protection were progressively marginalised in their financial size and functional scope. Sophisticated techniques (such as PAYGO financing for pensions) were invented and deployed in order to improve and rationalise the extraction of taxes and contributions, govern redistributive flows from the centre, and deliver benefits and services to the various clienteles. Finally, alongside the various insurance schemes for the standard risks, new non-contributory programmes of general social assistance were created, as well as increasingly complex health-care systems providing a wide array of medical services.

The *Trente Glorieuses* brought the social rights of citizenship (Marshall 1992) to full bloom, matching the saliency of the other two types of rights (civil and political) in shaping people's expectations and life chances. In this period social citizenship also reached its greatest degree of both external and internal *closure* (a point which tends to be neglected by historical accounts). The 'glory' of economic growth and social progress remained essentially linked to state-national institutions and circumscribed within their boundaries. For non-nationals, it was rather difficult to enter the solidarity spaces of other states, especially when it came to deriving benefits from them. During the first three post-war decades the 'principle of territoriality' dominated the most relevant aspects of social security that were strictly in the hands of national governments, putting non-nationals in conditions of systematic disadvantage (Holloway 1981; Cornelissen 1996; Ferrera 2005a). Nationals, on the other hand, were virtually 'locked in', that is obliged to be members of public schemes.

The 1970s marked the apex of the growth parabola of the welfare state as a real-world institution. This decade also witnessed the take-off of another parabola: that of systematic comparative analyses of the welfare state as an object of study. During the 1950s and 1960s there had been a rising academic interest in welfare programmes, especially in the UK. But the academic field of 'social policy' had remained primarily narrative and Anglo-centred, often displaying manifest normative preferences or biases. Starting from the 1970s welfare state research underwent a quantum leap, moving from the tranquil waters of history and idiography to the open seas of comparative social science.

The seminal works of this new phase appeared in the first half of the decade (e.g. Rimlinger 1971; Heclo 1974; Wilensky 1975). Their main explanatory focuses were the historical origins and subsequent expansion of welfare programmes. Broad research questions were posed (why were these programmes introduced? what were the main drivers of growth?) and the answers were sought through systematic comparisons. The comparative turn was indeed the most salient and fruitful characteristic of the new phase. Different authors resorted to different methods for their comparisons, however (the big divide being that between qualitative historical studies and quantitative statistical analyses), and adopted different approaches. As shown by Jens Alber, in the burgeoning literature of the 1970s two main theoretical juxtapositions were clearly recognisable: 1) conflictualist vs. functionalist approaches and 2) pluralist vs. Marxist approaches (Alber 1982). These two juxtapositions intersected with each other, giving rise to four basic 'clusters' of debates and interpretations, each characterised by distinct theoretical assumptions about the overall logic of social change and the hierarchy of its driving forces and actors. The confrontation (which at certain points became a true tug of war) between the various methodological strategies and theoretical approaches continued throughout the 1980s and part of the 1990s. In many respects the appearance of Esping Andersen's *Three Worlds of Welfare Capitalism* marked the apex of the academic discussion on the *Trente Glorieuses* (Esping Andersen 1990). This landmark book gave original contributions to the expansion debate on at least three fronts: it suggested looking not only at state policies, but at the overall welfare 'regime', consisting of the interaction between state and market (later extended to include the family as a third element (Esping-Andersen 1999); it contrasted three distinct types of regimes (liberal, corporatist-conservative and social democratic), tracing their historical origins and developmental trajectories during the golden age; it suggested extending the comparative analysis of regimes from outputs to outcomes in terms of stratification and de-commodification. Esping-Andersen's work sparked off a debate of its own, which would certainly deserve a dedicated survey.[3]

In the mid-1970s the developmental trajectory of the welfare state as a *thing* started to invert its direction. As mentioned, the EU countries entered the turbulent 1970s while still enjoying a high degree of closure and domestic autonomy, which had hitherto peacefully coexisted with an international economic order resting on 'embedded liberalism' at the global level (Ruggie 1982) and at the European level with a deepening market integration steered by benevolent supranational authorities. The oil price crises of the 1970s and the collapse of the Bretton Woods regime suddenly altered the nature of the international economic order, giving rise to an unprecedented 'stagflation' and to escalating monetary instability. Under such new conditions, the traditional strategies of fiscal and monetary demand management (which served as preconditions for autonomous domestic choices in the social policy sphere) became increasingly ineffective, if not altogether unviable (Scharpf 2000).

By the end of the decade it became clear, however, that 'the crisis' had not only external origins and dynamics. As a matter of fact, the European welfare states had started to be afflicted by a number of internal, increasingly troublesome challenges and dynamics (such as demographic ageing or the post-industrial transition). The seminal diagnoses of this internal side of the crisis appeared in the second half of the 1970s, within both the conflictualist-pluralist camp (e.g. Flora 1981) and the functionalist-Marxist one (e.g. Gough 1979, echoing O'Connor 1973). During the 1980s and 1990s the 'crisis' debate became a growth industry. We cannot offer here a systematic reconstruction of the expansion and crisis debates;[4] they will serve however as general backgrounds for the discussions that will be presented in the next three sessions.

From the *Trente Glorieuses* to Permanent Austerity: The External Challenges

The shift to permanent austerity has been mainly the result of exogenous pressures coming from the environment of the welfare state: the environment external to the nation-state (essentially globalisation and European integration) and the internal environment, i.e. changes in domestic economies and social structures. Let us briefly review the nature and impact of all these pressures, starting with the external ones.

Globalisation

Globalisation is generally understood as the international integration of markets as well as the internationalisation of production (see Genschel 2004: 616; Huber and Stephens 2005: 609–12). Both dynamics have undergone a rather dramatic acceleration in the last three decades in the wake of technological advances and policy liberalisation. Economic activities have become more and more specialised and dispersed across different areas and regions of the world, making it easier for goods and services to be subdivided and traded across countries. World trade has grown at an annual average rate of around 8.5 per cent over the period 1992–2005.

How exactly has globalisation affected the welfare state? Essentially by posing new constraints, by restricting the margins of manoeuvre that national governments enjoyed during the golden age in designing, managing and funding their social protection systems. The globalisation of finance (and in particular the emergence of offshore capital markets beyond the reach of central banks) has seriously weakened governments' control over national tax bases. The costs of deficit spending (a tenet of Keynesian demand management) have significantly increased due to the international rise of interest rates and the high risk premiums that need to be paid in case of lax spending. Economic opening has made firms in the exposed sectors more sensitive to the costs associated with social regulations. These firms have become 'price takers' and can no longer shift above-average costs to captive consumers or cross-subsidise the sheltered sectors of the economy. More generally investors compare post-tax rates of returns on an international scale and tend to demand higher returns on their investments, often resorting to strategies of production outsourcing and offshoring. These new 'exit options' for capitals, investors and firms have made it much more difficult for the state to steer the economy and the labour market and to reconcile the twin goals of economic competitiveness and social consensus. On the one hand, too much (or the wrong kind) of intervention on the side of the state risks to jeopardise competitiveness and/or generate employment losses. On the other hand, if the losers of economic internationalisation are not supported ('compensated') by adequate state policies, the social and political legitimacy of 'opening' as such risks to be undermined (Scharpf 2000).

A less reliable and controllable tax base has meant greater risks of financial disequilibria for those welfare state programmes that rest on entitlements (typically pensions). Governments have tried to counter the pressure of international tax competition by shifting welfare state funding onto consumption, income from labour or social security contributions. But such strategies have tended to cause negative effects on other macro-economic variables (such as inflation or growth as a whole) and to worsen the prospects of the employment base. Consumption taxes and social security contributions in particular tend to fall heavily on low-productivity service employment, crowding it out of the labour market and thus generating higher demand for social benefits; a vicious circle that has been identified as a prime cause of the rising unemployment and the financial crisis of the welfare state, especially in the big continental countries (Manow and Seils 2000; Palier 2000).

In the political debates of the 1980s and early 1990s globalisation was often portrayed as a subversive force, inevitably conducive to a 'race to the bottom' through regulatory competition.[5] During the last decade a number of serious systematic comparative analyses have however challenged these negative and pessimistic views. Far from being an irresistible destroyer of social protection institutions and a 'flattener' of country-specific preferences and diversities, globalisation is now seen as challenge that 1) is filtered through various elements of domestic political economy configurations and 2) can be more or less effectively contravened through politico-economic responses and institutional adaptations. The main factors that may determine the kind and level of globalisation's impact are political institutions (Huber and Stephens 2001; Swank 2002), the structure of industrial relations (Garrett 1998; Scharpf 2000), left-wing governments (Garrett 1998; Castles 2004) and the programmatic structure of specific social policies (Burgoon 2001). Several authors have noted that, if appropriately (re)configured, social policies can play a precious role in upholding the performance of domestic political economies in the new globalised environment: they can provide not only side-payments to the losers – thus avoiding potential anti-opening backlashes – but also spurs and resources for enhancing skills and productivity, thus boosting economic competitiveness more generally.[6]

European Integration

When it was launched in the 1950s, the project of European integration did not intend to challenge the institutional foundations of the nation-based welfare state. Quite the contrary, the Founding Fathers conceived of European integration as a project capable of creating and sustaining a virtuous circle between *open* economies and outward-looking economic policies on the one hand and *closed* welfare states and inward looking social policy on the other (Milward 2000). The limited competences assigned by the Rome Treaty to the supranational level in the social policy sphere reflected the explicit objective of a division of labour between national and EC rulers that was seen as virtuous for both the market and the welfare state; it also rested on an implicit *favour*, a positive orientation vis-à-vis social protection, high labour standards and full employment objectives, whose national scope and closure pre-conditions were taken for granted and thus assumed as inherently non-problematic for a project essentially aimed at creating a customs union. European integration and the welfare state were to remain only 'loosely coupled'.

The sudden change of the international economic order during the 1970s had a particularly marked effect on the European economies: the old institutional compromise of the 1950s ('Smith abroad, Keynes at home'; market making to the EC, market correcting to the member states) could not 'rescue' the nation-state this time around. The rapid and utter failure of Keynesian reflation and welfare state upgrading attempted by the French socialist government in 1982–83 only served to confirm this (Levy 2000).

As is well known, in the early 1980s this problematic background prompted an ambitious project for the 're-launching of Europe', based on two steps: completing the internal market and then move towards a fully fledged economic and monetary union (EMU). The Single European Act of 1986 unleashed a dynamic of 'market making' primarily through measures of negative integration (that is, the removal of national barriers to economic transactions), accompanied by some measures of positive integration (supranational harmonisation) aimed at safeguarding minimal standards and a level playing field. '1992' was indeed a huge market-building initiative in a double sense: cross-system boundaries were virtually erased, thus transforming the European market into a single, unified space of transactions; and the institutional buttresses of the market *as such* (that is, as an arena of transactions competing with other institutional arenas) were significantly strengthened by conferring on free movement provisions (in particular the free movement of goods) and competition law a 'supreme' status in the EC legal order (Poiares Maduro 1998). By setting fixed macroeconomic requirements and deadlines for admission, the Maastricht process imposed further constraints on the autonomy of national governments in the welfare state sphere.

Like globalisation, the EMU project was largely considered in the early debate of the 1990s as a subversive factor for national social contracts, in the wake of increasingly stringent market compatibility requirements, the new power of business, the hardening of budgetary constraints, and the impossibility of creating some sort of social Europe due to the institutional obstacles to positive integration.[7] Rescued in the 1950s, the national welfare state was now in serious danger of being slowly eroded if not entirely taken apart by the new phase of European integration.

Recent discussions have adopted a much more nuanced view. European integration has indeed forced several domestic adjustments, but not necessarily for the worse: the economic, fiscal, and monetary discipline enforced by supranational authorities has prompted or accelerated a dynamic of welfare state recalibration which was anyway appropriate and desirable for coping with a host of endogenous problems (Ferrera and Rhodes 2000; Ferrera and Hemerick 2003; Zeitlin and Trubeck 2003; Martin and Ross 2004). Liberalisations have made several goods and services more affordable to consumers, enhancing the range of options available to them; in certain areas (e.g. health and safety) market integration has also brought about more consumer protection and higher labour standards. Some regulatory competition has indeed taken place, but not necessarily towards the bottom (Scharpf 1999; Guillen and Matsaganis 2000). As in the case of globalisation, the literature has moreover highlighted a multitude of factors that mediate the impact of European integration on domestic redistributive arrangements, as well as the scope and intensity of their 'Europeanisation'.[8]

It must be noted, however, that European integration affects the welfare state not only in an *indirect* way, i.e. by posing constraints and altering the payoff matrix of the main social and political actors. The EU has also a *direct* impact on the boundaries of social citizenship and thus operates as a potentially more disruptive factor than globalisation.

We mentioned above that during the *Trente Glorieuses* social protection schemes reached their maximum level of closure. Since the mid-1970s the EU legal order has increasingly worked as an opening wedge for closure rules and practices (Bartolini 2005). The traditional link between rights and territory has become much looser:[9] for most civic and social rights, the filtering role of nationality has been neutralised. In the field of social insurance proper, a detailed set of regulations has been introduced for coordinating social security regimes in case of cross-border movements, while EU competition rules have started to affect certain aspects of these regimes at the national level (Leibfried and Pierson 2000; Sindbjerg Martinsen 2005). The exclusionary or discriminatory prerogatives of national governments vis-à-vis outsiders have been severely restricted and the very 'sovereignty to bound' of the nation-state in the social sphere has been put in question. Social insurance contributions and benefits have become portable across the Union; patients can seek medical treatment in any EU hospital; pension funds have been allowed not only to invest, but also to shop for clients and 'sponsors' in all member states; the treatment of legal immigrants (including third country nationals) has been harmonised across the Union, envisaging access not only to social insurance, but to means-tested social assistance as well; and private (third pillar) insurance has been almost fully liberalised. The principles of compulsory membership and of public monopoly over social insurance schemes are still shielded from the EU competition regime, but only to the extent that certain conditions apply (e.g. the adoption of PAYGO financing).

With respect to the *Trente Glorieuses*, the institutional framework which has emerged in Europe during the last 30 years represents a true quantum leap in terms of 'opening' for at least three reasons: 1) the extremely wide scope of coordination rules: both the material scope (i.e. the range of benefits and schemes covered by coordination rules) and its personal scope (i.e. the range of eligible groups and persons); 2) the 'tighter coupling' between social protection and the internal market, which have become increasingly intertwined with each other; 3) the high degree of 'juridification' of both the coordination and the competition regimes of the EU, a juridification emblematically represented by the powers of a supranational court enjoying supremacy over domestic courts.

The 'opening' of domestic social sharing arrangements on the side of the EU was well meant and has brought significant advantages, especially to migrant workers. But it has caused strains and problems too, originating a novel 'spatial politics' (see below). Traditional social and political equilibriums that had formed around national redistributive arrangements have been de-stabilised. Sizeable segments of the electorate have matured growing feelings of insecurity: about jobs, social benefits, rising immigration flows and generally intrusions from outside. According to recent Euro-barometer surveys, 20 per cent of respondents (EU15) consider their national economy as 'too open' and 26 per cent consider the European Union as 'too liberal' – with peaks of 34 per cent in France and Germany (European Commission 2004). Behind these numbers there is a hetero-geneous mix of socio-economic profiles and ideological orientations. But such numbers cannot be ignored: however desirable from an economic point of view, a policy platform predominantly centred on 'opening' risks generating various forms of 'political backlash', i.e. dynamics of defensive mobilisations around the status quo, increasingly framed in euro-sceptic terms and accompanied by anti-EU orientations (Ferrera 2006).

Internal Challenges: The Transformation of Domestic Economies and Social Structures

In addition to external pressures and constraints, welfare state programmes have also been facing growing challenges posed by the transformations of their domestic economic and social environments. The foundation and the expansion of such programmes had taken place in the context of 'industrialism' – understood as a general mode of organising the spheres of economic production and social reproduction. The last three decades have witnessed a rapid transition towards a new 'post-industrial' order, in the wake of the rising importance of services, changes in household patterns and behaviours, and population ageing.

The weakening of industrialism in OECD countries is a long-term process, which set in roughly at the beginning of the 1960s due to a saturation of markets and a declining price elasticity of demand for industrial goods (Iversen and Wren 1998). Since then the service sector has been the main driver of economic and occupational expansion, while employment in manufacturing has generally stagnated or declined. The emerging service economy is governed by a logic that is different from that of the industrial economy. The main contrast is that in services it is much harder to increase productivity – a problem that has huge consequences for the labour market. Rising productivity in the age of industrial expansion made it possible to combine wage increases with lower prices: the resulting rise in demand could be translated into new jobs. As in the service economy such a virtuous circle is impossible, employment creation in private services is highly sensitive to wage levels and dynamics (Baumol 1967; Iversen and Wren 1998; Esping Andersen 1999). In some countries (most notably in the Nordic area) this problem has been circumvented by creating public service employment on a large scale during the golden age. But the financial costs of this strategy are difficult to sustain if that historical window of opportunity was missed. As argued by Iversen and Wren (1998), post-industrial economies are thus faced with a challenging trilemma: only two out of the three traditional goals of 'welfare capitalism' (i.e. high levels of equality, employment and fiscal discipline) can be reconciled at any given time. And with the fiscal constraints posed by globalisation and European integration, during the last decade the trilemma has de facto reduced itself to the dilemma: maintaining equality vs. employment creation. Needless to say, slower productivity advancements have also meant lower growth rates in general.

The shift from an industrial to a post-industrial economy has caused serious upheavals in European occupational structures. 'Fordist' employment (i.e. stable and guaranteed jobs with permanent contracts) has been experiencing a steady decline since the 1970s, not fully compensated for by the rise of non-standard 'a-typical' forms of employment (such as temporary or part-time jobs). During the 1990s (and the problem is not solved) unemployment registered an alarming surge in Europe, especially in certain regions and among some categories (e.g. young people). Low wages and poor quality jobs have increased the numbers of 'working poor', systematically exposed to the risk of labour market and social exclusion (Gallie 2002; Saraceno 2002).

The second important change has involved family and gender relations. While in post-war industrial societies traditional families with a male breadwinner and a housewife predominated, the post-industrial age is characterised by a greater plurality of household forms: dual-earner families, single-parent households, de facto unions and so on (Lewis 2007). Average household size has declined, partly due to a fall in fertility rates, but also due to the greater number of single-person households and to a drastic drop in multi-generational households. In parallel with the increase of separations and divorces, these changes point towards a general 'precarisation' of social relations in European societies. Another important trend since the 1970s has been the increased participation of women in the labour market – a phenomenon that is closely connected to the rise of the service sector (Esping-Andersen 1999, Daly 2000; Orloff 2006). In some European countries the gender gap in participation rates has virtually disappeared and women's income now accounts for almost 50 per cent of all household income (Esping-Andersen 2002).[10]

The third significant transformation has been demographic ageing: due to lower birth rates and higher life expectancy the proportion of elderly people in the European societies has been constantly increasing in the last three decades. All projections point towards a dramatic intensification of this process in Europe. The OECD projects that in the EU-15 the ratio of people aged above 65 over the labour force will rise to 54.4 per cent by 2030 (OECD 2006). This means that for each elderly person there will be fewer than two workers. Largely due to the full maturation of the generous benefit formulas introduced in the past, these elderly will retire on average with higher pensions than current retirees: thus the real intergenerational transfer of resources will grow even more than just due to the shift in age group proportions. And a similar syndrome will affect the real expenditure on health care – a sector which is emblematically affected by the above-mentioned productivity problems and by the expansionary dynamics linked to medical progress.

These internal transformations have reinforced the pressures and constraints (especially in financial terms) linked to external changes and have brought delicate policy dilemmas. They have also generated a host of new social risks and needs: from new forms of poverty and social exclusion to personal dependency, from skills obsolescence (and thus 'un-employability') to situations of work–life 'imbalances' (Taylor-Gooby 2004; Bonoli 2006). Especially in the 'Bismarckian' systems of Continental and Southern Europe, these new risks have tended however to remain under-protected, if not totally neglected, due to the 'crowding out' effect of established programmes and their expansionary inertia even under conditions of budgetary austerity. The re-balancing of social expenditure towards the new risks and the more vulnerable social groups has clashed with the high 'stickiness' of the institutional status quo – a defining feature of that 'new politics of the welfare state' which has been the object of a lively debate in the literature of the last decade or so. Before turning to the politics of reform, let us briefly identify some common trends and key orientations of policy change that can be observed across systems, in response to environmental transformations.

Welfare State Recalibration at a Glance

Despite the gloomy prospects outlined by the early 'crisis' debate, European welfare states have not crumbled under the weight of the contextual changes described so far, and have actually given signs of at least some adaptive capacity (Kuhnle 2000). Quantitative indicators (e.g. various types of social expenditure ratios) show that there has been a *slowdown of growth* in respect of the golden age. But as concluded by a prominent scholar of the field, 'neither the race to the bottom predicted by the globophobes nor the expenditure blow-out predicted by the gerontophobes [has] apparently [taken] place on anything like the scale assumed by the crisis scenarios' (Castles 2004: 7). Institutional adaptation has been a complex incremental process, which has proceeded with different speed and success across the various countries and which has involved different policy areas: from macro-economic management and industrial relations to tax policy and labour market regulation (Hemerijck 2002). Limiting ourselves to the core elements of social protection, at least four key general trends of reform can be identified.

The first – and most significant – of these trends is constituted by structural adjustments in response to socio-economic developments. In the field of pensions the 1990s have witnessed a substantial wave of reforms that in some cases (e.g. Sweden or Italy) have altered the fundamental architecture of the system, promoting 'paradigmatic' change. Most countries though have kept within the boundaries of 'parametric' reform, moving within the logic of existing systems and taking steps in one or more of these directions: increasing the age of retirement, tightening qualifying conditions, restricting indexation rules or strengthening the link between contributions and benefits. Another important common trend in this area has been the growth of occupational and private pensions, giving rise to 'multi-pillar' systems combining PAYGO and funding as methods of financing.[11] In the field of health care reforms have been introduced with a view to enhancing efficacy and efficiency in the allocation of resources and in the provision of services through better incentives at both the macro and the micro levels (Freeman 2000; Freeman and Moran 2000; Guillen 2002; Steffen 2005). Social services and family policies have also witnessed some innovation in both substantive and organisational terms, with a view to responding to the rising needs of the elderly population, the changing gender division of labour and new forms of poverty and exclusion (Lewis 1993, 2007; Alber 1995; Anntonen and Sipila 1996; Saraceno 2002).

A second general trend has been a move to an *active* approach in the management of work incapacity (e.g. disability) and especially unemployment, with a view to preventing long-term dependency on income support.

In the course of the 1990s the 'job first' principle has gradually made its way throughout European (un)employment protection systems (Clasen and Clegg 2006). Access to benefits has been generally made more restrictive and conditional, but at the same time new networks of public and private employment services have been set up in order to promote and facilitate the labour market re-integration of workers without jobs. Activation strategies have proceeded hand in hand with wider exercises of labour market re-configuration, pioneered by the Netherlands in the 1980s under the banner of 'flexicurity' (Visser and Hemerijck 1997). Reforms in this field have received explicit spurs from the EU and in particular by the European Employment Strategy (EES), launched in 1997 (Zeitlin and Trubeck 2003; Zeitlin and Pochet 2005).

A third general trend – which cuts across various social protection programmes – has been greater 'targeting' or 'selectivity' of resources towards those most in need (Ferrera 1998), also in the wake of the policy recommendation of influential international bodies such as the OECD or the World Bank. Different strategies have been experimented with, depending on national preferences, constraints and opportunities (Kuhnle 2000): greater use of traditional means-testing; linking the amount of benefits received to income or means-testing from the top, clawing back transfer payments from those less in need via the tax system and so on. Alongside these strategies of 'vertical' targeting based on economic resources a trend is also observable towards 'horizontal' targeting based on social risk: reducing the generosity of some core transfer programmes (old age, disability and survivor pensions, for example) while increasing family benefits; introducing new subsidies for caregivers or categories with special needs, or expanding programmes against social exclusion. Despite the above-mentioned 'crowding out effect' of established programmes, some policy adaptations to the new structure of risks and needs have indeed taken place in a number of countries (Taylor-Gooby 2004; Armingeon and Bonoli 2006).

A fourth general trend has finally involved the financial side of social protection. We have already mentioned the promotion of funding as opposed to PAYGO in the area of pensions, with a double purpose: making income security at retirement less vulnerable to demographic imbalances and shifting some of the responsibility for its provision from the state to individual workers or the social partners. Another important development on the financing front has been the attempt at reducing charges on business and labour, particularly those in the form of non-wage labour. This development has been primarily motivated by competitiveness preoccupations, but also by the wish to neutralise the vicious circles generated by 'contribution-heavy' social insurance systems (discussed above). More generally – and, again, as recommended by the EES – most countries have reviewed the incentives of their tax/benefit systems in order to make them more 'employment-friendly'. In several countries these reviews have also offered the opportunity for putting in place a more transparent and rational 'division of labour' between social security contributions on the one hand and general taxation on the other in the overall financing of the welfare state (Palier 2002) .

We cannot offer here more detail on factual developments or provide an assessment of the extent and effectiveness of the institutional change that has already taken place. However, it might be interesting to raise a broader analytical (and partly normative) question: is it possible to identify the overall direction and 'flavour' of welfare state change since the late 1970s? Are there new concepts and analytical maps that can best capture the multifaceted and multidimensional dynamics of transformation?

The early 'crisis' debate tended to take a rather biased and restrictive view, interpreting change primarily in negative terms (both descriptively and normatively), i.e. as steps backwards from the golden age, assuming a sort of linear trajectory of evolution and progress. Cuts, retrenchment, roll-back of the state, these were the notions most commonly used to describe the new 'austerity' policies adopted by European governments since the late 1970s. Activation and targeting measures, in particular, tended to be seen as inherently coercive and punitive 'regressions' towards a conservative past or as undignified surrenders to the 'neo-liberal' orthodoxy, thus forgetting that 1) activation strategies had a long and honourable history as part of Swedish social democracy and 2) in the Continental and especially South European countries targeting and selectivity could pave the way for much needed distributive rationalisations, e.g. by shifting resources from over-protected insiders to under-protected outsiders (Ferrera 2005b). In merely descriptive terms, notions such as 'cuts' or 'retrenchment' did of course have some empirical grounding: traditional benefits were indeed reduced or even eliminated in certain sectors and in certain countries. But a lot of other things have been taking place – often in those very sectors and countries.

In order to escape from the traps of terminological (and at times ideological) reductionism, recent debates have suggested new and more neutral concepts in order to characterise the overall trajectory and rationale of institutional change after the golden age: *modernisation* (a term launched by the European Commission) (EC 1997), *recasting* (a term coined for a broad research Forum organised at the European University Institute in Florence in 1998–99) (Ferrera and Rhodes 2000), or *restructuring*. This latter term has been suggested by Pierson (2001a; 2001b), who has further articulated it on a number of sub-dimensions: *re-commodification* (which has to do with changes that restrict alternatives to labour market participation, either by tightening eligibility or by cutting benefits), *cost containment* (referring to changes primarily motivated by the urgency of reducing debts and deficits) and *recalibration* (involving both *rationalisation*, i.e. modifications of existing programmes in line with new ideas about how to achieve established goals and *updating*, i.e. specific initiatives in response to newly recognised social needs).

The notion of *recalibration* has been used also by Ferrera, Hemerijck and Rhodes (2000) for both descriptive and prescriptive purposes.[12] In the understanding of these authors, the metaphor is meant to suggest an act of institutional reconfiguration and re-balancing characterised by:

- the presence of a set of constraints conditioning policy choices and developments, stemming from the interaction between external and internal pressures and challenges;
- the interdependence between additions (or upgradings) and 'subtractions' in the social policy menu, as a consequence of such constraints; and
- a deliberate shift of weight and emphasis among the various instruments and objectives of social policy, in the wake of complex dynamics of social and institutional learning.

These authors have further articulated the concept of recalibration in a number of sub-dimensions:

- *functional* recalibration, which has to do with the social risks around which welfare provision has developed over time. It involves acts of re-balancing both *within* and *across* the established functions of social protection (e.g. 'less pensions and more social services and family benefits');
- *distributive* recalibration, which has to do with social groups and it refers to policy measures aimed at rebalancing social protection in favour of the most vulnerable, and at ironing out inequitable disparities between insiders and outsiders;
- *discursive* recalibration, which has to do with norms, arguments and justifications and denotes symbolic initiatives and new discourses addressing the functional and distributive dilemmas of the status quo and the future directions of policy;[13]
- *politico-institutional* recalibration, which has to do with the levels and actors that are be involved in the 'governance' of social protection, including supranational, trans-national and sub-national levels and actors.

Other conceptual maps can of course be used in order to interpret the logic and direction(s) of ongoing policy changes in the realm of social protection. For our purposes, however, it is important to highlight one general point: the factual transformation of their object of study has prompted scholars of the welfare state to modernise and update their analytical toolkit and to reconsider some of their established normative and cognitive assumptions. Since the comparative turn of the 1970s, the search for shared understandings of the *investigandum* and for 'conceptual deepening' has been a constant priority of the welfare state scholarship – as well as one of the keys to its 'success' relative to other fields of empirical social science (Amenta 2002). The advent of the Silver Age has definitely provided new spurs for this search, and thus for analytical and theoretical advances on how to describe and explain social policies, in their evolution through time and space.

Old and New: The Changing Politics of Welfare

'Politics' has always played a dominant role in explanatory arguments about the 'welfare state'. The causal link between the two has been theorised in a variety of ways, in the context of grand perspectives on social and political development as well as of more modest middle-range propositions on specific aspects or moments of change. At the risk of over-simplifying, we can identify four general and interrelated trends in the debate during the last three decades.

The first trend has to do with theoretical approaches. Referring back to Alber's map mentioned earlier, on this front there has been a shift from functionalist to conflictualist accounts and then from Marxism to pluralism. Initially seen as a by-product of 'late capitalism' or of 'industrial modernisation', the welfare state has come to be seen as the outcome of complex and largely contingent power struggles, with the participation of a plurality of actors moving within thick institutional configurations. Second, there has been a shift from society-centred perspectives, emphasising the role of classes and social conflict, to state-centred perspectives, highlighting the role of political structures/actors and institutional dynamics. This shift can also be interpreted in disciplinary terms, i.e. as a sign of the increasing contribution of political science relative to sociology. Third, causality links have become increasingly bi-directional: the welfare state is certainly a dependent variable of politics (however understood), but it can also be seen as an independent variable, i.e. a source of specific and distinctive types of politico-institutional dynamics which would not occur in its absence. Finally, there has been a gradual historicisation of the comparative politics of welfare, i.e. the recognition that structures, actors and dynamics of interaction are linked in developmental sequences and thus have different causal impacts, depending on space and time.

The expansion debate was largely dominated by the so-called power-resources theory, whose earliest formulation was offered by Korpi (1980, 1983). Distributional conflicts and outcomes – thus goes the theory – critically depend on the control of power resources. In capitalist democracies, the latter derive basically from two elements: the control over means of production and the organisation of the working class into collective action, through unions and political parties (typically social democratic parties). If the latter acquire strength in the wake of high levels of workers' mobilisation, then distributional outcomes will be shaped in the interest of wage-earners, leading to the formation of generous and universalistic welfare state programmes financed by progressive taxation (Stephens 1979; Hicks 1999). Empirically grounded in the Swedish experience, power resource theory has been the object of extensive theoretical specifications and refinements over the years and of equally extensive quantitative and qualitative testing, becoming a sort of standard model for interpreting observable welfare state variations, both cross-sectionally and cross-time (Hicks and Esping Andersen 2005). There were, of course, other voices in the expansion debate of the 1980s and early 1990s, rooted in state-centred and/or pluralist perspectives (e.g. Skocpol and Orloff 1986; Baldwin 1990). But power resources arguments (also known as 'social democratic/left-party', 'politico-organisational' or 'class mobilisation' arguments) remained firmly at the centre of the stage and provided the basic theoretical underpinnings for the welfare regimes literature initiated by Esping Andersen (1990).

As is well known, the advent of the 'Silver Age' was accompanied by the strengthening of neo-liberal ideologies and parties in many countries and by the rise to power of Reagan and Thatcher, two conservative leaders with ambitious pro-market agendas. According to power resource theory, this political configuration should have produced a significant degree of welfare state retrenchment. The work of Paul Pierson in the early 1990s (Pierson 1994) showed however that this was only partly the case: in both quantitative and qualitative terms the US and UK welfare states showed a much greater resilience than expected under conservative rule. Why was politics (essentially understood in terms of a power struggle between class-based collective actors) not producing the predicted distributional outcomes? This puzzle led Pierson to advance the idea that welfare retrenchment rests on (in fact: it creates) a 'new politics', driven by a different logic than the 'old politics' of welfare expansion.

Retrenchment (and more generally restructuring or recalibration) is qualitatively different than expansion: it implies 'taking away' rather than 'giving', subtractions rather than distributions. It thus hits the electorate, often concentrating subtractions (e.g. less generous pensions) on specific and concentrated groups of voters. As shown by political psychology and 'prospect theory' in particular, voters tend to be much more sensitive to losses than to gains (Kahneman and Tversky 1979; McDermot 2004). While the distributive politics of expansion was essentially about credit claiming, the subtractive politics of retrenchment is essentially about blame avoidance (Weaver 1986). Moreover, retrenchment takes place in an institutional context that is shaped by the social programmes that are already in place, in the wake of previous expansion. Large segments of voters benefit directly from the welfare state – a fact that has prompted the formation of several interest organisations in support of social programmes. Based as they are on codified entitlements, state commitments in the core schemes (pensions, health care) are inherently hard to transform, as they impinge directly on people's expectations and life plans. Changing the distributional status quo without suffering heavy electoral punishment is not impossible: but it requires shrewd and sophisticated political strategies. In his own work on the USA and the UK, Pierson identified a number of such strategies: obfuscation (i.e. restructuring by stealth, or in indirect ways), compensation (avoiding conflict and blame through various forms of *quid pro quo* and/or exempting from sacrifices certain groups of voters) and 'divide et impera' strategies (orchestrating conflicts of interest between various categories, i.e. consumers vs. producers of services). Pierson's pioneering analysis has paved the way for an articulated 'new politics' literature, which has identified additional strategies and political pathways to reform: e.g. the 'Nixon goes to China' strategy outlined by Ross (2000), or the 'vice into virtue strategy' unveiled by Levy (1999).[14] This literature has also discussed and explored the institutional, discursive, partisan and interest group configurations that facilitate or impede various forms of welfare state restructuring in different policy areas (e.g. Bonoli 2000; Schmidt 2000; Huber and Stephens 2001; Kitschelt 2001; Swank 2002; Immergut *et al.* 2007; for a review see Green-Pedersen and Haverland 2002; Starke 2006).

The new politics literature locates itself in many ways at the opposite end in respect of the debate of the 1970s: it tends to have a pluralist-conflictualist view of social policy actors and dynamics; it focuses on the fine grain of political processes and institutions, drawing heavily on political science; it treats the welfare state less as dependent than an independent variable, i.e. as a trigger of group formation, as an arena for policy-specific forms of political interaction, as a source of path dependence; it attributes great importance to timing and developmental sequences, taking history very seriously and suggesting phase-specific characterisations and explanations of welfare state trajectories. This literature has also problematised and articulated the very nature of its *explanandum*. As mentioned at the end of last section, restructuring and recalibration are seen as multifaceted phenomena, which can also bring about normatively desirable results in terms of equity and/or efficiency, e.g. by introducing measures in favour of vulnerable groups and/or addressing novel social risks. As a matter of fact, the 'new politics of new social risks' (i.e. the political configurations that affect functional and distributive recalibrations of the status quo) is one of the most interesting and promising frontiers of contemporary welfare state research (Taylor-Gooby 2004; Armingeon and Bonoli 2006).

It must also be acknowledged, however, that the new politics debate has tended at times to overstate its case, especially as regards the loss of explanatory potential of traditional variables (Scarbrough 2000). Power resource theorists have recently shown, for example, that the impact of left-wing power (the main causal variable of Golden Age development and regime variation) remains important if one looks specifically at 're-commodifying' reforms (e.g. reductions of replacement rates for unemployment benefits). A recent study by Korpi and Palme (2004) has demonstrated that the risk of such reform is indeed sensitive to partisan differences, being highest for right-wing incumbency, medium for Christian democratic incumbency and lowest for left-wing incumbency. Also Allan and Scruggs (2004) have found a significant impact of right-wing parties on the reduction of replacement rates after the early 1980s. The latest trend in the literature thus seems to be that of building new bridges between 'old' and 'new' political dynamics, through more sophisticated conceptualisations and operationalisations of the relevant variables as well as through more refined theoretical specifications.[15]

One final point deserves to be made about the political dimension of the welfare state. As mentioned earlier, one of the most significant trends of the last three decades has been the encounter between nation-based social programmes (in particular public insurance schemes) and the EU – the legal order of the EU. This encounter has posed serious challenges to national closure rules and practices, thus 'politicising' the issue of welfare state boundaries. The French referendum on the EU Constitutional Treaty (spring 2005) was largely centred on this issue: is European integration jeopardising domestic social sovereignty and the preservation of distinct national social models?

These developments have attracted scholarly interests towards the spatial dimension of the welfare state, understood as a political organisation linked to a geographical territory and consisting in a bundle of distinct membership spaces (the pension system, the health services and so on) characterised by their own regulations and surrounded by codified membership boundaries (Ferrera 2005a). Seen in this light, the welfare state has always had a 'spatial politics', that is, conflicts on inclusion and exclusion rules and on the relative positioning of different social groups within the bundle of sharing arrangements. But this 'old' spatial politics rested on a stable territorial basis whose boundaries were given and uncontested, and it unfolded in the shadow of a single ultimate hierarchy, that of the nation-state. European integration has changed the situation not only by redrawing the territorial boundaries of national welfare states but also by imposing new direct and indirect constraints on its internal membership boundaries, thus casting a new shadow of supranational hierarchy over domestic political interactions. For example, under the current EU legal order compulsory affiliation to social security schemes is legitimate only under certain conditions (e.g. the adoption of pay-as-you-go financing). National actors (workers, employers, insurance companies, and so on) can now challenge their governments on this issue before the European Court of Justice, that is, a higher-level hierarchical order. The impact of integration on the membership (as distinct from the territorial) boundaries of the welfare state is a relatively recent phenomenon. Its visibility is still low also because it is not uniform across the various risk-specific schemes, tiers, and pillars of provision. Nevertheless it has already prompted dynamics of interest articulation and aggregation at various levels of the Euro-polity. Exploring this new spatial politics of welfare – its origin, its logic, and its potential consequences for both national systems and the EU as a whole – is another very promising frontier of ongoing comparative research (Ewans and Moreno 2005; Obinger *et al.* 2005; for a review see Van Kersbergen 2006).

Conclusion

In a recent survey of the field, Amenta (2002) has argued that comparative welfare state research has made 'dramatic' progress in the last three decades and that, academically speaking, we can talk of a clear success story. Conceptual agreement on the nature of the *explanandum*, the ability to operationalise it in different and increasingly sophisticated ways, the availability of data thanks to the work and investment of both academic and international institutions, the open-minded methodological outlook of most scholars in the field, these are the main factors identified by Amenta for explaining this success. The presence of different disciplinary perspectives (and to some extent the competition between them) has also played an important role. But there is an additional factor that must be taken into consideration, which has less to do with the academic than the professional dimension of this field: the formation of a relatively integrated debate community, supported by dedicated organisational networks (such as Research Committee 19 of the International Sociological Association or, more recently, the European Social Policy Associations Network). Adam Przeworski perhaps exaggerated when he stated some time ago that scientific progress is less due to the compliance with methodological canons than to the exchange of experience between scholars and the appearance of 'exemplary' works (Przeworski 1987). But comparative welfare state research has indeed been blessed with intense scholarly exchanges and several exemplary works. And both were definitely very important for the scientific results that have been achieved during the last three decades.

Acknowledgements

I am grateful to Georg Picot for his valuable research assistance.

Notes

1. Our focus in this article will be almost exclusively on the 'old' Europe: a discussion of the problems and challenges of welfare state restructuring in the 'new' member states which joined the EU between 2004 and 2007 would deserve a separate article. The article will not deal with either the sub-national or the supra-national dimensions of social policy (i.e. EU social programmes), and will focus essentially on the national welfare states.
2. The late economic historian re-adapted the well-known French expression *les trois glorieuses*, used to indicate the Paris insurrection of 27, 28 and 29 June 1830, which caused the abdication of Charles X and paved the way for the rise to power of the 'liberal king' Louis d'Orleans.
3. For a discussion and references, see Castles and Obinger (this volume). A review of the voluminous literature on the various welfare regimes is contained in Arts and Gelissen (2002).

4. Good reviews can be found in Amenta (2002), Hicks and Esping Andersen (2005), and Manow and Van Kersbergen (2008).
5. For a discussion of such early debates and a critical analysis see Pfaller *et al.* (1991).
6. The 'virtuous' link between economic opening and high quality social provisions was originally noted by observing the experience of the smaller European states (e.g. Cameron 1978; Katzenstein 1982; for a restatement, see Rodrik 1998). This link has been the object of extensive analytical elaboration and empirical investigation within the literatures on 'neo-corporatism' and on the 'varieties of capitalism' (see Schmidt 2008).
7. For a discussion and review of this debate see especially Rhodes (1998) and – from a labour law perspective – Bercusson (1999).
8. For a discussion and review of the 'Europeanisation' debate, see Graziano and Vinck (2006).
9. For a discussion of territorial restructuring dynamics in Europe, see Keating (2008).
10. Pay gaps between men and women and occupational 'segregation' have not disappeared, however, not even in the Nordic countries. Higher rates of female participation to the labour market have had an ambivalent effect on the welfare state. On the one hand it has expanded the tax and contribution base for welfare state financing. On the other hand it has given rise to new risks and needs in the sphere of social reproduction, calling for an expansion of state programmes. For a discussion, see especially Daly (2000), Orloff (2006) and O'Connor *et al.* (1999).
11. For a systematic and updated comparative analysis of pension reforms in developed countries see Immergut *et al.* (2007).
12. As acknowledged also by Pierson, the concept of recalibration was originally suggested to all of us by Jonathan Zeitlin during the final seminar of the European Forum on 'Recasting European Welfare States', EUI, Florence, 18 June 1999. We are grateful to Jonathan for having broken this path of reflection.
13. For a thorough and pathbreaking discussion of this dimension, see Schmidt (2000).
14. For an updated discussion and new theoretical proposals on politcal strategies about unpopular reforms see Vis and Van Kersbergen (2007).
15. It is fair to say, however, that a number of dynamics and causal mechanisms identified by the recent new politics literature had already been highlighted by the expansion debate of the 1970s (e.g. by Flora 1981; and by the German debate on the new 'social clienteles' created by the welfare state: e.g. Baier 1977; Lepsius 1979).

References

Alber, Jens (1982). *Vonn Armenhaus zum Wohlfahrtsstaat.* Frankfurt: Campus.

Alber, Jens (1995). 'A Framework for the Comparative Study of Social Services', *Journal of European Social Policy*, 5:2, 131–49.

Allan, James, and Lyle Scruggs (2004). 'Political Partisanship and Welfare State Reform in Advanced Industrial Societies', *American Journal of Political Science*, 48:3, 496–512.

Amenta, Edwin (2002). 'What we Know About The Development of Social Policy: Comparative and Historical Research in Comparative and Historical Perspective', in James Mahoney and Dietrich Rueschemeyer (eds.), *Comparative Historical Analysis: Achievements and Agenda*. Cambridge: Cambridge University Press, 154–82.

Anttonen, A., and J. Sipila (1996). 'European Social Care Services: is it Possible to Identify Models?', *Journal of European Social Policy*, 6:2, 87–100.

Armingeon, Klaus, and Giuliano Bonoli, eds. (2006). *The Politics of Post-Industrial Welfare States: Adapting Post-War Social Policies to New Social Risks.* London and New York: Routledge.

Arts, Wilhelmus, and John Gelissen (2002). 'Three Worlds of Welfare Capitalism or More? A State of the Art Report', *Journal of European Social Policy*, 12:2, 137–58.

Baier, Horst (1977). 'Herrschaft im Sozialstaat', in Carl Farber and Franz-Xaver Kaufmann (eds.), *Soziologie und Sozialpolitik*. Opladen: Westdeutscher Verlag, 128–42.

Baldwin, Peter (1990). *The Politics of Social Solidarity*. Cambridge: Cambridge University Press.

Bartolini, Stefano (2005). *Restructuring Europe. Centre Formation, System Building and Political Structuring between the Nation State and the EU*. Oxford: Oxford University Press.

Baumol, William James (1967). 'Macroeconomics of Unbalanced Growth: The Anatomy of Urban Crisis', *American Economic Review*, 57:3, 415–26.

Bercusson, Brian (1999). 'European Labour Law in Context: A Review of the Literature', *European Law Journal*, 5:2, 87–102.

Bonoli, Giuliano (2000). *The Politics of Pension Reform*. Cambridge: Cambridge University Press.

Bonoli, Giuliano (2006). 'New Social Risks and the Politics of Post-Industrial Social Policies', in Klaus Armingeon and Giuliano Bonoli (eds.), *The Politics of Post-Industrial Welfare States: Adapting Post-War Social Policies to New social Risks*. London and New York: Routledge, 3–26.

Burgoon, Brian (2001). 'Globalization and Welfare Compensation: Disentangling the Ties that Bind', *International Organization*, 55:3, 509–51.

Cameron, David (1978). 'The Expansion of the Public Economy: a Comparative Analysis', *American Political Science Review*, 72:4, 1243–61.

Castles, Frank (2004). *The Future of the Welfare State: Crisis, Myths and Crisis realities*. Oxford: Oxford University Press.

Clasen, Jochen, and Daniel Clegg (2006). 'New Labour Market Risks and the Revision of Unemployment Protection Systems in Europe', in Klaus Armingeon and Giuliano Bonoli (eds.), *The Politics of Post-Industrial Welfare States: Adapting Post-War Social Policies to New Social Risks*. London and New York: Routledge, 192–210.

Cornelissen, Rolf (1996). 'The Principle of Territoriality and the Community Regulations on Social Security', *Common Market Law Review*, 33, 13–41.

Daly, Mary (2000). *Gendering Welfare States*. Cambridge: Cambridge University Press.

Esping-Andersen, Gøsta (1990). *The Three Worlds of Welfare Capitalism*. Cambridge: Polity Press.

Esping-Andersen, Gøsta (1999). *Social Foundations of Postindustrial Economies*. Oxford: Oxford University Press.

Esping-Andersen, Gøsta (2002). 'A New Gender Contract', in Gøsta Esping-Andersen et al., *Why We Need a New Welfare State*. Oxford: Oxford University Press, 68–95.

European Commission (EC) (1997). *Modernizing and Improving Social Protection*. Brussels: EC (COM 102/97).

European Commission (EC) (2004). *Eurobarometer no. 62*. Luxembourg.

Ewans, Nicola, and Luis Moreno, eds. (2005). *The Territorial Politics of Welfare*. Oxford: Routledge.

Ferrera, Maurizio (1998). 'The Four Social Europes: Between Universalism and Selectivity', in Yves Meny and Martin Rhodes (eds.), *The Future of European Welfare: A New Social Contract?* London: Macmillan, 81–96.

Ferrera, Maurizio (2005a). *The Boundaries of Welfare. European Integration and the new Spatial Politics of Social Protection*. Oxford: Oxford University Press.

Ferrera, Maurizio, ed. (2005b). *Welfare State Reform in Southern Europe – Fighting Poverty and Social exclusion in Italy, Spain, Portugal and Greece*. London: Routledge/EUI Studies in the Political Economy of Welfare.

Ferrera, Maurizio (2006). 'Friends, Not Foes: European Integration and National Welfare States', in A. Giddens, P. Diamond and R. Liddle (eds.), *Global Europe, Social Europe*. Cambridge: Polity Press, 257–78.

Ferrera, Maurizio, and Anton Hemerijck (2003). 'Recalibrating Europe's Welfare Regimes', in Jonathan Zeitlin and David Trubek (eds.), *Governing Work and Welfare in a New Economy: European and American Experiments*. Oxford: Oxford University Press, 88–128.

Ferrera, M., and M. Rhodes (2000). 'Building a Sustainable Welfare State', in M. Ferrera and M. Rhodes (eds.), *Recasting European Welfare States, West European Politics*, Special Issue, 23:2, 257–82.

Ferrera, Maurizio, Anton Hemerick and Martin Rhodes (2000). 'Recasting European Welfare States for the 21st Century', *European Review*, 8:3, 427–46.

Flora, Peter (1981). 'Solution or Source of Crises? The Welfare State in Historical Perspective', in Wolfgang J. Mommsen (ed.), *The Emergence of The Welfare State in Britain and Germany*. London: German Historical Institute, 342–89.

Flora, Peter, ed. (1986–87). *Growth to Limits: The European Welfare States Since World War II*. Berlin and New York: De Gruyter, vol.1 (1986), vols.2 and 4 (1987).

Flora, Peter *et al.* (1983). *State, Economy, and Society in Western Europe, 1815–1975*, vol.I. Basingstoke: Palgrave/MacMillan.

Flora, Peter *et al.* (1987). *State, Economy, and Society in Western Europe, 1815–1975*, vol.II. Basingstoke: Palgrave/MacMillan.

Fourastié, Jean (1979). *Les Trente Glorieuses*. Paris: Fayard.

Freeman, Richard (2000). *The Politics of Health in Europe*. Manchester: Manchester University Press.

Freeman, Richard, and Michael Moran (2000). 'Reforming Health Care in Europe', in Maurizio Ferrera and Martin Rhodes (eds.), *Recasting European Welfare States*. London: Frank Cass, 35–58.

Gallie, Duncan (2002). 'The Quality of Working Life in Welfare Strategy', in Gosta Esping-Andersen et al., *Why We Need a New Welfare State*. Oxford: Oxford University Press, 96–129.

Garrett, Geoffrey (1998). *Partisan Politics in the Global Economy*. Cambridge: Cambridge University Press.

Genschel, Philip (2004). 'Globalization and the Welfare State: A Retrospective', *Journal of European Public Policy*, 11:4, 613–36.

Gough, I. (1979). *The Political Economy of the Welfare State*. London: MacMillan.

Graziano, Paolo, and Christian Vinck, eds. (2006). *Europeanization: New Research Agendas*. Basingstoke: Palgrave.

Green-Pedersen, Christopher, and Marcus Haverland (2002). 'The New Politics and Scholarship of the Welfare State', *Journal of European Social Policy*, 12:1, 43–51.

Guillen, Ana Marta (2002). 'The Politics of Universalisation: Establishing National Health Services in Southern Europe', *West European Politics*, 25:4, 49–68.

Guillen, Ana Marta, and Manos Matsaganis (2000). 'Testing the Social Dumping Hypothesis in Southern Europe: Welfare Policies in Greece and Spain during the last 20 years', *Journal of European Social Policy*, 10:2, 120–45.

Heclo, Hugh (1974). *Modern Social Politics in Britain and Sweden*. New Haven, CT: Yale University Press.

Hemerijck, Anton (2002). 'The Self-transformation of the European Social Model(s)', in G. Esping Andersen et al., *Why We Need a New Welfare State*. Oxford: Oxford University Press, 220–63.

Hicks, Alexander (1999). *Social Democracy and Welfare Capitalism: A Century of Income Security Politics*. Ithaca, NY: Cornell University Press.

Hicks, Alexander, and Gosta Esping-Andersen (2005). 'Comparative and Historical Studies of Public policy and the Welfare State', in Thomas Janowski, Robert Alfors, Alexander Hicks and Mildred A. Schwartz (eds.), *The Handbook of Political Sociology*. Cambridge: Cambridge University Press, 509–25.

Holloway, John (1981). *Social Policy Harmonization in the European Community*. Westmead: Gower Publishing.

Huber, Evelyn, and John Stephens (2001). *Development and Crisis of the Welfare State: Parties and Policies in Global Markets*. London and Chicago: University of Chicago Press.

Huber, Evelyn, and John Stephens (2005). 'State Economic and Social Policy in Global Capitalism', in Thomas Janoski et al. (eds.), *The Handbook of Political Sociology: States, Civil Societies, and Globalization*. Cambridge: Cambridge University Press, 607–29.

Immergut, Ellen, Karen Anderson and Isabelle Schulze, eds. (2007). *The Handbook of West European Pension Politics*. Oxford: Oxford University Press.

Iversen, Torben, and Ann Wren (1998). 'Equality, Employment, and Budgetary Restraint: The Trilemma of the Service Economy', *World Politics*, 50, 507–46.

Kitschelt, Herbert (2001). 'Partisan Competition and Welfare State Retrenchment, When Do Politicians Choose Unpopular Policies?', in Paul Pierson (ed.), *The New Politics of the Welfare State*. Oxford: Oxford University Press, 265–302.

Kahneman, David, and Amos Tversky (1979). 'Prospect Theory: An Analysis of Decision under Risk', *Econometrica*, 47:2, 263–92.

Katzenstein, Peter (1982). 'Political Compensation for Economic Openness: Incomes Policy and Public Spending in the Small European States', in Kurt Steiner (ed.), *Tradition and Innovation in Contemporary Austria*. Palo Alto, CA: Society for the Promotion of Science and Scholarship, 99–108.

Korpi, Walter (1980). 'Social Policy and Distributional Conflict in the Capitalist Democracies: A Preliminary Comparative Framework', *West European Politics*, 3, 296–316.

Korpi, Walter (1983). *The Democratic Class Struggle*. London: Routledge.

Korpi, Walter, and Joachim Palme (2004). 'New Politics and Class Politics in the Context of Austerity and Globalization: Welfare State Regress in 18 Countries, 1975–95', *American Political Science Review*, 97:3, 425–46.

Kuhnle, Stein, ed. (2000). *Survival of the Welfare State*. London: Routledge.

Leibfried, Stephan, and Paul Pierson (2000). 'Social Policy', in Helen Wallace and William Wallace (eds.), *Policy-Making in the European Union*. 4th edn. Oxford: Oxford University Press.

Lepsius, Rainer Maria (1979). 'Soziale Ungleichheit und Klassenstrukturen in der Bundesrepublik Deutschland', in Hans-Ulrich Wehler (ed.), *Klassen in der Europaeischen Sozialgeschichte*. Goettingen: Vandenhoek & Ruprecht, 21–64.

Levy, Jonah (1999). 'Vice into Virtue? Progressive Politics and Welfare Reform in Continental Europe', *Politics and Society*, 27:2, 239–73.

Levy, Jonah (2000). 'France: Directing Adjustment?', in Fritz Scharpf and Vivien Schmidt (eds.), *Welfare and Work in Open Economies. Volume II. Diverse Responses to Common Challenges*. Oxford: Oxford University Press, 308–50.

Lewis, Jane, ed. (1993). *Women and Social Policies in Europe*. Cheltenham: Edward Elgar.

Lewis, Jane, ed. (2007). *Children, Changing Families and Welfare States*. Cheltenham: Edward Elgar.

Manow, Philip, and Eric Seils (2000). 'The Employment Crisis of the German Welfare State', in M. Ferrera and M. Rhodes (eds.), *Recasting European Welfare States*. London: Frank Cass, 137–60.

Manow, Philip, and Kees Van Kersbergen (2008). 'The Welfare State', in Daniele Caramani (ed.), *Comparative Politics*. Oxford: Oxford University Press.

Marshall, Thomas Humphrey (1992). 'Citizenship and Social Class', in Thomas Humphrey Marshall and Thomas Bottomore (eds.), *Citizenship and Social Class*. London: Pluto Press.

Martin, Andrew, and George Ross, eds. (2004). *Euros and Europeans. Monetary Integration and the European Model of Society*. Cambridge: Cambridge University Press.

McDermot, R. (2004). 'Prospect Theory in Political Science: Gains and losses from the First Decade', *Political Psychology*, 25:2, 289–312.

Milward, Alan (2000). *The European Rescue of the Nation State*. 2nd edn. London: Routledge.

Obinger, Herbert, Stephan Leibfried and Frank Castles, eds. (2005). *Federalism and the Welfare State: New World and European Experiences*. Cambridge: Cambridge University Press.

O'Connor, James (1973). *The Fiscal Crisis of the State*. New York: St. Martin's Press.

O'Connor, Julia, Ann Shola Orloff and Sheila Shaver (1999). *States, Markets, Families*. Cambridge: Cambridge University Press.

OECD (2006). *OECD Factbook 2006*, online edition: http://lysander.sourceoecd.org/vl=19385978/cl=11/nw=1/rpsv/factbook/

Orloff, Ann Shola (2006). 'From Maternalism to Employment for All. State Policies to promote Women's Employment Across the Affluent Democracies', in Jonah Levy (ed.), *The State After Statism*. Cambridge: Cambridge University Press, 230–68.

Palier, B. (2000). 'Defrosting the French Welfare State', in M. Ferrera and M. Rhodes (eds.), *Recasting European Welfare States*. London: Frank Cass, 113–36.

Palier, Bruno (2002). *Gouverner la sécurité sociale. Les réformes du systeme français de protection sociale depuis 1945*. Paris: PUF.

Pfaller, Anton, Ian Gough and Goran Therborn (1991). *Can the Welfare State Compete? A Comparative. Study of Five Advanced Capitalist Countries*. London: Macmillan.

Pierson, Paul (1994). *Dismantling the Welfare State? Reagan, Thatcher and the Politics of Retrenchment*. Cambridge: Cambridge University Press.

Pierson, Paul (1998). 'Irresistible Forces, Immovable Objects: Post-Industrial Welfare States Confronting Permanent Austerity'. *Journal of European Public Policy*, 5:4, 539–60.

Pierson, Paul (2001a). 'Coping with Permanent Austerity: Welfare State Restructuring in Affluent Democracies', in Paul Pierson (ed.), *The New Politics of the Welfare State*. Oxford: Oxford University Press, 410–56.

Pierson, Paul (2001b). 'Post-industrial Pressures on the Mature Welfare States', in Paul Pierson (ed.), *The New Politics of the Welfare State*. Oxford: Oxford University Press, 80–104.

Poiares Maduro, Miguel (1998). *We, the Court: the European Court of Justice and the European Economic Constitution*. Oxford: Oxford University Press.

Przeworski, Adam (1987). 'Methods of Cross-national Research 1970–1983: An Overview', in Meinolf Dierkes, Hans Weiler and Ariane Berthoin Antal (eds.), *Comparative Policy Research*. Aldershot: Gower, 31–49.

Rhodes, M. (1998). 'Defending the Social Contract', in David Hine and Hans Kassim (eds.), *Beyond the Market: The EU and National Social Policy*. London, Routledge, 36–59.

Rimlinger, Gaston (1971). *Welfare Policy and Industrialisation in Europe, North America and Russia*. New York: Wiley.

Rodrik, Dani (1998). 'Why do More Open Economies Have Bigger Government', *Journal of Political Economy*, 106:5, 997–1032.

Ross, Fiona (2000). 'Interests and Choice in the "Not Quite so New" Politics of Welfare', *West European Politics*, 23:2, 11–34.

Ruggie, Gerald (1982). 'International Regimes, Transactions and Change: Embedded Liberalism in the Post-War Era', *International Organisation*, 36, 379–415.

Saraceno, Chiara, ed. (2002). *Social Assistance Dynamics in Europe. National and Local Poverty Regimes*. Bristol: The Policy Press.

Scarbrough, Elinor (2000). 'West European Welfare States: The Old Politics of Retrenchment', *European Journal of Political Research*, 38, 225–59.

Scharpf, Fritz (1999). *Governing in Europe*. Oxford: Oxford University Press.

Scharpf, Fritz (2000). 'Economic Changes, Vulnerabilities, and Institutional Capabilities', in Fritz Scharpf and Vivien Schmidt (eds.), *Welfare and Work in the Open Economy. Volume I: From Vulnerability to Competitiveness*. Oxford: Oxford University Press, 21–124.

Schmidt, Vivien (2000). 'Values and Discourse in the Politics of Adjustment', in Fritz Scharpf and Vivien Schmidt (eds.), *Welfare and Work in the Open Economy. Diverse Responses to Common Challenges,* vol.2. Oxford: Oxford University Press, 229–309.

Sindbjerg Martinsen, Dorte (2005). 'With the European Court Towards an Internal Health Market', *West European Politics*, 28:5, 1035–56.

Skocpol, Theda, and Ann Shola Orloff (1986). 'Explaining the Origins of Welfare States', in Siedwark Lindenberg, James Coleman and Stefan Nowak (eds.), *Approaches to Social Theory*. New York: Russel Sage, 229–64.

Starke, Paul (2006). 'The Politics of Welfare State Retrenchment: A Literature Review', *Social Policy and Administration*, 40:1, 104–20.

Steffen, Monika, ed. (2005). *Health Governance in Europe: Issues, Challenges and Theories*. London: Routledge.

Stephens, John D. (1979). *The Transition from Capitalism to Socialism.* Urbana: University of Illinois Press.

Swank, Duane (2002). *Global Capital, Political Institutions, and Policy Change in Developed Welfare States.* Cambridge: Cambridge University Press.

Taylor-Gooby, Peter (2002). 'The Silver Age of the Welfare State. Perspectives on Resilience', *Journal of Social Policy*, 31:4, 597–621.

Taylor-Gooby, Peter, ed. (2004). *New Risks, New Welfare: The Transformation of the European Welfare State.* Oxford: Oxford University Press.

Van Kersbergen, Kees (2006). 'The Politics of Solidarity and the Changing Boundaries of the Welfare State', *European Political Science*, 5:4, 377–94.

Vis, Beatrice, and K. van Kersbergen (2007). 'Why and How Do Political Actors Pursue Risky Reforms?', *Journal of Theoretical Politics*, 19:2, 153–72.

Visser, Jelle, and Anton Hemerijck (1997). *'A Dutch Miracle': Job Growth, Welfare Reform and Corporatism in the Netherlands.* Amsterdam: Amsterdam University Press.

Weaver, Kent (1986). 'The Politics of Blame Avoidance', *Journal of Public Policy*, 6:4, 371–98.

Wilensky, Harold (1975). *The Welfare State and Equality. Structural and Ideological Roots of Public Expenditures.* Berkeley, CA: University of California Press.

Zeitlin, Jonathan, and Philippe Pochet, eds. (2005). *The Open Method of Coordination in Action.* Brussels: Peter Lang.

Zeitlin, Jonathan, and David Trubek, eds. (2003). *Governing Work and Welfare in a New Economy: European and American Experiments.* Oxford: Oxford University Press.

European Union?

LIESBET HOOGHE and GARY MARKS

Developments on the ground have provided a powerful reality check for research on European integration.[1] Harold Macmillan's response to a question about his greatest challenge in office: 'Events, dear boy, events', applies with special force to research on Europe. As the character of the European Union has changed, so has our understanding of it.

One might say that the object of research is unidentified and travels at great velocity. The EU is unidentified in that it escapes labels, such as nation, state, empire, region, federation, which form the conventional toolkit of political science. European integration challenges the long-standing division in political science between politics *within* countries – where justice, equality, freedom, and the rule of law are appropriate concepts, where executives, parliaments, and courts authoritatively legislate and arbitrate, and where interest groups and political parties intermediate interests – and politics *among* countries, where national governments express national preferences, and where relative economic or coercive power, arguably moderated by institutional and normative commitments, determine outcomes. Perhaps no field has spawned so much conceptual innovation as European integration; no field is so uncertain about what it is that needs to be explained.

Moreover, the EU travels at great velocity. The speed of institutional change is undeniable: from a consultative assembly to a powerful European Parliament, directly elected, and with veto power over a wide swathe of legislation; from a weak court to a formidable adjudicative and legislative body under the doctrines of supremacy and direct effect; from a trade-oriented regime involving six countries to a continental polity with responsibility stretching over monetary policy, environmental policy, structural policy, and much besides. Over the space of 50 years, the EU has increased two-and-a-half times in population, from 190 million to 493 million.[2] Has anything this big been created in so short a period? The answer is, of course, yes. Wars have produced large-scale political units in glimpses of historical time. What is distinctive about European integration is that the transformation has been deliberative; it has taken place in the absence of the coercion that has shaped and reshaped empires in the past. In the pantheon of deliberative regime creation, the EU is unique in its breadth and speed.

John Keeler (2005) identifies three eras in the development of EC/EU studies, and each corresponds with major shifts on the ground: the launch era, opened by the implementation of the Treaty of Rome and shaped theoretically by debates between neo-functionalists and intergovernmentalists; the doldrums era, a period of stagnation after the 'empty chair crisis' that induced scholars to turn away from grand theorising; and the renaissance/boom era, when rapid integration following the Single European Act (1986) revitalised grand theorising and led to unprecedented diversification of EU studies.

The first *West European Politics* issue echoed the disappointment of the doldrums era. Ralf Dahrendorf (1978: 9) observed bluntly that, 'After many years of progress in European unification, this process has now come to a halt'. The ardent federalist, Altiero Spinelli (1978), labelled his article 'Reflections on the Institutional Crisis in the EC'. When *WEP* – and political science – returned to European integration, the scholarly debate had changed. The purpose of this article is to sketch this change by engaging three substantive debates in the field of EU studies.

At the Margins

Europe has served as the laboratory for comparative research on democratic politics for the simple reason that most advanced industrial democracies are European. Researchers who wish to compare the authoritative institutions, public policies, party systems, and political economies of capitalist democracies are drawn to Europe.

The study of regional integration in Europe began in this genre as a distinctly comparative-historical enterprise. Ernst Haas (1958, 1961) examined the various forms of regional integration that were emerging in post-war Europe, including the Nordic Council, the Council of Europe, NATO, the Western European Union, and the European Coal and Steel Community. Haas' study (1964) of global forms of integration, such as the International Labour Organization, had a strong influence on the formulation of neo-functionalism. Karl Deutsch, another intellectual parent of regional integration studies, compared the creation of the European

Community to the Austro-Hungarian Empire, multinational states, such as Britain, Switzerland or Italy, and international organisations, such as NATO (Deutsch *et al.* 1957). Philippe Schmitter (1970) elaborated this comparative framework and took it to Latin America, and Joseph Nye (1970) sought to apply it to other parts of the world.

Events dealt a blow to this approach. By the end of the 1960s, efforts at regional integration outside Europe had regressed. The collapse of Bretton Woods ushered in a decade of national protectionism. At the same time, the resilience of European integration – despite the perception that it was in institutional crisis – highlighted the contrast between this enterprise and faltering integration elsewhere. The European Community stayed put, enlarged its membership, and in certain respects deepened.

One price of apparent stagnation was to induce comparativists and international relations scholars to exit the field. Of the ten contributors to the standard work on theorising regional integration (Lindberg and Scheingold 1970), only one, Donald Puchala, was still writing on the subject in the early 1980s (Schmitter 2005). Ernst Haas (1975) announced the obsolescence of regional integration theory, and began to study learning in transnational epistemic communities. Karl Deutsch turned to issues of security and modelling. Philippe Schmitter went on to discover neo-corporatism, a distinctly national phenomenon.

This exit was hastened by the theoretical problems that neo-functionalism, the only credible research programme until the early 1970s, was running into. While it generated a stream of empirical research, it also began to sprout findings and auxiliary hypotheses that looked suspiciously – in Imre Lakatos' (1970) terms – like a 'degenerating problem shift'. Neo-functionalism imploded under the weight of its own complexity, as much as, or perhaps more than, a result of competition with a rival theory. Subsequently, grand theorising took a back seat to implicit intergovernmentalism.

A small group of scholars (and practitioners), most of them committed to the idea of Europe, kept the field on the map. But the study of the European Community became a backwater of international relations, and European integration was regarded as a peripheral, one-off, phenomenon.[3]

In March 1982, the *Economist* featured on its cover a tombstone with the words 'EEC: born March 25th, 1957, moribund March 25th, 1982, *capax imperii nisi imperasset*'.[4] The problem was not that the Community had swum far from shore into deeper and more challenging waters (to use Stanley Hoffmann's metaphor[5]), but that it was incapable of making progress on the basic commitment of the treaty of Rome – to remove barriers to trade.

By the early 1980s it became clear that the elimination of the national veto was not merely a fantasy in the minds of European federalists. On the contrary, the national veto blocked trade. It allowed governments to avoid confrontation with domestic rent seekers who took advantage of the vagueness of the treaty of Rome to reap state aid, minimise competition in public procurement, and sit behind national product rules designed to keep foreign competitors at bay. Even committed defenders of national sovereignty, such as Prime Minister Thatcher, came to realise that some form of majority voting was necessary, as a practical matter, to achieve market integration. An unholy alliance of pro-marketeers and federalists produced the Single European Act. Political scientists renewed their acquaintance with a European Community led by an activist Commission President, Jacques Delors, with an ambitious legislative plan eliminating non-tariff barriers, empowering the European Parliament, and introducing a serious dose of majoritarianism in the Council of Ministers.

The Recasting of Europe – and Our Understanding of It

European integration has transformed the jurisdictional architecture of Europe. How has it done so, and with what implications? We review three debates, each of which has motivated major research programmes. Events have attracted some seasoned scholars and many novices, especially from comparative politics, to EU studies like bees to a honey pot. Renewed comparativist interest in European integration is arguably the most significant development in the field since the doldrums of the 1970s.

Dispersion of Authority or Central State Control?

The Single European Act reopened the debate about decision making in Europe. National governments had agreed to a treaty that imposed qualified majority decision making in the Council of Ministers on market legislation and gave the European Parliament the authority to pass amendments into law unless overridden by unanimous opposition in the Council. So instead of explaining why national sovereignty was immovable, researchers had to grapple with the question of why it had eroded.

The opening shot was fired by Wayne Sandholtz and John Zysman in a 1989 *World Politics* article that re-established the plausibility of neo-functionalism. The single market reform, they argued, was a response to exogenous international shocks – the decline of American hegemony and the economic rise of Japan – which threatened to further diminish European competitiveness. Sandholtz and Zysman (1989: 108) noted that 'any explanation of the choice of Europe and its evolution must focus on the actors – the leadership in the institutions of the European Community, in segments of the executive branch of the national governments, and in the business community (principally the heads of the largest companies)'. Rather than providing a blow by blow analysis of decision making, they examined how the views of these actors came to converge and, in particular, why national Keynesian policies were perceived as insufficient. The initiative, Sandholtz and Zysman argued, was taken by supranational entrepreneurs and transnational firms, often working against the inertia of national governments (see also Cowles 1995).

Sandholtz and Zysman eschewed causal models, and their interpretation had so many moving parts that it was almost immune to disconfirmation. James Caporaso, Wayne Sandholtz, and Alec Stone Sweet went on to hone neo-functionalist theory by elaborating a model in which societal groups press for reforms to lower cross-border transaction costs, and governments respond by establishing supranational institutions, which makes it easier for societal groups to increase cross-border interactions and press for further reform. This combines Karl Deutsch's insight that socio-economic transactions are a source of political reform, with Douglass North's idea that economic organisations press for institutions that lower their transaction costs. A powerful disconfirmable implication is that the demand for supranationalism will vary across groups in line with the density of their cross-border transactions, a pattern that has been confirmed in several empirical studies (Fligstein 2008; Sandholtz 1996; Sandholtz and Stone Sweet 1998). The theory placed the self-evident monopoly of national governments in the treaty process within a simple and powerful model of societal pressure. National governments negotiate and sign the treaties, but they are subject to functional pressures that shape their choice.

The revival of neo-functionalist theory highlighted the role of the European Court of Justice. Several studies confirmed the expectation that the greater the density of trade among EU countries and within a sector, the greater the demand on the part of firms for transnational dispute settlement (Caporaso 2006; Chicowski 2004; Conant 2006; Stone Sweet and Brunell 1998). In the process, a supranational legal system was emerging behind the backs of national states.

The intergovernmentalist response was that national governments retain control – individually, as well as collectively – by means of their monopoly over treaty making. Initially, intergovernmentalist Moravcsik (1993: 485), argued that collective EU decision making actually preserves, or even enhances, state control because national governments will only participate insofar as 'policy coordination increases their control over domestic policy outcomes, permitting them to achieve goals that would not otherwise be possible' (see also Milward 1992). This argument was criticised on the ground that it conflates the ability to control others with the ability to achieve goals, and consequently, does not allow meaningful statements about situations where an actor's best strategy for achieving a goal is to cede control to others. In his book, *Choice for Europe*, Moravcsik (1998) argued that member states make informed trade-offs between anticipated economic benefits through cooperation while minimising the loss of national control. That is to say, member states are both aware of, and capable of forestalling, undesirable transfers of authority to European institutions.[6]

The debate between neo-functionalism and liberal intergovernmentalism was interlaced with a discussion about the nature of the beast (Risse 1996) and, by implication, about the appropriate categories of analysis (Hix 1994, 1996; Hurrell and Menon 1996). Is European integration best conceived as a means for coping with international interdependence or is more to be gained from analysing the European Union as a federal polity? Should one use the language of international relations, or the language of comparative politics? Two volumes published in the early 1990s – one edited by international relations scholars Robert Keohane and Stanley Hoffmann (1991), and one by comparativist Alberta Sbragia (1992) – staked out contrasting positions. It is indicative of the changing times that two of the three editors of these volumes had not previously published on European integration. In the introduction to the Keohane/Hoffmann volume, Keohane writes that he had been 'paying little attention to current events in the European Community' and needed to tool up before he could co-chair a graduate seminar on European integration, where the foundation for the volume was laid (Keohane and Hoffmann 1991: vii). While Alberta Sbragia had written her Ph.D. on Italian politics with Leon Lindberg, she had never published on European integration when she was approached by the Brookings Institution to bring together a group of comparativists to analyse the European Community. Both projects viewed the European Community uninhibited by conventional theoretical lenses, though the editors were wise to employ as sounding boards policy makers, such as Peter Ludlow, Federico Mancini, and Shirley Williams, and respected EC scholars, such as Helen Wallace, William Wallace, and Wolfgang Wessels.

To understand Europe's jurisdictional architecture, scholars borrowed ideas from comparative politics (Caporaso 1996; Héritier 1996; Leibfried and Pierson 1995; Majone 1994; Marks and McAdam 1996; Peterson 1995; Pierson 1996; Pollack 1995; Sbragia 1993; Tarrow 1995; Tsebelis 1994). Fritz Scharpf was one of the first to do so in an influential article, published in 1988, in which he drew on his prior analysis of German federalism to show how divergent national interests under EU membership could lead to a joint decision trap, preventing national governments from making policy while blocking the European Union from taking joint decisions. Scharpf avoided taking a position on whether the EU was a state or an international organisation, but his analysis directly challenged the core tenet of intergovernmentalism, that national governments control policy outcomes.

By the late 1990s, the debate on Europe's jurisdictional architecture appeared settled in favour of the view that European integration had transformed a network of sovereign national states into a system of multilevel governance (Bache and Flinders 2004; Benz 2003; Hooghe and Marks 2001; Jachtenfuchs 2001; Kohler-Koch and Eising 1999; Marks *et al.* 1996; Scharpf 1997).[7] Even advocates of the staying power of national governments have come to accept that a 'multilevel governance system [is] prevailing in Europe' (Moravcsik 2004: 356).

There are (almost) as many definitions of multilevel governance as there are users of the term, but common to all is the idea that authority on a broad swathe of issues has come to be shared across EU institutions, national, and subnational governments.[8] The reason for this development lies in the benefits of adjusting the scale of governance to the scale of collective problems. Where the externalities that arise from a problem such as providing clean air, minimising transaction costs of monetary exchange, or reducing trade barriers, are transnational in scope, the most efficient level of decision making is similarly transnational. Where the externalities are local or regional, as for garbage collection or land-use planning, the most efficient level is subnational. However, there is no reason to believe that functional pressures translate directly into jurisdictional reform.

Multilevel governance in post-war Europe can be understood as a response to a shift in policy, a shift in regime, and a shift in geopolitics. First, during and immediately after World War II, authority was packaged in highly centralised states by the overriding need to mobilise resources for war and to survive scarcity. From the late 1940s, the policy portfolio of Western Europe came to encompass policies related to economic growth, trade, and welfare with widely varying externalities and economies of scale. Second, liberal democracies were established across Western Europe. Democracies divorce competition for office from the desire to centralise power in one's hands. Whereas autocratic rulers centralise to sustain their monopoly of power, democratic politicians face incentives to shift authority below or beyond the central state if this enables them to provide more goods for voters. Thirdly, the geopolitical tensions that had led to war centralisation and hyper-nationalism in Western Europe were transformed as the Cold War began and the United States pressed for European concertation. Rulers could focus on reducing barriers to trade in Western Europe because the nature of the coercive threats they faced had changed. National survival was aligned with, not against, European economic interdependence.

European integration is one outcome of a broader process of authority dispersion, which stretches beneath as well as above the central state. The two processes appear to be related. The existence of an overarching market lowers the cost of regional autonomy. One of the chief constraints on regional autonomy in the past has been the fear that it would lead to small, inefficient economic units that might be denied access to former markets. However, as rules about market access came to be determined at the European level, the meaning of decentralisation changed. Economic autarky was taken out of the equation.[9]

Figure 1 reveals how formal rules concerning national/EU decision making across 18 policy areas have evolved over six treaties, as charted by Tanja Börzel (2005).[10] *Breadth* of integration refers to the range of policies or tasks for which the EU plays a role; *depth* of integration refers to the supranational or intergovernmental character of the decision rules. There is

FIGURE 1
EVOLUTION OF EU AUTHORITY (POLICY BREADTH AND DEPTH) (1957–2004)

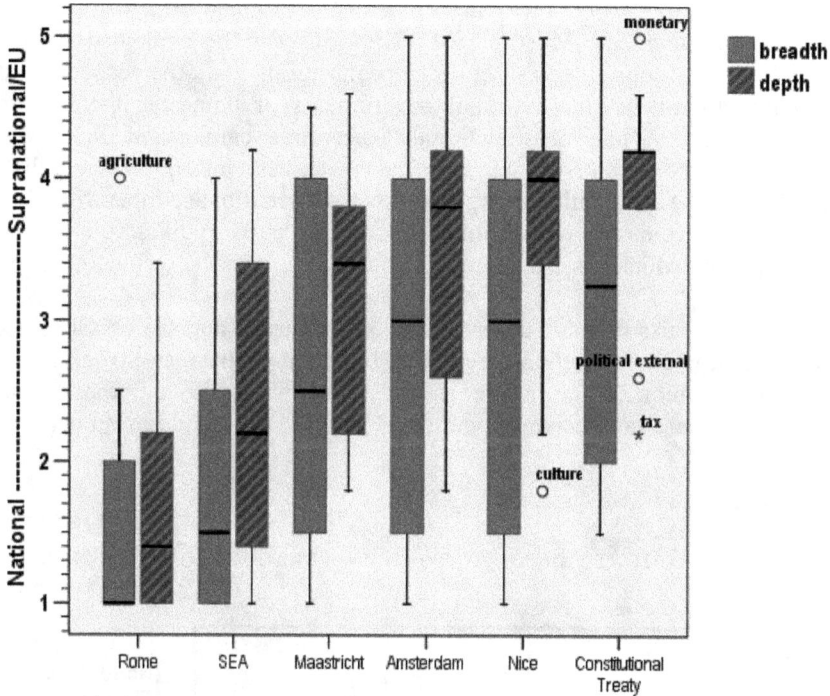

Note: Breadth (1–5) estimates the extent to which the EU plays a role in a policy (1–5); *Depth* (1–5) estimates the supranational or intergovernmental character of the decision rules. The boxes encompass the interquartile range for 18 policies, the horizontal line is the median, and the whiskers indicate the fifth and ninety-fifth percentiles. Starred policy areas are outliers, and white circles are extreme cases.
Source: Börzel (2005: 221–3).

wide variation across policy areas, as suggested in the size of the box plots representing the 5 to 95 per cent range for breadth and depth. As one would expect, policies that redistribute income among individuals are handled almost exclusively within national states, whereas policies having to do with trade and market integration are handled almost exclusively at the European level. A startling fact about the pattern revealed in Figure 1 is that there is not one case where a policy has been shifted from the European to the national level, nor is there a case where a policy that was supranational has become intergovernmental. At least up to this point in time, the formal development of European governance has been unidirectional.[11]

Most policy areas that have been shifted to the European level follow a functional logic rooted in the territorial scope of their externalities. This applies to policies concerned with trade, the environment, and movement of persons. But a functional logic gets us only so far. Some policy shifts involve political side-payments. These include structural and cohesion policy and agricultural subsidies. Moreover, Europeanisation does not encompass all policy areas for which there are collective functional benefits, such as defence procurement. Most of the exceptions can be explained by the distributional consequences of Europeanisation and the capacity of potential losers, be they national governments or domestic interests, to block reform. While neo-functionalist accounts emphasised functional pressures, albeit mediated by political processes, intergovernmentalists highlighted the distributional impediments to international cooperation. But neither predicted the constraining impact of mass publics – a recent development which, as we discuss below, has exerted a serious drag on integration.

Figure 2 charts regional decentralisation in Europe and the OECD since 1950. The increase in regional authority has been particularly strong in the European Union. The picture is consistent with the hypothesis that democracies are conducive to multilevel governance. It also supports the

FIGURE 2
EVOLUTION OF REGIONAL AUTHORITY (AVERAGE ANNUAL CHANGE)
(1950–2006)

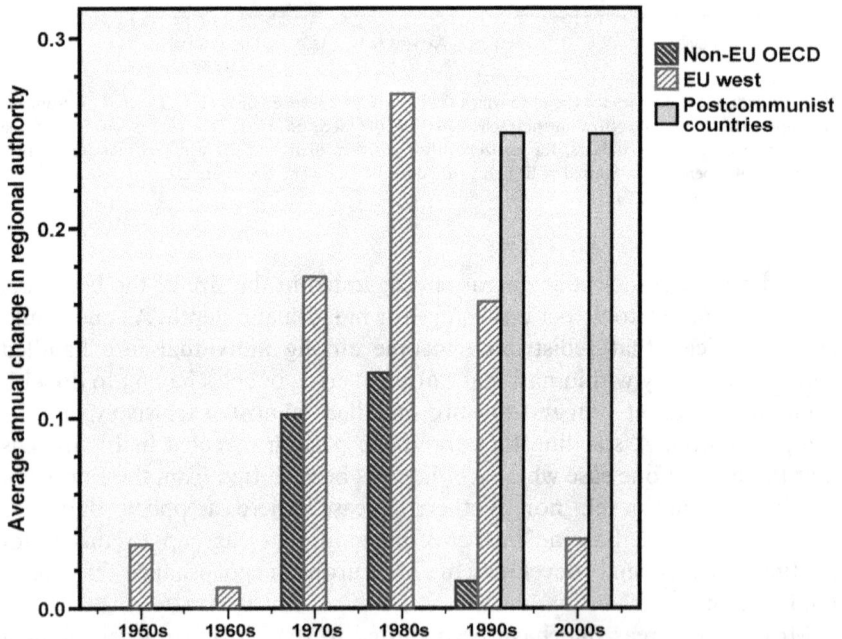

Note: Annual change in regional authority for 35 democracies, 1950–2006, averaged by decade. Regional authority is measured as an index of policy scope, taxation power, electoral representation, and power sharing in central government.
Source: Marks *et al.* (2008).

idea that decentralisation is less costly when it is detached from rules about market access, as is the case in the European Union. With minor exceptions, the regionalisation of Europe has been unidirectional. There are very few cases of recentralisation. So regionalisation is similar to Europeanisation in that it is a coherent process of change – not a series of independent bargains.

Figures 1 and 2 give credence to the claim that the jurisdictional architecture of the European Union has become multilevel. But what does this mean for politics in Europe? How has it affected Europeans' conceptions of their political communities? How has it influenced structures of political conflict? Over the past two decades research on Europe has engaged each of these questions.

Identity and Economic Interest

Political institutions that lack emotional resonance are unlikely to last. Economic interest and efficiency – the building blocks of social science research over the past 30 years – are arguably only part of the story of polity creation. Identity – emotional attachment to community – appears vital. The early theorists of European integration took identity seriously, and the topic has returned to the research agenda of Europeanists in this era of political populism.

Ernst Haas (1958: 16) defined integration as the 'process whereby political actors in several distinct national settings are persuaded to shift their loyalties, expectations, and political activities toward a new centre'. Karl Deutsch considered a 'sense of community' to be a key indicator of integration (Deutsch *et al.* 1957: 36). Would Europe become a focus of identity?

Ronald Inglehart (1967, 1970) believed that generational replacement was working in this direction. The underlying process was political socialisation: individuals socialised in a society where public goods are provided by supranational rather than national institutions would, Inglehart argued, develop loyalty towards supranational institutions. On the basis of his transaction theory of identity formation, Karl Deutsch disagreed. Deutsch and his collaborators found that national communication was expanding at a much faster pace than European communication. European institution building 'had not been matched by any corresponding deeper integration of actual behavior' (Deutsch 1966: 355; Merritt *et al.* 2001) When European integration appeared to grind to a halt in the 1970s, Deutsch seemed vindicated, and interest in identity as an outcome of integration withered away.

It was not until the late 1990s, in the wake of the Maastricht Treaty (1993), that the issue of identity resurfaced. The Treaty was a compendium of practical steps to Europeanise monetary policy and important aspects of environmental policy, social policy, cohesion policy, and much besides. Each step was designed to enhance efficiency by centralising decision making at the continental level, but the aggregate effect was to present citizens with a supranational polity. While scholars were debating whether or not national sovereignty was undermined, opinion leaders were debating whether or not they could tolerate a palpable authority shift to Europe.

The Maastricht Accord was negotiated by elites, but it was submitted to publics in four referendums which led to one defeat (in Denmark) and one near defeat (in France). Neo-functionalists and intergovernmentalists conceived European decision making as an elite affair, but now decision making appeared to be shifting in a populist direction. Seven referendums were held on European issues in the 25 years prior to the Maastricht Accord; in the 16 years following the Maastricht Accord, 27 referendums have been held on European issues.[12] At the very time that rulers subjected themselves to their publics, publics were inclined to withhold consent.[13] Governments and their allies have been defeated in six of these 27 referendums.

The mobilisation of mass publics has transformed the process of European integration. Whereas elites negotiated with an eye to efficiency and distributional consequences, publics appear to be swayed by identity as well as by economic concerns. Identity is no longer an inert outcome of jurisdictional reform, as Deutsch and Haas assumed, but has become a powerful constraint (Hooghe and Marks 2008).[14]

Many researchers who studied identity had an ear to the ground. Immigration had become a hot political issue, and populist right-wing parties, such as the *Front National* and *Vlaams Blok/Belang*, made emotional connections between immigration and loss of national sovereignty due to European integration. Elites who viewed Europe from the standpoint of Pareto benefits seemed to miss the point. As Eichenberg and Dalton (2007: 138) note in a recent survey of public opinion literature:

> [W]hen the post-Maastricht years are included in the analysis...the causal dynamic of previous periods is substantially altered. Through 1991, public opinion responded very much in the way that the existing literature would lead us to expect: support for integration responded positively to increased trade within the EU and to improvement in economic conditions. Since Maastricht, however, these relationships have essentially disappeared.

The theoretical underpinnings of research on identity were quite thin. In his presidential address to the American Sociological Association, Douglas Massey (2002) called for research on the interaction of emotion and rationality on the grounds that emotional responses antedated rationality in human evolution and are often causally prior in explaining social behaviour. Most articles on identity refer to social identity theory which posits that group identifications shape individual self-conception and that humans have an 'innate ethnocentric tendency' which leads a person to favour his or her own group over others (Brewer 1999; Druckman 1994). Whether this tendency breeds hatred or tolerance, or something in between, depends on answers to questions posed by political scientists. Three questions stand out. How are identities mobilised in political competition? How do multiple identities, to Europe, to nations, and to subnational communities, fit together? How are identities shaped by discourse?

Research on the first question engages the causal connection between being British or Slovenian or Dutch or Catalan and having an attitude over a particular political object. National identities do not speak for themselves in the world of politics, but must be *framed* (connected to a particular political object, as when a political party connects having a national identity to opposing immigration), *cued* (brought into play by instilling a bias, e.g. against foreign influence), or *primed* (made salient, e.g., when a political party highlights an identity in the context of an electoral campaign). A compelling example of framing is provided by Erica Edwards and Catherine de Vries who find that the extent to which individuals are Eurosceptic depends not only on the extent to which they see themselves as exclusively national (e.g. exclusively French and not European), but on whether this identity is framed by a populist right-wing party. The stronger the radical right party in a country, the more intensely individuals with exclusive identities oppose European integration (Edwards and de Vries 2008).[15]

The second question sets out from the basic psychological insight that most individuals have multiple identities (Brewer 1993).[16] Fifteen years of opinion polling reveal that most Europeans have some positive attachment to Europe and their nation, alongside subnational communities (Diez Medrano and Guttiérez 2001; Hooghe and Marks 2001). Moreover, these identities are not necessarily zero-sum. That is to say, strong identity and pride in one's nation do not, on average, predispose an individual against Europe (Citrin and Sides 2004). What is decisive is how identities fit together. Does an individual conceive of national identity as one among a set of attachments or as an exclusive attachment? Is national identity conceived as a civic characteristic that can be acquired, or as an ethnic characteristic that is inherent?

Mass surveys of public opinion have not provided the kind of in-depth information that would allow researchers to probe these issues. Analysing focus group discussions in a set of Welsh and Scottish communities, Richard Haesly (2001) has found that individuals in both countries see an affinity between being Welsh or Scottish and being European, but they conceive this in contrasting ways. Whereas most Welsh conceive of European identity as a marker that differentiates them from the Eurosceptic English, European-minded Scots are drawn to the pluralistic, overarching (and therefore non-British) character of Europe.

Research on multiple identities debunks the notion that European identity is homogenous across Europe, and it poses the question of how identities are shaped by discourse (Marcussen *et al.* 1999). How are identity frames constructed, and who does the construction? Whereas quantitative research highlights differences among individuals and suggests that identity is malleable, qualitative research emphasises national differences and describes how identities are refracted through durable patterns of discourse. Qualitative research has explored how history (and history lessons at school) and elite and media discourse reinforce particular national understandings (Diez Medrano 2003; Parsons 2003; Schmidt 2007). Such frames are durable and consequential. Puzzling over why some member states have consistently been more willing to cede sovereignty on common foreign and security policy than others, Thomas Risse (2005: 303–4) argues that this is best explained by

> the social constructions and collective understandings that come with federalism. . . . Countries whose elites and citizens are used to the notion that sovereignty can be divided and/or shared between various levels of governance, are also more prepared to include supranational levels of governance in these understandings. Once one is prepared to accept supranationalism over intergovernmentalism in general, this might also extend into questions of war and peace. Borrowing from neofunctionalism, one could call this ideational spill-over.

One of the strengths of the social identity approach is that it rejects the notion that one can read off a person's political views from her identity. The way identity bears on European integration depends on how it is framed, and it is framed in domestic political conflict.

Is European Integration a New Political Cleavage?

In the 1980s, researchers debated whether European union had shifted authority away from national states. When the Single European Act and the Maastricht Treaty made clear that this had happened, they began to ask questions about the effect of European union on democratic politics within and across member states. Was it still valid to conceive European integration as a broadly consensual elite project detached from domestic political competition?[17] Or had European integration begun to affect daily life in ways that made it salient and contestable for the public and for political parties? Once again, events intervened, this time in the form of referendums and a growing recognition that major European reforms were too important to be left to political elites.

When European integration moved into domestic arenas in the 1990s, comparativists moved into European integration. And they applied the stock of knowledge and techniques of comparative politics to the European level to shed light on conflict about Europe (Cowles *et al.* 2001; Hooghe and

Marks 1999; Imig and Tarrow 2001; Katz and Wessels 1999; van der Eijk and Franklin 1996).

Might European integration constitute a new political cleavage? In their classic analysis of the sources of party competition in Western Europe, Lipset and Rokkan (1967: 14ff) diagnose four key historical junctures over the past three centuries giving rise to a centre/periphery cleavage, a secular/religious cleavage, an urban/rural cleavage, and a class cleavage (see also Steenbergen and Marks 2002). In Lipset's and Rokkan's conception, a cleavage is not merely an ideological conflict, but is rooted in social structure and is expressed in organisations, such as churches or trade unions. So the hurdle is high, particularly in light of the apparent weakening of the connection between social structure and ideology in post-industrial societies, and a consequent increase in volatility of individual voting across elections. Past cleavages were rooted in massive social change which disrupted whole populations. The hurdle is high, but not, perhaps, impossibly high.

Two recent books boldly characterise European integration as a vital ingredient in a new cleavage pitting the winners of globalisation against the losers. Stefano Bartolini (2005) theorises that European integration reverses a centuries-long process of national boundary construction. Whereas the creation of national states replaced local or regional boundaries with national ones, European integration undermines national boundaries without replacing them with a meaningful European boundary.[18] The upshot is that individuals with mobile resources are no longer contained within national boundaries, but neither are they regulated within Europe as a whole. Individuals who lack the resources to take advantage of these new opportunities are stuck in weakened national states that are less able to provide economic security.

Hanspeter Kriesi, Edgar Grande and their colleagues write that, 'in a Rokkanean perspective, the contemporary process of "globalisation" or "denationalisation" can be conceived of as a new "critical juncture", which is likely to result in the formation of new structural cleavages, both within and between national contexts' (Kriesi *et al.* 2006: 921). Analysing public opinion and party positioning in six West European countries, they detect a new and powerful demarcation/integration dimension of conflict. European integration and globalisation have, they argue, given rise to three kinds of competition that are generating new sets of winners and losers: competition between sheltered and unsheltered economic sectors, cultural competition between natives and immigrants, and competition between defenders of national institutions and proponents of supranational governance. These conflicts cannot be absorbed in conventional left/right competition and are likely to provoke partisan realignment. Losers of globalisation (and European integration) flock to parties that propose to demarcate their society against external competition; winners support parties that advocate further integration. If mainstream parties fail to adjust, new parties arise to exploit social discontent.

These analyses build on recent research on public opinion and party competition to theorise the transformative effect of European integration. Both stress that European integration raises cultural as well as economic issues; both emphasise that conflict over Europe escapes conventional economic left/right competition; and both anticipate partisan re-alignment and a rise in radical-right populism.[19]

This cleavage perspective is challenged by a technocratic conception of European integration. Giandomenico Majone (1994) has conceptualised the European Union as a regulatory regime in which decisions are taken by experts and supranational officials in non-majoritarian settings. Christian Joerges and Jürgen Neyer (1997) have emphasised the deliberative, problem-solving character of decision making in comitology. And Helen and William Wallace (2006) have identified five different decision modes in EU decision making – only two of which envisage a significant role for partisan actors.

How might one square this with the view that European integration has become enmeshed with domestic political conflict? One response is that technocratic bargaining applies to a limited, perhaps shrinking, subset of decisions (Peterson 2001). While referendums and elections rarely determine particular policy outcomes, they do appear to constrain public policy within a zone of acquiescence (Stimson 1999). Majone (2005: 220) observes that 60 years of functionalist spillover have hit a brick wall: 'Integration by stealth is no longer a viable strategy. The latest European elections have shown that the efficiency and legitimacy costs of the traditional approach have become so high that popular hostility to the very idea of integration is no longer a phenomenon limited to a few member states of the Union'.

Conclusion

When *West European Politics* was launched in 1978, few would have predicted a bright future for the European Economic Community, or for the study of EEC. Just nine of 198 articles in the first 20 issues of *WEP* were concerned primarily with the EEC. Today, the EU is regarded as worthy of attention on both substantive and theoretical grounds. By a conservative estimate, the 20 most recent issues of *WEP* contain at least 70 articles (of 191 total) that are primarily concerned with the EU.

This is a field in motion. In the late 1970s, the European Economic Community was conceived as a declining intergovernmental regime, insulated from national politics, and determined largely by national governments and specialised economic interests. The research that we have described in this essay suggests that the European Union has become a multilevel polity resulting from a two-sided dispersion of authority away from the central state; EU decision making has become politicised in ways that mobilise identity as well as economic interest; and European integration is part of a broad process of national boundary deconstruction with profound consequences for the structure of political conflict.

We have observed that the European Union is a moving target. Theorising jurisdictional reform in Europe appears to be event prone – and therefore error prone. The twists and turns of the European Union have a habit of throwing up new and unexpected facts that wrong-foot extant theories. We write after a period of sustained politicisation, of public debates, mobilisation of populist parties, and referendums on Europe. But we doubt whether this can be extrapolated into the second and third decades of this century. European integration is self-reflexive in the sense that its causal processes are subject to purposeful manipulation. Rulers who have been burnt by referendums, or fear the heat of future referendums, want to change the process. Why not cut treaties up into smaller pieces that might escape broad public debate? Perhaps referendums could be avoided if European symbolism was downplayed? Why not shift decision making to agencies insulated from partisanship? The politicisation of European integration has intensified efforts to turn down the heat. Will these efforts be successful?

So we hear the owl of Minerva. Have we come to understand the wellsprings of European integration just as they are changing? European integration has a habit of confounding its students and its practitioners. This, at least, is one trend that we can boldly extrapolate into the remainder of this century.

Acknowledgements

We wish to thank John Erik Fossum, Klaus Goetz, John Keeler, and Peter Mair for comments and advice. The normal disclaimer applies.

Notes

1. *West European Politics* was born when the European Community, the European Union's predecessor, turned 20. European integration dominated *WEP*'s inaugural issue. Ralf Dahrendorf wrote a lead article on European–American relations; Altiero Spinelli outlined the EC's institutions; Wyn Grant tackled British lobbying in the EC. But the journal's first issue was its high point for the study of the EC. Over the next two decades, few articles on EC topics were published in *WEP*, or elsewhere. Not until 1995 did European integration re-emerge in the journal, with a special issue, edited by Jack Hayward, on 'The Crisis of Representation in Europe'. In the past half-decade, European integration has figured in around 30 per cent of the articles appearing in *WEP*.
2. At this rate of change the EU will encompass 3,188,000,000 people by 2107, and will cover the globe by the end of the twenty-first century. The virtue of this extrapolation is that it is patently absurd, whereas efforts to extrapolate the causal underpinnings of European integration as a linear function of the past are merely implausible. The notion that national governments will control outcomes in the future because they (arguably) have in the past is an example of inappropriate extrapolation.
3. See also Caporaso and Keeler (1995), and Niedermayer and Sinnott (1995: 12), who state that 'integration theory suffered near fatal asphyxia in the Euro-stagnation of the late 1970s'. However, Markus Jachtenfuchs (2001) points out that research in the 1970s and

1980s was going strong in the subfields of public opinion, political parties and elections, and EU policy making.

4. 'Capable of power until it tried to wield it.'

5. '[T]he limits of the functional method: its very (if relative) success in the relatively painless area in which it works relatively well lifts the participants to the level of issues to which it does not apply well any more – like swimmers whose skill at moving quickly away from the shore suddenly brings them to the point where the waters are stormiest and deepest, at a time when fatigue is setting in, and none of the questions about the ultimate goal, direction, and length of swim has been answered' (Hoffmann 1966: 886).

6. In contrast to Hoffman, Moravcsik argued that the European policies of member states are driven by commercial objectives rather than geopolitics. Lieshout, Segers and van der Vleute (2004) provide a detailed examination of the evidence that Moravcsik presents.

7. Many scholars have labelled the European Union a federation or a federal system (e.g. Burgess 2000; Kelemen 2004; McKay 1999, Nicolaidis and Howse 2001).

8. Among the unresolved issues in the study of multilevel governance in Europe are the extent to which non-public actors are involved in authoritative decision making, the extent to which networking (rather than hierarchy) is present in relations among governmental actors and between governmental and non-governmental actors, and the extent to which authority across levels of governance is fragmented or mutually interlocking (Goetz, this issue; see also Bache and Flinders 2004).

9. European integration has encouraged the presumption that authority can be broken into discrete pieces which can be allocated across multiple levels. Europe has been built piecemeal, in a series of deals pitched at the level of individual policy issues treated as units of decision making to be allocated and reallocated at will.

10. Börzel codes formal Treaty rules to gauge the proportion of issues in a given policy field subject to EU legislation (breadth) and the extent to which decision making on an EU issue is supranational or intergovernmental (depth). She condenses her evaluations in a five-point scale for breadth, ranging from 1 (exclusive national competence for all issues in a policy area) to 5 (exclusive EU competence for all issues in a policy area), and a six-point scale for depth, ranging from 0 (no coordination at EU level) to 5 (supranational centralisation) (see Börzel 2005: 221–3). To facilitate comparison we have recalibrated these dimensions on a five-point scale.

11. Formal rules may not capture the practice of policy in fields such as agricultural policy and cohesion policy where, arguably, there has been some renationalisation.

12. The figures in the text are for countries that were, or became, members of the EU. They do not include referendums in which Norwegian voters decided not to join the European Union (1972 and 1994), on EEA membership in Liechtenstein (1992), and five referendums in Switzerland (1992 on EEA membership, 2001 on EU accession negotiations, 2004 on Schengen, 2005 on freedom of movement for persons, and 2006 on the Swiss contribution to EU cohesion policy). Of these eight referendums, four were no-votes (Norway: 1972 and 1994; Switzerland: 1992 and 2001).

13. We seem to be living in an age when governments are pressured to ask citizens to legitimate constitutional reform. This has been the case for EU constitutional reform, for democratic transition in former communist societies in Central and Eastern Europe, and for regional devolution (e.g. in France, Italy, Portugal, and Switzerland). In the United Kingdom, the cradle of parliamentary sovereignty, devolution for Scotland, Wales, Greater London, and the North-East has been submitted to referendum.

14. Neil Fligstein builds on Haas' and Deutsch's interest in identity as an outcome of European integration. In his forthcoming book, Fligstein (2008) argues that Europeanisation, which he defines as the process of building European-wide social arenas where people and organizations . . . routinely interact, has been limited to the 20 per cent of the population who have benefited from cross-border transactions: managers, professionals, and other highly educated people. This finding is consistent with recent research on support for European integration (McLaren 2006).

15. De Vries and Edwards also find that radical left-wing parties frame attitudes over Europe among individuals who feel economically insecure. This effect is less pronounced than that of populist right-wing parties for individuals with exclusive national identity.
16. Deutsch and Haas were ambivalent on the question of whether European and national identity were mutually exclusive. Haas did not exclude the possibility that multiple overlapping sources of governance at different territorial levels would generate corresponding 'tiered multiple loyalties' (Haas 1971: 31), and he argued that 'shifts in the focus of loyalty need not necessarily imply the immediate repudiation of the national state or government' (Haas 1958: 14). Much depends on the meaning of the word 'immediate', but it seems fair to say that Haas did not conceive of identity as zero-sum (Risse 2005).
17. Functionalists, like Mitrany (1948), and neofunctionalists, like Ernst Haas, believed that the economic forces they described would ultimately prevail over politics. 'The end result would be a community in which interest and activity are congruent and in which politics is replaced by problem-solving' (Caporaso 1972: 27). European integration was conceived as a project that was going to overcome cleavages – not create one. This view was rooted in a theory of modernisation (Kerr *et al.* 1960), which espoused 'that modern societies, including their politics, were shaped by technological imperatives that left little or no choice with respect to alternative modes of social organisation or, indeed, ways of life. In fact, faced with the overwhelming dictates imposed by the unrelenting progress of technology and industry, politics had mutated into rational adjustment of social practices and institutions to indisputable universal constraints, dealing with which was best left to technocratic experts trained in the parsimonious pursuit of functionalist best practice' (Streeck 2006: 3.) This bold (but time-limited) vision underpinned the construction of the postwar international order, motivated economic planning across Europe and beyond, and inspired proponents of European integration.
18. This is consistent with the observation of John Pinder, Fritz Scharpf, Wolfgang Streeck, and others, that European integration has been primarily about negative integration.
19. This line of theorising constitutes a break with functionalist and neofunctionalist thinking, as Philippe Schmitter (2005: 268) has stressed:

> [T]he real impediment to a revived neofunctionalist dynamic comes from something that Ernst Haas long anticipated, but which was so slow in coming to the European integration process. I have called it 'politicisation'. When citizens begin to pay attention to how the EU is affecting their daily lives, when political parties and large social movements begin to include 'Europe' in their platforms, and when politicians begin to realise that there are votes to be won or lost by addressing policy issues at the regional level, the entire low profile strategy becomes much less viable. Discrete regional officials and invisible interest representatives, in league with national civil servants, can no longer monopolise the decision-making process in Brussels (known in Euro-speak as 'comitology'). Integration starts to generate visible 'winners and losers' within member states, and loses its perception of being an 'all winners' game. Haas had an idiosyncratic term for this. He called it 'turbulence' and there is no question in my mind that the regional integration process in Europe has become 'turbulent' It will take a major revision of his theory before anyone can make sense of its changing dynamics.

References

Bache, Ian, and Matthew Flinders, eds. (2004). *Multilevel Governance*. Oxford: Oxford University Press.

Bartolini, Stefano (2005). *Restructuring Europe: Centre Formation, System Building, and Political Restructuring between the Nation-State and the European Union*. Oxford: Oxford University Press.

Benz, Arthur (2003). 'Mehrebenenverflechtung in der Europäischen Union', in Markus Jachtenfuchs and Beate Koch (eds.), *Europäische Integration*. 2nd edn. Opladen: Leske and Budrich, 317–51.

Börzel, Tanja (2005). 'Mind the Gap! European Integration Between Level and Scope', *Journal of European Public Policy*, 12:2, 217–36.

Brewer, Marilynn (1993). 'Social Identity, Distinctiveness, and In-Group Homogeneity', *Social Cognition*, 11, 150–64.

Brewer, Marilynn (1999). 'The Psychology of Prejudice: Ingroup Love or Outgroup Hate?', *Journal of Social Issues*, 55, 429–44.

Burgess, Michael (2000). *Federalism and European Union: The Building of Europe, 1950–2000*. London: Routledge.

Caporaso, James A. (1972). *Functionalism and Regional Integration: A Logical and Empirical Assessment*. Beverly Hills, CA: Sage.

Caporaso, James (1996). 'The European Union and Forms of State: Westphalian, Regulatory or Post-Modern?', *Journal of Common Market Studies*, 34:1, 29–52.

Caporaso, James (2006). 'Polanyi in Luxembourg: Market Participation, Embeddedness, and Rights in the European Union', Paper prepared for a Conference of International Political Economy Society (IPES), Princeton, NJ, 17–18 November.

Caporaso, James, and John Keeler (1995). 'The European Union and Regional Integration Theory', in Carolyn Rhodes and Sonia Mazey (eds.), *The State of the European Union: Building a European Polity*. Boulder, CO: Lynne Rienner.

Cichowski, Rachel (2004). 'Women's Rights, the European Court, and Supranational Constitutionalism', *Law and Society Review*, 38, 489–512.

Citrin, Jack, and John Sides (2004). 'Can there be Europe without Europeans? Problems of Identity in a Multinational Community', in Richard Herrmann, Marilynn Brewer and Thomas Risse (eds.), *Transnational Identities: Becoming European in the EU*. Lanham, MD: Rowman and Littlefield, 161–85.

Conant, Lisa (2006). 'Individuals, Courts, and the Development of European Social Rights', *Comparative Political Studies*, 39, 76–100.

Cowles, Maria Green (1995). 'Setting the Agenda for a New Europe: The ERT and 1992', *Journal of Common Market Studies*, 33:4, 501–26.

Cowles, Maria Green, James A. Caporaso and Thomas Risse, eds. (2001). *Transforming Europe: Europeanization and Domestic Change*. Ithaca, NY: Cornell University Press.

Dahrendorf, Ralf (1978). 'Europe and America: A Reassessment', *West European Politics*, 1:1, 3–10.

Deutsch, Karl W. (1966). 'Integration and Arms Control in the European Political Environment: A Summary Report', *American Political Science Review*, 60:2, 354–65.

Deutsch, Karl W., S.A. Burrell, R.A. Kann, M. Lee, Jr., M. Lichterman, R.E. Lindgren, F.L. Loewenheim and R.W. Van Wagenen (1957). *Political Community and the North Atlantic Area: International Organization in the Light of Historical Experience*. Princeton, NJ: Princeton University Press.

Diez Medrano, Juan (2003). *Framing Europe: Attitudes to European Integration in Germany, Spain, and the United Kingdom*. Princeton, NJ: Princeton University Press.

Diez Medrano, Juan, and Paula Guttiérez (2001). 'Nested Identities: National and European Identity in Spain', *Ethnic and Racial Studies*, 24, 753–78.

Druckman, Daniel (1994). 'Nationalism, Patriotism, and Group Loyalty: A Social Psychological Perspective', *Mershon International Studies Review*, 38, 43–68.

Edwards, Erica, and Catherine de Vries (2008). 'Taking Europe to its Extremes: Extremist Parties and Public Euroskepticism', forthcoming in *Party Politics*.

Eichenberg, Richard, and Russell Dalton (2007). 'Postmaastricht Blues: The Transformation of Citizen Support for European Integration, 1973–2004', *Acta Politica*, 42:2, 123–52.

Fligstein, Neil (2008). *Euroclash: The EU, European Identity, and the Future of the EU*. Oxford: Oxford University Press.

Haas, Ernst B. (1958). *The Uniting of Europe*. Stanford, CA: Stanford University Press.

Haas, Ernst B. (1961). 'International Integration: The European and the Universal Process', *International Organization*, 15:4, 366–92.

Haas, Ernst B. (1964). *Beyond the Nation-State: Functionalism and International Organization*. Stanford, CA: Stanford University Press.

Haas, Ernst B. (1971). 'The Study of Regional Integration: Reflections on the Joy and Anguish of Pretheorizing', in Leon N. Lindberg, and Stuart A. Scheingold (eds.), *Regional Integration: Theory and Research*. Cambridge, MA: Harvard University Press.

Haas, Ernst B. (1975). *The Obsolescence of Regional Integration Theory*. Berkeley: University of California Press.

Haesly, Richard (2001). 'Euroskeptics, Europhiles and Instrumental Europeans: European Attachment in Scotland and Wales', *European Union Politics*, 2:1, 81–102.

Heritier, Adrienne (1996). 'The Accommodation of Diversity in European Policy-Making and Its Outcomes', *Journal of European Public Policy*, 3:2, 149–67.

Hix, Simon (1994). 'The Study of the European Community: The Challenge to Comparative Politics', *West European Politics*, 17:1, 1–30.

Hix, Simon (1996). 'Comparative Politics, International Relations and the EU! A Rejoinder to Hurrell and Menon', *West European Politics*, 19:4, 802–4.

Hoffmann, Stanley (1966). 'Obstinate or Obsolete? The Fate of the Nation-State and the Case of Western Europe', *Daedalus*, 95, 862–914.

Hooghe, Liesbet, and Gary Marks (1999). 'Making of a Polity: The Struggle over European Integration', in Herbert Kitschelt, Peter Lange, Gary Marks and John Stephens (eds.), *Continuity and Change in Contemporary Capitalism*. Cambridge: Cambridge University Press, 70–97.

Hooghe, Liesbet, and Gary Marks (2001). *Multi-level Governance and European Integration*. Boulder, CO: Rowman & Littlefield.

Hooghe, Liesbet, and Gary Marks (2008). 'A Postfunctionalist Theory of European Integration: From Permissive Consensus to Constraining Dissensus', forthcoming in *British Journal of Political Science*.

Hurrell, Andrew, and Anand Menon (1996). 'Politics Like Any Other? Comparative Politics, International Relations, and the Study of the EU', *West European Politics*, 19:2, 386–402.

Imig, Doug, and Sidney Tarrow, eds. (2001). *Contentious Europeans: Protest and Politics in the New Europe*. Boulder, CO: Rowman & Littlefield.

Inglehart, Ronald (1967). 'An End to European Integration?', *American Political Science Review*, 61:1, 91–105.

Inglehart, Ronald (1970). 'The New Europeans: Inward or Outward-Looking?', *International Organization*, 24:1, 129–39.

Jachtenfuchs, Markus (2001). 'The Governance Approach to European Integration', *Journal of Common Market Studies*, 39:2, 245–64.

Joerges, Christian, and Jürgen Neyer (1997). 'Transforming Strategic Interaction into Deliberative Problem-Solving: European Comitology in the Foodstuffs Sector', *Journal of European Public Policy*, 4:4, 609–25.

Katz, Richard S., and Bernhard Wessels, eds. (1999). *The European Parliament, the National Parliaments, and European Integration*. Oxford: Oxford University Press.

Keeler, John T.S. (2005). 'Mapping EU Studies: The Evolution from Boutique to Boom Field 1960–2001', *Journal of Common Market Studies*, 43:3, 551–82.

Kelemen, Daniel (2004). *The Rules of Federalism: Institutions and Regulatory Politics in the EU and Beyond*. Cambridge, MA: Harvard University Press.

Keohane, Robert O., and Stanley Hoffmann, eds. (1991). *The New European Community: Decision Making and Institutional Change*. Boulder, CO: Westview, 1–39.

Kerr, Clark, John T. Dunlop, Frederick H. Harbison and Charles A. Myers (1960). *Industrialism and Industrial Man: The Problems of Labor and Management in Economic Growth*. Cambridge, MA: Harvard University Press.

Kohler-Koch, Beate, and Rainer Eising, eds. (1999). *The Transformation of Governance in the European Union*. London: Routledge.

Kriesi, Hanspeter, Edgar Grande, Romain Lachat, Martin Dolezal, Simon Bornschier and Timotheos Frey (2006). 'Globalization and the Transformation of the National Political Space: Six European Countries Compared', *European Journal of Political Research*, 45, 921–56.

Lakatos, Imre (1970). 'Falsification and the Methodology of Scientific Research Programmes', in Imre Lakatos and Alan Musgrave (eds.), *Criticism and the Growth of Knowledge*. Cambridge: Cambridge University Press.

Leibfried, Stephan, and Paul Pierson, eds. (1995). *Fragmented Social Policy: The European Union's Social Dimension in Comparative Perspective*. Washington, DC: Brookings Institution.

Lieshout, Robert A., Matthieu Segers and Anna van der Vleuten (2004). 'De Gaulle, Moravcsik, and *The Choice for Europe*: Soft Sources, Weak Evidence', *Journal of Cold War Studies*, 6:4, 89–139.

Lindberg, Leon N., and Stuart A. Scheingold, eds. (1970). *Regional Integration: Theory and Research*. Cambridge, MA: Harvard University Press.

Lipset, Seymour Martin, and Stein Rokkan (1967). 'Cleavage Structures, Party Systems, and Voter Alignments: An Introduction', in Seymour Martin Lipset and Stein Rokkan (eds.), *Party Systems and Voter Alignments*. New York: Free Press, 1–64.

Majone, Giandomenico (1994). 'The Rise of the Regulatory State in Europe', *West European Politics*, 17:1, 77–101.

Majone, Giandomenico (2005). *Dilemmas of European Integration: The Ambiguities and Pitfalls of Integration by Stealth*. Oxford: Oxford University Press.

Marcussen, Martin, Daniela Engelmann-Martin, Hans-Joachim Knopf, Klaus Roscher and Thomas Risse (1999). 'Constructing Europe? The Evolution of French, British, and German Nation-State Identities', *Journal of European Public Policy*, 6, 614–33.

Marks, Gary, and Doug McAdam (1996). 'Social Movements and the Changing Structure of Political Opportunity in the European Community', *West European Politics*, 19:2, 249–78.

Marks, Gary, Liesbet Hooghe and Kermit Blank (1996). 'European Integration since the 1980s: State-Centric versus Multi-Level Governance', *Journal of Common Market Studies*, 34:4, 341–78.

Marks, Gary, Liesbet Hooghe and Arjan Schakel (2008). 'Patterns of Regional Authority', forthcoming in *Regional and Federal Studies*, 18:2.

Massey, Douglas (2002). 'Presidential Address: A Brief History of Human Society: The Origin and Role of Emotion in Social Life', *American Sociological Review*, 67:1, 1–29.

McKay, David (1999). *Federalism and the European Union: A Political Economy Perspective*. Oxford: Oxford University Press.

McLaren, Lauren (2002). 'Public Support for the European Union: Cost/Benefit Analysis or Perceived Cultural Threat?', *Journal of Politics*, 64, 551–66.

Merritt, Richard L., Bruce M. Russett and Robert A. Dahl (2001). 'Karl Wolfgang Deutsch: July 21, 1912–November 1, 1992', *Biographical Memoirs, volume 80 – National Academy of Sciences*. Washington, DC: The National Academy Press.

Milward, Alan (1992). *The European Rescue of the Nation-State*. Berkeley: University of California Press.

Mitrany, David (1948). 'The Functional Approach to World Organization', *International Affairs*, 24:3, 350–63.

Moravcsik, Andrew (1993). 'Preferences and Power in the European Community: a Liberal Intergovernmentalist Approach', *Journal of Common Market Studies*, 31, 473–524.

Moravcsik, Andrew (1998). *The Choice for Europe: Social Purpose and State Power from Messina to Maastricht*. Ithaca, NY: Cornell University Press.

Moravcsik, Andrew (2004). 'Is there a Democratic Deficit in World Politics? A Framework for Analysis', *Government and Opposition*, 39:2, 336–63.

Nicolaidis, Kalypso, and Robert Howse, eds. (2001). *The Federal Vision: Legitimacy and Levels of Governance in the United States and the European Union*. Oxford: Oxford University Press.

Niedermayer, Oskar, and Richard Sinnott, eds. (1995). *Public Opinion and Internationalized Governance*. Oxford: Oxford University Press.

Nye, Joseph (1970). 'Comparing Common Markets: A Revised Neo-Functionalist Model', in Leon N. Lindberg and Stuart A. Scheingold (eds.), *Regional Integration: Theory and Research*. Cambridge, MA: Harvard University Press, 192–231.

Parsons, Craig (2003). *A Certain Idea of Europe*. Ithaca, NY: Cornell University Press.

Peterson, John (1995). 'Decision-making in the European Union: Towards a Framework for Analysis', *Journal of European Public Policy*, 2:1, 69–93.

Peterson, John (2001). 'The Choice for EU Theorists: Establishing a Common Framework for Analysis', *European Journal of Political Research*, 39:3, 289–318.

Pierson, Paul (1996). 'The Path to European Integration: A Historical Institutionalist Analysis', *Comparative Political Studies*, 29:2, 123–62.

Pollack, Mark A. (1995). 'Creeping Competence: The Expanding Agenda of the European Community', *Journal of Public Policy*, 14:1, 97–143.

Risse, Thomas (1996). 'Exploring the Nature of the Beast: International Relations Theory and Comparative Policy Analysis Meet the European Union', *Journal of Common Market Studies*, 34:1, 53–80.

Risse, Thomas (2005). 'Neofunctionalism, European Identity, and the Puzzles of European Integration', *Journal of European Public Policy*, 12:2, 291–309.

Sandholtz, Wayne (1996). 'Membership Matters: Limits of the Functional Approach to European Institutions', *Journal of Common Market Studies*, 34: 403–29.

Sandholtz, Wayne, and Alec Stone Sweet, eds. (1998). *European Integration and Supranational Governance*. Oxford: Oxford University Press.

Sandholtz, Wayne, and John Zysman (1989). '1992: Recasting the European Bargain', *World Politics*, 42, 95–128.

Sbragia, Alberta M., ed. (1992). *Euro-Politics: Institutions and Policy-Making in the 'New' European Community*. Washington, DC: Brookings Institution.

Sbragia, Alberta M. (1993). 'The European Community: A Balancing Act', *Publius*, 23:1, 23–38.

Scharpf, Fritz W. (1997). 'The Problem-Solving Capacity of Multi-Level Governance', *Journal of European Public Policy*, 4:4, 520–38.

Scharpf, Fritz W. (1988). 'The Joint Decision Trap: Lessons from German Federalism and European Integration', *Public Administration*, 66, 239–78.

Schmidt, Vivien (2007). 'Trapped by their Ideas: French Elites' Discourses of European Integration and Globalization', *Journal of European Public Policy*, 14:4, xx–xx.

Schmitter, Philippe (1970). 'A Revised Theory of Regional Integration', *International Organization*, 24, 836–68.

Schmitter, Philippe (2005). 'Ernst B. Haas and the Legacy of Neofunctionalism', *Journal of European Public Policy*, 12:2, 255–72.

Spinelli, Altiero (1978). 'Reflections on the Institutional Crisis in the EC', *West European Politics*, 1:1, xx–xx.

Steenbergen, Marco, and Gary Marks (2002). 'Understanding Political Contestation in the European Union', *Comparative Political Studies*, 35:8, 879–92.

Stimson, James (1999). *Public Opinion in America: Moods, Cycles and Swings*. 2nd edn. Boulder, CO: Westview Press.

Stone Sweet, Alec, and Thomas Brunell (1998). 'Constructing a Supranational Constitution: Dispute Resolution and Governance in the European Community', *American Political Science Review*, 92:1, 63–81.

Streeck, Wolfgang (2006). 'The Study of Interest Groups: Before "The Century" and After', in Wolfgang Streeck and Colin Crouch (eds.), *The Diversity of Democracy: Corporatism, Social Order and Political Conflict*. Cheltenham: Edward Elgar, 3–45.

Tarrow, Sidney (1995). 'The Europeanisation of Conflict: Reflections from a Social Movements Perspective', *West European Politics*, 18:2, 223–51.

Tsebelis, George (1994). 'The Power of the European Parliament as a Conditional Agenda Setter', *American Political Science Review*, 88:1, 129–42.

Van der Eijk, Cees, and Mark Franklin, eds. (1996). *Choosing Europe: The European Electorate and National Politics in the Face of the Union*. Ann Arbor: University of Michigan Press.

Wallace, Helen, and William Wallace (2006). 'The European Union, Politics and Policy Making', in Knud Erik Jørgensen, Mark A. Pollack and Ben Rosamond (eds.), *Handbook of European Union Politics*. Oxford: Oxford University Press, 339–58.

Changing Values among Western Publics from 1970 to 2006

RONALD F. INGLEHART

More than 35 years ago, I suggested that 'a transformation may be taking place in the political culture of advanced industrial societies. This transformation seems to be altering the basic value priorities of given generations as a result of changing conditions influencing their basic socialization' (Inglehart 1971: 991). Survey evidence from six West European societies revealed large differences between the value priorities of older and younger generations. Among the older cohorts, 'materialist' values, emphasising economic and physical security, were overwhelmingly predominant – but as one moved from older to younger birth cohorts, 'post-materialist' values, emphasising autonomy and self-expression, became increasingly widespread. The differences were striking. Among those aged 65 or older, materialists were fully 12 times as numerous as post-materialists; among those born after World War II (who were under 25 in 1970), post-materialists were slightly more numerous than materialists.

If, as I argued, these age differences reflected intergenerational value change (and not simply a tendency for people to get more materialist as they aged), then we should expect to find a gradual shift from materialist to post-materialist values as younger birth cohorts replaced older ones in the adult population. The implications were far-reaching, for these values were closely linked with a number of important orientations ranging from emphasis on political participation and freedom of expression, to support for new issues and new types of political parties.

Intergenerational value change, by its very nature, moves slowly. But its long-term impact can be profound. More than 35 years have passed since the hypothesised shift from materialist to post-materialist values was published. Have the predicted changes actually taken place?

The implications of the underlying theory are clear. It holds that post-materialist values emerge as people come to place increasing emphasis on autonomy, self-expression and the quality of life. This shift is linked with changing existential conditions – above all, the change from growing up with the feeling that survival is precarious, to growing up with the feeling that survival can be taken for granted.

Throughout most of history, survival has been uncertain for the vast majority of the population. But the remarkable economic growth that occurred during the era following World War II, together with the rise of the welfare state, brought fundamentally new conditions in advanced industrial societies. The post-war birth cohorts spent their formative years under levels of prosperity that were unprecedented in human history, and the welfare state reinforced the feeling that survival was secure, producing major differences in the priorities of older and younger generations that became evident when the first post-war cohort emerged into political relevance two decades after World War II.

As we will see, a massive body of evidence demonstrates that an intergenerational shift from materialist to post-materialist priorities has been occurring. But it is only one aspect of a broader cultural shift from survival values to self-expression values, which is bringing new political issues to the centre of the stage and motivating new political movements.

This theory of intergenerational value change is based on two key hypotheses (Inglehart 1977):

1. *A scarcity hypothesis.* Virtually everyone aspires to freedom and autonomy, but people tend to place the highest value on the most pressing needs. Material sustenance and physical security are immediately linked with survival, and when they are scarce people give top priority to these 'materialistic' goals; but under conditions of prosperity, people become more likely to emphasise 'post-materialist' goals such as belonging, esteem, and aesthetic and intellectual satisfaction.
2. *A socialisation hypothesis.* The relationship between material conditions and value priorities is not one of immediate adjustment: to a large extent, one's basic values reflect the conditions that prevailed during one's pre-adult years and these values change mainly through intergenerational population replacement.

The scarcity hypothesis is similar to the principle of diminishing marginal utility. It reflects the basic distinction between the material needs for physical survival and safety, and non-material needs such as those for self-expression and aesthetic satisfaction.

During the past several decades, advanced industrial societies have diverged strikingly from the prevailing historical pattern: most of their population has *not* grown up under conditions of hunger and economic insecurity. This has led to a gradual shift in which needs for belonging, esteem and intellectual and self-expression have become more prominent. The scarcity hypothesis implies that prolonged periods of high prosperity will tend to encourage the spread of post-materialist values – and that enduring economic decline will have the opposite effect.

But there is no one-to-one relationship between socio-economic development and the prevalence of post-materialist values, for these values reflect one's subjective sense of security, not simply one's objective economic level. One's sense of security is shaped by a society's social welfare institutions as well as its income level, and is also influenced by the general sense of security prevailing in one's society. Furthermore, people's basic value priorities do not change overnight: the scarcity hypothesis must be interpreted in connection with the socialisation hypothesis.

One of the most pervasive concepts in social science is that one's basic personality structure crystallises by the time one reaches adulthood. A large body of evidence indicates that people's basic values are largely fixed when they reach adulthood, and change relatively little thereafter (Rokeach 1968, 1973; Inglehart 1977, 1997). If so, we would expect to find substantial differences between the values of the young and the old in societies that have experienced a rising sense of security. People are most likely to adopt those values that are consistent with what they have experienced first-hand during their formative years. This implies that intergenerational value change will occur if younger generations grow up under different conditions from those that shaped earlier generations – so that the values of the entire society will gradually change through intergenerational replacement.

These two hypotheses generate several predictions concerning value change. First, while the scarcity hypothesis implies that prosperity is conducive to the spread of post-materialist values, the socialisation hypothesis implies that fundamental value change takes place gradually; to a large extent, it occurs as younger generations replace older ones in the adult population. After an extended period of rising economic and physical security, one would expect to find substantial differences between the value priorities of older and younger groups, since they would have been shaped by different experiences in their formative years. But a sizeable time lag would occur between economic changes and their political effects. Fifteen or 20 years after an era of prosperity began, the birth cohorts that had spent their formative years in prosperity would begin to enter the electorate.

Per capita income and educational levels are among the best readily available indicators of the conditions leading to the shift from materialist to post-materialist goals, but the theoretically crucial factor is not per capita income itself, but one's sense of existential security – which means that the impact of economic and physical security is mediated by the given society's social security system.

In order to test the value change hypothesis, we asked people which goals they considered most important, choosing between such things as economic growth, fighting rising prices, maintaining order, and the fight against crime (which tap materialist priorities); and freedom of speech, giving people more say in important government decisions, more say on the job, and a society where ideas count (which tap post-materialist priorities). Representative national surveys in six West European countries in 1970 revealed huge differences between the values of young and old in all of these societies. As Figure 1 indicates, among those aged 65 and older, people with materialist value priorities outnumbered those with post-materialist value priorities by more than 12 to 1. But as one moves from older to younger cohorts, the balance gradually shifts towards a diminishing proportion of materialists and a growing proportion of people with post-materialist values. Among the youngest cohort (those from 18 to 25 years old in 1970) post-materialists outnumber materialists. If we assume that the value priorities of given birth cohorts are stable, this implies that in the 1930s, when the two oldest cohorts were in their 20s and 30s, materialists must have outnumbered post-materialists by at least a ratio of ten to one among the adult population of these countries. In that era, the Marxist model of politics being dominated by class conflict and economic issues provided a reasonably good first approximation of reality. But the cross-sectional evidence in Figure 1 also implies that as the four oldest birth cohorts die off during the four decades following 1970, we should observe a major shift in the motivations of these societies, with post-materialists becoming as numerous as materialists, bringing a corresponding shift away from economic issues toward increasing emphasis on quality of life and expressive issues.

But *are* these value differences stable? Do these age differences reflect enduring birth cohort effects or transient life-cycle effects? With data from just one time point, one cannot be sure – and the two interpretations have very different implications. The life-cycle reading implies that the young will become increasingly materialist as they age, so that by the time they are 65 years old they will have become just as materialist as the 65 year olds were in 1970 – which means that society as a whole will not change at all. The cohort-effects interpretation implies that the younger cohorts will remain relatively post-materialist over time – and that as they replace the older, more materialist cohorts, the prevailing values of society will change profoundly.

Cohort analysis provides the only conclusive way to answer this question and it requires: (1) survey data covering a long time period; (2) surveys carried out at numerous time points, enabling one to distinguish period effects from life-cycle and cohort effects; and (3) large numbers of respondents in each survey – because when one breaks a single national

FIGURE 1

VALUE TYPE BY AGE GROUP AMONG THE PUBLICS OF BRITAIN, FRANCE, WEST GERMANY, ITALY, BELGIUM AND THE NETHERLANDS IN 1970

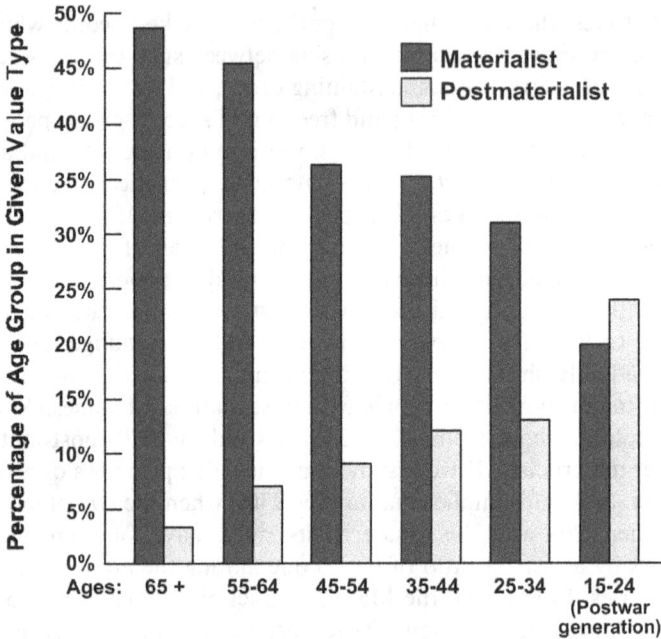

Source: European Community survey of February 1970, based on original four-item materialist/post-materialist values battery. Reprinted from Inglehart (1990: 76).

sample down into six or seven birth cohorts, the sampling error margin rises to the point where noise begins to drown out the signal.

Figure 2 shows the results of a cohort analysis that follows given birth cohorts over 35 years, using data from Euro-barometer surveys that included the materialist/post-materialist battery in almost every year from 1970 to 1997; supplemented with data from the fourth and fifth waves of the Values Surveys, carried out in 1999 and 2006.[1] This figure pools the data from Britain, France, West Germany, Italy, Belgium and the Netherlands in order to provide large samples and relatively stable estimates of each cohort's position at a given time – which is calculated by subtracting the percentage of materialists from the percentage of post-materialists. Thus, at the zero point on the vertical axis, the two groups are equally numerous. The proportion of post-materialists increases as one moves up; and the proportion of materialists increases as one moves down on Figure 2.

If the age differences shown in Figure 1 reflected a life-cycle effect, then each of the cohort lines would move downward, towards the materialist pole, with each cohort becoming more materialist as one moves across Figure 2, from 1970 to 2006. If the age differences reflect stable birth cohort

FIGURE 2
COHORT ANALYSIS: % POST-MATERIALISTS MINUS % MATERIALISTS IN SIX
WEST EUROPEAN SOCIETIES, 1970–2006

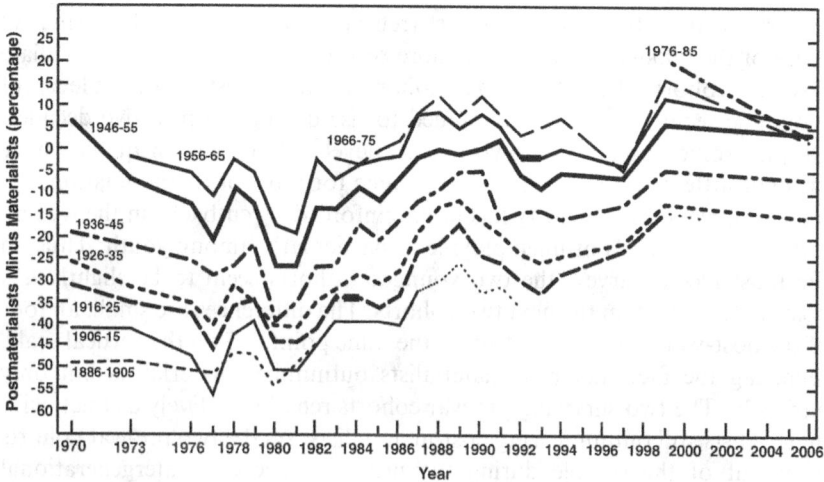

Source: Based on combined weighted sample of Eurobarometer surveys and World Values Surveys in West Germany, France Britain, Italy, the Netherlands and Belgium, in given years, using the four-item materialist/ post-materialist values index.

effects, the pattern would be horizontal, with each birth cohort remaining about as post-materialist at the end of the time series as it was at the start.

But we also need to take period effects into account. Our theory implies that negative short-term effects such as a major recession will tend to push all cohorts downward in response to current conditions; but with recovery, they will return to their former level, so that in the long run they will remain about as post-materialist as they were at the start. Over short periods, a period effect that pushed all the cohorts downward could give the misleading impression that the age differences reflected life-cycle effects. But in the long run, positive and negative fluctuations tend to cancel each other out.

Because we have data from numerous time points, we can see that period effects clearly *are* present. As Inglehart and Welzel (2005) demonstrate, they reflect current economic conditions, particularly inflation levels. But these period effects have no lasting impact: the younger cohorts remain relatively post-materialist despite short-term fluctuations, and over a period of 35 years we find no overall tendency for the members of given birth cohorts to become more materialist as they age – indeed most cohorts are slightly more post-materialist at the end of this time series than they were at the start.

But during this 35-year span the three oldest birth cohorts have left the sample: first the 1886–1905 cohort, then the 1906–15 cohort and finally the 1916–25 cohort disappeared as the number of surviving members in the cohort became too small to provide reliable estimates. These cohorts were replaced by three new ones, born in 1956–65, 1966–75 and, most recently, 1976–85. Although the 1956–65 birth cohort was significantly more post-materialist than the 1946–55 cohort (reflecting the fact that the formative years of the 1956–65 cohort were more secure than those of the immediate post-war cohort), the two youngest cohorts are *not*. West European levels of economic security have not continued to rise during the past two decades. Despite some economic growth, rising levels of income inequality have brought little or no increase in real income for most of the population; the impact on economic security has been reinforced by cutbacks in the welfare state and high levels of unemployment, particularly among youth. Thus, in the most recent survey, the two youngest cohorts seem to be slightly *less* post-materialist than the next two cohorts. The differences are small: all four of the post-war cohorts fall at about the same point, +5 on the vertical scale, reflecting the fact that post-materialists outnumber materialists but only narrowly. The two surviving pre-war cohorts remain relatively distinct, with materialists still outnumbering post-materialists. As the two pre-war cohorts drop out of the sample during the next two decades, intergenerational population replacement will still be conducive to a gradual shift toward post-materialist values, but (barring a reprise of rising existential security) the intergenerational shift would then come to an end. Already, the gap between the values of the oldest and youngest cohorts has dwindled to less than half the size that it had at the start of the time series in 1970.

The cohort analysis presented in Figure 2 shows no evidence whatever of life-cycle effects. Time series evidence covering 35 years makes it clear that the age-related differences that were found in 1970 reflect lasting cohort differences. This implies that as the younger, less materialist cohorts replace the older ones in the adult population, these societies should shift from materialist toward post-materialist values.

This is precisely what happened. Figure 3 shows the net shift from 1970 to 2006 among the five publics for which we have data from 1970 through 2006, plus the US. In every country, we find a substantial net shift toward post-materialist values. The vertical scale of this figure shows the mean score on the materialist/post-materialist index, with a mean of 2.0 indicating the point at which materialists and post-materialists are equally numerous. In the early 1970s, materialists heavily outnumbered post-materialists in all of these countries. In the six West European countries as a whole, materialists were four times as numerous as post-materialists (and 21 times as numerous as post-materialists among the oldest cohort). Similarly, in the US materialists were three times as numerous as post-materialists. During the next 35 years a major shift occurred. By 2006, post-materialists were slightly more numerous than materialists in Western Europe and post-materialists were twice as numerous as materialists in the US. Despite substantial short-term fluctuations and the negative economic conditions of recent years, the predicted shift toward post-materialist values took place.

FIGURE 3
THE CHANGING DISTRIBUTION OF MATERIALIST/POSTMATERIALIST
VALUES, 1970–2006

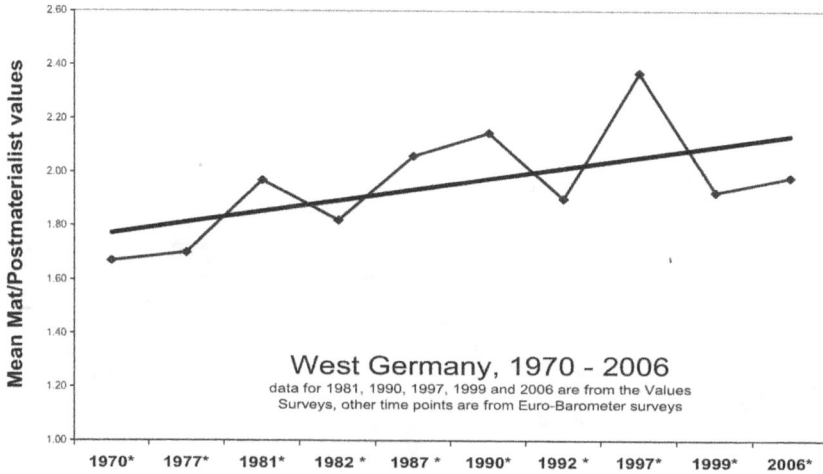

West Germany, 1970 - 2006
data for 1981, 1990, 1997, 1999 and 2006 are from the Values
Surveys, other time points are from Euro-Barometer surveys

Note: Graphs are based on mean scores where 1 = Materialist, 2 = Mixed, 3 = Postmaterialist. Thus if a country would have a mean score of 1 if 100% of the population were Materialists; with a mean score of 2, Materialists and Postmaterialists are evenly balanced; and the country would have a mean score of 3 if 100% of the population were Postmaterialists.

The shift toward post-materialist values has tapered off in the six West European countries first surveyed in 1970. But the logic of the underlying process remains relevant to much of the world. Though the rates vary widely from country to country, the world as a whole is experiencing unprecedented economic growth. India and China are currently experiencing annual growth rates of about 7 per cent and 10 per cent, respectively. For the time being, these countries are still in the phase of rising materialism that characterises early industrialisation. But if they continue on their present trajectories, they will eventually reach a stage where younger generations emerge that have grown up under conditions in which they take survival for granted. Many other countries from Mexico to Singapore are approaching or have already attained this level.

In the world as a whole, the ratio between materialists and post-materialists varies tremendously according to a society's level of economic development, as Figure 4 demonstrates. Low-income countries and strife-torn countries show an overwhelming preponderance of materialists, while prosperous and secure ones show a preponderance of post-materialists. Thus, materialists outnumber post-materialists in Pakistan by a ratio of 55 to 1, and in Russia by a ratio of 28 to 1; but in the US post-materialists outnumber materialists by 2 to 1, and in Sweden post-materialists prevail by 5 to 1. The world as a whole is currently experiencing the most rapid rate of

FIGURE 4
MATERIALIST/POST-MATERIALIST VALUES BY GNP/CAPITA

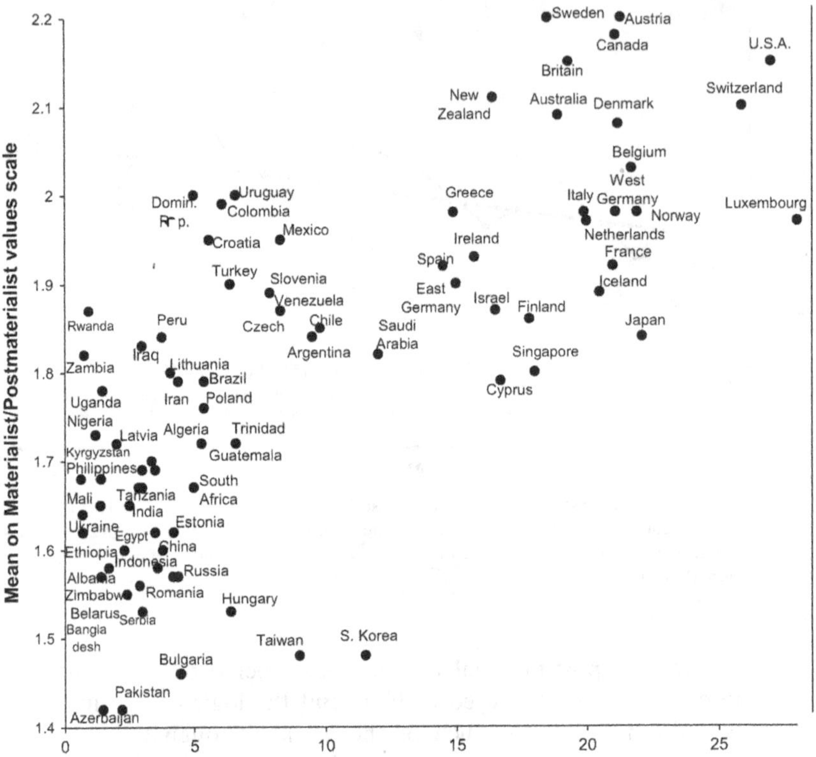

Note: 1 = 100% materialist; 2 = materialist and post-materialist evenly balanced; 3 = 100% post-materialist; GNP per capita in thousands, 1995 (PPP estimates) r = .64.

economic growth in recorded history. There is no guarantee that it will continue, but in those countries that do attain high levels of existential security, we would expect processes of intergenerational value change to take place.

Post-materialist Values: A Component of a Broader Cultural Change

The shift towards post-materialist values is itself only one aspect of a still broader process of cultural change that is reshaping the political outlook, religious orientations, gender roles, and sexual mores of advanced industrial society (Inglehart 1990, 1997; Inglehart and Welzel 2005). The emerging orientations place less emphasis on traditional cultural norms, especially those that limit individual self-expression.

In order to identify the main dimensions of global cultural variation, Inglehart and Baker (2000)[2] carried out a factor analysis of each society's mean level on scores of variables, tapping a wide range of values. The two most significant dimensions that emerged reflected: (1) a polarisation between *traditional* and *secular-rational* values and (2) a polarisation between *survival* and *self-expression* values.

Traditional values place strong emphasis on religion, respect for authority, and have relatively low levels of tolerance for abortion and divorce and have relatively high levels of national pride. *Secular-rational* values have the opposite characteristics. Agrarian societies tend to emphasise traditional values; industrialising societies tend to emphasise secular-rational values.

The second major dimension of cross-cultural variation is linked with the transition from industrial society to post-industrial societies – which brings a polarisation between *survival* and *self-expression* values. As Table 1 demonstrates, the polarisation between materialist

TABLE 1
ORIENTATIONS LINKED WITH SURVIVAL VS. SELF-EXPRESSION VALUES

Item	Correlation
SURVIVAL VALUES emphasise the following:	
Materialist/Post-materialist Values	.87
Men make better political leaders than women	.86
R. is not highly satisfied with life	.84
A woman has to have children to be fulfilled	.83
R. rejects foreigners, homosexuals and people with AIDS as neighbours	.81
R. has not and would not sign a petition	.80
R. is not very happy	.79
R. favours more emphasis on the development of technology	.78
Homosexuality is never justifiable	.78
R. has not recycled something to protect the environment	.76
R. has not attended a meeting or signed a petition to protect the environment	.75
A good income and safe job are more important than a feeling of accomplishment and working with people you like	.74
R. does not rate own health as very good	.73
A child needs a home with both a father and a mother in order to grow up happily	.73
When jobs are scarce, a man has more right to a job than a women	.69
A university education is more important for a boy than for a girl	.67
Government should ensure that everyone is provided for	.69
Hard work is one of the most important things to teach a child	.65
Imagination is not of the most important things to teach a child	.62
Tolerance is not of the most important things to teach a child	.62
Leisure is not very important in life	.61
Scientific discoveries will help, rather than harm, humanity	.60
Friends are not very important in life	.56
You have to be very careful about trusting people	.56
R. has not and would not join a boycott	.56
R. is relatively favourable to state ownership of business and industry	.54
SELF-EXPRESSION VALUES take opposite position on all of above	

The original polarities vary; the above statements show how each item relates to this values index.

and post-materialist values is a sensitive indicator of this dimension, for the conditions that give rise to post-materialist values are also conducive to self-expression values. But self-expression values encompass a number of issues that go well beyond the items tapped by post-materialist values. For example, self-expression values reflect mass polarisation over such issues as whether 'When jobs are scarce, men have more right to a job than women'; or whether 'Men make better political leaders than women'. This emphasis on gender equality is part of a broader syndrome of tolerance of outgroups, including foreigners, gays and lesbians. Self-expression values give high priority to environmental protection, tolerance of diversity and rising demands for participation in decision making in economic and political life.

The shift from survival values to self-expression values also includes a shift in child-rearing values, from emphasis on hard work toward emphasis on imagination and tolerance as important values to teach a child. Societies that rank high on self-expression values also tend to rank high on interpersonal trust and have relatively high levels of subjective well-being. This produces an environment of trust and tolerance, in which people place a relatively high value on individual freedom and self-expression, and have activist political orientations – the attributes that the political culture literature defines as crucial to democracy.

A major component of the rise of self-expression values is a shift away from deference to all forms of external authority. Submission to authority has high costs: the individual's personal goals must be subordinated to those of external authorities. Under conditions of insecurity, people are generally willing to do so. Under threat of invasion, internal disorder or economic collapse, people eagerly seek strong authority figures that can protect them from danger.

Conversely, conditions of prosperity and security are conducive to tolerance of diversity in general and democracy in particular. This helps explain a long-established finding: rich societies are much more likely to be democratic than poor ones. Under conditions of insecurity, people may be willing to submit to authoritarian rule, but with rising levels of existential security they become less willing to do so.

The rise of self-expression values brings an intergenerational change in a wide variety of basic social norms, from cultural norms linked with survival of the species, to norms linked with the pursuit of individual well-being. For example, younger birth cohorts are markedly more tolerant of homosexuality than their elders. And younger cohorts become increasingly permissive in their attitudes toward abortion, divorce, extramarital affairs, prostitution, and euthanasia. Economic accumulation for the sake of economic security was the central goal of industrial society. Ironically, their attainment set in motion a process of gradual cultural change that has made these goals less central – and is now bringing a rejection of the hierarchical institutions that helped attain them.

An Intergenerational Shift from Survival Values toward Self-expression Values

Throughout advanced industrial societies, the younger age cohorts emphasise self-expression values much more heavily than their elders do, in a pattern similar to that found with post-materialist values. As we have seen, given birth cohorts did not become more materialistic as they aged. This seems to hold true of the shift from survival to self-expression values as well, though we do not yet have a massive time series data base comparable to what is available with materialist/post-materialist values. But we do have evidence from five waves of the Values Surveys, carried out from 1981 to 2006. As Figure 5 demonstrates, from the start of this time series, younger birth cohorts have placed more emphasis on self-expression values than older cohorts did, and they did not move away from self-expression values toward survival values as they aged from 1980 to 2000. Throughout this period, younger birth cohorts continued to place more emphasis on self-expression values than older ones. And although each of the birth cohorts aged by 25 years during the period covered by the Values Surveys, none of them placed less emphasis on self-expression in 2006 than they did in 1981 – as would have happened if these age differences simply reflected life-cycle effects.

The inference that these age-related differences reflect intergenerational change rather than life-cycle differences gains further support from the fact that the populations of rich post-industrial societies show large

FIGURE 5
SELF-EXPRESSION VALUES BY BIRTH COHORT, 1981–2006

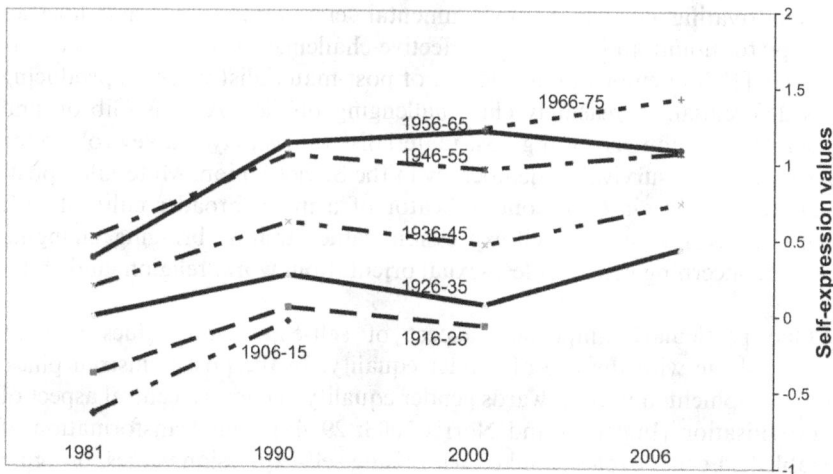

Note: Mean scores on self-expression values dimension combined data from France, Britain, W. Germany, Italy and Netherlands.

intergenerational differences, with the younger cohorts placing much stronger emphasis on self-expression values than do the older cohorts. But low income societies that have not experienced substantial economic growth during the past five decades do *not* display intergenerational differences – younger and older cohorts are about equally likely to display traditional values. This suggests that these intergenerational differences reflect historical changes, rather than anything inherent in the human life cycle.

The evidence suggests that major cultural changes are occurring through an intergenerational value shift linked with the fact that the younger birth cohorts have grown up under higher levels of existential security than those that shaped the formative years of the older cohorts.

The rise of post-materialism does not mean that materialistic issues and concerns will vanish. Conflicts about how to secure prosperity and sustainable economic development will always be important political issues. Nevertheless, if people's values are indeed shifting from survival to self-expression values, the implications are far-reaching. It implies that the main axis of political conflict should gradually shift from class-based issues such as income redistribution and state ownership of industry toward increasing emphasis on quality of life issues. As Inglehart (1971) predicted, social class voting has declined in most advanced industrial societies; in the last two US presidential elections, for example, the vote polarised much more strongly on life-style issues such as abortion and same-sex marriage than on social class, which had declined to the point where it had relatively little impact on voting.

The impact of changing values goes far beyond these changes in electoral behaviour. The central issues of political conflict have shifted, with the rise of environmentalist movements, the women's movement, gay liberation and other lifestyle movements. As Berry (1999) argues, post-materialist values are motivating consumer, environmental, civil rights, and civil liberties groups to mount an increasingly effective challenge to corporate power. As Nevitte (1996) demonstrates, the rise of post-materialist values is producing less deferential, increasingly elite-challenging publics. And as Gibson and Duch (1994) show, emerging post-materialist values played a key role in the emergence and survival of democracy in the Soviet Union. Materialist/post-materialist values are just one indicator of a much broader cultural shift from survival values to self-expression values that is bringing changing values concerning gender roles, sexual orientation, work, religion, and child-rearing.

One particularly important aspect of self-expression values is their close linkage with the rise of gender equality. In the post-industrial phase of development, a trend towards gender equality becomes a central aspect of modernisation (Inglehart and Norris 2003: 29–48). This transformation of established gender roles is linked with rising self-expression values, bringing increasing tolerance of human diversity and anti-discrimination movements on many fronts. Even today, women are confronted with societal disadvantages that make it more difficult for them than for men to develop their talents in careers outside the household. They have been socialised to accept these role limitations until very recently in history.

But history has recently taken a fundamentally new direction. In post-industrial societies, women no longer accept their traditional role limitations, and female empowerment has moved to a high place on the political agenda. Gender equality has become a central element in the definition of human development, for it is an essential aspect of human equality, like civil and political liberties and human rights. Never before in the history of civilisation have women enjoyed more equality and more freedom in choosing their education, their careers, their partners and their lifestyles than in contemporary post-industrial societies. This change is recent. Although it can be traced back to the introduction of female suffrage in some countries after World War I, female empowerment only recently became a pervasive trend. It is reflected in a massive tendency toward increasing female representation in national parliaments and in a shift towards gender equality that is closely linked with the rising emphasis on self-expression values.

The United Nations Development Programme has introduced a 'gender empowerment measure' that taps female representation in parliaments, in management positions and in administrative functions as well as gender equality in salaries. As Inglehart and Welzel (2005) have demonstrated, emphasis on self-expression values is strongly linked with the extent to which a given society actually approaches gender equality in political and social life (r = .85). Even more strikingly, as Inglehart and Welzel (2005) demonstrate, the shift toward self-expression values is conducive to good governance and the spread and flourishing of democratic institutions.

The intergenerational shift from survival values to self-expression values is contributing to substantial changes in West European publics' social and political orientations. It is linked with a shift toward rising support for gender equality, as Figure 6a demonstrates. In the 1990 Values Surveys, fully 34 per cent of the publics of France, Great Britain, West Germany, Italy and the Netherlands agreed with the proposition that 'When jobs are scarce, men have more right to a job than women'. A decade later, the proportion agreeing had fallen to 23 per cent and in 2006 it had dropped to 20 per cent. Similarly, in 1981, fully 44 per cent of these publics said that homosexuality is never justifiable – placing themselves at point 1 on a ten-point scale ranging from 'Never justifiable' to 'Always justifiable'. Twenty-five years later, in 2006, only 21 per cent still took this extreme position: the proportion viewing homosexuality as absolutely unacceptable was less than half what it had been in 1981. Intergenerational change is clearly not the only factor involved in these shifts, which do not move in a smooth linear fashion but are also affected by current conditions. Nevertheless, intergenerational population replacement seems to play a major role, and large intergenerational differences are present. For example, in the 1981

FIGURE 6
CHANGING ATTITUDES TOWARD (A) GENDER EQUALITY, 1990–2006, AND (B)
HOMOSEXUALITY, 1981–2006

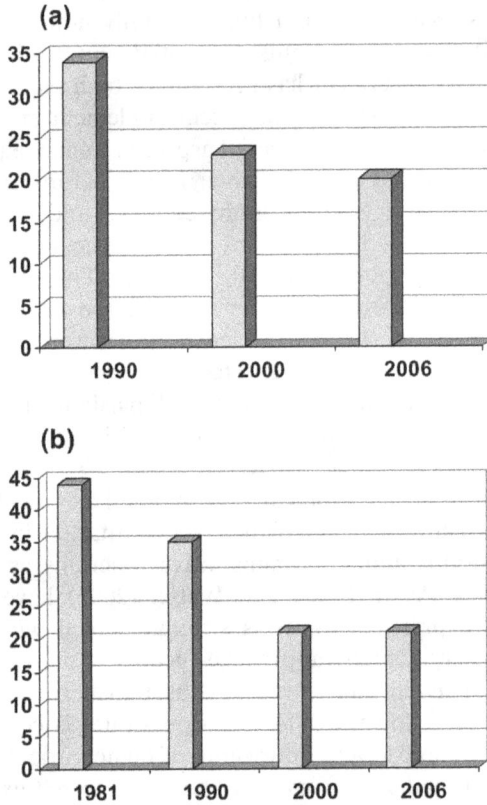

(a) (% agreeing that men have more right to a job than women among publics of France, Britain, W. Germany, Italy and Netherlands), (b) (% saying that homosexuality is 'never' justifiable among publics of France, Britain, W. Germany, Italy and Netherlands).

survey, among those 65 years and older fully 75 per cent of the respondents in these five countries agreed with the extreme position that homosexuality is never justifiable. Among those 18 to 24 years old less than half as many – only 34 per cent – took this position.

Conclusion

In 1971 it was hypothesised that intergenerational value changes were taking place. More than a generation has passed since then, and today it seems clear that the predicted changes have occurred. A large body of evidence, analysed using three different approaches – (1) cohort analysis; (2) comparisons of rich and poor countries; (3) examination of actual trends observed over the past 35 years – all points to the conclusion that major cultural changes are occurring, and that they reflect a process of intergenerational change linked with rising levels of existential security.

In the shift from materialist to post-materialist values, the massive differences between the values of young and old that were present in 1970 have dwindled. The birth cohorts born before World War II continue to place significantly more emphasis on materialist values than do the younger cohorts in Western Europe, but the post-war cohorts show relatively similar values. This means that intergenerational population replacement no longer exerts as strong a pressure towards post-materialist values as it once did. But with the broader survival/self-expression values dimension, large intergenerational value differences are still present, as Figure 5 demonstrates, which implies that West European publics will continue to show significant movement toward self-expression values as younger cohorts replace older ones in the adult population.

Intergenerational value change is not a uniquely West European phenomenon. It seems to occur whenever the formative experience of the younger birth cohorts are substantially different from those that shaped the older generations. In regard to both post-materialist values and self-expression values, a key factor is the extent to which a given generation grows up under conditions that permit it to take survival for granted. In Western Europe (together with North America, Japan and a few other countries), the economic miracles of the post-war era and the emergence of the welfare state contributed to long-term processes of inter-generational value change. There is no guarantee that other regions of the world will become prosperous, but the world as a whole is currently experiencing the highest rate of economic growth ever recorded. In so far as other countries attain high levels of existential security, the logic of value change developed here implies that they too will experience intergenerational shifts toward post-materialist and self-expression values.

Notes

1. The samples are weighted to reflect each country's population. Since the 2006 World Values Survey did not include Belgium, we used data from the 1999 Belgian survey in the pooled analysis. This tends to reduce the amount of change observed from 1999 to 2006, but the distortion is minimal since Belgium contains only 4 per cent of the population of the six countries.
2. For details on how these factor analyses were carried out, at both the individual and societal levels, see Inglehart and Baker (2000).

References

Berry, J.M. (1999). *New Liberalism: The Rising Power of Citizen Groups*. Washington, DC: The Brookings Institution.
Gibson, J., and R.M. Duch (1994). 'Postmaterialism and the Emerging Soviet Democracy', *Political Research Quarterly*, 47:1, 5–39.

Inglehart, R. (1971). 'The Silent Revolution in Europe: Intergenerational Change in Post-Industrial Societies', *American Political Science Review*, 65:4, 991–1017.

Inglehart, R. (1977). *The Silent Revolution: Changing Values and Political Styles among Western Publics*. Princeton, NJ: Princeton University Press.

Inglehart, R. (1990). *Culture Shift in Advanced Industrial Society*. Princeton, NJ: Princeton University Press.

Inglehart, R. (1997). *Modernization and Postmodernization: Cultural, Economic and Political Change in 43 Societies*. Princeton, NJ: Princeton University Press, 1997.

Inglehart, R., and W. Baker (2000). 'Modernization, Cultural Change and the Persistence of Traditional Values', *American Sociological Review*, February, 19–51.

Inglehart, R., and P. Norris (2003). *Rising Tide: Gender Equality in Global Perspective*. Cambridge: Cambridge University Press.

Inglehart, R., and C. Welzel (2005). *Modernization, Cultural Change and Democracy*. New York: Cambridge University Press.

Nevitte, N. (1996). *The Decline of Deference: Canadian Value Change in Cross-national Perspective*. Peterborough, Ont.: Broadview Press.

Rokeach, Milton (1968). *Beliefs, Attitudes and Values*. San Francisco: Jossey-Bass.

Rokeach, Milton (1973). *The Nature of Human Values*. New York: Free Press.

Political Mobilisation, Political Participation and the Power of the Vote

HANSPETER KRIESI

At the time when *West European Politics* was launched 30 years ago, a set of landmark studies was published that put the field of political participation on a new foundation. First, the 'Political Action' study by Barnes, Kaase and their co-authors (1979) extended the notion of political participation to include not only 'conventional' electoral or related forms of participation, but also 'unconventional' forms, i.e. different varieties of political protest. Since this path-breaking study, it has become common knowledge that unconventional, non-electoral forms of political participation have been on the rise in Western Europe.

The 'Political Action' study was a comparative analysis of political participation in five nations, but it had an individualistic bias and did not pay much attention to the political context of the different nations. It was another landmark study published by Verba, Nie and Kim in 1978 which explicitly took the mobilisation context into account. Verba and Nie (1972) had already studied the relationship between individual resources and political participation in the US, where they had found that political participation in various (conventional) forms increases considerably with individual resources. Applying the same model to a seven-country comparison, they were puzzled by the wide cross-national variation in the relationship between individual resources and political participation. In the search for a solution to this puzzle, they discovered the strength of institutions and group-level processes. Institutions, they found, can dominate political participation in two ways: they can dominate participation negatively by controlling and limiting access to channels of activity or positively by mobilising citizens. In countries like Austria and Japan, they identified some explicit basis for the mobilisation of lower status citizens to counteract the implicit bias built into a participatory system at the individual level. Negative institutional effects were pointed out by an influential contemporaneous theoretical piece by Offe and Wiesenthal (1979): according to the logic of collective action, they reasoned, the individually privileged also benefit at the level of group processes, since there are typically few of them, while the individually disadvantaged also suffer from the constraints imposed on large groups by the logic of collective action.

While these two studies have been very influential in the field of political participation, a third set of key studies from the days when *WEP* was first published has received much less attention from the specialists in political participation, although these works made a major contribution to the study of political protest. The reason is that these analyses were written in the field of social movement studies. They focused on the mobilisation of group resources (Gamson 1975; McCarthy and Zald 1977) and put these processes into their political context (Tilly *et al.* 1975; Tilly 1978; McAdam 1982). The crucial shortcoming of the classical model of social movements that these contributions put into sharp relief was not its individualistic bias, but its neglect of political mechanisms linking structural strain and individual reactions to such strain. Since the publication of this set of studies, the field of social movements has been dominated by what has come to be known as the 'political process approach', which accords prime importance to the organisational structure of aggrieved groups, their cognitive beliefs and frames, and the 'political opportunity structures' available to them (McAdam *et al.* 1996).

In spite of these developments 30 years ago, the study of political participation and social movement research have continued to lead somewhat separate lives, and, contrary to the social movement studies, the analysis of political participation, and especially that of electoral participation, continued to suffer from an individualistic bias. Mark Franklin (2004), whose important book analyses voter turnout in established democracies since 1945, starts out by criticising this bias in the current state of the art. Even the so-called mobilisation model (Rosenstone and Hansen 1993; Verba *et al.* 1995), he argues, focused on the individual and did not take into account the context of the election. Franklin distinguishes between institutional (electoral systems, policy consequences of elections), temporal or campaign-related (electoral competitiveness, size and nature of the stakes) and social (embeddedness in social networks) context elements and updates the calculus of voting on the basis of the kinds of information provided by the different types of contexts. In a similar vein, I propose a framework to recast our thinking about political participation, which focuses on what Franklin called the institutional and temporal or campaign-related aspects of the context of elections, and which makes an attempt to connect the study of electoral participation to the extended notion of political participation introduced by Barnes, Kaase *et al.* (1979) and by the social movement studies. This framework builds on a simple model of representative government and introduces some major changes that have modified its context over the last 30 years to set new conditions for conventional (electoral) and unconventional political participation.

The Institutional Context of Electoral Participation: Representative Government

It is a truism that, under modern conditions, government 'by the people' must for the most part be indirect, representative government. Elections of the political decision-makers at regular intervals constitute the key institution of this form of government (Manin 1995: 18; Powell 2000: 3). Such elections are instruments of democracy to the degree that they give the people influence over policy-making, i.e. to the degree that their representatives are *accountable* and *responsive* to the preferences of the citizens, considered as political equals (Dahl 1971: 1).

Individual representatives are usually members of collective actors, who organise the process of representation on their behalf. More specifically, with the extension of the suffrage, representative democracy has become party democracy, which means that the citizens have come to vote above all for a party and its agents instead of voting for individual personalities such as local notables. Parties have become the key intermediaries between citizens and government decisions, but they did not remain the only ones. Interest associations representing more specific preferences among the citizens have come to complement them, as have all sorts of social movement actors who also specialise in the articulation of specific interests. That is, the process of representation has become organised, and the collective actors and their agents who have come to control this process have become the key figures in democratic systems. Accordingly, Schattschneider (1975 [1960]: 138) defined democracy as 'a competitive political system in which competing leaders and organisations define the alternatives of public policy in such a way that the public can participate in the decision-making process...Conflict, competition, organisation, leadership, and responsibility are the ingredients of a working definition of democracy'. I shall call the individual agents of the collective actors who seek to control the democratic process 'the political elites'.

The citizens, in turn, constitute the mobilisation potential for the collective political actors who represent them in the political decision process. Each citizen individually controls a number of resources which may become available for a collective political actor. Mobilising these resources implies increasing the collective control over the individual resources; mobilisation is equivalent to the pooling of individual resources in the hands of a collective actor.[1] From the point of view of political mobilisation in a democratic regime, where elections constitute the decisive institution, the key resource of the citizen is his or her right to vote. In other words, mobilising in a democratic society, first of all, involves the mobilisation of electoral participation or the pooling of votes.

It is important to note that political mobilisation is not restricted to electoral campaigns, but takes place in between elections as well. Among other things, this has to do with the fact that, as Manin (1995) points out, it is the regular repetition of elections which constitutes the crucial mechanism allowing the voters in representative democracies to influence the decisions of those who govern. Based on this repetitive mechanism, the elected representatives are forced to take into account the retrospective (and, we should add, the prospective) judgement of the voters about the policies they have adopted. Repetition creates anticipatory pressure on elected representatives to take into consideration the preferences of the voters, which allows the voters to have an influence on their representatives on a daily basis. As Dick Morris (1999), a former political advisor to President Clinton, has observed, everyday is election day in the US today. In other words, voters do not make their choice of representatives between competing elites only once every so many years and then let their representatives govern, as suggested by Schumpeter's (1962 [1942]) 'realistic' theory of democracy, but they influence their representatives between elections, too. This means that, in the representative democracy, the elected officials have a strong incentive to adapt their decisions to the opinion of the mass public between elections.

This idea corresponds to Stimson *et al.*'s (1995) model of 'dynamic representation'. According to this model, at any given moment in time the elected politicians are highly responsive to the general mood in the population. According to this model, public opinion has a direct and an indirect effect on policy decisions (Figure 1): on the one hand, it influences policy decisions indirectly, by having an impact on the election outcome, which, in turn, leads to modifications in the policy decisions; on the other hand, it influences the policy decisions of the political authorities directly via their rational anticipations during a legislative period between elections.

In the model of 'dynamic representation', public opinion constitutes an exogenous factor. This implies, of course, a highly restricted view of what

FIGURE 1
THE MODEL OF DYNAMIC REPRESENTATION

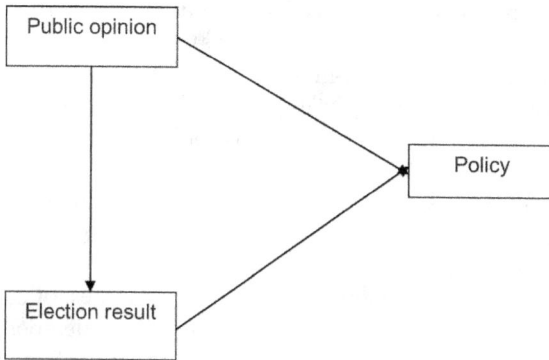

political mobilisation in a democracy is all about. In fact, in democratic systems the key issue for political actors is precisely to shape public opinion – on specific issues (and not with respect to the general mood, as suggested by Stimson's model). Public opinion is the product of the debate in the public sphere – a communication system involving a wide range of political actors. The public debate, its inclusiveness and its deliberative quality are essential for the quality of a democratic decision. This is Schattschneider's (1975 [1960]) view of democratic politics, for whom the expansion of conflict constitutes the essence of democracy. For Schattschneider, conflict is contagious and the larger the attentive public for a given conflict, the more democratic is the struggle in question.

Schattschneider's view corresponds to that of the agenda-setting approach (see Baumgartner and Jones 2002; Burstein 1998, 1999; Jones 1994). This approach distinguishes itself from traditional approaches to democratic representation by the fact that it does not focus on the representation of preferences, but on the information processing of citizens and decision-making authorities. It starts from the assumption that information is not a scarce good, but that the scarce factor is given by the attention to particular information. At any given moment, the attention of the public and the decision-makers can only be focused on a limited number of political problems. Both sides, however, are very sensitive with regard to new information. Viewed from the perspective of the agenda-setting approach, such information is always ambivalent, which is why the selection, presentation and interpretation of information by the media and the political elites plays a key role. There is always room for 'framing' of political problems. The processing of information, in other words, provides the baseline for the attention management of both the citizen-voters and the political elites.

Decision-makers are only one type of political actor involved in the struggle for the attention of the public. Any collective political actor may participate in this struggle – insiders (including government agencies, opposition parties and interest associations) as well as social movement actors challenging the decision-makers from the outside of the political system. Moreover, individual citizens may get involved as well – actors such as experts, writers of letters to the editor, or political entrepreneurs. Finally, the media become key political actors on their own, who are able to influence political decision-making processes by their presentation and selection activities, and, in rare instances, even as mobilising agents (Figure 2).

The extended model of dynamic representation implies, of course, that the political supply by the elite is crucial for the democratic process. Accordingly, the vote basically appears as a reaction of the citizens with regard to the terms proposed by the elite. This applies not only for representative forms of democracy, but, as I have tried to show (Kriesi 2005), for direct democratic procedures such as they exist in Switzerland as well. Given the crucial importance of the political supply, the key question with regard to the substantive orientation of the vote is to what extent it 'is largely not a genuine but a manufactured will', as Schumpeter (1942 [1962]) suggested in one of his devastating formulas a long time ago. The answer to this question largely depends on the quality of the debate in the public sphere, which, in turn, is a function of its inclusiveness, its openness to a

FIGURE 2
THE EXTENDED MODEL OF DYNAMIC REPRESENTATION

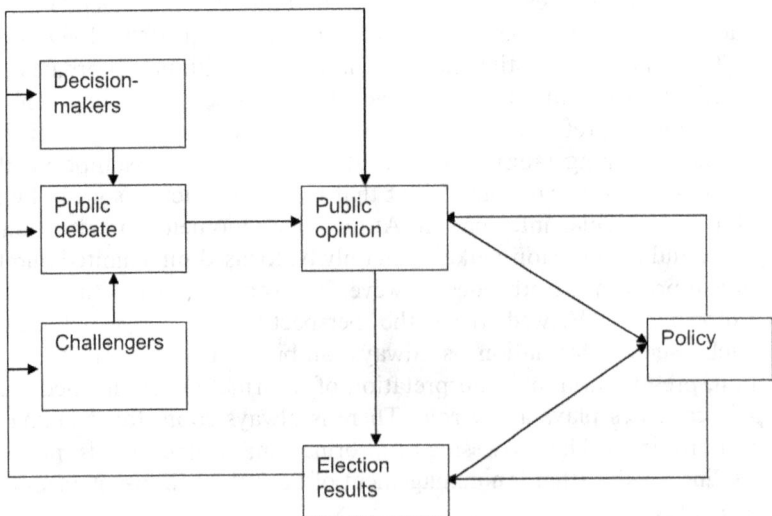

range of ideas and a range of styles of expression, as well as of its outcome (see Ferree *et al.* 2002: 205–31).

Implications for Electoral Participation

With regard to electoral participation, the modified and extended model of dynamic representation means that electoral participation essentially depends on the supply by the political elites. In other words, it essentially depends on the expansion of the scope of conflict by the political elite's mobilisation effort. The more intense the mobilisation effort by the elite, the larger the attentive public, the greater the potential electoral impact on the politicians, and the greater the electoral participation of the citizen public. As a corollary, the model implies that consensus makes for depoliticised, elitist politics. Citizens are not interested in political debates, where all participants agree. Thus, the ideological convergence of the mainstream parties to a centrist political position and their unresponsiveness to new political ideas (as in the Swiss all-party government, a case discussed in detail by Franklin 2004), the 'permissive consensus' at the level of European Union politics, and governments composed of technocrats all tend to reduce the scope of conflict, and, by implication, electoral participation.

In line with this approach, Franklin (1993) found 'electoral salience' to be the most potent factor for electoral turnout. A comparison of the turnout in European elections with that in the national elections of the European Union's member states confirms the importance of electoral salience (van der Eijk and Franklin 1996): in the 'secondary' European elections turnout is much lower than in corresponding national elections. In his more recent study, Franklin (2004: ch. 5) found that electoral competitiveness and long-term governmental responsiveness go a long way to explain turnout in 22 countries over the 1945–99 period. Both Franklin (2004) and Wattenberg (2002) confirm that voters vote when elections matter, and the recent falling turnout at national elections can to a large extent be explained by the fact that the elections involved are seen to count for less, particularly among the younger voters who then develop a habit of not voting. Whether elections matter, in turn, is to a large extent determined by elite mobilisation (electoral competitiveness), although it also depends on aspects of the institutional setting (such as government responsiveness or the electoral system). In a similar vein, I have been able to show (Kriesi 2005), that the citizens' participation in Swiss direct-democratic elections is largely a function of the intensity of the campaign preceding the vote, i.e. of the elite's mobilisation effort.

Intensive campaigns contribute both to the citizens' motivation and to their capacity to participate in the vote. They provide an incentive to participate by raising the stakes and they provide more information about the issues at stake. In addition, intensive campaigns increase the social pressure on the citizens: their personal environment urges them to vote in order to defend the common cause. Intensive campaigns also contribute to more normative and expressive motivations by reminding citizens of their duty to participate and providing them with occasions to reaffirm their identity as 'citizens', as 'partisans' of a good cause, or as 'patriots' (Pizzorno 1986: 353–4). Finally, intensive campaigns are also likely to contribute to the entertainment value of the vote. Just as taking sides for the 'home' team increases the thrill of a soccer match, taking sides by actively participating in the vote increases the thrill of finding out about its outcome.

The Increasing Role of the Media and the Decline of Party Control

So far, the reasoning presumed the continued existence of party democracy. But, according to the thesis defended by Manin (1995: 247–303), party democracy is on the decline and we witness a profound transformation of democratic systems of government today due to the greatly increased importance of the media-centred public sphere for democratic politics. According to Manin, after the classical parliamentarianism of the nineteenth century and the party democracy which was established at the beginning of the twentieth century, representative government currently takes the form of an audience democracy. The characteristics of this new form of government include the omnipresence of public opinion and the transfer of the political debate from the smoke-filled backrooms of parliamentary committees and the central offices of parties and associations to the public sphere. This leads to the transformation of both parties and political communication with important implications for the mobilisation of the vote. It also opens up new opportunities for the mobilisation of the public beyond electoral forms of participation.

Let us first look at the transformation of parties and political communication. On the one hand, party researchers have pointed to the rise of the 'catch-all party' (Kirchheimer 1966), the 'electoral professional party' (Panebianco 1988) or the 'cartel party' (Katz and Mair 1995). Central to each of these models is, among other aspects, the claim that the power of party leaders relative to that of members has been enhanced. On the other hand, media researchers noted that political communication is no longer party-centred but focused on the media, and they observed the increasing independence of the mass media from political parties (Hallin and Mancini 2004; Swanson and Mancini 1996). In the past, the European media systems had been closer to the world of politics than the North Atlantic systems but, under the impact of secularisation and commercialisation, they are shifting away from it and towards the world of commerce. Part of the parties' loss of control over the voters can be attributed to their loss of control over the media.

Commercial media create powerful new techniques of representation and audience creation. Two of the most important of these techniques are personalisation and the tendency to privilege the point of view of the 'ordinary citizen'. By highlighting the role of personalities, the media enhance the focus on party leaders and chief executives – a focus that is further reinforced by two additional structural changes in contemporary politics: the internationalisation of politics, which shifts power to the heads of governments, some of their ministers and key advisers, and the need for coordination of the institutional fragments of the state, which leads to the concentration of power in the hands of the core executive. This trend is not only observed in presidential systems, but also in parliamentary ones. Mény and Surel (2000: 111) speak of a growing 'de-parlamentarisation', i.e. a progressive erosion of the ties which linked the party and its leader in European democracies; Poguntke and Webb (2005) refer to this trend as the 'presidentialisation of politics in democratic societies' and they and their co-authors assemble strong evidence in support of a shift of power from organisational party power to individual power of chief executives and party leaders.

The increasing focus on the party leaders and chief executives, together with the tendency of the media to privilege the point of view of the ordinary citizen, gives rise to a relationship between voters and government that is unmediated by parties, i.e. to 'populist' forms of mobilisation within the channel of electoral participation (Mair 2002). Populism implies the mobilisation by charismatic personal leadership. Personalised leadership is a natural corollary of populism's reaction against politics-as-usual (Canovan 1999: 6). Accordingly, Mény and Surel (2000: 124) arrive at the conclusion that never before has charisma had as important a role as it has today, not only in politics, but also in economics and religion. At first sight, this trend reminds us of Max Weber's (1992: 44–9) vision of a 'plebiscitary democracy'. However, in Max Weber's view, which built on his observation of democratic politics in the early 1920s, the party leader was something of a 'plebiscitary dictator', because he was able to mobilise the masses by using the party apparatus (the 'party machine', including the foot soldiers of the regular party members). The contemporary party leader, by contrast, is able to mobilise the masses largely without the party apparatus, i.e. we are witnessing what Peter Mair has called the rise of a 'partyless democracy'.

The populist tendencies are rather likely to enhance the power of the vote: since the leaders and chief executives are no longer shielded by their parties, they directly depend on the voters' support for the implementation of their policies. By implication, other things being equal, the current populist tendencies can be expected to reinforce the stakes of elections, and, by implication, electoral participation.

Some other things tend to reinforce the effect of the populist tendencies. In party democracy, the vote was to a large extent not the result of an individual choice, but the expression of the voters belonging to a social category and of their corresponding social identity. The vote was under control of the party organisations and it was brought out by the party militants who canvassed their community. The loyalty of the voters reduced both party competition and the value of the vote for collective actors other than parties. By contrast, in the ideal-typical audience democracy, not only a much larger part of political action becomes public action, but a much larger part of public action escapes the control of the political organisations originally designed to mobilise the citizens as voters – the political parties (Kitschelt 2000). By increasing the role of the public sphere and by reducing the control over the vote by the political parties, the audience democracy increases the incentives for all kinds of political actors to directly appeal to the public and to mobilise it in order to influence the political process between elections.

The study by Barnes, Kaase *et al.* (1979) mainly attributed the expansion of the citizens' action repertoire to changing values in Western societies. Changing values, however, only provide the structural potential for the mobilisation by collective political actors. The changing role of the media and the declining control over the voters by the political parties provide the political opportunities for the mobilisation of this potential by a wide range of collective political actors, in particular for those actors, such as social movement organisations, who do not have regular access to the parliamentary or administrative decision-making arenas.

The direct mobilisation of the public by challengers gives rise to unconventional forms of political participation. Based on individual-level data about participation in modes of political action beyond voting, Topf (1995: 78) 'unequivocally' confirmed the thesis of a participatory revolution. In several countries, such as Britain, Norway, and Sweden, he found that 'well over two-thirds of their electorates are now participants in some mode or other of what, but recently, was labelled unconventional activity'. Studies of protest events by social movement scholars also show that – especially under the impact of the mobilisation by the so-called 'new social movements' – the number of protest events has considerably increased since the late 1960s in countries such as Switzerland (Kriesi *et al.* 1981), Germany (Rucht 1998, 2003) or the Netherlands (Koopmans 1996). As far as the number of participants is concerned, the results of these studies are, however, somewhat less clear-cut: in the German case, for example, in terms of protest participation, the 1950s surprisingly exceeded the mobilisation of the 1960s and 1970s (but not of the early 1980s and 1990s). The 1950s were dominated by relatively few but large protests, whereas the opposite holds for the later periods under study (Rucht 1998: 52). Koopmans (1996), who complements his longitudinal analysis of the Netherlands with a cross-sectional comparison of six Western European countries, concludes that the rise of the new social movements is as much reflected in the growth of conventional as in the growth of unconventional participation. Surveying the whole of the twentieth century, he suggests that the balance between the two forms of participation even seems to have shifted from unconventional to conventional participation.

What seems to have happened is that in the process of modernisation the new social movements have professionalised and institutionalised, the membership in the new associations that sprung from them has increased tremendously, and their repertoire of action has become more moderate (Koopmans 1996; Kriesi 1996). Accordingly, by the early 2000s non-electoral political participation in Western Europe most likely takes the form of donating money (i.e. 'check-book' activism), signing petitions, or of 'deliberately buying certain products for political, ethical or environmental reasons' (Teorell *et al.* 2007: 340). Social movement scholars summarise these trends by the term of the 'movement society' (Meyer and Tarrow 1998) – a term which serves to suggest that political protest has become an integral part of modern life; that protest behaviour is employed with greater frequency, by more diverse constituencies, and is used to represent a wider range of claims than ever before; and that professionalisation and institutionalisation may be changing the social movement into an instrument of conventional politics. As protest becomes a part of everyday politics, we assist at the 'normalization of the unconventional' (Fuchs 1991). At the same time, social movement organisations become rather like interest groups. Paradoxically, as unconventional forms of participation become increasingly accepted and political systems become more open to unconventional forms of mobilisation, these forms are likely to become more moderate and less prominent.

Finally, it is important to note that, ultimately, the effectiveness of mobilising the public in non-electoral forms of political participation tends to depend on the potential impact of the vote as well. In line with the extended model of dynamic representation, collective political actors such as social movements who resort to non-electoral forms of political mobilisation make an attempt to influence elected decision-makers indirectly, by attracting the attention of the public and increasing the public pressure on them. If the pressure is strong enough, elected representatives respond, because they anticipate the reaction of the citizen public at the next elections.

The Decreasing Electoral Accountability of Political Decision-makers

There are a number of contemporary institutional changes that reduce the electoral accountability of political decision-makers, i.e. which reduce the power of the vote, and, by implication, electoral participation. Policy-making takes place in policy subsystems which lack visibility and formal codification, and enjoy increasing autonomy. In combination with the increasing complexity of policy-making, these governance arrangements tend, as Papadopoulos (2002) has observed, to impede accountability regardless of whether or not incumbents behave responsively. Second, collectively binding decisions are to a growing extent also taken by courts or independent regulatory authorities such as central banks or regulatory boards. Judicialisation and delegation are both aspects of a continuing expansion of what Mény (2002) has called the 'constitutionalist element of democracy', inherited from the liberal approach to government, at the detriment of its popular element. All these tendencies limit the obligations of the incumbents to report on their acts and the possibilities of the voters to respond with electoral sanctions.

Third, collectively binding decisions are also made by supranational or international bodies composed of members who have either not been elected or who are at best indirectly legitimated by elections. The vote is territorially bound. Most importantly, voting power is bound to the nation-state and its subunits. As a voter, the citizen is 'locked in' (Bartolini 2005). Back in the 1960s, Schattschneider had considered the regional limitation of conflict in the US and compared it to the expansion of conflict to the national level. Such a nationalisation of conflict reinforced the power of the vote and was, as is well known, of crucial importance for the success of the civil rights movement (e.g. McAdam 1982): with the expansion of the racial conflict to the national level, the civil rights movement benefited crucially from the voting power of the black population outside of the South.

By contrast, the transnational expansion of conflict is constrained by the fact that voting power is limited to the nation-state. It is of course true that, in the particular case of the multi-level systems of governance of the EU, citizens have the right to vote in European elections, and that they also have an indirect impact on the supranational decision-makers via their national executives. However, as already pointed out, European elections are 'secondary elections' which are not really about representation at the European level (van der Eijk and Franklin 1996), nor are national electoral contests about the content or direction of EU policy (Mair 2000). European mainstream politicians have effectively organised EU issues out of the national political contests. As Follesdal and Hix (2005) argue, there is no electoral contest about the leadership at the European level or the basic direction of the EU policy agenda. In fact, as decision-making authority shifts to the EU level, there is an increasing lack of political accountability in the multi-level system of governance, which implies the devaluation of the individual citizen's voting resources.

The Mobilisation of Voice to Overcome the Declining Power of the Vote

The weakening of the value of the vote for the individual citizen and the declining power of the vote in democratic decision-making at the aggregate level have ambiguous implications for electoral participation. On the one hand, these trends reinforce the populist tendencies already described above. Populism is the indication of a democratic malaise that political actors and citizens would do well to take seriously (Mény and Surel 2002: 21). In this case, however, we are dealing with populism not in the sense of 'partyless politics', but in the sense of 'protest politics' (for the distinction of the two types of populism, see Mair 2002). Populist collective actors attempt to 'bring the voters back in', i.e. they mobilise the voters in the electoral channel in the name of the redemptive face of democracy. As is observed by Mény and Surel (2002: 11f.), the common denominator of populist movements puts an emphasis on the fundamental role of the people, claims that the people have been betrayed by those in charge, i.e. the elites are accused of abusing their position of power, and that the primacy of the people has to be restored. Populism is, as Taggart (2002: 67) has pointed out, hostile to representative politics and pleads for a more direct linkage of masses to elites. Ironically, however, populism expresses itself in the electoral channel of representative politics and in the way they mobilise, as already observed, populists often rely on charismatic leadership or at least on centralised political structures.

But it would be a mistake to view this populist challenge simply in terms of protest politics. As we have argued on the basis of a comparison of the transformation of six Western European party systems (Kriesi *et al.* 2006), the new populist parties of the radical right (or their functional equivalents of transformed mainstream parties) have become the driving force of this transformation by giving voice to the various groups of losers of the current processes of 'denationalisation' or 'globalisation'. They articulate the resistance against the opening up of the national borders mostly, but not exclusively, in terms of resistance against European integration or resistance against immigrants. As van der Eijk and Franklin (2004) have observed, European integration constitutes a political potential waiting out there to be mobilised by some political entrepreneur. If the mainstream parties in most countries have so far tried to shut out the issue from the national political contests, it has been taken up by more peripheral challengers. In Switzerland and the UK it has already become a key issue for mainstream parties and for the national political contest. In these two countries, the question of national sovereignty, which includes the question of national voting rights, is at the origin of widespread Euroscepticism (Kriesi 2007). Similarly, the French referendum on the EU Constitution in spring 2005 'was first and foremost a retrospective vote on the process of European integration itself, and the unilateral termination by a majority of voters of the "social welfare and economic growth" confidence pact that they had made with their national political elites on the occasion of the Maastricht Treaty referendum in 1992' (Ivaldi 2006: 49).

The French and Dutch referendums on the EU Constitution illustrate an additional point: the availability of direct-democratic institutions to vote on key issues reinforces the power of the vote and, accordingly, political participation in terms of voting. Thus, the participation rate in the French referendum on the European Constitution was 69.3 per cent, very similar to that of the 1992 referendum on the Maastricht Treaty (69.7 per cent), just below that of the first round of the 2002 presidential election (71.6 per cent), but much higher than turnout in the June 2004 European election in France

(42.8 per cent, in sharp decline since the first European ballot in 1979 where turnout reached 60.7 per cent) (Ivaldi 2006). Except for Ireland, the participation in referendums on European integration has been much higher than participation in the closest elections to the European parliament in all the countries where such referendums have been held.[2]

On the other hand, the citizens who perceive the declining value of the vote individually tend to take the exit option. To the extent that citizens exit from elections, the redemptive face of democracy is weakened. As Canovan (1999: 11) notes, elections are 'rituals of democratic renewal, and unless that ritual is taken seriously by a substantial proportion of voters and politicians, democratic institutions are weakened'. To the extent that citizens no longer participate in elections, the legitimacy of democratic decisions is reduced. The potential impact of citizens increasingly exiting from the electoral channel is compounded by the fact that the vote is tied to citizenship. The contemporary international migration leads to an increasing share of the local residents in any nation-state who do not have the right to vote.

Combined, the exclusion of the non-citizens and the exit of the disappointed or alienated citizens implies that, for relatively small minorities of highly motivated citizens, the value of the vote may, in fact, increase. They may use their voice and take advantage of the participatory opportunities provided by the exit of the many. Such minorities may be, as Fiorina (1999) fears, extreme voices who have less reason to moderate their commitments than in the past. In other words, paradoxically, as more of the citizens get disillusioned and increasing numbers of residents do not have the right to vote, the redemptive promise for power can be realised by small groups of people who believe in the continued power of the vote.

As far as non-electoral, unconventional forms of participation are concerned, the consequences of the weakening power of the vote are also ambiguous. On the one hand, collective political actors react to the weakening of the power of the vote by choosing to mobilise citizens in non-electoral forms to voice their concern. In other words, in addition to the 'pull' of the opportunities provided by the new media-centred forms of political communication, the 'push' of the declining power of the vote provides an incentive for collective actors to resort to the mobilisation of unconventional forms of participation. Piven and Cloward (1977) have noted the inverse relationship between the power of the vote and more radical forms of political protest a long time ago. As they observed, 'ordinarily, defiance is first expressed in the voting booth simply because, whether defiant or not, people have been socialised within a political culture that defines voting as the mechanism through which political change can and should properly occur' (Piven and Cloward 1977: 15). Accordingly, one of the first signs of popular discontent is sharp shifts in the voting patterns. Citizens only have recourse to more radical action forms when their vote has no impact.

The inverse relationship between voting and more unconventional forms of political mobilisation is illustrated by two studies of the action repertoires of social movements in Western Europe. In a comparative analysis of new social movements in four Western European countries (France, Germany, Netherlands, Switzerland), we have been able to demonstrate that the availability of direct democratic instruments has led to a very high aggregate level of mobilisation and a very moderate action repertoire of the social movement sector in Switzerland (Kriesi *et al.* 1995). In other words, the Swiss citizens put pressure on government mainly through direct-democratic campaigns, petitioning, and to some extent moderate unconventional forms like demonstrations. By contrast, the strong, exclusive French state, which provides little access to citizens beyond elections, is associated with protest characteristics diametrically opposed to those of the Swiss movements – the overall level of mobilisation is lower, but participation is heavily concentrated in rather radical unconventional forms. The importance of the availability and the institutional structuring of the voting resource for determining the actions of challengers is further illustrated by the analysis of the claims-making by migrants in five Western European countries (the four already mentioned, plus the UK) (Koopmans *et al.* 2005: 136f.). As this study shows, migrants face particularly unfavourable political conditions for the expression of their demands in Switzerland – the very same country that accords particularly favourable conditions to its own citizens. Accordingly, migrants' claims-making in Switzerland turns out to be characterised by a greater degree of radicalism than in the other four countries.

By mobilising in more radical forms of protest, collective political actors may not only attempt to mobilise public opinion in order to generate a response from policy-makers, as is suggested by the extended model of dynamic representation. In the less favourable circumstances of closed political systems they may also try to force political concessions from political elites by creating a crisis through massive use of disruption (Keeler 1993). A crisis can create a sense of urgency predicated on the assumption that already serious problems will be exacerbated by inaction. In addition, a crisis can create a sense of genuine fear predicated on the assumption that inaction may endanger lives and property or even result in a revolution or coup d'état. When either of these mechanisms comes into play, the government may feel propelled to adopt reform measures, and the opposition may be too intimidated to resist or may even feel compelled to lend reluctant support to the government. As Keeler (1993: 442) observes, this dynamic explains why 'some of the most radical innovations within democratic systems have been unanimously approved by the legislature'. Such reforms may, however, be turned back when the sense of crisis recedes. Examples of radical reforms introduced under great pressure by disruptive political action include the adoption of the New Deal (Jenkins and Brents 1989) and the civil rights reforms in the US (Haines 1989) as well as May 1968 and the *Loi d'Orientation* in France (Tarrow 1993).

But unconventional political participation is not only enhanced by the weakening of the vote. There is also a sort of 'exit option' for non-electoral, unconventional forms of political participation – an option that implies a shift with respect to the targets of the mobilisation effort away from political authorities. The weakening of the power of the vote is likely to incite collective political actors to shift the targets of their mobilisation efforts from political authorities to other types of actors. Alternative possibilities include litigation in courts and the mobilisation of consumer or investor power. Both of these alternatives have the advantage that, in contrast to electoral and the staple of unconventional forms of participation, they are not territorially bound. As consumers, investors, or legal litigators, citizens are less and less tied to the national boundaries and have ever more exit possibilities. As the national boundaries open up, we may, therefore, expect the collective political actors to increasingly mobilise individual resources which are less territorially bound than the vote.

As far as litigation in courts is concerned, Kolb (2007: 86) points out that courts can act in the face of public opposition because they are free from electoral accountability:

> In contrast to the normal policy making process, access to and influence in the court system is not dependent on connections or social and economic position, but on the strength of legal arguments.

In addition, judicial decisions can have important extra-judicial effects – such as creating publicity or increasing the bargaining power of social movements. Relying on courts for imposing reforms is, however, severely limited by the bounded nature of constitutional rights and by the fact that the judiciary is appointed by the other branches of government. Kolb argues that, in the case of the anti-nuclear movement, the bounded nature of rights dramatically curtailed the impact of its litigation in France, while the movement obtained temporary successes in German courts, which contributed to the slowing down of the construction process of nuclear power plants.

Among the resources that are less territorially bound, consumer purchasing power is a prime candidate for future political mobilisation. Beck (2002: 28) maintains that consumer protests are transnational as such: 'The consumers' society is the real existing world society.' Consumption knows no borders. As Beck also notes, however, the effective mobilisation of consumers depends on some constraining conditions. First, the bite of consumer protest depends on the purchasing power of the public. Without money, consumers cannot have an impact. One might add that their money can only make a difference when consumers have an alternative on the market, i.e. monopolists are hardly vulnerable to consumer power. Second, consumers are notoriously difficult to organise. This means that their mobilisation has to rely almost exclusively on the expansion of the attentive public via the media. So far, only relatively few corporate practices or policies – either positive or negative – have attracted significant public attention (Vogel 2005: 52). Finally, consumer power is also limited by considerations of costs: socially responsible products may be more expensive than their alternatives. This is certainly an important reason why there is a major gap between what consumers say they would do and their actual behaviour.

Capital is, of course, the quintessential mobile resource. At first sight, the mobilisation of citizens as investors does not seem like a very promising proposition. There is, however, a new type of collective political actor who attempts to do just that – socially responsible investment funds. These kinds of funds provide an efficient mechanism for investors to vote their values in the marketplace. In the US there are 200 social funds and in recent years the amount invested in them has grown substantially (Vogel 2005: 60). But the phenomenon of socially responsible investment is still of marginal importance. Remarkably few firms have been rewarded or punished by the financial markets for their social performance. Nonetheless, many firms act as if corporate social responsibility matters. For a few firms this appears to make business sense. It is a way for them to differentiate themselves from their competitors. A second category of firms are those that have been targeted by activists or who are concerned that they could be targeted, largely because of the visibility of their brands. As pointed out by Vogel (2005: 166), there are inherent limits for corporate social responsibility (CSR), however: if companies were to become more virtuous, the costs of CSR would become much more decisive. Most importantly, Vogel comes to the conclusion that CSR is not a substitute for effective government.

Conclusion

The approach to political participation adopted here insists on the role of collective actors and their agents – the political elites – in the democratic process. An updated version of competitive elitism, it makes an attempt to develop this theory by enriching it with insights from the theories of Schattschneider (1975) and Manin (1995), from agenda-setting theory, social movement research, and from empirical studies of the democratic process and alternative forms of mobilisation. At the core of this approach is the relationship between, on the one hand, the citizens with their equal right to vote in elections and their freedom to form an independent judgement about the representatives who govern in their name, and, on the other hand, the collective political actors and their agents who mobilise them in election campaigns as well as between elections in order to influence the decision-making process. From the point of view of the mobilising collective political actors and their agents, the citizens constitute various mobilising potentials which are supposed to react to their political supply and which they attempt to control as much as possible. From the point of view of the citizens, their representatives constitute agents whom they expect to exert political influence in their name. With regard to electoral participation, this approach implies that turnout essentially depends on the expansion of the scope of conflict by the political elites' mobilisation effort. The more intense this effort, the larger the attentive public, the greater the potential electoral impact on the politicians, and the greater the electoral participation of the citizens. A great deal of empirical evidence supports this claim.

Since mobilisation-related contextual factors are crucial determinants of electoral participation, the changing conditions of political campaigning and mobilisation linked to the rise of the audience democracy have important implications for the mobilisation of both electoral and non-electoral participation. The tendency towards 'partyless' populist forms of mobilisation within the electoral channel and the decreasing loyalty of the voters to their parties are likely to enhance the power of the vote and, by implication, electoral participation. The new opportunities for influencing the political process between elections give rise to increasing participation in non-electoral forms. It is important to note, however, that, paradoxically, the 'normalization of the unconventional' may above all mean that unconventional participation becomes more moderate and, possibly, even less prominent. Moreover, it is also important to keep in mind that, except for highly disruptive forms of mobilisation, the effectiveness of mobilising such non-electoral forms of political participation tends to depend, indirectly, on the power of the vote as well.

While the trends related to audience democracy tend to provide a campaign-related context which is rather favourable to both electoral and non-electoral forms of participation, a set of institutional changes, which reduce the accountability of political decision-makers and weaken the power of the vote, is expected to have more ambiguous consequences for both electoral and non-electoral forms of political participation. As far as electoral participation is concerned, it is reinforced by populist tendencies to 'bring the voters back in', but weakened by various forms of exit. Paradoxically, the latter may provide opportunities for the voice of small, intensive minorities in the electoral channel. Concerning non-electoral participation, given the weakening of the vote, collective political actors are expected to increasingly mobilise citizens in such forms, but they may do so with regard to targets outside of the realm of politics.

Notes

1. This definition comes from Amitai Etzioni (1968) and is approvingly cited by Charles Tilly (1978: 69).
2. Source: C2D-Centre d'études et de documentation sur la démocratie directe, Université de Genève, for turnout in referendums on Europe, EurActiv.com for turnout in elections to the European parliament.

References

Barnes, Samuel H., Max Kaase et al. (1979). *Political Action: Mass Participation in Five Western Democracies*. London: Sage.

Bartolini, Stefano (2005). *Restructuring Europe*. Oxford: Oxford University Press.

Baumann, Zygmunt (1998). *Globalization: The Human Consequences*. Cambridge: Polity Press.

Baumgartner, Frank R., and Bryan D. Jones (2002). 'Positive and Negative Feedback in Politics', in Frank R. Baumgartner and Bryan D. Jones (eds.), *Policy Dynamics*. Chicago: The University of Chicago Press, 3–28.

Beck, Ulrich (2002). *Macht und Gegenmacht im globalen Zeitalter. Neue werltpolitische Ökonomie*. Frankfurt: Suhrkamp.

Burstein, Paul (1998). *Discrimination, Jobs, and Politics. The Struggle for Equal Employment Opportunity in the United States since the New Deal. With a New Introduction*. Chicago: The University of Chicago Press.

Burstein, Paul (1999). 'Social Movements and Public Policy', in Marco Giugni, Doug McAdam and Charles Tilly (eds.), *How Social Movements Matter*. Minneapolis: University of Minnesota Press, 3–21.

Burstein, Paul (2002). 'The Impact of Public Opinion on Public Policy: A Review and an Agenda', *Political Research Quarterly*, 56:1, 29–40.

Canovan, Margaret (1999). 'Trust the People! Populism and the Two Faces of Democracy', *Political Studies*, 47, 2–16.

Dahl, Robert A. (1971). *Polyarchy: Participation and Opposition*. New Haven, CT: Yale University Press.

Etzioni, Amitai (1968). *The Active Society*. New York: The Free Press.

Ferree, Myra Marx, William A. Gamson, Jürgen Gerhards and Dieter Rucht (2002). *Shaping Abortion Discourse. Democracy and the Public sphere in Germany and the United States*. Cambridge: Cambridge University Press.

Fiorina, Morris P. (1999). 'Extreme Voices: A Dark Side of Civic Engagement', in Theda Skocpol and Morris P. Fiorina (eds.), *Civic Engagement in American Democracy*. Washington, DC: Brookings Institution Press.

Follesdal, Andreas, and Simon Hix (2006). Why there is a Democratic Deficit in the EU: A Response to Majone and Moravcsik', *Journal of Common Market Studies*, 44, 533–62.

Franklin, Mark N. (1993). 'Electoral Participation', in Lawrence LeDuc, Richard Niemi and Pippa Norris (eds.), *Comparing Democracies. Elections and Voting in Global Perspective*. London: Sage, 216–35.

Franklin, Mark N. (2004). *Voter Turnout and the Dynamics of Electoral Competition in Established Democracies Since 1945*. Cambridge: Cambridge University Press.

Fuchs, Dieter (1991). 'The Normalization of the Unconventional: New Forms of Political Action and New Social Movements', in Gerd Meyer and Frantisek Ryszka (eds.), *Political Participation and Democracy in Poland and West Germany*. Warsaw: Wydaeca, 148–69.

Gamson, William A. (1975). *The Strategy of Social Protest*. Homewood, IL: Dorsey Press.

Habermas, Jürgen (1992). *Faktizität und Geltung*. Frankfurt: Suhrkamp.

Haines, Herbert H. (1989). *Black Radicals and the Civil Rights Mainstream, 1954–1970*. Knoxville: University of Tennessee Press.

Hallin, Daniel C., and Paolo Mancini (2004). *Comparing Media Systems. Three Models of Media and Politics*. Cambridge: Cambridge University Press.

Ivaldi, Gilles (2006). 'Beyond France's 2005 Referendum on the European Constitutional Treaty: Second-order Model, Anti-establishment Attitudes and the End of the Alternative European Utopia', *West European Politics*, 29:1, 47–69.

Jenkins, Craig J., and Barbara G. Brents (1989). 'Social Protest, Hegemonic Competition, and Social Reform: A Political Struggle Interpretation of the Origins of the American Welfare State', *American Sociological Review*, 54, 891–909.

Jones, Bryan D. (1994). *Reconceiving Decision-making in Democratic Politics: Attention, Choice, and Public Policy*. Chicago: Chicago University Press.

Katz, Richard S., and Peter Mair (1995). 'Changing Models of Party Organization and Party Democracy: The Emergence of the Cartel Party', *Party Politics*, 1:1, 5–28.

Keeler, John T.S. (1993). 'Opening the Window for Reform. Mandates, Crises, and Extraordinary Policy-making', *Comparative Political Studies*, 25:4, 433–86.

Kirchheimer, Otto (1966). 'The Transformation of the Western European Party Systems', in Joseph La PaLombara and Myron Weiner (eds.), *Political Parties and Political Development*. Princeton, NJ: Princeton University Press, 177–200.

Kitschelt, Herbert (2000). 'Citizens, Politicians, and Party Cartellization: Political Representation and State Failure in Post-Industrial Democracies', *European Journal of Political Research*, 37:2, 149–79.

Kolb, Felix (2007). *Protest and Opportunities. The Political Outcomes of Social Movements*. Frankfurt: Campus.

Koopmans, Ruud (1996). 'New Social Movements and Changes in Political Participation in Western Europe', *West European Politics*, 19:1, 28–50.

Koopmans, Ruud, Paul Statham, Marco Giugni and Florence Passy (2005). *Contested Citizenship. Immigration and Cultural Diversity in Europe*. Minneapolis: University of Minnesota Press.

Kriesi, Hanspeter (1996). 'The Organizational Structure of New Social Movements in a political context', in D. McAdam, J.D. McCarthy and M.N. Zald (eds.), *Comparative Perspectives on Social Movements*. Cambridge: Cambridge University Press, 152–84.

Kriesi, Hanspeter (2005). *Direct Democratic Choice. The Swiss Experience*. Lanham, MD: Lexington Press.

Kriesi, Hanspeter (2007). 'The Role of European Integration in National Election Campaigns', *European Union Politics*, 8:1, 83–108.

Kriesi, Hanspeter, René Levy, Gilbert Ganguillet, and Heinz Zwicky, eds. (1981). *Politische Aktivität in der Schweiz, 1945–1978*. Diessenhofen: Rüegger.

Kriesi, Hanspeter, Ruud Koopmans, Jan Willem Duyvendak and Marco Giugni (1995). *New Social Movements in Western Europe. A Comparative Analysis*. Minneapolis: University of Minnesota Press.

Kriesi, Hanspeter, Edgar Grande, Romain Lachat, Martin Dolezal, Simon Bornschier and Tim Frey (2006). 'Transformation of the National Political Space. Western European Politics in the Age of Denationalization', *European Journal of Political Research*, 45:6, 921–57.

Mair, Peter (2000). 'The Limited Impact of Europe on National Party Systems', *West European Politics*, 23:4, 27–51.

Mair, Peter (2002). 'Populist Democracy vs Party Democracy', in Yves Mény and Yves Surel (eds.), *Democracies and the Populist Challenge*. Basingstoke: Palgrave, 81–98.

Manin, Bernard (1995). *Principes du gouvernement représentatif*. Paris: Flammarion.

McAdam, Doug (1982). *Political Process and the Development of Black Insurgency, 1930–1970*. Chicago: University of Chicago Press.

McAdam, Doug, John D. McCarthy, and Mayer N. Zald, eds. (1996). *Comparative Perspectives on Social Movements. Political Opportunities, Mobilizing Structures, and Cultural Framings*. Cambridge: Cambridge University Press.

McCarthy, John D., and Mayer N. Zald (1977). 'Resource Mobilization and Social Movements: A Partial Theory', *American Journal of Sociology*, 82:6, 1212–41.

McCarthy, John D., Clark McPhail and Jackie Smith (1996). 'Images of Protest: Dimensions of Selection Bias in Media Coverage of Washington Demonstrations, 1982 and 1991', *American Sociological Review*, 61:3, 478–99.

Mény, Yves, and Yves Surel (2000). *Par le peuple, pour le peuple. Le populisme et les démocraties*. Paris: Fayard.

Mény, Yves (2002). 'De la démocratie en Europe: Old Concepts and New Challenges', *Journal of Common Market Studies*, 41, 1–13.

Mény, Yves, and Yves Surel (2002). 'The Constitutive Ambiguity of Populism', in Yves Mény and Yves Surel (eds.), *Democracies and the Populist Challenge*. Basingstoke: Palgrave, 1–21.

Meyer, David S., and Sidney Tarrow (1998). 'A Movement Society: Contentious Politics for a New Century', in David S. Meyer and Sidney Tarrow (eds.), *The Social Movement Society*. Lanham, MD: Rowman & Littlefield, 1–28.

Morris, Dick (1999). *The New Prince. Machiavelli Updated for the Twenty-first Century*. Los Angeles: Renaissance Books.

Offe, Claus, and Helmut Wiesenthal (1979). 'Two Logics of Collective Action', *Political Power and Social Theory*, Vol. I, 67–115.

Panebianco, Angelo (1988). *Political Parties: Organization and Power*. Cambridge: Cambridge University Press.

Papadopoulos, Yannis (2002). 'Populism, the Democratic Question, and Contemporary Governance', in Yves Mény and Yves Surel (eds.), *Democracies and the Populist Challenge*. Basingstoke: Palgrave, 45–61.

Piven, Francis Fox, and Richard A. Cloward (1977). *Poor People's Movements. Why They Succeed, How They Fail*. New York: Vintage Books.

Pizzorno, Alessandro (1986). 'Sur la rationnalité du choix démocratique', in Pierre Birnbaum and Jean Leca (eds.), *Sur l'individualisme'*. Paris: Presses de la Fondation nationale des sciences politiques, 330–70.

Poguntke, Thomas, and Webb Paul, eds. (2005). *The Presidentialization of Politics: A Comparative Study of Modern Democracies*. Oxford: Oxford University Press.

Powell, G. Bingham, Jr. (2000). *Elections as Instruments of Democracy. Majoritarian and proportional visions*. New Haven, CT: Yale University Press.

Rosenstone, Steven J., and John Mark Hansen (1993). *Mobilization, Participation, and Democracy in America*. New York: Macmillan.

Rucht, Dieter (1998). 'The Structure and Culture of Collective Protest in Germany since 1950', in David S. Meyer and Sidney Tarrow (eds.), *The Social Movement Society*. Lanham, MD: Rowman & Littlefield, 29–58.

Rucht, Dieter (2003). 'The Changing Role of Political Protest Movements', *West European Politics*, 26:4, 153–76.

Schattschneider, E.E. (1975 [1960]). *The Semisovereign People*. New York: Wadsworth Thomson Learning.

Schumpeter, Joseph A. (1962 [1942]). *Capitalism, Socialism and Democracy*. London: Allen & Unwin.

Soule, Sarah A., and Susan Olzak (2004). 'When do Movements Matter? The Politics of Contingency and the Equal Rights Amendment', *American Sociological Review*, 69:4, 473–98.

Stimson, James A., Michael B. MackKuen and Robert S. Erikson (1995). 'Dynamic Representation', *American Political Science Review*, 89:3, 543–65.

Swanson, David L., and Paolo Mancini (1996). 'Patterns of Modern Electoral Campaigning and their Consequences', in David L. Swanson und Paolo Mancini (eds.), *Politics, Media, and Modern Democracy. An International Study of Innovations in Electoral Campaigning and their Consequences*. London:Praeger, 247–76.

Taggart, Paul (2002). 'Populism and the Pathology of Representative Politics', in Yves Mény and Yves Surel (eds.), *Democracies and the Populist Challenge*. Basingstoke: Palgrave, 61–80.

Tarrow, Sidney (1993). 'Social Protest and Policy Reform: May 1968 and the Loi d'Orientatoin in France', *Comparative Political Studies*, 25:4, 579–607.

Teorell, Jan, Mariano Torcal and José Ramón Montéro (2007). 'Political Participation: Mapping the Terrain', in Jan W. van Deth, José Ramón Montéro and Anders Westholm (eds.), *Citizenship and Involvement in European Democracies. A Comparative Analysis*. London: Routledge, 334–57.

Tilly, Charles (1978). *From Mobilization to Revolution*. Reading, MA: Addison-Wesley.

Tilly, Charles Louise Tilly, and Richard Tilly (1975). *The Rebellious Century 1830–1930*. Cambridge, MA: Harvard University Press.

Topf, Richard (1995). 'Beyond Electoral Participation', in Hans-Dieter Klingemann and Dieter Fuchs (eds.), *Citizens and the State*. Oxford: Oxford University Press, 52–92.

Van der Eijk, Cees, and Mark N. Franklin, eds. (1996). *Choosing Europe? The European Electorate and National Politics in the Face of Union*. Ann Arbor: Michigan University Press.

Van der Eijk, Cees, and Mark Franklin (2004). 'Potential for Contestation on European Matters at National Elections in Europe', in Gary Marks and Marco R. Steenbergen (eds.), *European Integration and Political Conflict*. Cambridge: Cambridge University Press, 32–50.

Verba, Sidney, and Norman H. Nie (1972). *Participation in America: Political Democracy and Social Equality*. New York: Harper & Row.

Verba, Sidney, Norman H. Nie and Jae-On Kim (1978). *Participation and Political Equality. A Seven Nation Comparison*. Cambridge: Cambridge University Press.

Verba, Sidney, Kay Schlozman and Henry Brady (1995). *Voice and Equality: Civic Voluntarism in American Politics*. Cambridge, MA: Harvard University Press.

Vogel, David (2005). *The Market for Virtue. The Potential and Limits of Corporate Social Responsibility*. Washington, DC: Brookings Institution Press.

Wattenberg, Martin P. (2002). *Where have all the Voters Gone?* Cambridge, MA: Harvard University Press.

Weber, Max (1992). *Politik als Beruf*. Stuttgart: Reclam.

State Feminism and Women's Movements

JONI LOVENDUSKI

Gender and European Political Science

This article is in two parts. The first is a brief reflection on the emergence of the study of gender and politics over the past 30 years and its influence on European political science. The second is a discussion of the early results of a recently completed comparative project, the RNGS project (Research Network on Gender and the State) on the influence of women's movements on public policy decisions. The two parts of the paper are not as disconnected as at first they may seem. The RNGS project reflects both developments in the sub-field of gender and politics and the influences of changes in approaches to the study of politics of the last 30 years or so.

The women's liberation movement that emerged in the 1970s in Western Europe generated new scholarly interest in women's social and political roles. However, it had little immediate impact on the study of politics. Political scientists were at best indifferent, at worst overtly hostile to the new scholarship. Most thought gender unimportant to explanations of political phenomena and to the extent that it was important, they were confident they understood it. Two reasons now seem to explain those attitudes. First, the mainstream European research agenda, although changing rapidly, was still dominated by old institutionalism, area studies and simplistic studies of voting behaviour, and hence offered little space for the study of the politically excluded. Second, the concerns raised by the feminist scholars, especially the claim that the invisible political roles of women merited investigation, found few sympathisers among the men who dominated the profession. In truth, European political science already taking up the challenges offered by new, innovative, systematic comparative work (Lipset and Rokkan 1967) which was advanced by a rising guard of scholars with an extensive research agenda. However, the new research questions were free of concerns about gender. Even so, despite resistance, gradually a study first of women and then of gender and politics became established in West European universities and research institutes. Today this is a thriving and varied sub-field with a significant research agenda and body of completed work. But mainstream European political science continues to ignore the study of gender, which is today mainly a separate endeavour. Most European political scientists tolerate but do not engage with the theories, concepts and research generated by feminist scholars. This is a mistake. It risks missing key developments in the understanding of political behaviour and, indeed, changes in political systems as important aspects of institutions and major dimensions of power go unnoticed. For example, most political scientists failed to appreciate emerging gender gaps in attitudes and behaviour as women shifted their traditional right-wing allegiances to the left and failed to notice differences among women despite being attentive to differences among men. Students of voting failed to realise that the rise of women and women's issues would alter policy agendas. Public policy analysts were taken by surprise when gaps in welfare policy arose from major gendered dimensions of demographic change (such as the provision of care for the aged, who were mainly women and poor) in ageing populations in which women are increasingly in paid employment, hence not available to perform unpaid caring duties. Such gender blindness, although costly in both knowledge and policy terms, continues even now.

The myopia of political scientists seems to stem from an aversion to the study of gender and politics, a phenomenon too large for an essay such as this to detail. It is well chronicled in a number of state of the art papers (Githens 1983; Sapiro 1991; Carroll and Zerilli 1993; Lovenduski 1998). Here I will mention four common explanations. First, the early feminist scholars were not themselves much interested in engaging the mainstream of political science, which pretty comprehensively returned the compliment. Second, the study of gender and politics began to be established at about the same time the discipline was fragmenting, and it was thus just one of many sub-fields competing for attention. The third reason is to do with methodological developments and hierarchies. The tidy and parsimonious models preferred by so many political scientists today are not suited to deal with embedded ubiquitous variables and complex, probably incomplete explanations of political phenomena. In addition, so much early and foundational work was necessarily descriptive, and description, however systematic and despite its importance, is out of fashion. Fourth, pervasive sexism and especially notions that the world of politics is male blinds many observers to the importance of gender.

During the period that the study of gender and politics became established, the discipline itself changed. For example, in the 30 years since the first issue of *West European Politics* the study of European politics has changed massively, grown in size, increased its access to resources and outlets, enlarged its research agenda, its repertoire of methods, and its ambit of study. Such changes are widely understood to reflect 'advances' in approaches to the study of politics, and the greater availability of data, but are also responses to the trinity of (1) challenges of democratisation after 1989, (2) long term processes of globalisation and (3) state reconfiguration and reconstruction in response to (2). When feminist political scientists try to influence the field, they are therefore both part of a process of change, and also trying to hit a moving target.

Nowadays, feminist scholars do want to engage with the mainstream of political science, not least to challenge its approaches and concerns. Indeed, the original objective of studies of women and politics was to correct previous biases. Early studies were critiques of the masculine biases, accompanied by excavations of lacunae, neglect and sexism in Western political theory (Pateman 1988). These were succeeded by analyses of the reasons for failure by the discipline to deal with women as political beings and systematic expositions of the ways in which political science and political theory were implicated in the exclusion of women from the public sphere. This literature is notable for the extent of its critique. The criticisms of empirical political science pointed out the neglect of women by traditional behavioural approaches which, authors claimed, described a stereotype of women's political roles – women were uninformed, unthinking bad citizens who, if they participated in politics at all, largely followed the lead of their husbands and other men in their families. They were thought of as political minors (Bourque and Grossholtz 1974; Goot and Reid 1975).

In the course of their project, feminists outlined a research agenda that would challenge that stereotype by contesting not only the data and the interpretations on which it was based, but also the way in which politics was practised and the manner in which it was understood. In so doing they demonstrated the importance of their sub-field, although large ambitions were inevitably limited by resource constraints and the need at first to concentrate on the exposition of women's political behaviour at elite and citizen levels. Even so, progress was soon being made. For example, although the huge expenses incurred in the administration of purpose-designed large-scale surveys prevented many scholars from making full investigations of women's political behaviour, they could and did learn from the re-analysis of data sets in which sex hitherto was a largely unexplored background variable.

How to overcome the limitations of the discipline became a central preoccupation in developing a feminist political science. The first step was to get rid of the 'bad science' of exaggerating and misconstruing differences between women and men, assuming a male political universe and using data without their original accompanying qualifications (Bourque and Gros-sholtz 1974; Goot and Reid 1975). As important was exposing the unspecified assumptions that the normal political actor was a man and that as far as politics was concerned the female was undifferentiated by age, class, employment or household type. This was a radical exercise, since many feminist political scientists were troubled by the distortions present in the mainstream of behavioural political science arising from an epistemology that separated facts and value and privileged so-called 'value free' factual accounts based on unreflective quantitative studies (Carroll and Zerilli 1993). The effect of concern only with putative facts was to allow political science to factor women out of consideration as political subjects. An over-emphasis on measurable political behaviour prevented recognition of 'not only the... exclusion of women from what is traditionally political, but also the inclusion of politics in what women have traditionally done' (Carroll and Zerilli 1993).

Feminists took account of developments in political science; indeed they made good use of developments in political science, which informed their scholarship. Especially social movement studies, the new institutionalism, network and advocacy coalition analysis and other techniques of policy studies were taken up by scholars who were also attentive to developments in the design requirements of qualitative and quantitative research (King *et al.* 1994; Brady and Collier 2004). The result was a diverse, well-theorised and insistent scholarship that created new research questions and extended existing understandings of politics.

This scholarship is distinctive in its acknowledgement of the important differences between the concepts of sex and gender. Although many political scientists continue to use the terms sex and gender interchangeably, this is not good practice. Gender is not the same as sex. The use of sex as a simple, dichotomous variable will distort research design and therefore findings, *unless* it is located in a gendered fame of reference, a theory of gender relations. Gender, as every sociologist knows, is embedded in individuals, relationships, institutions and organisations. In good research gender is always relational and is most simply measured on a continuum. With that proviso, of course, it is impossible to imagine how gendered research can do without the dichotomous variable of sex.

Inevitably, then, the feminist study of politics sought to expand the definition of politics, lending strength to other challenges to central concerns with electoral behaviour and elite participation, at the same time as examining differences and similarities in men's and women's political behaviour and taking advantage of the opportunities offered by inter-disciplinary study. They are thus part of a movement that eschews methodological monism. An example is the extensive discussion of the significance of the so-called public/private split and the accompanying confinement of women to the private realm. This is an important challenge to narrow definitions of politics as it draws on historical, sociological, philosophical and political research for its understandings and arguments.

In sum, the achievements of 30 years or so of feminist political science are typically characterised as moving from descriptive to more theoretical research, from the analysis of existing data, to innovative research design and the collection of new data and its analysis, from dichotomous concepts of sex, defined in terms of biological difference, to the continuum of gender defined as a (mainly) socially constructed parameter of masculinity and femininity (Hawkesworth 1994; Lovenduski 1998; Beckwith 2001, 2005; McKay 2004; Mazur 2006). The new feminist comparative politics emphasises especially the importance of intersectionality and the extent to which gender effects are intertwined with other inequalities, sometimes to the point where it is argued that no single basis of inequality (class, race, ethnicity, gender, disability, age etc.) has an independent effect (Weldon 2006). A recent essay by Amy Mazur (2006) on feminist scholarship in public policy finds more than 100 such scholars working in the field of comparative public policy, around three-quarters of whom are European. The feminist study of comparative public policy is European dominated, not least because of the sustenance provided by EU research funding which has resourced a number of major projects in the last ten years or so (MAGEEQ, http://www.mageeq.net; QUING, http://www.quing.eu; Walby 2005; Verloo 2006; Lister 2007).

Overall the sub-field of gender and politics has done well when assessed in terms of its research and output. It has made better use of developments in so-called mainstream political science than vice versa and, in its comparative form, has avoided the weaknesses of so much comparative political research, notably the failure to attend to context, to cultural specificity and to the meaning of politics in different settings that so often destroys its value.

The Impact of State Feminism on European Democracies

My sketch of the emergence of feminist political science establishes the context for the second part of this essay. The RNGS (Research Network on Gender and the State) project is a genuinely comparative collaborative study of women's substantive and descriptive political representation, which focuses not on countries, but on processes of policy-making. Members of this network are feminist scholars who together developed a comparative study of the impact of women's movements on state institutions in post-industrial democracies (http://libarts.wsu.edu.polisci.rngs). A central focus was the selection of appropriate methods for the study of the impact of social movements on states. The model of state feminism generated by the network draws on current approaches to the study of politics to combine the intellectual concerns of feminist and democratic theory. The research shows that for some 30 years women's movements in alliance with women's policy agencies supportive of movement concerns have been successful in expanding the political representation of women and hence have made post-industrial democracies more democratic (McBride and Mazur 2006).

That 'democratic' states were deficient in democracy was already well established. In terms of women, Anne Phillips (1995) pointed out that post-industrial democracies were deficient because they failed to represent women's interests and needs adequately. They neither included women in positions of power nor routinely incorporated gender perspectives in the policy process. Her observations are supported by feminist analysts in Europe and North America who show that the absence of women in positions of power may explain the extent to which public policies in many post-industrial democracies are gender biased and therefore discriminate against women (Haavio-Mannila *et al.* 1985; Lovenduski 1986; Bergqvist *et al.* 1999; Beckwith 2000). Phillips' arguments support her claim for *presence* in arenas of decision-making, arguing that women need women to represent them in decision-making, otherwise decisions will not reflect their interests and concerns. She reasons that without presence women will not be able to contribute to the detail of policy content that gets worked out during policy debates in legislatures. Phillips accordingly argues for more women's representation in legislatures. This is, of course, only one of several ways to increase the presence of women in policy debates. Other strategies include establishing women's advocacy and lobbying groups, maintaining women's presence in interest organisations and, relevant to this study, ensuring the presence of women and women's advocates in appointed executive and administrative official bodies that participate in the policy-making process.

Women's Policy Agencies

Since the last quarter of the twentieth century there has been a proliferation of (state) agencies established to promote women's status and rights, often called women's policy agencies (WPA). Examples include the UK Equal Opportunities Commission, the Dutch Emancipation Council, and the French Ministry of Women and the Spanish Institute of Women. What impact did these agencies have? Subject to considerable criticism and sometimes disdained by women's movements, their establishment changed the setting in which the women's movement activists, including feminists, could advance their aims, as it offered, in principle, the possibility to influence the agenda and to further feminist goals through public policies from inside the state apparatus. WPA could increase women's access to the state by furthering women's participation in political decision-making, and by inserting feminist goals into public policy. Thus WPA are a forum of representation in which women's advocates argue their interests in processes of state decision-making.

How do WPA know what are women's interests? The RNGS answer to this question is that WPA understands such interests through alliances with women's movements represented by women's movement actors, and more specifically through alliances with feminist movements. Women's movements are defined both as a form of collective behaviour and the ideas that inspire that behaviour. Women's movement actors are the women who present movement ideas in public and social life. Feminist movements are women's movements with a specific feminist discourse, and feminist movement actors present the ideas.[1]

How can we tell when successful alliances between women's movements and WPA have taken place? We can identify alliances and measure their success by analysing policy debates in terms of both outcome and participants. Policy-making can be construed as a set of arguments among policy actors about what problems deserve attention, how those problems are defined and what the solutions are (Schattschneider 1975; John 1999; Mazur 2001). In this conflict of ideas, only a few issues get taken up for action. Thus women's movement advocates must both gain attention for their ideas and ensure that the problem is defined in terms that are compatible with movement goals. The public definition of a problem is amongst other things a frame that affects how an issue is considered and treated. Frequently discussions of public policy issues with important gender implications are framed in gender-blind terms. One women's movement strategy therefore is to insert frames that highlight gender differences and expose the advantages and disadvantages of various policy options for women or for some groups of women into the debate in order to affect policy content and outcome. The aim is to 'gender' dominant frames of debates in terms that will highlight the status of women in order to bring about its improvement. Once successful, the movement may then act to maintain the frames so that the debate is conducted in feminist terms. In this account, gender becomes part of a process, *gendering*. Gendering a debate means drawing attention to the ways in which women and men are explicitly or implicitly treated in the discussion of the policy and by the policy itself. The strategy of gendering therefore draws attention to differences in interest and power among women and men in relation to the policy being debated. (Beckwith 2005).

Attempts to gender debates have varying degrees of success and successful gendering has varying degrees of impact. In most cases policies will not fully incorporate women's movement goals. However, attention to processes of gendering debates illuminates degrees of women's movement impact on public policies. Following this logic, the unit of analysis is not the country or the movement, but the *policy debate*. By examining *processes* of policy-making in a good sample of debates we are able to consider the extent to which women and women's preferences are considered and represented in the making of a particular decision and their preferences reflected in the resulting decision. In other words, attention to the emergence, development and resolution of a policy debate illuminates both the extent to and manner in which women's advocates (women's movement actors) participate in the decision and their success in securing the outcomes they advocate. These dimensions correspond to descriptive and substantive representation as described by Hannah Pitkin (1967).[2] Thus, the expansion of the representation of women in policy-making processes is an indicator of democratisation which can be assessed in terms of both substantive and descriptive representation by examining policy debates to discover how they are framed, who participates and what the outcome is.

When and why do policy decisions coincide with women's movement goals? Women's movement 'success' in a policy debate requires that its actors must have achieved both procedural access and policy change (Gamson 1975; Rochon and Mazmanian 1993). Procedural access occurs when movement actors are involved in deciding the outcome of a debate. They are therefore present in the debate and have achieved descriptive representation. Successful policy change occurs when the outcome of a debate coincides with the goals of the women's movement actors, an instance of increased substantive representation (McBride and Mazur 2006). So, to achieve full success in a policy debate two things are necessary – that the women's movement has participated in the debate and the outcome coincides with movement goals. For state feminism to exist, the relevant women's policy agency must have facilitated both of these.

To test these propositions the RNGS group examined policy debates across in different issue areas, in similar countries over the period of time in which WPA were in operation. The network chose five policy areas to examine: abortion, prostitution, job training, political representation and a 'hot issue', that is, priority issues of the 1990s. The debate selection includes therefore a range of issues, not all of which are likely to be explicitly gendered at the outset. It also includes a public/private (or body/institution for those who do not like the public/private terminology) dimension, crucial to feminist theory, whereby abortion and prostitution debates may be thought of as 'private' or 'body' issues, while job training, political representation and most of the 'hot issues' can be classified as 'public' or 'institutional'. In all, 130 debates on these issues were examined in 14 advanced democracies to assess women's movement success in inserting their interests into the debate. Here we consider those debates that were observed in 11 West European systems (see List of Debates, Appendix 1).

The Model of State Feminism

Drawing on theories of political representation, public policy-making, new institutionalism and social movements, the network developed a state feminist framework expressed in a model in which the units of analysis are policy debates.[3] The model is built on a set of classifications. We synthesised categories from democratic representation and social movement impact theories into typologies designed to measure the intervening and dependent variables: women's policy agency activities and women's movement impact. At the same time, these typologies separate analytically the variations in WPA activities from the state's policy and procedural responses to permit examination of the effects of one on the other in each debate. They also separate substantive representation from descriptive representation.

Each selected debate was traced to determine how it got to the public agenda, what frame dominated at the time and whether the debate was gendered. Researchers then determined whether or not new gender meanings were introduced into the debate and who inserted such new meanings. The endpoint of each debate (a law, or report, or other kind of decision) was described. In the course of debate tracing, close attention was given to the part played by the WPA and women's movement and the characteristics of movement, agency and policy environment were classified according to the schemes described below. The model is illustrated in Figure 1.

Movement Impact

The impact of the women's movement on the outcome is assessed using Gamson's (1975) two dimensions of substantive responses and procedural acceptance and is then classified in terms of a four-fold typology. When the state accepts individual women, groups and/or constituencies into the process and changes policy to coincide with feminist goals, it is a case of *dual response*. *Pre-emption* occurs when the state gives policy satisfaction but does not allow women, as individuals, groups or constituencies, into the process. When the state accepts women and women's groups into the process but does not give policy satisfaction, it is classified as *co-optation*. Finally, when the state neither responds to movement demands nor allows women or women's groups into the process, there is a *no response* (Figure 2).

WPA Activities

The debates were also classified according to agency activities within a four-fold typology based on two variables and illustrated in Figure 3: (1) whether or not the agency is an advocate of women's movement goals in the policy

FIGURE 1
RNGS MODEL

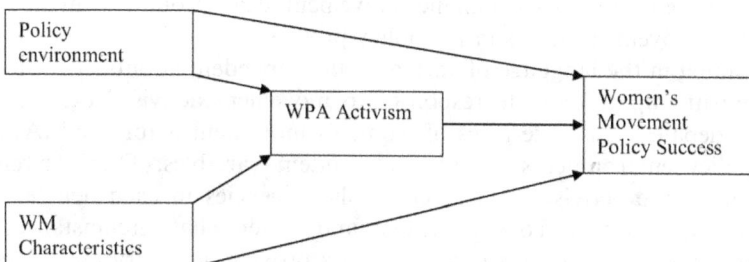

FIGURE 2
WOMEN'S MOVEMENT IMPACT/ STATE RESPONSE (WM IMPACT)

		Policy and Movement Goals coincide	
		Yes	No
Women involved in policy process	Yes	Dual Response	Co-optation
	No	Pre-emption	No response

FIGURE 3
TYPOLOGY OF WOMEN'S POLICY AGENCY ACTIVITIES (WPA ACTIVISM)

		WPA advocates movement goals	
		Yes	No
WPA genders frame of policy debate	Yes	Insider	Non feminist
	No	Marginal	Symbolic

process on the issue; (2) whether or not the agency was effective in changing the frame of the debate to one that coincides with movement interests. When the agency incorporates the goals of the movement and is successful in gendering, that is, inserts the gendered policy definitions into the dominant frame of the debate, it is classified as *insider*. If the agency asserts movement goals, but is not successful in gendering the policy debate, it is classified as *marginal*. When the agency is neither an advocate for movement goals nor genders the policy debate, it is classified as *symbolic*. Finally, when the agency is not an advocate for movement goals but genders or degenders the debate in some other ways, it is classified as *non-feminist*.

WPA Characteristics

In terms of characteristics, WPA and their activities and possible interventions were examined for each debate. The agency (or agencies in some cases) is described in terms of a number of characteristics, which may affect an agency's ability to enhance movement ideas, promote demands and facilitate movement actors in the policy process.

Restated in the language of variables, the dependent variable is women's movement impact or state responses to movement activists' demands in policy debates. Characteristics of women's movement actors (WMA) and the policy environments are the independent variables. The intervening variable is the activism of women's policy agencies in each debate. The research question is: To what extent and under what circumstances do different kinds of women's policy agencies provide necessary and effective linkages for women's movements in achieving substantive and procedural responses from the state?

Applying the Model: The Results of the RNGS Project

RNGS is a most similar systems comparison. The 14 countries included in the project are all post-industrial democracies. They are about half of the 23 countries that fall into this category of systems that have relatively similar and large levels of national wealth and, with the exception of Spain, relatively stable democratic political systems since 1945. All the countries have had stable democratic systems since the 1970s. Within this category they differ by type of democratic regime. Separate analyses of each issue have been published in a series of books produced by members of the network (Mazur 2001; Stetson 2001; Outshoorn 2004; Lovenduski *et al.* 2005; Haussmann and Sauer 2007).

The main findings were as follows:

- *Job training*: Only six of 25 debates resulted in the 'pure success' of a dual response. The nature of the policy environment was an important predictor of outcome. Country, women's movement characteristics, and time were also significant. WPA activism proved a strong predictor of an unfavourable outcome (Mazur 2001).
- *Abortion*: 16 of 32 debates resulted in a dual response. Women's movements became more successful over time in influencing abortion debate outcomes. WPA activism, high movement priority, movement cohesion and the openness of the policy environment were associated with movement success (Stetson 2001).
- *Prostitution*: 19 of 36 debates resulted in a dual response. Movement issue priority, movement cohesion, matching and compatible frame fits and WPA activism were associated with success (Outshoorn 2004).
- *Political representation*: 17 of 31 debates resulted in a dual response. Movement issue priority, movement cohesion, the openness of the policy environment, matching or compatible frame fit, strength of the counter-movement and WPA activism were associated with movement success (Lovenduski *et al.* 2005).
- *Hot issue*: Movement chances of success were most dependent upon policy environment variables, highest when they placed a high priority on the issue and the frame fit was compatible with the dominant issue frame in the policy subsystem (Haussmann and Sauer 2007).

The completion of the issue studies enables us to study the entire set of debates to assess the extent of state feminism, broadly defined as the advocacy of women's movement demands from inside the state in advanced industrial democracies. It is not possible, however, to read off full project results directly from the conclusions of the issue books, each of which treated only a small set of debates. To put the debates together, further coding and harmonisation was required. Independent scrutiny led to a major overhaul to quantify each qualitative variable and, as the project progressed, new codes were introduced and applied to all the debates (http://libarts.wsu.edu/polisci/rngs/). These changes standardise observations across all the debates, which were combined in a large dataset. It is now possible to analyse the full set of debates, using statistical techniques not available for the small-*n* individual issues. Moreover, there are some additional variables to consider, including issue type and of the level of women's legislative representation at the time of the debate decision (as part of the policy environment).

This essay reports findings from the 99 debates that were examined in the 11 West European countries in which a WPA was present during a debate. This is a 'first cut' of the aggregated, harmonised and expanded data.

Comparing the Debates

The results of the analysis are illustrated in Figure 4 which shows that 45 (46 per cent) of debates resulted in a dual response, full success for the women's movement and a further 27 (28 per cent) resulted in pre-emption, or the meeting of movement demands without accepting WMAs in the policy process. Insider (activist) WPA generally enhanced movement success

FIGURE 4
WPA ACTIVISM BY WOMEN'S MOVEMENT SUCCESS

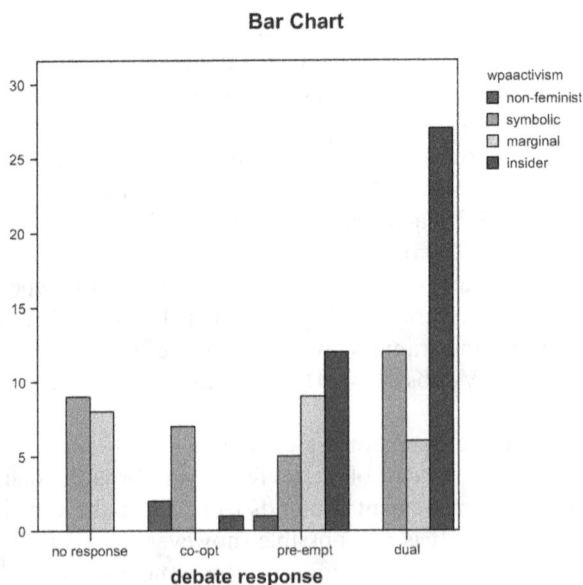

(68 per cent dual response). Of the 27 instances of policy failure (co-option and no response) for the women's movement, 16 (59 per cent) were associated with symbolic agencies. Overall, then, insider agencies are associated with policy success and symbolic agencies are associated (even more) with policy failure. Marginal agencies are more evenly distributed, with no clear pattern to the results. Present in 13 per cent of wholly successful debates, 33 per cent of partly successful debates and 50 per cent of policy failures, they are a little more associated with failure than success. Overall the data suggest that when WPA act on behalf of women's movements they enhance movement success in policy debates.

Explaining Women's Policy Agency Activism

Figure 4 indicates that, as the RNGS model predicts, WPA activities affect the success of women's movement actors in policy debates. The model predicts that the characteristics of women's movements and the policy environment at the time of each debate influence women's movement actors' success in policy debates directly and/or indirectly through an intervening variable of WPA activism. Accordingly, in this analysis, WPA activism is first treated as a dependent variable, after which it is entered into the explanation as an independent variable. The sample of 99 cases is large enough for some multivariate testing, but so small that such tests may miss some significant associations, hence bivariate tests are used to supplement and clarify the initial findings.

Following the logic of the model, the remainder of this paper falls into three parts. First, it examines the conditions for WPA activism; second it examines the patterns of debate outcomes in terms of women's movement and policy environment characteristics. Finally it examines the impact of WPA activism on movement success in relation to the other independent variables.

Accordingly, the first step is to examine the characteristics of WPA themselves. Institutional theory suggests that agencies with greater resources, scope, proximity to power etc. should be more effective. Although agencies might sometimes act on an issue outside their mandate, they should have greater capability when the issue is within their remit. We coded these predictions into five indicators. Administrative *capacity* refers to budgets, staff, and period of mandate, which range from temporary and small to permanent and large. The professional and political background of the *leadership* can determine the activities of the agency on the issue. Some agency heads are *feminist* and have close ties to the movement. Feminist theory indicates that agencies with feminist leadership are probably more representative of the women's movements. Agency leaders at the time of each debate are coded into three categories: those with neither women's movement nor feminist experience, those with women's movement but not feminist experience and those with feminist experience.[4] *Scope* refers to the policy mission of the agency; some are cross-sectional and others are single-issue agencies. *Proximity* refers to its location within the state system and the closeness to the major locus of power there. Finally, *policy mandate* indicates whether the debate issue falls within the remit and priorities of the agency.

TABLE 1
DETERMINANTS OF WPA ACTIVISM: CHARACTERISTICS OF WPA1

Model		Unstandardised coefficients		Standardised coefficients		
		B	Std. error	Beta	t	Sig.
1	(Constant)	3.205	.737		4.350	.000
	Capacity	−.076	.058	−.140	−1.307	.195
	Leadership1	.078	.118	.072	.659	.512
	Scope 1	.249	.202	.135	1.235	.220
	In mandate1	−.415	.569	−.078	−.729	.468
	Proximity1	−.085	.164	−.057	−.517	.606

a Dependent variable: wpaactivism N = 99 R square = .050.

Our data indicates that most agencies are political, multi-issue, in close proximity to centres of power, slightly under half are led by feminists and in almost all cases the debated issue was within their mandate. Table 1 presents simple OLS regression controlling for the effects of each of these indicators of agency activism for the most activist agency in each debate. It indicates that none of the agency characteristics is a significant predictor of activism.

What Kinds of Women's Movements are Associated with Activist WPA?

We next consider the relationships between WPA activism and women's movement characteristics. The research design proposes that the stage of the women's movement at the time of the debate (whether emerging, growing, in consolidation or decline), its closeness to the left, the priority of the issue and cohesion on the issue, and the strength of the counter-movement explain differences in WPA activism. Specifically we expected agencies to be most effective in assisting movements that were at stages of growth or consolidation, close to the left, cohesive or unified on the issue to which they gave a high priority and acting against a weak counter-movement. Women's movement actors were observed in order to identify the presence of characteristics that are considered to be important for mobilisation in policy debates. We hypothesised that characteristics such as stage of development, closeness to the left, priority of the debate issue on the movement agenda, cohesion of the movement on the issue, and the strength of a possible counter-movement were used to assess this first independent variable. Three *stages* of development, a combined measure of size, support and mobilisation (Rosenfield and Ward 1996) are employed: growth, consolidation and decline. *Ideological* closeness to the left refers to the overlap between the ideas of the movement and those of the parties and trade unions of the left. *Organisational* closeness refers to formal alliances between movement and the organisations of the left. They can be not close, close, moderately close or very close. *Cohesion* is a measure of the level of agreement among WMAs about policy proposals. In this paper cohesion can be either high or not high. *Priority* refers to the priority of the debate issue to movement concerns and is presented here in terms of whether or not the issue was one of the top five issues on movement agendas. *Counter-movement* is the strength of opposing movements, scaled in four categories from none to strong, and *institutionalisation* is a ten-point numeric scale of the density of presence of WMA in important decision-making institutions.

The issue analyses and initial counts of the aggregated results (cross-tabs) indicated that insider WPA are most associated with movements in stages of growth or consolidation that are very close to the left, cohesive and give high priority to the issue. Where the agencies are symbolic, movements are not so close to the left, tend to be less cohesive, do not give high priority to the issue. Marginal agencies operate in conditions in which counter-movements are weak, movements are perhaps less close to the left, movement cohesion is high, but movements do not give the issue high priority. Movement stage does not distinguish symbolic and insider agencies. However, when controlling for each variable in an OLS regression none of the indicators proved to be significant predictors of the activism of the agencies most active in the debate. Hence women's movement characteristics do not predict agency activism (Table 2).[5]

TABLE 2

WOMEN'S MOVEMENT CHARACTERISTICS AS DETERMINANTS OF WPA ACTIVISM

Model		Unstandardised coefficients		Standardised coefficients		
		B	Std. error	Beta	t	Sig.
1	(Constant)	3.489	.674		5.177	.000
	Priority	−.019	.227	−.010	−.084	.933
	Cohesion	−.286	.201	−.154	−1.423	.158
	Closeleftorg	−.277	.285	−.127	−.971	.334
	Closeleftideo	.172	.151	.149	1.133	.261
	Stage	−.086	.168	−.061	−.516	.607
	WMA Institutionalisation	.016	.059	.033	.268	.789
	Counter	−.049	.079	−.068	−.616	.540

a Dependent variable: wpaactivism N = 99, r square .068.

How does the Policy Environment affect WPA Activism?

The RNGS model predicts that success depends on movement character-istics in conjunction with characteristics of the policy environment, which

184   *J. Lovenduski*

influences both the characteristics of the women's policy agencies and the success of women's movements. We were also interested in whether levels of women's political representation at the time of a debate influence WPA activity and whether the type of issue had an influence. The characteristics of the policy subsystem in which each debate took place were divided into five indicators. First we examined the degree of *open- or closed-ness* of the policy environment and classified our observations. This classification is based on the patterns formed by three elements: common rules, accessibility by occasional participants and the chain of command. If there is a set of rules, a chain of command that governs the interactions of actors and there is no access for occasional participants, then the system is closed. If only two elements are present then the policy environment is moderately closed, if only one, it is moderately open and if none of the elements are present then the system is classified as open. Second, the dominant policy discourse is compared to that of the women's movement. The *frame fit* might match that of the women's movement, be compatible, mixed or threatening.[6] Third, the *party or coalition in power* was classified according to ideological position on the left–right spectrum of the country concerned. Fourth, *issues* were classified as either public or private. While RNGS is interested in levels of women's political representation in broader terms than their presence in legislatures, we nevertheless wanted to consider if different levels of legislative representation were associated with policy success. So, we identified the *percentage of women in the lower house* of the national legislature for each debate and entered it, with the other variables, into the OLS equation.

The results are presented in Table 3 which shows that the multivariate analysis of indicators of WPA activism does not identify significant relationships between these variables. However, the relationships examined in Tables 2 and 3 may be present but at a level that is not apparent from the strong multivariate test of significance, which may be affected by the sample size. I revisit these relationships in the final section of this article.

TABLE 3
POLICY ENVIRONMENT CHARACTERISTICS AS DETERMINANTS OF WPA ACTIVISM

Model		Unstandardised coefficients		Standardised coefficients		
		B	Std. error	Beta	t	Sig.
1	(Constant)	2.886	.406		7.100	.000
	Framefit	.304	.187	.217	1.628	.109
	Policy environment open	−.247	.158	−.218	−1.566	.123
	Issue type	−.047	.246	−.027	−.190	.850
	Left in power	.149	.119	.164	1.253	.215
	Percentage women legislators lh	.017	.010	.209	1.622	.111

a Dependent variable: wpaactivism N = 99 R square .168.

What Kinds of Women's Movements are Successful?

Having examined the relationships of women's movement and policy environment characteristics to agency activities we now turn to their relationship to movement success in policy debates. Accordingly, using the same coding, we checked women's movements characteristics against debate outcomes in order to determine if any of these characteristics had an impact on movement success. The OLS regression presented in Table 4 shows that, of women's movement characteristics, only the existence of a strong counter-movement predicts movement success.

In terms of policy environment, the OLS regression presented in Table 5 shows that the openness of the policy environment and the presence of women legislators are significant predictors of movement success and that issue type may have some impact on success as it is close to significance. Women's movement success increases both as levels of women's representation rise and with the openness of the policy environment.

TABLE 4

WOMEN'S MOVEMENT CHARACTERISTICS AS DETERMINANTS OF MOVEMENT SUCCESS

Model		Unstandardised coefficients		Standardised coefficients		
		B	Std. error	Beta	t	Sig.
1	(Constant)	.061	.755		.081	.936
	Priority	.272	.255	.114	1.067	.289
	Cohesion	−.005	.225	−.002	−.020	.984
	Closeleftorg	.062	.320	.023	.195	.846
	Closeleftideo	.283	.170	.200	1.667	.099
	Stage	.135	.188	.078	.720	.473
	WMA Institutionalisation	.100	.066	.168	1.515	.133
	Counter	.233	.089	.266	2.630	*.010*

a Dependent variable: debate response N = 99 R square .226

TABLE 5

POLICY ENVIRONMENT DETERMINANTS OF WOMEN'S MOVEMENT IMPACT

Model		Unstandardised coefficients		Standardised coefficients		
		B	Std. error	Beta	t	Sig.
1	(Constant)	2.312	.514		4.497	.000
	Framefit	.396	.236	.201	1.678	.099
	Policy environment open	−.551	.200	−.345	−2.758	*.008*
	Issue type	−.580	.312	−.234	−1.861	.068
	Left in power	.156	.151	.121	1.033	.306
	Percentage women legislators lh	.036	.013	.320	2.761	*.008*

a Dependent variable: debate response N = 99 R square .326.

Is WPA Activism Associated with Movement Success?

To summarise, the success of the women's movement in policy debates in Western Europe is affected by the level of women's representation and the openness of the policy environment. Neither women's movement nor policy environment characteristics predict women's policy agency activism, but aspects of each predict women's movement policy success. The next step in the analysis is to consider the impact of WPA activism on women's movement success.

As Figure 4 shows, in 63 debates WPA were *activist*, that is, insider or marginal and in 36 they were *non-activist*, that is symbolic or non-feminist. In 33 of the 45 debates in which WPA were activist, movements achieved a dual response. But does WPA activism predict movement success? To test this central question the WPA activism scale was entered as an independent variable into a regression equation along with the other indicators confirmed above as predictors or near predictors of movement success (Table 6).

Table 6 confirms that WPA activism, the openness of the policy environment, percentage of women legislators and strength of counter-movement are significant predictors of movement success in policy debates, as it seems that the activity of a WPA in a policy debate is the strongest predictor of movement success. Patterns of agency activism therefore warrant more exploration and discussion. The statistical tests used so far do not confirm the predictions of agency activism anticipated in the model. But before discarding this part of our model, we should re-evaluate the evidence in the light of the findings in Table 6. As well as confirming the importance of agency activism to movement success, Table 6 also alerts us to the significance of the policy environment and the proportion of women in the legislature as indicators of movement success, highlighting the sub-groups formed by the classification of these variables. Unfortunately, our sample is too small to permit meaningful use of the OLS regression equations to test

TABLE 6
PREDICTORS OF WOMEN'S MOVEMENT SUCCESS

Model		Unstandardised coefficients		Standardised coefficients		
		B	Std. error	Beta	t	Sig.
1	(Constant)	.898	.421		2.135	.035
	wpaactivism	.521	.094	.433	5.529	.000
	Policy environment open	−.405	.107	−.306	−3.778	.000
	Percentage women legislators	.025	.009	.224	2.862	.005
	Countermovement	.220	.072	.248	3.063	.003
	Issue type	−.230	.186	−.103	−1.235	.220

a Dependent variable: debate response N = 99, R square .434.

relationships within subgroups. Instead we use bivariate correlation tests for this part of the analysis.

Most policy subsystems are not open. In all, 84 debates took place in closed (61) or moderately closed (23) policy environments. Within this sub-group we found significant correlations between WPA activism and characteristics of the agencies and women's movements. In such debates WPA activism is positively associated with the scope (.319**) of the agency, with the ideological closeness to the left of the women's movement (.284*) and with the frame fit (.306*) between the dominant policy discourse and that of the women's movement on the issue, hence in closed policy environments the model explains WPA activism.[7]

Similar relationships appear to exist between agency activism and women's representation, although these associations are not statistically significant. To explore the impact of the presence of women legislators in more detail, we classified *women's representation* as high, low, or medium for each decade of the 30-year period.[8] Most observed WPA activity took place at times when women's representation was low, with only 17 debates in the sample occurring at times of 'high' women's representation. WPA activism in low periods is fairly evenly distributed between insider, marginal and symbolic agencies (40, 24 and 35 per cent respectively). However, symbolic agencies were present in only 18 per cent of debates which took place while levels of women's representation were high and no non-feminist agencies operated under high levels of women's representation. When levels of representation were high, agencies were more likely to be activist (47 per cent) or marginal (26 per cent). Hence the pattern of agency activism differed substantially between low and high periods of women's representa-tion. It seems that when levels of women's political representation are high, agencies are better positioned to act for women. The data indicate that the highest proportionate success rate for movements occurs in the high band of women's representation (11 of 17 debates or 64 per cent dual response). Concomitantly, the highest failure rates (18 of 27 or 66 per cent of debates resulting in co-optation or non-response) occur when women's levels of representation are low.

Returning to the relationship between WPA activism, policy environ-ment, women's representation and movement success described in Table 6, we note that insider WPA are more effective the more open are policy environments. However, it is likely that WPA activism is most important to movement success where policy environments are closed. In such circumstances the presence of an insider agency acts as an enabler of women's movement representation in the debates, while in open policy environments they are less important as WMA may have a range of means of entry into decision-making processes. This is confirmed by close examination of the outcomes of debates that took place in closed policy environments. Insider WPA were present in 23 of the 61 debates in which the policy environment was classified as closed. Of these, 22 debates resulted in full or partial movement success (13 dual responses and 9 pre-emptions.)

The research finds a small but significant relationship between the percentage of women in the legislature and the substantive and procedural success of women's movement actors in policy debates, evidence that the presence of women in legislatures matters for women's advocacy. However, the instances of debates taking place during periods of comparatively high levels of women's representation in the study were too few to permit more extensive statistical analysis. Future researchers in this area will have the benefit of a larger sample of instances of high levels of women's representation and will thus be able to confirm or refute this connection. The likelihood is that higher levels of women's representation enhance both agency activism and movement success, possibly through a policy triangle of cooperation among movement actors, legislators and officials working in WPA.

The type of issue being debated is not a predictor of movement success. The intuitively appealing argument for its inclusion is that movements are more likely to achieve full success over 'private/body' issues than over 'public/institutional' issues. The reasoning is that a political logic of appropriateness exists whereby gender has become a qualification for participation in decisions formulated in terms of the body or private sphere. However, this is not borne out by the research. More prosaically, the relationship between movement success and the presence of a strong counter-movement may be suggestive of processes of mobilisation that occur when debates are strongly contested. The impacts of issue type and counter-movement strength are tricky to interpret, as is the possible impact of frame fit. All require further in-depth analysis of the qualitative research conducted by RNGS.[9]

To conclude, the research confirms that WPA activism is a significant predictor of women's movement success. WPA activities make Western European democracies more democratic by contributing both to the participation of women's movement advocates in decision-making and to the meeting of women's movement demands. In other words activities within the state, by women's policy agencies, enhance the substantive and descriptive representation of women in policy debates. On this reckoning, agencies such as the Dutch Emancipation Council, the UK Equal Opportunities Commission, the Spanish Institute for Women or the French Ministry for Women do more good than harm.

Acknowledgements

I am grateful to Amy Mazur, Rosie Campbell, Mark Franklin, and the participants in the *WEP* 30th Anniversary Conference for their comments and suggestions on earlier versions of this paper. The analysis is based on the RNGS data set as at 1 July 2007.

Notes

1. Feminist discourse according to RNGS has five characteristics: (1) It expresses explicit identity with women as a group, a form of explicit gender consciousness (Tolleson 1992). (2) The language is explicitly gendered, referring to women as distinct from men. Gendered references include the following: images of women and what they are like; how women are different from men; how women are different from each other; the ways gender differences shape identities (Katzenstein 1995). (3) The ideas are expressed in terms of representing women as women in public life. (4) Because there is something wrong with the treatment and status of women, goals are presented that will advance the status of women. (5) Views expressed explicitly or implicitly challenge gender hierarchies and forms of women's subordination. To be considered feminist, discourse must include *all of these elements*: identity with women; be explicitly gendered; represent women; improve the status of women; challenge gender hierarchies.
2. It is customary to cite the work of Hannah Pitkin when defining political representation. Pitkin suggests four types of representation: *authorised*, where a representative is legally empowered to act for another; *descriptive* representation, where the representative stands for a group by virtue of sharing similar characteristics such as race, gender, ethnicity, or residence; *symbolic* representation, where a leader stands for national ideas; and *substantive* representation, where the representative seeks to advance a group's policy preferences and interests. Both descriptive and substantive representation are useful concepts for comparing the extent to which policy processes in democratic regimes are inclusive of women.
3. This discussion draws on and summarises the RNGS project description which sets out its theorisation in detail and describes the coding for each variable is available at http://libarts.wsu.edu/polisci/rngs/.
4. RNGS defines as feminist those women's movements actors who use feminist discourse as described in note 2 above. See project description for detailed discussion. http://libarts.wsu.edu/polisci/rngs/.
5. In some debates more than one WPA existed and was active. The observations reported here are of the most active, hence WPA1.
6. *Matching*: Issue frame that initially shapes the debate is expressed in terms that are similar to movement goals as expressed by activists. If two-sided, if WMA microframe is similar to one side of the debate, it may be matching.
   Compatible: Issue frame that initially shapes the debate is expressed in terms that are not similar but not in direct opposition to movement goals as expressed by activists
   Threatening: Issue frame that initially shapes the debate is expressed in terms that are in conflict with (oppose) movement goals the debate as expressed by activists.
   Mixed: Issue frame that initially shapes the debate is expressed in terms that are compatible with goals of some women's movement actors but challenge or threaten goals of other women's movement actors.
7. Spearmans Rho *significant at .05, **significant at .01.
8. The classification scheme was as follows: Based on the decade of the debate endpoint, we divided the range of the percentages of women in national legislatures into thirds in each decade and labelled them low, medium and high in order to create a women's legislative representation variable for each debate.
9. Such analysis will be forthcoming in the RNGS capstone volume, which is currently in preparation; see http://libarts.wsu.edu/polsci/rngs.

References

Beckwith, K. (2000). 'Beyond Compare? Women's Movements in Comparative Perspective', *European Journal of Political Research*, 37, 431–68.

Beckwith, K. (2001). 'Women's Movements at Century's End: Excavations and Advances in Political Science', *Annual Review of Political Science*, 4, 371–90.

Beckwith, K. (2005). 'A Common Language of Gender?', *Gender and Politics*, 1:1, 128–37.

Bergqvist, C., Anette Borchost, Ann-Dorte Christensen, Viveca Ramsted-Silén, Nina C. Raum and Auður Styrkársdóttir, eds. (1999). *Equal Democracies: Gender and Politics in the Nordic Countries*. Oslo: Scandinavian University Press.

Bourque, S.C., and J. Grossholtz (1974). 'Politics an Unnatural Practice: Political Science Looks at Female Participation', *Political Sociology*, 4, 128–57.

Brady, H.E., and D. Collier, eds. (2004). *Rethinking Social Inquiry: Diverse Tooks, Shared Standards*. Lanham, MD: Rowman and Littlefield.

Caroll, S.J., and M.G. Zerilli (1993). 'Feminist Challenges to Political Science', in A.W. Finifter (ed.), *Political Science: The State of the Discipline*. Washington, DC: American Political Science Association, 55–77.

Gamson, A.W. (1975). *The Strategy of Social Protest*. Homewood, IL: The Dorsey Press.

Githens, M. (1983). 'The Elusive Paradigmgender, Politics and Political Behavior: The State of the Art', in A.W. Finifter (ed.), *Political Science: The State of the Discipline*. Washington, DC: American Political Science Association, 471–99.

Goot, M., and E. Reid (1975). *Women and Voting Studies: Mindless Matrons or Sexist Scientism*. London: SAGE.

Haavio-Mannila, Drude Dahlerup, Maud Eduards, Esther Gudmundsdóttir, Beatrice Halsaa, Helga Maria Hernes, Eva Hänninen-Samelin, Bergthora Sigmundsdóttir, Sirkka Sinkkonen and Torild Skard, eds. (1985). *Unfinished Democracy: Women in Nordic Politics*. New York: Pergamon.

Haussmann, M., and B. Sauer, eds. (2007). *Gendering the State in the Age of Globalization. Women's Movements and State Feminism in Post Industrial Democracies*. Lanham, MD: Rowman and Littlefield.

Hawkesworh, M. (1994). 'Policy Studies within a Feminist Frame', *Policy Sciences*, 27, 97–114.

John, P. (1999). *Analyzing Public Policy*. London: Pinter.

Katsenstein, M.F. (1995). ,Faithful and Fearless: Moving Feminist Protest Inside the Church and Military', in M.M. Feree and P.Y. Martin (eds.), *Feminist Organisations*. Philadelphia, PA: Temple University Press.

King, G., R.O. Keohane and Sidney Verba (1994). *Designing Social Inquiry: Scientific Inference in Qualitative research*. Princeton, NJ: Princeton University Press.

Lipset, S.M., and S. Rokkan (1967). *Party Systems and Voter Alignment: Cross-National Perspectives*. New York: Free Press.

Lister, R., ed. (2007). *Gendering Citizenship in Western Europe*. Bristol: Policy Press.

Lovenduski, J. (1986). *Women and European Politics: Contemporary Feminism and Public Policy*. Brighton: Wheatsheaf Books.

Lovenduski, J. (1998). 'Gendering Research in Political Science', *Annual Review of Political Science*, 1, 333–56.

Lovenduski, J., C. Baudino, Marila Guadagnini, Petra Meier, and Diane Sainsbury, eds. (2005). *State Feminism and Political Representation*. Cambridge: Cambridge University Press.

Mazur, A.G., ed. (2001). *State Feminism, Women's Movements and Job Training: Making Democracies Work in a Global Economy*. New York and London: Routledge.

Mazur, A.G. (2006). 'Feminist Comparative Policy', *Encyclopedia of Public Administration and Public Policy*. Maurice Dekker. Available at: http://dx.doi.org/10.108.

McBride, D., and A.G. Mazur (2006). 'Women's Movements, Women's Policy Agencies and Democratisation', in Conference of Europeanists. Chicago: Council for European Studies.

McKay, F. (2004). 'Gender and Political Representation in the UK', *British Journal of Politics and International Relations*, 6, 99–120.

Outshoorn, J., ed. (2004). *The Politics of Prostitution. Women's Movements, Democratic States and the Globalisation of Sex Commerce*. Cambridge: Cambridge University Press.

Pateman, C. (1988). *The Sexual Contract*. Cambridge: Cambridge University Press.

Phillips, A. (1995). *The Politics of Presence*. Oxford: Clarendon Press.

Pitkin, H. (1967). *The Concept of Representation*. Berkeley: University of California Press.

Rochon, T.R., and D.A. Mazmanian (1993). 'Social Movements and the Policy Process', *Annals of the American Academy of Political and Social Science*, 583, 75–87.

Rosenfield, R.A., and K.B. Ward (1996). 'Evolution of Contemporary U.S. Women's Movement', *Research in Social Movements, Conflict and Change*, 19, 51–73.

Sapiro, V. (1991). 'Gender Politics, Gendered Politics: the State of the Field', in W. Crotty (ed.), *Political Science: Looking to the Future The Theory and Practice of Political Science*. Evanston, IL: Northwestern University Press, 165–87.

Schattschneider, E.E. (1975). *The Semi Sovereign People: A Realist's View of Democracy in America*. Hinsdale, IL: The Dryden Press.

Stetson, D.M., ed. (2001). *Abortion Politics, Women's Movements and the Democratic State: A Comparative Study of State Feminism*. Oxford: Oxford University Press.

Tolleson, R.S. (1992). *Gender Consciousness in Politics*. New York: Routledge.

Verloo, M. (2006). 'Multiple Inequalities, Intersectionality and the European Union', *European Journal of Women's Studies*, 13:3, 211–28.

Walby, S. (2005). 'Introduction: Comparative Gender Mainstreaming in a Global Era', *International Feminist Journal of Politics*, 7:4, 453–70.

Weldon, L. (2006). 'The Structure of Intersectionality: A Comparative Politics of Gender', *Gender and Politics*, 2, 235–48.

APPENDIX 1
LIST OF POLICY DEBATES IN DATASET

Job Training:
Spain

National plan on job training	1985
Creation of coordinating authority	1985–86
Management of programme delivery	1990–92

Italy

Job training and unemployment	1983–84
Job training and labour market reform	1993–97

France

Youth training and placement	1978–80
Representation of workers' interests	1982–84
Employer job training contribution	1990–91
Job training and reinsertion	1993
Job training and decentralisation	1993

Finland

Labour shortages and unemployment	1969–71
Adult further training reform	1971–75
State responsibility for training	1977–87
Training linked to unemployment benefits	1992–93

Ireland

Youth unemployment	1981
EU peripherality	1987–89
Training for globalisation	1995–97

Abortion:
Austria

Social Democratic Party draft liberalisation	1970–72
People's Initiative (anti-abortion) and National Council reaffirmation of legal abortion	1975–78
Regulation of mifegyne: abortion pill	1998–99

Belgium

State Commission for Ethical Problems	1974–76
Detiège bill to suspend prosecutions	1981–82
Reform of abortion law	1986–90

(continued)

APPENDIX 1
(*Continued*)

France	
Reaffirmation of legal abortion in the first trimester	1979
Reimbursement of abortion expenses	1981–83
Commando-IVG and *Loi Neiertz*	1991–93
Germany	
Legalisation of abortion	1969–74
Post-unification liberalisation	1990–92
Restoration of limited abortion law	1993–95
Great Britain	
White bill and Lane Committee	1970–75
Corrie bill to restrict abortions	1975–79
Human Fertilisation and Embryology Act: upper limit	1987–90
Ireland	
Constitutional amendment to protect the unborn	1981–83
X and Maastricht Treaty referendums on abortion and right to travel	1992
C and Green Paper on abortion policy	1997–99
Italy	
Legalisation of abortion	1971–78
Popular referendum to repeal legal abortion	1980–81
In vitro fertilisation and abortion	1996–99
Netherlands	
First cabinet proposal for limited reform	1971–73
Reform of abortion law	1977–81
Implementation of statute to register/ license abortion facilities	1981–84
Spain	
Abortion Act	1983–85
Implementation regulations	1986
Prostitution:	
Austria	
Penal Code amendment on pimping	1984
Vienna's prostitution law	1991–92
Social insurance for private enterprise	1997
Britain	
Abolition of prison for prostitutes	1979–83
Kerb crawling as an offence	1984–85
Maintaining a person in sexual servitude	2000–02
Finland	
Repeal of Vagrant Act	1984–86
New Sex Crime Act	1993–98
Helsinki's prostitution law	1995–99
France	
Prostitute rights and law enforcement	1972–75
Public health/AIDS	1989–90
Penal Code reform of pimping and solicitation	1991–92
Italy	
Protection for victims of trafficking	1996–99
Criminalising clients of underage prostitutes	1998
Funding projects to prevent sex trafficking	1998–99
Netherlands	
Bill 18202 repeal of brothel ban	1983–89
Bill on the trafficking of persons	1989–93
Bill 25417 on repeal of brothel ban	1997–2000

(*continued*)

APPENDIX 1
(Continued)

Spain	
Elaboration of the 1995 Penal Code	1994–95
1999 reform of the Penal Code	1997–99
2000 Immigrant Act	1998–2000
Sweden	
First Commission on Prostitution	1981–82
Proposal for violence against women act	1995–98
Law against purchasing sexual services	1997–99

Political Representation:

Austria	
Cabinet access	1979
Equal treatment for civil servants	1990–92
Gendering public party finances	1994–99
Belgium	
Quota for electoral lists	1992–94
Quota for advisory committees	1996–97
Quota for federal government	1996–98
Finland	
Change in electoral law	1972–75
Gender quotas in SKDL	1986–87
Quotas in Equality Act of 1995	1991–95
France	
Voting system for local councillors	1981–82
Voting system for parliamentary elections	1985–86
Parity Reform	1995–2000
Germany	
Quota in Social Democratic Party	1977–88
Second Equal Rights Law	1989–94
Reform of Nationality Law	1998–99
Italy	
Creation of the Democratic Party of the Left (PDS)	1989–91
Reform of Electoral law for Chamber of Deputes	1991–93
Constitutional Amendment on Equal Access	1999–2003
Netherlands	
Social Democratic Party	1966–77
Equality policy plan	1981–85
Corporatism	1989–97
Spain	
Endorsement of 25% quota in PSOE	1987–88
Endorsement of 40% quota in PSOE	1992–97
Bill for mandatory quotas in all parties	1998–2003
Sweden	
More women in politics	1967–72
Quotas for appointed positions	1985–87
Establishment of a women's party	1991–94
United Kingdom	
Reform of public bodies	1979–81
Candidate selection in Labour Party	1993
Parliamentary working hours	1997–2002

Hot Issue:

Austria	
Family policy for the sake of the children or the male breadwinner	1999–2001

(continued)

APPENDIX 1
(Continued)

Belgium	
Speedy Belgians: the new Nationality Law of 2000 and the impact of the women's movement	1999–2000
Finland	
Postponing implementation of universal day care	1991–94
France	
35-hour work-week reforms	1997–2000
Germany	
Biotechnology genetics debate	2000–02
Italy	
Debate on the reform of the state	1997–2001
Netherlands	
The 'home care gap': neoliberalism, feminism and the state in the Netherlands	1997–2001
Spain	
Unemployment insurance reform	2002
Sweden	
Child care allowance	1991–94
United Kingdom	
Constitutional change – House of Lords	1997–2003

The Changing Politics of Organised Interests

PHILIPPE C. SCHMITTER

'Interests' in *West European Politics* – in practice or in the journal – purport to explain everything and, therefore, they do not explain anything. Scratch the surface of almost any *WEP* article and you will find that the answer to 'why did he or she act politically?' will usually be: 'because it was in his or her interest to do so'. Ask 'why did he or she have such an interest in the first place?' or, even worse, 'why did he or she think that such an action or policy would eventually lead to the satisfaction of that interest?' and you will only rarely get a convincing answer.

Albert Hirschman (1977) has meticulously traced the origins of this concept and how it became such an omnipresent explanation for political action – despite the recentness of its usage and the ambiguity of its meaning. He argues that its rise in the political lexicon parallels the emergence of capitalism and, hence, has impregnated political thinking with analogies of market competition. It has become so commonplace that what used to be called 'greed' and regarded as a despicable vice by the ancients has become a universally expected and even benevolent motive among the moderns – so much so that those who still seem to be acting in the name of its antithesis, i.e. 'passions', are usually regarded as idiosyncratic and dangerous. National patriotism, religious zeal, moral certainty, family honour, tribal loyalty, personal glory and so forth are considered atavistic and more likely to lead to irresolvable conflicts and perverse outcomes than good old, prosaic but dependable, 'interests'.

Just because so many political analysts rely so much upon a notion of interests does not mean that they agree on how to define it. Following Hirschman, there seem to be three elements in common. First, interests are *self-regarding* in the sense that their pursuit is expected – rightly or wrongly – to produce a differential and favourable net benefit to the actor involved, despite the fact that quite frequently arguments in favour of them are phrased exclusively in terms of the benefit they would bring to a wider collectivity, e.g. the community, the nation, the public or the planet. Second, interests are *calculated by the actors* themselves – again, rightly or wrongly – to be of benefit rather than pursued instinctually or un-reflexively due to some prior and over-riding ethical indoctrination, social conditioning or cultural conformity, even though these same actors may include in their calculation the probability that others will react on such ethical, social or cultural grounds. Third, interests are *consciously recognised*, which follows from the previous two elements, in the sense that actors are aware of their existence (if often anxious to disguise them behind collective labels) and sufficiently concerned about their satisfaction that they are willing to act politically to obtain them (if also aware that it makes sense to 'free-ride' on the actions of others).[1]

Up to this point, the presumption seems to have been that the actors involved are exclusively individual human beings and, therefore, that a political science founded primarily on the pursuit of interests and the conflict among them has to be based on 'methodological' as well as 'epistemological' individualism. Not at all! 'Actors' as expressed above can just as well be collectivities – admittedly composed of individuals and dependent in varying degrees upon their contributions – but quite capable of regarding their own collective self-interests, making calculations about these interests and developing as well as inculcating interest consciousness in others. Indeed, one could argue that individuals would be incapable of recognising and evaluating their interests on their own, without the assistance of various collectivities in the workplace, social setting, cultural milieu and political environment that provide them with the reference points and identities that they need prior to making such an assessment. An isolated individual would be helpless without groups based on functional, territorial and/or symbolic identities.

Actual research on 'the politics of interests' as evidenced in WEP and the political science literature on Western Europe in general has focused overwhelmingly on *organisations* – permanently constituted and collectively governed – as its basic unit of observation and analysis. Of course, there exists a parallel literature on public opinion as formed by individual citizens and as measured by mass surveys, focus groups and media reports that attempts to assess its impact upon policy choices and electoral outcomes, but it would appear to be only of tangential relevance to the study of interest politics. Indeed, one often hears the accusation that 'special interests' have defeated or distorted some project that the public at large supports. What seems to count most when it comes to explaining 'who gets what, when and how' out of the competitive struggle in democratic polities depends on organised interests: political parties and factions, trade unions, professional and business associations, neighbourhood organisations, women's groups, environmental movements, advocacy groups, and so forth. Moreover, these organisations form more comprehensive systems of interest intermediation such that the influence of any one of them depends on its relationship with others.

After World War II, students of Western European politics tended to take their cues (and their premises) from such US scholars as Arthur Bentley and David Truman who had already elaborated a 'group theory of politics' that led to a natural configuration they eventually called 'pluralist'. These pioneers in the study of what was then called 'lobbying' or 'pressure group politics' such as Jean Meynaud, Allen Potter, Theodor Eschenbung, Henry Ehrmann, Graham Wootton, Samuel Finer, Roy Macridis, Harry Eckstein, Samuel Beer, Gerhard Braunthal and Joseph Lapalombara usually assumed the following:

1. Membership in all forms of interest organisation was a matter of voluntary choice by individuals.
2. These organisations were spontaneously formed and neither controlled, licensed nor sponsored by state agencies.
3. Interest associations and social movements would tend to be independent of each other and of political parties.
4. All of these organisational forms were themselves composed of 'interest groups' that coalesced and competed opportunistically in the formation of public policy.
5. Economic development would increase the division of labour and, hence, naturally lead to a multiplicity of autonomous and increasingly specialised associations competing with each other to represent the same interest category.
6. The predominant form of activity of these 'interest groups' was to exert external 'pressure' on those in elective office – whether this was accomplished in the 'lobby' of the parliament or elsewhere.
7. Whatever the existing differences, interest politics in the United States was more advanced than in Europe and the latter would eventually come to resemble the former.

As empirical research began to accumulate, these presumptions became increasingly questionable and something like a distinctive Western

European perspective on organised interest politics began to emerge. During the mid-1970s, this eventually took the form of a theoretical distinction between *pluralism* and *corporatism* as contrasting 'ideal-typical' organisational configurations. Both were compatible with capitalist development and liberal democracy, but each processed interests in quite different ways with quite different implications for public policy. Scholars began to treat Europe not as 'backward' but as 'different' with regard to the politics of interest in the United States.

According to the '*WEP* Model' (not exclusively of the journal but of the region as a whole), organised interests are especially crucial in this part of the world since they were historically and uniquely embedded in the civil societies of medieval city-states and since the later struggle for mass political democracy revolved around them. No other part of the world has developed such a dense network of class, sectoral and professional associations, such a variety of well-organised and disciplined political parties and such a historical legacy of social movements. Moreover, these units had often created relatively stable and encompassing hierarchies of collective action among themselves and had done so as the result of considerable intervention by state agencies. Rather than pressure politicians and civil servants from the outside, privileged and often monopolistic organisations were firmly entrenched inside the making of public policies and even accorded a role in their implementation.

The 'standard-revised' version of Western European politics as set out by Stein Rokkan and others presumes that these clusters of political organisations correspond to a varying set of social cleavages at the national level. Parties, associations and movements were composed of those who found themselves on different sides of these cleavages. The behaviour of these individuals could be predicted by their respective structural positions and, moreover, this behaviour of identity and loyalty tended to persist even after the original conflicts that generated them had weakened. Periodic compromises across these cleavages – often associated with war or depression – failed to dissolve their organisational expressions, precisely because they contributed so much to consolidating regimes of liberal democracy.

Some Descriptive Generalisations

Since the mid-1970s, Western European politics have undergone significant changes – and this has been particularly marked in the arena of 'interest politics'. Below, I will list 34 apodictic statements about these changes. Not all of them have been necessarily well documented in WEP (or in any other scholarly journal for that matter) and they are, for the moment, speculative observations that remain to be proven (or explained).

In presenting them, I will follow the conventional tripartite division into parties, movements and associations, even if the boundaries between them are fuzzy and changeable. Many political parties and interest associations had (and new ones continue to have) their origin in social movements. Many candidates nominated by parties have no chance of winning office or even participating in governing coalitions and are only on the ballot to attract attention to some corresponding movement. Associations make no overt attempt to nominate candidates or occupy elected positions and, thereby, to accept political responsibility for their actions, but they nevertheless may play a key role in the 'after-election' appointment process in order to place 'their people' in these offices. The key distinction between interest associations and social movements is supposed to be the self-regarding-ness of the former as they struggle to obtain selective goods only for their members and the other-regarding-ness of the latter as they promote the production of public goods that affect everyone. Needless to say, this analytical distinction may be of more rhetorical than practical difference.

While it is not inconceivable that individuals alone or spontaneous aggregations of individuals can affect policies or even bring down governments and regimes, these three types of organisations have become – certainly in Western Europe – the effective 'citizens' of their respective democracies. They offer the most reliable channels for influencing and holding accountable public authorities. The mix of their roles may differ across polities and over time, but together they constitute the civil societies that are so essential to the functioning of 'real-existing democracies' (REDs) – despite the fact that they are only rarely mentioned as such in their constitutions. As we shall now speculate, there is evidence to suggest that these organisations for representing interests (and passions) have changed a great deal in the past 25 to 30 years. This listing attempts to encompass the full variety of these changes.

Political Parties

1.　Decline in membership in and identification with political parties;
2.　Decline in trust in parties and their politicians/leaders;
3.　Decline in the role of parties in the process of forming governments;
4.　Increase in collusion between major parties and convergence in their programmes;
5.　Emergence of new parties at the fringe or take-over of pre-existing parties;
6.　Decrease in the margin of victory for winning parties or coalitions;
7.　Increase in the volatility of electoral choices by citizens;
8.　Increase in the rapidity of turnover of parties in power;
9.　Rise in the importance of public funding;
10.　Shift in organisational form from 'mass' to 'cartel' parties.

Social Movements

11. Increase in the number, variety, resources and visibility of social movements;
12. Attempts to convert some social movements into political parties, e.g. Greens;
13. Some increased recognition and access of movements as 'stakeholders';
14. Increase in the role of contributors/subscribers over members/militants;
15. Increase over time in the role of bureaucratic/professional staff;
16. Cross-national subsidisation of movements, especially from West to East;
17. Some shift in strategy from influencing public authorities to affecting the behaviour of private firms.

Interest Associations

18. Decline in membership of some traditional associations, especially trade unions;
19. Severance of long-standing connections between associations and 'sister' parties;
20. Decline in the role/capacity of encompassing peak associations;
21. Decline in resort to mechanisms of comprehensive policy concertation;
22. Shift to lower levels of inter-associational bargaining, even to micro or firm level;
23. Some increase in mergers between previously independent associations;
24. Increase in the provision of services to members as key organisational activity;
25. Steady level of membership in civil society organisations; but
26. Shift toward 'apolitical' forms of associability satisfying private interests; and
27. Shift away from 'political' forms oriented to influencing public policy decisions;
28. Challenges to well-established state practices of subsidisation and official recognition.

All Forms of Representation of Interests or Passions

29. Increase in trans-national connections between equivalent organisations;
30. Strong increase in formation of European-level associations and movements; but
31. Only modest rise in party organisation at the European or global level;
32. Spread of 'Western' organisational forms to 'Eastern' neo-democracies;

33. Increase in the role of professional staff/consultants and paid labour;
34. Persistently high level of 'interest in politics' (as measured by mass surveys) coupled with persistently declining level of participation in (electoral) politics.

An Inventory of Potential Explanations

Presuming that the observations are generally correct, what could have caused such numerous and significant changes? Even if only half of them were found to be correct, that would still leave a lot to be explained. One is tempted to claim that national civil societies in Western Europe have undergone a 'silent revolution' since the mid-1970s which has affected both the attributes of individual organisations and the configuration of their respective systems of party competition, social mobilisation and interest intermediation. And they have done this without regime discontinuity (except, of course, in Eastern Europe), widespread recourse to violence or enduring shift in the ideological orientation of governments.

Let us briefly examine the most likely suspects:[2]

1. *Impact of exogenous shocks*: The onset of the above-noted changes does correspond roughly with the two successive oil shocks of the mid-1970s. Together, they could have produced some major and lasting changes in the relations between economic sectors, but why would they have affected Left–Right party competition and capital–labour relations where most of the changes have taken place? The Southern and Northern enlargements of the EU were hardly very 'shocking', although the impact of the more recent (and much more significant) Eastern one has yet to be fully registered. The collapse of communist rule and the Soviet empire at the very end of the 1980s was certainly both unexpected and consequential. It helps to explain the convergence in programmes and collusion in behaviour of political parties (Item 4) and may have something to do with the proliferation of new 'fringe' parties (Item 5). But what might be the connection of this shock with organised interests and passions? Did it weaken the power of trade unions and of Social Democratic parties enough to bring about some of the observed transformations (Items 18 and 19)? Did the elimination of the 'Communist Menace' indirectly encourage the formation of 'radical' social movements, by freeing them of 'guilt by association' with real-existing communism (Item 11) and open up spaces on the fringe for their attempted conversion into new papers (Item 12)?

2. *Change in endogenous values*: What about the inverse causality? Is it plausible to sustain that a prior and gradual 'silent revolution' in Western European mass public opinion toward so-called post-materialist values – as documented by Ronald Inglehart and others – could be responsible for at least some of the observed changes? Many

of the new parties on the fringe (Item 5) profess such values. Items 11, 12 and 13 all refer to the surge in social movement activity which could be even more closely related to it – and, in a slightly more 'stretched' account so could the decline in membership in 'materialistic' self-regarding trade unions and employer associations (Item 18). But what about the shift towards services within associations and towards apolitical associations in general? Or the decline in the level at which bargaining between capital and labour takes place?

3. *Globalisation/liberalisation*: This is everyone's favourite suspect these days. The timing seems about right, although the process started long before the mid-1970s and gathered momentum during the 1990s. Removing political and technological barriers to the flow of goods, services, money, ideas and (to a lesser extent) people across previously more protected national or regional borders had a profound effect on the relative power of classes in the production system and the relative influence of 'exposed' as opposed to 'sheltered' sectors of the economy. Globalisation's 'twin' – the liberalisation of state ownership and regulation of private enterprises – has removed some highly contentious matters from the public agenda and even projected the image that no policy alternatives to it exist. This has repeatedly been credited with causing programmatic convergence between major parties (Item 4). Dialectically speaking, it could also be credited with promoting the shift in strategy noted in Item 17, not to mention the general rise in protest movements in response to the less regulated behaviour of private businesses (Item 11). Without a doubt, the demise of many macro-corporatist arrangements and the shift to lower level, even firm, bargaining was due to the defection of capitalists in larger multinational firms who had become more confident of their capacity to act unilaterally in defiance of trade unions (Items 21 and 22). Item 21 on the increase in transnational connections between associations and movements is a particularly direct result of globalisation, but it may well be that the shift toward service provision within associations is linked to processes of adaptation to greater competition and less protection (Item 23).

4. *Regional integration*: Western Europe has been the site of the most successful attempt at not just eliminating national barriers to exchange, but also at generating common rules to regulate transnational exchanges. Most observers have expressed surprise at its modest impact upon national political parties. My hunch is that much of the collusion among them (Item 4) and activity at the fringe (Item 5) can be attributed to the behaviour of major parties which have deliberately avoided making issues of European integration salient because these issues tend to divide their traditional supporters. The acceleration given to this process during the mid-1980s by the Single European Act must have contributed something to Item 28 since many practices of

business and professional associations violated the liberalising provisions of this treaty and subsequent EU directives. Item 30 on the formation of regional associations and movements was one clear and continuing impact of the EU. The number of business and professional interests with European representation in Brussels has reached the 1000s, although it should also be observed that direct representation of larger firms has increased even more proportionately – hinting at a process of circumvention of traditional 'corporatist' channels. The increase of inter-organisational exchanges at the wider continental or global level (Item 29) may also have been promoted by this variable, as well as globalisation. Much of the diffusion process whereby 'Western' practices moved East was closely linked to EU assistance programmes and the imperatives of adjusting to the *acquis communautaire* upon entry into the club (Item 32).

5. *Trans-continental migration*: Another process that began to affect Western Europe as a whole during this period, accelerating to crisis levels in recent years, is a massive increase in population flows from outside the region. EU treaties and directives had surprisingly little impact on intra-European labour flows. In fact, Southern enlargement seems to have produced more return flow than outflow and Northern enlargement seems only to have affected top-level professionals. Needless to say, Eastern enlargement has just begun to take hold and is already having a much more substantial effect. But it is the flows from the Middle East, Africa and Asia that have captured the political agenda and certainly stimulated the emergence of xenophobic fringe parties (Item 5). The manifest impotence (or unwillingness) of national governments to staunch these flows seems to be related to the decline in membership in governing parties and the prestige of governing politicians (Items 1 and 2). It may even be related to electoral volatility and frequency of turnover in power as citizens become more fickle in their perceptions of almost universally discredited politicians (Items 7 and 8). Presumably, the availability of low-cost foreign labour has some effect on the 'balance of class forces', but the response at the associational level is by no means obvious – and probably differs from one country to another. Macro-corporatism may be threatened (Items 20, 21 and 22) by such a shift in power, but not necessarily the other changes in associational structure and behaviour.

6. *Ageing population*: Western Europeans have been getting proportionately older during the past three decades, as birth rates and mortality rates have plummeted. The effect of this on associations and movements has received relatively little attention, but two aspects seem obvious. Older people have sustained their habits of associability and, indeed, have come to dominate specific organisational segments. For example, many trade unions in Europe today have more retired than active members, and the former demand more services (Item 24).

They also have more time to participate in recreational activities (Item 26). Moreover, associations catering to the aged have emerged and, in the East, one occasionally finds a Pensioners' Party or two. This may help to explain why youths entering the labour market find traditional trade unions less attractive (Item 18) and tend to express their interests (or, in some cases, their passions) more through social movements (Item 11).

7. *Lower economic growth*: Compared to '*Les Trente Glorieuses*' immediately after World War II, the last 30 years have been lean in terms of economic performance – and especially so for young people. The overall class and regional distribution of income in Western European democracies has been relatively constant, but job opportunities and salaries for those entering the labour market have been persistently lower than in the past. Since much of the reluctance to join established parties (Item 1) and the increase in electoral abstention have occurred among young people, it is tempting to lay the blame here. Stretching a bit further, the failure of governments of any of the major competing parties to perform markedly better may have something to do with narrowing the margins of victory (Item 6) and the subsequent consequences in terms of electoral volatility and turnover in office. Social movements have probably been boosted, especially among young people, by the failure of parties to perform when in office and by the appeal of 'alternative' solutions (Items 11, 12 and 17). High unemployment and downwardly flexible wages tend to reduce the incentives for capitalists to participate in policy concertation involving organised labour, especially at the macro-level (Items 20 and 21). They also give additional power to individual firms in the labour market (Item 22).

8. *Rapid pace of technological innovation*: The diffusion of major innovations, especially in information and communication technology, has become massive, unpredictable and uncontrollable. Some have originated within Western Europe; most have been thrust upon it from abroad. By now, it seems safe to say that not a single organisation in civil society has been unaffected by it – positively or negatively. Some have tried to resist, but once competitors have adopted them, they may have no choice but to conform. My suspicion is that most of its effect on parties, associations and movements shows up in their internal organisational structures – feeding pre-existing trends toward professionalised management, fund-raising, influence-peddling and voter-appealing (Item 33). At the extreme (admittedly, yet to be reached in Europe), political parties become little more than massive data-banks manipulated by paid specialists promoting messages generated by survey research or focus groups. Already the costs of campaigning have gone up – beyond what is covered by public funding (Item 8) – and this may have something to do with the replacement of voluntary

with paid labour and the shift to cartel forms of organisation (Item 10). Social movements have also used ICT more extensively and this seems to be reflected in Items 14 and 15: greater dependence on financial donors than upon active members and increased role for professional staff. Some use computerised schedules and professionally elaborated proposals to appeal for funds from individuals, corporations and foundations that share their cause, but never meet together – much less deliberate about the movement's goals and strategies. Those that have been recognised as bona fide 'stakeholders' (Item 13) have become even more reliant on technical expertise and data-gathering. Interest associations increasingly become electronic purveyors of specialised information and 'selective goods' to members who pay dues and fees but do not participate in their policy process (Item 24).

9. *Mediatisation*: No one doubts that mass media (and television, in particular) has become a much more important source of information and opinion about politics than civil society itself. The time when a citizen relied upon his or her party, trade union, neighbourhood organisation or 'social cause' to anchor their expectations about what public authorities should do seems gone. Survey evidence shows that, however residual this may be among older citizens, these identities and loyalties are not being passed on to sons and daughters. Each new generation seems to be starting with a blank slate – and filling it with the images and slogans it picks up from the media. Although it has emerged as a major force relatively late in the period we are considering, the use of the Internet as both a source of political information and a resource for coordinating political action has become pervasive. It is probably parties that have been most affected – negatively, in the sense of loss of members, trust and role in forming governments (Items 1, 2 and 3), but also positively in terms of the rising importance of public funding, the role of professional managers and consultants and the shift towards cartel forms of internal organisation (Items 9, 10 and 33). Social movements have also learned to exploit the media and to shift public attention away from 'the main ring of the electoral circus' towards 'the side rings of public corruption and private malfeasance'. This has not only increased their visibility (Item 11) and served to discredit parties and politicians (Item 2), but it has also helped them gain recognition (Item 13) and to shift their strategy to direct attempts to influence the behaviour of corporations. Interest associations typically operate in the shadow of public opinion and only rarely surface with 'institutional advertising' to promote the image/interest of their category. It is not clear what is the cause and effect, but the rupture between trade unions and their respective 'sister parties' has often been accompanied by a great deal of media attention (Item 19). Media promotion may also have had something to do with the shift towards more 'private-regarding' organisations in civil

society, just as well-publicised scandals may have discouraged membership and activism in more 'political-regarding' ones (Items 26 and 27).

10. *Declining capacity of the national state*: Objectively, in the context of globalisation and regionalisation, sovereign national states can no longer carry out effectively and autonomously the tasks assigned to them by their respective constitutions and expected of them by their respective citizens. Subjectively, the notion of sovereignty may still be comforting (and some even regard it as indispensable for RED), but many interests and passions can only be realised through cooperation or integration with other polities. Parties are still among the most 'national' of political organisations and even European integration has (so far) failed to affect them very much (Item 31). Both social movements and interest associations have 'Europeanised' themselves with greater ease (Items 16, 29 and 30). The fact that some, more specialised, class, sectoral and professional interests have found it easier to adapt to this trend has had a significant impact on the 'balance of socio-economic forces' that has historically been closely connected with the scope and level of collective bargaining (Items 20, 21 and 22).

11. *Increased sense of insecurity*: Much of the politics of immediate post-war Western Europe was rooted in the quest for regional security – first, in relation to potential armed conflict between Germany and France and, later, in relation to the threat of an invasion by the Soviet Union. By the mid-1970s, the region had become what Karl Deutsch called 'a security community' in which none of its members anticipated using force to resolve conflicts or interests or passions. Presumably, this helps to explain the persistently lower level of military expenditures and higher level of social expenditures in this part of the world when compared to other advanced industrial polities – and this must have had an impact on all three forms of interest organisations (and, probably, diminished the importance of 'passionate' nationalist, religious, class and moralistic organisations. It is probably too early to judge how and how much the rise in collective insecurity since 9/11 has affected such causes. So far, contrary to the United States, no specific political party has profited from this event, although it has given a boost to social movements advocating non-intervention in Iraq and resistance to limitations on civil rights.

12. *Individuation*: I have left this for last because I am convinced that it will have the longest lasting and most profound impact on the politics of interests in the future. This somewhat obscure sociological term refers to the trend for the individual to acquire – due to changes in working conditions, living situations, family structures, personal mobility and cultural contexts – a set of interests (or passions) that is increasingly specific to that individual. When and where this occurs (and the

evidence for it is less than compelling, I admit), the citizen should find it increasingly difficult to identify with those large collective categories that went into structuring what I called above the 'standard-revised WEP Model'. Those cleavages between classes, sectors, religions, ethno-linguistic groups, regions and nationalities that 'made' modern Europe do not go away – they still have plenty of mental and organisational residues left – but citizens find the identities attached to them by these cleavages much less convincing. Most importantly, they are reluctant to accept one of them as dominant and, hence, capable of exercising overarching control over all other interests or passions. Nationality may still be the most significant 'marker' in inter-state relations and class may predominate among all of the sources of intra-state conflict, but their invocation produces less predictable behaviour at the individual level and the organisations built upon these cleavages have declined in salience.

Another way of putting this point is that, in the past, what counted in determining the outcome of political struggle was the cumulative or cross-cutting distribution of interests and passions, and the emergence of some overriding identity among those involved. In the future, what will count is less the pluralism prevailing *between* collectivities within the unit as a whole than the pluralism prevailing *within* individual citizens – citizens who may grow increasingly indifferent concerning the identity of the unit as a whole and, hence, be willing to change one for another.[3] These pluralistic individuals will find it more difficult to assess what their 'real' interest or passion is in a given context – and they will be much less likely to rely on existing political parties, encompassing interest associations or comprehensive social movements to find out. They are going to change their view of politics frequently and shift their organisational allegiance more often. In the party arena, Europeans will finally act as Anthony Downs predicted long ago, switching indifferently around some 'mean' position on a uni-modal distribution of preferences depending on marginal appeals to the centre or the personality of candidates. In the arena of 'special interests' and 'passionate causes', the apposite model is pluralism. But the pending question is whether this will lead to moderation and compromise or, as I have suggested above, to populist mobilisation and intransigence.

While I am convinced that individuation (if it occurs on a significant scale) will have a major impact on interest politics, I am less capable of identifying the impact it has already had. One could blame it for decline in party membership and identification (Item 1) and trust in parties and politicians (Item 3) which, in turn, might be contributing to greater electoral volatility (Item 7), narrower margins of victory (Item 6) and greater turnover (Item 8). And why do parties depend increasingly on public funds? Because their traditional clienteles

(*Stammwähler*) have declined and others are no longer willing to contribute voluntarily (Item 9). The proliferation of types of social movements (Item 11) and the shift in their source of funding (Item 14) fits nicely within this line of reasoning. A lot of the movement among forms of organisation within civil society could also be attributed to individuation (Items 26 and 27), as could the increased resistance to semi-public status and funding for 'classic' corporatist associations (Item 28). But all of these are highly speculative connections – and none of them can be traced exclusively to this variable.[4]

Some Elements for a Conclusion

Interests furnish the primary raw materials for WEP, and that has not changed. Passions have not disappeared; indeed, there is some evidence that emotion-based and other-regarding causes have contributed to a renewal in the traditional role that social movements have played in the region. Parties, associations and movements share the task of 'processing' these materials in the REDs of Western Europe. Historically, parties with their capacity for aggregating a wide range of them into comprehensive platforms have played the predominant role. Movements may have played a role in their formation; associations representing class, sectoral and professional interests may have been penetrated by their ideologies – but, according to the standard revised model of WEP, it was political parties that best represented the cleavages, that formed the governments, that made the compromises, that produced the states, that made the politics of Europe so distinctive.

If the descriptive generalisations in this article have some accuracy and if the potential explanations drawn from contextual trends have some validity, then the hegemony of political parties is declining – which is not to say that they will be replaced by either associations or movements. The three forms of representation are not locked into a zero-sum game. In the past they have grown together and supported each other. Nothing says that they cannot also decline together in the present.

This implies a generalised loosening of the links between interests and organisations. Emile Durkheim (1997 [1883]) imagined something similar as a potential consequence of modernisation and gave it a label: *anomie*. In his scenario, the division of labour would advance more rapidly than the capacity of existing organisations to integrate individuals and inculcate in them stable identities and conceptions of interest. He envisaged serious consequences at the level of individual behaviour (suicide being the most dramatic), but said very little about its potential political implications.

My hunch is that it is something that we often label (and condemn) as *populism*. Elsewhere, I have defined this as 'a political movement that draws its support across or with disregard for the lines of cleavage that are embodied in existing political formations and does so by focusing on the person of its leader who claims to be able to resolve a package of issues previously believed to be unattainable, incompatible or excluded' (Schmitter 2006: 2). Could this be the face of the future for *WEP*? Will individuated citizens find themselves adrift without clear hierarchies of interest or passion and, therefore, choose their elected officials and interest representatives on the basis of cross-cutting promises and candidate personalities? Will they do so erratically on the basis of seemingly minor shifts in context or momentary events? There are already abundant signs of its emerging in EEP (Eastern European politics), but that could be dismissed as the product of a different point of departure where parties, associations and movements were either discredited or non-existent. Western Europe still has plenty of all three types of interest organisation, but if they are evolving as I have suggested and if individuation is such an inexorable 'developmental' trend, then populist movements-parties-associations could very well fill in part of the gap between more anomic citizens and less legitimate authorities.

The clue concerning the future lies in the last Item (34). Survey research seems to indicate that in Europe overall 'interest' in politics has not declined – even among those young citizens who are least connected with political organisations. Which raises the prospect, first suggested by Alexis de Tocqueville in his *L'Ancien Régime et la Révolution*, that the most vulnerable moment for any political regime exists when popular expectations increase or remain stable at the same time that regime performance (or, better, perception of regime performance) is in decline. Typically, this happens when political leaders attempt to introduce reforms that do not have immediate payoffs. This was later formalised by James Davies (1962) as the 'J-Curve' and connected with the hypothesis that it would produce increasingly violent collective action and, eventually, revolution. For contemporary Europe this projection seems highly exaggerated – either because the gap between expectations and performance is not (yet) so great or is too demographically concentrated, or because the capacity of social and economic institutions to absorb the disparity remains so great. My prognosis is, therefore, the periodic eruption of populist 'incidents' that do not threaten democracy as such and, in fact, may even have the benevolent effect of dissolving partisan collusions and oligarchic accumulations. As long as the electoral process remains 'free and fair' and basic political rights are constitutionally protected, the result of such incidents in Europe is quite predictable: the populists will be defeated eventually because they will have promised too much to too many – and failed to deliver even to those oppressed groups that they pretend to favour. They will exit peacefully (if noisily) from power probably leaving behind an economic mess and social confusion. It will be the task of a new (and hopefully rejuvenated) set of political interest organisations to reconnect citizens with their rulers and to hold them accountable for their exercise of legitimate authority.

Notes

1. Actually, some ambiguity with regard to this element has re-emerged in recent years. Rational choice analysts prefer to talk about 'preferences', presumably mimicking economists who have long used the concept of 'revealed preferences' in their theories. These are not expressions of conscious interests ('concerns') that actors give when asked why they acted or what they would like to gain from political action. Quite the contrary! These are the motives for action that can be imputed to actors on the basis of prior assumptions by theorists – regardless of whether the actors involved choose them in surveys, respond to them in interviews or express them in the course of acting. Indeed, such consciously articulated preferences are intrinsically suspect because actors have 'rational' reasons for not admitting to their 'true' preferences – especially when it comes to public goods. All this reminds me of an earlier debate over 'false consciousness', when Marxists – faced with identities and goals of proletarians that were not sufficiently revolutionary or even anti-capitalist – dismissed them on the grounds that such underlings could not be expected to recognise what their 'true' interests were due to the deliberate manipulation or inherent hegemony of dominant classes.
2. Except for the first two, the other variables come from an extensive list of trends in the external context in which 'real-existing' European democracies have been functioning over the last 30 years to be found in Schmitter and Trechsel (2004).
3. Consider what this could do to the so-called micro-foundations of the discipline. The individual no longer becomes the irreducible unit of action or analysis with a presumed fixed hierarchy of preferences. The individual is now a 'bundle' of interests (and passions) and the preference for any one of them depends on the context within which the choice is made.
4. One major change listed above (Item 10) that has passed under-explained (and un-defined) concerns internal party organisation, for which I plead lack of expertise. Richard Katz and Peter Mair (1995; also Mair this volume) have argued convincingly that significant changes in this condition have occurred during this period in the process of the shift from mass to cartel parties. Given the novelty of the concept, I have found it difficult to distinguish its causes, characteristics and effects.

References

Davies, James C. (1962). 'Towards a Theory of Revolution', *American Sociological Review*, 27:1, 5–18.
Durkheim Emile (1997 [1983]). *The Division of Labor in Society*. New York: The Free Press, originally published in 1893.
Hirshmann, Albert O. (1977). *The Passions and the Interests*. Princeton, NJ: Princeton University Press.
Katz, Richard S., and Peter Mair (1995). 'Changing Models of Party Organization and Party Democracy: The Emergence of the Cartel Party', *Party Politics*, 1:1, 5–28.
Schmitter, Philippe C. (2006). 'A Balance Sheet of the Vices and Virtues of Populism', EUI, unpublished article, April 2006 [translated and published as 'I populismi: vizi e virtù', *Aspenia*, 36 (2007), 71–9 and 'Los vicios y virtues de los "populismos": un balance general', *Revista Iberoamericana de Analisis Politico*, 3:4/5 (Novembre 2006), 208–15].
Schmitter, Philippe C., and Alexander H. Trechsel, eds. (2004). *The Future of Democracy in Europe: Trends, Analyses and Reforms*. Strasbourg: Council of Europe Publishing.

The Challenge to Party Government

PETER MAIR

Although the analysis of parties and party systems has proved an enduring concern within comparative European politics, the amount of attention that the topic has received has tended to ebb and flow over the decades. Just over 40 years ago, four path-breaking volumes were published that effectively defined the parameters of comparative party studies thereafter: Dahl's *Political Oppositions* (1966), LaPalombara and Weiner's *Political Parties and Political Development* (1966), Lipset and Rokkan's *Party Systems and Voter Alignments* (1967) and Epstein's *Political Parties in Western Democracies* (1967). These volumes represented a true explosion of capacity in the field, and effectively brought comparative party studies into the modern age. A decade later, and not long before the launch of this journal, this new wave of party literature reached the apogee marked by the publication of Sartori's *Parties and Party Systems* (1976;[1] see also Sartori 2005), perhaps the most important single contribution to the field. Thereafter, despite occasional high points (e.g., Janda 1980; Panebianco 1988), attention faded, such that within the European political science literature of the 1980s, in what was otherwise a period of major scholarly development, political parties tended to be deemed passé. This was partly because of the priority then being accorded to other closely related themes, most notably the study of corporatism, on the one hand, and the new social movements, on the other, with both phenomena being seen as more interesting or more important modes of interest intermediation than parties, and partly because the interest in parties in government had become absorbed into the burgeoning literature on coalition formation and public policy processes (see Katz and Mair 1992: 1).

Since the beginning of the 1990s, party studies have experienced a revival, such that by now even the highlights within the literature are too numerous to be specified (see Montero and Gunther 2002). There is now a successful and widely cited journal dedicated exclusively to the study of parties, *Party Politics*, launched in 1995, and, for the first time in the modern history of party studies, there is also a substantial empirical as well as theoretical literature on party organisations. All of this is to the good, of course, both for comparative politics scholars in general, and for students of party politics in particular. But there may also be an irony here, for at a time when the literature on parties in Europe is brimming with health and vitality, the parties themselves seem to be experiencing potentially severe legitimacy problems and to be suffering from a quite massive withdrawal of popular support and affection. In this paper, I intend to address one key aspect of the problems facing contemporary parties in Europe, which is the challenge to party government.[2] I begin by reviewing the changing pattern of party competition, in which I discuss the decline of partisanship in policy-making and the convergence of parties into a mainstream consensus. I then look again at the familiar 'parties-do-matter' thesis and at the evidence for declining partisanship within the electorate. In the third section of the paper I explore the various attempts to specify the conditions for party government, before going on in the final section to argue that these conditions have been undermined in such a way that it is now almost impossible to imagine party government in contemporary Europe either functioning effectively or sustaining complete legitimacy.

The Convergence of Parties

For a variety of inter-related reasons, the conflicts that divide political parties in the older democracies of Western Europe have attenuated substantially in the past 30 years. This has occurred at two different levels. In the first place, there has been a reduction in levels of ideological polarisation, in that formerly 'anti-system' parties – that is, parties that challenge the fundamental principles on which democratic regimes are founded, and that espouse a wholly alternative political settlement – have either moderated their demands and thus moved closer to the mainstream, or have experienced significant reductions in their electoral support. On the right, for example, the former anti-system alternative has now all but disappeared, being substituted instead by far-right parties, or national populist parties, which, though often espousing very radical and anti-consensual policy positions, do not claim to challenge the democratic regime as such (Mudde 2007). Indeed, in recent years it has often proved quite easy for mainstream parties of the centre-right to incorporate such parties into government – whether as full-fledged coalition partners, as in the case of the Austrian Freedom Party, the Italian National Alliance, or the Dutch Pim Fortuyn List; or as formal support parties for minority governments, as in the case of the Danish People's Party. Anti-system parties of the left have also tended to moderate or to fade away. In the wake of the collapse of the Soviet Union, for example, communist parties either gave up the ghost or transformed themselves into more widely acceptable social-democratic alternatives, and those that have chosen the latter route have also enjoyed access to government office. Even Sinn Fein, the political wing of what had been until recently a very active and highly visible terrorist group, the IRA, now shares power within the devolved government of Northern Ireland. Green parties, for their part, also quickly abandoned their pretensions to operate outside the system and became easily incorporated in broad-based centre-left coalitions. In a way that would have proved unthinkable in the 1950s and 1960s, therefore, more or less all West European parties have now entered the political mainstream and have become *salonfähig*. As far as electoral politics is concerned, it is only the democratic alternative that is now on offer.[3]

Although this new form of consensus might now be taken for granted, it represents quite a fundamental shift from the patterns that prevailed even as late as the 1970s, when *West European Politics* was first established. Consider the situation in Italy, for example, where the contrast can be most visibly marked. In the mid-1970s, the key dynamic in Italian politics was that associated with the so-called 'historic compromise', by which the powerful Italian Communist Party (PCI), then the strongest such party in Western Europe, had begun to knock on the door of cabinet office. The issue of communist participation in government had come to a head in January 1978, with the resignation of Giulio Andreotti's minority Christian Democrat (DC) government. This was the 35th DC-led government since 1946, and was the most recent in a long row of unstable governments that had been constructed on the basis of excluding both the PCI on the left, and the small neo-fascist Social Movement (MSI) on the right. By early 1978, however, it seemed that it would be impossible to reconstitute such a government again, leaving the only remaining option that of formally incorporating the PCI into the majority. For many commentators, both inside and outside Italy, this was an extremely worrying prospect. So much so, indeed, that it prompted an exceptional public warning from the US State Department, which on 12 January 1978, midway through the one-term Presidency of Democrat Jimmy Carter, issued the following statement:

Our position is clear: we do not favor [communist participation in Western governments] and would like to see Communist influence in any Western European country reduced...The United States and Italy share profound democratic values and interests, and we do not believe that the Communists share those values and interests. As the President [Carter] said in Paris last week: 'It is precisely when democracy is up against difficult challenges that its leaders must show firmness in resisting the temptation of finding solutions in non-democratic forces.'[4]

The same argument was echoed by the former US Secretary of State Henry Kissinger in a review of the electoral successes and potential successes of communist parties in Italy, France, Portugal and Spain. For Kissinger (1978: 184–5), 'the accession to power of Communists in an allied country would represent a massive change in European politics;...would have fundamental consequences for the structure of the postwar world as we have known it and for America's relationship to its most important alliances; and...would alter the prospects for security and progress for all free nations'. At the height of the Cold War, in other words, the communist electoral alternative was simply unacceptable. The ideological gap was too wide, and the strategic intentions as well as the legitimacy of the party itself were too suspect.

In the event, of course, the PCI never did win admittance to government. Andreotti went on to form a new minority administration and he continued to carve a successful career in US-friendly politics until his party collapsed in a wave of corruption scandals, and he himself was brought before the courts on charges of complicity in Mafia-related crimes. Indeed, it was not until 1996 that the more moderate successors to the PCI, the Party of the Democratic Left (DS), finally entered government as the then leading party in a broad-based centre-left coalition, under the leadership of Romano Prodi, later President of the European Commission. Three years later, this government again came into close contact with a US administration, this time led by Bill Clinton, the first Democrat to hold the Presidency since Carter. In November 1999, Clinton travelled to Florence in order to take part in an international gathering of various national political leaders. The idea of the meeting was to discuss their shared styles of politics, and its purpose was to sketch out a blueprint for a so-called 'Progressive Governance for the 21st Century'. Among the other national leaders taking part in these 'third way' discussions were Fernando Cardoso from Brazil, Tony Blair from the UK, Lionel Jospin from France and Gerhard Schröder from Germany. More strikingly, the meeting itself was hosted and chaired by Massimo d'Alema, then leader of the DS – that is, the former Communist Party – and by then also head of the new Italian centre-left government. Since the end of the Cold War his party was obviously no longer seen – by the Americans or by others – as a threat to the prospects for progress of all free nations. Instead, it was now being heralded as a component part of the supposed blueprint for progress. For d'Alema himself, meanwhile, 'the most "progressive" undertaking we [the Italian centre-left] have accomplished has been to get the national accounts in order and take the lira into the European currency by cutting inflation, lowering interest rates'.[5] This was a far cry from having threatened the future of the free world.

While times have changed for parties trying to survive outside the mainstream, they have also changed for those inside the boundaries of conventional politics. This is the second level at which major changes can be highlighted. Just three years before Kissinger and the US State Department were warning Italy about stretching its government too far, for example, the noted political scientist, S.E. Finer (1975), was mounting a major assault on what he called Britain's 'adversary politics'. Britain was then characterised by a highly competitive pattern of two-party politics. The Labour party had held government, with quite small majorities, from 1964 to 1970, and was then replaced by the Conservatives, also with a narrow majority, who held office until March 1974. Labour then returned as a minority government and, following a second election in late 1974, managed to retain power with a small overall majority. The party remained in office until 1979, when it was displaced by Margaret Thatcher's first Conservative government. From that point on, what had been a classic two-party system drifted towards what might better be seen as alternating predominant party systems, with the Conservatives holding power through three further elections, usually with massive majorities, and with Labour winning with its own overwhelming majority in 1997, and repeating this victory in 2001 and 2005.

In the mid-1970s, however, the pattern was obviously much more changeable, competitive and adversarial, and it was this which proved of particular concern to Finer. Not only did the politics of the time reflect a marked degree of polarisation and conflict, but it also see-sawed dramatically in terms of policy, with each newly incumbent government seeking to undo the policies that had been promoted by its predecessor. For Finer (1975: 3), British politics had deteriorated into 'a stand-up fight between two adversaries for the favour of the lookers-on . . . [and] what sharpens this contestation is that the stakes are extremely high'. Later in that same book he spoke disparagingly of 'the discontinuities, the reversals, the extremisms of the existing system' (Finer 1975: 32). A similar concern was voiced by Lord Hailsham, a former Conservative cabinet member, who complained about the British system becoming 'an elective dictatorship', in which the opposition was powerless and in which government programmes were based on strongly partisan considerations.[6]

Since the last years of the Thatcher governments, however, and in sharp contrast to this earlier pattern, the parties in Britain have rushed to the centre, with the win–win politics of New Labour's 'Third Way' in particular being promoted as a way of replacing the guiding role of ideology and partisanship in the process of policy-making. In place of the politics of party, and hence in place of the reversals and extremisms of the earlier system, there came what Burnham (1999, 2001) has identified as 'the politics of depoliticisation' – a governing strategy in which decision-making authority is passed over to ostensibly non-partisan bodies and in which binding rules are adopted which deny discretion to the government of the day. This was a politics that was couched in strictly non-party terms, and in the British case in particular it was presented as a new synthesis that rose above the traditional divisions of left and right and that therefore became non-contestable: the politics of 'what works'. As Britain's two-party system gave way to alternating periods of predominance, so too British adversary politics gave way to a new centrist consensus. The parties might still compete with one another for votes, sometimes even intensively, but they came to find themselves sharing the same broad commitments in government and being bound to the same ever-narrowing parameters of policy-making.

The increased sharing of commitments is also in evidence in other systems, particularly those in which there is a pronounced separation of powers, and/or those in which government is usually formed by a coalition of parties. In France, at least prior to the recent reform that shortens the presidential term, it had become quite common to see a form of US-style 'divided government', whereby left-wing presidents cohabited with right-wing parliaments and governments, or vice versa, with both sides being more or less obliged to find agreement, or consensus, on what government did. Across the continental European parliamentary systems, the basis for consensus and the sharing of commitments has also become more marked. In the Netherlands, for example, precedent was broken when, for the first time in Dutch history, a new government coalition was formed in 1994 that brought together in one cabinet the Labour Party and the right-wing Liberal Party, the two parties that, up to that point, had constituted the main alternative poles within the system. In Ireland, the traditional bipolar pattern of competition was irrevocably broken when Labour, long the traditional ally of Fine Gael, crossed the traditional 'civil war' divide to form a government with Fianna Fáil in 1993. In Germany, a new coalition in the late 1990s brought the Greens and Social Democrats together in government, and, as a result of the institutional constraints that operate in the German Federal Republic, forced both to work together with the opposition Christian Democrats, the party that held sway in the powerful upper house of parliament. In contemporary politics, in other words, it has become less and less easy for any one party or bloc of parties to monopolise power, with the result that shared government has become more commonplace.[7] As more or less all parties become coalitionable, coalition-making has become more promiscuous. This, together with the need for balance across separated domestic and European institutions, has inevitably led policy-making to become less partisan.

Do Parties Matter?

This last assertion is important and requires some justification. Since at least the late 1970s, a large number of political scientists from a variety of scholarly traditions have spent countless hours assessing, evaluating and debating research into the impact of parties on public policy, and discussing whether partisanship in government can be related to policy-making, policy choices and policy outputs (for an early assessment, see Rose 1980; Castles 1983). Initially, the balance of the argument seemed to favour the relevance of partisanship – the 'parties-do-matter' school. The radical conservative governments led by Ronald Reagan and Margaret Thatcher, and the sudden shift towards a neo-liberal consensus in the 1980s offered telling testimony in this regard, while over the course of the decades, a series of more or less sophisticated cross-national comparisons also emphasised the impact of parties, albeit in practice sometimes qualified by the role of other socio-structural, institutional or political determinants of outcomes (see Schmidt 1996; Keman 2002). In sum, the evidence suggested that partisan differences mattered.

This view also persisted even into the 1990s, despite the expectations that any residual partisan effects might have been undermined by the growing impact of globalisation. In a much cited analysis that incorporated evidence up to the late 1980s, for example, Garrett argued that globalisation had failed to erode either national autonomy (in the sense that it had not prevented nations forging their own policy solutions), or the capacity of left-wing or social democratic governments to pursue policies aimed at reducing market-generated inequalities. In other words, despite globalisation, countries and their governments – and hence also the parties in these governments – retained a major capacity for political control, suggesting that 'the impact of electoral politics has not been dwarfed by market dynamics' (Garrett 1998: 2). Garrett (1998: 10, 11) went on to advance two main reasons for this conclusion. First, far from disempowering partisan constituencies, globalisation had actually 'generated new political constituencies for left-of-centre parties among the increasing ranks of the economically insecure that offset the shrinking of the manufacturing working class'; second, globalisation offered new 'political incentives for left-wing parties to pursue economic policies that redistribute wealth and risk in favour of those adversely affected in the short term by market dislocations'. Even in the changed circumstances of late twentieth-century politics, therefore, party differences and left–right oppositions still played a major role in the policy-making process.

But although another highly authoritative analysis of the impact of partisan politics on macroeconomic policies by Carles Boix (1998) came to similar conclusions, in this case the most recent evidence appeared to suggest a weakening of the relationship over time. When first faced with pressure to liberalise financial markets in the 1980s, for example, non-socialist governments tended to act quite quickly, whereas socialist governments delayed or even resisted the process. By the end of the decade, however, these differences had evaporated, and 'an autonomous monetary policy became extremely hard to pursue' (Boix 1998: 70). Indeed, Garrett's later figures were also beginning to tell a different story. Looking at data that stretched into the 1990s, and in contrast to his earlier conclusions, he now found there was much more support for the idea that globalisation limited domestic autonomy and hence helped to force parties into common positions (Garrett 2000: 36–7). This conclusion was echoed in other contemporaneous analyses of policy profiles and outcomes. Within the traditionally contentious area of welfare policy, for example, Huber and Stephens' (2001: 321) exhaustive analysis showed ample evidence of the 'reduction and then the disappearance of partisan effects', while Caul and Gray's (2000: 235) analysis of party manifesto data showed a strong process of convergence between left and right, such that already by the end of the 1980s 'political parties across advanced industrial democracies increasingly find it difficult to maintain distinct identities'.

In itself, this drift towards declining partisanship is hardly surprising. Parties were always more likely to matter in the so-called 'Golden Age' of embedded liberalism, a period which lasted from the 1950s through to the early 1970s, and during which political parties were relatively unconstrained in shaping the policy outcomes that might matter to their electorates. As Scharpf (2000: 24; see also Ruggie 1982; Ferrera this volume) has put it, national governments and the parties that formed them could then easily shelter behind 'semi-permeable economic boundaries . . . [and] ignore the exit options of capital owners, tax payers and consumers'. By the late 1970s and early 1980s, however, the domestic capacity to control the economic environment was already going into decline, with the end of this Golden Age being signalled by the breakdown of the Bretton Woods system of fixed exchange rates and then by the first major oil-price crisis. By then, as Scharpf (2000: 27–9) goes on to point out, governments were not only losing their ability to shape the economy, but also their desire to do so, and it was this shift in attitude as much as circumstance that was later to provoke the widespread waves of deregulation, privatisation, and liberalisation. Ruggie (1997: 7) had come to similar conclusions, arguing in his reflections on the end of embedded liberalism that the expansion and integration of global capital markets in the 1990s had 'eroded traditional instruments of economic policy while creating wholly new policy challenges that neither governments nor market players yet fully understand let alone can fully manage'.

Declining Electoral Cohesion

It is not just the *supply* of partisan policy-making that determines whether parties make a difference. It is also a matter of what is *demanded* at the electoral level. Manfred Schmidt (2002: 168) has usefully pointed out that the very logic of the 'parties-matter' thesis builds from two core propositions: first, that the 'social constituencies of political parties in constitutional democracies have *distinctive preferences* and successfully feed the process of policy formation with these preferences'; and, second, that the 'policy orientations of political parties broadly *mirror* the preferences of their *social constituencies*' (see also Keman 2002). It follows that in the absence of such constituencies there is little by way of collective preferences that can be mirrored, even if the parties could or wished to mirror them, and hence the whole logic of the partyness of policy-making becomes difficult to sustain.

It is beyond dispute that the once distinct electorates of the various mainstream political parties in Western Europe have become markedly less cohesive in the past two to three decades. To be sure, it can be shown that traditional cleavages remain relevant to voting behaviour. For all the changes that have been wrought in the economy and in the polity over the past decades, for example, workers are still more likely than the middle class to vote for left-of-centre parties, and active church attenders are still more likely than secular voters to support religious parties. This is undeniable (e.g. Elff 2007). But what is also clear is that the relative weight of these voting determinants has declined. Church attenders might still vote along religious lines, but there are markedly fewer such citizens within the European electorates than was the case 30 years ago, and hence their capacity to shape electoral politics has eroded (Broughton and ten Napel, 2000). The shifts in class voting are even more pronounced. The core working class constituencies have experienced pronounced demographic decline, while the homogeneity of political preferences within the remaining class cohorts has dissipated. In the most comprehensive and nuanced comparative study to date, Knutsen (2007) points to a substantial decline in both absolute and relative class voting in Western Europe since the mid-1970s, with the falls being most pronounced in precisely those polities where class had once been a very strong predictor of political preference (see also Knutsen 2007).

It is also beyond dispute that, in responding to, and sometimes even provoking, the changes in their electoral alignments, parties have become electorally more catch-all, easing their grip on once core social constituencies while extending their appeal ever more broadly across traditional class and religious lines. In part, of course, this is the inevitable result of social change. Since the core constituencies themselves have begun to decline or to fragment, there is less within the social structure for the parties to grip (see also Freire 2006). Voters, as Mark Franklin and his colleagues (1992) already showed some time ago, have become more 'particularised'. But in coming to terms with this social change the individual parties have also had to learn to be more attractive to those segments of the electorate which were once seen as beyond the pale – religious parties have had to learn to appeal to secular voters, socialist parties to middle-class voters, liberal parties to working-class voters, and farmers' parties to urban voters. In other words, it is not only that the vote has become more free-floating and available, but so also have the parties themselves, with the result that political competition has become characterised by the contestation of socially inclusive appeals in search of support from socially amorphous electorates.

The tendency towards the decline of collective identities within Western electorates that had resulted from more or less common socio-economic or socio-cultural processes has therefore been further accentuated at the political level by the behaviour and strategies of the competing political parties, and one key consequence of this has been to undermine the key foundations of partisanship in policy-making and in government. Indeed, given the absence of coherent and relatively enduring social constituencies, there is little remaining on which parties can build or identify stable alignments. To be sure, the sort of ad hoc constituencies that are inevitably constructed in the process of electoral campaigning may also be marked by distinct sets of preferences, and such sets of preferences may be more or less sharply in competition with one another; but these are hardly likely to match the sort of enduring identities and interests that once characterised the traditional core constituencies of cleavage politics, and are therefore unlikely to be understood – or assumed – with the same degree of conviction by political leaders. It is in this sense that catch-allism, as well as the social conditions that foster it, proves anathema to partisan politics.

In fact, the decline of partisan identities is one of the most telling changes in European mass politics in the last 30 years. Dalton (2004: 31–4) has documented this in some detail, and has shown unequivocally that partisanship within European electorates has become significantly eroded in the past decades. In all but two of the 13 countries listed in the summary figures reported in Table 1 (Belgium and Denmark), the annual trend in

TABLE 1
TRENDS IN PARTY IDENTIFICATION IN WESTERN EUROPE, 1960s–1990s

Country	Per annum trend in:	
	% party identifiers	% strong party identifiers
Austria	−0.916	−0.663
Belgium	+0.090	−0.285
Britain	−0.202	−0.882
Denmark	+0.001	−0.207
Finland	−0.293	−0.147
France	−0.712	−0.329
Iceland	−0.675	−0.250
Ireland	−1.510	−0.767
Italy	−0.979	−0.770
Luxembourg	−0.317	−0.316
Netherlands	−0.329	−0.129
Norway	−0.542	−0.450
Sweden	−0.733	−0.543

Source: Dalton (2004: 33), as derived from Eurobarometer and election study data.

levels of party identification has fallen quite substantially. In all countries, this time without exception, levels of strong party identification have also fallen. As Dalton (2004: 32) suggests: 'If party attachments reflect citizen support for the system of party-based representative government, then the simultaneous decline in party attachments...offers a strong sign of the public's affective disengagement from political authorities.' Other strong signs are also readily visible (see Mair 2005a), including the recent growth to record high levels of aggregate electoral volatility, the recent decline to record low levels of electoral turnout, and the near universal and very marked drop in levels of party membership. Voters might still tend to line up behind one or other of the competing parties or coalitions of parties at election time, but who these voters are, or for how long they might remain aligned, becomes less and less predictable. There is greater uncertainty about whether any individual citizen will go to the polls, and, even if s/he votes, there is greater uncertainty about the preference s/he might reveal. In this sense, voting patterns have become less structured, more random, and hence also increasingly unpredictable and inconsistent. Thus in France in 2007, for example, in the space of a brief eight-week period, there occurred a presidential election that registered a record high turnout of 84 per cent, and

TABLE 2
GROWING BIPOLARISM AMONG THE LONG-STANDING EUROPEAN
DEMOCRACIES

	1950s–1960s N = 16	1990s–2000s N = 23
Bipolar Competition is Present	Denmark France Ireland Malta Norway Sweden UK	Austria Denmark France Germany Ireland Italy Malta Norway Sweden UK
	43.8% (N = 7)	**62.5% (N = 10)**
Bipolar Competition is Absent	Austria Belgium Finland Germany Iceland Italy Luxembourg Netherlands Switzerland	Belgium Finland Iceland Luxembourg Netherlands Switzerland
	56.2% (N = 9)	**37.5% (N = 6)**

Note: Table entries refer to countries that have experienced bipolar competition for government at either some elections or all elections in the given period.
Source: Mair (2008).

a legislative election that registered a record low turnout of 60 per cent (Sauger 2007).

Let me try to draw these strands together. In many different respects – including their patterns of incumbency, their policy commitments, and their electoral profiles – parties within the mainstream have become less easily distinguished from one another than was the case in the polities of the late 1970s. Despite the growing evidence of bipolar competition (Table 2; also see below), the parties now share government with one another more easily and more readily, with any lingering differences in policy-seeking goals appearing to matter less than the shared cross-party ambition for office. Policy discretion has become increasingly constrained by the imperatives of globalisation, and, within the much expanded EU and EFTA area, by the strictures imposed by the Growth and Stability Pact and the financial discipline demanded by the European Central Bank. Even when parties are in government, in other words, the freedom for partisan manoeuvre is severely limited, and this too makes the task of differentiating between parties or between governments more difficult. Finally, a combination of increasing social homogenisation – the blurring of traditional identity boundaries – and increasing individualisation has cut across differences in partisan electoral profiles, leaving most of the mainstream protagonists chasing more or less the same bodies of voters with more or less the same persuasive campaigning techniques. Through the sharing of office, programmes and voters, albeit sometimes as competing coalitions, the parties have become markedly less distinct from one another, while partisan purpose is itself seen as less meaningful or even desirable.

The Problem of Party Government

This also serves to undermine the notion of party government. Party government is a somewhat elusive concept which only began to receive attention in the European literature in the late 1960s, less than a decade before *WEP* was launched. By then, however, it was already a prominent theme within discussions of US politics, with the APSA 1950 Report *Towards a More Responsible Two-Party System* being at the centre of American debates on political and institutional reform. This much cited and later much criticised APSA report had been heavily influenced by the work of E.E. Schattschneider, a strong advocate of party government, who emphasised the need for effective choice and accountability in federal elections. As he argued in 1945:

> The major party in a two-party system is typically and essentially a mobiliser of majorities for the purpose of taking control of the government; it is the most potent form of democratic political organisation available for our use. The major party is the only

political organisation in American public life which is in a position to make a claim, upon any reasonable grounds whatsoever, that it can measure up to the requirements of modern public policy...It alone submits its claims to the nation in a general election in which the stakes are a mandate from the people to govern the country. (Schattschneider 1945: 1151)

In US practice, however, these arguments tended to fall somewhat flat, with many of the early responses to the APSA report suggesting that it was oriented towards a British style of cabinet government and majoritarian democracy, a system that was anathema to many American observers (see Kirkpatrick 1971). Nor did the arguments receive much support in Europe. In this case, it was again a British or perhaps Anglo-American two-party model that was seen to be favoured, and hence the arguments themselves were deemed largely irrelevant (see Daalder 1987).

The first substantial attempt to address the issue of party government in the European context was developed by Richard Rose (1969) and was also heavily biased towards the Anglo-American experience, although the analysis itself concluded with an attempt to draw more wide-ranging cross-national conclusions and to elaborate a series of hypotheses that could be tested in a wide variety of systems.[8] For Rose (1969: 413), party government is about the capacity of parties to 'translate possession of the highest formal offices of a regime into operational control of government'. And since this capacity varied from system to system, and also over time, his analysis sought to identify the more specific conditions that were required for parties to influence government. These are listed in Box 1, and may be summarised as requiring a winning party to have identifiable policies and to have the organisational and institutional capacity to carry these out through the people it appoints for that purpose. This is what constitutes operational control of government and hence what may be defined in these circumstances as the practice of party government. In the absence of these

BOX 1
ROSE CONDITIONS FOR PARTY GOVERNMENT

1. At least one party must exist and, after some form of contest, it must become dominant in the regime;
2. Nominees of the party then occupy important positions in the regime;
3. The number of partisans nominated for office is large enough to permit partisans to participate in the making of a wide range of policies;
4. The partisans in office must have the skills necessary to control large bureaucratic organisations;
5. Partisans must formulate policy intentions for enactment once in office;
6. Policy intentions must be stated in a 'not unworkable' form;
7. Partisans in office must give high priority to carrying out party policies;
8. The party policies that are promulgated must be put into practice by the personnel of the regime.

Source: Rose (1969: 416–18).

conditions, alternative forms of government may be identified, among which Rose (1969: 418) lists government by charismatic leadership, traditional government, military government, government 'by inertia', and in particular 'administrative government', whereby 'civil servants not only maintain routine services of government, but also try to formulate new policies'.

A similar but more parsimonious list of conditions for party government was later elaborated by Katz (1986: 43–4) in a more abstract analysis that was intended for application to a wide variety of parliamentary and presidential systems. For Katz, party government required three conditions. First, all major governmental decisions were to be taken by people chosen in electoral contests conducted along party lines, or at least by individuals appointed by and responsible to such people. Second, policy was to be decided within the governing party or by negotiations among parties in the case of coalition governments. In this sense policy was to be made on party lines 'so that each party may be collectively accountable for "its" position' (Katz 1986: 43). Third, the highest officials (ministers, prime ministers) were to be selected within parties and to be held responsible for their actions and policies through parties. Most importantly, this third condition implied that 'positions in government must flow from support within the party rather than party positions flowing from electoral success' (Katz 1986: 43). In a slightly later publication, Katz (1987: 7) adapted and summarised these condition into the five inter-related stipulations shown in Box 2. That is, party government is manifest when winning parties both decide and enact policies through officials who are recruited and held accountable by party. Katz also follows Rose (1969) in identifying a series of alternatives to party government, derived in this case from the concrete case analyses developing from his model: corporatist or neo-corporatist government, in which policies are set through negotiations between interests that are directly affected by the policies; pluralist democracy, in which each individual candidate and elected official is responsible to his or her own constituency, and in which party as such does not figure; and direct democracy, in which policies are determined by referendum and in which elections do not prove decisive for offering mandates or securing accountability (Katz 1987: 18–20).[9]

The decisiveness of the electoral process and a strong foundation of electoral accountability are also central to a more recent version of the party government model that has been elaborated by Thomassen (1994). In this

BOX 2
KATZ CONDITIONS FOR PARTY GOVERNMENT

1. Decisions are made by elected party officials or by those under their control;
2a. Policy is decided within parties which
2b. then act cohesively to enact it;
3a. Officials are recruited and
3b. held accountable through party.

Source: Katz (1987: 7).

case the emphasis is less on party government as such, and more on the role of elections as a mechanism of linkage and representation. Nevertheless, though differently oriented, the core conditions of Thomassen's party government model and, as he emphasises, of the 'responsible parties model', are quite similar to those of Rose and Katz (see Box 3) and are manifest when the will of the majority of the electorate is reflected in government policy.

All three sets of stipulations share much common ground, although the bias varies somewhat between an emphasis on policy-making in the case of Rose (1969), on recruitment in the case of Katz (1987), and on the electoral connection in the case of Thomassen (1994). If we try to synthesise them, bringing all three emphases together, then a single set of core stipulations can be suggested. Party government *in democratic polities* will prevail when a party or parties wins control of the executive as a result of competitive elections, when the political leaders in the polity are recruited by and through parties, when the (main) parties or alternatives in competition offer voters clear policy alternatives, when public policy is determined by the party or parties holding executive office, and when that executive is held accountable through parties. These stipulations are summarised in Box 4. Equally, party government will not prevail, or will certainly be severely weakened, should one or more of these conditions be absent.

It is the contention of this paper that, with time, these conditions are becoming marked more by their absence than by their presence in

BOX 3
THOMASSEN CONDITIONS FOR PARTY GOVERNMENT

1. Voters have a choice, in the sense that they can choose between at least two parties with different policy proposals.
2. The parties are sufficiently cohesive or disciplined to enable them to implement their policy.
3. Voters vote according to their policy preferences, that is, they choose the party that represents their policy preferences best. This in turn requires that:
    (a) Voters have policy preferences, and
    (b) Voters are aware of the differences between the programmes of different political parties.
4. The party or coalition winning the elections takes control of government.
5. Both the policy programmes of political parties and the policy preferences of voters are constrained by a single ideological dimension.

Source: Thomassen (1994).

BOX 4
SUMMARY CONDITIONS FOR PARTY GOVERNMENT

1. A party (parties) wins control of the executive as a result of competitive elections;
2. Political leaders are recruited by and through parties;
3. Parties offer voters clear policy alternatives;
4. Public policy is determined by the party (parties) in the executive;
5. The executive is held accountable through parties.

contemporary European politics. In short, as a result of long-term shifts in the character of elections, parties and party competition, it is precisely this set of conditions that is being undermined.[10]

The Waning of Party Government

Within the limited scope of this essay, it is impossible to offer a full account of the changing conditions of party government – indeed, much of what is relevant here is amply covered in many of the other contributions to this volume, including those on the executive, governance, regulation, interests, and values.[11] What can be done, however, is to identify a series of key changes which effect a number of the conditions listed above, and which together point towards a major shift in modes of government in Western Europe.

I will begin with the condition that has not faded, however, and which, if anything, has become even more evident with time: the condition by which a party or parties wins control of the executive as a result of competitive elections. This has obviously always been the case in two-party systems, in which elections are decisive and in which the winning party at the polls goes on to form the government. These are also responsive systems, with wholesale alternation in government being both a normal expectation and a relatively frequent occurrence. There are other systems, however, where the condition might seem less likely to be found, and these include in particular the more traditional 'continental' European systems, in which fragmented party groupings compete against one another in shifting multi-party coalitions, and in which a clear boundary between government and opposition has often proved difficult to identify. Wholesale alternation in these latter systems was also a relatively rare occurrence, at least traditionally, since one coalition usually overlapped with another, with the overall lines of responsibility and accountability being thereby often blurred.

With time, however, the balance of the European polities has appeared to shift in favour of the bipolar mode. This marks quite a substantial change in the functioning of European party systems, and has happened in two ways (Bale 2003; Mair 2008). In the first place, bipolarity has become the norm in the new democracies in southern Europe, with what are effectively two-party systems emerging and consolidating in Greece, Portugal and Spain, as well as in Malta. Second, bipolar competition is now also increasingly characteristic of many of the older multi-party systems (Table 2). That is, even in those systems that are marked by quite pronounced party fragmentation, party competition is now more likely to mimic the two-party pattern through the creation of competing pre-electoral coalitions which tend to divide voters into two contingent political camps. During the 1950s and 1960s, for example, the majority of European polities changed governments by means of shifting and overlapping centrist coalitions and rarely if ever offered voters a choice of alternative governments. During the

1990s, by contrast, almost two-thirds of these older polities had experienced at least some two-party or two-bloc competition, usually involving wholesale alternation in government. To these two sets of changes may also be added a third, albeit in a context of largely unstructured party systems, in that a number of the post-communist systems have also drifted towards more bipolar competition. In sum, if party government depends on electoral contests that can produce a clear distinction between winners and losers, then this condition was being met more frequently at the close of the twentieth century than was ever the case in the early post-war decades.

The other conditions listed in Box 4 have proved much less robust, however. Although political leaders continue to be recruited by party, for example, they are less likely to be recruited *through* parties, in that the choice of leader is now less often determined by the strength of a candidate's support within the party and more often by the candidate's capacity to appeal to the media and thence to the wider electorate. The choice of Blair above Brown in the leadership contest in the British Labour Party offered a clear example of this shift, as was the preference for Schröder above Lafontaine in the near contemporary debate about who was to be the SPD Chancellor candidate.[12] This, combined with the clear evidence of the 'presidentialisation' of political leadership in parliamentary democracies (Poguntke and Webb 2005), suggests the emergence of a more direct linkage between political leaders and the electorate that is now less strongly mediated by political parties as organisations. Moreover, as suggested above, the parties are also less able – and perhaps less willing – to offer clear policy alternatives to the voter. Whether circumscribed by global and European constraints, or whether limited by the inability to identify any clear constituency within the electorate that is sufficiently large and cohesive to offer a mandate for action, parties increasingly tend to echo one another and to blur what might otherwise be clear policy choices. To be sure, there is a choice between the competing teams of leaders and, given the growing evidence of bipolarity, that particular choice is becoming more sharply defined. But there is less and less choice in policy terms, suggesting that political competition is drifting towards an opposition of form rather than of content. Competition in these circumstances can be intense and hard-fought, but it is often akin to the competition enjoyed in football matches or horse races: sharp, exciting, and even pleasing to the spectators, but ultimately, as noted above, lacking in substantive meaning. Some 50 years ago, it was precisely this situation that Kirchheimer (1957) associated with the 'elimination' of opposition – the situation that prevails when polities experience government by cartel, and when no meaningful differences divide protagonists who sometimes compete very vigorously (see also Krouwel 2003).

Nor is public policy so often decided by the party, or even under its direct control. Instead, with the rise of the regulatory state, decisions are increasingly passed over to non-partisan bodies that operate at arms length from party leaders – the so-called 'non-majoritarian' or 'guardian' institutions (Majone 1994; see also Lodge this volume). Faced with increasing environmental constraints, as well as with the growing complexity of legislation and policy-making in a transnational environment, there is inevitably a greater resort to delegation and depoliticisation (Thatcher and Stone Sweet 2002). Moreover, the officials who work within these delegated bodies are less often recruited directly through the party organisation,[13] and are increasingly held accountable by means of judicial and regulatory controls. And since this broad network of agencies forms an ever larger part of a dispersed and pluriform executive, operating both nationally and supranationally, the very notion of accountability being exercised through parties, or of the executive being held answerable to *voters* (as opposed to citizens or stakeholders) becomes problematic. Party, in this sense, loses much of its representative and purposive identity and, by the same token, citizens forfeit much of their capacity to control policy-makers through conventional electoral channels.

Above all, it is here that we see the conditions for the maintenance of party government slipping away. This is also when the alternative forms of government identified by Rose (1969) begin to emerge with greater weight, including both government by inertia and 'administrative government'. Indeed, it is precisely such a shift that is identified by Lindvall and Rothstein (2006: 61) in their analysis of the decline of the 'strong state' model in Sweden, whereby 'the state... is no longer an instrument for the political parties that dominate the Riksdag to steer and change society. Instead, the administrative state is turning into another ideological battlefield, where sectoral interests seek power and influence... [and in which] the role of political parties as the main producers of policy-oriented ideology and ideas is challenged'.

There is also one other respect in which the conditions for the maintenance of party government are severely undermined, but which has received relatively scant attention in the literature. In Thomassen's (1994) account, summarised above (Box 3), a key condition for party government and for the responsible parties model is that both the policy programmes of the parties and the policy preferences of the voters be constrained by a single ideological dimension. The reasoning behind this argument is straightforward. Should two or more dimensions come into play, it would be impossible for either the voters or the parties to establish a relationship based on representation and accountability, since it would never be clear precisely which positions on which dimension had favoured support for one particular alternative over another. In other words, since the demands of popular control that are included in the various sets of conditions established by the other authors – 1, 5 and 6 in the case of the Rose set (Box 1); 1 and 3b in the Katz set (Box 2); 1, 3 and 5 in the summary set (Box 4) – require a shared recognition by both voters and parties of the policy choices that are on offer and of the commitment to implement these policies, they also require the sort of clarity which is intrinsically unavailable in a multi-dimensional space (Thomassen 1994: 252–7 and fn. 3). Moreover, as Thomassen goes on to suggest, and as is clear from the work of Sani and Sartori (1983) among others, the only possible single dimension that can afford this clarity is the Downsian left–right dimension. That is, the left–right dimension is the only dimension which is sufficiently elastic and pervasive to accommodate the various domains of voter identification, and which at the same time is sufficiently enduring to provide a stable reference point over time. In the absence of a left–right divide, however loosely defined, it is therefore difficult to imagine any other dimension that might offer the degree of coherence and clarity to the electorate and the parties taken as a whole. In the absence of a left–right dimension of competition, in other words, the entire foundation of the party government/responsible parties model is undermined.

It is here that the challenge to party government may be most sharply defined. Briefly put, and building on a variety of different arguments, it may be argued that the left–right divide, even in its simplest Downsian form, is now finally losing coherence (Mair 2007). Voters in contemporary Europe may still be willing to locate themselves in left–right terms, and they may even be willing to locate the parties along a similar dimension, but the meanings associated with these distinctions are becoming increasingly diverse and confused. In part, this is due to the policy convergence between parties that has already been discussed above. In part it is due to the often contradictory signals emerging from post-communist Europe, whereby the traditional left-wing position is often seen as the most conservative. In part it is also due to the new challenge of liberalism, and to the increasingly heterogeneous coalition that has begun to define leftness in primarily anti-imperial or anti-American terms, bringing together former communists, religious fundamentalists and critical social movements within a broad, loosely-defined camp. In this context, meanings are no longer shared and the implications of political stances on the left or on the right become almost unreadable.

This is also the essence of the argument developed by Hardin (2000) in an important essay on the problems of understanding political trust and distrust. Hardin argues that there have been two important changes in the way political issues have come to be understood and treated in contemporary democracies. The first is 'the essential end, at least for the near term, of the focus on economic distribution and the management of the economy for production and distribution' (Hardin 2000: 41–2). In other words, echoing Scharpf's (2000) and Ruggie's (1997) observations on the end of embedded liberalism (see above), he suggests that governments are no longer capable of purposefully managing the economy with a view to redistributing resources or responding to collective needs, and that this failing capacity has fundamentally altered traditional political discourse. The issue of planning versus markets has been settled – for now – in favour of the markets (Hardin 2000: 32), leaving much of conventional political debates at a loss. The second change is that problem-solving and decision-making in public policy have become substantially more complex, and hence less amenable to popular understanding or control (for a similar argument, see Papadopoulos 2003). Voters can no longer easily grasp the issues that are at stake, and find it difficult to evaluate the often quite technical alternatives that are presented to them. The result of both changes, claims Hardin (2000: 42), is to 'preclude the organization of politics along a single left–right economic dimension', leading to a situation in which the concerns of citizens become 'a hotchpotch of unrelated issues that are not the obvious domain of any traditional political party'.

In short, the left–right divide loses its capacity to make overall sense of mainstream politics, and is not replaced any alternative overarching paradigm. Demands become particularised and fragmented, while party policy and voter preferences evidence a lack of internal constraint or cohesion. In these circumstances, it is almost impossible to imagine party government functioning effectively or even maintaining full legitimacy – that is, it is almost impossible to imagine parties as such ruling effectively or enjoying an unchallenged right to rule.

Conclusion

Almost 30 years ago, in the anniversary issue of *Daedalus*, Suzanne Berger (1979: 30) argued that 'the critical issue for Western Europe today is the capacity of the principal agencies of political life – party, interest group, bureaucracy, legislature – to manage the problems of society and economy, and, beyond coping, to redefine and rediscover common purposes'. Today, it is not so much the management capacity of the traditional institutions that is the problem – as a number of the others paper in this volume testify, that is now being solved through expertise, delegation, regulation, and transnational cooperation and adjustment – but their legitimacy and, as such, their right to govern (Dalton and Weldon 2005; Mair 2005a). Parties, like the other traditional institutions of the European polities, might well be considered by citizens as necessary for the good functioning of politics and the state, but they are neither liked nor trusted. Indeed, as is clear from the comparative survey evidence, parties are the least trusted of any of the major political institutions in contemporary democracy. The argument of this paper is that we can better understand this change in perspective by recognising that although the trappings of party government might persist, the conditions for the maintenance of this form of government are being subject to a severe challenge.

Acknowledgements

I would like to thank Klaus Goetz, Jacques Thomassen and Rainer Bauböck for their help in clarifying a number of the arguments developed in this essay. For their sake in particular, the usual disclaimer applies.

Notes

1. This was the first of two proposed volumes, but for a variety of reasons Sartori's second volume was never published. In 2005, this journal published the section of the initial draft of that second volume dealing with party organisations and functions (see Sartori 2005; Mair 2005b).
2. I address the wider problems of party democracy in a separate paper (see Mair 2005a). For an earlier discussion of the changing notions of party democracy, see Katz and Mair (1995).
3. For a number of recent evaluations and analyses of these processes in the pages of *West European Politics*, see Downs (2001); Heinisch (2003); Minkenberg (2001); van Spanje and van der Brug (2007).
4. Quoted in Ranney (1978: 1).
5. The text of his contribution is reprinted in *Progressive Governance for the XXI Century: Conference Proceedings Florence, 20 and 21 November 1999*. Florence: European University Institute and New York University School of Law, 2000, p. 42.
6. Hailsham's speech is reprinted in *The Listener*, 21 October 1976. After the 1979 election, Hailsham went on to become a leading member in the unashamedly partisan governments of Margaret Thatcher.
7. See also Laver and Shepsle (1991) who discuss this in the context of minority governments.
8. Rose's 1969 article was later reprinted in his *The Problem of Party Government* (Rose 1974), although the book as a whole, despite its title, goes no further in dealing with party government as such than did the original article.
9. Laver and Shepsle (1994: 5–8) also briefly list a variety of alternatives to party government, including bureaucratic government, legislative government, Prime-ministerial government, cabinet government and ministerial government (see also Müller 1994).
10. For an earlier evaluation of these problems, see Smith (1986).
11. For a different approach to the issue of party government, focusing more attention on the link between parties and the governing institutions, see Blondel and Cotta (2000). In this essay, I focus mainly on the question of the power that might or might not travel from party to government. In the wider discussion of the cartel party (e.g. Katz and Mair 1995; Katz and Mair 2002), there is also a treatment of power that travels from government to party, and particularly to the party in public office.
12. The version of the German story as told by a clearly peevish Oskar Lafontaine (2000: 50–57) carries extraordinarily sharp echoes of the version of the British story that was reported by various allies of Gordon Brown to Andrew Rawnsley (2000). As Lafontaine (2000: 52) puts it, having admitted that Schröder cut the better figure on television, 'Is it permissible...for the media to have the decisive voice in a discussion over who shall lead a party into an election campaign? If the party were to answer this question in the affirmative, would it not be shedding too much of its own responsibility?'.
13. Although they may well be controlled by an autonomous political leadership, suggesting a 'party as network' notion that seems markedly different from the more traditional forms of party organisation.

References

Bale, Tim (2003). 'Cinderella and her Ugly Sisters: The Mainstream and Extreme Right in Europe's Bipolarising Party Systems', *West European Politics*, 26:3, 67–90.

Berger, Suzanne (1979). 'Politics and Antipolitics in Western Europe in the Seventies', *Daedalus*, 108:1, 27–50.

Blondel, Jean, and Maurizio Cotta, eds. (2000). *The Nature of Party Government: A Comparative European Perspective*. London: Palgrave.

Boix, Carles (1998). *Political Parties, Growth and Equality*. Cambridge: Cambridge University Press.

Broughton, David, and Hans-Martien ten Napel, eds. (2000). *Religion and Mass Electoral Behaviour in Europe*. London: Routledge.

Burnham, Peter (1999). 'The Politics of Economic Management in the 1990s', *New Political Economy*, 4:1, 37–54.

Burnham, Peter (2001). 'New Labour and the Politics of Depoliticisation', *British Journal of Politics and International Relations*, 3:2, 127–49.

Castles, Francis G., ed. (1983). *The Impact of Parties*. London: Sage.

Caul, Miki L., and Mark M. Gray (2000). 'From Platform Declarations to Policy Outcomes: Changing Party Profiles and Partisan Influence over Policy', in Russell J. Dalton and Martin P. Wattenberg (eds.), *Parties without Partisans*. Oxford: Oxford University Press, 208–37.

Daalder, Hans (1987). 'Countries in Comparative Politics', *European Journal of Political Research*, 15:1, 3–21.

Dahl, Robert A., ed. (1966). *Political Oppositions in Western Democracies*. New Haven, CT: Yale University Press.

Dalton, Russell J. (2004). *Democratic Challenges, Democratic Choices*. Oxford: Oxford University Press.

Dalton, Russell J., and Steven Weldon (2005). 'Public Images of Political Parties: A Necessary Evil?', *West European Politics*, 28:5, 931–51.

Downs, William M. (2001). 'Pariahs in their Midst: Belgian and Norwegian Parties React to Extremist Threats', *West European Politics*, 24:3, 23–42.

Elff, Martin (2007). 'Social Structure and Electoral Behavior in Comparative Perspective: The Decline of Social Cleavages in Western Europe Revisited', *Perspectives on Politics*, 5:2, 277–94.

Epstein, Leon D. (1967). *Political Parties in Western Democracies*. New York: Praeger.

Finer, Samuel E., ed. (1975). *Adversary Politics and Electoral Reform*. London: Anthony Wigram.

Franklin, Mark N., Thomas T. Mackie, and Henry Valen (1992). *Electoral Change*. Cambridge: Cambridge University Press.

Freire, André (2006). 'Bringing Social Identities Back In: The Social Anchors of Left–Right Orientation in Western Europe', *International Political Science Review*, 27:4, 359–78.

Garrett, Geoffrey (1998). *Partisan Politics in the Global Economy*. Cambridge: Cambridge University Press.

Garrett, Geoffrey (2000). *Globalization and Government Spending Around the World*. Working Paper 2000/155. Madrid: Instituto Juan March.

Hardin, Russell (2000). 'The Public Trust', in Susan J. Pharr and Robert D. Putnam (eds.), *Disaffected Democracies: What's Troubling the Trilateral Countries?* Cambridge: Cambridge University Press, 31–51.

Heinisch, Reinhard (2003). 'Success in Opposition – Failure in government: Explaining the Performance of Right-wing Populist Parties in Public Office', *West European Politics*, 26:3, 91–130.

Huber, Evelyn, and John D. Stephens (2001). *Development and Crisis of the Welfare State: Parties and Policies in Global Markets*. Chicago: University of Chicago Press.

Janda, Kenneth (1980). *Political Parties: A Cross-National Survey*. New York: Free Press.

Katz, Richard S. (1986). 'Party Government: A Rationalistic Conception', in Francis G. Castles and Rudolf Wildenmann (eds.), *Visions and Realities of Party Government*. Florence: EUI, and Berlin: de Gruyter, 31–71.

Katz, Richard S. (1987). 'Party Government and its Alternatives', in Richard S. Katz (ed.), *Party Governments: European and American Experiences*. Florence: EUI, and Berlin: de Gruyter, 1–26.

Katz, Richard S., and Peter Mair (1992). 'Introduction: The Cross-National Study of Party Organizations', in Richard S. Katz and Peter Mair (eds.), *Party Organizations: A Data Handbook*. London: Sage, 1–20.

Katz, Richard S., and Peter Mair (1995). 'Changing Models of Party Organization and Party Democracy: The Emergence of the Cartel Party', *Party Politics*, 1:1, 5–28.

Katz, Richard S., and Peter Mair (2002). 'The Ascendancy of the Party in Public Office: Party Organizational Change in Twentieth-Century Democracies', in Richard Gunther, José Ramon Montero and Juan J. Linz (eds.), *Political Parties: Old Concepts and New Challenges*. Oxford: Oxford University Press, 113–35.

Keman, Hans (2002). 'Policy-Making Capacities of Party Government', in Kurt Richard Luther and Ferdinand Müller-Rommel (eds.), *Political Parties in the New Europe: Political and Analytical Challenges*. Oxford: Oxford University Press, 227–45.

Kirkpatrick, Evron M. (1971). 'Towards a More Responsible Two-Party System: Political Science, Policy Science, or Pseudo-Science?', *American Political Science Review*, 65:4, 965–90.

Kirchheimer, Otto (1957). 'The Waning of Opposition in Parliamentary Regimes', *Social Research*, 24:1, 127–56.

Kissinger, Henry A. (1978). 'Communist Parties in Western Europe: Challenge to the West', in Austin Ranney and Giovanni Sartori (eds.), *Eurocommunism: The Italian Case*. Washington, DC: American Enterprise Institute, 183–96.

Knutsen, Oddbjørn (2006). *Class Voting in Western Europe: A Comparative Longitudinal Study*. Lanham, MD: Lexington Books.

Knutsen, Oddbjørn (2006). 'The Decline of Social Class?', in Russell J. Dalton and Hans-Dieter Klingemann (eds.), *The Oxford Handbook of Political Behaviour*. Oxford: Oxford University Press, 457–80.

Krouwel, André (2003). 'Otto Kirchheimer and the Catch-all Party', *West European Politics*, 26:2, 23–40.

Lafontaine, Oskar (2000). *The Heart Beats on the Left*. Cambridge: Polity.

LaPalombara, Joseph, and Myron Weiner, eds. (1966). *Political Parties and Political Development*. Princeton, NJ: Princeton University Press.

Laver, Michael, and Kenneth A. Shepsle (1991). 'Divided Government: America is not Exceptional', *Governance*, 4:1, 250–69.

Laver, Michael, and Kenneth Shepsle (1994). 'Cabinet Ministers and Government Formation in Parliamentary Democracies', in Michael Laver and Kenneth Shepsle (eds.), *Cabinet Ministers and Parliamentary Government*. Cambridge: Cambridge University Press, 3–12.

Lindvall, Johannes, and Bo Rothstein (2006). 'Sweden: The Fall of the Strong State', *Scandinavian Political Studies*, 29:1, 47–63.

Lipset, Seymour Martin, and Stein Rokkan, eds. (1967). *Party Systems and Voter Alignments*. New York: The Free Press.

Mair, Peter (2005a). 'Democracy Beyond Parties', *Center for the Study of Democracy*. Working Paper 05-06. Available at http://repositories.cdlib.org/csd/05-06

Mair, Peter (2005b). 'Introduction to Sartori's 1967 Manuscript on "Party Types, Organisation and Functions"', *West European Politics*, 28:1, 1–5.

Mair, Peter (2007). 'Left–Right Orientations', in Russell J. Dalton and Hans-Dieter Klingemann (eds.), *The Oxford Handbook of Political Behaviour*. Oxford: Oxford University Press, 206–22.

Mair, Peter (2008). 'Democracies', in Daniele Caramani (ed.), *Comparative Politics*. Oxford: Oxford University Press, forthcoming.

Majone, Giandomenico (1994). 'The Rise of the Regulatory State in Europe', *West European Politics*, 17:3, 77–101.

Minkenberg, Michael (2001). 'The Radical Right in Public Office: Agenda-Setting and Policy Effects in Germany, France, Italy, and Austria', *West European Politics*, 24:4, 1–21.

Montero, José Ramón, and Richard Gunther (2002). 'Introduction: Reviewing and Reassessing Parties', in Richard Gunther, José Ramón Montero and Juan J. Linz (eds.), *Political Parties: Old Concepts and New Challenges*. Oxford: Oxford University Press, 1–35.

Mudde, Cas (2007). *Populist Radical Right Parties in Europe*. Cambridge: Cambridge University Press.

Müller, Wolfgang C. (1994). 'Models of Government and the Austrian Cabinet', in Michael Laver and Kenneth Shepsle (eds.), *Cabinet Ministers and Parliamentary Government*. Cambridge: Cambridge University Press, 15–34.

234   P. Mair

Panebianco, Angelo (1988). *Political Parties: Organization and Power*. Cambridge: Cambridge University Press [originally published in Italian in 1982].
Papadopoulos, Yannis (2003). 'Cooperative Forms of Governance: Problems of Democratic Accountability in Complex Environments', *European Journal of Political Research*, 42:4, 473–501.
Poguntke, Thomas, and Paul Webb, eds. (2005). *The Presidentialization of Politics: A Comparative Study of Modern Democracies*. Oxford: Oxford University Press.
Ranney, Austin (1978). 'Introduction', in Austin Ranney and Giovanni Sartori (eds.), *Eurocommunism: The Italian Case*. Washington, DC: American Enterprise Institute, 1–5.
Rawnsley, Andrew (2000). *Servants of the People: The Inside Story of New Labour*. London: Hamish Hamilton.
Rose, Richard (1969). 'The Variability of Party Government: A Theoretical and Empirical Critique', *Political Studies*, 17:4, 413–45.
Rose, Richard (1974). *The Problem of Party Government*. London: MacMillan.
Rose, Richard (1980). *Do Parties Make a Difference?* Chatham, NJ: Chatham House.
Ruggie, John G. (1982). 'International Regimes, Transactions, and Change: Embedded Liberalism in the Postwar Economic Order', *International Organizations*, 36:2, 379–415.
Ruggie, John G. (1997). 'Globalization and the Embedded Liberalism Compromise: The End of an Era?', MPIfG Working Paper 97/1.
Sani, Giacomo, and Giovanni Sartori (1983). 'Polarization, Fragmentation and Competition in Western Democracies', in Hans Daalder and Peter Mair (eds.), *Western European Party Systems: Continuity and Change*. London: Sage, 307–40.
Sartori, Giovanni (1976). *Parties and Party Systems: a Framework for Analysis*. Cambridge: Cambridge University Press.
Sartori, Giovanni (2005). 'Party Types, Organisation and Functions', *West European Politics*, 28:1, 5–33.
Sauger, Nicolas (2007). 'The French Legislative and Presidential Elections of 2007', *West European Politics*, 30:5, 1166–75.
Schattschneider, E.E. (1945). 'Party Government and Employment Policy', *American Political Science Review*, 39:6, 1147–57.
Scharpf, Fritz W. (2000). 'Economic Changes, Vulnerabilities, and Institutional Capabilities', in Fritz W. Scharpf and Vivien A. Schmidt (eds.), *Welfare and Work in the Open Economy, Vol. 1: From Vulnerability to Competitiveness*. Oxford: Oxford University Press, 21–124.
Schmidt, Manfred G. (1996). 'When Parties Matter: A Review of the Possibilities and Limits of Partisan Influence on Public Policy', *European Journal of Political Research*, 30:2, 155–83.
Schmidt, Manfred G. (2002). 'The Impact of Political Parties, Constitutional Structures and Veto Players on Public Policy', in Hans Keman (ed.), *Comparative Democratic Politics*. London: Sage, 166–84.
Smith, Gordon (1986). 'The Futures of Party Government: A Framework for Analysis', in Francis G. Castles and Rudolf Wildenmann (eds.), *Visions and Realities of Party Government*. Florence: EUI, and Berlin: de Gruyter, 31–71.
Thatcher, Mark, and Alec Stone Sweet (2002). 'Theory and Practice of Delegation to Non-Majoritarian Institutions', *West European Politics*, 25:1, 1–22.
Thomassen, J.J.A. (1994). 'Empirical Research into Political Representation: Failing Democracy or Failing Models?', in M. Kent Jennings and T.E. Mann (eds.), *Elections at Home and Abroad: Essays in Honor of Warren Miller*. Ann Arbor: Michigan University Press, 237–65.
Van Spanje, Joost, and Wouter van der Brug (2007). 'The Party as Pariah', *West European Politics*, 30:5, 1022–40.

European Government(s): Executive Politics in Transition?

MORTEN EGEBERG

Standard portrayals of modern government tend to focus on the national and sub-national levels of government. The fact that modern governments for quite a long time have been involved in a multitude of international bodies across most policy areas does not seem to have changed this perspective profoundly. In this article, however, I argue that European governments, or, more correctly, *parts* of national governments, over the last couple of decades have to some extent become parts of a kind of European government as well. This is due to quite particular institutional developments at both the European and the national level.

At the European level, it is first and foremost the enhanced autonomy and consolidation of the European Commission which makes the difference: for the first time in the history of international organisations we can speak of a multi-purpose supranational executive with its own political leadership that is able to act relatively independently from national governments and councils of ministers. Being in charge of EU policy formulation as well as implementation, the Commission needs stable partners at the national level for both purposes. Arguably, those partners might be found among national (regulatory) agencies that during the same period of time have been created at arm's length from ministerial departments. Thus, the peculiar functional division of labour between the Commission and the Council of Ministers (Union Council) triggers centrifugal forces at the very heart of national governments. Such forces cannot be expected to emanate from classic international organisations in which all threads tend to be collected in councils of ministers. In the latter case national regulatory authorities will normally be held accountable to a particular ministry. In the EU case, on the other hand, a kind of dual loyalty, or 'double-hattedness', might be imposed on national agencies in the sense that they have to relate to both national ministries and the Commission.

The next section discusses what most students of government hold to be a key feature of development over the last couple of decades: 'agencification' and fragmentation of national governments. Interestingly, when dealing with the problems such a development might cause for democratic control and agency accountability, the focus tends to be on the relationships between agencies and various national stakeholders. Has a 'methodological nationalism' hindered us from seeing the emerging executive at the level above and the re-coupling of nationally decoupled agencies into multilevel and transnational networks of regulatory bodies? The following two sections try to show how the development of the EU takes quite another direction than intergovernmental cooperation and thus comes to challenge governments in a peculiar way. I draw on several case studies to illuminate how national agencies become parts of two administrations, a national as well as a Union administration. Finally, before concluding, the article deals with motors of change and the various attempts at explaining the major changes over the last couple of decades.

Fragmented Governments

There are many potential dimensions along which change in governments might be observed. Goetz (2006) proposes to focus on the relationship between the executive and the legislature, between governing parties and the government, between the prime minister, cabinet and ministers, and between executive politicians and ministerial officials. However, he tends to conclude that developmental trends are ambiguous and thus do not point in any clear direction. Scholars seem to agree, though, that as far as vertical and horizontal specialisation of the governmental apparatus are concerned, substantial reforms have indeed taken place over the last couple of decades (Pollitt and Bouckaert 2004; Christensen and Lægreid 2006). Along the vertical axis, a clearer separation of politics and execution has been formally installed, for example by 'hiving-off' regulatory tasks from ministerial departments to semi-independent agencies, i.e. 'agencification' (Kickert and Beck Jørgensen 1995). Thus, while the legal framework continues to stem from legislative bodies and the respective ministries, decisions on individual cases are to a considerable extent left to the agency itself and its expertise.

Along the horizontal axis, specialisation has also increased so that a range of 'single-purpose organisations' can be observed. While one previously could find rather complex public organisations, which, for example, combined the roles of regulator, service provider and infrastructure owner (as in transport and communication), the rule today is that these tasks have been split and assigned to separate bodies, including companies. Both 'agencification' and the formation of 'single-purpose organisations' belong to the 'New Public Management' (NPM) paradigm of public sector reforms. Together with corporatisation, privatisation, dismantling of public mono-polies and user/customer orientation they constitute key ingredients of the neo-liberal state. Although NPM elements can be traced in most countries, they tend to be more easily recognisable in Anglo-Saxon countries than in countries on the European continent or in Scandinavia (Christensen and Lægreid 2001). Non-Anglo-Saxon governments tend to reaffirm the role of the state, administrative law, distinctive public services and political accountability. They tend to complement rule orientation with user orientation and service standards (Pollitt and Bouckaert 2004). One of the founding editors of *West European Politics*, Vincent Wright, published in 1994 a pioneering article ('Reshaping the State: The Implications for Public Administration') on the NPM reform agenda in these pages (Wright 1994).

In general, splitting organisations horizontally – e.g., through the creation of 'single purpose bodies' – means to diminish the flow of information between former parts and to move processes of co-ordination and conflict resolution upward in a system, thus making it more likely that higher level leadership gets involved in such processes. Mergers, on the other hand, tend to push such processes downward, thus relieving higher levels of some of their workload but also of their control potential (Egeberg 2003). Splitting organisations vertically – as 'agencification' illustrates – also seems to have its clear effects. Officials in central agencies, in contrast to their colleagues in cabinet-level departments, exercise their discretion comparatively insulated from ongoing political processes at the cabinet level. They have relatively little contact with the political leadership of the ministry, with other ministerial departments than their 'own', and with parliament. They attach most importance to professional and expert considerations, and somewhat less importance to user and client interests. To assign weight to signals from the political leadership of the ministry is their third priority only (Egeberg 2003). Studies that explicitly focus on NPM-related 'agencification' seem to confirm that political control is, in general, undermined, although such a loss can sometimes be partly compensated for by informal contacts between ministers and agencies (Christensen and Lægreid 2006). In ministerial departments, on the other hand, officials give top priority to a 'steer' from the minister and also to professional concerns. Considerably less attention is paid to signals from user and client groups (Egeberg 2003; Page and Jenkins 2005).

The rationale behind setting up semi-detached national regulatory authorities and other agencies has often been to reduce the amount of political interference in daily decision-making and increase the scope for expert-based judgement (see below). Thus, 'agencification' seems to have delivered what many intended to achieve. Nevertheless, concerns about democratic accountability have been raised: to whom – if anybody – are these bodies accountable (Lodge 2004)? Interestingly, the discussion on principals and responsible political authorities focuses almost entirely on national bodies like the 'reporting ministry', the 'parent ministry', the treasury or the cabinet office (OECD 2002; Talbot 2004; Thatcher 2005; Rhodes 2006), a fact that might reflect the (sub-)discipline's overall 'methodological nationalism'.[1] Yet national agencies have increasingly become parts of transnational issue-specific networks of agencies in which the Commission or an EU-level agency constitutes the hub. Governments as such are responsible for implementing EU legislation at the national level, but in practice this has often been handed over to agencies that are in charge of policy execution in general. Precisely because these agencies are, as shown, to a considerable extent decoupled from other national bodies vertically as well as horizontally, they are exposed to being re-coupled into administrative webs that span national borders and levels of governance (see below).

An important lesson that can be drawn from the public administration literature is that significant reforms quite often trigger new reforms in the opposite direction (Hood and Jackson 1991). For example, subsequent to a period of extensive decentralisation, efforts of centralisation tend to follow. Thus, one has over the last years observed what Christensen and Lægreid (2006) have termed 'second generation NPM-reforms', aimed at compensating for some of the deficiencies caused by 'first generation reforms', such as reduced political control over agency activities and inadequate coordination across policy areas. However, reforms associated with the 'joined-up government' paradigm do not seem to replace former reforms. Similar to what has often be observed when established arrangements have reached a certain level of 'stickiness', new reforms tend to be layered around already existing structures (Thelen 2003). Thus, one aims at rectifying a lack of inter-sector coordination by setting up committees and task forces rather than by horizontal de-specialisation, and at counteracting undermined political control by expanding staff in ministerial departments rather than by 'de-agencification'. Although such compensating ('layered') devices cannot be expected to have the same impact on behaviour as more profound changes, they do have an effect (Egeberg 2003). As a consequence, national authorities might become less amenable to 'agency capture' by surrounding actors and networks. In other words, how one strikes the balance between the two loyalties or 'hats' (i.e., towards the parent ministry and the Commission) might be affected.

Thus, organisational changes at the national level seem to have affected executive politics significantly. The same might be true as regards such changes at the international level. Arguably, classic international governmental organisations (IGOs) do not challenge governments' sovereignty and coherence profoundly. They may increase the capacity for collective problem-solving and rule-making by establishing secretariats and committee structures, but could be said to underpin territorial lines of conflict at the international level and, thus, consolidating governments as such . Otherwise with the establishment of the European Commission: its 'emancipation' from national governments and the Council of Ministers, which has accelerated over the last couple of decades, may challenge governments deeply since the Commission could be seen to embody an alternative, competing executive centre (Bartolini 2005). Due to its independent position it triggers peculiar centrifugal forces at the very heart of national governments. From the multilevel governance literature it is already well known that the Commission may forge partnerships with regional governments, partly bypassing national governments (Marks *et al.* 1996; Bauer 2002).

The Development of International Governmental Organisations

Compared to the classic bilateral diplomacy, the multilateral diplomacy instituted by the Vienna Congress 1814–15 comes closer to an international organisation in the sense that representatives from more than two countries are exposed to each other simultaneously. However, the Concert of Europe and its Great Power conferences at ministerial as well as ambassadorial level did not meet on a regular basis and had no permanent location or secretariat (Schroeder 1994). Although this way of organising European politics did not challenge the Westphalian order, it may have contributed to transforming a system of states into a community of states (Schroeder 1994; Holsti 2004). Accordingly, the Concert decided on the admission of new members to 'Europe', as when it declared that Turkey was entitled to full status in the European system (1856), and when it accepted that Serbia could 'enter the European family' (1878) provided the country recognised religious freedom, described as one of 'the principles which are the basis of social organization in all States of Europe' (Claude 1964: 22).

It was the highly specialised sectoral or functional IGOs established during the second half of the nineteenth century – e.g. the International Telegraphic Union and the Universal Postal Union – that produced inventions like the permanent secretariat with a fixed location, the division of labour between a general conference and an executive council, and regular meetings (Claude 1964). The basic principle of organisational specialisation was territory. Thus, while the general conference was composed of representatives from all member states, only a few selected governments had a seat in the executive or governing council. Studies of decision-making processes within such organisations have shown that these organisations, notwithstanding their innovative character, did not challenge seriously the inherited state order. The power distribution and conflict pattern within these organisations seem to reflect very much the power distribution and territorial pattern of conflict found in the wider system (Cox and Jacobson 1973). Nevertheless, since the additional sectoral or functional specialisation of these organisations primarily engages non-diplomats as delegates from national administrations and also tends to partly sustain these officials' original sectoral or functional orientation, transnational coalitions along sectoral or functional lines are plausible within bodies structured in such a manner. Those attending meetings on a regular basis in comparable entities also display a considerable amount of loyalty to the international bodies in which they participate, although this loyalty is clearly inferior to their national loyalty (Egeberg et al. 2003; Beyers 2005). Moreover, expert-based permanent secretariats contribute significantly to task expansion at the international level and may be able to create transnational coalitions and arenas by linking previously discon-nected actors (Cox and Jacobson 1973; Barnett and Finnemore 2004; Trondal et al. 2005).

The Hague Conferences of 1899 and 1907 pointed in the direction of permanent location and staff, and thus regularity, also in the 'high-politics' area (Claude 1964). However, it was not until the establishment of the League of Nations (1919) that what had already been achieved organisationally in the sectoral or functional fields became realised in the security domain. Its founders approved the basic principles of the Westphalian order. They accepted the independent sovereign state as the basic entity and the great powers as the predominant actors. However, in the 'high-politics' area the League also represented a considerable organisational innovation: for the first time a central structure consisting of a general conference, a council and a secretariat with a fixed location had been created. According to Claude (1964: 175), 'nothing essentially new has been added by the multilateralization and regularization of diplomacy until the secretariat is introduced; this is the innovation that transforms the series of conferences into an organization'. In addition, the role of the Council president, the permanent missions of the member states in Geneva and numerous specialised committees in several sectoral and functional policy fields added a new dimension to the older forms of diplomacy (Steiner 2005).

A study of the role of the presidency in a comparable setting shows that the presidency's brokerage efforts can help governments avoid negotiation failure due to its privileged access to information about state preferences and its procedural control, although these resources are not only used for collective gain but also for pursuing national interests (Tallberg 2004). Research on the EU Council's Committee of Permanent Representatives (COREPER) unveils how the member states' resident ambassadors complement their pre-established national identities with collective, EU identities (Lewis 2005).

While the founders of the League of Nations had accepted Europe as the core of the world political system, the establishment of the United Nations (1945) clearly signalled a more global orientation. However, in organisational terms the United Nations could mainly be described as a moderately revised version of the League. It reformed somewhat the arrangement for collective security, for example by conferring upon the secretary general a more political role as regards policy formulation, and developed further the network of intergovernmental, specialised organisations, without, however, launching real innovations (Claude 1964). Other post-World War II organisations, like the Organization for European Economic Cooperation (OEEC) (1948), NATO (1949) or the Council of Europe (1949) did not deviate in their set-up from the territorially based decision structure inherited from the past, although the latter two incorporated consultative, indirectly elected parliamentary assemblies.

Arguably, significant organisational innovation did not take place before the establishment of the European Coal and Steel Community (ECSC) in 1952. For the first time, a state-like institutional system at the international level could be identified, consisting of an executive body organised separately from the council of ministers and with its own political leadership (the High Authority), two legislative bodies (the Council and the Assembly) and a Court of Justice. Thus, the four key institutions of today's EU, namely the European Commission, the Union Council, the European Parliament (EP) and the European Court of Justice (ECJ), were already operating from 1952 on, although in a nascent form. Equally important as regards the system's innovative character is the fact that individual core institutions have been structured on a non-territorial basis. Only the Council reflects in its composition and functioning parts of the legacy from the classical international organisation: contestation follows for the most part territorial lines although considerable attention is also devoted to systemic, sectoral and functional concerns (Egeberg *et al.* 2003; Thomson *et al.* 2004; Lewis 2005).

The European Commission: A New Executive Centre[2]

Autonomisation vs. Territorialisation

From its inception, the Commission was meant to be able to act independently of national governments. Since one of its main tasks was to take care of the common European interest – as it could be derived from the treaties – an autonomous and impartial role in the policy process might be legitimised. This construction seems to parallel to some extent the executive's role in the French republican state tradition (Elgie 2003: 149). The Commission's independence was clearly expressed in its formal structure, which forbids commissioners as well as officials from taking instructions from outside the organisation. To stress this, the first president of the High Authority, Jean Monnet, originally wanted a College of only five members – simply to underline the fact that commissioners were not to represent particular countries (Duchêne 1994: 240). The Commission has on several occasions, most recently in its proposal to the Convention on the future of Europe, emphasised the need for an independent and impartial body whose mission should be to serve the general interest of the Union.[3]

However, from the very start, it became fairly clear that running the Commission was indeed a balancing act between autonomy and dependence on the member states (Christiansen 1997; Lequesne 2000). From the point of view of the member states, a Commission with potential to become a genuine political actor and entrepreneur could not be allowed to act solely according to its own will, even if this will were defined as the community interest. The appointment procedure of the college – according to which member states nominate 'their' commissioner – and the national quota system – according to which the recruitment of officials should reflect the population size of the member countries – can be seen in this light. Member states' strong reluctance to give up their 'representation' in the College, as demonstrated during the Convention on the future of Europe, clearly illustrates this point.[4] Seen from the inside, a Commission that adopted an increasingly complex political agenda could not rely entirely on legitimacy derived from pursuing the common good in an impartial way. Additional legitimacy could be provided by co-opting key affected parties such as national administrations, for example by including them in policy preparatory committees.

Thus, from the beginning there have been organisational components that have underpinned autonomisation while others have supported territorialisation. Studies seem to indicate that commissioners, although more or less sensitive to the concerns of their country of origin, cannot in general be seen as representatives of 'their' governments (Nugent 2001: 115; Egeberg 2006). The same can be said of Commission officials: although they may serve as points of access for their compatriots (Michelmann 1978), and their attitudes on broad issues like capitalism and supranationalism may be linked to their nationality (Hooghe 2001), their actual behaviour is probably best accounted for by considering their bureaucratic role (Nugent 2001; Egeberg 2006). This seems to hold even for 'national experts' who are seconded from their governments to serve at the Commission for a limited number of years (Trondal 2006). Consistent with this, an overwhelming majority of national officials participating in Commission and Council committees considers Commission officials to act mainly independently of particular national interests (Egeberg *et al.* 2003).

Moreover, there is reason to believe that the Commission has gained more autonomy from national governments over time, at the political as well as the administrative levels. Concerning the College level, the Amsterdam Treaty assigned more leeway to the Commission president-elect as regards the selection of commissioners, and this leeway has been widened in the Constitutional Treaty. After Amsterdam the president also acquired the final say in how portfolios are allocated and even the right to reshuffle the team during the Commission's five-year term of office by redistributing dossiers, thus making it difficult to attach particular national flags to particular directorates general. Also, the president is authorised to dismiss individual commissioners. The Prodi Commission, furthermore, made *cabinets* more multinational in composition.[5] This has probably changed the role of entities previously portrayed as national enclaves (Michelmann 1978), or as being apparently sensitive to national interests (Spence 1994: 107–8; Cini 1996: 111–15).

Developmental trends and reform efforts pertaining to the services over the years all point in the same direction: territorial components in the organisation have continuously been weakened. In previous decades the community administration had to rely heavily on national civil servants on short-term contracts (Coombes 1970), while currently a large majority are employed on a permanent basis (Page 1997). While the Commission is supposed to maintain a broad geographical balance, nationality has been declared no longer to be the determinant in appointing a new person to a specific post.[6] A long-term trend seems to be that the Commission services have gradually enhanced their control of recruitment and appointment decisions (Peterson 1971). New procedures for appointing top officials have contributed to reducing the amount of interference by governments or commissioners in such processes (Egeberg 2006).

Sectorisation

Organisational devices such as the increased discretionary power conferred upon the president, the required multinational staffing of *cabinets*, more permanent administrative posts, as well as new rules of procedure for the appointment of senior officials have enhanced the autonomy of the Commission at the expense of national governments. However, while territorialisation has lost ground to autonomisation, sectorisation may simultaneously have challenged the autonomisation process. Since the Commission divides its work primarily according to the purpose or sector principle, it attracts in turn similarly structured societal interest groups (Kohler-Koch 1997). These organisations find clearer points of access to such structures than they would to structures arranged according to geography. At the same time, policy-makers in a sectorised bureaucracy may come to see co-optation or involvement of societal groups within their issue area as a route to legitimisation of policy proposals (Andersen and Eliassen 2001). According to the Commission's white paper on governance, 'with better involvement comes greater responsibility'.[7] Thus, understandably, the Commission has in fact encouraged the formation of EU-level interest organisations (Mazey and Richardson 1996).

While sectorisation, like territorialisation, may threaten institutional autonomy, sectorisation displaces territorialisation. The Commission might (in theory) have been organised primarily by territory so that each of the directorates general (DGs) corresponded to a particular member state. Each geographically-based DG could have been composed of officials seconded from the national administration of the country served by that particular DG. Each commissioner might have been in charge of the DG that was to serve the country from which he or she had been nominated. However, things are in fact arranged quite differently. Although there certainly are, as mentioned, some territorial components in the structure of the Commission, most are non-territorial: the division of labour among DGs reflects different sectors or functions rather than geographical areas. Most posts are permanent and filled – according to merit, with a view to geographical balance – by the Commission services themselves. Units and *cabinets* are staffed multinationally to avoid national clusters or enclaves. On this basis it makes sense that empirical studies portray decision-making at the Commission as more often politics among sectoral portfolios (or DGs) than politics between nation-states (Coombes 1970: 203; Cram 1994; Cini 2000; Hooghe 2000; Mörth 2000; Egeberg 2006).

Party Politicisation

It has been argued above that the Commission, at the political as well as the administrative level, has, over time, enhanced its autonomy in important respects in relation to national governments. One could, however, similarly assert that the College of Commissioners has become more dependent on the European Parliament. From the very inception of the ECSC, as forerunner of the EP, the Assembly had the power to dismiss the whole of the College, though not individual commissioners. The Maastricht Treaty codified the right of the EP to be consulted before the president of the Commission could be appointed and also that the College should be subject to a vote of approval by the EP. In 1999 the EP adopted as a resolution a report by its Committee on Institutional Affairs advocating a stronger link between the results of the European election and the nomination of the College of Commissioners and its programme for the parliamentary term. The Constitutional Treaty largely supported this resolution by stating that the European Council, when proposing its candidate for president of the Commission, should take into account the elections to the European Parliament. According to the Constitution, the candidate would be elected by the EP, not only 'approved' (Article I-26). In the meantime, some small steps towards a parliamentary system have already been taken. And in searching for a candidate to succeed Prodi as Commission president, the actors behaved as if the parliamentary principle had already come into force. In fact, a candidate who was not anchored in the winning party group seemed to be out of the question. Since the incoming president has been empowered to allocate the portfolios, the president might assign dossiers that he or she considers particularly important to commissioners belonging to the same political wing, thus giving the College a more consistent ideological profile. Moreover, there are indications of an increasingly stronger role for the European-level political parties in the process of selecting the person for the Commission presidency. Barroso had been a vice-president of the European People's Party, the biggest group in the EP, and was this party's candidate for the presidency (Ludlow 2004; Johansson 2005). It is probably too early to draw a firm conclusion as regards the robustness of this practice, however, it might indicate that the role of the nominating body, the European Council, could become more similar to the role of the monarch as regards the nomination of the prime minister in a parliamentary democracy.

Highly compatible with a development in a more parliamentary direction is also the growing proportion of genuine politicians rather than technocrats in the College so that the former have become completely dominant. Commissioners are also more often political heavyweights with experience as former ministers, often at a senior level (MacMullen 2000; Döring 2007). The fact that commissioners participate at their respective European political party meetings might be interpreted as a significant expression of the relevance of their partisan role.[8] Party politicisation would threaten autonomisation processes at the Commission. However, as with sectorisation, party politicisation would displace territorialisation: it would bring to the fore ideological lines of conflict and cooperation rather than politics among nations. It may represent an alternative route to legitimisation of the institution and its policy proposals.

Demarcating the Administrative and Political Levels

Self-management of the Services

From the point of view of organisation theory, one way of handling the tensions associated with the Commission's development is to separate more clearly the political and administrative levels. Autonomisation of the services could be justified on the grounds that they should be capable of impartially implementing, or monitoring the implementation of, common policies, and of providing reliable knowledge and 'Europeanised' policy expertise for the College of Commissioners. The College, on the other hand, obviously a genuine political body, could derive its legitimacy from being accountable to external bodies such as the directly elected EP or, as the Commission has proposed, to the EP as well as to the European Council.[9]

In fact, an emerging dual structure could be discerned at an early stage of the Commission's history. Monnet himself seems to have preferred a small, informal and integrated Commission (Duchêne 1994: 240). However, after his departure a larger gap opened between the High Authority's college and its officials than he had planned. For example, the growing difference between the two echelons as regards recruitment patterns pointed in such a direction (MacMullen 2000). And as we have seen, the services themselves gradually gained more control over their appointment processes, a feature indicating a more British or Scandinavian type of administration compared to the continental ones from which it had originated. Thus, while politicisation of civil service careers seems to have increased in most Western countries in the early twenty-first century (Rouban 2003: 316), the opposite trend has been observed at the Commission. Moreover, the Prodi Commission spelled out how *cabinets'* 'policy creep' should be stopped. They should be downsized and multinationally composed. They are to assist commissioners in particular in policy areas outside their portfolios, but should avoid interfering in departmental management.[10]

Agencification at the EU Level

During the 1990s a range of new EU-level agencies were established. The main function of some of these, such as the European Environment Agency, is to gather information in order to support EU policy-making and implementation across the Union. Others are entrusted with the responsibility to prepare decisions to be made by the Commission, as is the case for the European Agency for the Evaluation of Medicinal Products. Still others are assigned implementation tasks such as assisting the Commission in the management of EU programmes. In highly specialised areas such as trademarks or plant variety rights, or more recently aviation safety, such agencies come close to independent regulatory authorities since they are empowered to issue binding individual decisions (Dehousse 2002).

The arguments behind EU-level agencification are remarkably similar to those that have been advanced in relation to the establishment of agencies at the national level. Commission overload seems to be one important reason for delegation. Another is to ensure continuity and impartiality as regards (individual) regulatory decisions by organising such decision-making in bodies at arm's length from the respective ministries (Majone 1996; Everson *et al.* 1999). An increasingly party politicised Commission could make such reforms even more topical (Majone 2002).

In many respects most agencies are clearly connected to the Commission: they work closely with the Commission, the Commission has the organisational or budgetary responsibility for the agency and agency directors are usually appointed on a proposal from the Commission (Everson *et al.* 1999; Almer and Rotkirch 2004). As might be expected, though, given the character of the areas concerned, the European Defence Agency (for the development of defence capabilities) is supposed to work under Council authority and the police cooperation unit 'Europol' has to operate under 'European laws' (Constitutional Treaty, Article III-276). However, most agencies can be perceived as being situated somewhere between the Commission and the Council. Typically, there is a strong representation by the member states and a more limited representation by the Commission in the composition of supervisory boards (Almer and Rotkirch 2004: 58). Since some agencies may be seen as partly a functional alternative to comitology (Dehousse 1997) this 'double-headedness' makes sense: it reflects the legislator's willingness to sit in and monitor delegated law-making activities. More generally, the 'in-between status' mirrors a non-parliamentary, 'power-separated' polity. As in the US, agencies are part of the power struggle between executive and legislative branches (Shapiro 1997). Since the legislator cannot hold executive politicians fully accountable, it is instead eager to have some direct influence over regulatory agencies. A parliamentarised EU would not solve this problem, since the other legislative chamber, the Council, would not be part of such an arrangement.

A Multilevel Union Executive?

From the Commission's point of view, having to rely on national governments for implementation of EU policies makes community policies vulnerable to distortion. Studies show that implementing through national governments exposes common policies to considerable influence from national politics and administrative traditions (Goetz 2000; Heritier *et al.* 2001; Knill 2001; Olsen 2003, 2007; Sverdrup 2006a). In order to push standardisation of administrative practices across countries a bit further, some directives have contained specific requirements as to how national agencies should be set up (such as in the fields of communication and transport), with the underlying assumption of a close relationship between structure and actual implementation behaviour. Clearly, policy harmonisation would increase further if the Commission could run its own agencies at the national level. This is, however, entirely unrealistic and not even an objective for the Commission, which prefers to focus on policy development.[11] As an alternative to Commission-run agencies, the idea of a networked administrative system has been launched, according to which the Commission could partly 'dispose of' national agencies organised at arm's length from ministerial departments.[12]

There are studies within five different policy fields that examine the extent to which national agencies act in a 'double-hatted' manner. In all of these – competition (Barbieri 2006; Støle 2006), telecoms (Nørgård 2006), food safety (Ugland and Veggeland 2006), environment (Barbieri 2006; Martens 2006) and statistics (Sverdrup 2006b) – national agencies simultaneously constitute parts of national governments, while also being involved in European networks in which the Commission or an EU-level agency makes up the hub. Several observations are consistent across policy sectors: most typically, that as integral parts of national governments, national agencies assist their respective ministries at Council and comitology meetings. In these settings there is usually no doubt as to who is the leader of the delegation or who is entitled to instruct those attending; it is the ministry. Also, when EU directives are to be transposed into national legislation, national agencies often do much of the preparatory work, with which they are familiar from other legislative processes. Here again they seem to be relatively attentive to what the ministry wants. On all these occasions, though, it is the agencies that possess most of the necessary expertise.

When it comes to putting the transposed legislation into practice, however, the role of national agencies seems to shift remarkably. At this stage, they work in close cooperation with their respective directorates in the Commission and their respective 'sister agencies' in other member states, often through networks. This means that national agencies end up having to defend decisions that are in conflict with the intentions of their own governments. For example, while the Swedish government supported the attempted merger of Volvo and Scania, and even lobbied for its acceptance in Brussels, the Swedish competition authority advised against the merger (Støle 2006). Such clashes, do, of course, also occur at the national level, quite independently of the EU; they are inherently linked to fragmented governments. What is probably new is that the national agency, in a way, acts on behalf of a second master or centre, or at least on behalf of a transnational network of agencies in which the EU executive may constitute a node. The Commission may itself have initiated the creation of such a network, as in the telecom sector (Nørgård 2006) or in the education area (Gornitzka 2007). However, the EU executive has also successfully linked into existing networks that may have been relatively independent (Eberlein and Grande 2005: 101–2), but for which it has gradually taken over the coordinating functions, as seems to be the case for the implementation network of pollution authorities (Martens 2006). Like national ministries, the Commission might be perceived by national experts as a potential threat to their independence (Ugland and Veggeland 2006). In addition to playing a crucial role at the implementation stage, agency networks may also contribute in the policy formulation phase at the Commission. The case studies mentioned above show that ministries are usually informed about network activities. However, they tend to abstain from steering network activities, for example, by appointing and instructing participants. Interestingly, there are indications that such interference is deemed inappropriate, at least by the agency personnel themselves.

Motors of Change

We have so far dealt with new forms of executive organisation at the national as well as the international level and, from the perspective of organisation theory (Egeberg 2004), considered how these forms might have changed important elements of executive politics. Thus, it has been shown how agencification (vertical specialisation) and the establishment of 'single-purpose organisations' (horizontal specialisation) affect power relations between executive politicians and experts, the weight assigned to various concerns and considerations in decision processes and the degree of coordination among policy areas. As regards the Commission, we have seen how organisational devices such as its sectorally and functionally divided structure, have enhanced its actual autonomy from national governments and the Council by partly displacing territorial politics in the Commission. The peculiar institutional architecture of the EU, charac-terised inter alia by a separate executive body, triggers centrifugal forces at the heart of national governments, forces that cannot be expected to be created by classic IGOs. Thus, we see the contours of new patterns of executive politics across levels of governance and national borders in which the Commission, EU-level agencies and national agencies may to some extent circumvent ministerial departments and act relatively consistently within various policy fields as Union administration.

But how do these assumed organisational prerequisites for new patterns of executive politics themselves come about? How do we account for the fragmentation of governments and the formation of a new executive centre at the European level? As regards the former, the literature lists a range of explanatory factors without establishing a clear ranking among them. Agencification, which may simultaneously imply horizontal splits of formerly integrated bodies into, e.g., regulators, service providers and infrastructure owners, has variously been seen as the result of deliberate design, institutional fashion and isomorphism, institutional traditions and path dependence, and contingent events (Thatcher 2002; Christensen and Lægreid 2006). From the design perspective, principal–agent analysts have explained politicians' delegation of powers to non-majoritarian institutions in terms of insulation from political pressures, thus aiming at enhancing 'credible commitment' as well as efficiency by allowing experts to exercise a considerable degree of discretion. Another purpose may be to shift blame onto an agency for unpopular decisions (Thatcher and Stone Sweet 2002; Coen and Thatcher 2005).

However, in order to come to grips with the timing and pace of government reforms we have to look beyond principal–agent analysis. Why did the reforms we are focusing on spread almost worldwide since the 1980s and not 20 years before? And why were some governments reluctant reformers while others were vanguards? An answer to the first question is that this particular wave of organisational reforms probably has to be understood in the context of post-Keynesianism and neo-liberalism, the *Zeitgeist* (Majone 1996). The ideology's organisational expression was New Public Management, which rapidly became institutionalised in the sense that its prescriptions were deemed legitimate almost regardless of variation in local needs (Meyer and Rowan 1977; Wright 1994). An answer to the second question is that national institutional traditions constrain both reformers' scope of action and environmental impacts (Olsen 2007). Thus, as noted, NPM reforms have not been implemented to the same degree in countries in which administrative cultures are less compatible with the reform ideas (Pollitt and Bouckaert 2004; Christensen and Lægreid 2006).

How, then, do we account for the formation of a new executive centre at the European level? Taking as our point of departure the chronologically ordered empirical examples introduced above, the apparent 'stickiness' of the intergovernmental model is indeed a striking observation. The territorially based decision structure certainly seems to be the institutionalised model for organising politics at the international level. Since the first steps in the direction of a more regularised multilateral diplomacy happened in the wake of the Vienna Congress 1814–15, the model has survived until this day and seems indispensable and ubiquitous in all government arrangements at the international level (Schiavone 2005). In the EU, the classic model is, of course, primarily reflected in the set-up of the Council – probably the most important legislative body of the Union, a body that also has executive functions within the area of a common foreign and security policy. The fact that the Council has an intergovernmental structure somewhat similar to the second legislative chamber of the Federal Republic of Germany does not mean that the EU has copied the Germans' rather peculiar arrangement. Rather, it signals the institutional robustness of the classic model and the inherent path dependence as regards organising politics at the international level.

The second striking lesson that might be drawn from a simple chronology of organisational forms is that although there obviously is an enduring intergovernmental core, there has been a continuous expansion and refinement of structures. Over time, they have become more subtle and complex, perhaps endowed with more capacity for order and problem solving. Such developments may be interpreted as organisational learning processes which are inter alia mirrored in the growth of secretariats, buildings, procedures, role differentiation and committee systems.

Finally, the third remarkable observation is that some changes seem to have more the character of leaps or innovations than of incremental changes. According to historical institutionalists, critical junctures at which existing institutional arrangements may be placed on new paths or trajectories are often attributed to big, exogenous shocks such as war or economic crisis (Ikenberry 1998; Pierson 2004; Olsen 2007). Under such circumstances, 'steep learning' may take place and actors may come to accept solutions they would not otherwise accept. Thus, the Westphalian order can be seen as an innovative response at that time to the shock caused by the Thirty Years War. In the same vein, the Napoleonic Wars have constituted a catalyst for the qualitative changes that followed the Vienna Congress (Schroeder 1994). Moreover, World War I may have been a prerequisite for shifting track to a considerable extent as regards international security organisation (Steiner 2005). Finally, the new catastrophe in the years 1939–45 may have opened the door for the most radical reform of international organisation seen so far.

However, as shown, organisational innovations do not seem to replace existing arrangements; they are rather layered around existing bodies (Thelen 2003). Moreover, shocks do not necessarily lead to innovation: the UN, OEEC, NATO and the Council of Europe all inherited the territorially based structure at their core. So it is quite possible that the peculiar design of the EU and its predecessors has to be attributed to the entrepreneurship of Jean Monnet, adviser to the French foreign minister Schuman. Monnet had, among several things, been a deputy secretary general of the League of Nations and was convinced that politics at the international level had to be organised differently from the intergovernmental model which he saw as belonging to 'the old order' (Duchêne 1994: 241). Entrepreneurs provide skills beyond what follows from their organisational roles. On the other hand, without a relevant organisational platform and a window of opportunity such skills may never be translated into action.

Conclusion

There are indications of significant changes in patterns of executive politics in Europe over the last couple of decades. Most importantly, European governments, or more correctly, *parts* of national governments, have to some extent become parts of a European government as well. Case studies within various policy fields have unveiled the 'double-hattedness' of national (regulatory) agencies. On the one hand, they continue to serve national ministries; on the other, they take part in the formulation and implementation of EU policies in close cooperation with the European Commission or EU-level agencies, with relative independence from their respective ministerial departments. Needless to say, in the latter role they may have to defend positions not necessarily shared by their respective governments.

There are two major institutional prerequisites for this new pattern of executive politics across levels of governance and national borders to emerge, one at the European level and one at the national level. As regards the European level, the centrifugal forces present at the very heart of national governments cannot stem from classic IGOs. These forces occur due to the actual 'emancipation' of the Commission as a new executive centre outside the Council. Through organisational reforms it has become more similar to national governments both in terms of structure and functioning. While becoming more independent of national governments, it has at the same time involved interest groups and, increasingly, strengthened its ties with the European Parliament so that we might speak of a pre-parliamentary system at the EU level. The establishment of the Commission's predecessor, the High Authority, represented a genuine innovation as regards the organisation of executive politics at the international level. To explain this establishment mainly as governments' ('principals') delegation of powers to a supranational body ('agent') seems incomplete. Probably, this innovation cannot be properly understood without taking into account the accumulated experiences of past generations, including repeated fatal systemic breakdowns, over a very long period of time.

However, a new executive centre at the European level does not in itself result in new patterns of executive politics across levels that have been the focus of this article. After all, the original 'EU model' is based on 'indirect administration', which means that there should be a clear division of labour between the two levels: policies made at the EU level are (for the most part) to be implemented by national governments which enjoy a kind of 'administrative sovereignty' (Hofmann and Türk 2006). Therefore, an additional institutional prerequisite for the new patterns of multilevel executive politics to evolve is fragmented national governments. It is precisely when national agencies are vertically as well as horizontally decoupled that they are open to being re-coupled into new administrative configurations. Thus, the creation of semi-detached agencies and 'single purpose bodies', which enjoy considerable autonomy, has provided the necessary administrative infrastructure for this reconfiguration to take place. The motor of change in this case is also multifaceted; however, behind organisational reforms neo-liberal ideology seems to have played a crucial role, at least at an initial stage.

We started by contending that standard portrayals of modern government still tend to focus on the national and sub-national levels of government. And we asked if a kind of 'methodological nationalism' has hindered us from seeing the new emerging executive centre at the level above and the re-coupling of nationally decoupled agencies into a new multilevel Union administration. Drawing on insights from the study of international relations, and in particular from EU studies, may help to fill this gap. Students of EU politics and governance may learn from students of comparative government and public administration that things they tend to consider as given and stable, as for instance the existence of semi-independent national regulators (or regional governments), are much less so. The logic of public reform is that reforms often, after a while, trigger responses in the opposite direction. As shown in this article, organisational measures aiming at compensating for deficiencies caused by 'first generation NPM reforms' are already under way. 'Joined-up government' reforms might, if zealously implemented, change some of the conditions under which the new multilevel administrative order has developed.

Acknowledgements

I am grateful to Johan P. Olsen for his constructive comments on an earlier version of this article. Thanks also to the participants at the 30th anniversary conference of *West European Politics* at EUI, Florence, 18–20 January 2007, and to the participants at the ARENA seminar, University of Oslo, 27 February, 2007.

Notes

1. An important exception to this 'methodological nationalism' is Hayward and Menon (2003) in which 'governing Europe' clearly is a multilevel phenomenon.
2. This section draws on Egeberg 2006, chapter 3.
3. *European Governance. A White Paper*, COM (2001) 428 final, p. 8, and *For the European Union. Peace, Freedom and Solidarity. Communication of the Commission on the Institutional Architecture*, COM (2002) 728 final, p. 18.
4. For example, *European Voice*, 14–20 November 2002; 22–28 May 2003.
5. *European Voice*, 22–28 July 1999.
6. Press statement by Vice President Neil Kinnock, 29 September 1999.
7. *European Governance. A White Paper*, p. 15.
8. At least, this is the case for social democratic commissioners. Source: Espen Barth Eide, member of the presidency of the Party of European Socialists (PES).
9. *For the European Union. Peace, Freedom and Solidarity*, p. 18.
10. *European Voice*, 22–28 July 1999.
11. *Externalization of the Management of Community Programmes – including presentation of a framework regulation for a new type of executive agency* (COM (2000) 788 final).
12. Ibid., p. 6.

References

Almer, J., and M. Rotkirch (2004). *European Governance – An Overview of the Commission's Agenda for Reform*. Stockholm: Swedish Institute for European Policy Studies.

Andersen, S.S., and K.A. Eliassen (2001). 'Informal Processes: Lobbying, Actor Strategies, Coalitions and Dependencies', in S.S. Andersen and K.A. Eliassen (eds.), *Making Policy in Europe*. London: Sage.

Barbieri, D. (2006). 'Transnational Networks meet National Hierarchies: The Cases of the Italian Competition and Environment Administrations', in M. Egeberg (ed.), *Multilevel Union Administration. The Transformation of Executive Politics in Europe*. Basingstoke: Palgrave Macmillan.

Barnett, M., and M. Finnemore (2004). *Rules for the World. International Organizations in Global Politics*. Ithaca, NY and London: Cornell University Press.

Bartolini, S. (2005). *Restructuring Europe: Centre Formation, System Building, and Political Structuring between the Nation State and the European Union*. Oxford: Oxford University Press.

Bauer, M. (2002). 'The EU "Partnership Principle": Still a Sustainable Governance Device across Multiple Administrative Arenas?', *Public Administration*, 80, 769–89.

Beyers, J. (2005). 'Multiple Embeddedness and Socialization in Europe: The Case of Council Officials', *International Organization*, 59, 899–936.

Christensen, T., and P. Lægreid, eds. (2001). *New Public Management. The Transformation of Ideas and Practice*. Aldershot: Ashgate.

Christensen, T., and P. Lægreid, eds. (2006). *Autonomy and Regulation. Coping with Agencies in the Modern State*. Cheltenham: Edward Elgar.

Christiansen, T. (1997). 'Tensions of European Governance: Politicized Bureaucracy and Multiple Accountability in the European Commission', *Journal of European Public Policy*, 4, 73–90.

Cini, M. (1996). *The European Commission. Leadership, Organisation and Culture in the EU Administration*. Manchester: Manchester University Press.

Cini, M. (2000). 'Administrative Culture in the European Commission: The Case of Competition and Environment', in N. Nugent (ed.), *At the Heart of the Union. Studies of the European Commission.* Houndmills: Macmillan Press.

Claude, I.L. (1964). *Swords into Plowshares. The Problems and Progress of International Organization.* New York: Random House.

Coen, D., and M. Thatcher (2005). 'The New Governance of Markets and Non-majoritarian Regulators', *Governance: An International Journal of Policy, Administration and Institutions,* 18, 329–46.

Coombes, D. (1970). *Politics and Bureaucracy in the European Community.* London: George Allen and Unwin.

Cox, R.W., and H.K. Jacobson, eds. (1973). *The Anatomy of Influence. Decision Making in International Organization.* New Haven, CT: Yale University Press.

Cram, L. (1994). 'The European Commission as a Multi-organization: Social Policy and IT Policy in the EU', *Journal of European Public Policy,* 1, 195–217.

Dehousse, R. (1997). 'Regulation by Networks in the European Community: The Role of European Agencies', *Journal of European Public Policy,* 4, 246–61.

Dehousse, R. (2002). 'Misfits: EU law and the Transformation of European Governance', in C. Joerges and R. Dehousse (eds.), *Good Governance in Europe's Integrated Market.* Oxford: Oxford University Press.

Döring, H. (2007). 'The Composition of the College of Commissioners: Patterns of Delegation', *European Union Politics,* 8, 207–28.

Duchêne, F. (1994). *Jean Monnet. The First Statesman of Interdependence.* New York: W.W. Norton.

Eberlein, B., and G. Grande (2005). 'Beyond Delegation: Transnational Regulatory Regimes and the EU Regulatory State', *Journal of European Public Policy,* 12, 89–112.

Egeberg, M. (2003). 'How Bureaucratic Structure Matters: An Organizational Perspective', in B.G. Peters and J. Pierre (eds.), *Handbook of Public Administration.* London: Sage.

Egeberg, M. (2004). 'An Organisational Approach to European Integration: Outline of a Complementary Perspective', *European Journal of Political Research,* 43, 199–219.

Egeberg, M., ed. (2006). *Multilevel Union Administration. The Transformation of Executive Politics in Europe.* Basingstoke: Palgrave Macmillan.

Egeberg, M., G.F. Schaefer and J. Trondal (2003). 'The Many Faces of EU Committee Governance', *West European Politics,* 26, 19–40.

Elgie, R. (2003). 'Governance Traditions and Narratives of Public Sector Reform in Contemporary France', *Public Administration,* 81, 141–62.

Everson, M., G. Majone, L. Metcalfe and A. Schout, eds. (1999). *The Role of Specialised Agencies in Decentralising EU Governance.* Report presented to the Commission. Maastricht: European Institute of Public Administration.

Goetz, K.H. (2000). 'European Integration and National Executives: A Cause in Search of an Effect', *West European Politics,* 23, 211–31.

Goetz, K.H. (2006). 'Power at the Centre: The Organization of Democratic Systems', in P.M. Heywood, E. Jones, M. Rhodes and U. Sedelmeier (eds.), *Developments in European Politics.* Basingstoke: Palgrave Macmillan.

Gornitzka, Å. (2007). 'Networking Administration in Areas of National Sensitivity. The Commission and European Higher Education', in A. Amaral, P. Maassen, C. Musselin and G. Neave (eds.), *European Integration and the Governance of Higher Education and Research.* Dordrecht: Springer.

Hayward, J., and A. Menon, eds. (2003). *Governing Europe.* Oxford: Oxford University Press.

Heritier, A., D. Kerwer, C. Knill, D. Lehmkuhl, M. Teutsch and A.C. Douillet (2001). *Differential Europe. The European Union Impact on National Policymaking.* Lanham, MD: Rowman & Littlefield.

Hofmann, H.C.H., and A.H. Türk (2006). *EU Administrative Governance.* Cheltenham: Edward Elgar.

Holsti, K.J. (2004). *Taming the Sovereigns. Institutional Change in International Politics.* Cambridge: Cambridge University Press.

Hood, C., and M. Jackson (1991). *Administrative Argument.* Aldershot: Dartmouth.

Hooghe, L. (2000). 'A House With Differing Views: The European Commission and Cohesion Policy', in N. Nugent (ed.), *At the Heart of the Union. Studies of the European Commission.* Houndmills: Macmillan Press.

Hooghe, L. (2001). *The European Commission and the Integration of Europe. Images of Governance.* Cambridge: Cambridge University Press.

Ikenberry, G.J. (1998). 'Constitutional Politics in International Relations', *European Journal of International Relations*, 4, 144–77.

Johansson, K.M. (2005). 'The European Commission and the Growing Significance of Party Politics', paper prepared for the Connex conference in Oslo, 27–28 May.

Kickert, W.J.M., and T. Beck Jørgensen (1995). 'Introduction: Managerial Reform Trends in Western Europe', *International Review of Administrative Sciences*, 61, 499–510.

Knill, C. (2001). *The Europeanisation of National Administrations. Patterns of Institutional Change and Persistence.* Cambridge: Cambridge University Press.

Kohler-Koch, B. (1997). 'Organized Interests in European Integration: The Evolution of a New Type of Governance', in H. Wallace and A.R. Young (eds.), *Participation and Policy-Making in the European Union.* Oxford: Clarendon Press.

Lequesne, C. (2000). 'The European Commission: A Balancing Act between Autonomy and Dependence', in K. Neunreither and A. Wiener (eds.), *European Integration After Amsterdam. Institutional Dynamics and Prospects for Democracy.* Oxford: Oxford University Press.

Lewis, J. (2005). 'The Janus Face of Brussels: Socialization and Everyday Decision Making in the European Union', *International Organization*, 59, 937–71.

Lodge, M. (2004). 'Accountability and Transparency in Regulation: Critiques, Doctrines and Instruments', in J. Jordana and D. Levi-Faur (eds.), *The Politics of Regulation. Institutions and Regulatory Reforms for the Age of Governance.* Cheltenham: Edward Elgar.

Ludlow, P. (2004). 'The Barroso Commission: A Tale of Lost Innocence', *Briefing Note No 3.4/ 5.* Brussels: EuroComment.

MacMullen, A. (2000). 'European Commissioners: National Routes to a European Elite', in N. Nugent (ed.), *At the Heart of the Union. Studies of the European Commission.* Houndmills: Macmillan Press.

Majone, G. (1996). *Regulating Europe.* London: Routledge.

Majone, G. (2002). 'The European Commission: the Limits of Centralization and the Perils of Parliamentarization', *Governance*, 15, 375–92.

Marks, G., L. Hooghe and K. Blank (1996). 'European Integration From the 1980s: State-centric v. Multi-level Governance', *Journal of Common Market Studies*, 34, 341–77.

Martens, M. (2006). 'National Regulators between Union and Governments: A Study of the EU's Environmental Policy Network IMPEL', in M. Egeberg (ed.), *Multilevel Union Administration. The Transformation of Executive Politics in Europe.* Basingstoke: Palgrave Macmillan.

Mazey, S., and J. Richardson (1996). 'The Logic of Organisation. Interest Groups', in J. Richardson (ed.), *European Union: Power and Policy-Making.* London: Routledge.

Meyer, J.W., and B. Rowan (1977). 'Institutionalized Organizations: Formal Structure as Myth and Ceremony', *American Journal of Sociology*, 83, 340–63.

Michelmann, H.J. (1978). 'Multinational Staffing and Organizational Functioning in the Commission of the European Communities', *International Organization*, 32, 477–96.

Mörth, U. (2000). 'Competing Frames in the European Commission – The Case of the Defence Industry and Equipment Issue', *Journal of European Public Policy*, 7, 173–89.

Nørgård, G.H. (2006). 'National Limits to Transnational Networking? The Case of the Danish IT and Telecom Agency', in M. Egeberg (ed.), *Multilevel Union Administration. The Transformation of Executive Politics in Europe.* Basingstoke: Palgrave Macmillan.

Nugent, N. (2001). *The European Commission.* Basingstoke: Palgrave Macmillan.

OECD (2002). *Distributed Public Governance. Agencies, Authorities and other Government Bodies.* Paris: OECD.

Olsen, J.P. (2003). 'Towards a European Administrative Space?', *Journal of European Public Policy*, 10, 506–31.

Olsen, J.P. (2007). *Europe in Search of Political Order. An Institutional Perspective on Unity/ Diversity, Citizens/Their Helpers, Democratic Design/Historical Drift and the Co-existence of Orders.* Oxford: Oxford University Press.

Page, E.C. (1997). *People Who Run Europe.* Oxford: Clarendon Press.

Page, E.C., and B. Jenkins (2005). *Policy Bureaucracy. Government with a Cast of Thousands.* Oxford: Oxford University Press.

Peterson, R.L. (1971). 'Personnel Decisions and the Independence of the Commission of the European Communities', *Journal of Common Market Studies*, 10, 117–37.

Pierson, P. (2004). *Politics in Time. History, Institutions and Social Analysis.* Princeton, NJ: Princeton University Press.

Pollitt, C., and G. Bouckaert (2004). *Public Management Reform. A Comparative Analysis.* Oxford: Oxford University Press.

Rhodes, R.A.W. (2006). 'Executives in Parliamentary Government', in R.A.W. Rhodes, S.A. Binder and B.A. Rockman (eds.), *The Oxford Handbook of Political Institutions.* Oxford: Oxford University Press.

Rouban, L. (2003). 'Politicization of the Civil Service', in B.G. Peters and J. Pierre (eds.), *Handbook of Public Administration.* London: Sage.

Schiavone, G. (2005). *International Organizations. A Dictionary and Directory.* Basingstoke: Palgrave Macmillan.

Schroeder, P.W. (1994). *The Transformation of European Politics 1763–1848.* Oxford: Oxford University Press.

Shapiro, M. (1997). 'The Problems of Independent Agencies in the United States and the European Union', *Journal of European Public Policy*, 4, 276–91.

Spence, D. (1994). 'Structure, Functions and Procedures in the Commission', in G. Edwards and D. Spence (eds.), *The European Commission.* Harlow: Longman.

Steiner, Z. (2005). *The Lights that Failed. European International History 1919–1933.* Oxford: Oxford University Press.

Støle, Ø. (2006). 'Towards a Multilevel Union Administration? The Decentralization of EU Competition Policy', in M. Egeberg (ed.), *Multilevel Union Administration. The Transformation of Executive Politics in Europe.* Basingstoke: Palgrave Macmillan.

Sverdrup, U. (2006a). 'Policy Implementation', in P. Graziano and M. Vink (eds.), *Europeanization: New Research Agendas.* Basingstoke: Palgrave Macmillan.

Sverdrup, U. (2006b). 'Administering Information: Eurostat and Statistical Integration', in M. Egeberg (ed.), *Multilevel Union Administration. The Transformation of Executive Politics in Europe.* Basingstoke: Palgrave Macmillan.

Talbot, C. (2004). 'The Agency Idea: Sometimes Old, Sometimes New, Sometimes Borrowed, Sometimes Untrue', in C. Pollitt and C. Talbot (eds.), *Unbundled Government. A Critical Analysis of the Global Trend to Agencies, Quangos and Contractualisation.* London: Routledge.

Tallberg, J. (2004). 'The Power of the Presidency. Brokerage, Efficiency and Distribution in EU Negotiations', *Journal of Common Market Studies*, 42, 999–1022.

Thatcher, M. (2002). 'Delegation to Independent Regulatory Agencies: Pressures, Functions and Contextual Mediation', *West European Politics*, 25, 125–47.

Thatcher, M. (2005). 'Independent Regulatory Agencies and Elected Politicians in Europe', in D. Geradin, R. Munoz and N. Petit (eds.), *Regulation through Agencies in the EU. A New Paradigm of European Governance.* Cheltenham: Edward Elgar.

Thatcher, M., and A. Stone Sweet (2002). 'Theory and Practice of Delegation to Non-majoritarian Institutions, *West European Politics*, 25, 1–22.

Thelen, K. (2003). 'How Institutions Evolve. Insights from Comparative Historical Analysis', in J. Mahoney and D. Rueschemeyer (eds.), *Comparative Historical Analysis in the Social Sciences.* Cambridge: Cambridge University Press.

Thomson, R., J. Boerefijn and F. Stokman (2004). 'Actor Alignments in European Decision Making', *European Journal of Political Research*, 43, 237–61.

Trondal, J. (2006). 'Governing at the Frontier of the European Commission. The Case of Seconded National Experts', *West European Politics*, 29, 147–60.

Trondal, J., M. Marcussen and F. Veggeland (2005). 'Re-discovering International Executive Institutions', *Comparative European Politics*, 3, 232–58.

Ugland, T., and F. Veggeland (2006). 'The European Commission and the Integration of Food Safety Policies across Levels', in M. Egeberg (ed.), *Multilevel Union Administration. The Transformation of Executive Politics in Europe*. Basingstoke: Palgrave Macmillan.

Wright, V. (1994). 'Reshaping the State. The Implications for Public Administration', *West European Politics*, 17, 102–37.

Governance as a Path to Government

KLAUS H. GOETZ

Thirty years ago, at the time of the launch of *West European Politics*, the academic discussion of state and government in Western Europe was preoccupied with crises of governability, overload and legitimacy (the chief contributions are summarised succinctly in Kaase and Newton 1995: 17ff. and Birch 1984). Critics of both the left and the right agreed that the contemporary state was faced with ever-growing demands for the provision of services and benefits, which it was unable to meet. Analysts from the left pointed to a fundamental contradiction between the need for the democratic state to legitimate itself in the eyes of the voters through extensive service provision to be paid for through taxation; and the demands by capital to secure the highest possible returns. This theme, with variations, ran through the work of O'Connor (1973) on the *Fiscal Crisis of the State*, Offe (1972) on the *Structural Problems of the Capitalist State*, and Habermas (1973) on the *Legitimation Crisis*. Not only did the contradictory demands of capital and the mass of the population overstretch the state's capacity to deliver; the more the state's structural inability to meet the demands of both capital and the citizens at the same time became apparent, the more its popular legitimacy eroded.

Writers from conservative and liberal perspectives likewise highlighted the disparity between the demands placed on the state and its ability to satisfy them, making the business of government increasingly difficult, if not eventuating in a state of ungovernability. King (1975: 286), in his analysis of government overload, argued with reference to the British example that, first, 'the range of matters for which British Governments hold themselves responsible – and for which they believe that the electorate may hold them responsible – has increased greatly over the past ten or twenty years, as well as over the past fifty, and is still increasing at a rapid rate'; second, 'just as the range of responsibilities of Governments has increased, so, to a large extent independently, their capacity to exercise their responsibilities has declined' (King 1975: 288). Brittan (1975: 129), acknowledging King's contribution to his own analysis, noted that the two 'endemic threats' to liberal representative democracy: 'the generation of excessive expectations' and 'the disruptive effects of the pursuit of group self-interest in the market place' (ibid.: 129) led to an 'excessive burden (...) placed on the "sharing out" function of government (...) defined as the activities of the public authorities in influencing the allocation of resources, both through taxation and expenditure policies and through direct intervention in the market place' (ibid.: 130).

As Offe (1979) noted, there was much common ground between left and right in the analysis of problems of governability and legitimacy: 'There are a number of structural similarities between neo-conservative state and social theory, which centres on the problem of "ungovernability", and the socialist critique of late capitalist societal formations, which, understandably, neither side is keen to highlight' (Offe 1979: 294, my translation, KHG). Writers from different ideological perspectives offered stark warnings about the future. Brittan (1975: 155), for example, addressed the possibility that liberal democracy might disappear through a 'gradual process of disintegration of traditional political authority and the growth of new sources of power. Indeed, a continuation of present trends might lead to a situation where nothing remained of liberal democracy but its label'. Crozier (1975: 53), writing at the same time, acknowledged that 'The problems of European societies are difficult to solve but they are not intractable'; but he also suggested that crises from within and without could quickly lead to a situation in which 'the whole European system would crumble' and a 'disastrous drifting of Western Europe' might occur (ibid.: 54).

It is within this context of a widely shared sense of fundamental malaise and even pessimism about the prospects of democracy that detailed analyses of the conditions under which Western governments might go bankrupt (Rose and Peters 1979); of challenges to political authority through lack of effectiveness and popular consent (Rose 1980); or of the possible waning of the welfare state (Scharpf 1977) were undertaken. There were, of course, also cautiously optimistic voices, such as Kaase (1980: 190), who argued that 'political beliefs, attitudes and behaviours threatening ungovernability have not become clearly visible'. But the overall picture was one of gloom and, in some instances, doom.[1]

Crisis of Governability? Governance to the Rescue

Against this background of profound scepticism, the late 1970s and early 1980s witnessed sharply differing political responses to the widely perceived need for reform. In these responses, the lines between institutional reforms, focused on state and government, and policy reforms – the substance and instruments of public policy – were naturally blurred. The extremes were France, at one end, and the UK, at the other. In both, new incoming governments aimed at a rupture with past state and policy traditions. In France, the election of a socialist president and a parliament with a left-wing majority in May–June 1981 brought in a government intent on radical reform, which included, in particular, an 'extension of the public industrial sector' through large-scale nationalisation, 'greater state control over credit', 'an expansionary budgetary stance', 'an active industrial policy', 'a renovated planning system', 'a democratization of decision-making at plant level', and 'a decentralization of the decision-making process' (Machin and Wright 1985: 2). The 'crisis' of the state was, thus, to be tackled through state expansion (nationalisation, budgetary expansion, growth in public sector personnel, reinvigoration of state intervention in the economy) and its internal reconfiguration, notably through administrative and political decentralisation (Mény 1984, 1987).

The other extreme was marked by the reforms pursued by the Thatcher government in the UK, which had come into power in May 1979 on a Conservative manifesto

> generally regarded as the most ideological of the party's post-war manifestos (. . .) What the manifesto proposed included a shift towards monetarist policies as a means of controlling inflation, a reduction in the proportion of GNP taken in taxation and, above all, shifting the balance of society towards individual freedom and away from the tilt in favour of the state. (Douglas 1983: 69–70)

Combined with a policy of rigorous centralisation (Goldsmith and Newton 1983) and an onslaught on the power of the trade unions (Hague 1983), the UK's reform agenda constituted almost a mirror image of the French ambitions.

Neither case was, however, typical of Western European developments more broadly. In West Germany, the coming into power of Chancellor Kohl in late 1982, despite the proclaimed aim of a *Wende* (turnaround), did little to alter the main contours of the stable 'West German model' (Paterson and Smith 1981), whether in terms of state structures or state–society relations (Benz and Goetz 1996). Italy, although often regarded as a prime example of the twin crises of governability and legitimacy (Tarrow 1979; Graziano and Tarrow 1979), seemed to be 'in transition' at the end of the 1970s (Lange and Tarrow 1979) and continued to be in 'crisis and transition' two decades later (Bull and Rhodes 1997), but with little evidence, at least until the end of the 1980s, of any profound transformative ambitions amongst its ruling classes. Moreover, neither country pursued a policy of aggressive privatisation (as in the UK) or nationalisation followed by later privatisations, as in France (Vickers and Wright 1988).

With a focus on the reforms of the state and policy-making machinery, it seems, at least at first sight, paradoxical that in Europe the concept of governance first rose to prominence in analyses of the UK's political system. This occurred at a time when observers noted state centralisation – within the British central government and in intergovernmental relations – an ideological drive to shrink the state, and a determined attempt to minimise the role of organised interests in public policy-making. In reviewing his earlier work on policy networks – 'sets of organizations clustered around a major government function or department' – Rhodes (2003: 65) noted that the Thatcher government's intention to use the market to deliver public services had the unintended effect of increasing the role of policy networks. Thus, the corporate management and marketisation reforms:

> fragmented the systems for delivering public services and so created pressures for organizations to cooperate with one another to deliver services. In other words, and paradoxically, marketization multiplied the networks it was supposed to replace (...) Fragmentation not only created new networks but it also increased the membership of existing networks, incorporating both the private and voluntary sectors (...) In short, governance refers to the changing role of the state after the varied public sector reforms of the 1980s and 1990s. (Rhodes 2003: 65–6)

The driving forces behind the spread of governance were, of course, not uniform across Western Europe (see below). As far as developments at national level are concerned, chief factors commonly associated with the spread of governance arrangements include privatisation (Vickers and Wright 1988), which was one, though by no means the sole, factor behind the rise of the 'regulatory state' (Majone 1999; Lodge 2008); administrative reforms inspired by the New Public Management (Pollitt and Boukaert 2004; Wright 1994; Müller and Wright 1994a,b); and changes in intergovernmental relations and territorial politics (Keating 2008; Rhodes and Wright 1987). In the European context, the emergence of 'multi-level governance' (Hooghe and Marks 2001, with references to their earlier work) or 'European governance' (for an extensive review see Kohler-Koch and Rittberger 2006) were seen to reflect the extension of the powers of the European Union; the close interaction between public and private actors at

EU, national and subcentral levels in the EU policy process; and the concomitant progressive Europeanisation of national political systems (Goetz and Hix 2000).

It is scarcely surprising that there are many different conceptualisations of governance, as the concept has been used for different heuristic purposes and in diverse disciplinary and sub-disciplinary contexts (for reviews see, e.g., Benz 2004; Kjær 2004; Schuppert 2005). As far as comparative European government (and public administration) is concerned, most proponents of the concept would probably agree with Benz and Papadopoulos (2006a: 2–3) on the following 'major traits of governance': 'plurality of decision centres'; 'no clear hierarchy' between these centres; 'the core of decision structures consists of networks'; the boundaries of decision structures are fluid and defined primarily in functional terms; actors include experts, public actors and representatives of private interests; collective actors dominate; 'negotiation prevails'; and 'governance usually leads to less formal modes of decision-making' (quotations partly emphasised in the original). Benz and Papadopoulos also emphasise that amongst actors 'Elected politicians are deemed to play a secondary role' (ibid.: 3) and in 'governance the initiative and control functions of parliaments are expected to be weak, with parliaments instead being confined to the role of ratifying bodies' (ibid.: 3). In common with many other analysts, these authors stress the link between governability and governance, when they note that to 'to avoid ungovernability, the plurality of competing interests and preferences has to be organized through "horizontal" coordination and cooperative policy-making cutting across institutions, sectors and territories' (ibid.: 2).

Governance as Practice: The Challenge of Comparative European Government

What are the problems with governance that this article seeks to highlight? It would be facile to criticise what might appear as the inflationary use of the term or the fact that there are many different definitions to be found (though the latter certainly means that it is easy to dismiss any critique as being 'off target'). Similarly, there is not much to be gained from belabouring the obvious point that governance is not an integrated theory. It is certainly theory-applying, with prominent contributions from both rationalist and sociological-institutionalist perspectives, and, similar to the concept of Europeanisation, its main value may lie in serving as an 'attention-directing device' (Olsen 2002). Finally, it scarcely advances our understanding of either government or governance to ask whether the latter exists. Rather, my purpose here is to probe the oft-made claim that the past two decades or so have seen a decisive shift from government to governance.

The argument developed in the following can be briefly summarised as follows. Considered from the perspective of comparative European government, governance as a *practice* is less widespread and less consequential than talk about a major shift suggests. The propellants of governance are distributed unequally across the EU-27; the conditions upon which governance relies are in short supply in much of Europe; there is little, if any, evidence of weakened core executives, a downgrading of elected politicians and the progressive marginalisation of parliaments in the policy process; and neither EU policy-making nor Europeanisation provide compelling evidence of a strengthening of governance at the expense of government. Since governance as a *concept* is neglectful of political power, it is ill-positioned to capture how governments establish new needs for government intervention and build up institutional capacity – often in the face of fierce societal opposition – to deal authoritatively and hierarchically with these newly-identified needs. Viewed from this perspective, evidence of governance, which certainly exists, is not an indication of a shift *away* from government; rather, it signals a shift *towards* government, as problems and decision-making authority move from the societal to the state sphere.

Propellants of Governance

The forces that Rhodes (1996, 2003) and others have identified as propellants behind the rise of governance show a great deal of cross-national variation. This observation applies not only to the fragmenting effects of decentralisation, regionalisation and federalisation (Keating 2008), but also, and in particular, as regards the extent to which states have undergone administrative reforms that tend to be summarised under the label of the New Public Management. This NPM reform agenda has been linked to institutional fragmentation; regulation; competition within the public sector and between the latter and the private sector (e.g. privatisation, deregulation, marketisation, contracting out); hands-on management; management by objectives; output orientation; and customer orientation (Wright 1994).

Some commentators go as far as to suggest that NPM may now be intellectually 'dead' (Dunleavy *et al.* 2006), as its problematic side effects, 'radically increased institutional and policy complexity', have become more apparent, and NPM-inspired reforms are halted or even repealed. But although this may be an overstatement, comparative analysis shows convincingly that NPM has affected the EU-15 with very unequal force. Pollitt and Boukaert (2004), who have undertaken the most detailed comparative examination of public management reforms (including six European and four non-European countries), highlight the extent to which 'reform trajectories' have differed across nations as regards the scope and the major components of reform – including finance, personnel, organisation, performance measurement systems – and processes of implementation. A very similar conclusion is also reached in the recent comparative exploration of NPM practice by Pollitt *et al.* (2007), which highlights cross-European diversity in NPM practice, whether it concerns the use of performance indicators, personnel reforms, the creation and management of executive agencies, public–private partnerships, benchmarking and evaluations of the reforms.

For example, there is a great deal of cross-national variation in the degree to which governments have delegated tasks to non-majoritarian institutions, such as regulatory agencies, and the degree of independence, if any, which these enjoy (Thatcher and Stone Sweet 2002). Where, as in the UK, autonomisation through the setting up of agencies ('agencification') initially appeared to go very far, this seems to have been followed by a reassertion of the central Westminster bureaucracy (Richards and Smith 2004). Indeed, Christensen and Lægreid (2005) identify a more general dynamic where deregulation and agencification are followed by reregulation and a 'reassertion of the centre'. Even where, as, for example, in Norway, NPM reform has been influential and there has been major structural devolution – Christensen (2005: 728) notes that during 'the last 15 years, about 60 units have changed their organisational status and become formally more autonomous' – state and administrative traditions have proved highly resilient. Thus, Norway continues 'to have many of the features of the centralised state model, such as a hierarchical political-administrative system, a relatively large public sector, and structural homogeneity' (ibid.: 736).

When one turns to the ten new Central and Eastern European member states of the European Union, it is noticeable that post-communist administrative reforms have not been inspired by the NPM. In fact, as a World Bank expert noted towards the end of the 1990s, the CEE countries 'have stayed curiously clear of the NPM approach. The implicit systems and models adopted so far have been the centralized hierarchies of the Weberian tradition' (Nunberg 1999: 264). Later comparative analyses (Goetz 2001; Dimitrov *et al.* 2006, Meyer-Sahling 2004) have arrived at similar conclusions. This is not to suggest that strong central executives and administrations modelled on Weberian principles have taken deep root in post-Communist contexts; but nor has Central and Eastern Europe proved a fertile ground for the kind of state reforms that in Western Europe were seen as key drivers behind governance.

Conditions of Governance

Analysts of governance with a disciplinary background in comparative government (and public administration) typically recognise that governance cannot supplant government, but is, in fact, critically reliant on the latter. To set up state-government and governance in opposition to each other is, from this perspective, fundamentally misleading. This point of view is exemplified in the work of Pierre and Peters (2000). For them, the emergence of new patters of governance

> should not necessarily be seen as indications of a weakening of the
> state but rather a transformations of previous models of governance

into new ones (...) it is much too early to dismiss the state as a centre (if not *the* centre) of power and authority... Thus, the main issue is not so much whether the state is declining but rather how it transforms and what contending sources and models of governance seem to be emerging. (Pierre and Peters 2000: 94; emphasis original)

Elsewhere, they have noted that in 'retrospect it appears that if parts of the governance debate have attempted to move the state back *out* of governing into the relative oblivion it found itself during the heyday of the "behavioural revolution" (...) We believe that this movement is unfortunate, simply because it is an implicit argument that the state has lost empirical leverage' (Peters and Pierre 2006: 29; emphasis original). In particular, the core institutions of the state – law, executives, parliaments, courts – are critical in empowering and authorising governance. Even strong proponents of the governance paradigm acknowledge that political institutions 'define who is authorized to act and make collectively binding decisions, they make actors' behaviour predictable and visible, and they link those who hold power to those who are subject to decisions' (Benz and Papadopoulos 2006a: 4). The oft-invoked image of the 'shadow of hierarchy' as a necessary precondition of governance captures this point.

Governance is then state-dependent; it is also society-dependent in the sense that in order to work governance arrangements rely on the capacity of private interests to organise themselves effectively as collective actors. For public–private networks to function, private collective actors must, thus, be highly institutionalised, have considerable resources at their disposal and, crucially, must be seen as legitimate interlocutors for political actors. Clearly, these conditions are distributed very unequally across Europe, even if the analysis is restricted to the EU-27. Where state capacity is often seen as weak, organised civil society is typically also considered to be comparatively less developed. Thus, it has been pointed out that Southern European (Cassese 1993; Featherstone 2005; Sotiropoulos 2004) and Central and Eastern countries (Goetz 2001) suffer from administrative deficits, which have, amongst other things, been linked to their comparatively poor record in implementing EU law (Falkner *et al.* 2004); that organised civil society is less developed in these parts of Europe than in North-Western and Northern Europe; and that institutionalised cooperation between political actors and collective private actors is less extensive and intensive.

Recent work on the implementation of EU environmental policy in both Southern and Central and Eastern Europe highlights this mutual dependence as the key reason for the 'only limited evidence for the emergence of new modes of governance in the accession process. If at all, we find nascent forms of cooperation between state and non-state actors that hardly go beyond consultation' (Börzel 2007: manuscript). Where, as in the cases of Southern Europe and Central and Eastern Europe, both state and society are comparatively weak, governance is unlikely to emerge. Thus,

> state capacities have often been too limited to cast a credible shadow of hierarchy providing sufficient incentives for non-state actors to cooperate. Moreover, state actors that command only limited resources have been themselves reluctant to cooperate with non-state actors for fear of agency capture. Finally, weak states are mirrored by weak societies – like state capacities, the degree of societal organiza- tion is significantly lower in Southern Europe and Central and Eastern European (CEE) countries compared to the liberal democracies in North Western Europe. (ibid.)

Consequences of Governance

So far, the argument developed here suggests that outside the North- Western core of Europe both state and society have provided much less fertile grounds for the emergence of governance than proponents of a 'shift' from government and governance assume. But even if one restricts the analysis to those parts of Europe where governance could be expected to flourish, it becomes evident that central trends associated with the rise of governance – notably the weakening of central authority, the margin- alisation of elected (executive) politicians, and a loss of power for parliaments in the policy process – find little support in mainstream comparative European government.[2] The fact that these alleged conse- quences of governance have failed to materialise does not in itself suggest that governance arrangements do not play a central part in public policy- making; but it does cast doubt on the direction of the shift that many authors allege to have taken place. It supports the argument that governance complements or supplements government or, as is argued here, often leads towards government rather than away from it.

A weakening of central authority? Proponents of governance often assume that there has been a 'hollowing out' of the state, evidenced by 'a loss of capacity at the heart of the state – in the core executive' (Saward 1997: 17) and that this process also affects political leadership, notably chief executives, who are in danger of ending up wearing a 'hollow crown' (ibid.). With reference to the British core executive, Rhodes (2003: 69) has described this alleged 'hollowing out' as follows:

> The state has been hollowed out from above (e.g., by international interdependence), from below (by marketization and networks), and sideways (by agencies). Internally, the British core executive was already characterized by baronies, policy networks, and intermittent

and selective coordination. It has been further hollowed out internally by the unintended consequences of marketization which fragmented service delivery, multiplied networks, and diversified the membership of those networks (...) Externally, the state is also being hollowed out by membership of the European Union and other international commitments.

Curiously, this assessment runs counter to the argument put forward by Peters, Rhodes and Wright (2000: 7) in the context of a comparative study of core executives, where it is argued that 'over the last thirty to forty years there has been a steady move towards the reinforcement of the political core executive in most advanced industrial countries and, that within the core executive, there has been an increasing centralization of authority around the person of the chief executive – President, Prime Minister or both (as in France)'. More recently, Webb and Poguntke (2005: 21) have argued that Europe is experiencing a 'structurally induced presidentialization' of its politics, which reflects 'the growth of leadership power and autonomy within parties and political executives, and the greater prominence of leaders in electoral processes' (Webb and Poguntke 2005: 336). Surprisingly, given the emphasis by some influential writers on the importance of governance in the UK, the same country is also often regarded as a prime example of centralisation, giving rise to a 'British presidency' (Foley 2000). The evidence to support such statements is certainly open to question (see Goetz 2006); but comparative research into Western European governments and central ministerial administrations provides little evidence to support the notion of a 'hollowed out' central authority.

A marginalisation of elected politicians? In stark contrast to the expectations of proponents of governance, several recent comparative explorations of the relationships between elected politicians and their officials in Europe have found evidence of determined attempts by politicians to (re-)gain control over officials and to reassert their authority over the bureaucracy (Page and Wright 1999, 2007; Peters and Pierre 2004). Whilst in the 1960s and 1970 it was fashionable to warn against the dangers of 'technocracy' and 'government by experts', since the 1980s scholars have increasingly stressed the (re-)politicization of public policy-making. Amongst other developments, scholars have highlighted that executive policy-making has taken on an increasingly top-down character, as politicians and partisan advisors set policy priorities, with a much reduced scope for bottom-up bureaucratic leadership; that the sources of external policy advice in the forms of think-tanks and consultancies have multiplied, leading to an erosion of the erstwhile near-monopoly of the senior civil service in the provision of policy advice; that there has been a 'deinstitutionalization or personalization of political trust' in the relationship between political and bureaucratic elites (Page and Wright 1999: 277), which means that 'officials have to develop closer personal ties with political masters by acquiring political craft and confidence' (ibid.: 278); and that public management 'reforms meant to weaken the role of political leaders have resulted in greater political intervention in the day-to-day management of government' (Peters and Pierre 2004: 284).

Germany provides a prime illustration of the reassertion of political control. In a classical analysis of the German federal policy process published by Renate Mayntz and Fritz W. Scharpf (1975) some 30 years ago, they noted a pronounced weakness of political planning and control. As a result, a bottom-up policy process characterised by 'considerable decentralization' (ibid.: 67) predominated, with departmental 'working capacity (...) almost entirely concentrated at the lowest hierarchical level' (ibid.: 64), i.e. the section:

> It is obvious that the sections, the basic operating units of departmental organization, work out the proposals for new programs in detail. There is little institutionalized capacity for this work elsewhere in the department, and neither the departmental executive nor the divisional leadership are able to participate very actively in the drafting of proposals. In addition, however, the sections also play an important role in initiating policy proposals. In fact (...) most policy proposals in the federal departments are initiated by the sections, if by initiating we mean not simply to utter an idea but to decide that a more or less clearly conceptualized policy goal shall be transformed into a proposal for a new program or program change, and to sit down oneself to start work on it or direct somebody else to do so. (ibid: 67)

Thirty years later, on the basis of both own research and a review of the more recent literature, Goetz (2007a: 185) has argued that

> it is difficult to avoid the impression that top-down control rather than dialogue has gained the upper hand. The progressive erosion of the ideational foundations of civil service autonomy; organisational change in the ministerial administration; the growing strength of co-governing actors; and the proliferation of external sources of policy advice directed at the political executive have combined to curb the scope for policy leadership at the sectional level of the administration, in particular. The traditional decentralised, bottom-up policy process, with the expert civil servant at the its core, has been gradually replaced by a top-down process in which the civil service aides the preparation of, and executes, decisions taken elsewhere.

Thus, changes in Germany's federal policy process appear to have followed a path that Mayntz and Scharpf warned against 30 years ago: 'a more hierarchical, top-down model of executive control over policy-making'

(Mayntz and Scharpf 1975: 105), in which officials are the recipients of political directives rather than participants in a 'dialogue' (ibid.: 100ff.) with the political leadership. Comparative research (Page and Wright 2007) underlines that this development has been paralleled in other Western European countries.

A loss of parliamentary power? The third shift in institutional power that Benz and Papadopoulos associate with governance concerns the reduction in the policy-making powers of parliaments. Debates about the decline of the parliament do, of course, long precede the governance debate; but they have acquired a new momentum under the banner of the alleged rise of 'post-parliamentary' forms of democracy. Although the concept was already in use some 30 years ago – note the subtitle of Richardson and Jordan's (1979) book on 'governing under pressure' – it has gained greater prominence in mainstream comparative politics and comparative public policy over the last decade or so.

Again, however, scholars specialising in the study of parliaments seem much more optimistic about their power and influence than students of governance and have pointed to a reassertion of legislatures in public policy-making in countries as diverse as Norway (Rommetvedt 2005), Austria (Crepaz 1994) or Portugal (Leston-Bandeira 2001). In countries such as Italy, where the legislature has traditionally had a strong influence over policy, the growth in prime ministerial power does not appear to have led to a major weakening of parliament's policy-making function (Newell 2006). This is not to argue, of course, that Western European legislatures do not differ greatly in their policy powers (Norton 1990) or that formally increased powers translate easily into increased policy control (Raunio and Wiberg 2008). But it seems difficult to sustain the argument that the rise of governance has led to a decline in the policy-making functions of parliaments.

Europeanisation

Over the last decade or so, the impact of European integration, mostly in the form of the European Union, on domestic politics, government and public policy has emerged as a central concern in comparative political science (Goetz and Hix 2000; Goetz 2007b; Graziano and Vink 2007, Green Cowles *et al.* 2001; with further references). As concerns the impact on the core institutions of the state, this literature allows for no clear conclusions regarding the impact of integration on governance (for a detailed review that highlights the contradictory empirical findings see Goetz and Meyer-Sahling 2008, with full references). Thus, the argument that integration strengthens executives at the expense of parliaments and private interest groups co-exists side by side with accounts that reject the thesis of a progressive deparlamentarisation and even with the suggestion that integration might have been a driving force behind the 'reparlamentarisation' of the member states' political systems. Whilst some authors argue that within national executives integration strengthens the administration at the expense of political decision-makers ('integration promotes bureaucratisation'), others point to the growing involvement of national politicians in EU-related decision-making and a progressive restriction of bureaucratic discretion. Similarly, one finds both studies that associate EU integration with centralisation in national ministerial administrations in the form of privileged 'EU core executives' and arguments that stress the progressive diffusion of EU-related decision-making throughout the ministerial and non-ministerial administration, not least as new policy instruments, such as the Open Method of Coordination, encourage horizontal rather than vertical cooperation.

Europeanisation is certainly associated with major shifts in interinstitutional relations at the level of the member states; but there is no clear evidence to indicate that, at the level of the member states, European integration promotes governance at the expense of government.

EU Governance

Turning, finally, from national contexts to policy-making beyond state borders, it is in the context of European integration that the concept of governance has taken on special prominence. The online database on EU governance literature, GOVLIT, in mid-August 2007, contained some 3,345 entries and the search term 'governance' produced 1,006 entries (by contrast, 'government', 'governing' and 'govern' generated 266, 70 and 8 entries, respectively). Indeed, for many, it seems governing and public policy-making at the EU level and EU governance have become largely synonymous. A recent review article by Kohler-Koch and Rittberger (2006) on the 'governance turn in EU studies' underlines this fact. Although, as 'a concept, EU governance requires some considerable "stretching" to include all areas of EU policy-making activity' (ibid.: 33), central tenets of the EU policy process highlighted by Kohler-Koch and Rittberger – notably the importance of the 'Community method', the multi-level character of the decision-making system ('multi-level governance'), the inclusion of private actors ('network governance'), and 'under-politicisation' – are all taken as evidence of EU governance. EU enlargement has already been identified as a further spur towards 'more flexible, decentralized and soft modes of governance' (Zielonka 2007).

Again, as in the national context, my purpose is not to question the utility of the concept of governance for the study of the EU or, perhaps more quixotically, to deny the existence of central tenets of EU governance. It is, however, important to stress that a great – and arguably increasing – share of EU policy-making is resolutely centred on public institutions – EU-level and national. In many instances, EU policy-making processes show few signs of the pluralisation of decision centres and, in particular, the opening to collective private actors, which the notion of governance suggests. This point has been made with some force by Börzel (2005)

> Although it could be expected that the EU governs increasingly through non-hierarchical networks, one finds – compared to the national and international levels – surprisingly few structures in which public and private actors cooperate on equal terms in mixed public–private networks in decision-making and implementation. Tripartite negotiation systems and other forms of public–private partnerships, as they have existed for a long time in the member states and which increasingly also emerge in international politics, can only be found to a limited extent at the European level (...) Until now, there are no forms of public–private co-regulation at the European level comparable to those in the member states. Nor does one find multi-level cooperation between supranational decision-makers and private actors in the various member states and regions, which would involve the latter on equal terms in the determination and implementation of European policy programmes. (ibid.: 73–4; my translation, KHG)

Multi-level interactions are, then, often monopolised by governments – multi-level government. This is, of course, particularly the case in the second and third pillars of the EU – i.e. foreign and security policy and police and judicial cooperation in criminal matters – where the Council decides alone and member state governments traditionally enjoy considerable autonomy from domestic interest groups. The more second and, in particular, third pillar policies move centre-stage, the less EU policy-making and governance can be equated.

From Governance to Government: The Sharp Edges of the State

The argument advanced so far has been that governance constitutes part of the reality of how modern states are run, but that the traditional institutions, processes and means of governing associated with the concept of 'government' still prevail at national and probably also at EU levels. If parts of the governance literature make claims about a more general shift away from government to governance this is not just because they read empirical developments differently from what is suggested here. Rather, it is the result of two closely related shortcomings of the governance literature: first, the 'selectivity of the governance perspective', which, as Renate Mayntz has repeatedly highlighted (2002, 2004, 2005), lies in the 'problem-solving bias' of governance theories; and, second, the ahistorical nature of much governance research. These two shortcomings combined mean that the governance literature neglects how states progressively accrue the capacity for hierarchical intervention. Thus, what to many governance analysts appears as a shift *away from* government may turn out to be a path *towards* government.

Mayntz's critique focuses on the common understanding of governance as 'an action or process oriented towards the solution of collective problems' (Mayntz 2005: 17; my translation, KHG). This focus on 'successful or unsuccessful *regulation*', she argues, neglects the 'eminently political motive of gaining and maintaining political power for its own sake' (Mayntz 2004: 74; emphasis original; my translation, KHG). In reality, she adds, 'politics is not always and primarily about fulfilling tasks, producing benefits and problem-solving, but often primarily about gaining and maintaining political power'. But governance tends to reduce conflicts amongst political institutions and actors to disputes over policy priorities and preferences; it is largely oblivious to struggles for power that pervade the core state institutions and the business of government. For example, when Kohler-Koch and Rittberger (2006) identify 'under-politicisation' as one of the defining characteristics of EU governance, this characterisation tells us perhaps more about the governance perspective than about the EU policy process.

It is consistent with this perspective that questions of democratic legitimacy are also primarily viewed from the perspective of performance. As Peters and Pierre (2006: 39) have pointed out in the context of their analysis of 'governance, accountability and democratic legitimacy', from the governance perspective (...) legitimacy emerges as a problem because the state is underperforming. The raison d'être and legitimacy of the state in the governance debate is derived primarily from its performance in terms of outputs – services, decisions, and actions'. Even where it is explicitly acknowledged that 'governance is not only about participation, consensus or functional reorganization, but involves power' (Benz and Papadopoulos 2006b: 274), what is described as 'input-legitimacy' is understood as 'how the interests of citizens are transferred into policy-making, which procedures are applied, which interests are included and excluded and how this selection is justified' (ibid.: 275).

This narrow understanding of what motivates and drives political actors and institutions at the heart of the state, what shapes institutional settings and public policy profiles leaves out much of what students of comparative European government study routinely. Perhaps the most conspicuous weakness is the neglect of political parties in much of the governance literature, even though political parties are omnipresent in the central institutions of the state (Mair 2008). It is because of this neglect of politics and power struggles that analysts of governance are much better placed at studying how policy-making challenges are processed than at understanding the dynamics of how political problems emerge (or do not).

Yet how problems and state capacity materialise is critical to under-standing the relationship between governance and government. Two very well-known points are worth remembering here. First, state capacity takes time to evolve, so that in response to qualitatively or quantitatively new problems we would, at first, expect greater reliance on private and social actors as the capacity for hierarchical state intervention and/or state provision is build up over decades, if not centuries. Second, even under liberal-democratic conditions, state tasks and state capacity are often accrued in the face of strong societal opposition. Both points require brief elaboration.

When discussing governance it is worth remembering that the sharp edges of the state have taken time to emerge. In many parts of Europe, for example, private tax farming remained common Europe throughout the eighteenth century, as the state lacked the capacity to effectively monitor tax collection by state officials (Bonney 1999); this 'governance' arrangement was only discontinued when modern European states acquired a permanent career bureaucracy. Similarly, the collection of information on citizens moved from governance to government arrangements. Summarising the trajectory of information collection in England from 1500 to the present day, Higgs (2004: 196) writes that

> The (...) history of the English State can be seen not in terms of the expansion of power and authority from a central point outwards but as a contraction inwards. The state ceased to be a set of processes involving elites across the whole society undertaking tasks on an unpaid, amateur basis. Instead, it became the preserve of a centralised, salaried core of civil servants and party politicians.

Many other examples could be mentioned: the move from private, mercenary to state armies; the progressive introduction and nationalisation of education; or the nationalisation of welfare and the establishment of vast welfare bureaucracies. The point is that in each of those cases one can observe a progressive etatisation of tasks and the accumulation of the legal, financial, organisational and informational prerequisites for hierarchical state action, so that the 'shadow of hierarchy' progressively lengthened.

The governability literature understood this lengthening of the shadow of the state – in particular the massive expansion of the post-war welfare state – as a consequence of ever-increasing demands placed by citizens on the state. The same perspective dominates in the governance literature. Where governance is, furthermore, linked to the provision of 'common goods' (Héritier 2002), the assumption that governance is at heart about meeting voters' expectations and functional imperatives becomes even stronger, whether it concerns environmental protection, health care or education.

How is it such an apparently responsive state compatible with evidence of the continued erosion of political support and scepticism, if not cynicism, towards government in much of Europe (Dalton 2004; Dalton and Weldon 2005)? The gloomy scenarios of ungovernability reviewed at the start of the paper have not materialised. Public policy-makers have not run short of weighty problems to address, but the view that there is a systemic problem overload, the unresolvability of which progressively delegitimises the state in the eyes of the citizens, is not now widely held. Public deficits – perhaps the most tangible indication of a gap between expectations and capacity to deliver – have been brought firmly under control in much of Europe; there are no signs of major tax revolts; and on many indicators – e.g., public health, education, per capita GDP – at least Western European governments seem to perform much better than 30 years ago. Yet, and this does, at first sight, appear as a paradox, whilst the crisis of governability as understood then appears to have been countered effectively, the crisis of legitimacy appears to have persisted.

For the non-specialist what seems especially puzzling about this development, which is associated with phenomena such as increasing voter apathy and the rise of populist parties of the left and the right, is that it is also taking place in countries such as Austria, Denmark or Norway, which do very well on most public policy indicators. This raises the possibility – and nothing more is suggested here – that the crisis of governability may have partly mutated into a crisis of being governed. What does this mean?

The responsive state is also one that places ever-increasing demands and expectations on its citizens; moreover, in seeking to realise these demands and expectations, Europe's democratic states rely, as ever, if not more so, on (legitimate) coercion. In fact, the citizens in Europe are as tightly, if not more tightly, governed than ever before under conditions of democratic government; and the coercive powers of the state continue to be extended. This becomes clear if we remind ourselves of the state's demands on its citizens' income and wealth; their cultural tolerance; their sense of political identity and self-determination; or their civil liberties.

Thus, for the most Europeans, taxes and mandatory social contributions are on the increase, whilst relative entitlement levels tend to decline. Perhaps more importantly, in pursing their claims public agencies have progressively extended their rights to monitor, access and store private information, often without the knowledge, let alone consent, of those whose information is being used. Many European states pursue policies that test the cultural tolerance of at least parts of their citizenry. Such policies are often concerned with equality and minority rights and government does not shy away from creating new criminal offences so as to make sure that these new rights are vigorously enforced. But we also find instances of governments that appear to reject 'minority politics', yet, in doing so, rely on the same coercive methods, as when the French government, in 2004, outlawed the wearing of conspicuous religious symbols (such as kippot, headscarves or turbans) in state schools. The European integration process, in particular, places demands on citizens' sense of political identity and self-determination. To put it provocatively: it requires the citizens of Sweden to accept that the Romanian government and Maltese MEPs have a legitimate role in determining an ever-growing part of the laws to under which they live. Internally, traditional cultural identities are called into question through state-sanctioned mass immigration. Finally, under the banner of fighting crime and terrorism and maintaining law and order, European states have progressively extended their powers and, in particular, their access to technological abilities to keep their citizens under surveillance in their daily lives.

In short, the sharp edges of the state place growing demands on European citizens. The hierarchical state, relying on further reinforced means of coercion, seems alive and well. The extent to which this coercion is also recognised as legitimate by the people is at least open to debate. Certainly, previous historical experience would lead us to expect that that path from governance to government will not be a smooth one.

Notes

1. See also, e.g., the two influential volumes on *Regierbarkeit* (governability) edited by Hennis *et al.* (1977; 1979), which highlighted fundamental changes in the basic conditions of governing and noted that 'the colossus of modern statehood' stood 'on feet of clay' (Hennis 1977: 17; my translation, KHG).
2. This section draws on Goetz 2006.

References

Benz, A. (2004). 'Einleitung: Governance – Modebegriff oder nützliches sozialwissenschaftliches Konzept?', in A. Benz (ed.), *Governance – Regieren in komplexen Regelsystemen. Eine Einführung*. Wiesbaden: VS Verlag für Sozialwissenschaften, 11–28.

Benz, A., and K.H. Goetz, eds. (1996). *A New German Public Sector? Reform, Adaptation and Stability*. Aldershot: Dartmouth.

Benz, A., and Y. Papadopoulos (2006a). 'Introduction: Governance and Democracy: Concepts and Key Issues', in A. Benz and Y. Papadopoulos (eds.), *Governance and Democracy: Comparing National, European and International Experiences*. London: Routledge, 1–26.

Benz, A., and Y. Papadopoulos (2006b). 'Conclusion: Actors, Institutions and Democratic Governance: Comparing Across Levels', in A. Benz and Y. Papadopoulos (eds.), *Governance and Democracy: Comparing National, European and International Experiences*. London: Routledge, 273–95.

Berrington, H., ed. (1983). *Change in British Politics*, special issue *West European Politics*. 6:4.

Berrington, H., ed. (1998). *Britain in the Nineties: The Politics of Paradox*, special issue *West European Politics*, 21:1.

Birch, A.H. (1984). 'Overload, Ungovernability and Delegitimation: The Theories and the British Case', *British Journal of Political Science*, 14, 135–60.

Bonney, R., ed. (1999). *The Rise of the Fiscal State in Europe, c. 1200–1815*. New York: Oxford University Press.

Börzel, T. (2005). 'European Governance – nicht neu, aber anders', in G.F. Schuppert (ed.), *Governance-Forschung: Vergewisserung über Stand und Entwicklungslinien*. Baden-Baden: Nomos, 72–94.

Börzel, T. (2008). 'New Modes of Governance and Enlargement: The Paradox of Double Weakness', unpublished manuscript.

Brittan, S. (1989). '"The Economic Contradictions of Democracy" Revisited', *Political Quarterly*, 60, 190–208.

Bull, M.J., and M. Rhodes, eds. (1997). *Crisis and Transition in Italian Politics*, special issue *West European Politics*, 20:1.

Cassese, S. (1993). 'Hypotheses on the Italian Administrative System', *West European Politics*, 16:3, 316–28.
Christensen, T. (2005). 'The Norwegian State Transformed?', *West European Politics*, 28:4, 721–39.
Christensen, T., and P. Lægreid (2005). 'Autonomization and Policy Capacity: The Dilemmas and Challenges Facing Political Executives', in M. Painter and J. Pierre (eds.), *Challenges to State Policy Capacity: Global Trends and Comparative Perspectives*. Basingstoke: Palgrave, 137–63.
Crepaz, M.M.L. (1994). 'From Semi-sovereignty to Sovereignty: The Decline of Corporatism and the Rise of Parliament in Austria', *Comparative Politics*, 27:1, 45–65.
Crozier, M.J., S.P. Huntington and J. Watanuki (1975). *The Crisis of Democracy: Report on the Governability of Democracies to the Trilateral Commission*. New York: New York University Press.
Dalton, R.J. (2004). *Democratic Challenges, Democratic Choices: The Erosion of Political Support in Advanced Industrial Democracies*. Oxford: Oxford University Press.
Dalton, R.J., and S.A. Weldon (2005). 'Public Images of Political Parties: A Necessary Evil?', *West European Politics*, 28:5, 931–51.
Dimitrov, V., K.H. Goetz and H. Wollmann (2006). *Governing after Communism: Institutions and Policymaking*. Lanham, MD: Rowman & Littlefield.
Di Palma, G. (1979). 'The Available State: Problems of Reform', *West European Politics*, 2:3, 149–65.
Douglas, J. (1983). 'The Conservative Party: From Pragmatism to Ideology – and Back?', *West European Politics*, 6:4, 56–74.
Dunleavy, P., H.H. Mangetts, S. Bastow and J. Tinkler (2006). 'New Public Management is Dead – Long Live Digital-Era Governance', *Journal of Public Administration Research and Theory*, 16:3, 467–94.
Falkner, G., M. Hartlapp, S. Leiber and O. Treib (2004). 'Non-compliance with EU Directives in the Member States: Opposition through the Backdoor?' *West European Politics*, 27:3, 452–73.
Featherstone, K., ed. (2005). 'The Challenge of Modernisation: Politics and Policy in Greece', special issue, *West European Politics*, 28:2.
Flora, P. (1986). 'Introduction', in P. Flora (ed.), *Growth to Limits: The Western European Welfare States Since World War II*. Berlin: de Gruyter, xi–xxxvi.
Foley, M. (2000). *The British Presidency*. Manchester: Manchester University Press.
Goetz, K.H. (2001). 'Making Sense of Post-Communist Central Administration: Modernization, Europeanization or Latinization?', *Journal of European Public Policy*, 8:6, 1032–51.
Goetz, K.H. (2006). 'Power at the Centre: The Organization of Democratic Systems', in P.M. Heywood, H.E. Jones, M. Rhodes and U. Sedelmeier (eds.), *Developments in European Politics*. Basingstoke: Palgrave, 73–96.
Goetz, Klaus H. (2007a). 'German Officials and the Federal Policy Process: The Decline of Sectional Leadership', in E.C. Page and V. Wright (eds.), *From the Active to the Enabling State: The Changing Role of Top Officials in European Nations*. London: Routledge, 164–88.
Goetz, K.H. (2007b). *Territory, Temporality and Clustered Europeanization*. Vienna: Institute for Advanced Studies, Political Science Series 109. http://www.ihs.ac.at/publications/pol/pw_109.pdf
Goetz, K.H., and S. Hix, eds. (2000). *Europeanised Politics? European Integration and National Political Systems*, special issue, *West European Politics*, 23:4.
Goetz K.H., and J.-H. Meyer-Sahling (2008). 'The Europeanization of National Political Systems', forthcoming in *Living Reviews in European Governance*.
Goldsmith, M., and K. Newton (1983). 'Central–Local Government Relations: The Irresistible Rise of Centralised Power', *West European Politics*, 6:4, 216–33.
Graziano, L., and S. Tarrow, eds. (1979). *La crisi italiana*, 2 vols. Turin: Einaudi.
Graziano, P., and M. Vink, eds. (2007). *Europeanization: New Research Agendas*. Basingstoke: Palgrave.

Green Cowles, M., J. Caporaso and T. Risse, eds. (2001). *Transforming Europe: Europeaniza-tion and Domestic Change*. Ithaca, NY: Cornell University Press.

Hague, R. (1983). 'Confrontation, Incorporation and Exclusion: British Trade Unions in Collectivist and Post-Collectivist Politics', *West European Politics*, 6:4, 130–62.

Habermas, J. (1973 [1976]). *Legitimation Crisis*. London: Heinemann.

Hennis, W. (1977). 'Zur Begründung der Fragestellung', in W. Hennis *et al.* (eds.), *Regierbarkeit: Studien zu ihrer Problematisierung*. Stuttgart: Klett Cotta, 9–21.

Hennis, W., P. Kielmansegg and U. Matz, eds. (1977). *Regierbarkeit: Studien zu ihrer Problematisierung*. Stuttgart: Klett Cotta.

Hennis W., P. Kielmansegg and U. Matz, eds. (1979). *Regierbarkeit: Studien zu ihrer Problematisierung, Band II*. Stuttgart: Klett Cotta.

Héritier, A., ed. (2002). *Common Goods: Reinventing European and International Governance*. Lanham: Rowman & Littlefield.

Higgs, E. (2004). *The Information State in England: The Central Collection of Information on Citizens Since 1500*. Basingstoke: Palgrave.

Hooghe, L., and G. Marks (2001). *Multi-Level Governance and European Integration*. Lanham, MD: Rowman & Littlefield.

Kaase, M. (1980). 'The Crisis of Authority: Myth and Reality', in R. Rose (ed.), *Challenge to Governance: Studies in Overloaded Polities*. London: Sage, 175–98.

Kaase, M., and K. Newton (1995). *Beliefs in Government, Volume 5*. Oxford: Oxford University Press.

King, A. (1975). 'Overload: Problems of Governing in the 1970s', *Political Studies*, XXIII:2/3, 284–96.

Kjær, A.M. (2004). *Governance*. Cambridge: Polity Press.

Kohler-Koch B., and B. Rittberger (2006). 'Review Article: The "Governance Turn" in EU Studies', *Journal of Common Market Studies*, 44:Annual Review, 27–44.

Lange, P., and S. Tarrow, eds. (1979). 'Italy in Transaction: Conflict and Consensus', special issue, *West European Politics*, 2:3.

Leston-Bandeira, C. (2001). 'The Portuguese Parliament during the First Two Decades of Democracy', *West European Politics*, 24:1, 137ff.

Machin, H., and V. Wright (1985). 'Economic Policy under the Mitterrand Presidency, 1981–1984: An Introduction', in H. Machin and V. Wright (eds.), *Economic Policy and Policy-Making Under the Mitterrand Presidency 1981–1984*. London: Frances Pinter, 1–43.

Majone, G.G. (1993). 'The Rise of the Regulatory State in Europe', *West European Politics*, 17:3, 77–102.

Majone, G. (1999). 'The Regulatory State and its Legitimacy Problems', *West European Politics*, 22:1, 1–24.

Mayntz, R. (2002). 'Common Goods and Governance', in A. Héritier (ed.), *Common Goods: Reinventing European and International Governance*. Lanham: Rowman & Littlefield, 15–27.

Mayntz, R. (2004). 'Governance im modernen Staat', in A. Benz (ed.), *Governance: Regieren in komplexen Regelsystemen*. Wiesbaden: VS Verlag für Sozialwissenschaften, 65–76.

Mayntz, R. (2005). 'Governance Theory als fortentwickelte Steuerungstheorie?, in G.F. Schuppert (ed.), *Governance-Forschung: Vergewisserung über Stand und Entwicklungsli-nien*. Baden-Baden: Nomos, 11–20.

Mayntz, R., and F.W. Scharpf (1975). *Policy-Making in the German Federal Bureaucracy*. Amsterdam: Elsevier.

Mény, Y. (1984). 'Decentralisation in France: The Politics of Pragmatism', *West European Politics*, 7:1, 65–79.

Mény, Y. (1987). 'France: The Construction and Reconstruction of the Centre, 1945–1986', *West European Politics*, 7:1, 52–69.

Meyer-Sahling, J.-H. (2004). 'Civil Service Reform in Post-Communist Europe: The Bumpy Road to Depoliticisation', *West European Politics*, 27:1, 71–103.

Müller, W., and V. Wright (1994a). 'Reshaping the State in Western Europe: The Limits to Retreat', *West European Politics*, 17:3, 1–11.

Müller, W., and V. Wright, eds. (1994b). *The State in Western Europe; Retreat or Redefinition*, special issue *West European Politics*, 17:3.

Newell, J.L. (2006). 'Characterising the Italian Parliament: Legislative Change in Longitudinal Perspective', *Journal of Legislative Studies*, 12:3/4, 386–403.

Norton, P., ed. (1990). *Parliaments in Western Europe*, special issue, *West European Politics*, 13:3.

Nunberg B. (1999). 'Administrative Change in Central and Eastern Europe: Emerging Country Experience', in B. Nunberg (ed.), *The State After Communism: Administrative Transitions in Central and Eastern Europe*. Washington, DC: World Bank, 237–72.

O'Connor, J. (1973). *The Fiscal Crisis of the State*. New York: St Martin's Press.

Offe, C. (1972). *Strukturprobleme des kapitalistischen Staates*. Frankfurt a. M.: Suhrkamp.

Offe, C. (1979). '"Unregierbarkeit." Zur Renaissance konservativer Krisentheorien', in J. Habermas (ed.), *Stichworte zur "Geistigen Situation der Zeit", Band 1*. Frankfurt a. M.: Suhrkamp, 294–318.

Olsen, J.P. (2002). 'The Many Faces of Europeanization', *Journal of Common Market Studies*, 40, 921–51.

Page, E.C., and V. Wright (1999). 'Conclusion: Senior Officials in Western Europe', in E.C. Page and V. Wright (eds.), *Bureaucratic Elites in Western European States: A Comparative Analysis of Top Officials in Eleven Countries*. Oxford: Oxford University Press, 266–79.

Page, E.C., and V. Wright, eds. (2007). *From the Active to the Enabling State: The Changing Role of Top Officials in European Nations*. Basingstoke: Palgrave.

Peters, B.G., R.A.W. Rhodes and V. Wright (2000). 'Staffing the Summit – the Administration of the Core Executive: Convergent Trends and National Specifities', in B.G. Peters, R.A.W. Rhodes and V. Wright (eds.), *Administering the Summit*. Basingstoke: MacMillan, 3–22.

Peters, B.G., and J. Pierre (2004). 'Conclusion: Political Control in a Managerialist World', in B.G. Peters and J. Pierre (eds.), *The Politicization of the Civil Service in Comparative Perspective; A Quest for Control*. London: Routledge, 283–90.

Peters, B.G., and J. Pierre (2006). 'Governance, Accountability and Democratic Legitimacy', in A. Benz and Y. Papadopoulos (eds.), *Governance and Democracy: Comparing National, European and International Experiences*. London: Routledge, 29–43.

Pierre, J., and B.G. Peters (2000). *Governance, Politics and the State*. Basingstoke: Macmillan.

Pollitt, C., and G. Boukaert (2004). *Public Management Reform: A Comparative Analysis*, 2nd edn. Oxford: Oxford University Press.

Pollitt C., S. van Thiel and V. Homburg, eds. (2007). *New Public Management in Europe: Adaptation and Alternatives*. Basingstoke: Palgrave.

Putnam, W.E., and G. Smith, eds. (1981). 'The West German Model: Perspectives on a Stable State, special issue, *West European Politics*, 4:2.

Raunio T., and M. Wiberg (2008). 'Formally Stronger, Politically Still Weak? The Eduskunta and the Parliamentarisation of Finnish Politics', forthcoming in *West European Politics*, 30:3.

Rhodes, R.A.W. (1996). *Understanding Governance*. Buckingham: Open University Press.

Rhodes, R.A.W. (2003). 'What is New about Governance and Why Does it Matter?', in J. Hayward and A. Menon (eds.), *Governing Europe*. Oxford: Oxford University Press, 61–73.

Rhodes R.A.W., and V. Wright, eds. (1987). Tensions in the Territorial Politics of Western Europe, special issue, *West European Politics*, 10:4.

Richardson, J.J., and A.G. Jordon (1979). *Governing under Pressure: The Policy Process in a Post-Parliamentary Democracy*. Oxford: Robertson.

Rommetvedt, H. (2005). 'Norway: Resources Count, But Votes Decide? From Neo-Corporatist Representation to Neo-Pluralist Parliamentarism', *West European Politics*, 28:4, 740–63.

Rose, R., ed. (1980). *Challenge to Governance: Studies in Overloaded Polities*. London: Sage.

Rose, R., and G. Peters (1979). *Can Government Go Bankrupt?*. Basingstoke: Macmillan.

Saward, M. (1997). 'In Search of the Hollow Crown', in P. Weller, H. Bakvis and R.A.W. Rhodes (eds.), *The Hollow Crown: Countervailing Trends in Core Executives*. Basingstoke: Macmillan, 16–36.

Scharpf, F. (1977). 'Public Organization and the Waning of the Welfare State', *European Journal of Political Research*, 5:4, 339–62.

Schupperd, G.F., ed. (2005). *Governance-Forschung*. Baden-Baden: Nomos.

Sotiropoulos, D.A. (2004). 'Southern European Public Bureaucracies in Comparative Perspective'. *West European Politics*, 27:3, 405–22.

Tarrow, S. (1979). 'Italy: Crisis, Crises or Transition?', *West European Politics*, 2:3, 166–86.

Thatcher, M., and A. Stone Sweet, eds. (2002). *The Politics of Delegation: Non-Majoritarian Institutions in Europe*, special issue *West European Politics*, 25:1.

Vickers, J., and V. Wright, eds. (1988). *The Politics of Privatisation in Western Europe*, special issue *West European Politics*, 11:4.

Webb, P., and T. Poguntke (2005). 'The Presidentialization of Contemporary Democratic Politics: Evidence, Causes, and Consequences', in T. Poguntke and P. Webb (eds.), *The Presidentialization of Politics: A Comparative Study of Modern Democracies*. Oxford: Oxford University Press, 336–56.

Wright, V. (1994). 'Reshaping the State: The Implications for Public Administration', *West European Politics*, 17:3, 102–37.

Zielonka, J. (2007). 'Plurilateral Governance in the Enlarged European Union', *Journal of Common Market Studies*, 45:1, 198–209.

Regulation, the Regulatory State and European Politics

MARTIN LODGE

The term 'regulatory state' entered the vocabulary of students of European Politics over 12 years ago with the publication, in *West European Politics*, of Giandomenico Majone's seminal 'The Rise of the Regulatory State in Europe' (Majone 1994).[1] Underlying Majone's argument was the diagnosis of two key trends, one being an overall shift towards the use of legal authority or regulation over the other tools of stabilisation and redistribution, the other the European Commission's expansionist role through the use of influence over policy content in the absence of other, especially budgetary tools (see also Majone 1997a). Since then, it has become commonplace to state that we live in the age of the regulatory state, characterised by privatisation of public services, the establishment of quasi-autonomous regulatory authorities and the formalisation of relationships within policy domains (see Loughlin and Scott 1997; Moran 2002).

A special issue in 1986 on 'The Politics of Communications Revolution in Western Europe' arguably marked *West European Politics'* first major encounter with the theme of regulation. The regulation theme was developed further with the special issue on 'The Politics of Privatisation in

Western Europe' in 1988 (edited by Vickers and Wright); the 1994 'The State in Western Europe: Retreat or Redefinition' (edited by Müller and Wright); and the 2002 'The Politics of Delegation' (edited by Stone Sweet and Thatcher). These titles provide a good indication of the changing interest in regulation in the field of European Politics, moving from an initial curiosity about the impact of technological change, to the policy trend of the selling-off of public sector assets to the wider implications of the regulatory state for the organisation and nature of the state in itself. Other signs of the institutionalisation of regulation as part of the standard menu of political science have been the emergence of text books and edited volumes (Ogus 1994; Baldwin and Cave 1999; Jordana and Levi-Faur 2004; Black *et al.* 2005; Coen and Heritier 2005), the creation of postgraduate programmes and research centres, as well as, inevitably, the establishment of a journal with 'Regulation' in its title (*Regulation & Governance*).

A rough count points to an increase in absolute numbers of articles devoted to policy issues related to the regulatory state, although when seen in the context of an overall increase in articles within this subfield the trend is somewhat less impressive. Figure 1 charts the trend of regulation-related articles as a ratio of the total number of articles published in each calendar year since the inception of *West European Politics*. It looks at *West European Politics* on its own and at the overall trend by including also the *European Journal of Political Research, Journal of European Public Policy, Journal of Common Market Studies*, and *European Union Politics*.[2]

This paper enquires into four broad concerns. First, what are the sources of the supposed rise of the regulatory state in Europe and does it represent a distinct policy development? Second, what has been the 'value added' in terms of empirical and analytical insights? Third, does the age of the

FIGURE 1
REGULATION IN EUROPEAN POLITICS JOURNALS

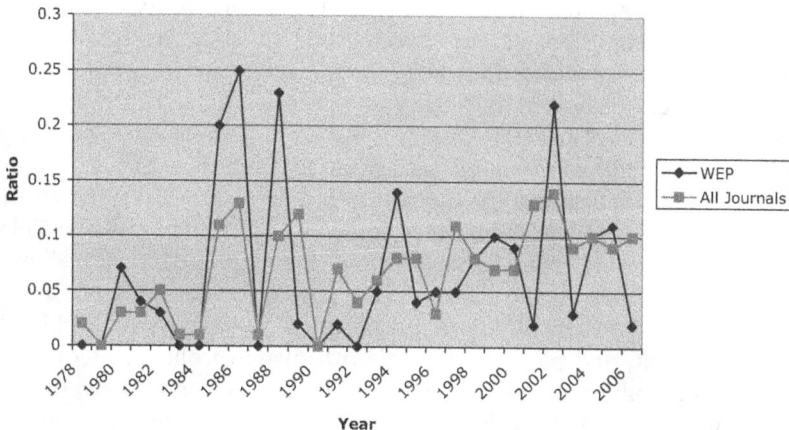

regulatory state constitute a new age of stability of the state in Europe? Fourth, and in conclusion, what is the future of (the study of) regulation? More specifically, will the study of regulation and the regulatory state qualify for inclusion as a central theme for the 50th anniversary issue of *West European Politics*?

The Rise of the Regulatory State in European Politics

As already noted, the emergence of the regulatory state in Europe has been linked to two developments. One is the diagnosed exhaustion of the 'positive' welfare state and the subsequent move towards the use of authority rather than the 'cheque book' as the preferred policy tool at the national level. The other is the attempts by the European Commission to maximise its influence over policy content given the absence of other substantial discretionary resources, and also the interest of member states in transnational policy responses to issues arising from the Single European Market. As a result of these two sources of change, member states are said to have embarked on three interrelated policy choices: the privatisation of activities formerly undertaken as part of state ownership, the emergence of quasi-autonomous agencies with quasi-legislative powers responsible for the economic regulation of private(-ised) activities, and the formalisation and contractualisation of relationships within the regulated policy domain. Linked to this formalisation has been the growing presence and importance of EU legislation for the provision of public services, for example for public tendering procedures or the cross-subsidisation of public services.

The 'rise of the regulatory state' has important implications for the study of European politics, for at least three reasons. First, policy developments such as the privatisation of essential 'infrastructures of power' are important given that these industries (telecommunications, electricity, railways, gas and water) have been widely seen as essential aspects of the modern state at least since the days of Max Weber. More broadly, the rise of the regulatory state in the form and instruments of the late twentieth century could be seen as a further extension of the powers of the state in the sense of 'standardisation, quantification, [and] public reporting' (Moran 2003: 7) Second, the establishment of regulatory agencies as separate and non-majoritarian parts of the state does not merely constitute a reallocation of power and a shuffling around of the institutional furniture of the state, but also has wider implications for the nature of liberal democracy, given that this implies an increased prominence for non-majoritarian politics. Third, the formalisation of relationships within the regulated policy domain suggests a reduction in the discretionary powers of the national level of government, due partly to the importance of European law within the national context, and partly to the role of private (profit-oriented) actors in providing public services. What have been the conditions for this perception of a rise of a regulatory state in Europe? And do the claims of a rise stand up in light of historical developments, both in the European and the international context? The rest of this section considers these two questions.

The conditions for the suggested contemporary rise of a regulatory state can be summarised by three factors: disappointment, strategic choice given structural constraints, and habitat change. Disappointment relates to the experience of the inability, at the macro-level, of the welfare state to achieve desired policy outcomes; at the micro-level, it points to the perceived failure of control over state-owned enterprises. Relationships between ministers/ministries and state-owned enterprises were said to have failed due to accusations of cheating, whether in terms of continuous political interference in managerial decision-making or in terms of control evasion by the services providers, or through simple 'capture' (Majone 1996a: 11–15; Tivey 1982).

Strategic choices in the light of these experiences of control 'exhaustion' via state ownership were also guided by the 'reality' of fiscal constraint, making a policy approach that shifts the costs of 'implementation' to third parties particularly attractive. In other words, the costs of deciding on rules as well as on monitoring and sanctioning are significantly less than the costs incurred by the regulated party that is required to alter its behaviour (or production process). In addition, 'delegation' to regulatory agencies has also been interpreted as a method of shifting blame away from politicians and towards 'defenceless' regulators as well as regulated companies (see Thatcher and Sweet Stone 2002). However, if such a blame-shifting strategy has indeed been present, then it arguably failed spectacularly in the UK, leading to a breakdown of the initial regulatory bargain between regulator and political system, with wider implications for the study and 'state' of the regulatory state in Europe.

Strategic choices within structural constraints have been a dominant theme in accounting for the emergence of the European Commission as an important party in regulatory policy-making. As already noted, the European Commission's interest in governing through rules requiring (costly) transposition and implementation in member states was one central part of Majone's original account. At the same time, member state governments were similarly interested in the 'supply' of EU-level provisions, largely in order to prevent electorally costly 'races to the bottom' in terms of social and environmental regulatory standards as part of competition across jurisdictions within the Single European Market. But they also sought to reduce the costs (to their national industries) of segmented national markets and to impose their own national solutions on other countries in order to minimise adjustment costs for their own industries. While, therefore, the emergence of rule systems at the supranational level was one source for the growing interest in regulation, the interaction between the EU and national levels provided for another. Transposition of rules in economic, environmental and social policy domains further facilitated the prominence of regulation as a policy tool and as a subject in search of academic interest, in terms of both rule change and rule accommodation within national systems.

Underlying the arguments diagnosing the rise of a regulatory state are more far-reaching 'habitat' changes. Changes in the international economy are said to have challenged traditional forms of social control and to have increased the potential benefits and costs of institutional choices (see Lodge and Stirton 2006). Majone (1996b) has suggested that the internationalisation of the economy and, more importantly, the increasing complexity of the modern economy have placed particular prominence on states to tackle the problem of 'credible commitment'. This problem arises from the 'time inconsistency' problem that is inherent in politics (as well as any other form of social relationship): governments face difficulties in providing safeguards that will protect benefit flows to constituents over time, in particular following changes in government.[3] This commitment problem arises in particular from the need of states to attract private investment to address large-scale modernisation issues (for example, in telecommunications infrastructure). Private investors will demand, so the argument goes, a particular risk surcharge in order to 'insure' themselves against the risk of political and administrative expropriation (for example through the imposition of social or environmental regulation) once the sunk investment has been made (see also Levy and Spiller 1994; Horn 1995).

In political contexts characterised by 'veto players',[4] non-majoritarian regulatory institutions provide a credible commitment device as they promise focused decision-making by experts rather than 'amateurs' in ministerial departments and a logic of decision-making that is dominated by policy rather than political motives. In Westminster systems, i.e. those where an 'elective dictatorship' is able to legislate on regulatory agencies without any major political constraint, a strategy of 'agencification' is not credible. Hence, alternative devices, for example licences, are required to provide for commitment.[5] In short, the institutional expressions of the 'regulatory state' as diagnosed by Majone and others are explained as strategic choices to signal 'credible commitment' to private investors, with a variety of institutional 'architectures' reflecting strategies to deal with the 'credible commitment' problem in different political institutional systems.

A variant of the above 'habitat' explanation points to the internationalisation of the economy as a source for the emergence of the regulatory state. Michael Moran (2003), for example, has suggested that the internationalisation and the social heterogenisation of the British economic elite has led to a part-collapse of traditional forms of 'club government' in which control was exercised through social norms and peer pressure. Such a world of informal control was also challenged by developments that Michael Power (1997) has diagnosed in his 'audit society' argument, namely that in a world of decreasing trust in experts and authority, programmatic ideas such as 'audit' are utilised to offer an illusion of assurance and control, often with tragic consequences (see also Rose 1994). In an even wider sense, a link can be drawn between the rise of an interest in regulation and the 'risk society' in which a society that anticipates and witnesses humanly created risks produces as a response a 'regulatory society' – with potentially disastrous consequences as rhetorical attempts of 'control' raise social expectations of control exactly at the same time in which social heterogenisation reduces collective identities and therefore problem-solving possibilities: we demand more hierarchical intervention exactly when the conditions for hierarchical intervention are no longer present.

So far, so normal: the interest in regulation and the regulatory state points to important contemporary phenomena. However, in order to qualify as a 'new' area of interest it needs to be shown that it represents a genuine 'new' development, either in Europe or in the wider international context. For example, Cento Veljanovski (1991: 4), argued that 'regulation is the border between the state and industry', representing the new 'battleground' in how the economy should be run (see Lodge 2002a: 176). As historical studies of regulation have shown, regulation has been a 'battleground' between the state and industry since at least the nineteenth century, for example in the economic regulation of the railways (see Lodge 2002a; Dobbin 1994; Moran 2003). Inspection, *Aufsicht* and licensing have been long-standing parts of European public administration over the centuries and debates on how to conduct control go to the heart of unresolved debates in the field of public administration. The railways safety provisions are widely seen to have been one of the key triggers for the 'growth in government', at least in the case of Britain (MacDonagh 1958; Parris 1965). In addition, in the age of state ownership, the 'godfather' of public corporations (in Britain), Herbert Morrison, suggested (in 1947) that eventually 'the minister's functions become more regulatory and supervisory in character'.[6] In other words, the technocratic dream of 'rational control' through depoliticised regulation instead of meddlesome organisation has been a recurring theme through the ages.

If regulation is therefore hardly a new idea in the study of European states, then it could nevertheless be argued that the 'newness' of contemporary regulation lies in the emergence of quasi-independent regulatory agencies on the lines of the United States and its regulatory commissions. However, the trends discussed above hardly represent a 'catching up' on the US by European states, in the sense of European states witnessing problems that the US was exposed to nearly a century earlier and which triggered the emergence of a 'regulatory state'. In brief, the dynamics of the growth of the US administrative (regulatory) state represented responses, first, to the growing perception that a country governed by 'parties and courts' could not sufficiently deal with the increases in corporate power, and therefore required free-standing regulatory agencies (the 'progressive era'); second, to the perils of economic depression and subsequent aspirations to provide for conditions for competition to take place (the 'New Deal era'); third, to the perception that market failures in the social and environmental field required regulatory activities (the 'new social regulation' era); and, fourth, to the perception that regulation was inherently associated with 'big government' and pathological policy outcomes (the 'deregulatory' era) (Eisner 2000; Glaeser and Shleifer 2001). Apart from different dynamics between European and US experiences, the institutional furniture of the European regulatory state, at least in the British case, represented an explicit rejection of the US experiences, despite the similarity of establishing free-standing regulatory offices. Taking the British case as an example, the initial choices in terms of price control (RPI-X; instead of 'rate of return' regulation) as well as single leadership ('director general', instead of boards) were taken in order to avoid what were perceived to be pathologies of the US regulatory process.

What unites European and US accounts is the diagnosed advocacy of regulation as a presumably technocratic and professional method of controlling social processes vis-à-vis the 'dirty' world of politics and business.[7] But the underlying processes that have led to the politics of regulation over the past three decades have been distinct. Even if one wants to draw similarities, then the case of the emergence of regulatory agencies in the 1980s–1990s across European states and the 1880s–1910s in the US seem to be a case of similar devices adopted for different motives. It is similarly questionable whether the dynamics of US federal–state relationships (Teske 2004) in the development of multi-level regulation can be read across to the level of EU–national systems relationships, despite the potential argument that in both cases these debates are driven by criticism of the legitimacy of the federal or the EU-level as an appropriate source for regulation. And the debates over the past two decades have seen 'regulation' largely as an outcome of a 'hollowing out' of the European state rather than as part of a problem of a (US-type) 'big government'.

The diagnosed rise of the regulatory state should therefore be seen within a historical context in which many arguments regarding the organisation of the state are being recycled and relived. The structural choices said to characterise the 'regulatory state' have important implications for the idea and nature of states in Europe. In addition, the conditions in which these debates take place have important implications for the study of European politics, as it centrally affects both aspects associated with the inherent idea of the (liberal democratic) state as well as the (institutional) space in which politics is taking place, across and between levels of government.

European Politics and the Study of the Regulatory State

The study of regulation in the broad field of European politics has been largely concerned with four interrelated fields, pointing, on the one hand, to an interest in the EU or the national level of analysis, and, on the other hand, to an interest in either the organisation of the 'regulatory state' (agencies and the wider institutional furniture) or processes of regulatory change. These four perspectives on the politics of the regulatory state in Europe are illustrated in Table 1. Apart from the search for the mechanisms that explain the emergence of a 'regulatory state' at the EU level, most of the literature has been largely concerned with establishing degrees of increasing similarity ('convergence') or differences across member states in the light of similar sounding broad policy trends or the penetration of EU laws into domestic policy domains. It is therefore mainly concerned with the question of whether the regulatory state in Europe can be regarded as a unified (unifying) phenomenon, whether the underlying developments suggest more diversity than similarity, and whether there has been any notable change over time in these dynamics.

TABLE 1
STUDIES OF REGULATION IN EUROPEAN POLITICS

	Organisation	Process
EU-level	EU-level regulatory agencies, role of the European Commission as regulator, modes of regulation	Emergence and evolution of EU regimes in economic, social and environmental regulation, 'soft law' and Open Method of Co-ordination
National level	Design and operation of national regulatory agencies, modes of regulation	Process of national regulatory change, impact of EU provisions on national systems ('Europeanisation')

In brief, most attention at the EU level has been paid to processes of regulatory change as well as their organisation. This includes processes of expansion of EU-level competence in economic and social regulation, driven by an interplay between supranational and member state interests (Eberlein and Grande 2005). Furthermore, the strategic role of the European Commission in areas such as competition policy as 'first supranational policy' (McGowan and Wilks 1995) or the re-regulation of diverse economic sectors through a process of 'subterfuge' (Héritier 1999) have been central to this discussion. In addition, the analysis of different regulatory domains has pointed to differential problem-solving capacities and dynamics across policy domains (see Scharpf 2001), none of which suggest a regulatory 'race to the bottom'.

The underlying message of the 'rise' of the regulatory state at the EU level also had a very functionalist logic: change in institutional forms sought to address functional pressures for differentiation. But whereas some aspects of EU regulation did indeed display the functionalist logic of market integration and spill-overs, in other areas of EU-level regulation, the limits of such a functionalist logic became evident. One limitation was the emergence of EU-level regulatory agencies that largely had a co-ordinative and informative rather than a traditional 'command and control' function (Majone 1997b, 2002). The establishment of agencies of a largely co-ordinative kind – ranging from pharmaceuticals, food safety, racism to railways – with strong member state 'oversight' could be seen as a way of building 'iron triangles' at the European level, allowing the European Commission to 'outsource' certain activities and expand jurisdiction at the European level, offering industries exclusive access, while granting member states oversight (also Keleman 2002; Demortain 2007).[8]

The other limitation was the constraints of European Union action, either because of lack of capacity, the absence of a variety of policy tools (i.e. the need to resort to regulation instead of a broader toolbox) and of national institutional variety that makes rule 'harmonisation' even at a minimum level problematic. As a response to capacity constraints, there was an increasing reliance on networks of national regulators in the areas of competition, communications and energy policy that were not merely to 'read across', but also to act as decentralised executive organs of the European Commission. In the case of dealing with national institutional variety, responses involved areas of social and fiscal 'co-operation', most prominently through the 'open method of co-ordination' (Hodson and Maher 2001; Chalmers and Lodge 2003; Zeitlin 2005; Lodge 2007). What emerged, however, was a diagnosis that neither the 'traditional' regulatory approaches nor the 'new' and 'soft' approaches seemed to provide satisfactory solutions – in terms of national acceptance and co-operation or in terms of improving policy outcomes.

Studies in national regulatory change have largely concluded that the direct impact of the EU has been rather limited. Change, especially its nature and extent, has largely emerged as a result of national political processes (Jordana *et al.* 2006). The role of EU developments has been said to constitute largely an additional source of legitimisation for national processes (Knill and Lehmkuhl 2003). This has been most evident in the way in which national regimes have been reformulated to appear compatible with EU provisions, even in those cases where Directives have been prescriptive in terms of institutional forms. Rather than policy transformation, Europeanisation of national rule systems is said to have led to differential policy accommodation among member states (see Héritier *et al.* 2001; Schmidt 2001). Related are those studies interested in the transposition patterns across member states, given the perception of uneven 'compliance' across member states with EU legislation (see Falkner *et al.* 2005).[9]

Similarly, while studies satisfied with diagnosing the existence of regulators and competition authorities have been able to argue that something along the lines of a 'regulatory state' has emerged across European countries, other studies highlighted formal differences in terms of institutional authority, autonomy and responsibilities (see Gilardi 2002; Thatcher 2002, 2005). A separate set of studies has focused on different modes of regulation. Early studies in environmental regulation already pointed to significant differences between Swedish or British 'co-operative' and US 'adversarial' regulatory relationships that also led to differences in the quality of regulation (see Kelman 1981; Vogel 1986). Studies of regulation *inside* government have also suggested that rather than finding convergence or at least similarity of regulatory developments, there have been significant differences within national systems as well as across states (see Hood *et al.* 1999, 2004). A more recent interest has focused on the growth of 'regulatory review' mechanisms across national states ('regulatory impact assessments) as well as their utilisation at the EU level (Radaelli 2004), again a development which parallels interest in the review activities of other transnational organisations, such as the OECD (see Schäfer 2004; Lodge 2005).

Four broad implications for understanding the nature of the state in Europe emerge from this brief review. One is that European states have responded in differential ways to what have been diagnosed as common challenges. The allocation of regulatory authority has witnessed both a move towards the EU level and 'sideways' to non-majoritarian institutions. However, the degree to which these shifts have taken place depends on sectors and on national experiences. The second implication is that far from a 'hollowing out' of the state, the regulatory state is said to have rearranged and not challenged or weakened the centrality of the European national state in the regulation of economic and social activities. The third is that far from a mere reliance on hierarchy, a diversity of modes of regulation has been and is being employed both at the EU and the national level.

Finally, the fourth implication is that the EU-level literature has pointed to substantial problem-solving capacities in regulation across the EU, but also to their limitations, whether in terms of 'discretionary' forms of transposition of EU provisions or in terms of adjusting 'voluntarily' in the face of high national electoral costs of policy change. In addition, the nature of responses across national systems to EU requirements has been shown to be less related to 'goodness of fit', but rather to a wider set of factors akin to more theoretically grounded studies of system responses to environmental turbulence.

However, has the focus on regulation added any analytical contribution to the study of European politics? As already noted, in the 2002 *WEP* special issue on 'non-majoritarian institutions', Mark Pollack suggested that in the study of delegation Europeanists were 'again' in a position to learn from the 'Americanists' (Pollack 2002). So has there been a dominant interest in coupling developments in regulation to approaches drawn from North American political science in general, or regulation in particular?

The seminal work by Majone arguably qualifies most strongly for the claim that the turn towards the regulatory state represented a direct drawing from American social science, even when leaving references to, and implications for, theories of democracy aside (see Moran 2003). As already noted, the importance attached to credible commitment draws on approaches emphasising strategic action within rule systems. It was therefore logical that the (US-focused) delegation literature, with its strong currents in the 'congressional dominance/abdication' debate, was taken up in the study of agencies across European states (see Gilardi 2002; Thatcher 2002). More broadly, the delegation approach was also utilised to study the 'delegation' of policy authority by member states to the European Commission as well as the control mechanisms that were said to have been deployed by member states to limit the discretion of the 'agent', the European Commission. While certainly worthwhile as an exercise in comparison, it is nevertheless important to put 'principals and agents' in their place. Regulatory agencies at the national level and the European Commission are hardly 'agents' in the strict sense, but have a fiduciary trusteeship function (Majone 2005: 74–82). In other words, the role is exactly *not* that of an agent that is at the beck and call of its principal(s) (see also Hood and Lodge 2006: ch. 2).

As noted above, the dynamics that are said to have facilitated the move towards the regulatory state at the EU level could also be associated with a functionalist logic – and the developments at the EU level shows signs both of the logic of functionalist integration and its limitations.[10] Similarly, it could be argued that the literature on the emergence of EU-level regulatory regimes, such as for telecommunications and electricity, have been shaped by traditional (North American) debates in the European integration literature over the sources for 'integration', namely those neo-functionalists with their claims of technologies creating spill-over pressures, the growth of European companies and the pressures of supranational authorities, or those liberal intergovernmentalists with their emphasis on national policy preferences (see Thatcher 2001). Cross-sectoral comparison has moved beyond such dichotomies. For example, Susanne Schmidt (1998) has shown how actor-centred institutionalism highlights the sector-specific conditions in which various actors are provided with different resources, motives and opportunities to initiate and shape regulatory change.

While in the above two cases the argument that the study of European politics has been shaped by *Americanists* could receive some qualified support, there has been a European 'rejection' of the early (US) regulation literature with its strong emphasis on the importance of private interests 'capturing' regulation in their own interest – either fully (Stigler 1971) or to some extent (Pelzman 1989) at the point of inception, or over time (see Bernstein 1955).[11] This absence of an interest in 'capture' is puzzling, even if only as a claim to be investigated (and dismissed) given the diagnosed close involvement of concentrated industry interests in the emergence of EU agencies.

One distinct European contribution to the study of regulation has been the concept of 'regulatory space' (Hancher and Moran 1989). While this term in itself is problematic, it nevertheless constitutes an important contribution in a number of senses. This variant of historical institutional analysis acknowledges the historical evolution and setting of regulation, in particular the distribution of regulatory authority across state, para-state and private actors. Rather than focusing on regulatory agencies, the study of regulation turns towards the distribution and fragmentation of regulatory authority across a diversity of actors. In addition, this 'lens' highlights the importance of being sensitive to national (and sectoral) difference. Given the historical embeddedness of regulation in national political economies, arguments about the spread of 'regulation' across European states should be treated with caution. As Marian Döhler (2002) has shown, while the language of 'regulation' may have travelled across national systems and regulatory agencies may have emerged, the way these are incorporated into national administrative law contexts leads to considerable formal differences, let alone differences in informal understandings that govern relationships within the 'regulatory space'.

Indeed, the way in which regulatory authorities were conceived and incorporated into national policy-making styles varied greatly, for example whether these agencies were conceived as part of a tradition within the policy domain or whether they were inspired by wider ideas regarding the appropriate organisation of the state in running parts of economic policy. Observers such as Michael Moran have therefore diagnosed an 'incomplete penetration' of the logic of regulatory state into the British policy-making process, leading to breakdowns. Similarly, others have noted a hybridisation between the 'old' and the 'new'; for example, in terms of rewards, in Britain traditional 'honours' were also part of the rations for the new breed of economic regulators, and not just for the traditional 'Whitehall' bureaucrats (Hood and Lodge 2006: 73). Given national variation, it is therefore not surprising that studies of 'Europeanisation' have noted the absence of immediate or inherent 'convergence' in policy approaches across policy domains, with Europeanisation mainly affecting the way in which domestic coalitions struggle over domestic policy change through normative support. At the same time, there has been some evidence of a growing presence of European-wide regulatory 'communities' that pursue a distinct regulatory 'conversation'.

Studies of regulation across European states employing grid-group cultural theory have also stressed the importance of moving beyond first-level approximations of the 'regulatory state' and its institutions (see Hood *et al.* 1999, 2004; Lodge and Wegrich 2005a, 2005b). Applying this particular analytical framework to the cross-sectoral and cross-national study of regulation 'inside' government makes at least two important additions to the study of regulation and the regulatory state. First, that the study of formal arrangements says very little about the way in which regulation *operates*; second, that studies that are sensitive to sectoral and national context present considerable challenges to widely held national stereotypes in public administration and regulation (see Hood 2004: 187–93).

In conclusion, the analytical contribution of the European politics literature to the field of regulation has been far more sophisticated than a mere cross-reading from the field of 'delegation studies' in the US, not only because of difficulties of transplanting US-centric approaches to regulatory regimes across European states. More positively, the interest in investigating whether contemporary macro-trends have triggered increased degrees of commonality or continuous difference has established not only the grounds for a careful analysis of casual mechanisms that affect regulatory change, but have also increased the sensitivity to the national specificity of regulation and the regulatory state. Thus, regulation may be regarded as similar activities divided by the same language. This may arguably not provide the grounds for parsimony or accommodation to contemporary hegemons in social science, but paves the way for a more helpful analysis of regulation as an empirical phenomenon.

Dilemmas of the Regulatory State

This paper has so far traced the origins of the contemporary interest in regulation and highlighted some dominant analytical and empirical themes that justify and stimulate this interest. The regulatory state is not only of interest as an empirical site for exploration, but also points to significant dilemmas affecting the nature of the European state. Again without seeking to explore this issue in any exhaustive way (and avoiding the long list of regulatory approaches that predict failure (see Lodge 2002b)), this section explores three dilemmas of the regulatory state which not only point to sources of policy instability, but more fundamentally highlight crucial issues affecting the state in contemporary Europe.

Legitimacy of state institutions is not only normatively desirable, but is also crucial for the effective and efficient use of administrative resources. Regulatory agencies, given their non-majoritarian nature, derive their legitimacy through the efficient achievement of the desired and prescribed states of the world – whether it is the control of economic monopolies, the safeguarding of the functioning of financial markets or the limitation of environmental pollution or health and safety-related incidents. In contrast, policy choices as to the nature and structure of the service, in terms of the allocation of responsibilities and financing, for example, should, so the argument goes, be decided by those who can be held to account for their decisions, whether in parliament or in elections. Therefore, regulatory agencies should have a single focus rather than be forced to undertake policy choices and engage in trade-offs (Foster 1992).

At least two counter-arguments suggest that such a narrow institutional focus is at best problematic, thereby creating dilemmas. One is that life is never that easy and even decisions that appear to be solely concerned with economic regulation – such as the setting of prices – inherently require value-choices that have far-reaching social (and hence redistributive) implications. The view of regulatory decisions being straightforward and 'narrow' becomes even less persuasive in the context of 'new social risk' regulatory arenas. The other counter-argument is that few regulatory agencies in Europe can be said to have a single and narrow focus. Instead, statutory obligations, imposed at the time of their inception as well as through a seemingly continual process of 'extensions', have increasingly come to resemble a 'smorgasbord' of regulatory values, ranging, in the case of the British energy regulator, across those of economic efficiency ('competition'), social welfare, security of supply and environmental protection. In other words, regulatory agencies have become policy-making departments in all but name, but without the 'normal' legitimating devices associated with liberal democracy.

The second dilemma emerges from the political dynamics of the regulatory process, which make the granting of autonomy from direct political interest an at best fragile construction. According to the naïve story of the conception of regulatory regimes, the initial regulatory bargain is something like this: politicians grant regulators full authority over specified decisions and promise more or less complete intergenerational 'abdication'. In exchange, they derive benefits from signalling the solution of the commitment problem to those constituents benefiting from this regulatory regime. If one accepts this characterisation of the bargain, both sides are likely to experience cheating or suspect cheating by other parties' behaviour.

In the case of the British railways in the early 2000s, this included the refusal of the British government to indicate what subsidy levels they were willing to provide for the continuation of services and at what level – thereby reducing the ability of the regulator to conduct a rate review of the railway infrastructure. Politicians then vilified subsequent regulatory decisions as unreasonable regulatory decision-making, leading to new legislation that significantly reduced the decision-space of the regulator. Earlier, decisions surrounding the bankrupting of the then railway infrastructure provider, Railtrack, represented for many the collapse of the idea of an autonomous regulator (see also Moran 2003: 115–19).

Apart from occasions of conflict, alterations to the initial legislation also suggest a continued politicisation of regulation. In the UK, changes in legislation allowed for the merging of regulatory bodies and the move from 'personal' to 'collective' organisational leadership. While justifications for these policy trends were functional ('convergence' and 'avoiding loose cannons'), these changes pointed to inherent instabilities within the organisation of the regulatory state per se, while also offering another encore of eternal argumentation across administrative doctrines about 'how to' organise administrative units.

In Britain, the selection of regulators was seen to reflect many tendencies of the previous age of public ownership, namely the selection not necessarily on the basis of party membership, but on the basis of broad policy congruence (and being a 'good chap'). In other countries, too, the idea of 'independent regulators' has either never really been embraced or has witnessed considerable neutering.[12] This is not to suggest that regulatory agencies do not matter or play no meaningful role in the processes of modern European states, but rather that they neither represent 'independence' or autonomy'. Nor do they represent a device that has depoliticised particular policy domains; in contrast, they have arguably allowed for increased complication and complexification of policy-making and thus politicisation.[13]

The third dilemma relates to the modern adage 'policies as their own cause', usually attributed to Aaron Wildavsky (1980: 62). In other words, self-exciting interactive effects do not facilitate mutual reinforcement, but rather contradiction and self-destruction. Regulation is about the achievement of the values of resilience, efficiency and equity and inherent trade-offs between these three values. And these decisions also take place in an environment that is not stable – systems inherently self-degrade. The past two decades have seen a trend towards liberalisation and 'economic' regulation that to some extent also contained components to address issues of 'equity'. However, as a consequence, 'resilience' is said to have been neglected. Dieter Helm (2004), for example, has argued that the emphasis on efficiency gains through the 'price cap' (RPI-X) has encouraged so-called asset sweating at the expense of investment in the UK. Such effects are inherent in particular policy choices.

In addition, given that the age of the regulatory state is characterised by decentralisation, in the sense of fragmented private providers offering services with government involvement being undertaken by a supposedly 'autonomous' economic regulator (raising issues noted above), then very few tools are left in the arsenal of governments to affect comprehensive policy decisions. This may be a good thing given what is known about the dysfunctionality of large-scale planning, but it is arguably nevertheless costly to co-ordinate or incentivise autonomous actors in the absence of elements of hierarchical authority. Similarly, in the area of food safety, the existence of competing logics, of risk and of anxiety, was said to place irresolvable problems at the door of EU-level food safety regulatory decision-making (Chalmers 2005).

This section did not seek to explore whether regulation can ever be complete in the sense of obtaining desired states of the world over time – and neither the 'high reliability systems' nor the 'normal accident' schools of organisation would suggest that the existence of rule-systems organised through an agency would achieve policy success in themselves. Nor did it point to empirical trends that suggest policy failure, such as the fact that despite increasing amounts of EU environmental legislation, the European environment has deteriorated. This section has pointed merely to the dilemmas arising from the institutional architecture of the regulatory state, whether in terms of implications for the democratic nature of the state, the impossibility of obtaining technocratic dreams of rational control by allowing differentiation of institutional forms to follow the process of differentiation of social processes, or the inevitability of dealing with side effects and problems in matching political demands for flexibility with the functional demands for non-discretion. Given the national specificity in which the infrastructure of the contemporary regulatory state has been adopted and adapted across states, the above dynamics are therefore both universal as well as particular to national states at the same time.

Towards the 50th Anniversary – Fading Away, Plodding Along, or Rejuvenation?

Although issues of 'control' and the organisation of state-owned enterprises had been well established in the field of public administration (see Robson 1962), the terms 'regulation' and 'regulatory state' hardly featured in the study of European politics 30 years ago. The language of regulation was reserved for students of US public policy. By 2008, regulation is firmly embedded across Europe. However, would an observer in 2028 still consider regulation an important topic, worthy of inclusion in a 50th anniversary issue of *West European Politics*, or is the area of regulation, especially in the area of European politics, about to go through a terminal mid-life crisis? The rest of this paper considers three potential scenarios, 'fading away', 'plodding along', and 'rejuvenation'.

A future of 'fading away' and eventual disappearance is not uncommon in the social sciences (and among social scientists). Concepts and terminologies are regularly 'invented', witness a rapid expansion in terms of academic interest and eventual forgetting, once academic interest has moved on to the next conceptual fad. Alternatively, social concerns may change suddenly or over time, therefore making the study of any particular field less relevant.

There are at least two reasons why regulation may fade away from academic interest. One is the lack of a definition and therefore of a clear boundary. While boundary issues are characteristic of (intellectual) adolescence, the traditional definition of regulation as 'the sustained and focused control exercised by a public authority over activities valued by the community' (as defined by Selznick 1985: 363) is only of limited value in the context of European politics, given varieties of 'public authority' ranging from the private, associational, the national state to the supranational and international. Nor does it address questions regarding decision-making rules establishing what is valued by the 'community', and problems arising from cross-border issues. Thus, while traditional definitions provide the literature with many of the initial points of departure for analysis, more contemporary definitions relying on 'intentional use of authority to affect behaviour of a different party according to set standards, involving instruments of information-gathering and behaviour modification' (Black 2002), risk endlessly extending the field of the regulation. One further but related criticism that could be launched at most of the literature on regulatory change in the context of European politics is that the meaning of the texts would hardly change if the word 'policy' were used instead of 'regulation'.

Similarly, 'regulation' and 'governance' could also be often used interchangeably.

A related reason for a potential fading away from academic attention is
exhaustion of intellectual effort. Regulation and 'regulatory state' have been
widely utilised to apply frameworks developed elsewhere and therefore have
been used as 'dependent variables'. Therefore, a distinct 'regulation' lens
has, as yet, not developed – neither has there been a significant debate
regarding the nature of the 'state' in the age of the 'regulatory state'. This is
not problematic as long as the field is relatively focused, and allows for
linkages to other key intellectual debates. However, given the uncertain
boundaries of regulation, the inherent risk is that regulation becomes the
study of 'everything', and therefore fades away from scholarly attention.

The above two arguments assumed a stable 'applied' regulation
background. But should those policy concerns as expressed in the earlier
section on dilemmas become more acute, then the language of regulation as
well as the organisation of regulatory activities may witness considerable
change, thereby leading to a displacement of academic interest over time.
However, even if such processes were to occur, it is unlikely that 'regulation'
as a policy activity in the wider sense, rather than as the institutional
arrangements of the 'regulatory state', will fade away because of social
irrelevance. Issues of control over economic and state activities (such as
energy and prisons) go to the heart of the nature of the state and its
capacities and are unlikely to disappear. Questions of how to deal with
emerging technologies require regulatory answers. In short, domains under
consideration may change, the language of regulation may move on and the
organisational infrastructure of the regulatory state may witness rearrange-
ment; but it is unlikely that the underlying issues and questions will
disappear, especially in an age where we are supposedly witnessing shifts
towards self- and co-regulation in some aspects (such as the environment)
and enhanced 'hierarchical' control in others (for example, in the area of
justice and civil liberties).[14]

Under the scenario of 'plodding along', interest in regulation expands
towards new fields and more cases. There are substantial areas in European
politics that are left to the regulation-interested student to explore, in
particular in the historical, cross-sectoral and cross-national perspective.
And it is unlikely, if only some aspects of the 'dilemmas' noted above were
to occur, that the field will be short of empirical stories to tell, whether in the
areas of the regulation of utility networks, social regulation or those of risk
management. Such a future of 'plodding along' (typical of 'normal science')
with studies exploring ever more niches that qualify as 'regulation' comes at
the risk of increasing marginalisation (through 'niche-isation) and the risk of
intellectual overextension and therefore exhaustion. By 2038 we may know
more and more about less and less.

Under the scenario of rejuvenation, regulation would be a strong
candidate for the *West European Politics* 50th anniversary issue. A decade

ago, Baldwin, Scott and Hood (1998) argued that such a future could lie in a stronger focus on the language, cultures and side effects of regulation. Apart from some studies (applying cultural theory), such a shift has not occurred, especially not in the pages of comparative politics journals. There is still need for an improved understanding of the rhetoric of regulation, its unintended consequences and its underlying cultures. In addition, these require advanced methodologies (despite these issues being long-standing concerns).[15] These concerns are not necessarily traditional, placing the field of regulation closer to other aspects of comparative public administration and public policy. If these issues were placed at the heart of European politics, the study of regulation in Europe could become leading, empirically as well as analytically.

Empirically, rejuvenation would provide for advances in the study of EU and national level regulation, different understandings of risk regulation in various domains and countries, competing logics within regulatory regimes as well as the evolution of regulatory regimes over time, in particular as we are said to move from an era of liberalisation and emphasis in efficiency towards an era of increased concern about resilience. Labour mobility is challenging established national approaches towards social regulation. In the area of risk, ongoing debates regarding the 'precautionary principle', popular distrust in new technologies and scientific applications to everyday things, such as food or human reproduction, have established policy environments that crystallise many of the above-mentioned dilemmas of the regulatory state. This field for future empirical studies allows for considerable cross-fertilisation between research in regulation and other fields in comparative European politics. Regulation in Europe is inherently about the politics of interest groups, societal values, and demand and supply of EU regulation across domains. Regulation is about the capacity of nation-states to regulate their economy and their society and narrow issues regarding the type of regimes that emerge at the EU level and at the national level. Issues such GM foods have triggered the search for alternative decision-making processes that relate to themes such as new social movements as well as alternative forms of representative politics.

This conclusion avoids any firm predictions as to the likely future of the study of regulation and the regulatory state. However, the fundamental issues that are at the heart of the study of regulation and the regulatory state are central to the understanding of the state, its relationship to business and its citizens, and the state's distribution of coercive authority; they also highlight the importance of supranational sources of regulation. Similarly, the issue of control over economic, social or technological activities is not something that is going to fade away. As a term, regulation may go out of fashion, but its central concern has been and remains fundamental to the very understanding of the state in Europe and, therefore, of politics in Europe.

Notes

1. According to 'google scholar', the article has been cited 224 times (last accessed: 24 April 2007).
2. JEPP articles since 1997 were included given the absence of electronic searches for its earlier volumes. WEP articles for the period up to 2002 were taken from the 25 year index. *Governance* and *Public Administration* were excluded as they are not European politics journals per se, their inclusion is likely to have increased the representation of 'regulation' in the overall population of articles. The peaks are attributable to special issues. The annual review of the EU volume of JCMS was excluded from the analysis.
3. The problem has therefore also been termed coalitional or political drift.
4. This modern parlance is used to comply with the contemporary logic of appropriateness (see Tsebelis 2002). More helpful would be 'a system with many powerful political actors'.
5. Gilardi (2002: 878) finds that, empirically, the lower the number of 'veto players', the greater the extent of 'independence'. This finding is in line with the lack of credibility of 'low veto point' systems, namely that given the lack of credibility, systems need to respond by creating (the illusion of) greater organisational distance.
6. H. Morrison, *Taking Stock*, PRO MT 47/15, S.I. (M) (47) (32), 18 July 1947.
7. The idea of 'regulation' as a mechanical process is arguably rooted in its etymology. Regulation emerged in the English language around 1630, drawing on the Latin *regulare* ('to control by rule') and *regula* ('law'), a *regulator* was established in 1687 as a member of a commission to manage county elections. By 1715, 'regulation' was defined as 'rule for management' and, by 1758, a 'regulator' was a 'clock by which other timepieces are set' (see www.etymonline.com).
8. There are, of course, differences across agencies given the timing of their establishment and the politics of the policy domain.
9. The European Politics literature has shown very little interest in engaging with the 'compliance' literature in regulation with its socio-legal research orientation. Compliance as utilised in European politics has been largely restricted to the study of formal transposition.
10. '...the practical case for delegating rulemaking powers to expert agencies has proved to be overwhelming' (Majone 2005: 83).
11. This view of a dominant interest capturing economic regulation in the US has been qualified (see Wilson 1980) and challenged (Eisner 2000).
12. In other words, the key problem has been the inherent trade-off between commitment and flexibility, or the reduced commitment and decision-making costs that politicians incur from establishing regulatory authorities and the increased 'agency costs' of monitoring and control.
13. At the time of writing, the Spanish stock market regulator, Manuel Conthe, resigned following calls for his resignation by the Spanish government over his conduct over a bid for the Spanish utility Endesa. Conthe in turn accused the Spanish government of eroding regulatory independence ('Spain's market regulator resigns over Endesa bid', *Financial Times*, 25 April 2007, p. 8 (London edition)).
14. It is also hardly imaginable that the dream of 'rational control' will fade away.
15. See, for example, Posner's provocative critique of the legal discipline (in the US) in being unable to deal with natural science complications arising from modern policy issues (Posner 2004).

References

Baldwin, R., and M. Cave (1999). *Understanding Regulation*. Oxford: Oxford University Press.
Baldwin, R., C. Scott and C. Hood (1998). 'Introduction', in R. Baldwin, C. Scott and C. Hood (eds.), *Reader on Regulation*. Oxford: Oxford University Press.
Bernstein, M. (1955). *Regulation of Business by Independent Commissions*. Princeton, NJ: Princeton University Press.

Black, J. (2002). *Critical Reflections on Regulation*, CARR discussion paper 4, January 2002. London: London School of Economics.

Black, J., M. Lodge and M. Thatcher (2005). *Regulatory Innovation*. Cheltenham: Edward Elgar.

Chalmers, D. (2005). 'Risk, Anxiety and the European Mediation of the Politics of Life', *European Law Review*, 30:5, 649–75.

Chalmers, D., and M. Lodge (2003). *The Open Method of Co-ordination and the European Welfare State*, CARR discussion paper No. 11. London: London School of Economics.

Coen, D., and A. Heritier (2005). *Redefining Regulatory Regimes*. Cheltenham: Edward Elgar.

Demortain, D. (2007). 'Regulation as a Source of Institutional Design', unpublished manuscript.

Dobbin, F. (1994). *Forging Industrial Policy*. Cambridge: Cambridge University Press.

Döhler, M. (2002). 'Institutional Choice and Bureaucratic Autonomy in Germany', *West European Politics*, 25:1, 101–24.

Eberlein, B., and E. Grande (2005). 'Beyond Delegation: Transnational Regulatory Regimes and the EU Regulatory State', *Journal of European Public Policy*, 12:1, 89–112.

Eisner, M.C. (2000). *Regulatory Politics in Transition*. 2nd edn. Baltimore, MD: Johns Hopkins.

Falkner, G., O. Treib, M. Hartlapp and S. Leiber (2005). *Complying with Europe*. Cambridge: Cambridge University Press.

Foster, C. (1992). *Privatisation, Public Ownership and the Regulation of Natural Monopoly*. Oxford: Blackwell.

Gilardi, F. (2002). 'Policy Credibility and the Delegation to Individual Regulatory Agencies', *Journal of European Public Policy*, 9:6, 873–93.

Glaeser, E.L., and A. Shleifer (2001). 'The Rise of the Regulatory State', Harvard Institute of Economic Research Discussion Paper No. 1934, http://post.economics.harvard.edu/hier/2001papers/2001list.html.

Hancher, L., and M. Moran (1989). 'Organizing Regulatory Space', in L. Hancher and M. Moran (eds.), *Capitalism, Culture and Economic Regulation*. Oxford: Oxford University Press.

Helm, D. (2004). *The New Regulatory Agenda*. London: Social Market Foundation.

Héritier, A. (1999). *Policy-Making and Diversity in the European Union*. Cambridge: Cambridge University Press.

Héritier, A., D. Kerwer, C. Knill, D. Lehmkuhl, M. Teutsch and A.C. Douillet (2001). *Differential Europe*. Lanham, MD: Rowman & Littlefield.

Hodson, D., and I. Maher (2001). 'The Open Method as a New Mode of Governance: The Case of Soft Economic Policy Co-ordination', *Journal of Common Market Studies*, 39:4, 719–46.

Hood, C. (2004). 'Conclusion: Making Sense of Controls over Government', in C. Hood, O. James, B.G. Peters and C. Scott (2004). *Controlling Modern Government*. Cheltenham: Edward Elgar.

Hood, C., and M. Lodge (2006). *The Politics of Public Service Bargains*. Oxford: Oxford University Press.

Hood, C., O. James, B.G. Peters and C. Scott (2004). *Controlling Modern Government*. Cheltenham: Edward Elgar.

Hood, C., C. Scott, O. James, G. Jones and T. Travers (1999). *Regulation Inside Government*. Oxford: Oxford University Press.

Horn, M. (1995). *The Political Economy of Public Administration*. Cambridge: Cambridge University Press.

Jordana, J., D. Levi-Faur and I. Puig (2006). 'The Limits of Europeanization: Regulatory reforms in the Spanish and Portuguese Telecommunications and Electricity Sectors', *Governance*, 19:3, 437–64.

Jordana, J. and D. Levi-Faur (2004). *The Politics of Regulation*. Cheltenham: Edward Elgar.

Keleman, R.D. (2002). 'The Politics of "Eurocratic" Structure and the New European Agencies', *West European Politics*, 25:4, 93–118.

Kelman, R.D. (1981). *Regulating America, Regulating Sweden*. Cambridge: MIT Press.

Knill, C., and D. Lehmkuhl (2003). 'The National Impact of European Union Regulatory Policy: Three European Mechanisms', *European Journal of Political Research*, 41:2, 255–80.

Loughlin, M., and C. Scott (1997). 'The Regulatory State', in P. Dunleavy, A. Gamble, I. Holliday and G. Peele (eds.), *Developments in British Politics 5*. Basingstoke: Macmillan.

Levy, B., and B. Spiller (1994). 'The Institutional Foundations of Regulatory Commitment', *Journal of Law, Economics and Organisation*, 10, 201–46.

Lodge, M. (2002a). *On Different Tracks: Designing Railway Regulation in Britain and Germany*. Westport, CT: Praeger.

Lodge, M. (2002b). 'The Wrong Type of Regulation?', *Journal of Public Policy*, 22:3, 271–97.

Lodge, M. (2005). 'The Importance of Being Modern: International Standards and National Regulatory Innovation', *Journal of European Public Policy*, 12:4, 649–67.

Lodge, M. (2007). 'Comparing New Modes of Governance in Action: The Open Method of Co-ordination in Pensions and Information Society', *Journal of Common Market Studies*, 45:2, 343–65.

Lodge, M., and L. Stirton (2006). 'Withering in the Heat? In Search of the Regulatory State in the Commonwealth Caribbean', *Governance*, 19:3, 465–95.

Lodge, M., and K. Wegrich (2005a). 'Governing Multi-level Governance: Comparing Domain Dynamics in German Land–Local Relationships and Prisons', *Public Administration*, 83:2, 417–42.

Lodge, M., and K. Wegrich (2005b). 'Control over Government: Institutional Isomorphism and Governance Dynamics in German Public Administration', *Policy Studies Journal*, 33:2, 213–33.

MacDonagh, O. (1958). 'The Nineteenth-Century Revolution in Government: A Reappraisal', *The Historical Journal*, 1:1, 252–67.

Majone, G. (1994). 'The Rise of the Regulatory State in Europe', *West European Politics*, 14:3, 77–101.

Majone, G. (1996a). 'Regulation and its Modes', in G. Majone (ed.), *Regulating Europe*. London: Routledge.

Majone, G. (1996b). 'Public Policy and Administration: Ideas, Interests and Institutions', in R.E. Goodin and H.D. Klingemann (eds.), *A New Handbook of Political Science*. Oxford: Oxford University Press.

Majone, G. (1997a). 'From the Positive to the Regulatory State', *Journal of Public Policy*, 17:2, 139–67.

Majone, G. (1997b). 'The New European Agencies: Regulation by Information', *Journal of European Public Policy*, 4:2, 262–75.

Majone, G. (2002). 'Delegation of Regulatory Powers in a Mixed Polity', *European Law Journal*, 8:3, 319–39.

Majone, G. (2005). *Dilemmas of European Integration*. Oxford: Oxford University Press.

McGowan, L., and S. Wilks (1995). 'The First Supranational Policy in the European Union', *European Journal of Political Research*, 28:2, 141–69.

Moran, M. (2002). 'Review Article: Understanding the Regulatory State', *British Journal of Political Science*, 32, 391–413.

Moran, M. (2003). *The Regulatory State in Britain*. Oxford: Oxford University Press.

Ogus, A. (1994). *Regulation*. Oxford: Oxford University Press.

Parris, H. (1965). *Government and the Railways in Nineteenth-Century Britain*. London: Routledge and Kegan Paul.

Pelzman, S. (1989). 'The Economic Theory of Regulation after a Decade of Deregulation', *Brookings Papers on Economic Activity (Microeconomics)*, 1–44.

Pollack, M. (2002). 'Learning from the Americanists (Again): Theory and Method in the Study of Delegation', *West European Politics*, 25:1, 200–219.

Posner, R. (2004). *Catastrophe: Risk and Response*. Oxford: Oxford University Press.

Power, M. (1997). *The Audit Society*. Oxford: Oxford University Press.

Radaelli, C. (2004). 'The Diffusion of Regulatory Impact Assessment – Best Practice or Lesson-drawing', *European Journal of Political Research*, 43:5, 723–47.

Robson, W. (1962). *Nationalized Industry and Public Ownership*. London: George Allen & Unwin.

Rose, N. (1994). 'Governing by Numbers: Figuring Out Democracy', *Accounting, Organisations and Society*, 16:7, 673–92.

Schäfer, A. (2004). 'A New Form of Governance? Comparing the Open Method of Coordination to Multilateral Surveillance by the IMF and the OECD', Max Planck Institute for the Study of Societies, working paper 5.

Scharpf, F.W. (2001). 'What Have We Learnt? Problem-solving Capacity of the Multi-level European Polity', Max Planck Institute for the Study of Societies, working paper 4.

Schmidt, S. (1998). *Liberalisierung in Europa*. Frankfurt/M: Campus.

Schmidt, V. (2001). 'Europeanization and the Mechanics of Economic Policy Adjustment', *European Integration online papers*, 5:6.

Selznick, P. (1985). 'Focusing Organizational Research on Regulation', in R. Noll (ed.), *Regulatory Policy and the Social Sciences*. Berkeley and Los Angeles: University of California Press.

Stigler, G. (1971). 'The Theory of Economic Regulation', *Bell Journal of Economic and Management Science*, 2:1, 3–21.

Teske, P. (2004). *Regulation in the States*. Washington, DC: Brookings Institution Press.

Thatcher, M. (2001). 'The EU Commission and National Governments as Partners', *Journal of European Public Policy*, 8:4, 558–84.

Thatcher, M. (2002). 'Delegation to Independent Regulatory Agencies: Pressures, Functions and Contextual Mediation', *West European Politics*, 25:1, 125–47.

Thatcher, M. (2004). 'Varieties of Capitalism in an Internationalized World: Domestic Institutional Change in European Telecommunications', *Comparative Political Studies*, 37:7, 1–30.

Thatcher, M. (2005). 'The Third Force? Independent Regulatory Agencies and Elected Politicians in Europe', *Governance*, 18:3, 347–74.

Thatcher, M., and A. Sweet Stone (2002). 'Theory and Practice of Delegation to Non-Majoritarian Institutions', *West European Politics*, 25:1, 1–22.

Tivey, L. (1982). 'Nationalised Industries as Organised Interests', *Public Administration*, 60, 42–55.

Tsebelis, G. (2002). *Veto Players*. Princeton, NJ: Princeton University Press.

Veljanovski, C. (1991). 'The Regulation Game', in C. Veljanovski (ed.), *Regulators and the Market*. London: Institute of Economic Affairs.

Vogel, D. (1986). *National Styles of Regulation*. Ithaca, NY: Cornell University Press.

Wildavsky, A. (1980). *The Art and Craft of Policy Analysis*. Basingstoke: Macmillan.

Wilson, J.Q. (1980). 'The Politics of Regulation', in J.Q. Wilson (ed.), *The Politics of Regulation*. New York: Basic Books.

Zeitlin, J. (2005). 'Introduction: The Open Method of Co-ordination in Question', in J. Zeitlin and P. Pichot with L. Magnusson (eds.), *The Open Method of Co-ordination in Action: The European Employment and Social Inclusion Strategies*. Brussels: PIE Peter Lang.

European Political Economy: Labour Out, State Back In, Firm to the Fore

VIVIEN A. SCHMIDT

Had a latter-day European Rip Van Winkle gone to sleep in 1978 only to have awakened in 2008, he would have found the European political economy barely recognisable. Having closed his eyes to the power of labour, strong state action, and the subordination of business to the needs of society, he would have opened them to the power of business, a much diminished state, and the subordination of labour to the needs of the market. Moreover, whereas he would have commenced his slumber surrounded by staunch believers in Marxian ideas about class conflict whose discourse centred around the fight between labour and capital, he would have ended it encircled by equally staunch believers in neo-liberal ideas whose discourse was all about free markets and global trade. Most immediately, however, he would have been hard put to buy himself a cup of coffee with the national coins in his pockets, given European Monetary Union, while the croissant he would have had with his coffee might have been from a French bakery, the sugar from a German beet grower, the orange juice from a Spanish orchard, the coffee cup from China, and the coffee itself from a well-known American chain, all thanks to the Single Market.

The political economic story behind this transformation begins in the late 1970s, with the policy responses to the economic crises of the period – in particular the extreme currency volatility following the end of the Bretton Woods System and the exponential increase in the competitive pressures in the capital and product markets linked to the two oil shocks. The responses to these crises produced major changes in the monetary, industrial, and labour policies of all West European countries over the course of the following decades. While the late 1970s and early 1980s were characterised primarily by the shifts in monetary policy from neo-Keynesian 'pump-priming' to monetarist austerity budgets, the mid-1980s saw the beginnings of the end of interventionist industrial policy and public ownership as states started deregulating business, privatising public enterprise, and liberalising financial markets. Changes in labour policy through deregulation of labour markets and decentralisation of wage bargaining systems, by contrast, came at different junctures in different countries with differing effects. Last but certainly not least, European integration, which took off in the mid-1980s, had the twin effects of building a European economic space – ever-deepening through the Single Market and the Single Currency and ever-widening through enlargement – as it pushed an ever-increasing Europeanisation of national economies.

Along with these changes in policies came changing ideas and discourse about the changing economic realities. In the late 1970s and early 1980s, the rise of neo-liberalism in particular offered a new set of ideas about the kinds of economic policies appropriate for capitalist systems: a free market based on competition and individualism, limited government intervention and a regulatory state, economic openness and free trade. By the late 1980s and early 1990s, the fall of communism had left no alternatives to capitalism, and East European countries embarked on their own conversion to capitalism, influenced by neo-liberal ideas as well as by the foreign multinationals investing in their countries and the EU accession demands for free and open markets underpinned by the *acquis communautaire*. In Western Europe, across this entire time period, moreover, the internationalisation of national economies and businesses was increasing in scope and intensity. But while discourse about the challenges of internationalisation was widespread in the 1970s, it largely disappeared in the 1980s only to resurface with even greater resonance by the early 1990s, although now called globalisation. The concerns about globalisation, both in the 1970s and the early to mid-1990s, focused mainly on the rise of multinational business as a harbinger of the decline of the nation-state. By the late 1990s and early 2000s, however, globalisation's impact on labour and the welfare state had become the main worry, with 'off-shoring' the latest buzzword.

In response to these changes in the power and influence of the state, business, and labour in the face of globalisation and Europeanisation, scholarly attention has itself shifted over time. Political economists went from a major focus on labour in the 1970s, with corporatist analyses of the power of unions and their role in macroeconomic policymaking, to a renewed emphasis on the state in the 1980s, as it liberalised financial markets, privatised and deregulated business, and decentralised labour markets. State-centred analyses themselves, however, transmogrified into approaches that by the early 1990s denied the centrality of the state either directly, by charting its decline in the face of globalisation and Europeanisation, or indirectly, by disaggregating the state into its component parts, in particular through historical institutionalist accounts of the evolution of political economic institutions and practices. What is more, by the late 1990s and early 2000s the state was totally eclipsed, displaced by business as the primary object of study in the firm-centred analyses of the 'varieties of capitalism' school. Most recently, however, the state has been brought back in yet again while labour has been making a comeback.

At the same time that the objects of inquiry in European political economy may have shifted from labour to state to firm, the focus of inquiry has expanded, growing in richness and complexity as the study of national economies has been joined by the study of an integrated regional European economy, of clusters of capitalist economies, of sectors, and of sub-national regional and local economies. Differences in how scholars approach the explanation of European political economy are also questions of analysis, interpretation, and methodology. The main analytic questions ask whether European countries are moving toward convergence or divergence, and whether the drivers of such change are the external pressures of globalisation and Europeanisation or the internal pressures of politics and economics. The interpretive questions speak to whether the directions of change and/or their drivers are good or bad. The methodological questions address how to study European political economy.

The methodological answers can be roughly boiled down to the differing approaches of the four 'new institutionalisms'. These include the three older ones: rationalist, historical, and sociological (see Hall and Taylor 1996; Immergut 1998; Thelen 1999; Campbell 2004) and the latest one, 'discursive institutionalism' (see Schmidt 2002: ch. 5, 2006a; see also Campbell and Pedersen 2001). Rationalist approaches have tended to develop institutionalist models of firm coordination or quantitative macro-statistical analyses of the impact of globalisation. Historical institutionalist approaches have tended to describe the path-dependent trajectories of state institutions or the incremental changes in labour practices. Sociological institutionalist approaches have tended to evoke the culturally-framed ideas and practices of government, business, or labour. And discursive institutionalist approaches have tended to detail the influence of ideas in neo-liberal policy change or of discourse in political leaders' legitimisation of economic reform.

The article proceeds by time periods, beginning with the late 1970s into the 1980s to discuss the decline of labour both as a powerful actor in

European political economy and as the main object of inquiry. It then considers the early 1980s into the 1990s, when the state is brought back in as an autonomous actor only to fade from view as the disaggregating and weakening effects of its liberalising actions make it appear in decline, especially in comparison to the forces of globalisation and Europeanisation. The article follows with the early 1990s into the 2000s, as the firm is put front and centre not only by the convergence theorists of globalisation but also by the divergence theorists of the 'varieties of capitalism' school. The article concludes with current trends, as both the state and labour are coming back into their own as objects of inquiry in tandem with business.

Taking Labour Out

Labour was central to the study of European political economy in the 1970s and on into the 1980s, as corporatism became the main research programme of political economists. It faded as a major focus of mainstream political economy by the late 1980s. This reflected material realities, in particular the shift in balance of power from labour to capital, as well as theoretical developments, as corporatism seemed to explain fewer and fewer macro-level (national) interrelationships, even if meso (sectoral) and micro (firm) level relationships continued to attract attention (Cawson 1986; Schmitter 1989).

As a theory of political economy, corporatism was the European answer to the American pluralist theories of economic interest organisation and representation that had predominated in the 1950s and 1960s. Against this, corporatist theories based themselves on the model of interest organisation of the smaller European democracies such as the Netherlands, Sweden, Denmark, and Austria, with Germany as a more complicated case (see Katzenstein 1985; Lehmbruch and Schmitter 1982). In corporatist polities, organised interests remain central to the policy process, but the policy-making process is cooperative rather than competitive, and closed to all but certain 'privileged' interest groups, mainly business and labour, which participate with government not only in the formulation of policy but also in its implementation as 'an integral part of administration' (Cawson 1986: 37; see also Schmitter and Lehmbruch 1979).

Just as pluralism had been the measure against which all countries were evaluated as to their 'democratic' potential in the 1950s and 1960s, so corporatism became the measure against which all national political economies were evaluated for their 'democratic corporatist' potential in the 1970s and 1980s. As such, those countries which lacked the prerequisites – including an ideology of social partnership, relatively centralised interest groups organised in peak associations which exercised power over a relatively compliant base, and bargaining between government and organised interests that was voluntary, informal, and continuous – were lower on the comparative scale than those which fulfilled the prerequisites.

Leaving aside the most pointed contrast, with the United States, the less democratically corporatist countries included Britain, which had strong craft-based unions, adversarial business–labour relations, and voluntaristic negotiations which made corporatist agreements difficult to reach and almost impossible to sustain (Lehmbruch 1982); France, which had weak unions, adversarial business–labour relations, and state-imposed negotiations which obviated corporatism (Hayward 1986; Schmidt 1996); and Italy, which time and again seemed close to attaining corporatism, but which failed over and over again due to fragmented unions, weak employers' associations, and a paralysed state (Lange and Regini 1989; Ferrera and Gualmini 2004).

The problem for corporatist theory is that just as it was at its peak of popularity in the 1980s, corporatist reality was encountering more and more difficulties as wage-bargaining systems and cooperative labour–management relations broke down in more and more countries, including even the most ideal-typical of corporatist systems. The Netherlands was the first to go, with a period of almost total breakdown in effective tripartite bargaining during the 1970s, although corporatism returned in the early 1980s, but reinstated on a new, more subordinate footing (Visser and Hemerijck 1997). By contrast, Sweden experienced the end of macro-level corporatism in the early 1980s, when the employers pulled out of the national centralised concertation process, although they continued in the sectoral (Pontusson and Swenson 1996; Blyth 2002). But equally significantly, whereas in the 1970s some could still hope that Britain or even France would develop corporatism, by the 1980s such hopes were dashed. This came first with a bang in Britain through Thatcher who smashed the unions in the early to mid-1980s and then with a whimper in France as the Socialist government failed to generate a German-style concertation system through laws creating direct management–worker dialogue and subsequent governments simply gave up on organising centralised labour–management wage negotiation (Howell 1992, 1995; see also Schmidt 2002: ch. 2). In the cases of both Britain and France, the radical decentralisation of wage bargaining ensued.

It should be no wonder, then, that scholarly interest slowly drift away from corporatist theory, even if studies of labour relations continued. This shift was also understandable in a context in which the state had returned to centre stage beginning in the 1980s, not only in scholarly theory but also in economic practice.

Bringing the State Back In

The state has also had its ups and downs in European political economy. After taking centre stage up until the late 1960s, it faded out as an object of study only to return with vigour in the late 1970s and early 1980s, and then to disappear again. This was not only the result of material events linked to the rise of globalisation and Europeanisation, which reduced the autonomy of the state, but also an outgrowth of theoretical developments related to the rise of the 'new institutionalisms', which disaggregated the state into its constituent institutional parts.

When Andrew Shonfield (1965) published his seminal work on capitalism, the three models he described – liberalism, typical of Britain; statism, typical of France, and corporatism, typical of Germany – were all largely defined by the state and its role in the economy. Beginning in the 1970s, this state-focused approach to European political economy was supplanted by corporatist approaches. By the late 1970s and early 1980s, however, as corporatism seemed to be breaking down in even the most ideal-typical of corporatist countries, the state came 'back in' as governments began increasingly taking decisions on their own, with or without the acquiescence or even participation of labour or business.

Importantly, governments that in the 1960s and 1970s might have sought to coordinate policymaking with labour and business began in the 1980s to act more autonomously in the face of crisis. But different countries took different paths even as they all sought to loosen labour markets, liberalise financial markets, and deregulate business (Schmidt 2002: ch. 2). The UK was the first and certainly the most radically neo-liberal, as Prime Minister Margaret Thatcher, fuelled by neo-liberal ideas that had developed in the 1970s (Hall 1993), abruptly turned to monetarism, brutally opened business to competition, and broke the back of labour (Gamble 1985; King and Wood 1999). France, by comparison, experienced the most extreme shifts in reform initiatives, going from a massive programme of nationalisation and industrial restructuring by a Socialist government in the early 1980s to a major programme of privatisation in the mid-1980s by a newly neo-liberal right-wing government under Prime Minister Jacques Chirac (Hall 1986; Schmidt 1996). Germany, Sweden, and Italy, by contrast, experienced comparatively little change in the 1980s, Germany and Sweden because their economic dynamism meant they did not need to reform, Italy because its state paralysis meant that it could not reform, although it desperately needed to. All of these countries, however, engaged in significant reforms in the 1990s, as economic crisis spurred Sweden to join the EU, as the costs of unification plus the pressures of globalisation pushed Germany to begin liberalising reform efforts, and as the fall of the Berlin wall enabled the Italian state finally to shed its post-war paralysis (Scharpf and Schmidt 2000).

Even more dramatically, the fall of the Berlin Wall led to the economic transformation of Central and Eastern Europe (CEE), with the transition from command economies to capitalist economies. Here, rather than speaking of a renewal of autonomy, we would need to speak of a new role for the state. But unlike in Western Europe, where the state's renewed autonomy beginning in the 1980s continued to be for the most part balanced out by reasonably strong non-state actors in business and labour, in Central and Eastern Europe the state's transformation in the 1990s into a strong regulative power was not balanced out by non-state actors, as unions and business associations tended to be weak and fragmented. This entailed that market-making reforms in Eastern Europe often came without the market-correcting social policies found in the West (Bruszt 2002). But while privatisation, deregulation, and liberalisation became the watchwords across the CEEs, states proceeded in different ways at different paces. Some, like Poland, engendered a 'big bang' in political economic reform, liberalising prices and shifting macroeconomic policy very quickly, while others were slower – some so slow, in fact, that they experienced an anti-democratic backlash, as in Bulgaria (Aslund 2002; Ekiert 2003).

Over this same time period the EU got a new lease on life, as national leaders came to recognise that only together could they effectively respond to the economic crises that began in the 1970s. The EU's resurrection started with the European Monetary System in 1979, which was to diminish currency volatility while promoting convergence in European countries' monetary policies. This was followed by the Single Market Act in the mid-1980s, which led to tremendous state-promoted, business-oriented activity to get national firms ready for the '1992' completion of the Single Market, along with more concerted efforts regarding the harmonisation and standardisation of products (Egan 2001). It was followed by the Maastricht Treaty's agreement for European Monetary Union (EMU) in 1992, which was to underpin the single market with a single currency (Dyson 2002; Martin and Ross 2004). And it culminated (at least insofar as political economy is concerned) with enlargement, as the EU exerted massive leverage – both passive, through its power of attraction, and active, through the requirements of the *acquis communautaire* – in Central and Eastern European countries in the transition from communism to capitalism (Vachudova 2005).

While European states were taking a leadership role in reorganising national economies and building the EU, scholars were reassessing their own explanations of the European political economy. These were the earliest of the 'new institutionalists' who, concerned that the role of the state as an autonomous actor in the organisation of the economy was being forgotten, sought to 'bring the state back in' (Evans *et al.* 1985). Significantly, the Europeanists among these scholars tended to focus on countries where the state was more active and in evidence in structuring economic relations, such as in France or Britain (Zysman 1983; Hall 1986) and the small European states (Katzenstein 1985). However, almost as soon as it began, the focus on the state *qua* state began to fade away, the result of two reinforcing developments, one in scholarly research itself, the other in material reality.

In academic research, the very scholars who had brought the state back in began to disaggregate it into its component parts. In their new 'historical institutionalist' approach, institutional actors are seen to be shaped by the path-dependent development of their institutions, understood as regularised practices (see Steinmo *et al.* 1992). The upshot of this new approach in comparative political economy has not so much been that the state was thrown 'back out' as that instead of remaining in the foreground of political economic research as an autonomous actor it ended up in the background, significant mainly through the effects of its variegated institutional structures and practices.

The changing realities of national political economies in an increasingly Europeanising region and internationalising world also conspired to devalue the state as a focus of research. But even more central to this was the fact that the state had engineered its own retreat, having divested itself of the very instruments that had ensured its autonomy. This came in the macroeconomic sphere through the turn to monetarism; in the micro-economic sphere through deregulation, privatisation, and liberalisation; and in the supranational sphere with the rise of international and regional trade organisations – most notably the European Union. Countries that were emblematic of state direction like France transformed themselves, with a *dirigiste* end to *dirigisme* as public ownership dropped precipitously, Chief Executive Officers (CEOs) gained a tremendous amount of autonomy, and top state civil servants came to 'colonize business' (Schmidt 1996, 2002). Even countries like the UK, where the state intervened less, or at least less effectively, significantly reduced the state's direct involvement by slashing state subsidies, and creating a regulatory state (King and Wood 1999; Wood 2001). Only in countries like Italy or Greece could one talk about an increase in state capacity, but this was largely due to greater incapacity in the past, and the role of the EU as a '*vincolo esterno*' (external constraint) (Featherstone 1998; Radaelli 2002).

The retreat of the state did not mean the end of the state, however, since deregulation signalled not an end to regulation, just a different kind of regulation (Vogel 1996). But the switch from state action to more independent public action nonetheless suggested to scholars at this time that the state remained little more than a regulator of markets, ensuring that it was no longer a central player in capitalism.

The Rise of Business and the Decline of the Nation-State?

The retreat of the state, combined with the rising importance of the international financial markets that fuelled increasingly mobile capital, underpin the escalating attention to globalisation beginning in the 1990s and peaking in the early 2000s (see Busch 2000). For many scholars, globalisation signalled the rise of business and the decline of the nation-state (see Schmidt 1995). But how meteoritic the rise of business and how deep the decline of the state was the main focus of scholarly debate.

For some, whom we will call the convergence theorists of globalisation, the demise of the nation-state was imminent, with multinationals having become so footloose and fancy-free that they could no longer be contained or controlled either by their countries of origin or those in which they invested. This echoed the discussions of the 1960s and early 1970s, in which multinationals were seen as escaping nation-state control, but which scholars quickly came to agree overestimated the power of multinationals and underestimated the ability of nation-states – home and host countries alike – to regain control through a wide range of constraints on doing business (Vernon 1971, 1985). Those predictions appeared more relevant by the 1990s. This is when convergence theorists argued that the exogenous pressures of globalisation – through financial market internationalisation and capital mobility fuelled by government policies of liberalisation, privatisation, and deregulation – meant one thing alone: convergence to a neo-liberal model of capitalism, the demise of the state as a key actor in global capitalism, and the end of any significant differences between governments of the left and the right as both sought to liberalise, leading to a regulatory 'race to the bottom' (e.g., Cerny 1994; Strange 1996; see discussion in Schmidt 2002: ch. 1).

But much as in the 1970s, the convergence theorists' arguments about the demise of the nation-state and the end of any differences among national capitalisms were exaggerated. They were countered by divergence theorists who argued that there were few signs of convergence, and that national diversity continued to matter (Berger and Dore 1996; Boyer and Drache 1996). This they demonstrated through studies of individual countries' differing political economic trajectories, whether that of Britain as 'globalization in one country' (Hirst and Thompson 2000), France as a country in which the liberalised state nevertheless continued to play an influential role (Schmidt 1996), Italy as a country in which industrial districts were the key to success (Locke 1995), or Germany in which the social market economy still predominated (Streeck 1997). But they also showed that deregulation in the financial markets produced different rules (Moran 1991; Vogel 1996); that tax policies remained highly differentiated (Steinmo 1993), without any necessary race to the bottom with regard to the welfare state (Swank 1998); and that governments of the left were largely still able to pursue their traditionally redistributive goals (Garrett 1998). Moreover, they provided evidence for continuing country-based differences in regulatory regimes (Lütz 1998a; Thatcher 1999; Coen and Héritier 2005); in industrial production systems (Hollingsworth et al. 1994); in labour relations and training systems (Thelen 1993, 2001); and in local economies (Crouch et al. 2004). Finally, they revealed that evidence for such differences appeared not only in the economic statistics or in the institutional practices but also in the differing impact of neo-liberal ideas and the discourses of globalisation in Britain and Ireland (Hall 1993; Hay 2001; Hay and Smith 2005) as opposed to those in Sweden and other Scandinavian countries (Blyth 2002; Campbell and Pedersen 2001; Campbell 2004) or France and Germany (Schmidt 2002: ch. 6).

Whereas divergence theorists of globalisation divide largely between those who argue for convergence and those who insist on divergence, theorists of Europeanisation seem to opt for convergence *and* divergence at the same time. This is because while Europeanisation acts as a conduit for globalisation, by pressing for greater openness in capital and product markets, it also serves as a shield against it, by reducing macroeconomic exposure to the vagaries of the currency markets and enhancing microeconomic economies of scale through the single market. Moreover, in exchange for state losses in autonomy and control are gains in shared state authority and joint control (Schmidt 2002: ch. 1). Many of the very same above-named theorists who posit divergence in terms of globalisation are much more circumspect with regard to Europeanisation, seeing convergence and divergence at the same time in, say, the financial markets (Lütz 1998b) or telecommunications (Thatcher 1999). This stands to reason, of course, given the role of the EU in generating policies that all then must transpose and implement into national law. With European integration again, moreover, the role of ideas and discourse is important in demonstrating the development of EU policies, whether with regard to EMU (McNamara 1998; Verdun 2000) or the Single Market (Fligstein and Mara-Drita 1996; Jabko 2006).

Putting the Firm Front and Centre

Divergence theorists have 'converged' most recently around the Varieties of Capitalism (VOC) school, as proponents and critics alike share the conviction that there are different varieties of capitalism in Europe, although they differ on the number of varieties – two, three, four, or more; where to look for them – at national, sectoral, or subnational regional levels; which variables to emphasise – the firm, labour, or the state; and how to organise them.

The VOC school takes a 'firm-centred' approach to political economy with a binary division of capitalism into two main types, Liberal Market Economies (LMEs) and Coordinated Market Economies (CMEs). The only thing these divergence theorists have in common with the convergence theorists is the equally minimal role of the state and the subordination of labour. VOC theorists' primary focus is how firms coordinate with their environment. In LMEs the market coordinates interactions among socioeconomic actors whereas in CMEs socioeconomic actors engage in non-market coordination (see Hall and Soskice 2001). The state, if considered at all, plays at most a supportive role in creating a positive regulatory environment.

Although this binary division of capitalism is highly seductive because of its parsimony, it has been the subject of many critiques, including the very basic one that a binary division into ideal-types tends to be too reductive, squeezing much too much into much too rigid a set of categories (see

Crouch 2005). Another problem is that the explanation is overly functionalist, with its emphasis on complementarity and positive feedback effects from coordination. This makes the system static, overly path-dependent, and unable to account for institutional change, in particular in light of the very real disaggregating forces coming from globalisation pressures and neo-liberal policies (see Schmidt 2002, ch. 3; Crouch 2005; Morgan *et al.* 2005; Hancké *et al.* 2007). Moreover, VOC has great difficulty dealing with country cases that are treated as outliers because they do not fit well into either ideal-type (Schmidt 2002) and because they seem plagued by intra-system contradictions, misfits, and perverse spillovers (Molina and Rhodes 2007).

Scholars have responded in various ways to these problems. Some have attempted to counter the functionalist bias of the approach by positing open rather than closed systems, with multilayered reference frames and relatively autonomous components, as in the Netherlands (Becker 2006), or even different patterns of interdependence in different subsystems, as in Germany (Deeg 2005). Others have sought to inject more dynamism into the system by positing incremental change in the institutional components of loosely connected, historically evolving varieties of capitalism, which change at different rates in different ways through different processes, including layering in of new elements, conversion through reinterpretation, or even exhaustion (Thelen 2004; Streeck and Thelen 2005). In either case, however, the binary nature of VOC is undermined, as open systems or incremental evolution create hybrids and/or point to the disaggregation of the variety of capitalism.

Yet others have argued that rather than the binary division of capitalism into two basic varieties, there are at least three varieties of capitalism (Rhodes and Apeldoorn 1997; Coates 2000; Schmidt 2002), if not four (Boyer 2004; Whitley 2005), five (Amable 2004) or more, including national varieties (Crouch and Streeck 1997), sectoral varieties (Hollingsworth *et al.* 1994), or regional and local varieties (Crouch *et al.* 2004). Importantly, even those who seemingly accept the binary division increasingly talk about mixed market economies (MMEs) with different logics of interaction (Molina and Rhodes 2007) or 'hybrids' in the cases of Eastern European countries as well as Germany, despite its status as the ideal of the ideal-type (Jackson 2003).

The differences among political economists on how many varieties of capitalism there are can be seen as depending mainly upon whether, as Colin Crouch puts it, one takes a 'labelling' approach to create country groupings for the purpose of theoretical comparison or an 'analysing' approach concerned more with empirical realities (Crouch 2005). Another way of looking at it would be to differentiate between those who prefer parsimony, which makes for ideal-typical models and difficulties in applying to specific cases, and those who accept complexity, which may be more empirically valid but, naturally, suffers from its specificities (Deeg and Jackson 2006: 21).

Yet another way to explain the differences is to take note of how political economists prefer a particular set of features in arriving at their ideal-typical models and country ideals. Convergence theorists tend to take finance and globalisation as defining factors – with all that that means in terms of the internationalising trends in capital ownership, corporate governance, and the emphasis on profits – making for convergence to a neo-liberal model epitomised by the United States and the United Kingdom (e.g. Lane 2005). Divergence theorists in the VOC school, by contrast, take firms and their coordinating mechanisms as the defining factors – with all that that entails in terms the binary division of capitalism into LMEs, epitomised by the US, the UK, and Ireland, and CMEs, epitomised by Germany, the Scandinavian countries, the Netherlands, Austria, and Switzerland (i.e. Hall and Soskice 2001). Those countries that do not fit have been termed, variously 'mid-spectrum' economies (Hall and Soskice 2001) or 'mixed market economies' (MMEs) (Hall and Gingrich 2004), which will necessarily under-perform because they lack the complementarities (Amable 2003; Hall and Gingerich 2004). These misfits include France, Italy, and Spain, all three countries in which the role of the state has traditionally been more pronounced. For another set of divergence theorists, such countries represent a third variety of capitalism.

Bringing the State Back In Yet Again

In recent years, political economists across the spectrum have begun to bring the state back in yet again. This has been particularly the case for those who argue for a third variety of capitalism clustered around the cases of France, Italy, and Spain, but it lately includes historical institutionalists who in the 1990s had disaggregated the state and even VOC scholars. There are a whole range of scholars, however, who never abandoned the study of the state, but now show the ways in which changes in polity, policy, and politics continue to make public action key to understanding national political economies.

For divergence theorists who see at least three varieties of capitalism, state action is the defining feature that serves to differentiate liberal and coordinated market economies from the third variety – which I call 'state-influenced' market economies (SMEs) (see Schmidt 2006b). SMEs encompass countries in which the state played a distinctive role in the post-war period, intervening more, and differently, for better or for worse, than in LMEs and CMEs; and in which the state retains significant influence over business and labour, playing a more active, and different, role in the economy than the state in LMEs or CMEs, even subsequent to the state's retreat beginning in the mid-1980s. In Europe, country cases include France, which has moved from 'state capitalism' to 'state-enhanced' capitalism (Schmidt 2002) and Mediterranean countries like Italy, which until changes in the 1990s was seen as a 'dysfunctional state capitalism' (Della Sala 2004) or 'failed state capitalism' (Schmidt 2002). But Italy and Spain have also been classified as part of 'Latin capitalism' (Rhodes and Appeldoorn 1997) and Mediterranean 'mixed market economies' (Molina and Rhodes 2007) along with Portugal and Greece.

In state-influenced market economies, the role of the state is theorised very differently from its role in LMEs and CMEs, such that we come up with three very different categories of states for the three varieties of capitalism. Unlike the 'liberal' state in LMEs, which is identifiable by its arms-length relations (King and Wood 1999; Hall and Soskice 2001; Wood 2001) or the 'enabling' state in CMEs, which is typified by its coordinating and facilitating activities (Streeck 1997; Hall and Soskice 2001), the 'influencing' state in SMEs – although a pale shadow of its former interventionist self – is nonetheless exemplified by its capacity to intervene where it sees fit, either 'enhancing' business and labour activity or 'hindering' it (see Schmidt 2002, 2006b).

If it were only state action that serves as justification for the third variety of capitalism then one might still be tempted to argue that all states intervene, some more, some less, and dismiss the claim that there is a third variety. But bringing the state back in is not just about recognising the differential role of the state. It is that in SMEs, in which the state has long played an influential role, business interactions and labour relations also differ in character and in logic of coordination, leading to different mechanisms of adjustment from LMEs and CMEs. In the liberal market economy of Britain, adjustment is driven by the financial markets and led by autonomous firms acting unilaterally, with comparatively little input – whether positive or negative – from the state or labour. In the coordinated market economy of Germany, adjustment is led by firms and jointly negotiated cooperatively between business, labour, and the state.

In the state-enhanced market economy of France, adjustment is firm-led in those domains where business now exercises autonomy – in business strategy, investment, production, and wage bargaining – but adjustment is still state-driven in those domains where neither business nor labour can exercise leadership – in labour rules, pension systems, and the like – or where the state sees a need to reshape the general economic environment to promote competitiveness. In either case, the logic of interaction is one of hierarchical authority rather than joint-decision or unilateral action (Schmidt 2002: 144). A similar logic of adjustment can be found in Italy and Spain when applied to the sphere of industrial relations in particular (see Molina and Rhodes 2007), where 'top-down conflict governance' is very close to the logic of hierarchical authority noted above for France once we add into the equation the conflictual politics that such hierarchical authority often generates.

But taking state action seriously means considering the distinctive role of the state not only in 'state-influenced' market economies – as a distinguish-ing feature – but also in liberal and coordinated market economies. This, however, requires going beyond the 'labelling' approach to an 'analysing' one, and pushes us to consider state action in all its complexity, by deconstructing state action into its component parts in terms of policy, 'polity', and politics (see Schmidt 2006b).

We have already covered much of this above, in the review of divergence theorists' arguments about the differential impact of globalisation and Europeanisation beginning in the 1990s. But it is important to highlight developments in scholarship in the 2000s that draw attention to the continuing significance of the state even in countries where it has been assumed to be largely absent. In the UK, for example, the 'steering state' which has emerged from the regulatory reforms of Thatcher, Major, and Blair engages in much more public intervention than in the past (Moran 2003). In Sweden, moreover, where the state has always been more present, public institutions, imbued with trust by the public as a result of 'collective memories', continue to be a key sustaining factor for the Swedish welfare state and the collective bargaining system (Rothstein 2005: ch. 1, 7). Finally, in countries as diverse as the Netherlands, France, Britain, Germany, and the UK and in sectors as different as the digital economy and the global services market, scholars have shown that the state continues to structure markets in significant ways, developing new missions, and making critical choices that are the 'product of power and politics, not just path-dependence and employer "coordination"' (Levy 2006: 26).

To be fair, VOC does not entirely neglect state action (e.g. Thelen 2001; Wood 2001; Martin and Thelen 2006), in particular with regard to responses to international challenges (e.g. Hall and Thelen 2006). Importantly, however, most VOC scholars still do not take the state-like role of the EU sufficiently into account. The role of the state in European varieties of capitalism cannot be fully explained without considering the ways in which national state action comes into play at the EU level, through the 'bottom-up' process of European integration by which national actors participate in EU policymaking, and the ways in which EU 'state' action comes into play at the national level, through the 'top-down' process of Europeanisation, as member states implement policies jointly decided in Brussels.

Labour's Comeback

During the same time that the state was being brought back in, labour was making a comeback. Already in the 1990s, in response to the convergence theorists' claims, some scholars insisted that the unions' decline was better explained by technological changes (Pontusson and Swenson 1996), and that the unions had in any event declined significantly only in some countries (Goldin *et al.* 1999). Although France and Britain both radically decentralised their wage-bargaining systems, corporatism seemed reborn in a number of the least likely countries. In an LME like Ireland and even SMEs like Italy and Spain, social pacts became the order of the day (Rhodes

1997; Royo 2002; Ferrera and Gualmini 2004). Moreover, traditionally corporatist CMEs like the Netherlands and Denmark revised the old compromises and systems of coordination (Visser and Hemerijck 1997). The renewal of corporatism, moreover, came largely from employers' own need to maintain the cooperative labour relations essential to producing high-quality products on a just-in-time basis in tightly coupled production networks (Thelen and Kume 1999; Thelen 2001). Thus, rather than globalisation leading toward convergence to a single neo-liberal, deregulated model of industrial relations, it has brought continuing if not increasing divergence. This means that labour remains a force to be reckoned with, albeit differently in the different varieties of capitalism.

The latest turn taken by globalisation, moreover, with regard to the 'off-shoring' of jobs to the Far East and 'near-shoring' of jobs to Eastern Europe is increasing the political salience of labour. Public responses, however, depend not so much on the amount of off-shoring per se as on how countries' work and welfare systems cushion its effects and on how the public has come to perceive globalisation generally and off-shoring more specifically. Winners and losers vary with the state of the economy and type of work and welfare system. But national publics' perceptions of who is winning or losing are also influenced by national leaders' legitimising discourses about globalisation and Europeanisation (Schmidt 2007).

Conclusion

European political economic scholarship, in summary, has moved from a focus on labour to the state to the firm and now back to a more balanced emphasis on all three. The questions today are contemporary versions of the ones that have bedevilled scholars throughout this period: will globalisation lead to convergence now, given that off-shoring represents a major challenge to production systems and labour regimes, even if the internationalisation of financial markets alone did not produce the expected convergence? Can we still talk about national varieties of capitalism in Europe, whether two, three, or more, not only because of the very real disaggregating trends as a result of the forces of globalisation and even more of Europeanisation, but also because these forces also have a tendency to create supranational sectoral or even subnational regional varieties of capitalism that challenge national varieties. And finally, is it not time to bring welfare states into the mix? But if we do so, then it becomes all but impossible to stick with two, three, or even four varieties. Labelling may indeed have to give way to analysing.

References

Amable, Bruno (2003). *The Diversity of Modern Capitalism*. Oxford: Oxford University Press.
Aslund, Anders (2002). *Building Capitalism: The Transformation of the Former Soviet Bloc*. Cambridge: Cambridge University Press.

Becker, Uwe (2006). 'Open Systemness and Contested Reference Frances. A Framework for Understanding Change in the Varieties of Capitalism', Paper delivered at the Center for European Studies, Harvard University, 6 February.

Berger, Suzanne, and Ronald Dore, eds., (1996). *National Diversity and Global Capitalism*. Ithaca, NY: Cornell University Press.

Blyth, Mark (2002). *Great Transformations: Economic Ideas and Institutional Change in the Twentieth Century*. New York: Cambridge University Press.

Boyer, Robert (2004). 'How and Why Capitalisms Differ', MPIfG Discussion Paper 04/5. Cologne: Max Planck Institute for the Study of Societies. http://www.mpifg.de/pu/mpifg_dp/dp05-4.pdf

Boyer, Robert, and Daniel Drache, eds. (1996). *States against Markets: The Limits of Globalization*. London and New York: Routledge.

Bruszt, Laszlo (2002). 'Making Markets and Eastern Enlargement: Diverging Convergence?', *West European Politics*, 25:2, 121–41.

Busch, Andreas (2000). 'Unpacking the Globalization Debate: Approaches, Evidence and Data', in David Marsh and Colin Hay (eds.), *Demystifying Globalization*. London: Macmillan.

Campbell, John L. (2004). *Institutional Change and Globalization*. Princeton, NJ: Princeton University Press.

Campbell, John L., and Ove K. Pedersen, eds. (2001). *The Rise of Neoliberalism and Institutional Analysis*. Princeton, NJ: Princeton University Press.

Cawson, Alan (1986). *Corporatism and Political Theory*. Oxford: Basil Blackwell.

Cerny, Philip (1994). 'The Dynamics of Financial Globalization', *Policy Sciences*, 27, 319–42.

Coates, David (2000). *Models of Capitalism*. Cambridge: Polity Press.

Coen, David, and Adrienne Héritier (2005). *Redefining Regulatory Regimes: Utilities in Europe*. Cheltenham: Edward Elgar.

Crouch, Colin (2005). *Capitalist Diversity and Change*. Oxford and New York: Oxford University Press.

Crouch, Colin, and Wolfgang Streeck, eds. (1997). *Political Economy of Modern Capitalism*. London: Sage.

Crouch, Colin, Patrick LeGalès, Carlo Trigilia and Helmut Voelzkow (2004). *Changing Governance of Local Economies*. Oxford: Oxford University Press.

Deeg, Richard (2005). 'Path Dependence, Institutional Complementarity, and Change in National Business Systems', in G. Morgan, R. Whitley and E. Moen (eds.), *Changing Capitalisms?* New York and Oxford: Oxford University Press.

Deeg, Richard, and Gregory Jackson (2006). 'How Many Varieties of Capitalism?', MPIfG Discussion Paper 06/2. Cologne: Max Planck Institute for the Study of Societies. http://www.mpifg.de/pu/mpifg_dp/dp06-2.pdf (14 March 2006).

Della Sala, Vincent (2004). 'The Italian Model of Capitalism: On the road between globalization and Europeanization', *Journal of European Public Policy*, 11:6, 1041–57.

Dyson, Kenneth, ed. (2002). *European States and the Euro*. Oxford: Oxford University Press.

Egan, Michelle (2001). *Constructing a European Market*. Oxford: Oxford University Press.

Ekiert, Georgz (2003). 'Patterns of Post-Communist Transformation in Central and Eastern Europe', in G. Ekiert and S.E. Hanson (eds.), *Capitalism and Democracy in Central and Eastern Europe*. Cambridge: Cambridge University Press, 89–119.

Evans, Peter, Dietrich Reuschemeyer and Theda Skocpol (1985). *Bringing the State Back In*. New York: Cambridge University Press.

Featherstone, Kevin (1998). '"Europeanization" and the Centre Periphery: The Case of Greece in the 1990s'. *South European Society and Politics*, 3:1, 23–39.

Ferrera, Maurizio, and Elisabetta Gualmini (2004). *Rescued by Europe?* Amsterdam: Amsterdam University Press.

Fligstein, Neil, and Iona Mara-Drita (1996). 'How to Make a Market: Reflections on the Attempt to Create a Single Market in the European Union, *American Journal of Sociology*, 102, 1–32.

Gamble, Andrew (1985). *Britain in Decline*. London: Macmillan.

Garrett, Geoffrey (1998). 'Global Markets and National Politics: Collision Course or Virtuous Circle?', *International Organization*, 52, 787–824.

Goldin, Miriam, Michael Wallerstein and Peter Lange (1999). 'Postwar Trade-Union Organization and Industrial Relations in Twelve Countries', in Herbert Kitschelt, Peter Lange, Gary Marks and John Stephens (eds.), *Continuity and Change in Contemporary Capitalism*. New York: Cambridge University Press.

Hall, Peter (1986). *Governing the Economy*. New York: Oxford University Press.

Hall, Peter (1993). 'Policy Paradigms, Social Learning and the State: The Case of Economic Policy-Making in Britain', *Comparative Politics*, 25, 275–96.

Hall, Peter, and Daniel Gingerich (2004). 'Varieties of Capitalism and Institutional Complementarities in the Macroeconomy', Max Planck Institute for the Study of Societies. Discussion Paper 04/5.

Hall, Peter, and David Soskice (2001). *Varieties of Capitalism*. Oxford: Oxford University Press.

Hall, Peter, and Rosemary Taylor (1996). 'Political Science and the Three New Institutionalisms', *Political Studies*, 952–73.

Hall, Peter and Thelen Kathleen (2006). 'Institutional Change in Varieties of Capitalism', paper prepared for presentation to the Europeanists Conference, Chicago, March.

Hancké, Bob, Martin Rhodes and Mark Thatcher (2007). 'Introduction', in Bob Hanké, Martin Rhodes and Mark Thatcher (eds.), *Beyond Varieties of Capitalism*. Oxford: Oxford University Press.

Hay, Colin (2001). 'The "Crisis" of Keynesianism and the Rise of NeoLiberalism in Britain: An Ideational Institutionalist Approach', in John L. Campbell and Ove Pedersen (eds.), *The Rise of NeoLiberalism and Institutional Analysis*. Princeton, NJ: Princeton University Press.

Hay, C., and N.J. Smith (2005). 'Horses for Courses? The Political Discourse of Globalisation and European Integration in the UK and Ireland', *West European Politics*, 28:1, 125–59.

Hayward, Jack (1986). *The State and the Market Economy*. New York: New York University Press.

Hirst, Paul, and Grahame Thompson (2000). 'Globalization in One Country? The Peculiarities of the British', *Economy and Society*, 29:3, 335–56.

Hollingsworth, Roger, Philippe Schmitter and Wolfgang Streeck, eds. (1994). *Governing Capitalist Economies*. Oxford: Oxford University Press.

Howell, Chris (1992). *Regulating Labor: The State and Industrial Relations Reform in Postwar France*. Princeton, NJ: Princeton University Press.

Howell, Chris (1995). 'Trade Unions and the State: A Critique of British Industrial Relations', *Politics and Society*, 23, 149–83.

Immergut, Ellen (1998). 'The Theoretical Core of the New Institutionalism', *Politics and Society*, 26:1, 5–34.

Jabko, Nicolas (2006). *Playing the Market: A Political Strategy for Uniting Europe, 1985–2005*. Ithaca, NY: Cornell University Press.

Jackson, Gregory (2003). 'Corporate Governance in Germany and Japan', in Kozo Yamamura and Wolfgang Streeck (eds.), *The End of Diversity*. Ithaca, NY: Cornell University Press.

Katzenstein, Peter J. (1985). *Small States in World Markets*. Ithaca, NY: Cornell University Press.

King, Desmond, and Stewart Wood (1999). 'The Political Economy of Neoliberalism: Britain and the United States in the 1980s', in H. Kitschelt, Peter Lange, Gary Marks and John Stephens (eds.), *Continuity and Change in Contemporary Capitalism*. New York: Cambridge University Press.

Lane, Christel (2005). 'Institutional Transformation and System Change', in Morgan Glenn, Richard Whitley and Eli Moen (eds.), *Changing Capitalisms?* New York, Oxford: Oxford University Press.

Lange, Peter, and Marino Regini, eds. (1989). *State, Market and Social Regulation: New Perspectives on Italy*. Cambridge: Cambridge University Press.

Lehmbruch, Gerhard (1982). 'Neo-Corporatism in Comparative Perspective', in G. Lehmbruch and P. Schmitter (eds.), *Patterns of Corporatist Policy-Making*. Beverly Hills, CA: Sage Publications.

Lehmbruch, Gerhard, and Phillipe C. Schmitter, eds. (1982). *Patterns of Corporatist Policy-Making*. Beverly Hills, CA: Sage Publications.

Levy, Jonah, ed. (2006). *The State after Statism*. Cambridge, MA: Harvard University Press.

Locke, Richard M. (1995). *Remaking the Italian Economy*. Ithaca, NY: Cornell University Press.

Lütz, Susanne (1998a). 'The Revival of the Nation-State? Stock Exchange Regulation in an Era of Internationalized Financial Markets', *Journal of European Public Policy*, 5, 153–69.

Lütz, Susanne (1998b). 'Convergence within National Diversity: The Regulatory State in Finance', *Journal of Public Policy*, 24:2, 169–97.

Martin, Andrew, and George Ross (2004). *Euros and Europeans*. Cambridge: Cambridge University Press.

Martin, Cathie Jo, and Kathleen Thelen (2006). 'Varieties of Coordination and Trajectories of Change: Social Policy and Economic Adjustment in Coordinated Market Economies', unpublished manuscript.

McNamara, Kathleen (1998). *The Currency of Ideas: Monetary Politics in the European Union*. Ithaca, NY: Cornell University Press.

Molina, Oscar, and Martin Rhodes (2007). 'Conflict, Complementarities and Institutional Change in Mixed Market Economies', in B. Hancké, M. Rhodes and M. Thatcher (eds.), *Beyond Varieties of Capitalism*. Oxford: Oxford University Press.

Moran, Michael (1991). *The Politics of the Financial Services Revolution: The U.S., U.K., and Japan*. New York: St. Martin's Press.

Moran, Michael (2003). *The British Regulatory State*. Oxford: Oxford University Press.

Morgan, Glenn, Richard Whitley and Eli Moen, eds. (2005). *Changing Capitalisms? Internationalization, Institutional Change, and Systems of Economic Organization*. New York, Oxford: Oxford University Press.

Pontusson, Jonas, and Peter Swenson (1996). 'Labor Markets, Production Strategies and Wage-Bargaining Institutions', *Comparative Political Studies*, 28, 117–47.

Radaelli, Claudio M. (2002). 'The Italian State and the Euro', in K. Dyson (ed.), *The European State and the Euro*. Oxford: Oxford University Press.

Rhodes, Martin (1997). 'Globalization, Labour Markets, and Welfare States: A Future of "Competitive Corporatism?"', in Martin Rhodes and Yves Meny (eds.), *The Future of European Welfare*. London: Macmillan.

Rhodes, Martin, and Bastiaan Van Apeldoorn (1997). 'Capitalism versus Capitalism in Western Europe', in Martin Rhodes, Paul Heywood and Vincent Wright (eds.), *Developments in West European Politics*. London: St. Martin's Press.

Rothstein, Bo (2005). *Social Traps and the Problem of Trust*. Cambridge: Cambridge University Press.

Royo, Sebastián (2002). *A New Century of Corporatism?*. Westport, CT and London: Praeger.

Scharpf, Fritz W., and Vivien A. Schmidt eds. (2000). *Welfare and Work in the Open Economy*, 2 vols. Oxford: Oxford University Press.

Schmidt, Vivien A. (1995). 'The New World Order, Incorporated: The Rise of Business and the Decline of the Nation-State', *Daedalus*, 124:2, 75–106.

Schmidt, Vivien A. (1996). *From State to Market?* Cambridge: Cambridge University Press.

Schmidt, Vivien A. (2002). *The Futures of European Capitalism*. Oxford: Oxford University Press.

Schmidt, Vivien A. (2006a). 'Give Peace a Chance: Reconciling the Four (not Three) New Institutionalisms', Paper prepared for presentation for the National meetings of the American Political Science Association (Philadelphia, PA, 31 August–1 September).

Schmidt, Vivien A. (2006b). 'Bringing the State back into the Varieties of Capitalism and Discourse into the Explanation of Change', Paper prepared for presentation for the National meetings of the American Political Science Association (Philadelphia, P PA, 31 August–1 September).

Schmidt, Vivien A. (2007). 'Social Contracts under Siege: National Responses to Globalized and Europeanized Production', in Eva Paus (ed.), *Global Capitalism Unbound: Winners and Losers of Offshore Outsourcing*. Basingstoke: Palgrave Macmillan (forthcoming).

Schmitter, Philippe C. (1989). 'Corporatism is Dead! Long Live Corporatism', *Government and Opposition*, 24:1, 54–73.

Schmitter, Philippe, and Gerhard Lehmbruch, eds. (1979). *Trends towards Corporatist Intermediation*. London: Sage.

Shonfield, Andrew (1965). *Modern Capitalism: The Changing Balance of Public and Private Power*. Oxford: Oxford University Press.

Steinmo, Sven (1993). *Taxation and Democracy*. New Haven, CT: Yale University Press.

Steinmo, Sven, Kathleen Thelen and F. Longstreth, eds. (1992). *Structuring Politics Historical Institutionalism in Comparative Analysis*. Cambridge: Cambridge University Press.

Strange, Susan (1996). *The Retreat of the State*. Cambridge: Cambridge University Press.

Streeck, Wolfgang (1997). 'German Capitalism: Does It Exist? Can It Survive?', in Colin Crouch and Wolfgang Streeck (eds.), *Modern Capitalism or Modern Capitalisms*. London: Pinter.

Streeck, Wolfgang, and Kathleen Thelen (2005). 'Introduction', in Wolfgang Streeck and Kathleen Thelen (eds.), *Beyond Continuity*. Oxford: Oxford University Press.

Swank, Duane (1998). 'Funding the Welfare State: Globalization and the Taxation of Business in Advanced Market Economies', *Political Studies*, 46: 671–92.

Thatcher, Mark (1999). *Politics of Telecommunications*. Oxford: Oxford University Press.

Thelen, Kathleen (1993). 'West European Labor in Transition: Sweden and Germany Compared', *World Politics*, 46, 23–49.

Thelen, Kathleen (1999). 'Historical Institutionalism in Comparative Politics', *Annual Review of Political Science*, vol. 2. Palo Alto, CA: Annual Reviews, Inc.

Thelen, Kathleen (2001). 'Varieties of Labour Politics in the Developed Democracies', in Peter A. Hall and David Soskice (eds.), *Varieties of Capitalism*. Oxford: Oxford University Press.

Thelen, Kathleen (2004). *How Institutions Evolve*. New York: Cambridge University Press.

Thelen, Kathleen, and Ikuo Kume (1999). 'The Effects of Globalization on Labor Revisited: Lessons from Germany and Japan', *Politics and Society*, 27, 477–505.

Vachudova, Milada (2005). *European Undivided*. Oxford: Oxford University Press.

Verdun, Amy (2000). *European Responses to Globalization and Financial Market Integration*. Basingstoke: Macmillan and New York: St. Martin's Press.

Vernon, Raymond (1971). *Sovereignty at Bay*. New York: Basic Books.

Vernon, Raymond (1985). 'Sovereignty at Bay: Ten Years After', in T. Moran (ed.), *Multinational Corporations*. Lexington, MA: D.C. Heath.

Visser, Jelle, and Anton Hemerijck (1997). *A Dutch Miracle*. Amsterdam: Amsterdam University Press.

Vogel, Steven K. (1996). *Freer Markets, More Rules: Regulatory Reform in Advanced Industrial Countries*. Ithaca, NY: Cornell University Press.

Whitley, Richard (2005). 'How National are Business Systems?', in G. Morgan, R. Whitley and E. Moen (eds.), *Changing Capitalisms?* New York and Oxford: Oxford University Press.

Wood, Stewart (2001). 'Business, Government, and Patterns of Labor Market Policy in Britain and the Federal Republic of Germany', in P. Hall and D. Soskice (eds.), *Varieties of Capitalism*. Oxford: Oxford University Press.

Zysman, John (1983). *Governments, Markets, and Growth*. Ithaca, NY: Cornell University Press.

Worlds, Families, Regimes: Country Clusters in European and OECD Area Public Policy

FRANCIS G. CASTLES and HERBERT OBINGER

The idea that the politics and policies of states and nations are distinctively clustered in terms of enduring affinities is as old as type construction in comparative political inquiry. The clustering concept has two strong variants: one where policy affinities are seen as being closely associated with aspects of territoriality – a shared language, a common geography or a common culture – and another where the basis of commonality is manifested in a logic of policy coherence deriving from relatively unchanging structural characteristics, often, but not exclusively, of a socio-economic nature. In other words, national policy profiles are seen as being clustered into different and distinctive 'worlds' either because they share distinct 'family' resemblances – they have similar territorial origins – or because common structures give rise to distinct types of policy 'regime' – they are informed by qualitatively different policy logics. In what follows, the technical term 'clusters' is often preferred to the more metaphorical 'worlds'.

Regime and family variants should not be regarded as mutually exclusive. There is no reason, in principle or in practice, why clustering resulting from territorially derived characteristics should not co-exist with structurally determined policy logics, with the policy effects of the first-past-the-post electoral systems of the English-speaking world a possible example. There is also a much weaker clustering notion, with the term 'world' or 'model' sometimes used to designate membership of a type without any notion of common origins or logically coherent and structured outcomes and, hence, with no implication that such worlds or models will be anything more than evanescent. This article does not discuss worlds or clusters in this much weaker sense.

Of the two strong variants, the regimes concept is, arguably, the most venerable, with a case to be made that such a notion informs Aristotle's classification of constitutional forms in Book IV of *The Politics*, where he suggests that differences in class structure shape diverse constitutional orders with distinctive outcomes in terms of distributive justice. Similar notions of clustering tend to occur wherever an attribution of qualitatively different policy arrangements or outcomes is seen as resulting from deep laid and persistent structuring and it is no accident that the classification of diverse regime types in recent policy research often emerges in the context of analysis informed by class and gender perspectives. It is also no accident that the debate on the proper definition of regime types is most intense where class and gender perspectives intersect, as in the social policy arena.

The territorial conception is of more recent provenance. Its heyday was the late nineteenth and early twentieth centuries, when, in an era in which the nation-state progressively became the paramount focus of political identity, historians, political scientists and popular commentators increasingly made distinctions amongst countries in terms of possession of a common language, a common culture or relationship to a 'mother country' or 'fatherland'. Although modern scholars rarely see such affinities as sufficient explanations for cross-national policy differences, collective proper nouns with territorially specified designations, i.e. 'English-speaking', 'Southern European', 'Nordic', etc., are frequently used in the literature to identify recognised differences in the character of policy outcomes in different groups of nation-states.

Neither the idea of resemblance on the basis of shared national attributes nor that of policy logics proceeding from deep underlying structures prospered in the social sciences in the decades immediately following World War II. The functionalism informing the 'comparative politics movement' of the 1950s and 1960s (Almond 1968) explicitly rejected explanation in terms of institutional forms and legal rules of a kind transparently attributable to territorial transmission mechanisms. Attributions of similarity designated by collective proper nouns were clearly not a part of what was seen as the proper task of comparative analysis: namely, to 'reduce proper names to explanatory variables' (Przeworski 1987: 38–9) and, on those grounds, area studies had to be regarded as being pre-scientific. Moreover, a scientific study of politics had little time for an analysis that could be easily construed as endorsing the kind of national character attributions featuring widely in the rhetoric of pre-war authoritarian politics. Nor, although the causal programme of comparative analysis gave a prominent role to socio-economic causation, was the immediate post-war period particularly hospitable to the kind of class and gender analysis that implied persistent and qualitatively diverse patterning of social and economic relationships over substantial periods of time. The mindset of the structural-functional analysis from which the comparative politics movement was born was initially almost exclusively focused on the factors driving the process of industrial modernisation and not on the factors shaping diverse national 'routes to and through modernity' (Therborn 1995: 5).

The notion that it might be worth investigating the possibility of the existence of a distinctive and enduring clustering of national public policy outcomes only became a part of the comparative public policy mainstream in the early 1990s. While previous research – particularly that emanating from the 'politics matter' school and what remained of area studies after a generation of structural-functional analysis – had frequently noted similarities in the policy patterns of particular groupings of nations defined in terms of their territorial and/or structural attributes,[1] two studies now appeared which provided reasonably exhaustive classifications of advanced Western nations in terms of country clusters with distinctive public policy profiles. The first was Esping-Andersen's *The Three Worlds of Welfare Capitalism* published in 1990, which used measures of the degree of 'decommodification' of pension, sickness and unemployment benefit programmes to identify 'liberal', 'conservative' and 'social democratic' welfare state regimes in 18 advanced Western nations. The second was an edited volume entitled *Families of Nations* published in 1993, in which Frank Castles, Manfred Schmidt, Göran Therborn and a number of other colleagues explored the heuristic value of analysing national public policy patterns in terms of family resemblances between English-speaking, German-speaking and Scandinavian nations.

Both strands of analysis had precursors outside the comparative public policy field. Regime analysis started its life as a political economy response to the prevailing realism of international relations theory, seeking to explain international cooperation amongst groups of nations as the consequence of the existence of regimes defined as 'sets of implicit or explicit principles, rules and decision-making procedures around which actors' expectations converge in a given area of international relations' (Krasner 1982: 186). During the past two decades, 'regime theory' in this sense has become a prominent strand of international relations theory. A similar development took place in urban politics, where 'urban regimes', defined 'as the collaborative arrangements through which local governments and private actors assemble the capacity to govern' (Mossberger and Stoker 2001: 812), are now widely seen as a key to understanding the incorporation of interests in local politics.

An explicit notion of family affinities has not been nearly so prominent in the recent literature. Nevertheless, through the seminal work of Stein Rokkan (1970), the idea that modern nation-states manifest greater or lesser resemblances in virtue of characteristics deeply embedded in their historical trajectories of development and differentiation is one quite familiar to those coming to comparative public policy analysis with a background in comparative politics. In Rokkan's account of the evolution of European nation-building, socio-economic cleavages and centre–periphery relationships have shaped a territorial clustering of European nation-state types, each characterised by distinctive political structures and distinctive patterns of political conflict. If the presumption is that politics matters, it takes but one further step to see these structures and cleavage divisions combining to generate a distinctive policy dynamic that continues to unfold up to the present day.[2]

Because regime analysis in the broad area of policy studies seeks to locate distinctive logics of policy provision, its focus tends to be on specific dependent variables. The main emphasis is on showing that policy arrangements and/or outcomes in a given area of policy are distinctively clustered, with greater or lesser attention paid to the factors conducive to the emergence of such regime clusters. In addition to Esping-Andersen's original welfare regimes typology, which continues to be the topic of the most extensive debate (see Abrahamson 1999; Arts and Gelissen 2002), the comparative public policy literature now includes a wide variety of other regime classifications including 'social assistance regimes' (Gough 2001), 'health policy regimes' (Altenstetter 1992), 'gender policy' (Sainsbury 1999) and 'gender regimes' (Pascall and Lewis 2004), 'production regimes' (varieties of capitalism) (Hollingsworth *et al.* 1994; Soskice 1999; Hall and Soskice 2001), 'labour market regimes' (Traxler and Woitech 2000) and 'tax regimes' (Wagschal 2001). In the realm of economic policy proper, where professional economists often use the regime concept to denote little more than the existence of distinctive sets of policy options, we encounter analyses of 'monetary policy regimes' (a topic with its own very extensive literature), 'competition policy regimes', 'inflation regimes' and 'regulatory regimes'.

Family of nations' attributions are necessarily less policy specific, with the implicit or explicit assumption that territorial clustering shapes policy arrangements and outcomes across a wide spectrum.[3] Despite this lack of specificity, there is, in principle, considerable room for diverse attributions of family resemblance based variously on similarities deriving from affinities of descent, imperial ties, common legal or religious cultures, diffusion and deliberately chosen membership of political and economic unions such as the EU (see Therborn 1993). However, with the exception of this last, many of these potential sources of resemblance overlap to a greater or lesser degree and, at least as far as OECD and European policy comparisons are concerned, usually come down to a fourfold distinction between English-speaking, Scandinavian, continental European and Southern European families of nations initially elaborated in Castles (1998)[4] or to variations on that theme.[5] Widening the perspective somewhat, there has been some speculation that the 2005 enlargement of the existing EU membership to include a new family of Central and East European states may be a barrier to further pan-European policy development (see Goetz 2006), that the relationships of Spain, France and Britain with their former colonies constitute something analogous to family of nations type identities (Brysk *et al.* 2002), and that 'varieties of capitalism' have distinctive families of nations attributes (Amable 2004).

Apart from the elaboration of diverse regime types and diverse bases of family resemblance, the main issues of concern in the clustering literature have tended to relate to the number, defining characteristics and membership of clusters. Arguably, greater effort should have gone into establishing their coherence and persistence. After some 15 years of debate on how many worlds of welfare there might be, whether their dimensions are properly captured by Esping-Andersen's measure of 'decommodification' and how individual countries should be classified, questions are now beginning to be asked about the extent to which the different welfare programmes Esping-Andersen analysed are interrelated and whether patterns of policy outcomes observed a quarter of a century previously (Esping-Andersen's data were from 1980) persist into the present. Those questions do not yield reassuring answers. A paper by Scruggs and Allan, replicating Esping-Andersen's data and bringing it up to date, suggests that 'clustering is, at best, very weak' and that 'there are not elective affinities within countries' social insurance programmes, an assumption on which the whole notion of distinctive regimes rests' (Scruggs and Allen 2006: 68–9). Another paper replicating Esping-Andersen's findings points out that the identification of three rather than some other number of worlds of welfare is a statistical artefact of the classificatory method employed[6] and that an updated decommodification index does not suggest similar clustering today (see Bambra 2006).

Since the majority of elaborations of regime types in the policy literature pay no more attention to issues of coherence and persistence than the Esping-Andersen study,[7] undue confidence in their findings is unwarranted. There has, however, been a replication study of Castles' four families' typology identifying distinctive English-speaking, Scandinavian, continental European and Southern European patterns of outcomes across a wide range of policy areas. This study explicitly employs cluster analysis techniques to establish the existence of coherent policy profiles using a combination of social policy, labour market and tax policy indicators as outcome variables for the 1960–73, 1974–95 and 1960–95 periods covered by Castles' research. The study concludes not only that 'the hypothesised families of nations can be shown to exist', but also that 'they are quite robust and stable over time' (Obinger and Wagschal 2001: 99).

These findings confirm the existence, coherence and persistence of country clusters of a family of nations' kind during much of the post-World War II era. They leave open, however, two important questions, which this article seeks to explore. First, whilst the persistence of 1960–73 policy clusters into the period 1974–95 demonstrates the longevity of these families of nations patterns, it offers no guarantee that such patterns continue to exist into the first decade of the twenty-first century. There are, of course, strong theoretical arguments that the joint influences of globalisation, convergence and Europeanisation have diminished cross-national policy differences over recent decades. One question, then, is whether distinctive country clusters have survived such ostensibly massive levelling influences. Second, the political and economic boundaries of Europe have changed appreciably since the mid-1990s. Of the 21 countries classified into families of nations in Castles' (1998) analysis and revisited in the Obinger and Wagschal (2001) replication study, five were from outside Europe and only 12 were members of the EU. Since that time EU membership has more than doubled, with the largest influx of new members coming from the former communist nations of Central and Eastern Europe. A further question, then, is whether the four cluster pattern of public policy outcomes characterising Europe in the immediate post-war decades is in the process of being modified or superseded either by the addition of new family clusters or by the disappearance of old ones.

In the remainder of this article we investigate the extent of clustering of public policy outcomes and the persistence of such clustering over time. We also examine the further question of whether there is a correspondence between the clustering of policy outcomes and of economic, social and political antecedents as presumed in the regimes literature, but here manifested across a very much wider range of policies than implied in that literature, i.e. we ask whether there are worlds of structural antecedents as well as worlds of public policy. Finally we examine the extent of policy clustering in the EU-25. In the next section, we discuss briefly the strategy of comparison that informs our analysis and the methods and data on which our findings are based.

Strategy, Methods and Data

We base our investigation of the presence and persistence of distinct worlds of public policy on comparisons of 20 advanced OECD democracies[8] over two separate time periods using the techniques of hierarchical and k-means cluster analysis. We use averaged data for separate time periods rather than single years in order to reduce the risk of distortions resulting from exogenous shocks or country-specific idiosyncrasies.

The logic informing our strategy of comparison is as follows. First, we seek to establish the existence of policy clusters for the period 1960–75, often referred to as the 'golden age' of post-war capitalism and of the welfare state. Next, and using the same set of variables, we repeat this exercise for the early years of the new millennium. Hence, we have a time span of approximately 25 years between the two periods of observation over which to test for the persistence of country clustering. During this period, the international political economy and the political landscape of Europe have undergone fundamental transformations. More specifically, this period has witnessed the collapse of communism, a deepening European integration, a marked societal modernisation and an ever increasing economic globalisation. These remarkable changes have undoubtedly led to new challenges for public governance that could very well have contributed to a Rokkanian 'unfreezing' of distinct worlds of public policy.

A potential mechanism for such a blurring of worlds might be a process of policy convergence, clearly demonstrated as occurring across a wide range of public expenditure arenas over the past quarter of a century (see Castles 2007), but not evenly across all areas of public policy (see Starke *et al.*, forthcoming). Reasons for increasing similarity in policy outcomes are not difficult to discern and include (i) the legal harmonisation resulting from EU integration, (ii) the regulatory competition induced by globalisation, (iii) the similarity of problem pressures fuelled by societal modernisation (e.g. 'new social risks' and changed demographics), (iv) the imposition of policies by international organisations (e.g. in Eastern Europe) and (v) policy diffusion triggered by increasing transnational communication (see Holzinger and Knill 2005). It should be noted, however, that policy convergence, even where it does occur, does not automatically produce a diminution in the distinctiveness of country groupings. If country clusters become more internally homogeneous with the passage of time, they may persist – and acquire a greater distinctiveness – as countries in general become more alike in their policy outcomes.

European integration has been accompanied by a substantial increase in the number of EU member states. Leaving aside the intrinsic virtues of greater integration, a major advantage of enlargement for public policy comparison has been the increase in the number of countries for which comparative data on policy outcomes are available. This means that we can now go beyond the limits of the normal OECD policy comparison, using Eurostat data to locate patterns of policy affinity in a wider Europe. Unfortunately, we cannot fully replicate our OECD two-period comparison due to lack of data for the earlier period. However, our analysis of contemporary policy patterns in the EU-25 does allow us to investigate the extent of policy clustering in the new Europe.

A further issue we seek to address concerns the nature of the mechanisms underlying country clustering. Our conclusions here will be admittedly tentative. Regimes theory suggests a correspondence between structural antecedents and specific policy outcomes. The family of nations hypothesis suggests that the range of policy similarities is much wider, but does not deny the possibility that these similarities are mediated via structural similarities nations may have in virtue of language, culture, history and geography. Here, we seek to establish whether OECD policy clusters correspond with a similar clustering of political, societal and economic circumstances in the immediate post-war decades. A demonstration that such a correspondence exists is not a decisive test of whether regimes theory or a family of nations interpretation provides the most persuasive account of clustering patterns. Certainly, such a correspondence would show that the structural determination of policy outcomes is plausible, but over a much wider ambit than generally presupposed in much of the regimes literature. Assuming that the clustering identified has strong territorial characteristics, an appropriate conclusion might be that family of nations affinities are frequently manifested through structural mechanisms that are conducive to the emergence of cognate regime clusters in different policy areas.

The method we use to establish the existence of worlds is hierarchical cluster analysis, which is an exploratory data analysis tool for solving classification problems. The main goal of this method is to discover a structure within a given data set that can be visualised by means of a dendrogram. This technique is a simple heuristic tool which seeks to discern clusters showing great internal homogeneity – or what, in the context of this discussion, we label as worlds, families and regimes. In other words, the goal is to identify a set of clusters such that units of observations within a cluster are more similar to each other than they are to cases in other clusters. The advantage of hierarchical cluster analysis compared to non-hierarchical k-means cluster analysis is that we do not have to predetermine the number of clusters. In consequence, the clustering obtained by this method is exclusively data-determined and therefore fits the underlying purpose of this article to identify clustering as it occurs or fails to occur in the real world.

A disadvantage is that this method is sensitive to the set of variables used. Therefore, in order to avoid the accusation that we have predetermined our findings by our prior selection of variables, we have selected outcomes variables featuring prominently in the international discussion of policy regimes and families of nations and antecedents variables identified by the main schools of thought of comparative public policy research (see Castles 1998; Schmidt 1996). Another disadvantage is that the hierarchical clustering technique does not tell us which variables contribute most to the distinctiveness of the clusters identified in the analysis. To gain some leverage on this issue, we also undertake k-means analyses, using F-tests as a means of identifying the variables driving the clustering of outcomes.

Hierarchical cluster analysis proceeds as follows. In a first step, z-scores for all variables subject to cluster analysis are computed in order to standardise the data. Next, either a measure of similarity or a distance measure for all variables and all units of observation (in our case countries) is calculated. We have chosen a distance measure, namely the squared Euclidean distance, which is the sum of the squared differences between the scores for any pair of cases on all variables. Based on the resulting distance matrix, the units of observations are then combined (fused) into clusters in an iterative process until all cases have been assigned to a particular cluster.

The logic of fusion is determined by a clustering algorithm. We use the Ward method which determines cluster membership on the basis of the total sum of squared deviations from the mean of a cluster.

In order to improve the coherence of the findings, we have used the same set of variables for our initial inquiry of policy clusters and their persistence over time. In total, we use 16 outcome variables to examine the existence of worlds of public policy in 20 OECD nations and 15 variables for the 25 EU countries. The variables selected map the size of government, distinct spending priorities of governments (e.g. spending on education, industrial subsidies, welfare and defence), the mode of public expenditure financing, economic and labour market performance and gender-related outcomes. This final policy dimension is measured by female labour market participation and the total fertility rate.

The analysis that aims to identify the factors shaping policy clusters is also based on a substantial number of variables (15 for the first period; 14 for the second) derived from the major schools of thought of comparative public policy research. More specifically, the variables reflect social and cultural characteristics (demographics, ethno-linguistic fractionalization and religious adherence), levels of economic development (GDP per capita, agricultural employment), the distribution of power resources (partisan complexion of government, party system fractionalisation, union density), the system of interest mediation and the institutionally mediated horizontal and vertical division of power. Definitions and sources for all the data used in analysis of policy antecedents are to be found in Appendices A3 and A4.

Findings

Patterns of Public Policy (1960–75)

We commence our analysis with a cluster analysis of cross-national public policy outcomes for the period from 1960 to 1975. The cluster tree (or dendrogram) for these outcomes is displayed in Figure 1.

The cluster tree should be interpreted as follows. The more one moves to the right on the x-axis, the more dissimilar are the clusters. Hence, long cluster lines indicate marked dissimilarities between the clusters. Figure 1 strongly supports the idea of the existence of distinct worlds of public policy. First, there is a cluster consisting of all continental countries plus Italy. The three – at the time less developed and less democratic – countries of Southern Europe make up a cluster of their own, which is quite distinct from all other groups of nations. A third cluster is composed of the Nordic countries plus the UK, whereas Ireland is an outlier that joins this group at a later stage. The location of the UK in the Nordic cluster is, at first glance, surprising. However, Britain's similarity to the Nordic countries can be explained by the policy legacy of the post-war Labour government and the fact that the Nordic policy cluster appears rooted in a Lib–Lab power constellation that, at the time, was also prevalent in Britain. The

FIGURE 1
PATTERNS OF PUBLIC POLICY (ca. 1960–75)

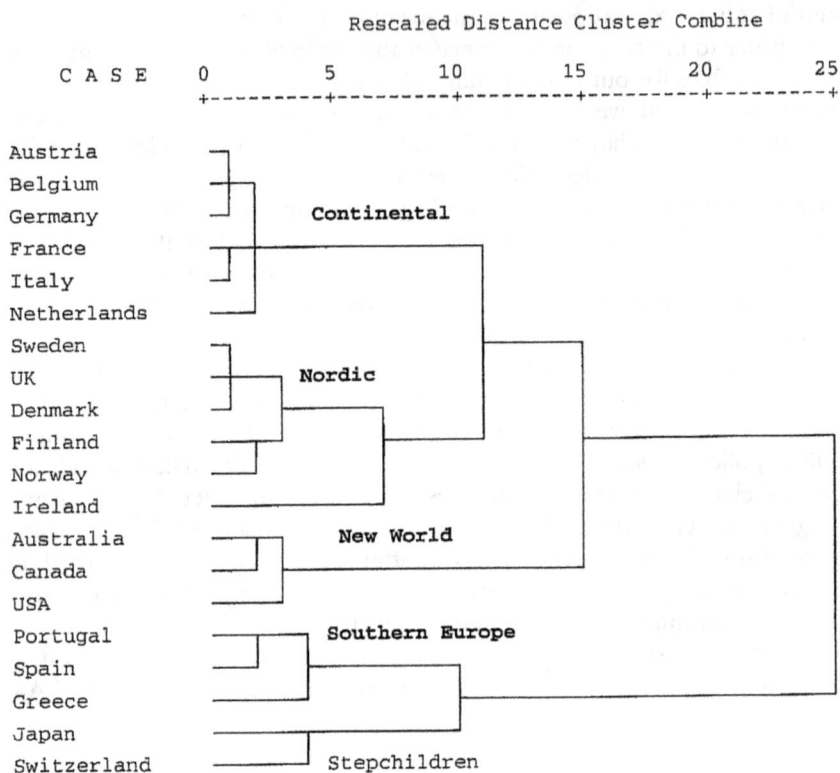

Notes: Dendrogram using Ward Method and squared Euclidean Distances; Variables are listed in Appendix A1.

British settler colonies, by contrast, form a quite distinct cluster. Finally, and fully in accordance with a families of nations interpretation, Switzerland and Japan are clear outliers that do not belong to any of the particular families. That said, these countries' closest resemblance is to the policy profile of the countries of Southern Europe characterised by a non-interventionist stance in economic and social affairs and by a focus on rapid economic development.

Patterns of Public Policy (early 2000s)

The second step in our analysis is to undertake a cluster analysis of public policy patterns at the turn to the twenty-first century. Using the same set of variables as in the previous analysis allows us to examine whether or not the clustering of nations has changed over time. Figure 2 reveals several striking results. To begin with, there is no evidence of a blurring of regimes or families of nations. Rather the contrary is true since the boundaries between the distinct worlds of public policy have become even more clear-cut over

FIGURE 2
PATTERNS OF PUBLIC POLICY (ca. 2000–2004)

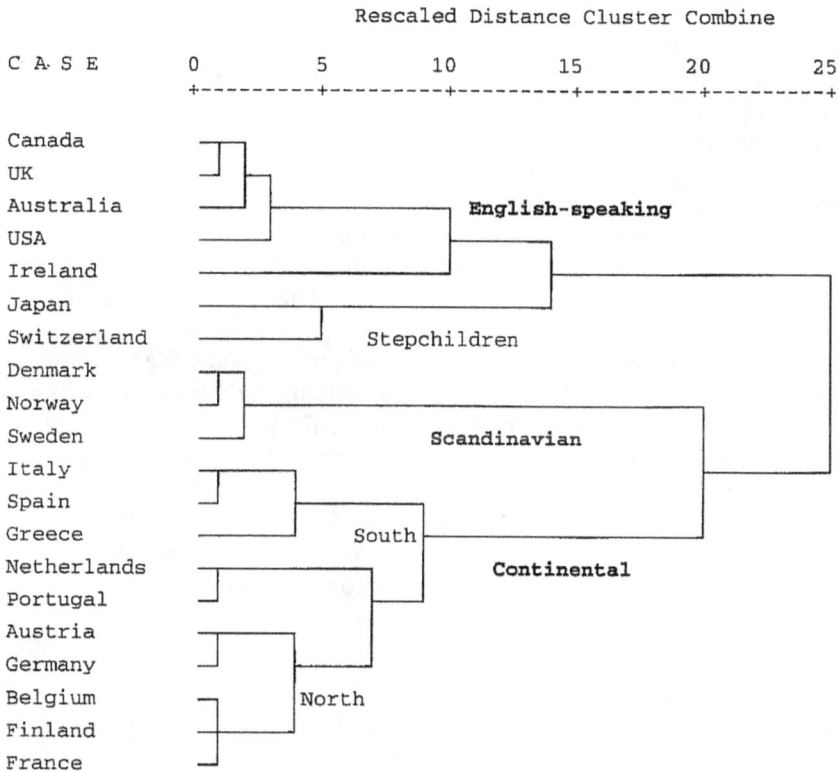

Rescaled Distance Cluster Combine

```
C A S E       0       5      10      15      20      25
              +--------+--------+--------+--------+--------+

Canada        ┐┐
UK            ┘│
Australia      │         English-speaking
USA            │
Ireland
Japan
Switzerland            Stepchildren
Denmark       ┐┐
Norway        ┘│
Sweden         │         Scandinavian
Italy         ┐┐
Spain         ┘│
Greece         │   South
Netherlands   ┐┐          Continental
Portugal      ┘│
Austria       ┐┐
Germany       ┘│
Belgium       ┐  North
Finland       ┤
France        ┘
```

Notes: Dendrogram using Ward Method and squared Euclidean Distances; Variables are listed in Appendix A2.

time, with convergence within clusters exceeding that of the sample as a whole. The UK and Ireland are now part of the English-speaking cluster, albeit Ireland clearly deviates from the remaining English-speaking countries. A comparison between Figures 1 and 2 is strongly supportive of a remarkable persistence of distinct policy regimes or families of nations.

A caveat of some significance, however, is the fact that the countries of Southern Europe have become more similar in their policy outcomes to those of continental Western Europe, There nevertheless remains a visible divide between the northern and southern countries located in the cluster. Two further changes are also worth mentioning. First, in the new millennium Finland is, in policy terms, no longer part of the Nordic family, but has become a member of the continental family. Thus, the distinctive policy family of North-Western Europe is now exclusively Scandinavian in character. Second, Switzerland and Japan remain outliers, but now show greater similarities with the policy profile of the English-speaking than the continental countries.

In sum, the clustering of nations identified in Figure 2 is not only highly congruent with the families of nations concept, but also with Esping-Andersen's 'three worlds' classification (Esping-Andersen 1990). Figure 2 displays a continental or conservative world of policy, a Scandinavian or social democratic cluster and an English-speaking or liberal world to which Japan and Switzerland are affiliated. A four family account rests on the fact that Southern Europe is not yet fully assimilated into the continental Western Europe cluster; a three worlds account on the fact that the Southern European and continental European clusters are clearly now converging. Irrespective of the account that is preferred, what is most remarkable is the persistence of the clustering of nations over time despite fundamental transformations of the international and domestic political economy over the past quarter of a century.

Figure 2 suggests three distinct clusters of public policy. We now use this information to run a k-means analysis specifying a three-cluster solution. Table 1 reports the cluster centres by variable for the final cluster solution. Note that the clustering is more or less identical to the results obtained by hierarchical cluster analysis.

The F-test statistics indicated by asterisks in Table 1 tell us which variables are significant in accounting for differences between the clusters. Interestingly, most of the indicators of economic performance as well as the

TABLE 1
CLUSTER CENTRES BY VARIABLES (K =3)

Variable	Cluster centres by variable		
	1 English (liberal)	2 Continental (conservative)	3 Scandinavian (social democratic)
Total fertility rate*	1.7	1.4	1.6
Military spending	1.6	2.0	1.7
Subsidies	1.3	1.4	1.8
Public education expenditure*	4.7	4.9	6.5
Total tax revenues*	31.2	40.2	47.8
Taxes on income and profits*	43.8	29.3	45.7
Taxes on goods and services	26.3	29.9	29.7
Social security contributions*	19.0	33.6	20.2
Total disbursements of government*	37.2	48.2	52.3
Inflation	2.0	2.5	2.0
Unemployment	5.2	7.7	5.7
Female labour market participation*	68.4	59.8	76.0
Male labour market participation*	86.2	79.2	82.5
Government employment*	14.8	15.4	29.6
Economic growth	2.13	1.87	1.95
Social security transfers*	11.1	15.6	16.5

Notes: English = Australia, Canada, Ireland, Japan, Switzerland, UK, USA.
Continental = Austria, Belgium, France, Germany, Greece, Italy, Netherlands, Portugal, Spain.
Nordic = Denmark, Finland, Norway, Sweden.
Variables that are marked with an asterisk indicate that the ANOVA F-test is significant at a level p ≤ .05. Variables are listed in Appendix A2.

measures of military and subsidy spending do not differ significantly between the different groups of nations. What really matters in shaping the distinctiveness of clusters is the overall size of government, educational and social spending levels, labour market outcomes, the tax structure and the fertility rate. Among the various tax variables, the major watershed between clusters is the relative share of social security contributions and of taxes levied on income and profits. Many, although not all, of these variables feature in various adumbrations of Esping-Andersen's three worlds account and it therefore comes as little surprise that the patterns of public policy identified in Figure 2 closely resemble those specified by his regimes classification.

The Origins of Public Policy Patterns (1945–75)

The next step in our analysis is to investigate similarities between patterns of OECD policy outcomes and their antecedents. As noted previously, the demonstration of an isomorphic relationship between underlying structures and broad patterns of policy outcomes is not sufficient to distinguish between family of nations and regime interpretations, precisely because the assumption of the territorial approach is that territorial contiguities are likely to have structural and institutional consequences that feed into policy outcomes. What such an isomorphic relationship between territorially defined clusters and structural antecedents would demonstrate is the plausibility of regime theory's insistence on the structural determination of policy outcomes and the strength of the family of nations argument that territorially distinctive structural antecedents produce territorially distinctive policy outcomes across a broad front.

To investigate a possible correspondence between the clustering of structural antecedents and of policy outcomes in the immediate post-war period, we have used the 15 variables listed in Appendix A3. The data cover the period from 1945 to 1975, building in an element of time-lag for the determination of outcomes. The nations of Southern Europe are excluded from the analysis due to gaps in the data for this period. However, given the marked divergence in the developmental status of these countries during these years, there can be absolutely no question that they would constitute a distinct cluster in economic, social, cultural and political terms until the mid-1970s at least.

The resulting cluster tree shown in Figure 3 manifests a striking resemblance to the dendrogram depicting policy outcomes in the period 1960 to 1975 (see Figure 1 above). Once more we can identify an English-speaking cluster (plus France), a continental group of nations (which now includes Switzerland) and a Scandinavian cluster. There is, however, an additional cluster consisting of a territorially heterogeneous group of nations. What these countries (Japan, Italy, Finland and Ireland) have in common is that they have all been laggards in economic development terms.

FIGURE 3
CLUSTER ORIGINS (1945/60–75)

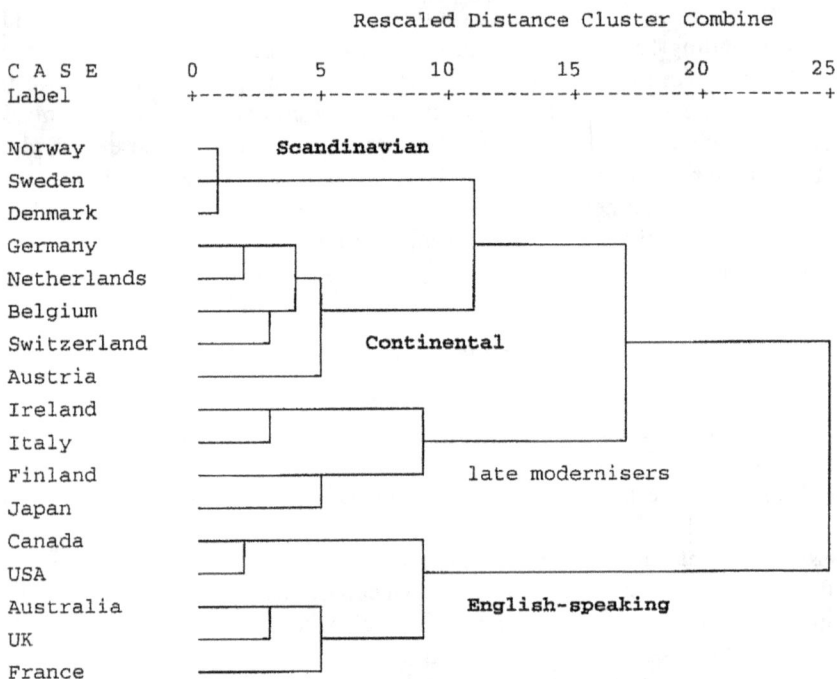

Rescaled Distance Cluster Combine

```
C A S E        0         5        10        15        20        25
Label          +---------+---------+---------+---------+---------+

Norway           ─┐    Scandinavian
Sweden            ├┐
Denmark          ─┘│
Germany        ─┐  │
Netherlands    ─┤ ─┤
Belgium         │  │
Switzerland    ─┘  │   Continental
Austria         ───┤
Ireland        ─┐  │
Italy          ─┤  │
Finland        ──┤      late modernisers
Japan          ──┘
Canada         ─┐
USA            ─┤
Australia      ─┤      English-speaking
UK             ─┘
France         ───
```

Notes: Dendrogram using Ward Method and squared Euclidean Distances; Variables are listed in Appendix A3.

Interestingly, as the previous analysis has shown (see Figures 1 and 2), three of these countries have switched between different outcomes clusters over time, presumably as a consequence of the rapid economic development resulting from their delayed modernisation.

Overall, the analysis demonstrates a strong affinity between antecedents and outcomes. A major exception is France, which manifests structural similarities to the countries of the English-speaking cluster, while the country's policy profile shows strong continental traits. Arguably, this discrepancy results from the continuing legacy of the French Revolution, manifested in the absence of characteristically continental, Christian democratic parties, low union density, and the presence of a highly centralised state structure. A second exception is Switzerland, which is part of the continental cluster in terms of structural antecedents, but shows an affinity to a different world of public policy. Obinger and Wagschal (2001) have argued that this pattern is likely to have been influenced by Switzerland's unique political institutions, notably the far greater importance of referendums than in any of the other countries of the OECD.[9]

We now move on to examine policy antecedents for the period from 1985 to 2004 with a view to establishing whether the clustering of structural antecedents we have just identified persists over time and whether it continues to correspond with outcomes clustering. With the exception of the variable measuring ethno-linguistic fractionalisation, which is only available for the early 1960s, we use the same set of variables as in the previous analysis. The resulting cluster tree is reported in Figure 4. A comparison with Figure 3 shows that the contemporary clustering of regime origins is now more clear-cut and almost perfectly in line with the notion of families of nations. The late modernisers, which had formed a distinct group in the immediate post-war period (see Figure 3), have been absorbed by the 'correct' family of nations, whereas the 'stepchild' Japan has been adopted by the English-speaking family. Note that the former autocracies of Southern Europe, which were not included in the previous analysis, form a cluster of their own. Even more important, however, is the fact that the patterns identified again point to a close correspondence between structural antecedents and patterns of public policy.

FIGURE 4
CLUSTER ORIGINS (1985 – ca. 2004)

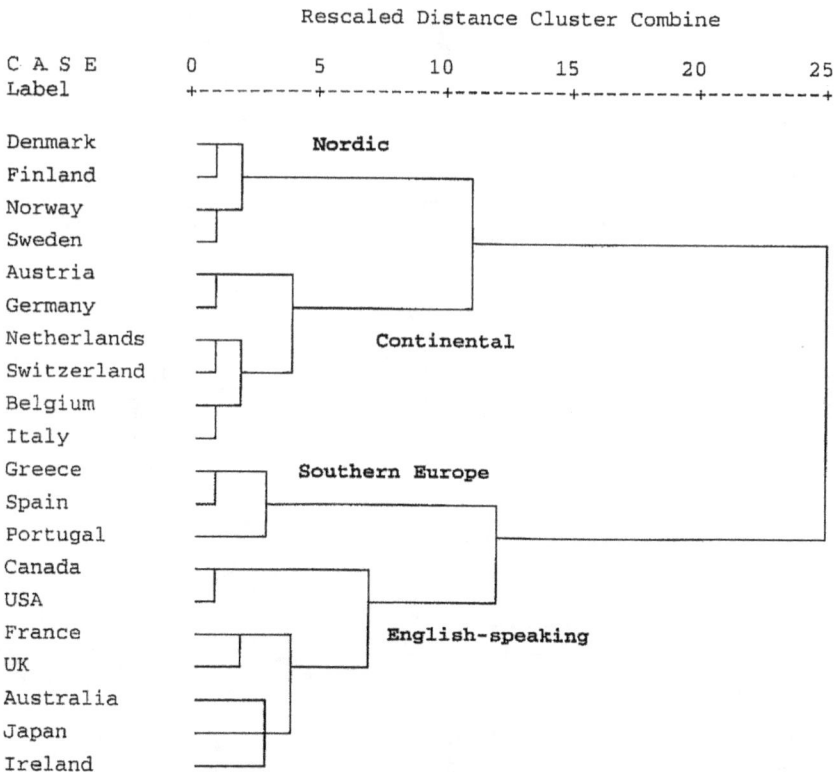

Notes: Dendrogram using Ward Method and squared Euclidean Distances; Variables are listed in Appendix A4.

Patterns of Public Policy in the EU-25

In this final section of our findings, we examine the existence of worlds of public policy amongst the 25 member states of the European Union. With the exception of military expenditure, we use similar (but not always identically defined) variables as those featuring in our previous analysis of the OECD democracies. Hence, our cluster analysis is based on 15 variables and covers the period between 2000 and 2005.

The cluster tree reported in Figure 5 suggests that the recent eastern enlargement of the EU has added a quite distinctive new world of public policy to the already existing country clusters of Western Europe. Leaving Malta and Cyprus to one side, the new member states form a coherent policy cluster that may appropriately be described as 'post-Communist'. Interestingly, within this cluster may be distinguished two distinct

FIGURE 5
PATTERNS OF PUBLIC POLICY IN THE EU-25 (CA. 2000–2005)

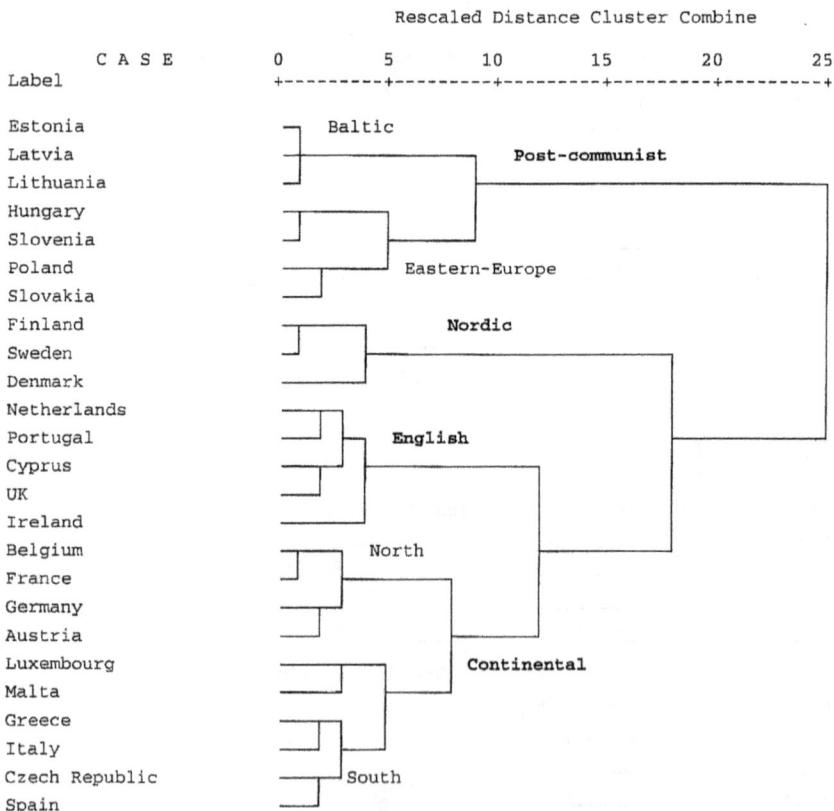

Notes: Dendrogram using Ward Method and squared Euclidean Distances; Variables are listed in Appendix A5.

sub-worlds. Very much as one might expect on the basis of a families of nations approach, we may identify a Baltic cluster consisting of Latvia, Estonia and Lithuania and another cluster comprising the countries of Eastern Europe with the notable exception of the Czech Republic. Together these groupings form a super-cluster exhibiting marked policy contrasts as compared to other EU members.

The cluster groupings of the remaining countries are, in most respects, similar to those identified in Figure 2. Once again, it is possible to locate a distinct Nordic cluster and a continental cluster, again consisting of distinguishable northern and southern sub-clusters. The fact that the Czech Republic is part of the continental cluster should come as little surprise, given policy origins owing much to cultural diffusion from Germany and Austria in the late nineteenth and early twentieth centuries. That the country is now a member of the southern sub-cluster is a legacy of a suppressed modernisation stemming from the Communist period. One important difference from Figure 2 that should be noted and which is discussed further below is that, while England and Ireland still feature as part of a distinctive cluster, that cluster now also includes Portugal, Cyprus and the Netherlands and is defined less in territorial terms than by emergent policy similarities.

The final step in the analysis is to attempt to identify the factors contributing to the distinctiveness of the EU-25 clusters located in Figure 5. Again, we use k-means cluster analysis and F-tests for this purpose, specifying a five-cluster solution as shown in Table 2. It should be noted, however, that, in this instance, the k-means analysis produces a somewhat changed composition of clusters as compared to that resulting from the hierarchical cluster analysis on which Figure 5 is based (see country clusters as specified in the notes to Table 2).

The most notable finding of Table 2 is the very clear distinctiveness of a somewhat attenuated post-Communist family of nations manifesting extreme values in respect of nearly all the variables shaping the clustering of EU-25 policy patterns. These nations are the least statist in the EU (low outlays, low transfers, low subsidies and low direct taxes), manifest the greatest economic and social problems (low male labour force participation, high inflation, massive unemployment and low fertility), but, at the same time, exhibit much the highest rates of economic growth. An optimistic interpretation might suggest that high growth rates may ultimately be the key to diminishing some of these other aspects of policy distinctiveness in much the same way as occurred in the New Southern Europe in the years following the EU enlargement of the 1980s.

The other interesting point to note is that Table 2 provides empirical substance for the source of distinctiveness of the wider grouping to which the English-speaking nations now belong. In Table 1, the English-speaking countries of the old and new worlds are clustered together as the nations exhibiting much the lowest degree of statism (the lowest levels of public disbursements, social security transfers, low educational spending and low

TABLE 2
CLUSTER CENTRES BY VARIABLES (K = 5)

	Cluster centres by variable				
	1 Continental (north)	**2** Continental (south)	**3** Scandinavian	**4** English	**5** Post- Communist
Total fertility rate*	1.51	1.34	1.71	1.60	1.28
Employment public sector	7.37	7.67	5.78	7.39	6.44
Social security contributions*	32.77	29.02	14.70	25.92	30.71
Direct taxes*	26.24	26.83	43.08	29.20	20.92
Indirect taxes	29.91	32.16	29.60	32.64	34.31
Inflation	3.13	2.91	1.81	2.74	3.86
Unemployment*	7.31	9.24	5.35	4.89	14.32
Education expenditure*	5.66	4.34	7.88	4.94	5.28
Subsidies	1.69	1.04	1.93	1.31	.96
Male employment*	69.62	72.47	77.33	76.72	62.96
Social transfers*	16.80	14.52	17.01	11.95	11.35
Total tax revenues*	43.39	37.63	50.63	36.09	31.49
Female employment*	57.67	41.30	71.43	59.12	54.42
Outlays of government*	49.47	45.14	55.87	42.05	38.20
Economic growth*	2.56	2.59	2.19	3.23	6.15

Notes: Continental (north) = Austria, Belgium, Germany, Finland, France, Hungary, Slovenia.
Continental (south) = Greece, Italy, Spain, Malta.
Scandinavian = Denmark, Sweden.
English = Ireland, UK, Czech Republic, Portugal, Netherlands, Luxembourg, Cyprus.
Eastern Europe = Estonia, Latvia, Lithuania, Poland, Slovakia.
Variables that are marked with an asterisk indicate that the ANOVA F-test is significant at a level $p \leq .05$; Variables are listed in Appendix A5.

government employment). In Table 2, with the new world English-speaking countries no longer in the picture, England and Ireland still find themselves in a grouping characterised by a degree of statism lower than in the majority of continental and Scandinavian countries, but at least marginally greater than that of the countries of the post-Communist EU periphery and without these latter countries' economic and social problems or growth rate performance. In the EU of 25, the 'awfulness of the English' (see note 3) has been replaced by post-Communist exceptionalism and post-Communist malaise.

Conclusion

In the introduction to this article we argued that there were two outstanding questions raised by the literature on policy clustering in advanced nations: first, whether the strong family of nations patterns clearly discernable amongst OECD nations up to the mid-1990s had persisted into the early years of the new millennium and, second, whether the latest stage in the enlargement of the EU had led to the addition of new families of nations or the disappearance of old ones. The answers provided by our cluster analysis are unequivocal. Within the OECD, and despite convergence trends in respect of many variables, families of nations have, if anything, become more distinct with the passage of time, with only the diminishing distinctiveness of continental and Southern European outcomes patterns suggestive of a blurring of cluster boundaries already clearly defined in the early pre-war decades. Within the new boundaries of the EU, all the previously existing families of nations are present, but are now joined by a still more distinctive post-Communist family, with clearly defined Baltic and Eastern European sub-types. Convergence trends including European integration may have made nations more alike in certain respects, but the evidence presented here suggests that they have not succeeded in extinguishing policy differences between groups of nations stemming directly or indirectly from characteristics shaped by aspects of territoriality.

The direct evidence of territorial or family of nations clustering is simply the fact that that groups of nations we know to be linked by language, history, culture and geography are so frequently identified as falling into the same clusters by a technique that is exclusively data-determined, that these clusters persist over time and that they are replicated for policy outcomes and for policy antecedents. That said, the very fact of the strong correspondence between outcomes and antecedents demonstrated here does vindicate an important aspect of regime theory; namely that the persistence of policy clusters is, to a significant degree, a function of the persistence of underlying structural characteristics. However, we do not consider the fact that outcome clusters are often structurally determined as evidence against a family of nations interpretation, since the very fact that structural differences cluster in much the same way as outcomes provides further strong indirect evidence of the shaping influence of territorially linked variables. As we have insisted throughout, regime interpretations and family of nations interpretations are not necessarily in conflict, with the most sensible ordering of concepts, given that most regime attributions are policy specific and that family of nations' attributions have a much wider policy span, being that regimes are specific policy manifestations of structurally mediated family of nations differences. The coherence and persistence of family of nations patterns and their structural determination have been amply demonstrated in this article.

Notes

1. An instance is the article by Castles (1978), appearing in the first number of *West European Politics*, which sought to identify the political antecedents of the Scandinavian countries' outstanding welfare state performance.
2. See, for an explicitly Rokkanian analysis of contemporary European welfare state development, Ferrera (2005).
3. For instance, Castles (1993) identifies commonalities amongst the English-speaking nations in respect of poor economic performance, low welfare spending and high divorce rates justifying an earlier attribution of the 'awfulness of the English(-speaking nations)' in Castles and Merrill (1989).

4. Essentially, Esping-Andersen's three worlds of welfare plus Southern Europe. The debate on whether there is a distinctive Southern European welfare state type has been an important theme in the comparative social policy literature since the early 1990s (see Leibfried 1993; Esping-Andersen 1993; Castles 1995; Ferrera 1996).
5. See, for instance, Stockard and O'Brien's (2006) distinction between 'English-speaking', 'Romanist', 'Germanic' and 'Nordic' families.
6. Outcomes are grouped according to whether they are within one standard deviation of the mean, more than one standard deviation above or more than one below.
7. Exceptions are studies like those of Gough (2001) and Powell and Barrientos (2004), which use cluster analysis techniques to test for coherence. The latter study of types of 'welfare mix' focuses on different dimensions and measures of welfare from those featuring in the three worlds typology, but derives a very similar regime clustering and one which is shown to be persistent over time.
8. Australia, Austria, Belgium, Canada, Denmark, Finland, France, Germany, Greece, Ireland, Italy, Japan, Netherlands, Norway, Portugal, Spain, Sweden, Switzerland, United Kingdom and United States.
9. Note that direct democracy is not included in the set of variables underlying the analysis of regime origins.

References

Abrahamson, P. (1999). 'The Welfare Modelling Business', *Social Policy and Administration*, 33:4, 394–415.
Almond, G.A. (1968). 'Comparative Politics', in *International Encyclopedia of the Social Sciences*. New York: Macmillan, 13, 331–6.
Altenstetter, C. (1992). 'Health Policy Regimes and the Single European Market', *Journal of Health Politics, Policy and Law*, 17:4, 813–46.
Amable, B. (2004). *The Diversity of Modern Capitalism*. Oxford: Oxford University Press.
Armingeon, K., P. Leimgruber, M. Beyeler and S. Menegale (2006). *Comparative Political Data Set (1960–2004)*. Bern: Institut für Politikwissenschaft, Universität Bern.
Arts, W., and J. Gelissen (2002). 'Three Worlds of Welfare Capitalism or More? A State-of-the-Art Report', *Journal of European Social Policy*, 12:2, 137–58.
Bambra, C. (2006). 'Decommodification and the Worlds of Welfare Revisited', *Journal of European Social Policy*, 16:1, 73–80.
Brysk, A., C. Parsons and W. Sandholtz (2002). 'After Empire: National Identity and Post-Colonial Families of Nations', *European Journal of International Relations*, 8:2, 267–305.
Castles, F.G. (1978). 'Scandinavian Social Democracy: Achievements and Problems', *West European Politics*, 1:1, 11–29.
Castles, F.G., ed. (1993). *Families of Nations: Patterns of Public Policy in Western Democracies*. Aldershot: Dartmouth, 31–49.
Castles, F.G. (1995). 'Welfare State Development in Southern Europe', *West European Politics*, 18:2, 291–313.
Castles, F.G. (1998). *Comparative Public Policy: Patterns of Post-war Transformation*. Cheltenham: Edward Elgar.
Castles, F.G. (2003). 'The World Turned Upside Down: Below Replacement Fertility, Changing Preferences and Family-friendly Policies in 21 OECD Countries', *Journal of European Social Policy*, 13:3, 209–27.
Castles, F.G., ed. (2007) *The Disappearing State? Retrenchment Realities in an Age of Globalisation. Cheltenham*: Edward Elgar.
Castles, F.G., and V. Merrill (1989). 'Towards a General Model of Public Policy Outcomes', *Journal of Theoretical Politics*, 1:2, 177–212.
Cusack, Thomas R. (2007). 'Sinking Budgets and Ballooning Prices: Recent Developments Connected to Military Spending', in F.G. Castles (ed.), *The Disappearing State? Retrenchment Realities in an Age of Globalisation*. Cheltenham: Edward Elgar.

Esping-Andersen, G. (1990). *The Three Worlds of Welfare Capitalism*. Oxford: Polity Press.

Esping-Andersen, G. (1993). 'Budgets and Democracy: Towards a Welfare State in Spain and Portugal, 1960–1986', in I. Budge and D. McKay (eds.), *Expanding Democracy: Research in Honour of Jean Blondel*. London: Sage.

Ferrera, M. (1996). 'The "Southern Model" of Welfare in Social Europe', *Journal of European Social Policy*, 6:1, 17–37.

Ferrera, M. (2005). *The Boundaries of Welfare: European Integration and the New Spatial Politics of Social Protection*. Oxford: Oxford University Press.

Goetz, K.H. (2006). 'Territoriality, Temporality and Clustered Europeanization', *Political Science Series*, No. 109, Institute for Advanced Studies, Vienna.

Gough, Ian (2001). 'Social Assistance Regimes: A Cluster Analysis', *Journal of European Social Policy*, 11:2, 165–70.

Hall, P.A., and D. Soskice, eds. (2001). *Varieties of Capitalism. The Institutional Foundations of Comparative Advantage*. Oxford: Oxford University Press.

Hollingsworth, J.R., P. Schmitter and W. Streeck, eds. (1994). *Governing Capitalist Economies*. New York: Oxford University Press.

Holzinger, K., and C. Knill (2005). 'Causes and Conditions of Cross-national Policy Convergence', *European Journal of Public Policy*, 12:5, 775–96.

Krasner, S.D. (1982). 'Structural Causes and Regime Consequences: Regimes as Intervening Variables', *International Organization*, 36:2, 185–205.

Leibfried, S. (1993). 'Towards a European Welfare State?', in C. Jones (ed.), *New Perspectives on the Welfare State in Europe*. London: Routledge.

Lijphart, A. (1999). *Patterns of Democracy*. New Haven, CT: Yale University Press.

Maddison, A. (2001). *The World Economy. A Millennial Perspective*. Paris: OECD.

Mossberger, K., and G. Stoker (2001). 'The Evolution of Urban Regime Theory: The Challenge of Conceptualization', *Urban Affairs Review*, 36:6, 810–35.

Obinger, H., and U. Wagschal (2001). 'Families of Nations and Public Policy', *West European Politics*, 24:1, 99–114.

Obinger, H., P. Starke and F.G. Castles (2007). 'Convergence Towards Where: In What Ways, If Any, Are Welfare States Becoming More Similar?', *Journal of European Public Policy*, 14.

Pascall, G., and J. Lewis (2004). 'Emerging Gender Regimes and Policies for Gender Equality in a Wider Europe', *Journal of Social Policy*, 33:3, 373–94.

Powell, M., and A. Barrientos (2004). 'Welfare Regimes and the Welfare Mix', *European Journal of Political Research*, 43:1, 83–105.

Przeworski, A. (1987). 'Methods of Cross-National Research, 1970–83: An Overview', in M. Dierkes, H.N. Weiler and A.B. Antal (eds.), *Comparative Policy Research*. Aldershot: Gower.

Rokkan, S. (1970). *Citizens, Elections, Parties*. New York: McKay.

Sainsbury, D., ed. (1999). *Gender and Welfare State Regimes*. Oxford: Oxford University Press.

Schmidt, M.G. (1996). 'When Parties Matter. A Review of the Possibilities and Limits of Partisan Influence on Public Policy', *European Journal of Political Research*, 30, 155–83.

Schmidt, M.G. (2007). 'Testing the Retrenchment Hypothesis: Educational Spending, 1960–2002', in F. G. Castles (ed.), *The Disappearing State? Retrenchment Realities in an Age of Globalisation*. Cheltenham: Edward Elgar.

Siaroff, A. (1999). 'Corporatism in 24 Industrial Democracies: Meaning and Measurement', *European Journal of Political Research*, 36, 175–205.

Soskice, D. (1999). 'Divergent Production Regimes: Coordinated and Uncoordinated Market Economies in the 1980s and 1990s', in H. Kitschelt, P. Lange, G. Marks and J.D. Stephens (eds.), *Continuity and Change in Contemporary Capitalism*. Cambridge: Cambridge University Press, 101–34.

Scruggs, L., and J. Allan (2006). 'Welfare-state Decommodification in 18 Countries: A Replication and Revision', *Journal of European Social Policy*, 16:1, 55–72.

Stockard, J., and R.M. O'Brien (2006). 'Cohort Variations in Suicide Rates among Families of Nations', *International Journal of Comparative Sociology*, 47:1, 5–33.

Therborn, G. (1993). 'Beyond the Lonely Nation-State', in F.G. Castles (ed.), *Families of Nations: Patterns of Public Policy in Western Democracies*. Aldershot: Dartmouth, 329–40.
Therborn, G. (1995). *European Modernity and Beyond: The Trajectory of European Societies, 1945–2000*. London: Sage Publications.
Traxler, F., and B. Woitech (2000). 'Transnational Investment and National Labour Market Regimes', *European Journal of Industrial Relations*, 6:2, 141–59.
Wagschal, U. (2001). 'Deutschlands Steuerstaat und die vier Welten der Besteuerung', in M.G. Schmidt (ed.), *Wohlfahrtsstaatliche Politik: Institutionen, politische Prozess und Leistungsprofil*. Opladen: Leske und Budrich, 124–60.
Welzel, C., R. Inglehart and H.-D. Klingemann (2003). 'The Theory of Human Development: A Cross-cultural Analysis', *European Journal of Political Research*, 42, 341–79.

APPENDIX A1

List of variables (Figure 1)

1. Total fertility rate 1960; Castles (2003: 212)
2. Military spending as a percentage of GDP 1960–69; Cusack (2007)
3. Total economy subsidies as a percentage of GDP 1960–75; Denmark = 1971–75; Economic Outlook Database
4. Public education expenditures (average 1960/74); Castles (1998: 177)
5. Total tax revenue as a percentage of GDP (average 1965/1970/75), OECD Revenue Statistics 1965–2003, Paris
6. Taxes on income and profits as a percentage of total taxation (average 1965/70/75), OECD Revenue Statistics 1965–2003, Paris
7. Taxes on goods and services as a percentage of total taxation (average 1965/70/75), OECD Revenue Statistics 1965–2003, Paris
8. Social security contributions as a percentage of total taxation (average 1965/70/75), OECD Revenue Statistics 1965–2003, Paris
9. Total outlays of government 1960–73, Spain = average 1968/74; OECD Historical Statistics 1960–93, Paris
10. Inflation (CPI) 1963–73; OECD Historical Statistics 1960–93, Paris
11. Unemployment 1960–74; OECD Economic Outlook Database
12. Female labour force as a percentage of the female population 15–64, Norway = average 1960/86/1974; OECD Historical Statistics 1960–93, Paris
13. Male labour force as a percentage of the male population 15–64, Norway = average 1960/68/1974; OECD Historical Statistics 1960–1993, Paris
14. Government employment as a percentage of total employment 1960–74, OECD Economic Outlook Database
15. Economic Growth in Geary-Khamis dollars, 1960–75; Maddison (2001)
16. Social security transfers as pct of GDP 1960–73; OECD Historical Statistics 1960–93, Paris

APPENDIX A2

List of variables (Figure 2, Table 1)

1. Total fertility rate 1998; Castles (2003: 212)
2. Military spending as a percentage of GDP 2000–03; Cusack (2007)
3. Total economy subsidies as a percentage of GDP 2000–04, OECD Economic Outlook Database
4. Public education expenditures 2002; Schmidt (2007 Table 7.1)
5. Total tax revenue as a percentage of GDP 2000-2002; OECD Revenue Statistics 1965–2003

6. Taxes on income and profits as a percentage of total taxation 2000–02; OECD Revenue Statistics 1965–2003
7. Taxes on goods and services as a percentage of total taxation 2000–02; OECD Revenue Statistics 1965–2003
8. Social security contributions as a percentage of total taxation 2000–02; OECD Revenue Statistics 1965–2003
9. Total disbursements of government 2000–04, OECD Economic Outlook Database
10. Inflation (CPI) 2000–04; OECD Economic Outlook Database
11. Unemployment rate 2000–04; OECD Economic Outlook Database
12. Female labour force as a percentage of the female population 15–64 2000–04; OECD Labour Force Statistics 2006 online edition
13. Male labour force as a percentage of the male population 15–64 2000–04; OECD Labour Force Statistics 2006 online edition
14. Government employment as a percentage of total employment 2000–04; Switzerland and Australia = 1999
15. Economic growth 1990–01, OECD Economic Outlook Database
16. Social security transfers as a percentage of GDP 2000 (or late 1990s); OECD Historical Statistics 1970–2000

APPENDIX A3

List of variables (Figure 3)

1. Ethno-linguistic fractionalization in the 1960s (= probability that two randomly selected individuals in a country will belong to different ethno-linguistic groups); Soviet data
2. Percentage of population aged 65 and over in 1960; Castles (1998: 50)
3. Trade union membership as a percentage. of wage and salary earners 1960; Castles (1998: 68)
4. Employment in agriculture as a percentage of civilian employment 1960–73, Denmark and Norway = average (1960/68/74); OECD Historical Statistics 1960–93, Paris
5. Cabinet share of left parties [Social Democrats and Communists] (1945–75); data provided by Manfred Schmidt
6. Cabinet share of liberal and non-Christian centre parties (1945–75); data provided by Manfred Schmidt
7. Cabinet share of secular conservative parties (1945–75); data provided by Manfred Schmidt
8. Cabinet share of Christian Democrats (1945–75); data provided by Manfred Schmidt
9. Catholics (percentage of population baptised into a non-Protestant Christian faith); Castles (1998: 56)
10. Level of GDP per capita in 1990 international Geary-Khamis dollars (average 1950/60/ 75); Maddison (2001: appendix C)
11. Integration score late 1960s; Siaroff (1999: 198)
12. Division of power (executives-parties dimension) 1945–75; Lijphart (1999: 312)
13. Division of power (federal-unitary dimension) 1945–75; Lijphart (1999: 312)
14. Index of interest pluralism 1945–75; Lijphart (1999: 313)
15. Effective number of parties in parliament (1960–75); Armingeon *et al.* (2006)

APPENDIX A4

List of variables (Figure 4)

1. Percentage of population aged 65 and over, early 1990s, Castles (1998: 50)
2. Trade union membership as a percentage of wage and salary earners, early 1990s; Castles (1998: 68)

3. Employment in agriculture as a percentage of civilian employment (1970–2000); OECD Historical Statistics 1970–2000
4. Cabinet share of left parties (Social Democrats + Communists), 1985–2004; data provided by Manfred Schmidt
5. Cabinet share of liberal an non-Christian centre parties, 1985–2004; data provided by Manfred Schmidt
6. Cabinet share of Christian Democrats, 1985–2004; data provided by Manfred Schmidt
7. Cabinet share of secular conservative parties 1985–2004; data provided by Manfred Schmidt
8. Catholics (percentage of population baptised into a non-Protestant Christian faith); Castles (1998: 56)
9. Level of real GDP per capita (1985–2000); Penn World Table 6.1.
10. Integration score mid-1990s; Siaroff (1999: 198)
11. Division of power (executives-parties dimension) 1971–96; Lijphart (1999: 312)
12. Division of power (federal-unitary dimension) 1971–96; Lijphart (1999: 312)
13. Index of interest pluralism 1971–96; Lijphart (1999: 313)
14. Effective number of parties in parliament (1985–2003); Armingeon *et al.* (2006)

APPENDIX A5

List of variables (Figure 5, Table 2)

1. Total fertility rate, 2000–05; EUROSTAT
2. Employment in the public sector (administration, defence, social insurance) as a percentage of total employment, 2002–05; EUROSTAT
3. Social security contribution as a percentage of total government revenue, 2000–05; EUROSTAT
4. Direct taxes as a percentage of total government revenue, 2000–05; EUROSTAT
5. Indirect taxes as pct of total government revenue, 2000–05; EUROSTAT
6. Inflation (CPI), 2000–05; EUROSTAT
7. Unemployment rate, 2000–05; EUROSTAT
8. Education expenditure as a percentage of GDP, 2000–03; EUROSTAT
9. Subsidies as a percentage of GDP, 2000–05; EUROSTAT
10. Male employment as a pct of male population 15–64, 2000–05; EUROSTAT
11. Social transfers (cash) as pct of GDP, 2000–05; EUROSTAT
12. Total tax revenue as a percentage of GDP 2000–04; EUROSTAT
13. Female employment as a percentage of female population 15–64, 2000–05; EUROSTAT
14. Total outlays of government as a percentage of GDP, 2000–05; EUROSTAT
15. Growth of real GDP, 2000–05; EUROSTAT

Historical Institutionalism and West European Politics

ELLEN M. IMMERGUT and KAREN M. ANDERSON

The 'new institutionalism', and in particular, the branch of the new institutionalism known as 'historical institutionalism' has not only influenced the study of West European politics, but indeed, in some respects, this approach emerged out of the study of West European politics itself. As the editors point out in the introduction to this volume, the field of West European politics in the founding days of *West European Politics* was very much concerned with the institutions of West European politics. In contrast to a much earlier generation's concern with institutions in the inter-war period – that termed 'formalist' in the field of domestic politics, and 'idealist' in the field of international politics – the focus of the new generation of West Europeanists was not in the main on formal political institutions, such as constitutions, but on institutions understood as the informal rules of the game, organisational patterns of political behaviour, and organisational structures both within and outside of government.

The world of West European politics also contrasted, however, with the post-war successors to the formalists and the idealists – the behaviouralists and the realists, respectively – in several respects. First, the state was neither ignored nor treated as either a neutral arena or as just another interest group, as in the behaviouralist perspective. Nor was it reified to be viewed as a unified actor and the sole source of political activity as in the realist view. Second, the geographic range of interest was restricted considerably by comparison to the 'grand theories' and search for universal generalisations that had characterised comparative politics in the immediate post-war period and especially the 'political development' or 'modernisation' approach. This reduced range, with its greater respect for historical context and particularity, was also counterposed to the enthusiasm for Marxist theory in the late 1960s and early 1970s. Thus, in place of functionalist universals of modernisation or an ineluctable logic of capitalism, the focus was on the unique and conflictual pattern of political and economic development in Western Europe, and the institutional legacies that these political crises had left in place. Consequently, the preferred methodology was one of comparative-historical analysis, and the level of theoretical generalisation was focused on the middle range, or even on the peculiarities of a single case, viewed in comparative perspective. Furthermore, the regional focus allowed sustained interdisciplinary cooperation, for example with sociology (Goldthorpe 1984) and history (Maier 1987). The following sections will detail, first, the influence that the field of West European politics has had on the new institutionalism; second, some problems that have emerged; and third, it will point to potential solutions and avenues for future research.

Founding Ideas of the 1970s and Early 1980s

The Artefactuality of Politics

In turning from the class struggle to corporatist theories and studies of trade unions as organisations in a historical and institutional context, the field of West European politics put the issue of interest representation (or interest intermediation, to use Gerhard Lehmbruch and Philippe Schmitter's term; Schmitter and Lehmbruch 1979) at the centre of its research agenda. Not just the study of economically based interests, but also that of political parties and social movements, emphasised institutions of interest representation and institutional factors that affected the articulation of political preferences, and their expression in politics. As Suzanne Berger put it, institutions for representing interests were no longer viewed as neutral 'transmission belts' for relaying citizens' preferences to political decision-makers, but as relatively stable institutional fixtures that modified the process of interest representation by amplifying some definitions of interest and attenuating others (Berger 1981). At the same time, it should be noted that Berger's work stands out not just for her institutionalist focus on institutions of interest representation, but also for her emphasis on the role of individuals in interpreting their own interests; as well as the role of political contestation in deciding which one of multiple potential constructions of interest will prevail (Berger 1972). In some ways, then, Berger should be considered as 'constructivist' as well as 'institutionalist'.

The corporatism literature addressed the ways in which the same basic class interests could be organised in different ways, and how this influenced politics and public politics (citizen unruliness and governability, for example, in part expressed as demonstrations, strikes and inflationary pressures; Schmitter 1981). Indeed, in contrast to the conservative focus in the 1970s on the 'democratic distemper' and 'government overload' (Crozier *et al.* 1975), corporatist theory viewed institutions as potentially helpful for public policy, and as in Lijphart's institutionalist approach to political systems, viewed West European consensus democracies with their systems of social partnership as a 'kinder, gentler model' (Lijphart, 1999; and Hayward 1980; Heidenheimer 1980). To be sure, there was also a leftist critique of corporatism that viewed corporatist institutions as a tool for repressing, rather than modulating, the expression of class interests (Panitch, 1977).

Similarly, the parties literature focused both on the existence of different social cleavages, and the translation of these cleavages into party systems that became 'frozen' in the 1920es – the same inter-war period held responsible for the 'recasting of bourgeois Europe' into a corporatist mould (Maier 1975). A key question was whether these parties would – as Kirchheimer and Downs predicted – start to converge on a 'catch-all' model, or whether their social and ideological distinctiveness would remain intact. Would the 'end of ideology' prevail (Bell 2000 [1960]) or the 'resurgence of class conflict in Western Europe' (Pizzorno and Crouch 1978) prove enduring? (See for example Wright 1978; Lange and Tarrow 1979.)

The field of social movements was very much influenced by the 'Tilly model' which viewed the emergence of social movements as a product of resource mobilisation on the part of challengers from 'below', and chinks in the armour of repression from 'above'. The latter 'political opportunity structures' were good examples of the role of states as actors and structures. As actors, states actively intervene to shape the landscape of social groups as in the Tocquevillian approach, at the same time that their structural features provide distinct opportunities and constraints, as in the Weberian model (Kitschelt 1986; Skocpol 1985; Tarrow 1994). More generally, this period saw an upsurge of interest in the state, as well as in the relationship between states and social structures (Evans *et al.* 1985).

What these studies and approaches share as a whole is a recognition of what one could call the 'artefactuality' of politics. That is, they all view politics as being (in part) artefacts of political institutions. Institutions of interest representation intervene in the process whereby citizens can express their interests, and thus shape what appears as a political interest in public arenas. The particular institution in question may vary – be it a state structure, party system or pattern of interest intermediation – but the basic point is the same: the interests that come to be expressed in politics are shaped by those institutions. Indeed, these institutions may even affect whether these interests come to be expressed at all. Thus, the focus on individual attitudes, so stressed by the political culture framework, took insufficient account of the role played by institutions in mediating between individuals and the politicised visions and organisational forms of their interests.

Because there is some confusion on this issue, it is important to state here that the value of the institutions for expressing interests does not mean that interests do not exist or that they are creations of institutions. Instead, this 'artefactual' approach calls for an examination of the empirical relationship between individual preferences and the organisational structures of politics. Interests are expressed through institutions – just as behaviour takes place within an institutional context – making it extremely difficult to separate the impact of institutional conduits from the 'raw' preferences or interests of individuals and groups. Both the organisation of interests and the political structures within which they organise shape the demands and issues that are put on the political agenda, and whether or not they even get there. This is what Steinmo (1993) called (using Schattschneider's term) 'the mobilization of bias', and Hall (1986) referred to as 'the impact of organizational factors on politics'. Thus the need to focus on institutional variation within Western Europe is part and parcel of a theoretical focus on the impact of institutions on the articulation of interests.

Historical Legacies

A second general tendency of the study of West European politics that has influenced the new institutionalism, and especially historical institutionalism, is the impact of historical legacies. In response to modernisation theorists' efforts to delineate a universal pattern of political development consisting of a standard set of crises and functions, conflict theory understood historical development – in particular the emergence of capitalism and the rise of the modern nation-state – both in terms of class conflicts and as a result of struggles for political domination. Though some strands of this historical approach were initially engaged with a Marxist focus on the transition from feudalism to capitalism, this developmental approach quickly turned to variation within Europe and historical particularism (Moore 1966; Beer and Ulam 1972; Anderson 1974; Tilly 1975). As the larger scholarly debate was beginning to ebb by the time *WEP* was founded at the end of the 1970s, this focus on the rise and development of the modern state was not quite as central to contributors to *West*

European Politics. Nevertheless, the debate was indeed an important precursor to the *WEP* agenda, and in fact integral to it, as the impact of history remained implicit in the institutional analysis referred to above. This broader engagement with the long-term development of the state is a central point, for example, in the corporatism literature, which views the role of the state and the historical development of state–interest group relationships as key factors in explaining differences in contemporary neo-corporatist institutions of interest intermediation. Similarly, the Rokkan model, so central to an understanding of party systems, was based on the historical sequence and particular alliances chosen during conflicts leading to the incorporation of new cleavages into institutions of political representation. Indeed, the political system as a whole came to be seen as a product of historic conflicts, whose outcomes depended upon both political choices and pre-existing structures, which in turn reflected a previous set of past choices, and thus could be understood only through a sort of 'political archaeology'. In the words of Suzanne Berger:

> [P]olitical modernization does not clear the political terrain of all vestiges of the past and raise a new house on bare earth. Rather, modern states have been built on top of and with the half-collapsed, half-standing institutions of the past. States differ, however,... because [political elites] make different choices about how much of the past to preserve in the modern political system. (Berger 1973: 334)

These institutional sediments are particularly important for understanding the relationship between religion and politics (Berger 1982), and the territorial dimension of European politics (Rhodes and Wright 1987). Thus, again, as with the issue of the artefactuality of politics, one can observe a selective affinity between the turn to detailed, historically grounded case studies and the theoretical interest in the impact of institutions and institutional legacies on contemporary politics.

The State and Capitalism

Finally, the substantive focus on states and class structures was also critical background for WEP's approach to understanding governmental structures and public policies. A major paradigmatic work was Schonfeld's (1965) comparison of the role of the state in various political economies, which was followed up by decades of discussion of convergence versus divergence in modern political economies (Berger and Piore 1980; Zysmann 1983; Hall 1986; Berger and Dore 1996; Crouch and Streeck 1997; Hollingsworth and Boyer 1999). Here a key insight was on the impact of politics – and in particular of state power – on the organisation of the economy. One influential framework that emerged from this 'macro' approach to political economy was Katzenstein's (1978, 1985) focus on 'strong' versus 'weak' states and societies in explaining foreign economic policies, and domestic institutions. Building on Alexander Gerschenkron's work, Gourevitch (1985, 1995 [1977]) developed a 'producer groups' analysis, which focused on specific sectors and their relationship to the international economy, but also on culturally specific histories of economic ideas. Thus, ideas, interests and institutions interacted over time to produce nationally and even regionally distinct political economies, whose development was subject to political contestation rather than functionalist imperatives. Again, only historical-comparative analysis sensitive to the contextual particularities of Western Europe as a unique region could meet the challenge of understanding patterns of continuity and change in these embedded economies, including tendencies of dualism and discontinuous development (Berger and Piore 1980).

Evolution of the Foundational Ideas in the 1980s and Early 1990s

While a coherent set of empirical and theoretical concerns led to an interest in a regional focus, the emphasis on institutional structures with their historical burdens was also, in a sense, set on shifting foundations. For just at this time West European politics and their institutions were undergoing change, and perhaps moving towards disequilibrium. The two oil shocks of the 1970s were arguably the first portent of the phenomenon later to be termed 'globalisation', with their destabilising effects both on domestic social and political institutional arrangements, and on international economic institutions. Institutional structures were looked at as important explanatory variables for differences in the ability of national political economies to come to terms with these exogenous shocks; at the same time, corporatist institutions were becoming less effective, and party systems suffering from 'decomposition' and electoral 'de-alignment'. The ten years subsequent to *WEP*'s founding saw the rise of right-wing radicalism – but also Green parties; the democratisation of Southern Europe; the neo-conservative attack on neo-corporatist arrangements and the post-war welfare state in Northern Europe; and the beginning of a renewed intensity of European integration.

While these developments are addressed in greater depth elsewhere in this volume, here the important question is about the impact of this concern with crisis and transition on theories and approaches to West European politics. In dealing with stability and change in West European political institutions, scholars began to drop the last vestiges of the older concern with states and classes, and to reject these reified concepts, focusing more stringently on human agency and the exact links between individuals and collective action, including the perceptual lenses of individuals, and the shared understandings of members of groups. Further, perhaps spurred by the rise of feminism and other new social movements on both the left and the right, a much more diverse range of dimensions of interest beyond the basic economic duality of capital and labour became prominent in research on Western Europe States and political systems came to be disaggregated into concrete institutional configurations, with their own (and sometimes conflicting) logics. As voters dislodged themselves from their social origins, the role of parties as strategic actors became more obvious. By the end of the 1980s, a concern with the 'new institutionalism' had replaced the older emphasis on states and social structures (March and Olsen 1984; Steinmo *et al.* 1992; Hall and Taylor 1996). In the area of political economy, this took the form of an even greater recognition of the role of political conflict and ideas in economic and technological development (see for example Piore and Sabel 1984; Hall 1993; Ziegler 1997). In the area of welfare state research, this meant more fine-grained analysis of particular instances of policy-making in their historical context in place of a more structural approach (cf., e.g., Weir and Skocpol 1985 to Skocpol 1992 or Weir 1992). In the areas of political development and interest representation, it meant greater recognition of the role of strategic choices by political actors, such as party and interest group leaders, and political contingency, in place of historical constraints and state structures (Kitschelt 1989; Bartolini and Mair 1990; Thelen 1991).

From Structures to Institutional Configurations

As stated at the outset, the branch of the new institutionalism most centrally associated with West European politics is historical institutionalism. This approach relies heavily on the insights generated by this regional, qualitative focus on the artefactuality of politics, historical legacies, and the specific development of states and economies in Western Europe. Yet, in order to pin down the effects of institutions and history, historical institutionalists have tended to further narrow the range of analysis, focusing on explaining specific political or policy outcomes, and performing what has sometimes been called a problem-oriented type of research (for positive views, see Scharpf 1997; Steinmo 2007; more critically, Katznelson 1997; Schmidt forthcoming). At centre stage have been interest groups, parties, governments and public policies, rather than capital, labour, states and the long-term sweep of history. The puzzles to be explained are generally empirical: why was one policy chosen rather than another? How can we explain the greater popularity of right-wing populism in one country rather than another? The preferred method is generally historical-comparative analysis.

To be sure, the influence of historical institutionalism has not been evenly distributed amongst all areas of interest in *WEP*. In fact, while the range of research can be said to have narrowed over the course of the 1980s, the theoretical perspective can be said to have become more diverse and varied. That is, in the early days of *WEP* an interest in political economy understood in terms of states and classes, and a critique of the modernisation approach to comparative politics provided a common set of questions. With the later efforts to deepen the institutional and political dimensions of analysis, however, we can observe further diversification. The parties literature kept a much stronger behaviouralist focus on individual preferences and the socio-economic basis of interest cleavages, but also focused on the role of party strategies (that is, on institutionalised actors) in mediating electoral change (see for example Mair and Smith 1989). Work on political economy maintained an emphasis on unions, producer groups and interest coalitions, but also focused to a greater extent than previously on the role of historical contingency and the specifics of institutional development, with some authors probing the borders of historical sociology (see for example Sabel and Zeitlin 1985, 1997; Thelen 1991; Herrigel 1995; Locke 1995; Ziegler 1997). And work on public policies – particularly that concerned with 'privatisation' and 'liberalisation' – was concerned with non-state decision-making and new forms of interest representation, such as policy networks and epistemic communities, (e.g. Dyson and Humphries 1986; Vickers and Wright 1988).

Nevertheless, despite the eclecticism of both historical institutionalism and *WEP*'s approaches in the 1980s and early 1990s, one can nevertheless observe a concern with a coherent range of issues, even if these issues are not united by a single theory or methodology. One important idea – the one selected by Thelen and Steinmo (1992) as perhaps 'the' unique characteristic of historical institutionalism – was the 'endogeneity' of preferences. This was the insight that institutions may influence the formation of preferences by political actors. It is linked to the foundational idea that institutions for representing interests affect the politicisation of interests, but goes one step further by looking more intensively at interactions between preferences, interests and institutions – a scrutiny that was made more intense by dropping any assumption of objective economic interests. Steinmo (1993), for example, shows how political institutions affected the strategies used by groups to pursue their interests in different polities, and hence changed their interpretations of their preferences. This idea has a parallel in the discussions of changes in West European party systems and the rise of right-wing populism, which also stress the strategic role of parties in redesigning political space (von Beyme 1988).

A second, related, idea was the importance of political actors' subjective interpretations, not only of their own interests and preferences, but of their identities, beliefs and capacities. For example, whether union members identified as 'producers' or 'workers' in the nineteenth century, Hattam (1993) argues, determined whether they allied with farmers and craftsmen in a producers' alliance against banks, or whether they viewed their interests as industrial workers to be contrary to those of property holders. This focus on identities as a key to actors' perceptual lenses is relevant to contemporary European politics as well, and has been central to research on both social movements and right-wing populism, as a corrective to the somewhat overly materialist 'resource mobilisation' perspective (Knutsen 1990; Finger and Sciarini 1991; Reiter 1993; Fuchs and Rohrschneider 1998).

A third common theme is the idea of 'contextual causality'. The causal workings of institutions may depend upon their historic contexts, which include the interpretations that political actors bring to institutions. Constitutional choices made in the context of the transition from state socialism to capitalist democracy in Eastern Europe, for example, were very much influenced by interpretations of the past (Elster *et al.* 1998). Such narratives of the past seem to be crucial as well for the creation of the institutional coordination needed to sustain such complex institutions as 'industrial districts' (Sabel and Zeitlin 1985, 1997). Finally, historical institutionalism is often characterised by attention to historical contingency: accidents of history with long-term consequences, such as, for instance, the choice of the administrative structure for unemployment insurance, which it turns out has substantial consequences for levels of union density (Rothstein 1992).

Radical Revision of the Foundational Ideas in the 1990s and Early 2000s

Whereas political analysis of West European politics of the 1980s could take a combination of stability and change as its point of departure, the 1990s were undoubtedly a period of rapid and radical change in Western Europe. With the signing of the Maastricht treaty, European integration took on new speed and intensity – and entered onto *WEP*'s agenda for the first time, having previously been left (relatively speaking) mainly to the field of international relations (Goetz and Hix 2000). Whereas privatisation, deregulation and welfare state retrenchment had been associated with the Reagan and Thatcher governments in the 1980s, in the 1990s all European political economies and their patterns of consensus politics underwent significant restructuring – including the previously stable German and Swedish 'models', (Lane 1991, 2001; Luther and Müller 1992; Bull and Rhodes 1997; Kitschelt and Streeck 2003). Indeed, Social Democracy itself entered into a period of redefinition and repositioning, both in terms of electoral positioning and policy stances, and in terms of party structures and links to unions (see for example Gillespie and Patterson 1993; Merkel 1993, 2006; Kitschelt 1994). Further, new issues, such as immigration, attained new prominence in this era of change and upheaval (Baldwin-Edwards and Schain 1994).

Given this changing landscape, the working definition offered by Thelen and Steinmo (1992: 2) for historical institutionalism as 'an emphasis on how pre-existing institutions structure contemporary political conflicts and outcomes' seemed to need revision or amendment. How could one account for both stability and change? This effort took several forms, ranging from specifying more clearly the impact of history on contemporary politics to developing more thoroughly the two frontier issues flagged from the beginning by Thelen and Steinmo, namely institutional change and the role of ideas. A third frontier issue, the origins of institutions, has also been the basis for important contributions to recent historical institutionalist scholarship, as well as the basis for a rapprochement between historical institutional and rational choice scholarship.

Pinning Down History

Paul Pierson's recent work (2004) explicitly addresses the role of history in political-institutional analysis. Pierson cautions scholars not to over-emphasise initial institutional choice points and moments of substantial reform to the neglect of long-term processes of institutional development. In Western Europe, many, if not most formal political institutions and important public policies (especially social policies) are mature enough that they are more or less permanent features of the political landscape. Given these constraints, the most important and relevant analytical task is to explain the sources of institutional resilience rather than to search for immediate sources of institutional change, for institutional development may be better understood, Pierson argues, from the vantage point of the *longue durée*. This perspective allows one to examine various feedback links, demographic developments, threshold effects, and the like, which may be more important than short-term political decisions. Thus Pierson has suggested that the role of history can be better specified by three 'historical' effects: increasing returns and path dependence; the role of timing and sequence; and attention to long-term processes.

Although models of path dependency were first developed to explain sociological phenomena such as segregated residence patterns, and economic phenomena such as the inefficient spread of technological innovation, Pierson points out the fruitfulness with which path dependency may be applied to political phenomena. The very nature of politics, with its need for collective action, institutional constraints on behaviour, scope for political authority and power asymmetries, and lack of both transparency and mechanisms for restoring efficiency, such as competition and learning, makes the political sphere rife with opportunities for path dependency. To the extent that a political outcome is the product of path dependency, political analysis must adopt a much longer time frame than that generally assumed by multivariate quantitative approaches or game theoretic models. One must move, as Pierson puts it, from a 'snapshot' to a 'moving picture' analysis; this is what it means concretely to place 'politics in time' and to move beyond vague assertions that 'history matters' in order to conduct what Pierson calls 'genuine' *historical* research. In examining sequential effects, such as the relative timing of the introduction of democracy and the emergence of a professional civil service, or the emergence of cleavages in party systems, Pierson argues that more analytic purchase can be had by re-analysing these effects in terms of positive feedback mechanisms, similar to those so important to path dependency. Similarly, long-term, slow-moving processes and even sharp reversals in the direction of such processes, can be more compellingly explained if one replaces evocation of 'History' with more precise analysis of the feedback mechanisms at the micro-level that explain both stagnation and shifts at the macro-level.

One of the strengths of Pierson's framework is that it goes beyond the claim that 'history matters' and gives us the tools to analyse the ways in which temporal context matters – that events unfold differently in different historical contexts, the order in which events occur matters very much (think of democratisation in Eastern Europe compared to countries that democratised at other points in time), and increasing returns over time help to explain why institutional change is often incremental. Pierson's insights provide the starting point for much research published in *WEP*, especially his path-breaking work on the 'new politics of the welfare state' (Pierson 1994, 2001; Ferrera and Rhodes 2000). Nevertheless, despite the inclusion of feedback effects that can induce changes, such as threshold effects, the emphasis on feedback effects results in far more sustained focus on institutional resilience than on institutional change. Further, although mapping feedback more precisely may be analytically rigorous, in practice, it is extremely difficult to measure feedback effects in politics, particularly if one is using qualitative methods. How would one apply these ideas using a case study research design? Are the methods and measures traditional for West European politics up to this task? Indeed, in order to make progress on this agenda, it would seem to be most feasible to return to the variable approach rejected by Pierson at the outset, and indeed to focus on the political variables that lend themselves easily to precise measurement: electoral results, parliamentary representation, and legislative behaviour. Yet these standard features of political life tend to be downplayed by this take on historical institutionalism, despite the inclusion of chapters in Pierson's book on institutional change and institutional design. Even more disturbingly, the focus on pinning down history has resulted in the neglect of two basic features of both politics and history: political contestation and actor reflexivity. For it is precisely in the moments when individuals find the courage to contest the status quo that we witness historically relevant change in political behaviour and political structures. Thus, the search for social scientifically relevant regularities should not lead one away from the very stuff of politics: conflict, contestation and power.

Analysing Institutional Change

Recent work by Thelen (2004), Streeck and Thelen (2005) takes up Pierson's (2004) call for a nuanced view of institutional change by investigating the kinds of long-term processes of institutional development that Pierson emphasises, but places much more emphasis on political processes in accounting for both stability and change. The key point here is that what

Thelen (1999) calls 'mechanisms of reproduction' are central elements in any account of institutional development. All institutions – and here Streeck and Thelen (2005) focus in their edited book *Beyond Continuity* on sets of institutions that are backed by political legitimacy and legal sanctions, and can thus be thought of as institutional regimes – are continually renegotiated and reinterpreted, for none can provide complete and unambiguous guides to action. Moreover, as circumstances change, this room for 'play' in institutional enforcement is necessary for the successful adaptation of such institutional regimes. Thus, the view of institutions provided by Streeck and Thelen can be termed 'Artistotelian': not theoretical models of institutions, but existing historical formations must be the starting point for institutional analysis. This historical residue includes the ideas and practices people bring to the institution as it has developed over time. Thus, like Schumpeter (1975 [1942]) and Polanyi (2001 [1944]), Streeck and Thelen's claim is that without continual renegotiation and reinterpretation, as well as the support of ancillary institutions, such as customs, beliefs and assumptions, institutions would lose their social embeddedness, and hence cease to function at all. In stark contrast to the more 'Platonic' varieties of capitalism (Hall and Soskice 2001) approach, this view on institutions does not assume coherent institutional complementarities which result in continual return to equilibrium. Instead, institutional regimes arise from historical coincidences in combination with the efforts of human agents to solve changing problems – much as in the perspective of Sabel and Zeitlin (1997), which so stresses 'accidents in the struggle for power'.

Streeck and Thelen (2005) construct a typology of institutional change that encompasses different types of mechanisms through which change occurs.[1] Their central claim is that much transformative institutional change takes place gradually, so we need to analyse the ways in which these processes unfold. This framework is a major step forward for historical institutionalism because it provides the conceptual tools for analysing and categorising different types of institutional change. One of the great virtues of *Beyond Continuity* is that agency plays a much greater role than in earlier research that largely attributed incremental institutional change to a path dependent process in which political actors seemed almost to be onlookers in a self-reinforcing process; now institutional change is much more directly related to *politics*. Nevertheless, perhaps precisely for this reason, the book stops short of offering a causal theory for the various types of institutional change. In other words, Streeck and Thelen have done an enormous service by elaborating a typology for distinguishing and understanding different types of institutional change, but they tell us more about how to categorise outcomes and to understand the logics associated with them than how to explain path-breaking institutional change. In fact, it is not their ambition to produce such a theory. As such, the book is typical of the challenges associated with historical institutional research: it is exceedingly difficult (if not impossible) to develop theoretical frameworks powerful enough to explain more than a few cases, if one is serious about paying sufficient attention to the particularities of historical context, the role played by political contestation, and the intervening impact of human perception and reflection.

Despite these challenges, several recent works represent important advancements in this area. Lynch's (2006) research on the 'age orientation of welfare states' combines qualitative case studies with quantitative analysis to understand why some welfare states privilege programmes for the aged at the expense of measures to help families and younger workers. She shows that the dynamics of party competition within different types of political systems (programmatic versus patronage) lock in decisions taken in the late nineteenth and early twentieth centuries, precluding welfare state modernisation and adaptation to new needs in 'occupational welfare states'. What makes these processes path dependent is the style of political contestation, and the key mechanism of path dependence is the mechanism that links politicians' competitive strategies to institutional structures. So path dependence is a decidedly political process. Morgan's (2006) book on family policy shows how church–state relationships and political conflicts over religion affected both ideologies of gender roles and the incorporation of religiosity in political life, thus shaping the politics of family policy at several critical junctures. Political contestation sets policies on a specific 'path' but the steps on the path are continuously renegotiated in an ongoing political process.

Both of these books put political contestation back into the centre of institutional analysis, thus helping the authors better to account for both stability and change. Further, each is sensitive to the role played by political beliefs in political conflict and institutional innovation, and, hence, provides a more 'historical' account of welfare state development, in the sense of respecting actor-reflexivity.

The Role of Ideas

Indeed, despite the historicist and idiographic stance of historical institutionalist scholarship, one must fault this approach for its general neglect of the non-material sources of actor preferences. Actor preferences originate in the ways in which policy feedbacks such as lock-in and policy drift shape the organisation of interest groups and their definition of interest; there is little scope for the impact of cognitive framing and ideational processes. This focus on the material sources of preferences was never the exclusive focus of historical institutionalism, however, so the recent 'ideational turn' in historical institutionalism is in some ways a return to origins. For example, both Hall (1993) and Rothstein (1998) incorporate the importance of ideas and cognitive understandings into their analyses, and it is worthwhile returning to these ideational/cognitive foundations.

Hall's (1993) conception of 'policy paradigms' incorporates cognitive understandings into his explanation of preference formation. According to Hall (1993: 279) a policy paradigm is 'a framework of ideas and standards that specifies not only the goals of a policy and kind of instruments that can be used to attain them, but also the very nature of the problems they are meant to be addressing'. Policy paradigms are the world views of bureaucrats, politicians, and other key political actors about the nature of policy problems and the range of potential and appropriate solutions. These paradigms constitute roadmaps that provide actors with cognitive tools and directions about how to interpret how key macro-institutions (like the economy) function. These cognitive understandings, in turn, shape the range of policy alternatives that come into focus.

Rothstein extends these studies' focus on the ideas and cognitive understandings held by political elites within political parties, unions and public bureaucracies by focusing on the normative dimension of policy feedback. Rothstein (1998) argues that institutions, particularly welfare state institutions, influence the development of social norms; social policies have consequences for how citizens view notions of fairness, solidarity, equality, and trust. Universal welfare state institutions generate strong norms of social trust because no one is cheating (getting more than their 'fair' share) and everyone who can, works (and pays taxes). Thus institutional choices shape the emergence of both a 'political' and 'moral' logic. The 'political logic' is similar to Pierson's (1994, 2001, 2004) conception of path dependence: public policies generate incentives for interest group activity, influence adaptive expectations and generate distinctive patterns of public support. Office-seeking politicians are aware of the electoral constraints that path dependence produces and pursue strategies designed to avoid blame for unpopular policies. The 'moral logic' of path dependence is closely bound up with the 'political logic' but is decidedly normative. This moral logic suggests why people support institutions when their self-interest would dictate otherwise.

More recent work extends and enlarges this focus on ideas and cognitive processes as sources of actor preferences, but their link to historical institutionalism's original focus, that is the interplay of temporal and institutional factors to explain political processes and outcomes, is weak. Two examples of influential works will suffice to illustrate this. First, Berman (1998) explains divergence in the Swedish and German Social Democratic parties' responses to democratisation and economic crisis in the inter-war period with reference to differences in the parties' ideas. As Berman argues, different ideas produce different policy responses even when the nature of political and economic pressures is similar (ibid.: ix). Divergent responses are explained by 'each party's long-held ideas and the distinct policy legacies those ideas helped create' (ibid.: 4). The German and Swedish Social Democratic Parties each developed their own nationally distinct definitions of what constituted social democracy. The basic line of argument is that ideas shape political behaviour in ways similar to what Weir (1992), Hattam (1993) and Hall (1986, 1993) have argued (although ideas have more causal weight), but the institutional focus is missing.

Like Berman, Blyth (2002) emphasises the causal impact of ideas on policy choice, specifically Swedish economic policy-making. Blyth conceptualises ideas as roadmaps, weapons in political struggles, and cognitive 'locks', stressing the ways in which 'ideational contestation' shapes institutional development. Despite his historical focus, Blyth's account of ideational impact rests on exogenously generated ideas. The neo-liberal ideas that came to dominate thinking on economic policy did not originate in Sweden; the ideas were transposed to the Swedish context by influential 'carriers'.

These two recent studies share with earlier historical institutionalist research a focus on the impact of ideas and cognitive understandings, or what Berman calls 'programmatic beliefs', on policy choices. Berman's study has more affinities with historical institutionalism's focus on temporality than Blyth's because her focus is on ideational/cognitive legacies. The programmatic beliefs of social democratic parties produced policy legacies in much the same way that Pierson (1994) conceives them. Unlike Pierson's more material focus, however, Berman's policy legacies are ideational and cognitive (see also Cox 2001; Schmidt forthcoming). Newer work by younger scholars departs from earlier efforts to understand the impact of ideas by examining the available discourse space for new ideas (Naumann 2005), and ways in which framing dynamics construct corridors for action in policy-making (Daviter 2007).

The Origins of Institutions

Not only ideas, but standard political institutions are now becoming more central both to historical institutionalist work and to studies of West European politics. This represents the influence of the rational choice approach's emphasis on the impact of institutions viewed as formal rules. Thus, the impact of electoral systems, party regulations, and the formal division of powers is increasingly being brought into the study of political parties and public policy-making (Rogowski 1987; Cusack *et al.* 2007; Scarrow 2006). Further, as discussed above, the feedback effects of political institutions may be an important aspect of historical legacies (Lynch 2006; Morgan 2006). At the same time, however, the recognition of the importance of institutions has prompted scholars to investigate the origins of institutions. And here we see that the process of choosing institutions has generally been far from far-sightedly rational, but instead resembles more the models of bounded rationality and 'non-rationality' proposed by cognitive psychologists and 'sociological' institutionalism (Powell and DiMaggio 1991; Gigerenzer 2001).

Further, the effects of constitutional structures depend upon the political content with which they are filled: this depends upon partisan preferences, the ways in which electoral formulas translate votes into seats, the strategies of political parties and on political culture, as well as the beliefs of leaders. Skach (2005), for example, shows how the semi-presidential constitutional designs adopted in the French Fifth Republic and Weimar Germany resulted in very different democratic outcomes because of the ways in which the electoral and party systems, as well as the actions and beliefs of political leaders, worked to aggregate or fragment political majorities. Ziblatt's (2006) combination of detailed comparison of the politics of German and Italian unification nested within a broader sample of 18 cases belies rational accounts of institutional design, and instead indicates that pre-existing structures and expectations shaped the politics of state formation. Thus, a look at the actual history of the origins of institutions uncovers a messy politics of muddling through, in which assumed structures and ideas play an important role in institutional outcomes.

Taking Stock in the 2000s

What are the achievements of historical institutionalism, the challenges that remain, and what do these suggest about the future of research published in *WEP*? First, historical institutionalism's greatest achievement is probably its contribution to our understanding of how interests are constructed. A central analytical concern has always been to investigate the sources of actor interests, and the cumulative achievements of historical institutionalism in this area are considerable. We now know quite a bit about how institutions constitute actors and their interests, as well as the ways in which cognitive and ideational factors shape interests. Second, historical institutionalist scholarship has achieved much in terms of conceptualising and explaining actor behaviour. One of historical institutionalism's core insights is that the 'rules of the game' matter. This analytical precision concerning the workings of institutions has generated powerful insights into how the institutional context structures not just interests but behaviour. Third, historical institutionalism constitutes a powerful, historically based analytical framework for investigating institutional genesis and change. Eschewing the 'snapshot' view of politics prevalent in much political science research, historical institutionalism emphasises the ways in which institutions are the product of political contestation and compromise, how they are renegotiated and reformed over time, and how institutions take on forms, functions, and meanings that their creators never intended. Finally, historical institutionalism provides powerful insights into policy-making. *WEP* has published many articles that analyse the politics of reform in distinct policy areas, and much of this research draws heavily on historical institutionalist insights.

These considerable achievements should not obscure the challenges that remain. First, we currently live in an unsettled period, and our theoretical tools for understanding the causes and consequences of this fluidity are inadequate. Given historical institutionalism's core claim that institutions mediate behaviour, the current political context is problematic because it is so fluid. One obvious sign of this instability is the breakdown of corporatism. Across Western Europe, union membership has declined, new social movements have emerged, and new political issues have reached the political agenda. This has occurred in the context of greater voter volatility, the emergence of new political parties, and the breakdown of once-stable institutions for interest intermediation. These developments challenge the viability of corporatism at the same time that they call into question the theoretical frameworks that dominated research published in *WEP*. Despite the widespread recognition that corporatism is waning ('new social pacts' notwithstanding), there is no successor for corporatist theory in sight. It is worthwhile considering whether theoretical insights drawn from regions that are less stable than Western Europe may provide a starting point for reconceptualising interest intermediation in a post-corporatist Europe. If post-war political stability was indeed an anomaly and West European politics is becoming more like politics in other regions marked by more cleavages and higher volatility, i.e. Eastern Europe or Africa, it is worth examining whether models based on these political conditions offer insights for the study of Western Europe.

Second is the challenge of building middle-range theory. One of the strengths of *WEP* is that it provides an outlet for qualitative research aspiring to particular or middle-range theoretical explanations. Single or comparative case studies of particular policy areas or types of political behaviour provide much of the substance in *WEP*, much of it informed by historical institutionalism. But even after 30 years it is fair to say that progress in theory-building has been disappointing. Even the most sophisticated attempts to combine analytical rigour with historical institutionalist analysis are prone to some of the same problems prevalent in the 1970s when *WEP* was founded: theoretical concepts that are difficult to apply consistently to empirical cases, contradictory hypotheses generated by the same theory, theoretical over-determination, the biases of case choice, the problem of measuring both independent and dependent variables, and the like. Whereas the 'variable' approach so criticised by historical institutionalists has its shortcomings, the 'historical' approach needs to find new ways of addressing theory-building without sacrificing the gains that have been made by increased sensitivity to context and perception. Some steps in this direction have been the increasingly prevalent efforts to combine quantitative and qualitative methods, as well as innovations such as the 'Ragin method' (Ragin 1987). Nevertheless, much theoretical, conceptual and methodological work remains.

The third challenge concerns the regional identification of *WEP*. Is there still today a need to focus on Western Europe? Or is this simply a remnant of Western Europe's rapidly declining economic and political dominance? Analysis of the particular political-institutional development of Western

Europe may perhaps regain greater contemporary relevance by more emphasis on cross-regional comparison. In a way, this is somewhat of a return to the early focus on states and capitalism, and the foundational period's focus on broad comparative-historical analysis on an international scale as carried out by Barrington Moore (1966) Reinhardt Bendix (1969), Shmuel N. Eisenstadt (2003), and other historically oriented comparativists. At the same time, some of the focus on general theory and quantitative methods of the post-war political development and modernisation schools might be reasonably brought to bear on problems of comparative analysis, without, however, ignoring the lessons of conflict theory and multiple routes of modernisation, as has been increasingly the case, for example on the topic of democratisation. Here, the work of Samuel A. Huntington (1966, 1968, 1971, 1991) may serve as an outstanding example of an effort to synthesise acknowledgment of historical particularity and a search for general causal relationships.

What do these challenges suggest for the future of *WEP*? Even as we attempt cross-regional comparisons and middle range theory-building, the tension between an 'Aristotelian' focus on historical and cultural context, and in which there is little or no regular logic apart from historical forces, versus a 'Platonic' search for logical, empirical regularities is likely to remain. We cannot solve this basic dilemma of the social sciences, but we can point to three different strategies for grappling with this inherent tension. The first entails a basic acceptance of the limits of social science explanation, and an embrace of 'plain old history'. There may be many things that we cannot explain, but that does not mean that it is not worth trying to find out what happened. We may not be able to identify all causally important variables, or even to be able to demonstrate a particular causal link or causal model, but we can find out what political actors intended as they framed legislation, joined social movements, or started a war. Indeed, political actors constantly document what they are doing, and there are innumerable sets of historical documents that provide rich detail that can be mined to test competing hypotheses to explain political phenomena. As Lijphart (1971), Hall (2003) and Rueschemeyer (2003) have argued, when historical investigation is embedded in a set of competing hypotheses, the results of this kind of work can be theoretically valuable, even if it does not necessarily provide a universal or general explanation. Thus, accepting the limits of explanation does not have to mean abandoning all ambition of providing an explanation: the key parameter is the research design.

And this brings us to the second strategy: improving qualitative inquiry. While discussions of the philosophy and methods of social science are far from new, one can point to an increasing trend in efforts to address the nuts-and-bolts problems of research on politics, particularly at the dissertation level (King *et al.* 1994; Van Evera 1997; Geddes 2003; George and Bennett 2005; Parsons 2007). These efforts are all valuable, but some may have perhaps overshot their mark. King *et al.*, for example, pay a great deal of attention to problems that arise in statistical analysis and extend these to qualitative studies. Yet they neglect the side of positive prescription: how do we compensate for these problems in a small-*n* study? How many paired comparisons are necessary? Should one focus on outliers? Or more directly on the cases that best fit a proposed explanation, in order to process-trace the causal links? What is needed is more focused guidance on paired case study design in comparative politics (as opposed to international relations), and on combining information on a complete universe of cases with more sustained focus on a smaller set of cases. Furthermore, for all the focus on research design and methodology, in an area where data collection is imprecise, and dependent upon the talents and instincts of the investigator, we may gain more mileage in better coverage of the basics of the historical method (again, 'plain old history'), and in the guidelines of common sense. After all, there are many classics that have been based on biased case selection but yet remain read because they convince the sceptical reader despite their methodological weaknesses. And there are other studies that, while perfectly executed, do not address a substantive issue of compelling importance, and hence fail to convince.

And this brings us to the final point: the need for substance in the analysis of West European politics in international comparison. Theoretical and methodological quandaries aside, the most important factor in keeping *WEP* alive and vibrant will be its ability to continue to focus on issues of substantive importance to West European politics. Recent research on varieties of capitalism, constitutionalism and democracy, political integration and cultural diversity shows a return to substantive issues like 'state and capitalism' that animated so much of *WEP*'s early research. What direction is capitalism developing in? What is the role of the state in this process? Are there just and unjust forms of capitalism? How does political development affect the workings of democracy? What are its social, political, cultural and economic underpinnings? This kind of substantive controversy is precisely the kind of niche that *WEP* has filled in the past and should continue to address in the future. At the same time, however, this conceptual and theoretical work is impossible without the kind of fine-grained qualitative research that *WEP* publishes. Thus we insist on the centrality of the historical method, case studies, and process tracing. The historical record is as close as we get to observing political behaviour directly, that is 'politics in action'. Without meaning to diminish the value of alternative approaches, we only want to emphasise the unique potential for historical research in addressing important research questions.

Note

1. The five types of incremental, potentially transformative institutional change are: layering, conversion, displacement, drift and exhaustion.

References

Anderson, Perry (1974). *Lineages of the Absolutist State*. London: Verso Editions.

Baldwin-Edwards, Martin, and Martin A. Schain, eds. (1994). *The Politics of Immigration in Western Europe* (Special Issue), *West European Politics*, 17:2.

Bartolini, Stefano, and Peter Mair (1990). *Identity, Competition and Electoral Availability – The Stabilisation of European Electorates 1885–1985*. Cambridge: Cambridge University Press.

Beer, Samuel H., and Adam B. Ulam, eds. (1972). *Patterns of Government*. 3rd edn. New York: Random House.

Bell, Daniel (2000 [1960]). *The End of Ideology: On the Exhaustion of Political Ideas in the Fifties*. 2nd new edition. Cambridge, MA: Harvard University Press.

Bendix, Reinhard (1969). *Nation-Building and Citizenship. Studies of Our Changing Social Order*. Garden City, New York: Anchor Books.

Berger, Suzanne (1972). *Peasants Against Politics: Rural Organization in Brittany, 1911–1967*. Cambridge, MA: Harvard University Press.

Berger, Suzanne (1973). 'The French Political System', in Samuel H. Beer and Adam B. Ulam (eds.), *Patterns of Government*. 3rd edn. New York: Random House, 333–463.

Berger, Suzanne (1981). 'Introduction', in Suzanne Berger (ed.), *Organizing Interests in Western Europe: Pluralism, Corporatism and the Transformation of Politics*. Cambridge: Cambridge University Press, 1–23.

Berger, Suzanne, ed. (1982). *Religion in West European Politics* (Special Issue), *West European Politics*, 5:2.

Berger, Suzanne, and Ronald Dore, eds. (1996). *National Diversity and Global Capitalism*. Ithaca, NY: Cornell University Press.

Berger, Suzanne, and Michael J. Piore (1980). *Dualism and Discontinuity in Industrial Societies*. Cambridge: Cambridge University Press.

Berman, Sheri (1998). *The Social Democratic Moment Ideas and Politics in the Making of Interwar Europe*. Cambridge, MA: Harvard University Press.

Blyth, Mark (2002). *Great Transformations: Economic Ideas and Institutional Change in the Twentieth Century*. Cambridge: Cambridge University Press.

Bull, Martin J., and Martin Rhodes, eds. (1997). *Crisis and Transition in Italian Politics* (Special Issue), *West European Politics*, 20:1.

Cox, Robert H. (2001). 'The Social Construction of an Imperative', *World Politics*, 53:3, 463–98.

Crouch, Colin, and Wolfgang Streeck, eds. (1997). *Political Economy of Modern Capitalism*. London: SAGE.

Crozier, Michel, Samuel P. Huntington and Joji Watanuki (1975). *The Crisis of Democracy*.

Cusack, Thomas R., Torben Iversen and David Soskice (2007). 'Economic Interests and the Origins of Electoral Systems', *American Political Science Review*, 101:3, 373–91.

Daviter, Falk (2007). 'Policy Framing in the European Union', *Journal of European Public Policy*, 14:4, 654–66.

Downs, Anthony (1957). *An Economic Theory of Democracy*. New York: Harper & Row.

Dyson, Kenneth, and Peter Humphreys, eds. (1986). *The Politics of the Communications Revolution in Western Europe* (Special Issue), *West European Politics*, 9:4.

Eisenstadt, Shmuel N. (2003). *Comparative Civilizations and Multiple Modernities*. Boston: Brill.

Elster, Jon, Claus Offe and Ulrich K. Preuß (1998). *Institutional Design in Post-communist Societies: Rebuilding the Ship at Sea*. Cambridge: Cambridge University Press.

Evans, Peter B., Dietrich Rueschemeyer and Theda Skocpol, eds. (1985). *Bringing the State Back In*. Cambridge: Cambridge University Press.

Ferrera, Maurizio and Martin Rhodes, eds. (2000). *Recasting European Welfare States* (Special Issue), *West European Politics*, 23:2.

Finger, Matthias, and Pascal Sciarini (1991). 'Integrating "New Politics" into "Old Politics": The Swiss Party Elite', *West European Politics*, 14:1, 98–112.

Fuchs, Dieter, and Robert Rohrschneider (1998). 'Postmaterialism and Electoral Choice before and after German Unification', *West European Politics*, 21:2, 95–116.

Geddes, Barbara (2003). *Paradigms and Sand Castles: Theory Building and Research Design in Comparative Politics*. Ann Arbor: University of Michigan Press.

George, Alexander L., and Andrew Bennett (2005). *Case Studies and Theory Development in the Social Sciences*. Cambridge, MA: MIT Press.

Gerschenkron, Alexander (1962). *Economic Backwardness in Historical Perspective: A Book of Essays*. Frederick A. Praeger Publishers.

Gerschenkron, Alexander (1966). *Bread and Democracy in Germany*. New York: Howard Fertig, Inc.

Gigerenzer, Gerd (2001). 'Decision-Making: Nonrational Thories', in N.J. Smelser and P.B. Baltes (eds.), *International Encyclopedia of the Social and Behavioral Sciences*. Vol. 5. Amsterdam: Elsevier, 3304–9.

Gillespie, Richard, and William E. Patterson, eds. (1993). *Social Democracy in Western Europe*, (Special Issue), *West European Politics*, 16:1.

Goetz, Klaus H., and Simon Hix, eds. (2000), *Europeanised Politics? European Integration and National Political Systems* (Special Issue), *West European Politics*, 23:4.

Goldthorpe, John H., ed. (1984). *Order and Conflict in Contemporary Capitalism: Studies in the Political Economy of Western European Nations*. Oxford: Clarendon Press.

Gourevitch, Peter A. (1986). *Politics in Hard Times. Comparative Responses to International Crises*. Ithaca, NY: Cornell University Press.

Gourevitch, Peter (1995 [1977]). 'International Trade, Domestic Coalitions, and Liberty: Comparative Response to the Crisis of 1873–1896', in Ronald Rogowski (ed.), *Comparative Politics and the International Political Economy I*. Aldershot: Edward Elgar Publishing Limited, 96–128.

Hall, Peter A. (1986). *Governing the Economy: The Politics of State Intervention in Britain and France*. New York: Oxford University Press.

Hall, Peter A. (1993). 'Policy Paradigms, Social Learning, and the State: The Case of Economic Policymaking in Britain', *Comparative Politics*, 25:3, 275–96.

Hall, Peter A. (2003). 'Aligning Ontology and Methodology in Comparative Politics', in James Mahoney and Dietrich Rueschemeyer (eds.), *Comparative Historical Analysis in the Social Sciences*. Cambridge: Cambridge University Press, 373–404.

Hall, Peter A., and David Soskice, eds. (2001). *Varieties of Capitalism*. New York: Oxford University Press.

Hall, Peter A., and Rosemary C.R. Taylor (1996). 'Political Science and the Three New Institutionalisms', *Political Studies*, 44:5, 936–57.

Hattam, Victoria C. (1993). *Labor Movement Visions and State Power*. Princeton, NJ: Princeton University Press.

Hayward, Jack, ed. (1980). *Trade Unions and Politics in Western Europe* (Special Issue), *West European Politics*, 3:1.

Heidenheimer, Arnold, ed. (1980). *Public Policy Comparisons: Scandinavia* (Special Issue), *West European Politics*, 3:3.

Herrigel, Gary B. (1995). *Industrial Constructions: The Sources of German Industrial Power*. Cambridge: Cambridge University Press.

Hollingsworth, Roger J., and Robert Boyer, eds. (1999). *Contemporary Capitalism: the Embeddedness of Institutions*. Cambridge: Cambridge University Press.

Huntington, Samuel P. (1966). 'Political Modernization: America VS. Europe', *World Politics*, 18:3, 378–414.

Huntington, Samuel P. (1968). *Political Order in Changing Societies*. New Haven, CT and London: Yale University Press.

Huntington, Samuel P. (1971). 'The Change to Change', *Comparative Politics*, 3:3, 283–322.

Huntington, Samuel P. (1991). *The Third Wave: Democratization in the Late Twentieth Century*. Norman and London: University of Oklahoma Press.

Katzenstein, Peter J. (1985). *Small States in World Markets: Industrial Policy in Europe*. Ithaca, NY: Cornell University Press.

Katzenstein, Peter J., ed. (1978). *Between Power and Plenty: Foreign Economic Policies of Advanced Industrial States*. Madison: The University of Wisconsin Press.

Katznelson, Ira (1997). 'Structure and Configuration in Comparative Politics', in Mark Irving Lichbach and Alan S. Zuckerman (eds.), *Comparative Politics: Rationality, Culture, and Structure*. Cambridge: Cambridge University Press, 81–112.

King, Gary, Robert O. Keohane and Sidney Verba (1994). *Designing Social Inquiry: Scientific Inference in Qualitative Research*. Princeton, NJ: Princeton University Press.

Kirchheimer, Otto (1966). 'The Transformation of the Western European Party Systems', in LaPalombara, Joseph and Weiner Myron (eds.), *Political Parties and Political Development*. Princeton: Princeton University Press, 177–200.

Kitschelt, H., and Wolfgang Streeck, eds. (2003). *Germany: Beyond the Stable State* (Special Issue), *West European Politics*, 26:4.

Kitschelt, Herbert (1986). 'Political Opportunity Structures and Political Protest: Anti-nuclear Movements in Four Democracies', *British Journal of Political Science*, 16:1, 57–85.

Kitschelt, Herbert (1989). *The Logics of Party Formation: Ecological Politics in Belgium and West Germany*. Ithaca, NY: Cornell University Press.

Kitschelt, Herbert (1994). *The Transformation of European Social Democracy*. New York: Cambridge University Press.

Knutsen, Oddbjørn (1990). 'The Materialist/Post-Materialist Value Dimension as a Party Cleavage in the Nordic Countries', *West European Politics*, 13:2, 258–74.

Lane, Jan-Erik, ed. (1991). *Understanding the Swedish Model* (Special Issue), *West European Politics*, 14:3.

Lane, Jan-Erik, ed. (2001). *The Swiss Labyrinth: Institutions, Outcomes and Redesign* (Special Issue), *West European Politics*, 24:2.

Lange, Peter, and Sidney Tarrow, eds. (1979). *Italy in Transition: Conflict and Consensus* (Special Issue), *West European Politics*, 2:3.

Lijphart, Arend (1971). 'Comparative Politics and the Comparative Method', *American Political Science Review*, 65:September, 682–93.

Lijphart, Arend (1999). *Patterns of Democracy: Government Forms and Performance in 36 Countries*. New Haven, CT: Yale University Press.

Locke, Richard (1995). *Remaking the Italian Economy: Policy Failures and Local Successes in the Contemporary Polity*. Ithaca, NY: Cornell University Press.

Luther, Kurt Richard, and Wolfgang C. Müller, eds. (1992), *Politics in Austria: Still a Case of Consocialtionalism?* (Special Issue), *West European Politics*, 15:1.

Lynch, Julia (2006). *Age in the Welfare State: The Origins of Social Spending on Pensioners, Workers, and Children*. Cambridge: Cambridge University Press.

Maier, Charles S. (1975). *Recasting Bourgeois Europe: Stabilization in France, Germany, and Italy in the Decade After World War I*. Princeton, NJ: Princeton University Press.

Maier, Charles S., ed. (1987). *Changing Boundaries of the Political: Essays on the Evolving Balance between the State and Society, Public and Private in Europe*. Cambridge: Cambridge University Press.

Mair, Peter, and Gordon Smith, eds. (1989) *Understanding Party system Change in Western Europe* (Special Issue), *West European Politics*, 12:4.

March, James G., and Johan P. Olsen (1984). 'The New Institutionalism: Organizational Factors in Political Life', *American Political Science Review*, 78:3, 734–49.

Merkel, Wolfgang (1993). *Ende der Sozialdemokratie? Wählerentwicklung, Machtressourcen und Regierungspolitik im westeuropäischen Vergleich*. Frankfurt: Campus.

Merkel, Wolfgang, with Christoph Egle, Christian Henkes, Tobias Ostheim and Alexander Petring (2006). *Die Reformfähigkeit der Sozialdemokratie. Herausforderungen und Bilanz der Regierungspolitik in Westeuropa*. Wiesbaden: VS Verlag für Sozialwissenschaften.

Moore, Barrington Jr. (1966). *Social Origins of Dictatorship and Democracy: Lord and Peasant in the Making of the Modern World*. Boston: Beacon Press.

Morgan, Kimberly J. (2006). *Working Mothers and the Welfare State: Religion and the Politics of Work-Family Policies in Western Europe and the United States*. Stanford, CA: Stanford University Press.

Naumann, Ingela (2005). 'Child Care and Feminism in West Germany and Sweden in the 1960s and 1970s', *Journal of European Social Policy*, 15:1, 47–63.

Panitch, Leo (1977). 'The Development of Corporatism in Liberal Democracies', *Comparative Political Studies*, 10:1, 61–90.

Parsons, Craig (2007). *How to Map Arguments in Political Science*. Oxford: Oxford University Press.

Pierson, Paul (1994). *Dismantling the Welfare State*. Cambridge: Cambridge University Press.

Pierson, Paul, ed. (2001). *The New Politics of the Welfare State*. Oxford: Oxford University Press.

Pierson, Paul (2004). *Politics in Time: History, Institutions, and Social Analysis*. Princeton, NJ: Princeton University Press.

Piore, Michael J., and Charles F. Sabel (1984). *The Second Industrial Divide: Possibilities for Prosperity*. New York: Basic Books.

Pizzorno, Alessandro, and Colin Crouch, eds. (1978). *The Resurgence of Class Conflict in Western Europe since 1968*. London: The MacMillan Press.

Polanyi, Karl (2001 [1944]). *The Great Transformation: The Political and Economic Origins of Our Times*. 2nd edn. Boston: Beacon Press.

Powell, Walter W., and Paul J. DiMaggio, eds. (1991). *The New Institutionalism in Organizational Analysis*. Chicago: The University of Chicago Press.

Ragin, Charles C. (1987). *The Comparative Method: Moving Beyond Qualitative and Quantitative Strategies*. Berkeley: University of California Press.

Reiter, Howard L. (1993). 'The Rise of the "New Agenda" and the Decline of Partisanship', *West European Politics*, 16:2, 89–104.

Rhodes, R.A.W., and Vincent Wright, eds. (1987). *Tensions in the Territorial Politics of Western Europe* (Special Issue), *West European Politics*, 10:4.

Rogowski, Ronald (1987). 'Trade and the Variety of Democratic Institutions', *International Organization*, 41:2, 203–23.

Rothstein, Bo (1992). 'Labor-Market Institutions and Working-Class Strength', in Sven Steinmo, Kathleen Thelen and Frank Longstreth (eds.), *Structuring Politics. Historical Institutionalism in Comparative Analysis*. Cambridge: Cambridge University Press, 33–56.

Rothstein, Bo (1998). *Just Institutions Matter*. Cambridge: Cambridge University Press.

Rueschemeyer, Dietrich (2003). 'Can One or a Few Cases Yield Theoretical Gains?', in James Mahoney and Dietrich Rueschemeyer (eds.), *Comparative Historical Analysis in the Social Sciences*. Cambridge: Cambridge University Press, 305–36.

Sabel, Charles F., and Jonathan Zeitlin (1985). 'Historical Alternatives to Mass Production: Politics, Markets and Technology in Nineteenth-Century Industrialization', *Past and Present*, 108:August, 133–76.

Sabel, Charles F., and Jonathan Zeitlin (1997). *World of Possibilities – Flexibility and Mass Production in Western Industrialization*. vol.1. Cambridge: Cambridge University Press.

Scarrow, Susan (2006). 'Party Subsidies and the Freezing of Party Competition: Do Cartels Work?', *West European Politics*, 29:4, 619–39.

Scharpf, Fritz W. (1997). *Games Real Actors Play: Actor-Centered Institutionalism in Policy Research*. Boulder, CO: Westview Press.

Schattschneider, E.E. (1960). *The Semisovereign People: A Realist's View of Democracy in America*. New York: Holt, Rinehart & Winston.

Schmidt, Vivien A. (forthcoming). 'Give Peace a Chance: Reconciling the Four (not Three) New Institutionalisms', in Daniel Béland and Robert H. Cox (eds.), *Ideas and Politics in Social Science Research*.

Schmitter, Phillippe C. (1981). 'Interest Intermediation and Regime Governability in Contemporary Western Europe and North America', in Suzanne Berger (ed.), *Organizing Interests in Western Europe*. Cambridge: Cambridge University Press, 285–327.

Schmitter, Philippe C., and Gerhard Lehmbruch, eds. (1979). *Trends Towards Corporatist Interest Intermediation*. Beverly Hills, CA: Sage.
Schumpeter, Joseph A. (1975 [1942]). *Capitalism, Socialism and Democracy*. New York: Harper Torchbooks.
Shonfield, Andrew (1965). *Modern Capitalism: The Changing Balance of Public and Private Power*. Oxford: Oxford University Press.
Skach, Cindy (2005). *Borrowing Constitutional Designs: Constitutional Law in Weimar Germany and the French Fifth Republic*. Princeton, NJ: Princeton University Press.
Skocpol, Theda (1985). 'Bringing the State Back In: Strategies of Analysis in Current Research', in Peter B. Evans, Dietrich Rueschemeyer and Theda Skocpol (eds.), *Bringing the State Back In*. Cambridge: Cambridge University Press, 3–43.
Skocpol, Theda (1992). *Protecting Soldiers and Mothers: The Political Origins of Social Policy in the United States*. Cambridge: Harvard University Press.
Steinmo, Sven (1993). *Taxation and Democracy. Swedish, British, and American Approaches to Financing the Modern State*. New Haven, CT: Yale University Press.
Steinmo, Sven (2007). 'Historical Institutionalism', Unpublished paper, European University Institute.
Steinmo, Sven, Kathleen Thelen and Frank Longstreth, eds. (1992). *Structuring Politics: Historical Institutionalism in Comparative Analysis*. Cambridge: Cambridge University Press.
Streeck, Wolfgang, and Kathleen Thelen, eds. (2005). *Beyond Continuity: Institutional Change in Advanced Political Economies*. Oxford: Oxford University Press.
Tarrow, Sidney (1994). *Power in Movement: Collective Action, Social Movements and Politics*. Cambridge: Cambridge University Press.
The Trilateral Commission Task Force Report #8. New York: New York University Press.
Thelen, Kathleen A. (1991). *Union of Parts: Labor Politics in Postwar Germany*. Ithaca, NY: Cornell University Press.
Thelen, Kathleen (1999). 'Historical Institutionalism in Comparative Politics', *Annual Review of Political Science*, 2, 369–404.
Thelen, Kathleen (2004). *How Institutions Evolve: The Political Economy of Skills in Germany, Britain, the United States and Japan*. Cambridge: Cambridge University Press.
Thelen, Kathleen, and Sven Steinmo (1992). 'Introduction', in Sven Steinmo, Kathleen Thelen and Frank Longstreth (eds.), *Structuring Politics: Historical Institutionalism in Comparative Analysis*. Cambridge: Cambridge University Press.
Tilly, Charles, ed. (1975). *The Formation of National States in Western Europe*. Princeton, NJ: Princeton University Press.
Tilly, Charles (1978). *From Mobilization to Revolution*. London: Addison-Wesley Publishing Company.
Van Evera, Stephen (1997). *Guide to Methods for Students of Political Science*. Ithaca, NY: Cornell University Press.
Vickers, John, and Vincent Wright, eds. (1988). *The Politics of Privatisation in Western Europe* (Special Issue), *West European Politics*, 11:4.
Von Beyme, Klaus, ed. (1988). *Right-Wing Extremism in Western Europe* (Special Issue), *West European Politics*, 11:2.
Weir, Margaret (1992). *Politics and Jobs: The Boundaries of Employment Policy in the United States*. Princeton, NJ: Princeton University Press.
Weir, Margaret, and Theda Skocpol (1985). 'State Structures and the Possibilities for "Keynesian" Responses to the Great Depression in Sweden, Britain, and the United States', in Peter B. Evans, Dietrich Rueschemeyer and Theda Skocpol (eds.), *Bringing the State Back In*. Cambridge: Cambridge University Press, 107–63.
Wright, Vincent, ed. (1978). *Conflict and Consensus in France* (Special Issue), *West European Politics*, 1:3.

Ziblatt, Daniel (2006). *Structuring the State: the Formation of Italy and Germany and the Puzzle of Federalism*. Princeton, NJ: Princeton University Press.

Ziegler, J. Nicholas (1997). *Governing Ideas: Strategies for Innovation in France and Germany*. Ithaca, NY: Cornell University Press.

Zysman, John (1983). *Governments, Markets and Growth: Financial Systems and the Politics of Industrial Change*. Ithaca, NY: Cornell University Press.

Capacities: Political Science in Europe

HANS-DIETER KLINGEMANN

This article portrays the capacities of political science in Western as well as in Central and Eastern Europe. The discussion is divided into four subtopics: the political and social context in which European political science developed after World War II; its degree of institutionalisation as an academic discipline; its professional organisation and communication structure; and, finally, its capacity to represent the discipline's education and research interests in the European area.[1]

Our definition of Europe includes all countries that are members of the Council of Europe – with the addition of non-member Belarus. There are no comprehensive data covering the development of political science in the Central and Eastern European countries. However, political science has become a respected academic discipline in these new democracies. Their place in European higher education and research and their capacities in political science should not be ignored.

Data comparability problems also exist with respect to the Western European countries, making it difficult to assess developments across countries and over time. Available country reports are summarised in Table 1a. Table 1b shows the situation regarding Central and Eastern Europe. Together, the seven volumes to which the tables refer provide a wealth of detailed information; however, as the tables show not all European

TABLE 1A
MAJOR REPORTS ON THE DEVELOPMENT OF POLITICAL SCIENCE IN WESTERN
EUROPEAN COUNTRIES

Country	UNESCO 1950	Andrews 1982	Easton *et al.* 1991	Newton & Vallès 1991	Quermonne 1996	Klingemann 2007b	N
France	X	X	X	X	X	X	6
Germany**	X	X	X	X	X	X	6
Sweden	X	X	X*	x*	X	X	6
United Kingdom	X	X	X	X	X	X	6
Austria	X	X		X	X	X	5
Belgium	X	X		X	X	X	5
Denmark		X	X*	X*	X	X	5
Finland		X	X*	X*	X	X	5
Italy	X		X	X	X	X	5
Netherlands	X	X		X	X	X	5
Spain	X		X	X	X	X	5
Norway		X		X	X	X	4
Switzerland	X	X		X		X	4
Greece				X	X	X	3
Iceland		X			X	X	3
Ireland				X	X	X	3
Portugal				X	X	X	3
Cyprus						X	1
Luxembourg					X		1
Turkey							0
Andorra							0
Liechtenstein							0
Malta							0
Monaco							0
San Marino							0

*Part of a general review of the Nordic countries.
**Andrews (1982) has a chapter both on the Federal Republic of Germany and the German Democratic Republic. Easton *et al.* (1991) and Newton and Vallès (1991) carry chapters on West Germany while the volumes by Quermonne (1996) and Klingemann (2007b) describe the situation after reunification.

countries are covered in each of these books, whilst some countries are not covered at all.

As mentioned earlier, the overwhelming part of the information gathered on Central and Eastern Europe is country-specific and difficult to summarise. That is why we shall mainly rely on the comparative tables provided by Klingemann *et al.* (2002) for Central and Eastern Europe, by Klingemann (2002a) for Western Europe, and on material provided by the German Social Science Infrastructure Services. In addition, we consult relevant websites where appropriate.

The Political and Social Context of the Development of Political Science after World War II

Political science has been growing across post-World War II Western Europe. Change from autocratic to democratic rule constituted one of the

TABLE 1B

MAJOR REPORTS ON THE DEVELOPMENT OF POLITICAL SCIENCE IN CENTRAL
AND EASTERN EUROPEAN COUNTRIES

Country	UNESCO 1950	Andrews 1982	Klingemann *et al.* 2002b	Kaase *et al.* 2002	N
Poland	X	X	X	X	4
Bulgaria			X	X	2
Czech Republic			X	X	2
Hungary			X	X	2
Romania			X	X	2
Slovenia			X	X	2
Slovakia			X	X	2
Estonia			X	X	2
Latvia			X	X	2
Lithuania			X	X	2
Albania					0
Bosnia-Herzegovina					0
Croatia					0
Macedonia					0
Montenegro					0
Armenia					0
Azerbaijan					0
Georgia					0
Russia					0
Belarus*					0
Ukraine					0
Moldova					0
East Germany		X			1
Former Yugoslavia		X			1
Former Soviet Union	X	X			2

*Currently not a member of the Council of Europe.

most fundamental preconditions for this development. Mackenzie (1971) summarised the argument as follows: 'Political science cannot develop except in certain limited intellectual and social conditions; there must be an established practice of debate based on analysis and observation, and it must be accepted that there exist political questions open to settlement by argument rather than by tradition or by authority. In this sense, political science is conditioned by political society.' Thus, the spread of representative democracy after World War II offered fertile ground for establishing political science as an academic discipline. Italy (1946), (West) Germany (1949), and Austria (1955) turned democratic after military defeat. Portugal (1974/76), Spain (1975), and Greece (1974) joined the ranks of representative democracies in the mid-1970s by overthrowing autocratic governments. After the mid-1970s, all West European countries were ruled by democratically elected governments.

The breakdown of the Communist regimes in Central and Eastern Europe likewise offered a new political context hospitable to political science. Today political science is a recognised academic discipline in most of the 22 Central and Eastern European members of the Council of Europe. This constitutes the first critical juncture.

In the 1960s and 1970s, growing Western European prosperity, the need for an academically trained workforce, and a demand for equal access to higher education led to the broadening of old and the building of new universities. These economic, social, and political changes – which constitute a second critical juncture – helped to establish political science. In many of the old universities the faculties of law, philosophy, history, or economics thought that they covered all the objects the new discipline claimed for itself. Obviously, these old faculties tended to resist the institutionalisation of a competitor. However, this resistance was much lower in the newly established, reform-oriented universities or polytechnics. In addition, the introduction of required civics courses as an integral part of the curriculum of the primary and secondary school systems increased demand, thus lessening the competitive pressure.

While history does not repeat itself, there are indications of the same developments in recent Central and Eastern European experience. There, too, the old institutes of philosophy and history have been suspicious of modern political science, a situation that is quite different in the new (often private) reform-oriented universities. However, a solid database on political science in Central and Eastern Europe to detail this claim is still lacking.

The third critical juncture European political science is facing is linked to the 'Bologna Process' (Reinalda and Kulesza 2006). The Bologna Process started with the Sorbonne Declaration and can justifiably be regarded as the most important politically induced effort to harmonise the systems of higher education and research in Europe. Its main goal is the implementation of a system of easily readable and comparable degrees for all academic disciplines, including political science. The action lines promoting this goal have been worked out in a number of meetings of an intergovernmental conference of Europe's ministers of education. In 2007, this conference comprised 47 countries, including all European countries except Belarus, Monaco, and San Marino. The Bologna Process reaches well beyond the borders of the European Union. Thus, the Bologna challenge must be confronted by Western, Central, and Eastern European universities alike. West European political science has reacted by working out and recommending minimum requirements for the degree of a Bachelor of Arts (Reinalda and Kulesza 2006: 224). This, however, is only a first step. It must be followed by similar recommendations regarding M.A. and Ph.D. degrees.

Professionalisation and Institutionalisation of Political Science as an Academic Discipline

Richard Rose (1990) has pointed out that the pioneers of political science were necessarily amateurs. Their subject simply did not exist in the universities. Needless to say, most of these amateurs were professionals in other disciplines such as law, economics, history, or philosophy. However, today political science has become a collective enterprise, a profession with well-defined standards for training and employment, based institutionally on national university systems. As described above, the process of professionalisation of political science in Europe is a post-World War II phenomenon. This process was much aided by immigrants returning to Europe from exile after World War II. A similar development has occurred in the new democracies of Central and Eastern Europe.

Today, there is rather widespread agreement in Europe that the following subfields are the core components of the political science curriculum:

- Political theory and the history of political ideas,
- Political system of one's own country and of the European Union;
- Public administration and policy analysis;
- Political economy and political sociology;
- Comparative politics;
- International relations; and,
- Methodology (including statistics).

However, even today, different epistemological positions surface when it comes to particular methodological skills. One camp stresses the importance of analytic theory and quantitative data analysis. The other camp prefers a historical approach and hermeneutics. However, both the analytical and the historical perspectives have their own potential to contribute to a better understanding of 'the way in which decisions for a society are made and considered binding most of the time by most of the people' (Easton 1953: 129–48).

Today's research products reveal a broad definition of political science. This breadth has become somewhat centrifugal as subfields try to create disciplines of their own, as is the case with International Relations, European Studies, Public Administration, or Political Communication – just to mention a few examples. The ensuing variety of political science related disciplines makes rather fragile the overarching discipline at both the national and at the European levels.

In order to practise their profession, political scientists need an economic base, and this normally requires a job at an institution (Rose 1990: 582). Country reports indicate that there are differences in the institutionalisation of European political science in these terms. As a discipline, political science has gained access to universities more easily in the north than in the south of Europe. For example, political science in France had initially profited from its incorporation in the curriculum of the law faculties. However, while this might have been an advantage in the early period after World War II, it subsequently created a gap between France and the rest of the European countries. Because of the strong alliance with the teaching of law at the level of universities, political science has been organised as Institutes of Political Studies (IEP). Until today, only one French university has a political science department.

European systems of higher education are largely dominated by central governments. Thus, most of the data we present describe the institutionalisation of political science in a system of state-supported universities. This is a serious restriction because the number of private universities is currently rising across all of Europe. This is also true for non-university based political science research institutions such as the Austrian Academy of Sciences, the Social Science Research Centre Berlin (WZB), the Juan March Institute in Madrid, or the Swedish Institute for Social Research, to name just a few. And, again, it seems that private universities or independent research institutes are playing an increasingly important role in Central and Eastern Europe, too.

How many political scientists do we have in Europe? How many institutions are there to employ them? There is no easy answer to these questions. Quermonne (1996: 15) estimated that in the mid-1990s, 3,500 political scientists were active in Western Europe. About ten years later Klingemann (2007: 20) counted 1,526 full or associate professors in the 18 West European countries he had surveyed around the year 2005. His estimate is more conservative than the one by Quermonne because it is restricted to professors and associate professors and not aiming to account for the total academic staff. Adjusting for this more conservative measurement, Klingemann (2007: 20) comes up with a figure of roughly 4,600 political scientists around the year 2005.

Exactly comparable data are not yet available for the Central and Eastern European countries. For 1999/2000, Klingemann *et al.* (2002a) have counted 41 state universities offering political science in the ten new EU Central and Eastern European countries. These universities occupy an academic staff of 550 professors and full-time lecturers (Klingemann *et al.* 2002a: 12–17). A first rough sorting of information for all 22 Central and Eastern European countries for the years around 2005 counted 351 organisational units devoted to teaching and/or research of political science located at 168 state universities.[2] This count does not include the sometimes very large political science institutes of the Academy of Sciences, institutes catering to the needs of governments, private universities or non-profit institutes. We were unable to estimate the number of political science professors or the more comprehensive academic staff for a point in time comparable to the West European situation around the year 2005. However, if we were to assume a West European average of 4.4 professors per organisational unit we would come up with an estimate of 1,544 professors in that region. And if, as in Western Europe, we multiply this figure by three to calculate the total size of the academic staff the resulting estimate would suggest about 4,600 political scientists. These estimates rest on shaky ground. But we can accept the figures as reasonable approximations, marking but the lower end of the scale. This is because a first look at personnel figures seems to justify the conclusion that the overall size of the academic staff is larger in Central and Eastern Europe than our estimate for Western Europe.

One last statistical observation deserves mention. The ratio of political science institutes (organisational units) per university is twice as high in Central and Eastern Europe (Central and Eastern Europe: 2.01; Western Europe: 1.13). We can only speculate about the causes. Size of Central and Eastern European state universities may be a prime cause. However, it is also a plausible assumption that 'new' political science has sought its own organisational identity apart from the 'old' institutes once committed to studies of Marxism-Leninism and Scientific Communism.

The above description portrays the supply-side of European political science. What about the demand-side? Again, reliable figures of the number of political science students are hard to come by. Klingemann (2007: 23) tried to estimate the number of undergraduate, graduate, and doctoral political science students for mid-2005. Relying on country reports, which, however, are notoriously difficult to aggregate, he counts more than 150,000 students of political science in Western Europe. There is much variation between countries, reflecting differences in population (United Kingdom: 33,000; Cyprus: 129). For the time being let us accept these figures as a first approximation of student numbers in Western Europe. If we extrapolate this figure to Central and Eastern Europe, we get a total of approximately 300,000 students in the larger Europe taking at least some courses in political science. This, too, is a conservative estimate because so many students take political science as a minor subject. Unable to make a proper distinction along these lines, Klingemann *et al.* (2002a: 17) report 160,000 political science students in the ten EU accession countries alone. Future research is needed to arrive at a more solid estimate of student numbers.

TABLE 2

INSTITUTIONALISATION OF EUROPEAN POLITICAL SCIENCE AROUND THE YEAR 2005

Europe	N universities	N of political science units	Total N of academic staff
Western Europe	307	347	4600 (est.)
Central and Eastern Europe	168*	351*	4600*
Europe	575*	698*	10,000*

*First estimates.

Professional Organisations, Journals, and Data Archives

In this section, we will describe capacities of European political science in terms of organisation, communication, and data supply. This includes national political science associations and their various modes of international cooperation; European organisations and networks set up to study European politics: professional journals, and data archives catering to the needs of empirical political science.

National Political Science Associations and their International Cooperation

The emergence of national political science associations is a good indicator of the discipline's professionalisation and institutionalisation. By organising meetings and supporting professional journals on a national level, these organisations provide the infrastructure for a critical debate over new insights from political inquiry. Reports differ about the year of foundation of the various national political science associations, but it is clear that, compared to other disciplines, political science associations are latecomers. Trent (1982: 34) reports that political science associations were founded prior to World War II only in the United States (1903), Canada (1913), Finland (1935), and India (1938). The Finnish association started off in the 1930s as a voluntary organisation for the promotion of democratic political life rather than as an interest organisation for academic political science (Anckar 1991: 240). With this exception, all Western European political science associations were organised after World War II, starting with France and the United Kingdom in 1949. Disregarding the very small countries, this process was completed in the 1990s when Spain and Portugal established their national political science associations. Although all seven of the smallest member countries of the Council of Europe support a university, only the University of Iceland and the University of Cyprus have, in recent years, institutionalised political science as an autonomous academic discipline. The University of Luxembourg is in the process of following up. The University of Malta, founded in 1769, has developed an Academy of Diplomatic Studies as well as various area study programmes that include political science. However, no report on the state of the discipline in this country is available to this author.

Most of the Central and Eastern European political science associations were founded before the breakdown of the Communist regimes. The UNESCO Report (1950: 413) mentions that political science associations were active as early as 1950 in Poland, 1954 in Yugoslavia, and 1960 in the USSR (Smirnov 1982: 351). Bibic (1982: 403) reports that a Union of the Political Science Associations of Yugoslavia was founded in 1954. However, it was not until 1968 that political science associations emerged in the individual Yugoslav Republics of Slovenia (Bibic 1994: 148), Croatia, and Macedonia (Zajc, personal communication). The Soviet Political Science Association was founded in 1960 under the auspices of the Social Sciences Section of the USSR Academy of Sciences. We know little about the development of political science in the various Soviet Republics, except that territorial sections of the association were established in six cities of the Soviet Union (Smirnov 1982: 351–4). Political Science Associations were founded in 1964 in the Czech Republic (Mansfeldova 2002: 72), followed by a Slovakian Political Science Association in 1968/69 (Szomolanyi 1994: 141), in Romania in 1970 (Barbu 2002: 235), in Bulgaria in 1974 (Karasimeonov 2002: 41), and in Hungary in 1982 (Ágh 1994: 83).

TABLE 3A
YEAR OF FOUNDATION AND IPSA MEMBERSHIP OF POLITICAL SCIENCE
ASSOCIATIONS IN WESTERN EUROPE

Country	Year of foundation
Finland (IPSA)	1935 (Berndtson 2007: 125)
France (IPSA)	1949 (Blondiaux & Déloye 2007: 154)
United Kingdom (IPSA)	1949 (Goldsmith & Grant 2007: 382)
Netherlands (IPSA)	1950 (Andrews 1982: 413); reorganisation 1966 (IPSA 2000: 107)
Belgium (IPSA)	1951 (DeWinter et al. 2007: 66)
Flemish	1979 (IPSA 2000: 98)
Walloon	1996 (IPSA 2000: 98)
Germany (IPSA)	1951 (Schüttemeyer 2007: 181)
Greece (IPSA)	1955 (1975) (Contogeorgis 2007: 212)
Norway (IPSA)	1956 (Kuhnle, personal communication)
Switzerland (IPSA)	1959 (Freymond et al. 2007: 373)
Denmark (IPSA)	1961 (Pedersen 2007: 98)
Turkey (IPSA)	1963 (Turan, personal communication)
Austria (IPSA)	1970 (Appelt & Pollak 2007: 52)
Sweden (IPSA)	1970 (Berglund & Ekman 2007: 355)
Italy (IPSA)	1973 (Freddi & Giannetti 2007: 270)
Iceland	1982 (Hardarson 2007: 238)
Ireland (IPSA)	1982 (Coakley & Laver 2007: 252)
Spain (IPSA)	1993 (Etherington & Morata 2007: 335)
Portugal	1998 (Moreira 2007: 319)
Cyprus	In the process of formation (Agapiou-Josephides 2007: 85)
Andorra	n.a.
Liechtenstein	n.a.
Luxembourg	n.a.
Malta	n.a.
Monaco	n.a.
San Marino	n.a.

Note: The Handbook of the International Political Science Association (cited in Tables 3a and 3b as IPSA 2000) mentions political science associations which have preceded the ones given in Table 3.1 for Switzerland (1950), Sweden (1950), Austria (1951), Italy (1952), and Spain (1958).

This list is likely to be incomplete. More research is needed to monitor the foundation and subsequent fate of political science associations in Central and Eastern Europe during Communist rule. Marxism-Leninism and Scientific Communism dominated the agenda of what was called political science in these days. However the degree of freedom to develop and communicate with Western political science differed significantly across countries. In the former Soviet Union, all academic disciplines were centrally controlled. This began to change during the period of Glasnost and Perestroika. A similarly rigid situation could be observed Czechoslovakia (after 1956), Bulgaria, East Germany, and Romania. The more moderate and open socialist regimes such as Poland or Yugoslavia offered the relatively best conditions for the development of political science among the Eastern Bloc countries.

Political science in Central and Eastern Europe has to come to grips with its legacy from Communist times. After the breakdown of the old regime, new national political science associations were created in some countries; in others they were reorganised or – in the open socialist regimes – simply continued. Often dual associations were formed, typically with one representing the interests of the 'old guard' and the other those of the 'newcomers'. However, as seen by the number of 'not ascertained' in Table 3b, more information is needed about the institutionalisation of political science in Central and Eastern Europe.

TABLE 3B

YEAR OF FOUNDATION AND IPSA MEMBERSHIP OF POLITICAL SCIENCE ASSOCIATIONS IN CENTRAL AND EASTERN EUROPE

Country	Year of foundation 'old'	Year of foundation 'new'
Poland (IPSA)	1950 (IPSA 2000: 109)	continued*
Croatia (IPSA)	1966 (IPSA 2000: 100)	continued
Montenegro	1968 (Zajc, personal communication)	continued together with Serbia
Serbia	1968 (Zajc, personal communication)	continued together with Montenegro
Slovenia (IPSA)	1968 (Bibic 1994: 148)	continued
Romania (IPSA)	1968 (IPSA 2000: 109), 1970 (Barbu 2002: 235)	1970 continued*
Hungary (IPSA)	1968 (IPSA 2000: 103), 1982 (Agh 1994: 83)	1982 continued
Bulgaria (IPSA)	1968, 1973 (IPSA 2000: 99)	1989 (Karasimeonov 2002: 41)
Czech Republic (IPSA)	1964 (IPSA 2000: 101)	1989 (Mansfeldova 2002: 72)
Slovakia (IPSA)	1968	1990 (Szomolanyi 1994: 141)
Lithuania (IPSA)	n.a.	1991 (Alisauskiene 1994: 118)
Ukraine	n.a.	1991 (Shestopal, personal communication
Russia (IPSA)	1960 (IPSA 2000: 109)	1991 (IPSA 2000: 109)
Belarus	n.a.	1993 (Ukhanov 1994: 48)
Estonia	n.a.	1993 (Vetik 1994: 75)
Albania	n.a.	n.a.
Armenia	n.a.	n.a.
Azerbaijan	n.a.	n.a.
Bosnia-Herzegovina	n.a.	n.a.
Georgia (IPSA)	n.a.	n.a.
Latvia	n.a.	n.a.
Macedonia	n.a.	n.a.
Moldova	n.a.	n.a.
Central European Political Science Association (Austria, Croatia, Czech Republic, Hungary, Lithuania, Poland, Slovakia, Slovenia)		1994 (CEPSA website)
German Democratic Republic	1974 (Andrews 1982: 413)	–
Soviet Union	1960 (Smirnov 1982: 351)	–
Yugoslavia	1954 (UNESCO Report 1950: 413)	–

*More than one association.

Around 2005, the 18 national political science organisations in Western Europe had a total of about 8,900 members (including Turkey's 150 members, but excluding the British International Studies Association). The numbers for the Central and Eastern European countries add up to a total of 1,858 political scientists who are members of a national political science association.[3] No membership information is available for the other countries.

Two regional political science associations deserve mention. First, the Nordic Political Science Association (NOPSA) founded on the initiative of Stein Rokkan in 1975. NOPSA organises joint meetings of Danish, Icelandic, Norwegian, and Swedish political scientists. Second, the Central European Political Science Association (CEPSA), founded in 1994, brings together political scientists from Austria, the Czech Republic, Croatia, Hungary, Lithuania, Poland, Slovakia, and Slovenia. In addition, the Flemish- and French-speaking political science associations seek closer cooperation with their Dutch, French, and Swiss counterparts. Cooperation between national science associations such as these is particularly important for political scientists from smaller countries who do not find an audience of sufficient size on the national level.

Challenged by the Bologna Process, the major national political science associations formed the European Conference of National Political Science Associations (ECNPSA) in 2001. 'Its first role...is to provide in so far as possible a united voice for political science in Europe, to enable us, in conjunction with ECPR and epsNet, to come to an agreed view about what is best for our discipline as a collaborative enterprise, and to promote that vigorously' (Furlong 2007: 403).

By 2006, all West European political science associations, with the exception of Portugal and Iceland, were members of the International Political Science Association (IPSA). In Central and Eastern Europe, 11 national political science associations are members of IPSA (Tables 3a and 3b). IPSA was founded in September 1949 at an international conference on political science held under the auspices of United Nations Educational, Scientific and Cultural Organisation (UNESCO) in Paris. With members on all continents, IPSA organises triennial World Congresses (starting in 1950), sponsors research committees, periodicals, and a book series (Trent 1982).

Genuinely European Political Science Organisations

In addition to the national political science associations, many other organisations and networks have emerged to promote political science in Europe. The wide variety of topics pursued by these various organisations reflects the ever-growing differentiation and specialisation of political science.

There is no dispute that the European Consortium for Political Research (ECPR) is the most important of all European political science associations.

It is hard to overstate the ECPR's contribution to the development and integration of European political science. Founded in 1970 by eight member institutions, it has now grown to well above 330 collective members, extending beyond Europe's borders. In 2006, 280 departments or institutes of political science from 32 European countries had joined ECPR, among them 14 Central and Eastern European countries representing 35 member institutions. ECPR members comprise about 8,000 political scientists (plus graduate students), which makes ECPR the second largest political science association in the world (Berg-Schlosser 2007: 413).

Since 1973, ECPR has held annual Joint Sessions of Workshops bringing together in small groups both senior and junior scholars. Each participant is obliged to present a paper. Lasting for almost a week, these workshops

TABLE 4

NUMBER OF INSTITUTIONAL MEMBERS OF THE EUROPEAN CONSORTIUM FOR POLITICAL RESEARCH IN EUROPEAN COUNTRIES IN 2006

Country	Number of institutional members
United Kingdom	58
Germany	44
Spain	18
Italy	15
Sweden	15
France	14
Norway	14
Netherlands	13
Turkey	9
Denmark	8
Belgium	7
Austria	6
Finland	5
Hungary	5
Ireland	5
Switzerland	5
Czech Republic	4
Greece	4
Poland	4
Russia	4
Bulgaria	3
Lithuania	3
Portugal	3
Romania	3
Croatia	2
Estonia	2
Latvia	2
Cyprus	1
Georgia	1
Iceland	1
Slovakia	1
Slovenia	1
Total	280

*Source: http://www.essex.ac.uk/ecpr/membership/currentmembers.aspx.

allow sufficient time for a detailed discussion and mutual assessments of research results. The ECPR (co-)sponsored methods summer schools at Essex, Lille, and Ljubljana have helped to improve significantly skill levels in quantitative data analysis. Starting in 2003, ECPR has offered biannual General Conferences that regularly attract more than 1,000 participants. A Graduate Conference alternates with the General Conference (Berg-Schlosser 2007: 411–13). English is the lingua franca. Thus, communication in the framework of ECPR has paved the way for an English language based discourse in European political science.

The European Political Science Network (epsNet) was launched in June 2001 as an association of political scientists devoted to discussion, exchange and cooperation in the field of political science teaching. Since its foundation, epsNet has engaged in a systematic programme of research into curriculum development and the state of the profession (Topf 2007: 418). The organisation had its origins in the European Thematic Network in Political Science founded in 1997. It has provided opportunities for many Central and Eastern European political scientists to cooperate with Western European colleagues.

These two organisations deal with the full range of topics as far as research (ECPR) and teaching (epsNet) of political science are concerned. In addition, however, there are a large number of active networks and organisations focused on particular subfields of political science. We know of no study trying to describe this development systematically. To illustrate the point, we sampled 47 European networks related to issues in political science from a list compiled by the German Social Science Infrastructure Services (2007). Table 5 shows that policy issues attract most of the attention (22), followed by networks connecting research on political institutions (12), organisations promoting the integration of research and teaching (9), and area studies groups (4). All these networks will contribute their share to the development of a genuine European political science.

The sprouting network of cooperation between political and other social scientists in Europe – mostly focused on European politics – has been actively supported by the European Union. The Socrates programme helped launch many thematic networks; the EU Commission's framework programmes have become a major source of research funding; and Jean Monnet Chairs were granted to many departments of political science and research institutes. Their number increased from 46 in 1990 to 623 in 2005.

Interest in European politics is by no means restricted to scholars working in Europe. There has long been widespread international fascination with many aspects of European politics. A large part of this research community is based in the United States of America. The 'European Politics and Society' section of the American Political Science Association (APSA) counted 525 members in 2007, and many of the 1,593 political scientists dealing with problems of European politics are also organised in the APSA

TABLE 5
THE EMERGENCE OF EUROPEAN NETWORKS RELATED TO POLITICAL
SCIENCE*

Field/acronym	Name
Policies	
01 TEPSA	Trans-European Policy Studies Association
02 EPIN	European Policy Institutes Network
03 NPN	New Politics Network
04 NESPA	Network for European Social Policy Analysis
05 ASPEN	Active Social Policies European Network
06 TSEP	Third Sector European Policy Network
07 WeAVE	European Gender Studies Network
08 ATHENA	Advanced Thematic Network in Activities in Women's Studies in Europe
09 RNGWSEE	Regional Network for Gender and Women's Studies in South-Eastern-Europe
10 ESA	Research Network Gender Relations in the Labor and the Welfare State
11 EMES	European Network – Building Europe's Knowledge on the Social Economy and Social Entrepreneurship
12 CENYR	Central European Network of Youth Research
13 EEPN	European Education Policy Network
14 ESREA	European Society for Research on the Education of Adults
15 GENIE	The Globalization and Europeanization Network in Education
16 ENDIPP	European Network on Drugs and Infection Prevention in Prison
17 EUROFOR	European Research Forum on Migration and Ethnic Relations
18 IMISCOE	International Migration, Integration, and Social Cohesion
19 ENRHCA	European Network for Research into Historical and Current Antisemitism
20 FUTURE	Urban Research in Europe. Research Network to Meet Future Challenges in the Cities of Europe
21 ENSHLD	European Network for Self-Help and Local Development
22 NRTEFP	Network of Research and Teaching on European Foreign Policy
Political institutions	
01 ECSA	European Community Studies Association
02 ESN	European Studies Network
03 EUG	European Governance
04 CONNEX	Connecting Excellence on European Governance
05 EGN	European Governance Network
06 Eurela	European Election Law Association
07 EPERN	European Parties, Elections and Referendum Network
08 EGOS	European Group for Organizational Studies
09 EPAN	European Public Administration Network
10 CiSoNet	European Civil Society Network
11 CINEFOGO	Civil Society and New Forms of Governance in Europe
12 EIN	European Ideas Network
Organisations promoting research and teaching	
01 ESSE	Network for a European Research Space in the Social Sciences
02 ECPR	European Consortium for Political Research
03 epsNet	European Political Science Network
04 NESSIE	Network of Economic and Social Science Infrastructures in Europe

(continued)

TABLE 5
(*Continued*)

Field/acronym	Name
05 PRIME	Policies for Research and Innovation in the Move towards the European Research Area
06 SEEERANET	Integrating and Strengthening the European Research Area in South Eastern Europe
07 SSN	Social Science Network
08 TransEurope	Social Sciences Research Network
09 UACES	University Association for Contemporary European Studies
Area studies	
01 EEN	Eastern Europe Network
02 BSRN	Black Sea Research Network
03 EUB	EU-Balkan Working Group
04 NDN	Northern Dimensions Network

*Selected from a list compiled by the German Social Science Infrastructure Services.

'Comparative Politics' section. In addition, European Studies are promoted by the inter-university Council for European Studies based at Columbia University. There are ten European Union Centers of Excellence located at high ranking US universities and funded by the EU. There are six Centers of German and European Studies established by the German government at Georgetown, Brandeis, Berkeley, Harvard, Université of Montréal and York, and the University of Toronto. The European Union Studies Association (EUSA) is probably the most comprehensive US based association of scholars focusing on the European Union. Its 2007 website claims 480 members in North America. The US government-sponsored Center for West European Studies counts ten member institutes and other select centres. Finally, in 2006 the ECPR counted 43 associate member institutions in the United States and Canada. Thus, capacities to investigate European politics reach well beyond European borders.

Political Science Journals

Development and support of infrastructure for professional communication is one of the major functions of academic professional associations. Publication in professional journals is the central medium for communication and criticism of research results. Kaase (2007) estimates that 40,000 political scientists around the world publish their findings in more than 1,000 political science journals, mostly in their native language.

All national political science associations in Europe provide a journal as a major part of their services to members. The same is true for the regional political science associations (e.g., NOPSA: *Scandinavian Political Studies*; CEPSA: *Politics in Central Europe. The Journal of the Central European Political Science Association*, formerly the *Central European Political Science Review*) and international associations such as IPSA (*International Political Science Review*) or the International Studies

Association (*International Studies Quarterly*). These general periodicals are often complemented by more specialised journals. Klingemann (2007: 32–3) has monitored political science journals in 19 Western European countries and found 56 significant journals in addition to the official journals of the various national political science associations. Coakley and Doyle (1998) have included political science journals from Bulgaria, Croatia, the Czech Republic, Hungary, Lithuania, Poland, Romania, Russia, Slovenia, and Yugoslavia. They concluded that most journals that existed in the Communist period have disappeared and new ones have entered the stage. A first count based on data provided by the German Social Science Infrastructure Services yields a total of 76 journals. The same source justifies the conclusion that Western social science journals devoted to problems of Central and Eastern Europe have increased significantly.

The flagship journal of European political science remains ECPR's *European Journal of Political Research* (EJPR), founded in 1972 with Arend Lijphart as its first editor. In 2001, ECPR launched a second professional journal, *European Political Science* (EPS). It includes original articles, symposia, progress reports on areas of current research and news of the profession. The *European Journal for International Relations* has followed since. epsNet has established an electronic journal *THE NET Journal of Political Science* which contains articles about epsNet projects, the profession, teaching and training, as well as reviews, an Open Forum, and the doctoral students' platform called Nethesis. Coakley and Doyle (1998) note the rapid increase in number and importance of web based publications, such as *THE NET Journal of Political Science*. This development makes the world of political science journals ever more complex and difficult to follow.

To consider their impact is one way to evaluate the importance of professional journals. The impact factor is regularly measured for a great number of professional journals, including political science journals, by the Thompson Institute of Scientific Information (ISI) and published in their Journal Citation Reports (www.sciencegateway.org/impact). The index is calculated by taking the number of all current citations to sources published in a journal over the previous two years and dividing by the number of articles published in the journal during the same period (www.in-cites.com/research). This index should be used with caution as it is sensitive to single articles, which can lead to wide variation over time. Thus, it should be carefully evaluated in the context of total cites and number of articles. Despite these precautions, ranking of journals by their impact factor has become the norm. We will follow this norm, but we will also provide total cites and number of articles. Data are available for Political Science and International Relations (which we count as a subfield of political science at large). Table 6 takes into account journals of both fields ranked one to ten by their respective impact factors. What is the general picture? How do 'European' journals fare?

TABLE 6
THE 20 GLOBALLY MOST IMPORTANT PROFESSIONAL JOURNALS IN POLITI-
CAL SCIENCE AND INTERNATIONAL RELATIONS AS MEASURED BY THEIR
IMPACT FACTOR, 2005*

Impact factor	Total cites	N articles	Journals
3.233	4628	44	American Political Science Review
2.630	883	21	International Security**
2.148	1196	42	American Journal of International Law**
2.060	1911	30	International Organization*
2.058	1110	69	Foreign Affairs**
1.845	3123	60	American Journal of Political Science
1.812	87	3	Stanford Journal of International Law**
1.783	928	69	European Journal of Political Research
1.686	291	20	Journal of Theoretical Politics
1.509	1700	34	Public Opinion Quarterly
1.500	226	17	European Journal for International Relations**
1.079	1327	39	Journal of Conflict Resolution
1.415	718	30	International Studies Quarterly**
1.493	621	35	Political Geography
1.308	1129	5	World Politics**
1.292	613	37	Journal of Peace Research**
1.286	147	22	Conflict Management/Peace Studies**
1.273	189	20	European Union Politics
1.261	347	27	Political Communication
1.254	527	41	Political Psychology
1.239	1645	54	Journal of Politics

*The *Journal of Peace Research* was part of both groups. The *Journal of Politics* was ranked 11 in the Political Science group and more important than the 11 ranked journal in the International Relations group. Thus, the *Journal of Politics* was incorporated as number 20 in Table 6.
**International Relations journals.

Table 6 carries several messages. The first one is crystal clear, all major journals in the fields of Political Science and International Relations (as defined by Thompson ISI) are published in English. The second message removes any doubt that US based journals, such as the *American Political Science Review* and *International Security*, dominate the scene. However, thirdly, it is interesting to note that the *European Journal of Political Research* and the *European Journal for International Relations* come in respectable positions (8 and 11). Both journals are backed by the ECPR and are truly Europe based. Fourth, many other journals cannot easily be classified as 'US' or 'European' such as *International Studies Quarterly*, *European Union Politics*, or *Political Psychology* – to name just a few. And it is probably to this type of journal, transcending regionally defined borders, that the future belongs.

Journals in the various mother tongues are indispensable both for professional communication and to provide links to society at large. However, we have to take note that the first non-English language journal, the German *Politische Vierteljahresschrift* (impact factor: 0.238, total cites: 59, number of articles: 22), ranks 67. Thus, the growth of English language journals cannot be overlooked, and the number of political scientists publishing both in their mother tongue and in English is on the rise. It seems fair to say that today command of English is a precondition for any political scientist who wants to participate in European or global professional discourse.

Data Archives for Empirical Political Research

'To take up the behavioral approach in the 1960s and 1970s was to distinguish political science from law, philosophy, history, and economics. . . . At the same time, to use the methods and approaches of empirical research and surveys required the academic apparatus of survey centers, computers, research teams, specialised techniques, and data archives' (Newton and Vallès 1991: 236). Thus, the build-up of social science data archives in particular was a corollary to political science's development as an empirical discipline. These archives provided individual-level survey data – the main source for an analysis of political behaviour – which, if only for reason of costs, would have been otherwise inaccessible to the broad research community.

The University of Cologne based *Zentralarchiv für empirische Sozialforschung*, set up by Günther Schmölders, an economist, in 1960 became Europe's first social science data archive. The survey archive of the University of Essex followed in 1967. As in so many other enterprises, Stein Rokkan was one of the major figures supporting the archive movement. Over the years, many such archives have been set up. Today, there are 21 major national data archives in Europe cooperating in the Council of European Social Science Data Archives (CESSDA). They provide a common internet portal which allows easy access to their collections. These collections consist of more than just sample surveys. They also include aggregate data, data describing institutions, or data sets derived by quantitative content analysis. In addition there are seven other non-profit, social science data archiving organisations in five countries marked with a '**' in Table 7.

Services provided by data archives have become indispensable for political research. This is true for students looking for research data as well as for research teams working on large scale comparative projects. In a division of labour, major ongoing studies have been adopted by specific archives. For example, the German *Zentralarchiv* documents and distributes the European Commission's Eurobarometer surveys; the Norwegian NSD does the same with the European Social Survey study. Mochmann (2002) and Caul-Kittilson (2007) provide valuable reports of the resources for empirical research currently available in the various social science data archives. We want to note, however, that more and more data sets are made available by research institutes or individual researchers on their various websites. This does not mean that data

TABLE 7
EUROPEAN SOCIAL SCIENCE DATA ARCHIVES, 2007*

Country	Name and acronym
Austria	Wiener Institut fuer Sozialwissenschaftliche Dokumentation und Methodik WISDOM
Belgium	Archives Belges en Sciences Sociales BASS
Bulgaria**	Social Science Data Archive at REGLO
Czech Republic	Sociological Data Archive SDA
Denmark	Danish Data Archives DDA
Estonia	Estonian Social Science Data Archive ESSDA
Finland	Finnish Social Science Data Services FSD
France	Réseau Quetelet
Greece	Greek Social Data Bank GSDB
Germany	Zentralarchiv fuer Empirische Sozialforschung ZA (GESIS)
Hungary	Social Research Informatics Center TARKI
Ireland	Irish Social Science Data Archive ISSDA
Italy	ADPSS Sociodata
Luxembourg	CEPS/INSTEAD
Netherlands	Data Archiving and Networked Service DANS
Norway	Norwegian Social Science Data Services NSD
Poland**	Archive of Sociological Data ADS
Romania	Romanian Social Science Data Archive RODA
Russia**	Russian Sociological Data Archive, Independent Institute for Social Policy
	Data Bank of Social Research at the Institute of Sociology of the Russian Academy of Sciences DBSR
Slovakia**	Slovak Archive of Social Data
	Data Archive of the Institute for Sociology SAV
Slovenia	Social Science Data Archives ADP
Spain	Archivo de Estudios Sociales ARCES, CIS
Sweden	Swedish Social Science Data Services SSD
Switzerland	Swiss Information and Data Archive Service for the Social Sciences SIDOS
Ukraine**	Ukrainian Sociological Archive, Kiev International Institute of Sociology
United Kingdom	UK Data Archive UKDA

*Source: CESSDA website.
**Not members of CESSDA.

archives are superseded by this development. Rather, it is just one more indication that the world of political science is not exempt from growing complexity.

Interest Representation of Political Science in the European Context

Political scientists do not live in an ivory tower. As individual scientists, they are committed to preserve academic freedom and to garner resources in support of research. In their various countries national political science associations have successfully fought many battles on both fronts. However, there are four reasons why political science is ill-prepared for representation of its interests in the broader European context.

First, the identity problem comes back again (Stein 2006). The political pressure caused by the Bologna process to implement a common European degree structure has-again-started a discussion about the nature of political science and its core elements. Thus, the proposition for the structure of a BA in political science, handed to the Bologna conference of ministers in Berlin on behalf of European political science, rests on shaky grounds (Reinalda and Kulesza 2006: 223–5).

Second, in addition to the identity problem, European political science is confronted with the general problem of specialisation and differentiation. Practitioners within such subfields as International Relations, Public Policy, Public Administration, Political Communication, or Political Sociology often seem to act as though they would be better off in acquiring resources if they were separate disciplines. This may sometimes work for a particular subfield. However, it is definitely counterproductive if it comes to interest representation of political science as a whole. Group size is an important variable, suggesting that political success sometimes benefits from economies of scale.

Third, country-specific development of systems of higher education, coupled with the problem of specialisation and differentiation, have made it almost impossible to document and compare even the most fundamental facts, such as academic staff or number and type of students. The label 'Political Science' is only one among many names for numerous subfields that are often treated as if at the same level. Thus, any information sought for political science as a discipline in Europe must be extracted from parts of a variously labelled maze.

Fourth, European political science does not speak with a common voice. Currently, there are at least three organisations which would have to agree on common positions: the European Conference of National Political Science Associations, the European Consortium for Political Research, and the European Political Science Network. And no decision can be regarded legitimate if the positions of the various national political science associations are not taken into account. Therefore, affiliates of ECNPSA must cooperate. epsNet aggregates a clientele interested in teaching political science at the European level. And the ECPR is the undisputed leader in promoting European comparative research. They must be heard, too. To reach common positions is a long and tedious process.

Europe has developed strong capacities in the field of professional political science. Entering a new stage of the integration of Europe's higher education and research, it would certainly help to represent the discipline's interests if it could speak with one voice.

Summary Assessment of the Capacities of Political Science in Europe

Political science in Western Europe has developed rapidly since the 1960s. After the breakdown of the Communist regimes, Central and Eastern

Europe is catching up. The total number of the academic staff employed by
the 575 universities in East and West is at about 10,000 political scientists.
This indicates a rather high degree of institutionalisation of political science
as an academic discipline.

About 31 national political science associations that also cooperate
regionally (e.g. NOPSA, CEPSA) and internationally (e.g. IPSA) provide
communication opportunities for a total of about 10,000 members. They
organise meetings and support journals, mostly on the national level. More
and more political science organisations have been founded at the European
level. The most visible among them is the European Consortium for
Political Research. ECPR has become the leader in integrating European
political science. The more recent and much smaller European Political
Science Network has taken up the task of helping to integrate curricula and
teaching; a task rapidly gaining importance with the ongoing Bologna
Process.

Prestigious professional journals at the regional and European levels
encourage English language contributions. English is by now the dominant
language at important meetings and conferences. Many political science
departments outside the UK and Ireland offer English language courses.
This is especially true for the most prestigious universities. Data archives
have spread and cooperate at the European level. They, too, document
major parts of their holdings in English.

In short, conditions for integrated development of political science
in Europe have never been more promising. And the use of the English
language has an additional advantage: It opens the door to the most
competitive markets of political science in North America and around
the world. Thus, there is hope that quality of teaching and research
will increase and come closer to the universities that lead the pack
today.

Quality indicators are hard to come by, especially on a global scale.
Simon Hix (2004) has proposed a global ranking of political science
departments based on publication record. As could have been predicted,
results are disputed on various grounds. We do not want to engage in that
dispute. We accept his results as a rough indicator of what one would get
in any other replication. What does Table 8 say about European political
science as compared to other parts of the world? Eighty-five (43 per cent)
of the top 200 universities are located in Europe and 101 (51 per cent) are
located in the United States. The UK is very well represented. Only 14 (7
per cent) from the rest of the world make the list. This means that
European universities are represented quite well compared to their
counterparts in the US. However, political science in Europe still has a
lot of catching up to do. The growing number of English language
publications in the non-English speaking countries is a sign of hope for
them to reach the level of representation the universities of the United
Kingdom have already achieved.

TABLE 8
THE PERFORMANCE OF EUROPEAN POLITICAL SCIENCE DEPARTMENTS IN
THE GLOBAL RANKING OF THE TOP 200 POLITICAL SCIENCE DEPARTMENTS,
1998–2002, ACCORDING TO SIMON HIX (2004)

European rank	Global rank	University	Country
01	005	European University Institute	Italy (EU)
02	015	London School of Economics	UK
03	016	University of Essex	UK
04	019	Oxford University	UK
05	022	University of Birmingham	UK
06	023	Cambridge University	UK
07	025	University of Sheffield	UK
08	034	University of Bristol	UK
09	037	Cardiff University	UK
10	039	University of Aberystwyth	UK
11	040	Trinity College Dublin	Ireland
12	043	University of Geneva	Switzerland
13	046	UCL	UK
14	052	University of Oslo	Norway
15	055	University of Leiden	Netherlands
16	063	University of Hull	UK
17	071	University of Warwick	UK
18	074	Mannheim University	Germany
19	075	University of Strathclyde	UK
20	078	Aarhus University	UK
21	079	University of Sussex	UK
22	082	University of Aberdeen	UK
23	083	Newcastle-Upon-Tyne University	UK
24	085	Glasgow University	UK
25	086	University of Leicester	UK
26	087	University of Manchester	UK
27	090	Birkbeck University	UK
28	096	University of Bradford	UK
29	097	Humboldt University Berlin	Germany
30	099	University of Edinburgh	UK
31	099	University of Leeds	UK
32	101	Durham University	UK
33	103	Queen Mary and Westfield College, University of London	UK
34	108	Max-Planck-Institute for the Study of Societies, Cologne	Germany
35	110	University of Groningen	Netherlands
36	111	University of Southampton	UK
37	114	University of Liverpool	UK
38	116	University of Amsterdam	Netherlands
39	117	Manchester Metropolitan	UK
40	121	University of Kent	UK
41	122	University of Exeter	UK
42	123	University of Helsinki	Finland
43	126	University of Nottingham	UK
44	127	Liverpool John Moores	UK
45	131	University of East Anglia	UK
46	133	University of Konstanz	Germany
47	134	Queens University Belfast	UK
48	135	University College Dublin	Ireland
49	135	St. Andrews University	UK
50	137	University of Twente	Netherlands

(continued)

TABLE 8
(*Continued*)

European rank	Global rank	University	Country
51	140	University of Bremen	Germany
52	142	Keele University	UK
53	145	Norwegian University of Science and Technology, Trondheim	Norway
54	147	University Nijmegen	Netherlands
55	148	Uppsala University	Sweden
56	153	University of the West of England	UK
57	155	University of Copenhagen	Denmark
58	157	University of Bern	Switzerland
59	158	University of Vienna	Austria
60	162	Nottingham Trent	UK
61	166	Stirling University	UK
62	168	Reading University	UK
63	169	Lancaster University	UK
64	170	Sciences Po Paris	France
65	170	University of Bath	UK
66	172	INSEAD	France
67	173	Technical University Darmstadt	Germany
68	175	GIIS	Switzerland
69	176	Gothenburg University	Sweden
70	177	University of Westminster	UK
71	178	De Montford University	UK
72	181	University of Lund	Sweden
73	182	University of Leuven (KUL)	Belgium
74	183	UCLAN	UK
75	184	University of Tübingen	Germany
76	186	University of Frankfurt, Viadrina	Germany
77	188	University of Florence	Italy
78	189	Central European University Budapest	Hungary
79	190	University Erlangen-Nürnberg	Germany
80	191	Staffordshire	UK
81	192	Fernuniversität Hagen	Germany
82	194	University of York	UK
83	195	University of Bergen	Norway
84	198	The Juan March Institute	Spain
85	200	University of Ulster	UK

This all is – potentially – good news. The bad news is that European political science is unable to provide quantitative data about even basic indicators such as students or academic staff. This is caused not only by country-specific differences but also by the desire of subfields of the discipline to be statistically represented as disciplines in their own right. Thus, political science does not speak with a single voice in European higher education or research. It is a sign of hope that national political science organisations have set up a European Conference of National Political Science Associations to negotiate common policy positions with ECPR and epsNet. The likelihood is significant that ECPR and epsNet are merging. Thus, there is hope that those responsible for creating a genuine European Political Science Association will not fall short of their task.

Acknowledgements

I owe thanks to Russell J. Dalton, Richard I. Hofferbert, Ute Klingemann, and Christian Welzel who critically read this essay. Klaus H. Goetz and Peter Mair offered valuable editorial advice. Ulrike Becker, Brigitte Hausstein, and Natalija Schleinstein, German Social Science Infrastructure Services, Service Agency Eastern Europe, were helpful in providing much needed data about the situation of political science in Central and Eastern Europe.

Notes

1. This selection leaves out a number of other important topics such as research funding or academic career structures. To deal properly with research funding would require an essay of its own and the same is true for an analysis of academic career patterns. Recently Holzinger (2007), Schneider (2007), and Steunenberg (2007) have contributed to a better understanding of these issues.
2. This information was kindly provided by the Berlin-based Service Agency Eastern Europe, a unit of the German Social Science Infrastructure Service (GESIS).
3. Country-specific figures are: Bulgaria 60, Czech Republic 200, Estonia 30, Hungary 350, Lithuania 80, Slovakia 130 (Karasimeonov 2002, Mansfeldova 2002, Vetik and Avikson 2002, Szabó 2002, Krupavicius 2002, Malová and Miháliková 2002), Croatia 100, Poland 200, Romania 188, Russia 300, Slovenia 220 (International Political Science Association 2000).

References

Agapiou-Josephides, Kalliope (2007). 'The Current State of Political Science in Cyprus', in Hans-Dieter Klingemann (ed.), *The State of Political Science in Western Europe*. Opladen and Farmington Hills: Barbara Budrich Publishers, 73–86.

Agh, Attila (1994). 'Hungary', in Hans-Dieter Klingemann, Ekkehard Mochmann and Kenneth Newton (eds.), *Political Research in Eastern Europe*. Bonn-Berlin: Informationszentrum Sozialwissenschaften, 77–105.

Alisauskiene, Rasa (1994). 'Lithuania', in Hans-Dieter Klingemann, Ekkehard Mochmann and Kenneth Newton (eds.), *Political Research in Eastern Europe*. Bonn-Berlin: Informationszentrum Sozialwissenschaften, 115–18.

Anckar, Dag (1991). 'Nordic Political Science: Trends, Roles, Approaches', in Kenneth Newton and Josep M. Vallès (eds.), *Political Science in Europe, 1960–1990*. *European Journal of Political Research*, 20, 239–62.

Andrews, William G., ed. (1982). *International Handbook of Political Science*. Westport, CT: Greenwood Press.

Appelt, Erna, and Johannes Pollak (2007). 'The Current State of Political Science in Austria', in Hans-Dieter Klingemann (ed.), *The State of Political Science in Western Europe*. Opladen and Farmington Hills: Barbara Budrich Publishers, 43–55.

Barbu, Daniel (2002). 'Political Science in Romania', in Hans-Dieter Klingemann, Ewa Kulesza and Annette Legutke (eds.), *The State of Political Science in Central and Eastern Europe*. Berlin: edition sigma, 229–52.

Berg-Schlosser, Dirk (2007). 'European Political Science – The Role of the European Consortium of Political Research (ECPR)', in Hans-Dieter Klingemann (ed.), *The State of Political Science in Western Europe*. Opladen and Farmington Hills: Barbara Budrich Publishers, 409–15.

Berglund, Sten, and Joakim Ekman (2007). 'The Current State of Political Science in Sweden', in Hans-Dieter Klingemann (ed.), *The State of Political Science in Western Europe*. Opladen and Farmington Hills: Barbara Budrich Publishers, 341–60.

Berndtson, Erkki (2007). 'The Current State of Political Science in Finland', in Hans-Dieter Klingemann (ed.), *The State of Political Science in Western Europe*. Opladen and Farmington Hills: Barbara Budrich Publishers, 103–36.

Bibic, Adolf (1982). 'Yugoslavia', in William G. Andrews (ed.), *International Handbook of Political Science*. Westport, CT: Greenwood Press, 383–412.

Bibic, Adolf (1994). 'Slovenia', in Hans-Dieter Klingemann, Ekkehard Mochmann and Kenneth Newton (eds.), *Political Research in Eastern Europe*. Bonn-Berlin: Informationszentrum Sozialwissenschaften, 145–72.

Blondiaux, Loic, and Yves Déloye (2007). 'The Current State of Political Science: Report on the Situation in France', in Hans-Dieter Klingemann (ed.), *The State of Political Science in Western Europe*. Opladen and Farmington Hills: Barbara Budrich Publishers, 137–62.

Caul-Kittilson, Miki (2007). 'Research Resources in Comparative Political Behavior', in Russell J. Dalton and Hans-Dieter Klingemann (eds.), *The Oxford Handbook of Political Behaviour*. Oxford: Oxford University Press, 865–95.

Coakley, John, and John Doyle (1998). 'Developments in European Political Science Journal and Electronic Literature During 1997', *European Journal of Political Research*, 33, 525–47.

Coakley, John, and Michael Laver (2007). 'The Current State of Political Science in Ireland', in Hans-Dieter Klingemann (ed.), *The State of Political Science in Western Europe*. Opladen and Farmington Hills: Barbara Budrich Publishers, 243–54.

Contogeorgis, Georges (2007). 'Political Science in Greece', in Hans-Dieter Klingemann (ed.), *The State of Political Science in Western Europe*. Opladen and Farmington Hills: Barbara Budrich Publishers, 187–228.

DeWinter, Lieven, André-Paul Frognier, Karolien Dezeure, Anne-Sylvie Berck, and Marleen Brans (2007). 'Belgium: From One to Two Political Sciences?', in Hans-Dieter Klingemann (ed.), *The State of Political Science in Western Europe*. Opladen and Farmington Hills: Barbara Budrich Publishers, 57–71.

Easton, David (1953). *The Political System. An Inquiry into the State of Political Science*. New York: Knopf.

Easton, David, John G. Gunnell and Luigi Graziano, eds. (1991). *The Development of Political Science*. London: Routledge.

Etherington, John, and Francesc Morata (2007). 'The Current State of Political Science in Spain', in Hans-Dieter Klingemann (ed.), *The State of Political Science in Western Europe*. Opladen and Farmington Hills: Barbara Budrich Publishers, 325–39.

Freddi, Giorgio, and Daniela Giannetti (2007). 'The Current State of Political Science in Italy', in Hans-Dieter Klingemann (ed.), *The State of Political Science in Western Europe*. Opladen and Farmington Hills: Barbara Budrich Publishers, 255–74.

Freymond, Nicolas, Christophe Platel and Bernard Voutat (2007). 'The State of Political Science in Switzerland in Teaching and Research', in Hans-Dieter Klingemann (ed.), *The State of Political Science in Western Europe*. Opladen and Farmington Hills: Barbara Budrich Publishers, 361–79.

Furlong, Paul (2007). 'The European Conference of National Political Science Associations: Problems and Possibilities of Co-operation', in Hans-Dieter Klingemann (ed.), *The State of Political Science in Western Europe*. Opladen and Farmington Hills: Barbara Budrich Publishers, 401–7.

Goldsmith, Michael, and Wyn Grant (2007). 'British Political Science in the New Millennium', in Hans-Dieter Klingemann (ed.), *The State of Political Science in Western Europe*. Opladen and Farmington Hills: Barbara Budrich Publishers, 381–98.

Hardarson, Olafur T. (2007). 'The Current State of Political Science in Iceland', in Hans-Dieter Klingemann (ed.), *The State of Political Science in Western Europe*. Opladen and Farmington Hills: Barbara Budrich Publishers, 229–42.

Hix, Simon (2004). 'A Global Ranking of Political Science Departments', *Political Studies*, 2, 293–313.

Holzinger, Katharina (2007). 'Career Incentives', *European Political Science*, 6, 177–84.

International Political Science Association (2000). *Handbook of the International Political Science Association*. Dublin: IPSA.

Kaase, Max (2007). 'Political Participation', in Russell J. Dalton and Hans-Dieter Klingemann (eds.), *The Oxford Handbook of Political Behaviour*. Oxford: Oxford University Press, 783–96.

Kaase, Max, Vera Sparschuh and Agnieszka Wenninger, eds. (2002). *Three Social Science Disciplines in Central and Eastern Europe. Handbook on Economics, Political Science, and Sociology (1989–2001)*. Bonn, Berlin and Budapest: Social Science Information Centre (IZ)/ Collegium Budapest.

Karasimeonov, Georgi (2002). 'Political Science in Bulgaria', in Hans-Dieter Klingemann, Ewa Kulesza and Annette Legutke (eds.), *The State of Political Science in Central and Eastern Europe*. Berlin: edition sigma, 37–51.

Klingemann, Hans-Dieter (2002). 'Political Science in Central and Eastern Europe: National Development and International Integration', in Max Kaase, Vera Sparschuh and Agnieszka Wenninger (eds.), *Three Social Science Disciplines in Central and Eastern Europe. Handbook on Economics, Political Science, and Sociology (1989–2001)*. Bonn, Berlin and Budapest: Social Science Information Centre (IZ)/Collegium Budapest, 206–12.

Klingemann, Hans-Dieter (2007a). 'A Comparative Perspective on Political Science in Western Europe around the Year 2005', in Hans-Dieter Klingemann (ed.), *The State of Political Science in Western Europe*. Opladen and Farmington Hills: Barbara Budrich Publishers.

Klingemann, Hans-Dieter, ed. (2007b). *The State of Political Science in Western Europe*. Opladen and Farmington Hills: Barbara Budrich Publishers.

Klingemann, Hans-Dieter, Ewa Kulesza and Annette Legutke (2002a). 'Political Science in the Countries of EU Enlargement', in Hans-Dieter Klingemann, Ewa Kulesza and Annette Legutke (eds.), *The State of Political Science in Central and Eastern Europe*. Berlin: edition sigma, 11–33.

Klingemann, Hans-Dieter, Ewa Kulesza and Annette Legutke, eds. (2002b). *The State of Political Science in Central and Eastern Europe*. Berlin: edition sigma.

Klingemann, Hans-Dieter, Ekkehard Mochmann and Kenneth Newton, eds. (1994). *Political Research in Eastern Europe*. Bonn and Berlin: Informationszentrum Sozialwissenschaften.

Mackenzie, W.J.M. (1971). 'The Political Science of Political Science', *Government and Opposition*, 6, 277–302.

Mansfeldova, Zdenka (2002). 'Political Science in the Czech Republic', in Hans-Dieter Klingemann, Ewa Kulesza and Annette Legutke (eds.), *The State of Political Science in Central and Eastern Europe*. Berlin: edition sigma, 71–95.

Mochmann, Ekkehard (2002). *International Social Science Data Service: Scope and Accessibility*. Cologne: International Social Science Council.

Moreira, Adriano (2007). 'Political Science in Portugal', in Hans-Dieter Klingemann (ed.), *The State of Political Science in Western Europe*. Opladen and Farmington Hills: Barbara Budrich Publishers, 311–23.

Newton, Kenneth, and Josep M. Vallès, eds. (1991). 'Political Science in Europe, 1960–1990', *European Journal of Political Research* (Special Issue), 20.

Newton, Kenneth, and Josep M. Vallès (1991). 'Introduction: Political Science in Western Europe, 1960–1990', in Kenneth Newton and Josep M. Vallès (eds.), *Political Science in Europe, 1960–1990. European Journal of Political Research*, 20, 227–38.

Pedersen, Mogens N. (2007). 'Denmark: Political Science – Past, Present and Future', in Hans-Dieter Klingemann (ed.), *The State of Political Science in Western Europe*. Opladen and Farmington Hills: Barbara Budrich Publishers, 87–102.

Quermonne, Jean Louis, ed. (1996). *La Science Politique en Europe: Formation, Coopération, Perspectives. Rapport Final. Projét realize avec le soutien de la Commission Européenne (DG XII)*. Paris: Institut d'Études Politiques de Paris.

Reinalda, Bob, and Ewa Kulseza (2006). *The Bologna Process – Harmonizing Europe's Higher Education*. 2nd edn. Opladen: Barbara Budrich.

Roeder, Karl-Heinz, and Jürgen Franke (1982). ‚German Democratic Republic', in William G. Andrews (ed.), *International Handbook of Political Science*. Westport, CT: Greenwood Press, 177–84.

Rose, Richard (1990). 'Institutionalizing Professional Political Science in Europe: A Dynamic Model', *European Journal of Political Research*, 18, 581–603.

Schneider, Gerald (2007). 'The Search for the Holy Grant: (Mis)allocating Money in European Political Science', *European Political Science*, 6, 160–68.

Schüttemeyer, Suzanne S. (2007). 'The Current State of Political Science in Germany', in Hans-Dieter Klingemann (ed.), *The State of Political Science in Western Europe*. Opladen and Farmington Hills: Barbara Budrich Publishers, 163–86.

Smirnov, William (1982). 'The Soviet Political Science Association', in William G. Andrews (ed.), *International Handbook of Political Science*. Westport, CT: Greenwood Press, 351–4.

Stein, Michael B. (2006). 'Is There a Genuinely International Political Science Discipline? An Overview of Recent Disciplinary Historical Trends', Paper Prepared for Presentation at the XXth World Congress of the International Political Science Association, Fukuoka, Japan, 9–13 July.

Steunenberg, Bernard (2007). 'Move or Perish: Increasing Professional Mobility in European Academia', *European Political Science*, 6, 169–76.

Szomolanyi, Sona (1994). 'Slovak Republic', in Hans-Dieter Klingemann, Ekkehard Mochmann and Kenneth Newton (eds.), *Political Research in Eastern Europe*. Bonn and Berlin: Informationszentrum Sozialwissenschaften, 135–43.

Topf, Richard (2007). 'The European Political Science Network', in Hans-Dieter Klingemann (ed.), *The State of Political Science in Western Europe*. Opladen and Farmington Hills: Barbara Budrich Publishers, 417–24.

Trent, John (1982). 'Institutional Development', in William G. Andrews (ed.), *International Handbook of Political Science*. Westport, CT: Greenwood Press, 34–46.

Ukhanov, Victor (1994). 'Belarus', in Hans-Dieter Klingemann, Ekkehard Mochmann and Kenneth Newton (eds.), *Political Research in Eastern Europe*. Bonn and Berlin: Informationszentrum Sozialwissenschaften, 43–9.

UNESCO (1950). *La Science Politique Contemporaine. Contribution à la recherche, la méthode et l'enseignement*. Paris: UNESCO Publications.

Vetik, Raivo (1994). 'Estonia', in Hans-Dieter Klingemann, Ekkehard Mochmann and Kenneth Newton (eds.), *Political Research in Eastern Europe*. Bonn and Berlin: Informationszentrum Sozialwissenschaften, 71–6.

Internet Sources

Bologna Process: ec.europa.eu/education/policies/educ/bologna
Centres for German and European Studies: www.cges.cla.umn.edu
Centre for West European Studies: www.jsis.washington.edu.cwes
Central European Political Science Association: www.cepsa.cz
Council of Europe: www.coe.int
Council of European Social Science Data Services: www.nsd.uib.no/cessda
Council on European Studies: www.councilforeuropeanstudies.org
European Consortium for Political Research: www.essex.ac.uk/ecpr
European Political Science Network: www.epsnet.org
European Union Studies Association: www.ucis.pitt.special.eusa475
German Social Science Infrastructure Services: www.gesis.org/eastern_europe
International Political Science Association: www.ipsa.com
Journal Citation Reports: www.sciencegateway.org/impact; www.in-cities.com/research
Minda de Gunzberg Center for European Studies: www.ces.fas.harvard.edu
Network of European Union Centres of Excellence: www.unc.edu/euce
Nordic Political Science Association: www.nopsa.org
The American Political Science Association: www.apsanet.org

Index

Pierre, J. 264–5, 272
Pierson, P. 47–8, 83, 95, 98, 99, 354–5, 358, 359
Pim Fortuyn List (Netherlands) 213
Pitkin, H. 176
Piven, F.F. 160
Poguntke, T. 155, 267
Polanyi, K. 356
policy paradigms 358
political economy *see* European political economy
political participation 54–5, 147–64; and consumer power 162–3; and declining power of vote 158–63; and decreasing electoral accountability 157–8; electoral participation 149–54, 164; and protest 148, 156–7, 160–1; representative government 149–53; and role of media 154–7; and social movements 148, 156–7, 161; unconventional forms of 147, 149, 156–7, 160–3, 164, *see also* democracy
political parties 199, 211–30, 347, 349, 350, 351; convergence 212–16, 218, 219, 222, 347; declining electoral cohesion 218–22; divergence 358–9; focus on party leader 155; and globalisation 217–18; 'parties-do-matter' thesis 212, 217–18, 219; and single ideological dimension 228–30; transformation of 154–5, *see also* party government
Political Psychology 386
political science 370–92; associations 377–84, 390, 392; data archives 387–9, 390; development after World War II 371–3, 389–90; European networks 380–4, 392; institutionalisation of 374–6, 390; interest representation 388–9; journals 384–7, 390; professionalisation of 373–4; specialisation and differentiation 374, 380, 389
Pollack, M. 289
Pollitt, C. 263–4
populism 155, 159, 208–9
Power, M. 284
power resources theory 97–8

privatisation 261, 282, 303, 304, 307, 309, 353
Prodi, Romano 214, 243, 244, 246
Przeworski, A. 61, 101
public policy 27, 55, 74, 261, 352, 354, 358; and gender 169, 173, 174, 175, 176; and parties 217, 225, 227, 359, *see also* country clusters in public policy; governance
Puchala, D. 110

Quermonne, J.L. 375

Railtrack 293
Reagan, Ronald 98, 353
regime change, theory of 47–51
regional integration theory 110
regionalism 69–75; Central and Eastern Europe (CEE) 74–5; globalisation and European integration 71–3; new regionalism 69–71; regional government 73–5
regulatory state 280–97, 309; and 'audit society' 284; and autonomy of regulator 293–4; dilemmas of 292–5; in European politics 286–92; future interest in regulation 295–7; 'regulatory space' 290–1; rise in Europe 282–6; and 'risk society' 285
religion, decline in Europe 35–6
Rhodes, M. 96
Rhodes, R. 68, 261, 263, 266–7
Richardson, J.J. 269
Ringen, S. 43
Risse, T. 120
Rittberger, B. 270, 272
RNGS project (Research Network on Gender and the State) 169, 173–4, 176–7, 183–4, 188; list of policy debates 191–4; results 179–81
Rokkan, Stein 63, 65–6, 121, 198, 211, 324, 380, 387
Rokkanian analysis 27, 73, 75, 327, 349
Rome Treaty 88, 109, 110–11
Rose, R. 223–5, 228, 373
Ross, F. 99
Rothstein, B. 228, 357, 358
Rouquié, A. 44

For Product Safety Concerns and Information please contact our EU
representative GPSR@taylorandfrancis.com
Taylor & Francis Verlag GmbH, Kaufingerstraße 24, 80331 München, Germany

www.ingramcontent.com/pod-product-compliance
Lightning Source LLC
Chambersburg PA
CBHW060131280326
41932CB00012B/1487

9 780415 602136